WHO WILL
ROLL AWAY
THE STONE?

WHO WILL ROLL AWAY THE STONE?

Discipleship Queries
for First World Christians

CHED MYERS

And they were saying to one another,
"Who will roll away the stone
for us from the door of the tomb?"
Mk 16:3

ORBIS BOOKS

Maryknoll, New York 10545

Copyright © 1994 by Ched Myers
Published by Orbis Books, Maryknoll, NY 10545
Manufactured in the United States of America

Acknowledgments:

"On Your Shore," on p. 372, by Enya: Lyrics by Roma Ryan, SBK Songs Ltd., Dublin, 1989.

Grateful acknowledgment is made to the following for permission to quote from previously published material: Ecumenical Program on Central America and the Caribbean for "Revelation" by Julia Esquivel; West End Press for "Chumash Man" by Georgiana Sanchez; for lines from "On the Pulse of the Morning" by Maya Angelou, copyright © 1993 by Maya Angelou, reprinted by permission of Random House, Inc.

Library of Congress Cataloging-in-Publication Data

Myers, Ched.
    Who will roll away the stone? : discipleship queries for First
World Christians / Ched Myers.
      p. cm.
    Includes bibliographical references and index.
    ISBN 0-88344-947-1 (paper)
    1. Christian life—1960– 2. Church and social problems.
3. Liberation theology. 4. Bible. N.T. Mark—Criticism,
interpretation, etc. I. Title.
BV4501.2.M94   1994
270′.09172′2—dc20
                               94-4445
                                CIP

To my father, who never impeded my questioning.

I wish you would not have left so soon
when all I had were questions.
My heart still reaches out to yours,
scattered in the waters I love.
I will try to tend what is left,
golden poppies and oak trees, my inheritance.

I feel almost unbearable anguish when faced by the fact that only the word recovered from history should be left to us as the power for stemming disaster. Yet only the word in its weakness can associate the majority of people in the revolutionary inversion of inevitable violence into convivial reconstruction.

Ivan Illich, *Tools for Conviviality*

Contents

Part One
CONTEXT

Part Two
DENIAL

Part Three
DECONSTRUCTION

Part Four
RECONSTRUCTION

Part Five
REFLECTION

Acknowledgments

The final stage of this project, proofing the copyedited manuscript, was delayed by the wildfires of late October/early November 1993, which in a week burned almost two hundred thousand acres of southern California and destroyed more than a thousand structures. I joined many other community volunteers to try to help with evacuation and consolation in north Altadena and south Laguna. It was difficult to see places I love burning again. Then, while the flames were still spreading, six boys aged thirteen and fourteen were gunned down in Northwest Pasadena, where I work with the American Friends Service Committee. We scrambled to organize a response to that tragedy as well.

I mention this because such "interruptions" have been more the rule than the exception during the writing of this book. The process over the past three years has been anything but contemplative: I have had to set this project aside for the Gulf War, my father's sudden death, and the Los Angeles uprising and its long series of legal epilogues. My theological reflection has been deeply impacted by these events. But perhaps that is appropriate given my conviction that theology should not be detached from context and history.

These essays also reflect fifteen years of work within the radical Christian movement of the First World, our heartbreaks and failures as well as our experiments with the gospel. This circle of people are family to me, and I hope I have done our story some justice here. My perspective has also been shaped by countless other local, regional, national, and international retreat groups, communities, churches, and organizations committed to the work of justice and peace. First on the list would be my colleagues in the AFSC locally and around the country, and particularly the community folk we work with in Northwest Pasadena. Friends in the East Los Angeles Theological Reflection group and many others around town have also helped along the way, as has my family. Others who have contributed specific ideas, references and/or constructive criticisms to this book, often without knowing it, include: Dan Berrigan, David Bremer, Vince Cobb, Danny Collum, Steve Commins, Jim and Pat Corbett, Jeff Dietrich, Jim and Shelly Douglass, Tricia Farris, Bruce Frederick, Douglas Hall, John and Carol Hirt, Wes Howard-Brook, Neil and Denise Jacobsen, Bill Kellermann, Mike Kennedy, Ross and Gloria Kinsler, Lisa Kiser, Karen Lattea, Sandy Lejeune, Joe Lynch, Jim McClendon, Charlotte Myers, Paul Ojibway, Glenn Omatsu, Ciaron O'Reilly, Jonathan Parfrey, Ardath Platte, Marlee Powell, Frank Rogers, Richard Rohr, Julie Salvorsen, Richard Shaull, Ladon Sheats, Pat Simmons, Sandra Stevenson, Mark K. Taylor, Stuart Taylor, Marsha Timmel, George Tinker, Orlando Tizon, Leonardo Vilchis, Louis Vitale, Jim Wallis, and Jeanie Wylie. Thank you each, and the many others not mentioned. I am grateful to Robert Ellsberg, editor in chief at Orbis Books, for his patience, and Holly Elliott for her fine job editing the manuscript. The love and support offered by Robbie Diaz Brinton over several long years of labor is woven into these pages.

The title of this book is taken from the last question uttered by Jesus' disciples in Mark (16:3). I hope these chapters reflect the honest anguish and stubborn hope of that Markan moment of truth. We typically seek to hurry past such moments, anxious to construct less ambiguous ideological scaffolding. There is, however, for Christians, no other ground on which to stand than the rocky, uneven soil of assayed faith. A theology and practice of radical discipleship must be about honest self-examination, as befits repentance, and clear-eyed assessments about our world, as required for resistance and reconstruction. I am all too aware that this is a long and in some ways complex book that demands a lot of the reader. Several people advised me against making this entire argument at once, fearing it might be too overwhelming or imposing. I nevertheless stayed with my original intent to survey the landscape, and to offer what I hope can be a resource to those who are struggling with the issues and questions I have tried to grapple with here.

This book is at its core a theology of repentance because that is the central theme of Mark's story of Jesus. But in the biblical tradition, the demand for change arises from compassion, not contempt. *Jesus looked at the rich man and loved him* (10:21). It is my conviction that we of the First World must come to terms with the social architecture of our privilege and our legacy as oppressors. This does *not* mean I believe our story as a people is a seamless tale of duplicity and betrayal, however. Demonizing is, after all, merely the flip side of idealizing. In fact there is much to be redeemed and preserved from the social ideas, experiments, and institutions of European America. The invitation to "turn around" assumes there is something important and precious we have left behind. It is an invitation to deconstruct what is wrong about our way of life and to reconstruct one that is more characterized by justice and dignity.

"It's a funny thing," wrote Zora Neale Hurston in *Moses, Man of the Mountain,* "the less people have to live for, the less nerve they have to risk losing — nothing" (1984:17). I believe there is much to live for and much to lose in our struggle against the imperial Dream. There are subversive memories to be recovered; dissonant notes to sound against the orchestrated anthems of the dominant culture; multicultural treasures to celebrate; common folk to cherish. I would not want to live in a world without baseball and Magic Johnson, stand-up comedy and Max Fleischer animation, street rappers and Ursula LeGuin, straight-ahead jazz and Flaco Jimenez, gumbo and flapjacks. I long for the redemption of the world, but more specifically for the places I call home: *Los Angeles,* city of my birth, which though oppressed by the hucksters of overdevelopment and quick profit and scorched by the fires of rage erupting from the nightmare of empire, yet holds my affection; *California,* where five generations of my ancestors have lived, from the Sea of Cortez to the Trinity Alps a place of unmatchable beauty and unfathomable betrayal; *Aztlán,* the ancient name of the American Southwest, the place wherein my bioregional loyalties lie, a wilderness of mystical power that invites us to the vision quest; and *Turtle Island,* a great land which patiently offers hospitality to the United States, a country still haunted by its own ideals of "liberty and justice for all" and the unrealized promise of *nuestra* America. My love for this world and for Mark's Word join in the circle of Story to which I am devoted as a disciple-reader. May what follows help the church to continue the narrative of biblical radicalism.

Los Angeles, All Saints Sunday, 1993

[handwritten margin note: Read: "Appalachia". Read: Midwest]

Introduction

I will tell you something about stories,
[he said]
They aren't just entertainment.
Don't be fooled.
They are all we have, you see,
all we have to fight off illness and death.

You don't have anything
if you don't have stories.

Their evil is mighty
but it can't stand up to our stories.
So they try to destroy the stories
let the stories be confused or forgotten.
They would like that
They would be happy
Because we would be defenseless then...

Leslie Marmon Silko
Ceremony

And Gabriel said to me...
"Consider the word and understand the vision..."
Daniel 9:23

A. PROLOGUE

Third Sunday after Pentecost (Father's Day), 1993
Los Angeles

I open this circle of Story with a story. Last night Jonathan, Robbie, and I stayed up late talking about the matters that concern this book, quietly celebrating its long-overdue completion. The first subtropical front of the summer moved in during the night; the morning breaks bright and muggy. It is already warm and clear under a thin canopy of high clouds as we begin driving toward the Angeles National Forest in the San Gabriel Mountains. In less than an hour we are heading down a trail crisscrossing the east fork of the San Gabriel River, still swollen from the heavy rains of late winter. Around us is a cacophony of blooming yucca and sage, oak and sycamore trees clinging to the river bank, bleached arroyo stones below, and circling hawks above. Our communion is disturbed only by the occasional weekend prospector, swigging beer and intently panning for the gold they believe has been dislodged by the rains.

As we walk Jonathan explains the story of this place. It seems that during the Great Depression the state of California had a grandiose dream of connecting the rapidly suburbanizing San Gabriel Valley with the high desert to the east by building a highway up this normally dry river canyon. Subsidized by the old Federal Works Progress Administration, construction was completed all the way up to the base of nine thousand–foot mountains, a beautiful arched bridge spanning the last gorge. The next step was to build the highway over Blue Ridge, but it never commenced. In 1938 a massive flash-flood wiped out the highway, and the project was abandoned. Today the Progressive-era bridge stands alone, a road to nowhere in the heart of the magical San Gabriel wilderness (J. Robinson, 1991:234ff).

San Gabriel. According to ancient apocalyptic tradition, Gabriel was the angel who explained the meaning of history to those trying to resist empire (Dan 8:15ff; Lk 1:11ff).

At noon we stop under a magnificent old oak, seven great branches spreading from its trunk in the Four Directions. Among acorns, in dappled sunlight, we sit, awed by the power of this grandmother oak, this *roble santo*. It represents the spirit and strength of this canyon, which, though barely thirty miles from a world Metropolis, has survived the assault of Progress. My heart burns with gratitude, and I offer silent prayers to San Gabriel that this river canyon might forever be spared from the imperial follies of big construction and little gold fever.

I lay my head upon an arroyo stone and think of Jacob's dream of angels (below, 13,C). *Surely God is in this place and I did not know it!* (Gen 28:16). I take the stone and fashion a simple altar at the base of grandmother's trunk. *This stone which I have set up for an altar shall be God's house* (28:22). I gaze for a long moment at the sycamore reaching across the river, almost touching grandmother oak. Jacob was right, I muse. *This is the gate of heaven*...

B. STORY, THEOLOGY, DISCIPLESHIP

This book is the promised sequel to *Binding the Strong Man: A Political Reading of Mark's Story of Jesus* (1988:xxvii, 450), another attempt to "understand the vision by considering the Word." Maintaining vision is no simple task for those of us who dwell at the heart of the *locus imperii* ("situation of empire"; ibid:6f) in the last decade of the twentieth century (below, 2,A). It is difficult for many reasons, but I believe Native American author Leslie Silko has given us the most fundamental one in the oracle that opens her acclaimed novel *Ceremony*. Though not written for or about the church, we Christians would do well to heed its wisdom.

Stories, Silko's elder says, *are all we have to fight off illness and death.* Christians find such Stories in scripture — what I call the narrative of biblical radicalism. The problem is, the North American church has *been fooled* into thinking our Stories are *just entertainment,* or it *has forgotten* them altogether. At the same time we have been seduced by stories spun by the imperial Dream: the official narratives of the National Security Council and the six o'clock news, the fabulations of Madison Avenue and Hollywood. These tales promise prosperity, power, and prestige, but deliver only captivity. Worst of all, we Christians have confused our Stories with the narrative of empire, thus allowing scripture to be expropriated into the service of oppression. Pablo Richard, a Latin American theologian, underscores this betrayal by citing an open letter sent by a delegation of indigenous peoples organizations to the pope on a recent visit to Peru:

> John-Paul II, we, Andean and American Indians, have decided to take advantage of your visit to return to you your Bible, since in five centuries it has not given us love, peace or justice. Please, take back your Bible and give it back to our oppressors, because they need its moral teachings more than we do. . . . The Bible came to us as part of the imposed colonial transformation. It was the ideological weapon of this colonialist assault. The Spanish sword which attacked and murdered the bodies of Indians by day at night became the cross which attacked the Indian soul. (1991:66)

This is the judgment of history: When the church allows the narrative of the cross to be *destroyed* by the narrative of the sword, we become *defenseless* against the spirituality of empire and consequently complicit with its *mighty* evils.

Richard insists, however, that the challenge for Christians today is "not to *give back* the Bible, but to *make it our own*" (ibid). I agree. Despite our painful legacy of apostasy, it remains the case that imperial evil *can't stand up to our Stories.* The fact that the Bible is still read in our churches makes it at least possible for them to be places where we who are members of the dominant culture can find the courage to face our illusions of noble innocence and learn how to live responsibly, places where the Dream can be unmasked and the vision reclaimed. Indeed I would contend that churches are among the last genuinely popular spaces left in North America where, as Cornel West puts it, we can engage the "public conversation" with nonmarket values (Clayton, 1993). My hope lies in the fact that throughout the history of the church, whenever the Stories have been taken seriously Christians have been animated to repent, to resist evil, and to help reconstruct a more humane world.

Bible study alone is not enough, of course. In their fine study *Reading in Communion: Scripture and Ethics in Christian Life,* Stephen Fowl and Gregory

Jones write: "For Christians, interpreting Scripture is a difficult task... not because one has to be a specialist in the archaeology of the ancient Near East, an expert in linguistics, or a scholar of the literature of the Greco-Roman world... [but] because it is, and involves, a life long process of learning to become a wise reader of Scripture capable of embodying that reading in life" (1991:29). This volume addresses the task of embodying my reading of Mark's gospel. While I hope these essays stand on their own merit, they are predicated upon *Binding the Strong Man* (hereinafter referred to as *BSM*), to which I will often allude. There my aim was to interpret the text of Mark's story of discipleship through the lens of my world and Christian practice. The necessary second part of the project is to interpret the interpretation — the inverse, and more demanding, task of reflecting on contemporary Christian practice in the First World through the lens of Mark. I offer this book then in the spirit of the ancient Jewish tradition of midrash; as Jacob Neusner puts it, "Everyday life forms a commentary on revealed Scripture... and Scripture... provides a commentary on everyday life; life flows in both directions" (1990:141).

Whereas *BSM* was an exercise in *exegesis,* this is an exercise in *theology.* Now theology, wrote Walter Benjamin earlier in this century, has become like a troll, which though wise is "small and ugly, not risking itself to be seen in public" (Lamb, 1980:188). The days are indeed long past when theology was royalty in the court of critical disciplines, a fact that cuts two ways. On the one hand, theological discourse has been relieved of the untenable burden of presuming *always* to speak universally and comprehensively. On the other, many contemporary theologians, unsure of their role in secular postmodernity, are clearer about what theology can no longer claim to do than about what its task might legitimately be. Fortunately for me, what little theological method I know I learned from James W. McClendon, Jr., who does understand how the task is both legitimate and important. McClendon has taught me that theology has four essential characteristics, each of which this book tries to reflect (see his *Ethics,* 1986:36ff; on postmodern theological method see also M. Taylor, 1990:23ff).

Theology is pluralistic. With analytic precision McClendon defines theology as "the discovery, understanding, and transformation of the convictions of a convictional community, including the discovery and critical revision of their relation to one another and to whatever else there is" (ibid:23). Convictions here are understood literally as *what one lives by* ("a persistent belief... [that] cannot be relinquished without making X a significantly different person [or community] than before"). This definition brings theology from perceived irrelevance back to the center of modern life, since everyone lives by certain values (however unacknowledged) and participates in communities of conviction (for example, a church, a political party, a PTA, a peasant union, a relief organization, a Pueblo kiva society, a corporate board of directors, a black student union). I speak from and to the determinate constituency of the Christian church. More specifically, I address convictional communities within the church who are struggling with the concrete problems and prospects of radical discipleship in the *locus imperii.*

I am well aware that the rubric "radical discipleship" rings dissonantly on both counts, which is in part why I persist in using it. *Radical* is a term as unfashionable today as it was trendy in the 1960s, but its etymology (from the Latin *radix,* "root") is the best reason not to concede it to nostalgia. As Gore Vidal says, "If you want to get to the root of anything you must be radical. It is no accident that the word has now been totally demonized by our masters, and no one in politics dares even to use the word favorably, much less track any problem to its root" (1992:54).

I am concerned both with *exposing* the roots of our socio-political and historical pathologies in the First World and *recovering* the roots of our discipleship tradition. In the gospels, discipleship (in English related to *discipline,* another decidedly unpopular notion today) connotes the journey of learning or, in the peripatetic rabbinic tradition, being a "follower" (Segovia, 1985). In the world of narcissistic capitalism, few wish to be disciplined followers (Lasch, 1979). But our autonomous individualism is illusory: "We're all disciples of something," says Atallah Shabazz, echoing her father, Malcolm X (Christon, 1992:84). To the extent we are not consciously pursuing alternative disciplines we are being socially and spiritually formed by the dominant culture. Seeking roots requires discipline, and sustaining discipline requires rootedness — that is why I stubbornly continue to use the term *radical discipleship* to describe the ideology of the faith communities with whom I identify and work.

"Radical Christian discipleship" is a strongly delimiting notion; it is not, however, meant to be an exclusionary one. I recognize that the convictional community I am in conversation with here is one among many; pluralism is a central fact of our social existence and should be affirmed and nurtured by the church (below, Chapter Ten). Theology, notes McClendon, is also the "means by which those of one community encounter those of other communities . . . for mutual witness and critical correction" (ibid:36). Sometimes that encounter is a polite dialogue, sometimes a fierce war of myths contesting for hearts and minds. It is the intent of this book to maintain the utmost respectfulness toward other communities within and outside the Christian tradition even as I offer witness and criticism from my own.

Theology is narrative-based. Our convictions are shaped by high fictions, popular storytelling, and the plots of our own life-experience, from the grand public tale of Manifest Destiny to the smallest, most private memory of childhood. Contemporary theology's method of working from within specific narrative traditions is sometimes called correlation (see M. Taylor, 1990:24ff). Christians correlate their experience to the Bible, but this is a stumbling block, warns McClendon:

> The church's story will not interpret the world to the world's satisfaction. Hence there is a temptation (no weaker word will do) for the church to deny her "counter, original, spare, strange" starting point in Abraham and Jesus and to give instead a self-account or theology that will seem true to the world on the world's own present terms. Surely, it will be said, the

salvation of the world must rest on some better foundation than tales about
an ancient nomad and stories of a Jewish healer? (1986:17)

Silko's elder, however, wisely reminds us that we depart from our stories at great
peril; Christian theology must abide by the fact that the narrative of biblical
radicalism "is not the world's accepted story" (McClendon).

My approach here is to correlate our experience of discipleship today with
Mark's narrative. *BSM* focused on how we read Mark's story; this sequel, on
how that story *reads us*. I mean this plainly. Mark's gospel has profoundly
shaped my character and continually leads me to reinterpret the text of my life.
I have, for example, structured this book in three major sections (Parts Two,
Three, and Four), which correlate to Mark's narrative strategy of three calls
to discipleship. This is in part because I have experienced these moments in
my own journey of discipleship. A Markan theology will not interpret North
America in a way pleasing to most North Americans; Christians whose political agenda centers around "keeping America strong" will not be pleased
either. This is just as Mark's Jesus said: "The strong have no need of a physician" (Mk 2:17). Only those who recognize the need for radical change in the
U.S. — understanding themselves and their society to be "sick and sinful" — will
take interest in Mark's narrative of repentance and discipleship. Similarly, those
trained in philosophical theology will no doubt find my approach too narrative-
based, as if innocent of the demands of logical argument. But I believe that
while logic can often persuade us to change what or how we think, only the
circle of Story has the power to transform *what we live by*.

Theology is rational. While theology is narrative-based, McClendon reminds
us that it must also strive to be a rational venture, accountable but not beholden
to other disciplines of inquiry (1986:39f). I prefer to refer to this as the *critical* and *careful* character of theology. Theology is careful not in the sense of
being timid so as to avoid offense, or discreet so as to evade possible heresy,
or equivocal so as to be acceptable, but in testing its own internal coherency
and its relation to competing discourses and claims. This distinguishes theology
from sheer ideological advocacy, ad hominem editorial commentary, or ad hoc
journalism, all of which enjoy considerably more poetic license. I have tried to
exercise care in this project, within the constraints of my life-situation. I do not
work from the site of academia, and I struggle to read and write amid the demands of social justice work, with little opportunity to immerse myself in the
ever-expanding literature concerning each of the many fields I venture into. I
am, in other words, a "layperson." Like Robert Bellah, I "acknowledge my amateur status as an Americanist, though not, I hope, as an *American*" (1975:vii),
and similarly my amateur status as a theologian, though not, I hope, as a member of a convictional community. The guild of professional theologians will
consider this work more homiletic than systematic; I am writing, however, to
or for not primarily them but communities that practice radical discipleship.

Theology also demands we reflect critically not only on the world but on
our own convictional tradition. McClendon thus likens theology to performing

surgery on living flesh. As Cornel West puts it, "Criticism is about discomfort —
it's unsettling, it's about being transgressive in the sense of calling what one has
assumed into question. America does not take well to that. Socrates said that
the unexamined life is not worth living. But we could say the examined life is
painful" (1993:M3).

Radical Christians involved in the work of justice and peace rarely take
enough time and space to engage in self-critique or analysis. Our movement
is notorious for allowing the demands of the political moment to dominate our
agenda, and we tend to do our work in isolation without seeing how things inter-
relate. This explains why contemporary radical Christians, like others belonging
to what McClendon calls the "baptist" tradition in general, have produced so
little theology (1986:20ff).

This book does not pretend to be a comprehensive articulation of the issues that concern us. It touches only briefly on such crucial matters as sexuality,
family, and the arts, for example. Nor does it offer an overall portrait of radical discipleship today. Indeed many of the essential arguments herein have
been made elsewhere in much more detail. I hope only to lay out some basic issues germane to our historical moment, which can be developed further
through ongoing reflection and refinement within our circles and, I hope, the
wider Christian community. It is a "political reading" of theology in the way
BSM was a political reading of Mark: It gives hermeneutical priority to the
actual relations of power in the world. I therefore tend to draw more on social-
scientific disciplines — such as political economy, social psychology, cultural
criticism, and history — than I do on traditional theological ones.

I do not imagine that I can suggest blueprints or formulaic answers for all
the problems I raise. The pedagogy of Jesus, and the difficult complexity of this
moment in which we straddle the millennia, make it far more appropriate to
try to present the reader with questions than answers (below, 2,C). To "speak
plainly," as Quakers would say, about the quandaries of discipleship today is
not bleak pessimism but open-eyed realism, the true basis of hope. Thus I offer partly a controversy with dominant culture theology, partly what Catholic
Workers call an exercise in "clarification of thought," and partly a debate with
my own community of conviction about where we go from here.

Theology is self-involving. Individuals and communities are formed in national, cultural, class, race, and gender contexts, which influence and to some
extent determine what and how we see, think, and act. Theological discourse
cannot pretend to be neutral, as if it were "above" these contexts — though
it still sometimes does. "In convictional work self-involvement is natural
and appropriate, while disengagement requires to be explained" (McClendon,
1986:33). Theologies of liberation have sharpened this mandate: They understand theology to be critical reflection on the *practice* in which a community is
already engaged (see Gutiérrez, 1973; Ferm, 1986b:17f). Practice here means
more than any community's experience; it denotes the specific historical struggle of the oppressed and their allies to humanize their lives. Christian theology
is committed theology, and I trust my own alliances will be clear throughout.

Finally, I have tried to be explicit about my own social location of dominant cultural privilege and my struggle for dis-location (below, 2,A). The questions I raise are in every case directed first to *my* practice, which is why I have felt free to draw from my own situation: Desert Storm and the Los Angeles uprising, my family history and my work with the American Friends Service Committee, moments of revelation in the Pacific islands and in the San Gabriel wilderness. But this is a methodological commitment as well: I argue that in order for our theology to be more contextual and literate we must learn to take the texts of our own lives at least as seriously as we do official narratives about the world (below, 3,D; 4,E; 5,D). Moreover I contend that reclamative theology must "re-place" itself on real land and within real cultural traditions (below, 11,A,E). Thus, while self-involved theology is not autobiography, it does exhibit a more specific character than the abstract discourse of classical theology. I believe this to be a good thing; communion in the church is predicated not upon conformity to disembodied doctrine but upon conversation between genuine embodiments of our common tradition in diverse contexts.

I hope what follows maintains the essential character of theology: proceeding from the modest but authentic perspective of a determinate community of faith and practice (*constituent*); interpreted in terms of the specific narrative tradition of Mark (*correlative*); respectful yet critical of both my own community and the dominant traditions (*careful*); and concrete in its understanding of my social location and our historical moment (*contextual*). Like all theology, it is a conversation in progress. Though there is a small body of literature exploring issues related to a contextual First World theology, I believe we are only beginning to formulate the questions and approaches appropriate to the demands and dilemmas of liberative practice within the dominant culture of the U.S. There is plenty of room and reason to continue inquiring into the meaning of the narrative of radical discipleship for the *locus imperii*.[1]

C. A SYNOPSIS OF THIS BOOK

Each chapter explores a discipleship query that is developed along the lines of a correlate theme. These parts contribute to the overall architecture of the book, though seeing the whole may require more than one reading. I am aware that such a long book presents difficulties for many readers and can be intimidating. I encourage readers to reflect together in small groups on discrete sections of this book, feeling free to pick and choose. Though there are no "suggestions for discussion" at the end of each chapter, it should not be difficult to relate the themes I work with to your own situation. I have used inclusive language throughout my text but yielded to Orbis policy not to change language in texts I cite.

Part One maps out my "site and strategy" for doing theology. **Chapter One** is a meditation on Peter's denial in the palace courtyard, which I propose as a major situative theme for First World theology. **Chapter Two** discusses my own social location and dis-location with the *locus imperii* and notes the challenges by theologies of liberation and the recent *Kairos* documents to traditions of the Metropolitan center. In considering whether the theological discourse of confession is appropriate to our moment, I look at Mark's portrait of Jesus as Interlocuter. I then examine the traditions of Critical Theory and the Quaker tradition of "Queries, Advices, and Testimonies" in order to explore the prospects for an "interrogatory" theology.

Part Two is the first of three major sections (each containing three chapters) that explore respectively the "three calls to discipleship." Jesus first calls us to repent, to see reality as it is and change it. The fact that concerned and capable First World Christians — who are politically free, socially mobile, and information- and resource-rich — typically feel unable or unwilling to struggle for social change is symptomatic of denial, understood both in the ancient and modern sense. According to the gospel story, our avoidance of the *via crucis* is a denial of the Human One. According to contemporary psychotherapy, our refusal to face the truth about ourselves and our history leaves us stuck in destructive and addictive patterns. The chapters in this section attempt to diagnose (literally, "to discern") the three Markan symptoms of denial, or what traditional theology calls *Sin* — blindness, deafness, and hardness of heart — through a recent historical "text." They suggest in turn a reinterpretation of three traditional Christian disciplines that can help us confront and overcome our problems of perception.

Chapter Three, "Have You Never Read?...?", examines the pervasive sense among First World Christians that the causes of oppression are too complex to understand and therefore to engage. I use the text of the 1992 Los Angeles uprising to illustrate barriers to "seeing," such as our dependence upon "mediated" reality and our confusion about the war of myths in a world of sophisticated sign-systems. These dominant cultural discourses mystify vast globalized social, economic, and ideological systems (as Bob Dylan put it, "the face of the executioner is well hidden"); but Marx reminds us that these systems were humanly constructed and can be analyzed, understood, and changed. This, however, requires a popular pedagogy that uses our practical knowledge of the world and empowers us to identify contradictions and to act for transformation. The church's practice of Bible study is our best vehicle for developing disciplines of "critical literacy."

Chapter Four, "Why Could We Not Cast It Out?" moves from *objective* conditions to *subjective* ones. Using the text of the 1991 Gulf War and the dynamics of political silencing that resulted, I illustrate how we carry within us a repressed consciousness of the human oppression that predicates our dominant culture entitlement. Unresolved guilt and internalized social anxieties reside in our "political unconscious" as shame, as we internalize the imperial culture's cycles of grandiosity and depression and its remarkable susceptibility to self-delusion. "Conscientized" activists are not free from these pathological symptoms; as the African American proverb puts it, "It is easier to get the people out of Egypt than to get Egypt out of the people." Liberation from this repetitive-compulsive cycle of socially introjected and militarily projected violence requires that we integrate the insights of political and therapeutic analysis. I then suggest an interpretation of prayer as the discipline of "dis-illusionment."

Chapter Five, "Do You Not Remember?" explores the third basic form of denial: our intergenerational suppression of history. Freud's psychological dictum ("What is unconscious is bound to be repeated") here becomes Santayana's "Those who do not learn from history are doomed to repeat it." I reflect on the text of the 1992 Columbus Quincentenary as an invitation to understand how the stories of the oppressed have been dismembered and devised by the dominant culture. Our hearts can be unhardened only through remembering and revising history and its traumas. The church in the *locus imperii* must follow Jesus in undertaking a vision quest to find out where and how we have gone wrong as a people. Our practice of liturgy-as-memory can help pave the way for a theology and politics of reparation and healing.

Part Three addresses the second stage of the discipleship journey: the move from denial to response-ability, from social location to dis-location, in order to deconstruct the systems that hold us captive.[2] Referred to as conversion by traditional theology, this call is predicated upon the judgment that our life-constructs are fundamentally flawed when measured against the kingdom of God. The dominant ideology, however, would persuade us that real change is impossible, and it demands conformity to economic and political imperatives while encouraging all manner of private distractions. The three chapters of this section discuss repentance as individual and collective "dis-continuity." This involves concrete practices that seek to break the addictions of entitlement, to defy the social architecture of division, and to resist the imperial culture of violence. These practices are illustrated with texts from the First World radical discipleship movement — our experiments with strategies of economic repentance, social relocation, and nonviolent politics — which are then critically assessed.

Chapter Six, "Who Then Can Be Saved?" begins by inquiring how and why the First World church has abandoned the discourse of the kingdom of God, or what I will call (following Wendell Berry) the Great Economy. I conclude this has to do with the seductions and illusions of capitalist culture for those privileged within it. Like the rich man in Mark's story, our entitlement is an addiction — we cannot imagine life without it. Its power (both as a social fact and a form of "false consciousness") can be broken only through the long-term struggle of recovery, which must be sustained through "spiritual disciplines of dis-continuous lifestyle." I then examine the way our experiments with alternative Christian community have been constrained by class- and race-based assumptions, which limit their usefulness in the wider struggle for political change. I conclude with a reflection on repentance as the concrete practice of redistributive reparation.

Chapter Seven, "Do You See These Great Structures?" looks at the greatest barrier preventing Palace Courtyard Christians from taking the "option for the poor": our structural insulation from the real lives of those who are oppressed. Social and ideological architecture keeps the disenfranchised invisible — whether in the Horn of Africa or around the corner — and prevents us from experiencing compassion and acting in solidarity. This geography of isolation also functions to keep potentially kindred groups "divided and conquered." The gospel invites us to become gender, race and class defectors in the struggle to "tear down the walls of our own House." First World Christians have experimented with strategies of social relocation, or "ap-proximation" to the oppressed, through exposure programs, especially to Third World countries where liberation movements are underway. But insofar as we have responded to injustice only in direct proportion to its distance from our own neighborhood, our solidarity politics are too exotic, and we must bring them home.

Chapter Eight, "What Will Be the Sign?" identifies the central sociopolitical characteristic of the *locus imperii* as domination and its central ethos (following Walter Wink) as the myth of redemptive violence. Sensing the bankruptcy of the political orthodoxy of violence as a means for social change in a world of escalating militarism, the radical discipleship movement has committed itself to nonviolent practices. Inspired by the apocalyptic understanding of the cross, we have experimented with what Gandhi called *satyagraha* and the "somatic politics" of symbolic direct action. But our nonviolence is still politically marginalized; we need to examine the degree to which our practices may be sectarian, precluding broader alliances that could lead to a genuinely subversive and militant peace and justice movement in the U.S. and abroad.

Part Four examines the third call to discipleship, which pits Jesus' vision of a "house for all peoples" against the reality of a house built upon privilege and profit. Traditional theology calls this redemption or sanctification. In many ways the greatest challenge facing radicals is to move beyond negation to the practical exploration of alternatives, not only naming Babylon but invoking the New Jerusalem. This section looks at how the church can participate in the struggle for a world more characterized by politico-economic and socio-ecological justice, self-determination, and reclamation of identity based on cultural and geographic re-place-ment. Each chapter then suggests a theological theme that arises out of the work of reconstruction.

Chapter Nine, "Who Are My Kin?" takes up the challenges of embodying the church as a "redeemed community" in a world of persistent gender, race, and class oppression. True solidarity demands that Christians move from charity and paternalism to role-specific partnership with women, people of color, and the poor in their struggles for empowerment. But the church must never lose sight of its special vocation to stand also with those who never receive public attention — the sick, the "unacceptable" outcast, and the forgotten. We need to develop a *minjung* theology for North America.

Chapter Ten, "Why Don't Your Disciples Live according to Tradition?" considers the vocation of the church to be truly "ecumenical" in light of changing demographics resulting from the forces of global capitalism. The rising tide of exploitation and scapegoating of new immigrants should be a key issue of solidarity with the "outsider," particularly given our own immigrant pasts. In postmodern societies, the pull from above toward technocratic monism battles the push from below for cultural pluralism. By repudiating its old fear of pluralism, the church can work to heal its own internal divisions through unity in diversity even as it advocates for a multicultural justice in the body politic. For the richness of genuine cultural diversity represents the Promise of *nuestra* America.

Chapter Eleven, "How Shall We Describe the Great Economy?" argues that our displacement and alienation from the land and our own cultural roots impoverishes the church's symbolic life, stunts our political imagination, and leads to environmental destruction. What are the prospects for "re-grounding" the church in local knowledge and culture and in a beloved land? I suggest that Christians should advocate revisioning economics within the limits of the land; should recover the biblical wisdom of "retribalizing" society through the anarchistic demand to decentralize power and decision making; and should support a more fundamentally bioregional politics of self-determination. I close with a hymn to theological re-place-ment in the Pacific Southwest.

Part Five offers reflections on what traditional theology calls eschatological hope and divine grace. Deconstruction and reconstruction are the work of generations. With our world balanced on the scales in so many ways, will history allow radical change, or will the explosive power inherent in our social contradictions cause us to self-destruct?

Chapter Twelve, "Are You Not Strong Enough to Stay Awake?" asks what it means to hope for historical redemption without the delusions of Progress, the unifying principle of modernity. Against the pendulum of imperial optimism and pessimism I propose the "bifocal vision" of apocalyptic faith as "staying awake" to the realities of history *and* the vision of the kingdom of God. The discipleship journey will take us deeper into the storms of our time, not away from them into the safe confines of religion. But it is there that we encounter Jesus and the true Lord of history.

Chapter Thirteen, "Who Will Roll Away the Stone?" concludes, like Mark, with a meditation adapted from a homily I delivered at the Great Vigil of Easter at St. John's Episcopal Church in 1992. It reflects on the final Markan quandary before Jesus' tomb — that moment in which we are terrified the discipleship narrative cannot be reopened yet equally uncertain whether we really want it to continue. I have chosen this quandary for the title of this book because Christians in the *locus imperii* are so often paralyzed before the formidable obstacles that impede us in our desire to follow Jesus. Apocalyptic faith invites us to "look again and see that the stone is rolled away," and to discover that the Jesus we abandoned in the palace courtyard is our faithful companion on the Way of radical discipleship.

NOTES

1. Among male European-American academics, the concerns of radical Christianity can be found in the work of, e.g., Jim McClendon, Robert McAfee Brown, and Douglas John Hall. Neill Hamilton (1981) deserves mention as an earlier effort to do a "synoptic reading" of Mark's gospel and the North American story. King, Maynard, and Woodyard

(1988) is a recent attempt to reflect theologically on the social aspects of Christian faith in the context of the dominant culture in the U.S. A number of dear friends who are similarly situated in the radical Christian movement have published important contributions, such as: Jim Douglass, Bill Kellermann, Jim Wallis, Jack Nelson-Pallmeyer, Jim McGinnis, Jim Corbett, Robert Aldridge, John Dear, Dan and Phil Berrigan, and Dick Shaull in the U.S.; Chris Tremewan and George Armstrong in New Zealand/Aotearoa; and in Australia, John Hirt's dissertation on radical discipleship in Mark and especially the work of the late Athol Gill. Their influence is evident throughout this book.

There are, thanks in no small measure to Orbis Books, numerous books by women and people of color articulating theologies of liberation within the U.S. A good sampling can be found in the recent collection edited by Peter-Raoul, Forcey, and Hunter (1990). One can find topical reflections by Third and First World Christian activists in the pages of *Sojourners, Christianity and Crisis, The National Catholic Reporter, The Witness, The Other Side, Catholic Worker* papers, and other periodicals of similar outlook.

2. I use the term "deconstruction" with some hesitation, because I do not want it to be confused with the current intellectual fad of deconstructionism. It seemed best, however, to engage the issue head on rather than avoiding it. Thus I use deconstruction to connote a political practice of repentance from, relocation in, and resistance to oppressive social structures. This seeks to re-politicize the term deconstruction, which in most academic circles is limited to a critique of discourse and social constructs at the level of superstructure. See below, Chapter Two, note 6.

Author and other volunteers tearing down rubble of burned out buildings in South
Central Los Angeles in the aftermath of the uprising, Saturday, May 2, 1992

Part One

Context

In the end, whether or not we will find a way to carry on with this story of biblical radicalism, this way of living and dying together, this way into a new heaven and earth, depends upon our understanding and acceptance of the tragedy and hope of our own failures. For it is there that our discipleship will either truly end or truly begin.

*BSM:*457

The interpretive work of Christian theology properly begins at the intersection of biblical and historical narrative. Reentering the Markan circle of Story where I left off in *BSM,* I imagine First World Christians standing with Peter in the Palace Courtyard, anguishing about denial. Chapter One offers this Markan theme as a beginning point for theology in the *locus imperium.* Chapter Two begins by elaborating my social location and dis-location and then confronts the challenge from the Third World church to the First in the recent *Kairos* documents. In a brief methodological consideration I then weigh the appropriateness of "confessional" discourse for our historical moment in light of Mark's portrait of Jesus as one who offers us hard questions instead of theological certainty. With help from the traditions of Critical Theory and Quaker "Testimonies, Advices, and Queries," I explore possibilities for recovering a more "interrogative" character for theological discourse.

1

Opening Meditation

"I Do Not Know What You Are Talking About!"

This we do know: Our cause is just; our cause is moral; our cause is right.

President George Bush, January 29, 1991,
State of the Union address during the Gulf War

People, I just want to say, can we all get along? Can we stop making it horrible for the older people and the kids?... We're all stuck here for awhile. Let's try to work it out.

Rodney Glen King, May 1, 1992,
press statement during Los Angeles uprising

In our America it is imperative to know the truth about the United States.

José Martí,
Patria, March 23, 1894

Peter had followed Jesus at a distance, right into the courtyard of the high priest (Mk 14:54). Twilight. The fisherman finds himself standing in the palace courtyard, of the Holy City, a very long way from home. It is the end of the line for him. Jesus has just been arrested by the Jerusalem authorities. His *compañeros* have fled for their lives. Peter, however, is trying to fulfill his vow to follow Jesus "to the end" (14:29). Having managed to slip into the courtyard he mingles incognito with armed security guards and expressionless functionaries. He is just outside the courtroom where Jesus is being arraigned, where he will shortly be charged and convicted of heresy and treason (are they not the same crime?). Near enough to hear Jesus' screams from the holding cell where he is being tortured during interrogation.

3

He was sitting with the guards, warming himself at their fire. With each howl of pain the veteran soldiers shake their heads. Peter winces, shivering. Shoulder to shoulder with them, the hood of his cloak obscuring his face, Peter tries to shake the chill. He stands, gazing into the coals. Numb with shock, terrified at this turn of events, he is uncertain what he is waiting for. We can only imagine the despair this villager from the north must feel at the fast and brutal descent of Metropolitan justice. What is he thinking? *The new order is dawning, he told us.* Tears well up, his stomach tightens. *And it has all come to this.* He wonders if he might be dreaming.

Dusk turns to deep night. The howls of pain from inside have stopped. A prevaricatory court has convened, and imperial justice is being dispensed. Like a drunk in a dark alley, history-as-usual stumbles forward, unaware that a corner is about to be turned.

"You too were with that Nazarene?!" (14:67). Suddenly, at the very moment Jesus is summarily condemned to the via crucis inside the palace, Peter's cover is blown outside in the courtyard. It is a servant to the high priest who recognizes him, no doubt from earlier Temple skirmishes. Peter is nailed, trying to do the next best thing to the via crucis. This is his moment of truth, and consequences, the one Jesus promised would sooner or later present itself to those invited to discipleship (8:34; 13:11; 14:37). He inches slowly backward toward the gate.

"I do *not* know what you are talking about!!" (14:68). Squeezed by conflicting loyalties in the imperial vise, Peter makes the fateful choice — he seeks refuge in the shadow world of Denial. To forfeit the truth about ourselves in order to save our asses: This is the deal the *locus imperii* teaches us to cut, the Faustian bargain Jesus warned us against (8:35f). Jesus understood perfectly the unforgiving psychological and political character of Denial: If we flee from the consequences of discipleship, it is into the arms of ignominy (8:38). And in the end, Peter's country drawl betrays what the flickering shadows had hidden. "A Galilean!" snort those around the fire; for them, guilt by association is enough to convict (14:70). Peter's desperate backpedal does not work. Unable to follow Jesus, neither can he pass as an innocent bystander.

And he began to curse his life (14:71). Who wouldn't curse their life at such a dead end? Curse religion, or politics, or history, or one's parents, or friends, or one's own choices — curse everything that conspires to bring us to such moments. Finally, cornered and cowering, Peter swears his oath of dissociation — the inevitable fruit of Denial. It is almost dawn. A rooster's hoarse croon drifts hauntingly in the sudden stillness. Then, slowly, like a stake being driven into his heart, Peter's soul begins to implode, and he breaks down in bitter weeping.

His inconsolable sobbing echoes through the ages, resonating whenever believers have betrayed the vision they held dearest. Throughout the two millennia of the "Christian era" it has continued to well up, as the church struggles with its own apostasy, our Trail of Tears. Today, in the waning years of the twentieth century, that bloodiest of epochs, in the twilight of a different imperial courtyard, this lament again lodges in our Christian hearts. In the *locus imperii* we too have tried to "follow Jesus at a distance." We too are being confronted by the ignominy of our conflicted loyalties. We too are realizing our Denial.

Here, in this moment, paralyzed and ashamed before *our* Wailing Wall, we are invited to "look again" to the narrative of biblical radicalism. This sacred circle of Story invites us to fight off the illness and death of Denial and to continue the journey of discipleship.

A. END OR BEGINNING?
FACING DENIAL IN THE COURTYARD TWILIGHT

I write from where I live and work: Los Angeles, California, U.S.A. My country exports war against the poor around the world, covertly from Nicaragua to Mozambique and overtly from Grenada to Iraq. My city built its prosperity manufacturing the military tools of that trade (see Didion, 1993). My country seeds a homegrown war against its own poor, from Miami to Watts and from the Rio Grande Valley to Akwesasne. My city cultivates the seeds of oppression every day at Florence and Normandie and Pico-Union — and has reaped the bitter fruit of its harvest twice in the last quarter century.

In other words, I live in a war zone, where violence is a way of life, a wildfire raging across the world and a tree smoldering steadily at its core. According to the dominant culture's Dream of itself, however, it is not a war zone at all. The official story portrays my country through fantasies of grandiosity: land of the free, home of the brave, hope of the democratic world. The Dream Factory portrays my city through fantasies of whimsy ("La-La-land," "Lifestyles of the Rich and Famous") and law and order (from "Dragnet" to "L.A. Law"). But I know differently. I know my country and city are each defined by two things: by a *gulf* and by *guns.*

The ever-deepening gulf between rich and poor is illustrated by two voices already cited, one belonging to George Bush, a man who abusively policed the world, the other belonging to Rodney King, a man who took a world of abuse from the police. They articulate the divergent perspectives on reality from either side of the gulf. Bush's proclamation from *above,* uttered while Iraq burned, envisions history as *conquest:* "Our cause is right." Rodney's question from *below,* offered while Los Angeles burned, suggests a vision of history as *conscience:* "Can we all get along?" The gulf represented by the distance between these two testimonies is in turn maintained and intensified by guns. The inexhaustible proliferation of guns is the inevitable legacy of a country founded upon the "freedom" to exploit upheld by the "right" to bear arms, at home and abroad (see Hull, 1993).

I live in a war zone, but unlike Rodney King, I can choose whether or not the cross fire affects me at all. People like me — inheritors of entitlement and gender, race, and class privilege — are not pulled over for erratic driving and beaten, *ever.* We rarely feel vertigo from the economic gulf, we are rarely disturbed by the pop of guns. The country's wars are not fought on our soil — their carnage is distant. The urban uprisings leave our houses untouched — their fires are over the hill. Above all, we can choose whether or not to tune in to such events. This is life in the *locus imperii,* and for those of us trying to be disciples in the lengthening shadows of its twilight, it is our moment of truth. To which voice will we pay attention? The gulf and the guns are what Bush believes to be "just and moral and right"; they are what King identifies as "making it horrible for the older people and the kids." These are choices of great consequence: to stay in the Dream, which obscures the way things really are, or to struggle for the Promise of what this country, this city, could be. We can, as Mark's gospel would put it, choose to "see" or "hear" or "understand" the factors that make wars and uprisings inevitable. Or we can live in Denial.

This is why the story of Peter in the palace courtyard "speaks to our condition," as Quakers would say. "The whole scene is indelibly fixed in the consciousness of the Western world," wrote C. G. Montefiore concerning this Markan story (Taylor, 1963:571f). Is this because the story of the U.S. is somehow *named* by this tragic biblical episode? Deep inside our national soul is the haunting sense that most of our high ideals have been betrayed by our historical practice. But this becomes clear only when our national story is interpreted not through Bush's lens of imperial arrogance but through the questioning lens of King. From the perspective of the poor, our history is a litany of noble intentions of justice subverted by self-serving ambitions, of professed democratic values sold out in the drive toward empire. Would that we as a people could heed the invitation of Guatemalan Julia Esquivel, in her poem "Revelation" (1993):

> The cry of the poor
> is clear water
> that rinses off our makeup;
> we can let the mask fall.
> The eyes of the poor
> are two mirrors,
> we need not be afraid
> to see ourselves there.

But we are unwilling to confront this truth about ourselves. Unable to bear the travesties of justice occurring in the Palace Courtroom, we, like Peter, have sought refuge in Denial out in the Palace Courtyard.

We are in Denial about our past. The 1992 Columbus Quincentenary (below, Chapter Five) reminded us that we have suppressed the dark subtext of exploitation lurking below each chapter of our story as a people. Our long imperial project of colonization and domination — which first reached across the Atlantic sea, then stretched from "sea to shining sea," and now has spread to the Seven Seas of the world — has left countless victims in its wake. In a Quincentenary interview Creek writer and poet Joy Harjo made the following diagnosis of our condition: "To name colonization is to recognize it, and to recognize it is a deeply painful thing for everyone involved. The psychic wound is deep in the land, in all of us in this land — both the colonized and the colonizer. . . . The denial in the colonial world is vast, so deep, so overwhelming, the stink is hiding the sun" (in Dunbar-Ortiz, 1990:20, 23). Such suggestions, however, enjoy no hospitality in the culture of domination. The ideological architects of empire forever endeavor to banish self-doubt with appeals to the primal myths upon which European-American identity has been constructed. In the seventeenth century these were myths of "discovery"; in the eighteenth century, nationhood; in the nineteenth century, Manifest Destiny; and in the twentieth century, the Manichaean struggle with communism. The continuing vitality of such imperial mythology is evident from its efficacy during the Reagan-Bush era.

To be sure, there have been prophetic European-American movements that called for repentance, but few were able to resist the myths and practices of domination for very long. Early on Great Awakening preachers such as Jonathan Edwards detected betrayal, complaining that ideals of a godly Commonwealth were slowly but surely giving way to the politics of greed (McClendon, 1986:113ff). But Puritan religion was no match for the Enlightenment faith of Adam Smith: The gold and silver produced by Spanish mines and the enterprising aggressiveness of the Hudson's Bay Co. proved more compelling than the moralistic visions of Jesuit or Methodist reformers. The possibilities of a pluralistic republic were eclipsed by the expansionist designs of nineteenth-century wars, and the hopes of huddled immigrant masses yearning to breathe free were betrayed by the imperatives of industrial robber baron profiteering. Today we still cannot name the sin of colonization and so cannot attend to its profound psychic wound.

We are in Denial about our present. Ours is perhaps the most indebted, stratified, and violent society in the world today. As the U.S. empire, unrivaled in its global reach and military strength, has come to full flower in the second half of the twentieth century, our duplicity has become increasingly evident. Evident, that is, to those viewing the world from the killing fields of Guatemala or Mozambique or East Timor, or from the housing projects of south Los Angeles ganglands or the refugee trails through Sonora borderlands or the health clinics in Lakota badlands. It is not as evident, however, to those of us who by reason of race, class, and/or gender are inheritors of the imperial system. And it is certainly not evident in our official narratives about ourselves — whether in religion, education, entertainment, mass media, or government — according to which the U.S. epitomizes the grand design of Progress, the engine driving history, the *Pax Americana.* Nevertheless the contradictions we strive so hard to mask are surfacing with a rapidity few could have imagined. Around the globe our government's support for dictators, its opposition to movements for self-determination, and its wars for control of resources make us cynical about our alleged national commitment to freedom and democracy, as made excruciatingly clear by the Gulf War. At home a persistent recessionary economy, deteriorating race relations, and growing class polarization destroys our hopes for socio-economic prosperity, as made equally plain by the Los Angeles uprising. And yet any suggestions of imperial hubris are ruthlessly dismissed in

Denial about our present

our public discourse. Has any people ever been as convinced of its own benev-
olence and innocence? This is the power of our culture of Denial. No wonder
psychologist-theologian M. Scott Peck (1983) has diagnosed us as "People of
the Lie."

The malaise at the heart of the *locus imperii* is deeper than the Vietnam
Syndrome so excoriated by Reagan and Bush. As the fissures in the imperial
edifice widen, exposing our illusions, they engender an unprecedented anxiety
and fear among us. These doubts have been reflected back to us by modern
iconoclasts such as novelist Ken Kesey, of whom Charles Bowden writes:

> Like George Bush, he is a prisoner of the '50s, a man struck by the order,
> dullness, dumbness, suicidal tendencies and pointlessness of mid-century
> America, the America of the empire, the America that was going to put its
> stamp on a century, the America with its arteries clogged with things and
> its soul left at some pawn shop along the way in order to raise the cash
> for guns.... He asks questions and can't give us answers. But he has these
> bothersome questions, the main one being: What are we going to do about
> this emptiness, this lack of dreams, ambitions, visions. We no longer have
> promises to keep, miles to go before we sleep, so we just content ourselves
> with meeting the mortgage payments on a continental empire we seem to
> have inherited.... We've still got this hollow feeling, this emptiness as
> we go slowly insane in our treasure house and putter around the mansion
> dusting off our large collection of things. Jesus, sometimes this feeling
> gets so bad we need a little war just to perk ourselves up. (1991:17)

So were North Americans perked up by Desert Storm, only to become again
discouraged almost immediately afterward about the economy (see below, 4,A).
We continue to ride a murderous roller coaster of manic-depression, unable to
awaken from the imperial Dream in the deepening twilight of the twentieth
century. "I do *not* know what you are talking about!" screamed Peter when
confronted with the truth about himself in the palace courtyard.

We are in Denial about our future. Perched as we are on the cusp of the
second and third millennia of the Christian era, we are presented with unprecedented opportunities to reckon with the truth about ourselves, to make different
choices, and to forge new beginnings. We are witnessing at least four significant
global shifts that unarguably represent major historical crossroads:

[margin annotation: Denial about the future]

· the collapse of bipolar East-West politics and realignment along North-South
lines;
· the replacement of nationalist economic strategies by regional trade blocs,
migratory capital, and the globalization of markets;
· the restructuring of U.S. militarism from strategic deterrence to low-intensity
interventionism;
· the growth of the environmental crisis from a peripheral concern of industrialized countries to a central international struggle.

To an entire generation these relatively sudden and dramatic shifts represent sea changes. If the fall of Saigon and the oil crisis were defining symbols for my generation in the 1970s, for young people today it is the fall of the Berlin Wall and the free trade crisis.

In the wake of these developments has come vigorous talk of a New World Order. Rather than reassessing their tradition of empire in order to explore new possibilities, however, U.S. leaders are busily resurrecting their old, pre–Cold War Dream of unrivaled power and global management. About this fact, if not about its desirability, commentators on the political left and right agree. Archconservative apologist Charles Krauthammer, for example, put the matter succinctly in his ringing endorsement of a 1992 Pentagon strategy paper: "It starts with the fact that this is a one-superpower world. It proceeds on the assumption that for us, for our friends and for our values this is a good thing. It then offers a program for keeping things that way" (1992:5). Senator Phil Gramm in turn offered this remarkable imperial skewing of a well-known biblical text in his speech to the 1992 Republican National Convention: "Even in a world where the lion and the lamb are about to lie down together, we Republicans are committed to the principle that the United States of America must always be the lion" (Gramm, 1992).

Council on Foreign Relations senior analyst Shafiqul Islam has a somewhat more sober assessment of this New World Order. The challenge now, he argues, is to "manage the breakdown of the postwar bipolar order and prevent the deadly fallout of a capitalist conflict from derailing the transition to a new multipolar world" (Silk, 1992). Columnist Daniel Singer goes further, warning that the world is now *more* dangerous: "Limited as it was, the threat of Russian retaliation was the only brake on the American-dominated expansion in the Third World, while current Soviet abdication in this sphere is the only real novelty in President Bush's otherwise very old order" (1992:31). And *Christianity and Crisis* writer Tom Kelly compares the determination of the elite "to compel all who can be compelled to conform their political economies to the slogans and nostrums of the Free Market" with the first European conquistadors who encountered a new world by seeking to dominate it:

> The pursuit of "comparative advantage" leads to the inevitable downward spiral of cheaper labor, shrinking markets, marginalized majorities, and a state of ungovernability in the poorer Two-thirds World — as the victorious system produces the "instability" it has installed as its new prime demon.... Once again, those who assert the power to define the dimensions of the new are so wedded to the old — institutionally, ideologically, rhetorically — that they can conceive of the new energies of a world freed from the struggle of superpowers only as a means of immortalizing their own "side" in the late, unlamented contest. (1992:403)

"Curious, isn't it," Kelly concludes, "how those who see themselves as making history so rarely seem to learn from it?"

Just when there was a chance to back down from the historical ultimatums of the East-West conflict, with its omnipresent threat of Mutual Assured Destruction, the architects of the New World Order began to follow a new recipe for Armageddon (see Peters, 1992). The weapons this time, according to Filipino political scientist Walden Bello (1992a) of the Institute for Food and Development Policy, are policies of North-South economic warfare. The U.S.-dominated World Bank has used "structural adjustment loans" to force struggling Third World countries to adopt austerity measures, which include "reducing the state's role in the economy, lowering barriers to imports, removing restrictions on foreign investment, eliminating subsidies for local industries, reducing spending for social welfare, cutting wages, devaluing currency, and emphasizing production for export rather than for local consumption" (Bello, 1992a:37). This has accelerated the global stratification of rich and poor: "Draconian policies of debt collection produced a staggering net transfer of financial resources — $155 billion — from the South to the North between 1984 and 1990" (ibid:36). And as the gulf widens the guns are re-deployed: U.S. military forces find new tasks in Somalia, in Latin American drug wars, and in domestic border enforcement.

As social, economic, and political conditions throughout the Third World have deteriorated, the predictable result has been massive human displacement. This is no abstract matter: The ever-increasing flow of undocumented immigrants has profoundly transformed the economy and socio-cultural face of Los Angeles and other North American cities. "Perhaps," writes Bello, "it is the migrants who most clearly perceive the truth about structural adjustment: it was intended not as a transition to prosperity but as a permanent condition of economic suffering to ensure that the South would never rise again to challenge the North" (ibid:38). But the grim prospect is that this could result in what a French official envisioned as "a war unlike any seen in modern times, [one that] will resemble the barbarian raids of the seventh and eighth centuries" (ibid:39). The ultimatum of the twenty-first century, concludes Bello, will be between solidarity with the victims of global economic warfare or permanent apocalypse.

The turning of the millennium is, then, truly a time of reckoning. Those who see no future for the *locus imperii* are increasingly polarized from those who see no future without it. Will our generation face Denial and struggle to bring the imperial Zeitgeist to an end, or will we join the imperial celebration of a new beginning to a very old world order? This is the quandary of Christians in the Palace Courtyard twilight.

B. "PETER BROKE DOWN AND WEPT":
JESUS, *ABANDONADO*

On May 1, 1992, the fires of the Los Angeles uprising had finally burned out as the National Guard occupied the streets of my city. On May 1, 1993, Boris Yeltsin's police beat back rioting Communist demonstrators in Moscow. One would have thought, remarked one Russian observer, one was in Los Angeles (C. Goldberg, 1993). Mayday, Mayday, indeed. Are we going down? Dread and uncertainty are awash in the "Brave New World Order" (Nelson-Pallmeyer, 1992).

It is doubt, however, that provides a wedge with which biblical theology can begin to work, argues Canadian theologian Douglass John Hall:

A dimension within North American historical experience to which the Christian community may turn for an entree in its attempt at contextualization . . . is the incipient disillusionment of a people which has given itself long and wholeheartedly to the modern illusion. In this hesitant but no longer dismissable skepticism and disbelief, perhaps a point of contact can be found for a gospel that dares to pronounce that real hope can begin where illusions end, and real life where death is tasted. (1989:44)

Will our churches help the people of the *locus imperii* confront disillusionment, or will we remain co-captives to the Denial, hedging our bets until it is too late to offer hope?

In such circumstances, Mark's circle of Story beckons our own. Peter, as the first (1:16) and last (16:7) disciple in the story, is archetypal: We are meant to identify with him. His life runs the gamut of human emotion, bouncing between grandiosity (14:29) and depression (14:37f). His story is ours. Given the benefit of the doubt, we love Jesus and have vowed, perhaps even stridently, to follow him. We have recognized him as Messiah — it is just that we don't understand what that really means. Of course, we First World Christians are more comfortable in the Palace Courtyard than Peter could ever have been. We participate obediently in its political mechanisms (and machinations). Presidents and military leaders sit in our churches. In the Courtyard we are proximate to Palace power, although perhaps we feel frustratingly impotent. If we listen hard enough, we can hear the screams of the victims of imperial justice; we know Jesus stands with them, but we can't seem to bridge the distance between us and him — or them. It is easier to enjoy the distractions of petit bourgeois pleasures, to retreat to the comfort of Palace Courtyard religion. And when the evening shadows of history chill us to the bone, we huddle around the fire tended by the imperial police — chagrined, yellow ribbons pinned to our lapels.

We may be well intentioned, but we are not innocent. Our true allegiances, which shape our social practice and determine our net worth and career aspirations, will sooner or later be revealed. Perhaps, as with Peter, it will be functionaries in service of the Palace Courtyard who unmask us; they always seem to have the best nose for our vulnerabilities and contradictions and are able to recognize the conflict in our souls by our trembling voice. We want to follow Jesus, but we also want to stay on good terms with the Palace. And so, often unwittingly, we end up betraying our own convictions about what is good and just and compassionate.

So it is that in the Courtrooms of empire, Jesus and all those who accompany the poor in their struggle for justice lose-and-therefore-gain their lives by embracing the via crucis (Mk 8:35). Mohandas Gandhi and Martin King, nineteenth-century Maori prophet Te Whiti and twentieth-century Palauan activist Alfonso Kabokal, the religious martyrs of El Salvador, and the secular martyrs of Matewan—these and countless others, named and unnamed, famous and forgotten, form a cloud of witnesses to the Passion piling up on the horizon of history, an epiphany of redemptive suffering we find too bright to behold (see Cassidy, 1991; Wallis and Hollyday, 1991; Sobrino and Ellacuría, 1990). Meanwhile, outside in the Courtyard, we gain-and-therefore-lose our lives by choosing to live in Denial. Unable to distinguish the emperor's voice from our Lord's, *we* become the "adulterous and sinful generation" that refuses to "see the Human One" revealed on the cross (8:38f). Jesus in turn becomes *el abandonado,* abandoned by a church that will believe in him only if he comes down off the cross (14:32). And when we realize the truth, we are ashamed.

"And Peter broke down and wept" (14:72). These are the most tragic words in the gospel. For our Denial of Jesus is in the end a Denial of our true selves. Those who internalize the colonial reality, wrote Frantz Fanon in *The Wretched of the Earth,* suffer a "systematic negation" of personhood: "Colonialism forces the people it dominates to ask themselves the question constantly: 'In reality, who am I?' The defensive attitudes created by this violent bringing together of the colonized man and the colonial system form themselves into a structure which then reveals the colonized personality" (1968:250). Denial is the consequence of colonization by the *locus imperii;* if we do not face it, our humanity, like that of imperial victims, will be eroded and ultimately erased.

A century ago Cuban patriot José Martí contended that the future of *our* America—the America that belongs not to the imperial Dream but to the Promise of liberty and justice for all—depended upon our ability to know the truth about the United States. Today his words could not be more to the point. For those citizens of imperial America who are Christians, the story of Peter's Denial in the Palace Courtyard best captures the dilemma of our discipleship in this historical moment. Dietrich Bonhoeffer knew something about such moments. In *The Cost of Discipleship,* penned during the dark days of the Third Reich, he admitted, "We are no longer sure that we are members of a Church which follows its Lord. . . . The issue can no longer be evaded. It is becoming clearer every day that the most urgent problem besetting our Church is this: How can we live the Christian life in the modern world?" (1959:60). The hard truth about our America confronts Christians with hard choices. Conscience or conquest? Solidarity or apocalypse? The Dream or the Promise? End or beginning?

Jesus and the victims of empire stand in the dock, *abandonados.* We tarry, anguished, warming ourselves by the imperial fire. What separates us is the gulf and the guns. Palace Courtyard functionaries are pressing us to reveal our allegiances. If we are identified with the Nazarene, two options remain: discipleship or Denial.

2

"I Will Ask You a Question"

Interrogatory Theology

The moral duty of the free writer is to begin his work at home: to be a critic of his own community, his own country, his own government, his own culture. . . . It [is] not merely heretical but treasonous to question our own government's policies, to doubt the glory of planetary capitalism, to object to the religion of endless economic growth, or to wonder about the ultimate purpose, value, and consequences of our techno-military-industrial empire. Those who persist in raising doubt and question are attacked by defenders of order as the "adversary culture." Very well: let us be adversaries.

Edward Abbey,
"A Writer's Credo"

The primary theological task of an indigenous theology in North America is to provide a frame of reference for the prolonged and intense experience of negation. We have concentrated on being an answering theology, and this is our undoing in an age when answers can have only a hollow ring. Now we must concentrate on providing a place to which to refer the questions.

Douglass John Hall,
"Towards an Indigenous Theology of the Cross"

"By what authority are you doing these things; and *who gave it to you?"* (11:28). At a crucial juncture in his mission, in another carefully staged Markan moment, Jesus was confronted by members of the ruling Jerusalem establishment, who demanded that he present his political credentials (*BSM*:306f). "These things" refer to Jesus' dramatic challenges to the scribal status quo: his

13

theatrical, militant march into the capital city, followed by his public disruption of commerce in the Temple (11:1–25). As far as the guardians of civic order were concerned, things had gone far enough. It was one thing for this Nazarene to have made a name for himself playing the prophet in distant provinces, quite another to create a protest spectacle in the city of David — especially during the feast days, that tension-ridden season in the nation's life when old symbols of liberation, uneasily latent, always threatened to erupt again. It was time to force this country preacher to divulge just what he was up to.

By what authority, and who gave it to you? In all times and places, this is the central challenge put by governments to dissidents. Those in power recognize no authority they have not defined, brokered, or mediated. Conversely, any who would contest their arrangement must justify themselves before the bench. It is the circular genius of State logic: There can be no protest except by permission. How will Jesus counter? He pauses, eyeing his antagonists. He understands that defending his practice is a losing proposition as long as they are framing the issue. Measuring his words carefully, he decides to go on the offensive.

"I will ask you one question; answer me, and I will answer you" (11:29). Here is Jesus' most powerful weapon, with which he lays siege to the citadel of self-referential authority: questions that drive a sharp wedge of inquiry into the cracks of the status quo in order to pry open its internal contradictions.

Where do you think John's authority came from? Jesus' opponents stiffen, gulp hard, huddling. The case of the recently martyred rebel prophet John is a delicate political matter indeed. They can hardly delegitimize the work of so popular a national hero; yet if they eulogize John, their own duplicity — as the administration that consented to his execution — will be unmasked (11:30–32). Jesus has, in effect, thrown the challenge back in their faces: *Tell me whose side you are on, and we'll talk.* The breeze shifts, and an awkward silence settles heavily over the scene.

"We do not know" (11:33).

Like all official spokespeople under pressure, they issue no comment, refusing either to confirm or deny. So Jesus shrugs, and walks. The moral of the story: If we want to know what Jesus stands for in the conflict-ridden world, we had better be prepared to be questioned by him about our own alignments.

A. "WARMING OURSELVES AT THEIR FIRE": SOCIAL LOCATION AND DIS-LOCATION

What are the basic characteristics of the social and political context in which I do theology?

This chapter examines my interpretive site and strategy for doing theology in the First World and defines some of the terms I use throughout this book. Readers less interested in theological method may find parts of the following sections too dense. If so, they are encouraged to move on to Chapter Three, where my argument begins.

My context remains *locus imperii,* the "space of empire" (*BSM:*6ff). I use this metaphor not for rhetorical flourish but in order to take sides in what Enrique Dussel calls "contested political space":

> Space as a battlefield . . . is very different from the abstract idealization of empty space of Newton's physics or the existential space of phenomenology. Abstract spaces are naive, nonconflictual unrealities. The space of a world within the ontological horizon is the space of a world center, of the organic, self-conscious state that brooks no contradiction — because it is an imperialist state. . . . I am speaking of political space, which includes all existentially real spaces within the parameters of an economic system in which power is exercised in tandem with military control. (1985:1f)

I believe that empire is determinative of our collective reality in the U.S., and that its primary characteristic is hegemonic capitalism.[1] It is not, however, a necessary, immutable, or divinely created human condition; quite the contrary, as a historical "production" it can — and in my opinion must — be deconstructed.

The "irreducible meaning" of empire is the "geopolitical control of the periphery by the center" (*BSM:*6). I have chosen to use the broad rubrics "First World" (representing the center) and "Third World" (representing the periphery) throughout this book to reflect this fundamental geopolitical tension.[2] More specifically, my site is that of the dominant culture of the United States, within which I am distinctly privileged by race, class, and gender inheritance.[3] In terms of the Markan metaphor introduced in the last chapter, the dominant culture is warmed and comforted by the hearth of an imperial fire intended for and tended by those loyal to the Palace Courtyard.

I am using the first person plural — *we warm ourselves* — not as a presumptive royal we, as if I speak for everyone, but rather to identify myself specifically as part of a determinate social group. This is what Mark Kline Taylor calls "the necessary and intersubjective act of hermeneutical self-implicature — necessary because no longer can we write books, in this view, without attending to the located selves entailed in the writing, and intersubjective because selves (contrary to much North American popular culture) are not just individual, discrete egos, but distinctive beings produced at the centers of various intersubjective dynamics" (1990:16). To put it more simply: *I* am not the subject of this book, but I am the *subject* who writes it, a subject with a social location and history that shapes the writing. Both I and the reader can and should take into account the particular perspectives, biases, and blindness that attend to this location.

The highly polarized public struggle over multiculturalism — trivialized by the ideological right and by the popular press as "political correctness" (Berman, 1992) — has ironically made it both easier *and* more difficult to be self-conscious about social location. It is easier because class, racial/ethnic, and gender identification is rightly expected as it becomes more widely accepted that such matters necessarily shape one's perspective. The presumption, for example, that a professional discursive community made up of predominantly white male theologians could speak for everyone in the church has, gratefully, been thoroughly discredited. It is more difficult, however, because identifying social location necessarily entails certain cultural, economic, and political generalizations that can easily degenerate into one-dimensional stereotypes or, worse, caricatures of one's own group or others. Nevertheless the task is a necessary one; theology, like other forms of public discourse, must come to terms with multicultural realities and the promise and problems of genuine social pluralism (see below, 10,A).

I am an educated, middle-class male of predominantly European-American origin, socialized within the dominant culture (below, 5,D). Defining the "middle class" in the U.S. is complicated, as has often been pointed out.[4] But the essential characteristic of this social location is what I will call "entitlement": a pervasive system, inherent to capitalism but also characteristic of other socioeconomic models, that enfranchises some and disenfranchises most others. In the U.S. it is constructed according to race, class, and gender privileges and structural advantages, all of which overlap and commingle. The mechanisms of dominant culture entitlement are so embedded within institutions and practices at every level of society that they are sometimes difficult to pin down, though they obviously seem more mysterious to the beneficiaries than to the disenfranchised (below, 7,B). Because it is supremely important that this term not be construed as a slippery abstraction, let me cite a recent attempt to characterize concretely the "taxonomy," assumptions, and ethos of entitlement.

Frustrated with men who would not face male privilege, feminist scholar Peggy McIntosh decided to try to identify some of the daily effects of white privilege. She writes: "I have come to see white privilege as an invisible package of unearned assets which I can count on cashing in each day, but about which I was 'meant' to remain oblivious. White privilege is like an invisible weightless knapsack of special provisions, maps, passports, codebooks, visas, clothes, tools and blank checks" (1989:10). Her list of special circumstances and conditions that obtain for this privilege includes the following examples:

- I can arrange to be in the company of people of my race most of the time;
- If I should need to move I can be pretty sure of renting or purchasing a dwelling in an area I can afford and in which I would want to live...;
- I can turn on the television or open to the front page of the paper and see people of my race widely represented;
- When I am told about our national heritage or about "civilization" I am shown that people of my color made it what it is;
- I can be sure that my children will be given curricular materials that testify to the existence of their race...;
- Whether I use checks, credit cards or cash I can count on my skin color not to work against the appearance of financial reliability...;
- I can swear, or dress in second hand clothes, or not answer letters, without having people attribute these choices to the bad morals, the poverty, or the illiteracy of my race...;

- I can do well in a challenging situation without being called a credit to my race;
- I am never asked to speak for all the people of my racial group;
- I can remain oblivious to the language and customs of persons of color who constitute the world's majority without feeling in my culture any penalty for such oblivion . . . ;
- I can go home from most meetings of the organizations I belong to feeling somewhat tied in, rather than isolated, out-of-place, outnumbered, unheard, held at a distance, or feared . . . ;
- I can take a job with an affirmative action employer without having coworkers on the job suspect that I got it because of race. (Ibid:10f)

McIntosh notes that "in proportion as my racial group was being made confident, comfortable, and oblivious, other groups were being made proportionately inconfident, uncomfortable and alienated" (ibid:11). The question, she concludes, is "whether we will get truly distressed, even outraged, about unearned advantage and conferred dominance" (ibid:12). While her list deals with race privilege, the "pattern of assumptions" it represents clearly extends to class and gender advantage as well.

Entitlement is, of course, the *unacknowledged* space within which most European-American theology in this century has been generated. The task is to break its unconscious control of my perspective through what Paulo Freire called conscientization. This pedagogy helps people "develop their power to perceive critically the way they exist in the world with which and in which they find themselves; they come to see the world not as a static reality, but as a reality in process, in transformation" (1992:70f; below, 3,D). The existing relations of power must be articulated, analyzed and "problematized" in order to animate the struggle to change them. For Christian theology, the privileged space of entitlement is first and foremost problematized by the gospel itself, which contends that its truth is better perceived by those on the margins than by those at the center. This stands to reason: Those who have been *dispossessed* by a social system are by definition *less possessed* by that system's illusions about itself. We have seen this very point illustrated in Mark's palace courtyard episode. Jesus' courtroom defense questions the omnipotent claims of empire (14:62; 15:2), while Peter's courtyard denial cowers before those same claims. These symbolize two contrasting practices within imperial space: resistance versus conformity. Only the former can reveal the contradictions of the latter. This is the dilemma of the entitled in the *locus imperii.*

The contrast between what we might call the "poor perspective of the privileged" and the "privileged perspective of the poor" is articulated throughout the Bible (see, e.g., Lohfink, 1987; Tamez, 1982). In Mark's story of Jesus, that foundational narrative of the gospel tradition, it is clear from the outset. Mark's prologue unveils three unequivocal and unapologetic assertions about reality, calculated to disturb every religio-philosophical explanation of life's meaning or God's existence and to undermine every socio-political pretension to power.

The first assertion is that the story of human liberation — the subject of the exodus God's intervention in history — is not finished: the "way" has been re-opened (Mk 1:2). The second assertion, however, immediately problematizes the expectations generated by this "good news": This reanimation takes place at the margins of the social order ("the wilderness"), not at its *center* (1:3f). The third assertion then utterly subverts the dominant relations of power: Those in the Metropolitan center are directed to the margins, where they are challenged to repent, that is, to reorient their lives in a radically different direction (1:4f; *BSM:*121ff).

How then can we at the center be subjects of a gospel tradition that was itself generated from and for the margins? This dilemma is addressed by Jon Sobrino, who correctly notes that the gospel tradition makes a basic distinction between what Jesus asks of the poor and what he demands from the entitled:

> Jesus sees people's relationship to the kingdom exemplified in two types: the "poor" or "lowly" person on the one hand and the "follower of Jesus" on the other. Faith and hope is demanded of the first, practical service to the kingdom and behavior akin to that of Jesus is demanded of the second.... Hope in God gives expression to the gratuitous nature of the kingdom. Following the praxis of Jesus gives expression to the concrete obligation to fight for love and justice among human beings. (1978:59)

This thesis certainly holds up in Mark. The poor (represented by the "crowds"; *BSM:*156f) and the disciples (represented by the "twelve"; *BSM:*132f) are both subjects of Jesus' teaching and demonstrative practice. But the poor are healed by their faith (5:34; 10:51f) while the entitled are called to discipleship (2:14; 10:21ff). This gospel distinction is the single most compelling reason why First World theology must focus on *discipleship.*

If entitlement represents my social location within the political/historical space of the *locus imperii,* discipleship represents my social dis-location. The radical discipleship movements of the First World — those struggling for church renewal and fundamental social change — are the communities of conviction with which I identify. While we will always be privileged within the dominant social system, we are attempting to live in ways incongruous with and even defective from the expectations of our gender, race, and class location (below, Chapter Six). Our admittedly modest attempts to practice solidarity with Third World communities of struggle, sustained resistance to the culture of violence, and service among the poor can in the long run empower us to ever deeper discontinuity with the dominant culture and realignment with the disenfranchised.

Because our efforts are never free of our class/race/gender illusions and constraints, however, we must exercise the "hermeneutics of suspicion" on ourselves first and last in order to remain critically aware of the geography, forms, and functions of our entitlement. Therefore a basic task of this book is to understand how entitlement is both the cause and result of Denial (Part Two). Our participation in the struggle to deconstruct systems of domination (Part Three) and reconstruct a more just world (Part Four) depends on our willingness and ability to come to terms with the fire that warms us. It is true that by making *our* social location and dis-location a central issue of our theology we run the risk of slipping into just another form of bourgeois subjectivity — placing ourselves at the center of the universe. But the bigger risk is that we First World Christians will remain in the privileged role of being mere spectators, commentators on, or vicarious boosters of the practice of others rather than subjects in the work of transformation. Thus a focus on the dilemmas of denial and discipleship in the Palace Courtyard is appropriate to First World theology.

B. "YOU TOO WERE WITH THAT NAZARENE?!"
THE *KAIROS* CHALLENGE TO FIRST WORLD CHRISTIANITY

How do efforts by Third World Christians to "name" their historical situation and moment influence our attempts to do the same in the Palace Courtyard?

The political geography of Mark's prologue carries on the legacy of Exodus and Exile. The story of God's epiphany at the margins of empire is not only axiomatic, it is axial — upon it should turn all truly Christian theology and practice. Today the distance between center and periphery has never been more daunting, and thus the task of trying to do theology from a Metropolitan site, never more problematic. Fortunately in our time voices have again appeared in the wilderness to witness to the truth of the *locus imperii* from the periphery, addressing pathologies of domination and envisioning transformed relations of power.

1. Responding to Liberation Theologies

The voices of the marginalized — long suppressed or ignored by the discourses of the center — are today finding expression in diverse theologies of liberation: feminist, black, Latino, Asian, Pacific, and indigenous (see, e.g., Hennelly, 1990; Abraham, 1990; Ferm, 1986a, b; R. M. Brown, 1993, 1979). But although this good news from below is slowly "trickling up" to our First World churches, it is exceedingly difficult for us to hear since we have long assumed that theological truth was, by definition, handed down from above. This assumption corresponds with the centrist worldview into which we have been socialized: Wealth, political power, knowledge, indeed history itself are all created, organized, and controlled by the rich, the powerful, and the educated, the true subjects of history, and trickle down to the masses. We have believed, with unassailably circular logic, that God was on our side because we were successful and powerful, and that we were successful and powerful because God was on our side. But according to the biblical geography of faith, centrist theology is fundamentally wrong, and innumerable crimes small and large have followed from its error. This is why the gospel — if we dare to leave the insular walls of Fortress Metropolis to encounter it on the periphery — still demands repentance (Mk 1:14f).

A small but growing number of First World Christians have come to see liberation theologians as our primary dialogue partners. But what kind of a conversation are we having with them? Our partners are rightly concerned at the way their work can (and has) so easily and subtly become a novel (even exotic) commodity in First World ecclesial and theological marketplaces. We "consumers" too often respond only with our critical evaluations of these Third World theological "products." Are they up to our intellectual standards? Have they covered all the territory? Are they too ideological? Critical assessment of liberation theologies (or any theology) is both legitimate and important, of course (see McGovern, 1989). Yet theologies of liberation claim to be reflection on practice, and mere commentary on someone else's practice deftly sidesteps the question of our own. Even if we sympathize with theologies of liberation, we are in constant danger of expropriating their rhetoric without engaging their methods. A midweek Bible study group in our local parish does not become a "base community" just because it is so renamed, nor are we in solidarity with the poor simply by declaring we are. This is why liberation theologians have become more insistent that we who claim to understand and concur with their basic assertions must discern our own context, respond with our own practice, and reflect critically on that.

The conversation we wish to have is also precarious because it takes place amid the painful contradictions of a world order in which the very structures that enfranchise First World Christians disenfranchise our Third World sisters and brothers. This explains why some Third World liberation theologians began during the 1980s to address their discourse more directly to us (rather than about us, as in earlier works). This development is best viewed through the recent series of *kairos* theological consultations.[5] The original South African *kairos* process struggled to undomesticate theological discourse in the context of an apartheid system sponsored by both church and state. A subsequent Central American consultation tried to do the same in terms of the ongoing U.S.-backed, low-intensity war against popular resistance movements in that region (cf Nelson-Pallmeyer, 1989). The most recent *kairos* process included African, Central American and Asian theologians and church activists and produced "The Road to Damascus: *Kairos* and Conversion."

The "Road to Damascus" calls First World Christians to reflect on the meaning of faithfulness in a time of increasing global socio-economic disparity and ideological polarization between North and South. It indicts the legacy of colonialism as the cause of a "litany of woes: our children die of malnutrition and disease, there are no jobs for those who want to work, families break up to pursue employment abroad, peasants and indigenous communities are displaced from their land, most urban dwellers have to live in unsanitary slums, many women are forced to sell their bodies, too many die without having lived a life that human persons deserve" (R. M. Brown, 1990:117). Asking hard questions about idolatry and apostasy, hypocrisy and blasphemy, the Damascus document seeks to "lay bare the historical and political roots of the conflict...between two antagonistic forms of Christianity":

> Christian faith has now been introduced into the political conflict. Both oppressor and oppressed seek religious legitimation....The Church itself has *become a site of struggle.* Some sectors of the Church align themselves with the status quo and defend it passionately, while others align themselves with the oppressed and struggle for change. There are yet others who claim to be neutral. In fact neutrality plays into the hands of those in power because it enables them to continue, and to discredit the Christians who oppose them. (Ibid:120f)

Then, in the tradition of liberation theology, the authors of "The Road to Damascus" attempt to name this situation biblically. They draw from the story of Saul of Tarsus, the persecutor of those who "wished to turn the world upside down" (Acts 9). Saul was struck blind by the revelation that the God he purported to serve was in fact suffering alongside those he stalked. "This *kairos* on the road to Damascus must be taken seriously by all who in the name of God support the persecution of Christians who side with the poor" (ibid:1990:135). Indeed the story of Saul is without doubt compelling for our context; Protestant churches in particular, having historically identified with the apostle Paul in their missionary zeal, would do well to reflect on the fact that Saul required dramatic conversion before he "saw" the Jesus who was in solidarity with those he victimized.

But if it will not do for us simply to expropriate the rhetoric of liberation theology, neither can we reflexively adopt their characterizations of our situation. During the 1960s and 1970s some Latin American theologians began to understand their "sinful situation" — characterized by structures of socio-economic domination and dependency — in terms of the Exodus story and the liberation from slavery in imperial Egypt (Gutiérrez, 1973:155ff). First World theologians who have tried to appropriate this theme for their own work, however, have found it an awkward fit (King, Maynard, and Woodyard, 1988:154ff). Too often the language of liberation has been emptied of its political-economic specificity, degenerating into gratuitous talk of "liberating" middle-class people from the anxieties of affluent urban lifestyles. It occurred to some therefore to reverse the Latin American equation: If the poor were trying to break free of Pharaoh's hegemony, we in the First World were stuck trying to do theology in Pharaoh's house (Soelle, 1979:178). This is certainly a more accurate (if essentially derivative) theme, suggesting the frustrating and even compromised nature of our task. Still, if we wish to have a dialogue, we must name our own theme, taking into account the triple challenge of the gospel, theologies of liberation, and the historical moment. I have suggested Mark's story of Peter's denial as such a theme for First World theology. The *kairos* demands of liberation theologians are here represented in the voices of those who observe Peter warming himself by the imperial fire, noting the contradictions between our social location and our alleged loyalties. "You too were with the Nazarene?!" is both a question and an accusation as to why we are in the Palace Courtyard alongside the imperial guard and not with Jesus in the courtroom confronting the Powers.

2. Questioning Authority? From Confession to Quandary

Third World *Kairos* Documents have stimulated renewed interest in "confessional" theology in the U.S. In his groundbreaking *Seasons of Faith and Conscience: Kairos, Confession, Liturgy* (1991) Bill Wylie Kellermann describes this tradition:

> In church history, especially Protestant tradition, it is recognized that there are extraordinary times when the church's very identity is imperiled. If its confession is not made unequivocally clear, nothing less than the meaning of the gospel with the church and before the world is at risk. This special time, a *status confessionis,* is brought on by a historical crisis within the church or without. It is incumbent on the community of faith to discern and name the crisis and to distinguish, as clearly as it possibly can, between truth and error, even between life and death. (1991:36)

He points to two such historical moments in the twentieth century: the Barmen Declaration in Germany under Hitler and (less successful) attempts in the U.S. and Europe to make nuclear weaponry a confessional issue (see Yoder, 1970:133). Following his mentor, the late William Stringfellow, Kellermann has argued the need for a confessional theology in the U.S. church today, accompanied by a practice of public witness (Kellermann, 1989b). For two decades he and a small circle of other First World theologian-activists have been pursuing this very task. Recently a number of national ecumenical peace and justice groups have taken up this challenge, promoting a call to a *kairos* process in the U.S. (see R. M. Brown, 1990:143ff; Agne et al, 1991).

But is confession the discourse most appropriate to our situation in the Palace Courtyard? Kellermann rightly points out that confession is precisely what is called for at the plain level of the Peter narrative. Clearly the integrity of the gospel in the world demands that the church declare its allegiances in critical historical moments — the 1992 Los Angeles uprising was, in my opinion, a recent case in point (see Lejeune et al, 1992). Yet declaring our allegiance is just what we First World Christians have been consistently unable to do. The nineteenth century abolitionist movement, for example, so split the churches that it eventually had to secularize. More recently, efforts to forge an "abolitionist covenant" around the issue of nuclear weapons remained at the margins of the church. And even if we could come to unity, declaring "Here we stand," such pronouncements always run the risk of being tainted with triumphalism in the context of the *locus imperii.* But what if we *questioned* rather than *confessed?*

"Question Authority." This is the slogan, emblazoned on bumper stickers and banners, of my friends at the Resource Center for Nonviolence in northern

California. It offers straightforward counsel to think critically about matters of power and decision making in society, to pause before we obey the law. This would seem a good rule of thumb for any truly democratic culture. Yet for most North Americans, this slogan represents a disturbing, anarchist notion that is received with suspicion and contempt (below, 11,C). Of course, its shock value is intentional, seeking precisely to unmask that peculiar constellation of dread and reverence — so deeply lodged in our political unconscious — with which we apprehend public authority.

The courage and commitment to question authority lay at the heart of Jesus' mission. Conversely, the dread of and reverence for authority lay at the root of Peter's denial in the palace courtyard — and ours in the *locus imperii*. Unlike the Markan story with which I began this chapter (11:27ff), State officials have no reason to question by what authority we First World Christians act, because our actions do not question their authority! Our churches, liberal and conservative, are like Mark's scribes — essentially noncommittal about their political alignments in the historical moment. Indeed they tend to view religious movements that *do* challenge the State — whether Christians for Socialism in Chile or Islamic "fundamentalism" in Algeria — with utmost wariness.

There are many reasons why we have sought refuge in political ambivalence. We experience enough worldly comfort and privilege, and are sufficiently insulated from those for whom "the system" does not work, to be relatively content with the social order, comparatively untroubled by its contradictions. We assume that our socio-political structures, though flawed, are nevertheless the lesser of evils — at least we cannot think of a better alternative. And sometimes we just figure that contemporary political issues are too complicated for the church to deal with. But at the root of our ambivalence lies an ideological bargain Christian theology has struck with secular capitalism: It has conceded authority over the public sphere to the State in hopes of retaining a modicum of authority over the private sphere.

Many complex historical forces have created and sustained theology's agreement to rationalize rather than problematize social reality. McClendon and Murphy (1989) have shown how the philosophical forces of the Enlightenment moved theological concern away from traditional problems of collective character ("What is expected of us?") to problems of personal existence ("Who am I?") and epistemological doubt ("How can I know?"). The socio-economic forces of capitalism have facilitated the steady privatization of consciousness and disintegration of community ("I am what I produce/consume"). And the political forces of bureaucratic centralization have removed religion to the margins of influence, while sacralizing the State (a drift clearly evident in twentieth-century state socialism, but no less the case in the West's democracies).

In the U.S. this ideological bargain was reified from the beginning by the Deist architects of our oligarchic republic in the Constitutional "separation of church and State." In the eighteenth century this was understandably attractive to minority Christian traditions fleeing the oppressive, neo-Constantinian arrangements of Old Europe. But by the end of the nineteenth century the forces of the secular, monist faith of Progress and the national ideology of Manifest Destiny had thoroughly displaced older Puritan or Baptist visions of how to build a moral and plural society (Lasch, 1991). Thus, whereas allegedly this separation was intended to protect church and State from each other, it has functioned over time to make the former increasingly irrelevant to the latter.

However gradual and complex the evolution of this bargain with modernity has been, its outcome has been every bit as Faustian for Christian theology as was the ancient deal the church cut with Constantine.[6] The social contract that trades off public for private is a deal with the devil not because the social power of the institutional churches has been broken, or because postmodernity has brought theological pluralism — those are promising features of our post-Constantinian situation. No, it is a deal with the devil because the church, by making faith a private matter severed from public life, has undermined its critical vocation at a time when technocratic totalitarianism is rapidly dehumanizing every aspect of life, public and private. Religious ethics in the *locus imperii* is preoccupied with personal morality or individual choice, while equivocating on socially or politically contested issues. Conservative theologians need not question the social order because Jesus is "the answer" to all personal dilemmas; their Jesus shrugs at public crimes while obsessing about sexual behavior. In reaction, theologies of liberation too often simply reverse the equation, emphasizing political struggle and dismissing individual piety as irrelevant. And in between liberal theologians forever find it easier to question the existence of God than the authority of the State.

The wedge driven between the private and the public is a central problematic of First World theology and thus of this book. I will refer to it as the alienation of our "political bodies" from our "body politic" (see below, 4,B). Our churches have exchanged their messianic commission to question public authority for government sanction to peddle private answers. Like Peter in the palace courtyard, we are comforted by imperial certainties even as we are surrounded by protracted historical quandaries. We make our confession too soon and realize our Denial too late.

Because we live in a socio-political universe of high mystification, however, we cannot afford *not* to question authority. A couple of relatively random items in today's news (December 4, 1992) can serve to illustrate why. This morning President George Bush delivered a brief speech from the Oval Office announcing the deployment of U.S. troops to Somalia under the auspices of the United Nations. Legitimizing Operation Restore Hope as a humanitarian mission, Bush invoked "images of starving people we've all seen," denounced "armed thugs" and "anarchy," and appealed to the American people's compassion "for the children of Somalia." This was already a familiar refrain in the New World Order, the soundbytes virtually interchangeable: Grenada, Panama, Kuwait, Bosnia, and perhaps next Zaire, or Peru, or Moldavia, or Myanmar. A credulous U.S. audience, scrambling for maps to locate such obscure outposts of empire, was given little context, history, or analysis concerning Somalia. There was no discussion of its colonial history, or of the competition between the U.S. and Soviet

Union for naval basing rights there because of its strategic geopolitical location at the mouth of the Gulf of Aden or even of why people starve. There were no questions raised about why human tragedies of equal scope in Kampuchea, Mozambique, or East Timor did not merit U.S. initiative or about the emerging pattern of U.S. military intervention as a strategy for global management. There was only Bush's assurances that the soldiers being deployed to Somalia are "doing God's work." The evening paper's headline read: "Bush Sending Troops to Help Somalia's Hungry Millions." Alongside it were EZ graphics of troop deployments and photos of departing Marines clutching pictures of their children.

Also today the radio broadcasted an interview with the military crew of the space shuttle orbiting the earth on a mission to deploy a top-secret satellite. What was not of concern to the media was the fact that this satellite would further enable pinpoint targeting for strategic missiles (advancing the continuing dream of unanswerable First-Strike capacity) or the implications of such technology for post–cold war disarmament and the "peace dividend." The subject of this dramatic live-in-space interview? The crew's allegiances and predictions concerning the upcoming annual Army-Navy football game.

These two news items from a day in the life of the *locus imperii* show why Palace Courtyard theology must question authority. The convolutions and duplicities of foreign intervention, or the militarization of space, deserve the highest level of critical apprehension and response from the church. But the public discourses of empire are designed to preclude such reflection, so that we would remain mired in the culture of credulity (below, 3,B). We First World Christians have dwelled too long in the shadow of our tradition's long legacy of scribe-like equivocation. We have too often taken refuge in political agnosticism in the face of Jesus' challenge to declare where we stand. We need a theological discourse that can empower us to question authority while remaining cognizant of our own complicity in empire.

C. THE AUTHORITY OF QUESTIONS:
JESUS AS INTERLOCUTOR OF CHURCH AND WORLD

Should First World theology be organized around "the right answers" or "the right questions"?

Douglass John Hall has been arguing for two decades that a contextual theology for North America must proceed from a discourse of negation rather than affirmation. In a 1976 essay entitled "Towards an Indigenous Theology of the Cross" he wrote:

Our culture is sick, and because it is also very powerful, its sickness infects the whole world. On the brink of overt nihilism in our public life, and neurotically clinging to the positive in our private existences, we fear

an open confrontation with the contradiction between our optimistic expectations and our increasingly depressing experiences. The repression of
this contradiction is costly in life and truth. Its repression at home inevitably means that it breaks out in strange places with names which
quickly become household words: Vietnam, Bangladesh, Chile.... There
can therefore be no more responsible theology than one which tries to
provide a climate in which men and women in this society may feel able
to expose themselves to that contradictory state. Is it possible to discover
in the tradition of Jerusalem a way through which we may enter into our
own darkness? (1976:162)

Hall has recently developed this approach in *Thinking the Faith,* the first of
his three-part systematic theology, contending that "the malaise of modernity is
the legacy of Promethean optimism which did not take into account the limits of
human power and the ubiquity and subtlety of evil" (1989:37). We have become
"a people wondrously afraid of the dark," Hall believes; "there is no greater
public task for theology in North America today than to help to provide a people
indoctrinated in the modern mythology of light with a frame of reference for the
honest exploration of its actual darkness" (ibid:36).

I agree with Hall. But what kind of theological discourse can best promote
such exploration? I believe Mark's gospel offers us clues. More than three-
quarters of the episodes in his gospel are composed around questions to, by,
or about Jesus — from his inaugural challenge to scribal authority (1:24) to the
story's closing quandary (16:3). Jesus is presented not as a sage who explains
life's mysteries but as the great interlocutor of reality. His queries lay bare the
"inner conflicts" of disciples and opponents alike (Gk *dialogizesthai;* 2:8; 8:16f;
9:33f; 11:31). Sometimes they are sharply rhetorical: "Can Satan exorcise Satan?" (3:23); "What will the owner of the vineyard do?" (12:9). Other times
they are wrapped in metaphor or parable: "Is a lamp brought indoors to be put
under a basket?" (4:21); "Should wedding guests fast while the bridegroom is
with them?" (2:19). But always they challenge both the ideology of the dominant culture ("How can the scribes say...?" 12:35) and the theology of disciples
("Do you not yet understand?" 8:21). Above all, they call into question our biblical literacy: "Have you never read...?" (2:25; 12:10); "Is it not written...?"
(9:12; 11:17).

Jesus questions the world. In the tradition of the Hebrew prophets, Jesus is
a relentless interrogator of those in power. With deadly rhetorical aim he exposes the duplicity behind official piety: for instance, theological legitimations
of elite social power that appeal to heaven (8:12), or to intellectual traditions
(10:3) or to Temple State nationalism (12:35). When challenged by the authorities, Jesus turns the tables with brilliantly crafted counterquestions that unmask
their ideological agenda, such as their attempts to control the economy of redemption (2:9) or their subservience to Roman interests (12:16). Even when in
legal jeopardy and cornered in a public showdown, Jesus acts as prosecutor, not
defendant: "Is it lawful to do good or to do harm on the Sabbath, to save life or

to kill?" (3:4). So skillful is he at relativizing the authorities before the sovereignty of God that in the end, Mark tells us, Jesus' opponents stopped debating with him: "When Jesus saw that the scribe had answered wisely, he said to him, 'You are not far from the kingdom of God.' After that no one dared anymore to press questions to him" (12:34).

Jesus' actions too question the dominant arrangements of power. His practice of exorcism names the very demons of empire who seek to name and control him (5:7–9). It challenges a "House divided" (3:23) and symbolically enacts the denouement of an ancient prophetic plot:

> The Lord whom you seek will suddenly come to his temple.... But who can stand when he appears?... Then I will draw near to you for judgment, to bear witness against sorcerers and adulterers, against those who swear falsely and who oppress hired workers in their wages, against those who thrust aside the alien, the widow and orphan.... (Mal 3:1ff)

In his direct action in the Temple (*BSM*:297ff) Jesus assumes the role of a divine litigator indicting public crimes: "Is it not written, 'My house shall be called a house of prayer for all the peoples?' But you have made it a 'den of thieves' " (Mk 11:17). Jesus cross-examines Israel's most inured institution before the bar of Yahwist justice and finds it wanting: "Do you see these great buildings? There will not be one stone left upon another" (13:2). Mark's Jesus is thus portrayed not as the *answer* to our private questions but as the *question* to our public answers.

Jesus questions the church. Mark's Jesus offers his disciples not certitude but queries that force us to question our own assumptions:

> Who is my mother and my brother? (3:33)
> What is the kingdom of God like? (4:30)
> Why are you afraid? (4:40)
> Why do you bother arguing with the scribes? (9:16)
> Can you be baptized with my baptism? (10:38)
> Why do you bother this woman's good deed? (14:6)
> Could you not keep watch with me? (14:37)

Jesus' questions open up painful and awkward uncertainties for disciples: "Do you have eyes, and fail to see? Do you have ears, and fail to hear? And do you not remember?" (8:18). But does this mean that he is merely playing the Grand Inquisitor or the Devil's advocate?

His teaching and practice are meant to provoke the incredulity of his disciples (10:24, 32). This is his pedagogical strategy — to break the spell of credulity the dominant order casts over its subjects, to force a crisis of faith. Incredulity can be subversive, for doubt about the world is a necessary condition to joining the struggle to transform it. In other words, Jesus is practicing what Paulo Freire calls "conscientization" (below, 3,C). Freire's work in promoting

literacy among the poor showed him that the empowering teacher provides the
right question, not the right answer: "The educator's role is to propose problems
about the codified existential situation in order to help the learners arrive at a
more and more critical view of their reality" (1971:264). Mark's Jesus is indeed such a pedagogue, problematizing the worldview of his followers and his
opponents because it is problematic from the vantage point of the Kingdom.

We see this discursive strategy best in another vignette featuring Peter, one
so important that Mark places it at the structural center of his story. Here Jesus
poses his famous double question to his disciples, upon which all Christian
theology turns:

> "Who do the people say that I am?...
> Who do *you* say I am?" (8:27, 29a)

Mark is boldly transforming the foundational declaration of Hebrew faith —
"God said to Moses, 'I am who I am!' " (Ex 3:14) — into a query. The Exodus
God's absolutely self-defining prerogative suddenly assumes the vulnerability
of an inquiry.

Peter, however, sees this remarkable solicitation only as a happy occasion
for confession — and so has Christian orthodoxy ever since (8:29b). "You are
the Christ!" was, let us not forget, the creed of the churches to which Mark
wrote and that still read him today. That is why it is so disturbing that Jesus
responds as if Peter were yet another demon attempting to "name" him (8:30; cf
1:25; 3:12; 9:25). He *silences* Peter, precipitating what I have called the "confessional crisis" (*BSM:*241ff). Jesus repudiates Peter's messianic triumphalism
by invoking the political vocation of the Human One (8:31). Horrified, Peter in
turn rejects such a negating theology (8:32). Jesus then utterly problematizes the
matter by aligning Petrine orthodoxy with Satan (8:33)! The struggle concludes
with Jesus' invitation to a practice of the cross (8:34ff). In other words, Mark
here displaces Peter's confession with Jesus' quandary about losing life in order
to save it. The later trial episode reiterates this theological displacement by narrating it conversely. Jesus is "not ashamed" and confesses the Human One in
the courtroom (14:62ff), while at the very same moment Peter is "ashamed" of
Jesus as he faces his quandary in the courtyard (14:66ff).

Interlocutees become interlocutors. The disciples do not say much in
Markan theater. Their few lines function to reveal the shadowy hues of their
humanity — duplicity (10:39), equivocation (14:19), or plain foolishness (9:5).
Their incredulity does, however, cause them to ask questions of their own, even
if they are leery (5:31), leading (10:35), or pleading (4:38) ones. Their quandaries resound perhaps most sharply in the hollows of our readerly stomachs,
for in them our own deepest anxieties about discipleship are laid bare. Who of
us has not wondered why Jesus seems absent in the midst of storms that threaten
to sink us (4:41)? Have we not many times puzzled resentfully over how to respond to the overwhelming needs of the poor, given our meager resources (6:37;
8:4)? Awed by the legitimacy of the rich and powerful, do we not constantly

check our bearings according to their maps (9:11), unable to imagine a history freed from their control (10:26)? Do we not rage against our impotence (9:29) and doubt in our innermost selves whether the world can really ever be changed (13:4)? Battered by disappointment and failure, do we not agonize over our own betrayal (14:19) and too often despair that we have come to the end of the line (16:3)? In the disciples' questions, inspired by Jesus' own, we encounter our individual and corporate darkness.

The subversive genius of Mark's theological discourse engages the disciple/ reader with disturbing and disrupting quandaries that animate rather than with logically satisfying answers that pacify. This does not mean, however, that we are left with an endless labyrinth of unresolve. As Kellermann rightly points out: "In the end the questions leading to more questions distill down to the big one: What am I willing to die for? And the answer to that is probably not another question." But the problem for us in the Palace Courtyard is that we do not know what we are willing to die for because we are not asking the right questions.

Jesus has been variously named by the church — Christ, Sophia, Suffering Servant, Good Shepherd, Word of God. Whatever else he may be, however, he is our Lord only insofar as he is our Interlocutor. Mark's gospel, the prototype of Christian narrative theology, suggests that the church's own theological discourse should also be interrogatory. But if we wish to recover such a discourse, our reconstructive task is formidable, for ecclesial doctrine long ago buried the voice of Jesus the Interlocutor. When the early church struck its deal with Constantine, it moved decisively away from questioning reality and began its long theological orbit around the propositional discourse of dogma, institutionalized in the great declarative confessions.[7] As long as the church understood Christ to be mysteriously present among the poor, and Christians inhabited the margins, no ruler's authority was beyond question, no social system beyond critical scrutiny. But once Christ was located on a heavenly throne, and Christians were advisers in earthly courts, the grounds upon which theology could (or dared) challenge the authority of emperor, pope, or king narrowed considerably.

Today, in the twilight of the Palace Courtyard, recovering an interrogatory discourse in the spirit of Jesus, the Interlocutor of church and world, could not be more important. Below I suggest two discursive traditions that I believe can help us do just that. One is a philosophical and prophetic tradition that spared no question of the world. The other is an ecclesial and pastoral tradition that models how the church can persistently question itself.

D. PROPHETIC NEGATION: CRITICAL THEORY

How can Critical Theory help Christian theology to problematize *rather than* rationalize *the structures of human existence?*

"A refusal to cut off further relevant questions even when they lead us into the darkness of negativity" — this was the central thrust of the mid-twentieth-century intellectual tradition known as Critical Theory, according to its foremost North American theological interpreter Matthew Lamb (1980:186; 1982). Critical Theory was founded by the "Frankfurt School" of philosophy: Max Horkheimer, Theodor Adorno, Walter Benjamin, and, best known in the U.S., Herbert Marcuse. It "emerged from a distinct crisis in European bourgeois culture" in the aftermath of World War I, writes Paul Mendes-Flohr, which deepened through the experience of the Third Reich and the Cold War: "The modern world had indeed witnessed the creation of a splendid, majestic edifice, but it was held to be a Trojan horse hiding within insidious forces bent on humanity's spiritual and psychic emasculation" (1983:631).

Adherents of Critical Theory articulated a profound disillusionment with the optimistic creeds of modernism — Enlightenment rationalism, technocracy, and, above all, history-as-Progress (below, 12,A). They were among the first to understand that these *positivistic* myths could be countered neither by pessimism nor skepticism but only by a thoroughgoing discourse of *negation*. Through its so-called negative dialectics, Critical Theory challenged the most basic assumptions of modernity:

> In their *Dialectic of Enlightenment,* Adorno and Horkheimer develop the antithetical or "inverse" insights into how scientific reason is mythic, how enlightened liberal morality is barbaric, how technological progress is retrogression. Benjamin caught this inverse insight imaginally: "Marx says, revolutions are the locomotives of world history. But perhaps... revolutions are the grasp by the human race travelling in this train for the emergency brake." ... If the twentieth century vaunts an ideology of life, liberty, and the pursuit of happiness, then critical theory poses the uncomfortable question of why no other century has witnessed such massive destruction of human life by human beings. (Lamb, 1980:186)

In the well-known dictum of Walter Benjamin: "There is no record of civilization that is not also a record of barbarism" (see Smith, 1989).

If the Frankfurt School set its face against modernity, however, it was nevertheless squarely within the Enlightenment tradition of rational criticism, in much the same way that Anabaptists were within the spirit of the Reformation. In both cases these radical minorities refused to suspend their criticism once the reformist movements that spawned them began to compromise with systems of domination.

The modern era began when the "Age of Reason" overthrew the sacred totalism of the "Age of Faith" through scientific inquiry into how the physical universe was ordered, breaking the grip of the old cosmologies. At the same time, nascent industrial capitalism sought to transform traditional economic culture while the emerging bourgeoisie questioned the divine right of kings and launched new republican experiments in democracy. But once the old feudal order was shattered, liberal thought became increasingly unable or unwilling to turn criticism back upon its own constructs. "The old order of sacral hierarchy gave way to a new order of secular bureaucracy in which the myth of identity between reason and reality would be legitimated by an empirical science increasingly constituted by 'value-free' observation and quantification as the only valid form of rationality" (Lamb, 1980:190). New totalist and instrumentalist theories of the universe, society, and the human being were now legitimating colonial projects and advancing military technologies and industrial profiteering.

Marx launched a second phase of criticism by challenging the absolute claims of liberal capitalism. He formulated his theory of human alienation by studying how an uncontrolled economy controlled all social relations, "practicing a new form of dialectical analysis which exposed the basic economic contradiction inherent in capitalist relations of production" and introducing the notion of class struggle (ibid:191). Marx thus inspired a new round of struggle for freedom and justice throughout the industrializing world, though his theory of revolution ironically found its most dramatic expression in semifeudal Russia. Again, however, once Marxist criticism was reified and canonized in state socialism, its revolutionary power atrophied, as Leninism yielded to Stalinism. Hegemonic Marxism, like liberalism before it, became a legitimating ideology for bureaucratic totalism.

By the mid-twentieth century, then, history seemed to offer only "the cynical choice between monopoly-controlled states or state-controlled monopolies" (ibid). The Frankfurt School thus launched a third phase of the critical tradition, arguing that the mass cultures of Western and Eastern blocs were more alike than different. The "conveyors of packaged images and symbols" — Soviet propagandists and Madison Avenue hucksters alike — were strangling social and political imagination (ibid:202). Marcuse understood clearly that the "death of politics" was itself a highly political agenda:

As a technological universe, advanced industrial society is a *political* universe, the latest stage in the realization of a specific historical *project* — namely, the experience, transformation, and organization of nature as the mere stuff of domination. As the project unfolds, it shapes the entire universe of discourse and action, intellectual and material culture. In the medium of technology, culture, politics, and the economy merge into an omnipresent system which swallows up or repulses all alternatives. The productivity and growth potential of this system stabilizes the society and contains technical progress within the framework of domination. (1964:xvi)

Negative dialectics attempted to resist this totalism by deconstructing its foundational myths and interrogating its social and intellectual conventions in order to free political imagination and reanimate the struggle for human liberation.

Critical Theory was, predictably, berated from the political Right for its "sour grapes" about modern society. But there were objections from the Left as well, the most telling complaint being that thoroughgoing negativity undermined efforts to construct concrete social alternatives. Indeed many Critical Theorists were leery of political activism, with the notable exception of Marcuse. Yet during the 1960s Critical Theory was rehabilitated as part of the intellectual underpinning of the New Left, student antiwar protests, and the counterculture. But as these movements began to unravel in the 1970s, doubts were again raised about the politics of negation.

A notable chapter in this debate was the often-heated dialogue between North Atlantic political theologians inspired by Critical Theory and Latin American liberation theologians influenced primarily by Marxism-Leninism (*BSM:*20f; see Moltmann, 1976; Abayasekera et al, 1975; Bancroft, 1982). Political theology, disillusioned by the atrophy of human rights in Eastern Europe, rejected socialist positivism and "every identification of utopian thinking with Christian eschatology" (Richardson, 1974:1). Writing from the perspective of insurgent Latin America, Juan Luis Segundo countered that this seemed "much more akin to the Cartesian theoretical revolution based on methodic doubt than to real practical revolution . . . it does not choose between one system and another" (1979:246f).

An analogous debate rages in current cultural theory, which is awash in Deconstructionism. Deconstructionists rightly insist that the mystifying discourses of capitalist culture must be dismantled (see, e.g., Barthes, 1972). But the exclusive focus on discourse leads Marxists such as Raymond Williams to dismiss them as merely "textual revolutionaries" who posit "the universality of alienation, the position of a closely associated bourgeois idealist formation" (1977:168). "It is remarkable how parallel deconstructionism is," notes Terry Eagleton in his sympathetic study of Benjamin, "to the later Frankfurt school [in its] rage against positivity, the suspicion of determinate meaning *as such,* the fear that to propose is to be complicit" (1981:141). He contends that this tendency can be traced to the failure of radical student politics in Europe in the late 1960s: "Unable to break the structures of state power, post-structuralism found it possible instead to subvert the structures of language" (1983:142).[8]

A theology of discipleship must indeed be leery of theoretics that give primacy to discourse-critique over practice and that are reluctant to make political choices and forge constructive social programs. At the same time, the political developments of the last decade suggest that neither our practice nor our criticism has been nearly critical enough. On one hand, the failure of many Third World revolutionary movements has chastened theologies of liberation. A group of Nicaraguan Christian base community coordinators, reflecting on the collapse of the Berlin Wall and the electoral defeat of the Sandinistas, wrote in November 1990: "The real faults and sins committed in the construction of socialism . . . [are] very clear now in the case of Eastern Europe, with its bureaucracy, apathy, authoritarianism, dogmatism, rigidity, corruption, inefficiency, lack of creativity, fear of freedom, and absence of a healthy social competitiveness. . . . Many certainties which were held as 'scientific' clearly have to be revised. . . . To be honest with reality we need to accept humbly what experience teaches" (Delegates of the Word, 1990:4f,6). On the other hand, First World political theologians have had to come to terms with the fact that "freedom" for former Communist countries is rapidly translating into peonage to the most totalitarian system of all. This is what Marcuse called "society without opposition" — the iron rule of mercenary capital. In the New World Order the ideology of global open markets and open shop is destroying the hard-fought gains of organized labor, while the triumphant military machine of the West is unobstructed in its war on the poor, from Panama to Somalia (Nelson-Pallmeyer, 1989, 1992).

If indeed we are seeing the steady ascendancy of what Bertram Gross (1980) calls capitalist technocracy's "friendly fascism," Critical Theory and its legacy, despite its shortcomings, offers encouragement to our quest for interrogatory theology in at least three respects. First, Critical Theory's uncompromising emphasis on philosophical "nonidentity" with totalist ideologies echoes the First Testament's prohibition of images and the exodus God's refusal to be named (Ex 3:13ff). This caused some to refer to the Frankfurt School as "theological Marxism." Critical Theory also encouraged both political and liberation theologians to rediscover the "negativity of the cross," which, Sobrino contends, "calls into question all knowledge of God based on natural theology": "God on the cross explains nothing [but] criticizes every proffered explanation. The cross is not a response; it is a new form of questioning.... It is not so much people asking questions about God; rather it is primarily people being called into question concerning themselves and their self-interest in trying to hold and defend a specific form of the deity" (1978:222). Critical Theory thus helps free theology from its self-imposed obligation to *rationalize* reality by answering questions to *problematizing* reality by questioning answers.

Second, Critical Theory rediscovered biblical eschatology in its critique of history-as-Progress (below, Chapter Twelve). This, in turn, inspired a whole generation of philosophers (e.g., Ernst Bloch) and theologians (e.g., Jürgen Moltmann) to rediscover apocalyptic hope as "brushing history against the grain" (Mendes-Flohr, 1983). Challenging modernism's sacred assumptions of social Darwinism and redemptive historicism, from Adam Smith's "invisible hand" to Marx's "historical necessity," liberates the future from the tyranny of the present. As Marcuse put it: "The possibilities of the new society are sufficiently ... removed from and incongruous with the established universe to defy any attempt to identify them in terms of this universe" (1969:86). Indeed if the self-justifying theoretics of both orthodox Marxism and laissez-faire capitalism have been discredited, there is fresh discursive space for genuinely different alternatives to emerge (below, Chapter Eleven). In the *locus imperii* there is a desperate need for Christians to offer hope and reignite the fires of political imagination and social innovation.

Third, Critical Theory helped reestablish the philosophical ground for conversionist theology. "The innocence of secularist faith can no longer be sustained, any more than the innocence of a sacralist faith could be sustained," writes Lamb; both "have given abundant evidence of a *hubris* all too guilty of crucifying both God and humankind" (1980:206). Critical Theory asserted the universality of historical guilt and, in its own way, called for repentance. Marcuse, for example, argued that people can "find their way from false to

true consciousness...only if they live in need of changing their way of life"
(1964:xiiif; below, Chapter Six). In its rejection of modernity's pretensions
to nobility, and its exhortation to resistance, Critical Theory moves from the
detachment of denunciation to the engagement of alternative practices.

In sum, Critical Theory's insistence on toppling the idols of modernity, its
nonprogressive historical hope, and its conversionist orientation can help a First
World theology recover an interrogatory discourse, and with it the prophetic
vocation of the church. "Those who persist in raising doubt and question are attacked by defenders of order as the 'adversary culture,'" wrote Edward Abbey;
"Very well: let us be adversaries." Jesus the Interlocutor was such an adversary
and faced its consequences. Can the church do differently? It will take courage.
It takes just as much courage, however, to turn our criticism of the world back
on ourselves. There is no room for self-righteousness, for Jesus is also the ques-
tioner of the church. Where can we find resources for an interrogatory theology
that also insists on self-examination?

E. PASTORAL INQUIRY: QUAKER "QUERIES"

*How can a pastoral discourse of self-examination empower ordinary
people to persevere in the work of transformation?*

As a historical generalization it is fair to say that the more social status and
privilege the church has assumed in a given social order, the more its theological discourse has taken on a defensive, apologetic, and abstract character.
Conversely, when the church has had less status, or was willing to risk losing
it, its theology has tended to be more offensive, critical, and practical. We see
this, for example, in the Reformation. Luther and Zwingli began as "protest"
theologians, first questioning and then breaking with the Roman church. Once
they decided to forge political alliances with governments, however, the tone
of their discourse quickly became apologetic concerning matters of civil order,
as evidenced by Luther's decision to side with the princes during the peasant uprisings and even more so by second-generation magisterial Calvinism
(Chadwick, 1964:59ff). Meanwhile Catholic theology, awakened from its complacency by the Protestant threat, recovered an offensive zeal in the Jesuit
Counter-Reformation.

The most consistently evangelical, prophetic, and eschatological discourse
of the period, however, belonged to the various movements of the Radical Reformation. Anabaptists were persecuted by Catholic and Protestant magistrates
alike for their radical practical and theological challenges to religious, economic,
and political orthodoxies. Walter Klaassen (1971, 1981) has rightly characterized theirs as the most concerted attack on the Constantinian arrangement in
the history of the church. As McClendon has pointed out, the descendants of
the Radical Reformation continued to give priority to discipleship over dogma
(1986:20; see also Bender, 1950, Rutschman, 1981). It is not surprising, therefore, that in this family tree we find a branch that came closest to adopting an

explicitly interrogative theological discourse: the Religious Society of Friends, or Quakers.[9]

A discourse of "Testimonies, Advices, and Queries" takes the place of doctrine among Quakers. Leonard Kenworthy calls this a "cluster of practices intended to encourage Friends, individually and as groups, to hold up their lives to the Light" (1981:71). This discourse, according to Quaker historian T. Canby Jones, first appeared in 1682 in three questions posed by London Yearly Meeting to determine the "state of the Meeting":

> What friends in the Ministry, in their respective countries, departed life since last Yearly Meeting?
> What friends imprisoned for their Testimony have died in prison since last Yearly Meeting?
> How has the Truth prospered among friends since last Yearly Meeting and how do they fare in relation to peace and unity? (1988:8)

Meant to inspire reflection on costly discipleship, these *Queries* were institutionalized in 1723, and others were added over time. A century later London Yearly Meeting developed *Advices,* which Jones calls "short counsels and positive suggestions for the improvement of the life, conduct and witness of Friends...conceived of as supplementary and subsidiary to the Queries" (ibid:9). *Testimonies* were in turn developed to articulate "corporate convictions, concerns which we are committed to put into action as a community of faith" (ibid:2).

Jones thus defines the three elements of this discourse as follows:

> A Testimony is a standard of faith, ethical behavior or Gospel Order which a group of people covenants together to observe....
> A Query is a sharply focused question designed to challenge persons or a group to live up to a corporately adopted standard of faith and behavior....
> An Advice is friendly counsel from the group on what it means to live by a commonly accepted testimony. (1988:1)

Friends look to Queries to help clarify the meaning and requirements of the various Testimonies. "Meetings were asked to read out the Queries and have their members examine their consciences in regard to such questions as the taking of oaths...the witness against paying tithes...the keeping of slaves...the penal system...[and] whether they held their lives free enough from the excessive cumber of acquisitive vocations" (Steere, 1984:22f). But Queries are not "loaded" questions; their purpose is to facilitate an examination of the community's conscience. "Suited to the searching mood of Friends at their best, they are broad, open-ended questions to promote self-examination under the leadership of the Spirit. They are non-dogmatic, non-hortatory...not intended to discourage but to encourage" (Kenworthy, 1981:72).

Unfortunately this desire not to condemn has often diffused efforts by Quaker meetings to take a firm position. Herb Lape points out that John Woolman's long campaign to get Friends to reject slavery "would not have gotten very far if the framework for...deliberations had been 'love and tolerance' rather than discerning the 'will of God'" (1988:29). Indeed it was Woolman's opponents who appealed to meeting unity in their arguments against excluding slaveowners from fellowship (Woolman, 1989:3ff).

As the vehicle for community self-assessment, then, Queries try to preserve a delicate balance. They are questions to our life, not accusations, yet they are hard questions, not merely rhetorical ones (Loukes, 1968:1ff). Advices grow from the community's experiences of fidelity (and infidelity) to its Testimonies. They are eminently practical encouragements, not legalisms. Pacific Yearly Meeting's current *Faith and Practice* does not require silence during meeting for worship, for example, but rather urges Friends "to give adequate time to study, meditation, prayer, and other ways of preparing for worship, and to arrive at meeting with an open and expectant spirit."

To see the contrast between this interrogatory, practice-centered approach to theology and traditional dogmatic discourse, let us look briefly at a concrete social issue. The most well known, and probably first, Quaker Testimony was the Peace Testimony, articulated by George Fox in his Declaration of 1660: "We do utterly deny all outward wars and fighting, whether for the kingdoms of this world or for the kingdom of Christ, and this is our testimony to the whole world." This practice is understood by Friends to express their conviction that "there is that of God in every person." This radically egalitarian notion was applied by early Friends to small matters as well as large, including both dress and address (Plain Dress and Plain Speech). It represented a direct threat to established seventeenth-century conventions of social hierarchy as well as political conformity, and for this Friends were fiercely persecuted.

In today's democratic cultures, the notion of the divine in each individual, as an abstract theological proposition, has become palatable; indeed it would be affirmed by most Christian traditions. These other churches would not, however, predicate the idea upon an ethical practice, so resistance to militarism does not necessarily follow. Thus, outside the opinions of professional ethicists or the dictums of pastoral letters, mainstream Catholic and Protestant churches offer few vehicles for community self-examination on weighty matters such as war.[10] In contrast, the Peace Testimony has anchored a long Quaker tradition of active nonviolence and noncooperation with authority (Brock, 1968). Indeed mainstream church acceptance today of the individual right of conscientious objection is attributable largely to Mennonite and Quaker advocacy.

Pacific Yearly Meeting's *Faith and Practice* includes the following Query concerning the Peace Testimony: "Do we live in the virtue of that life and power which takes away the occasion of all war? Do we refrain from taking part in war as inconsistent with the spirit of Christ? What are we doing to remove the causes of war and to bring about the conditions and instruments of peace?" To be sure, one could argue that this traditional language is too vague. Given our present context of technological militarism and the brutality of economic oppression, we might sharpen this Query as follows: "How are we complicit in structural violence without ever taking aggressive personal action? How can we resist institutions of domination politically while still seeing that of God in those who control them? What does it mean to be in solidarity with victims of violence despite the fact that they may seek just redress through violent methods?" Though Advices concerning the Peace Witness have not always been clear and courageous, historically Friends have formulated some quite specific ones. Woolman is again a good example. On the eve of the French and Indian wars in 1755, he and twenty-one others issued an epistle arguing that paying tax monies for military purposes was "inconsistent with our peaceable testimony" (Brock, 1968:122ff). War tax resistance has been an arena of struggle for many Friends ever since (Durland, 1982).

We need not idealize the discursive practices of Testimonies, Queries, and Advices. Friends, like every other community of faith, have compromised the best of their own tradition. There are two notable problems. One is the fact that this tradition, like any other, can and has degenerated into a formalized discourse that inspires the memorialization of discipleship rather than the reproduction of it. Jones points out that by the third generation of the Quaker movement, after the Toleration Act of 1689 halted official persecution, Advices and Queries began to function more to encourage sectarian conformity than practical formation, and that in the nineteenth century, under the influence of evangelical pietism, they became increasingly devotional (1988:9f). Today much of the discourse one hears in meeting strikes me as vague and overly solicitous. For example, London Yearly Meeting's 1964 Advices on peace sound more like sanctimonious exhortation than practical counsel: "Seek, through his power and grace, to overcome in your own hearts the emotions which lie at the root of conflict. In industrial strife, racial enmity and international tension, stand firmly by Christian principles, seeking to foster understanding between individuals, groups and nations." First World Quakers know well how the sharp edge of community self-examination has been dulled by prosperity and comfort.

A second problem is the tendency of contemporary liberal Quakers to disconnect their discursive tradition from its biblical moorings. Unprogrammed Friends have too often ignored Rufus Jones's warning that the authority of the Inner Light should not replace "the slow verification of truth by historical process; nor is it a substitute for Scripture" (Lape, 1988:24). The result over time has been theological ambivalence, followed by confusion of identity, followed by ethical drift. When our Queries arise only from within ourselves, there is a danger they will be confined by our own fearful horizons, cut off from the unboundaried questions of Jesus the Interlocutor and the radical biblical vision of the kingdom of God.

Still, we non-Quaker Christians would do well to consider this tradition. How different our churches might be if, as part of our regular worship, we reflected on queries concerning war, peace, and Christian witness rather than reciting ancient theological creeds! We can note three characteristics in the discourse of Testimonies, Queries, and Advices that can serve as a help for interrogatory theology. First, it puts the concrete before the theoretical; like liberation theology, it seeks unity in orthopraxy rather than orthodoxy. Second, it puts the communal before the private. Indeed it depends upon the vitality of corporate discernment, which is why Friends have developed a patient (if painfully slow) process of coming to "unity" (Sheehan, 1983). Third, this discourse relies on the reflective rather than the declarative and is thus open to constant rearticulation. In the words of Philadelphia Yearly Meeting's *Faith and Practice,* Testimonies, Queries, and Advices represent "landmarks, not campsites." Testimonies endure but should be reinterpreted into new contexts. Queries stand ever in need of honing so they do not become rote or irrelevant. Advices, by definition, must be revised as the times change so they will be practical, not rhetorical.

There remain, of course, broader issues of community formation, discipline, and decision making; but these are beyond my scope here (see Hauerwas, 1981; below, 6,D,1). Of particular interest to me is the way queries offer a pastoral corrective to the prophetic negations of Critical Theory. Self-examination prevents us from imagining we can somehow stand apart from the ambiguities of the world, smugly reproaching the compromises of practical politics, and reminds us how compromised we ourselves are. Sadly, hypercritical attitudes are widespread among radical Christians today and represent the biggest reason why our movement is so fragmented. It is a great irony that we who are deeply critical of the "great" orthodoxies of the established church end up constructing only "little" orthodoxies to replace them. We then relentlessly apply litmus tests to each other, thus succumbing to the grand sectarian tradition of the First World Left — defining ourselves according to our differences with those closest to us.

It is a good thing to talk about our own work and witness — this is the stuff of testimonies — as long as this is not held up as the only legitimate expression of discipleship (below, 8,F). We need to offer each other practical suggestions about how to live more simply or nonviolently or justly — this is the stuff of advices — as long as this does not deteriorate into a kind of purity code (below, 6,E,1; 7,E). We who would be radical Christians should center our discourse above all around queries, because we all stand under the questioning — at once prophetic and pastoral — of Jesus the Interlocutor. The query that ought to circulate among us is not "Who is the most faithful?," but rather "How can we deepen our journey of discipleship — *wherever* we are starting from?" In the narrative of biblical radicalism, radical *judgment* is accompanied by radical *grace,* and this should also characterize the church's interrogatory theology.

Jesus the Interlocutor is prophet and pastor, standing before history asking the right questions of us and the world, inviting his disciples to do the same. The church must rediscover the authority of questions through interrogatory theology. In the spirit of that task, I have shaped the chapters that follow around questions that arise from Mark's gospel and aimed them squarely at my church and world.

NOTES

1. As I go I will try to fix my rhetorical bearings (or in the parlance of post-modernism, plot out my discursive space). Marxist philosopher Henri Lefebvre writes the following about the varying ways of defining capitalism:

> What some have in mind is "money" and its powers of intervention, or commercial exchange, the commodity and its generalization, in that "everything" can be bought and sold. Others are concerned rather with the actors in these dramas: companies national and multinational, banks, financiers, government agencies, and so on. In either case both the unity and the diversity — and hence the contradictions — of capitalism are put in brackets. It is seen either as a mere aggregate of separate activities or else as an already constituted and closed system which derives its coherence from the fact that it endures — and solely from that fact. Actually capitalism has many facets: landed capital, commercial capital, finance capital — all play a part in practice according to their varying capabilities, and as opportunity affords; conflicts between capitalists of the same kind, or of different kinds, are an inevitable part of the process. These diverse breeds of capital, and of capitalists, along with a variety of overlapping markets — commodities, labour, knowledge, capital itself, land — are what together constitutes capitalism.... Distinct from these precisely because it is dominant... is the hegemony of one class.... It is exercised over society as a whole, culture and knowledge included, and generally via human mediation: policies, political leaders, parties, as also a good many intellectuals and experts. It is exercised, therefore, over both institutions and ideas. (1991:10)

2. I risk employing generalizing terms, despite their obvious limitations and minimization of complexity and diversity, because the alternative is the tedium of constant qualification. I use generalizations as "lexical provisions" — they provide a specific perspective but are clearly provisional to the discourse of my argument. I have chosen here to use "First" and "Third World" precisely because they are still highly contested in the debate over political semantics. Instead of the usual associations stemming from their origins in Cold War discourse, however, I understand them in terms of the center-periphery model. Thus "Third World" refers to all persons and groups who have been structurally marginalized and/or exploited within the context of the global culture of late capitalism. It therefore includes most people of color, women, ethnic minorities, and the poor, as well as those discriminated against because of sexual orientation or physical abilities. "First World," conversely, refers to those who enjoy privilege and power (what I will call entitlement) within this same global system: e.g., the broad middle and upper classes, consisting predominantly (but not exclusively) of those of European ancestry or adaptation. By choosing these rubrics I am emphasizing class distinctions over those of geography or ethnicity; First World excludes poor whites just as Third World excludes elites of color (hence there are First and Third World people inside both the U.S. and El Salvador). We must keep in mind, however, that in the U.S. racial/ethnic distinctions are deeply embedded within those of class, while gender and gender-specific divisions of labor cut across both.

3. Within U.S. society we must distinguish between the dominant culture, historically defined by an Anglo-American bourgeois ethos, and myriad "minority cultures." Obviously there are those within the dominant culture who are seeking a different ethos, just as there are those within minority cultures striving to acculturate to the dominant

ethos. But the generalization is a meaningful one, as I try to argue at length below in Chapters Seven and Nine.

4. King, Maynard, and Woodyard offer the following summary of the definitional problem:

> There are three basic positions that attempt to interpret the place of the new middle sectors. 1) The middle sectors are a distinct new class, separate from both the working class and the elite. There are definable middle class interests that are in opposition to the interests of both the workers and owners. 2) The middle sectors are not a distinct class, but instead are located with one foot in the working class and the other foot in the owning classes. Interests are sometimes aligned with the working class, sometimes with the owners. 3) The middle sectors are a part of a single larger class. In fact, the middle layers, working proletariat, and the poor are three class fractions belonging to a general laboring class. All its members earn their income through wages or salaries; though there are internal differences, they have much more in common with each other than they do with the elites. (1988:27)

While each of these definitions is in part true, the authors lean toward the third: "With the centralization of the economy, the rise of transnational corporation, and the coming of the information revolution, there is a growing similarity in the interests of all fractions of the laboring class ... particularly evident in an increasing economic precariousness and sense of powerlessness" (ibid:40). I however lean toward the first definition of a " 'professional-managerial class' made up of technicians, managers, and 'culture producers' " (ibid:27).

5. The Greek word *kairos,* used in Mark 1:15 and elsewhere, connotes a "critical moment" in which people must choose and act. The three *kairos* documents are chronicled and discussed in R. M. Brown (1990).

6. It can hardly be accidental that the sixteenth-century tale of Dr. Faustus (Eliot, 1910), who sold his soul to the devil in exchange for knowledge and power, has become as archetypal in Western culture as the story of Peter's denial.

7. The Greek terms *dogma/dogmatizō* appear only a few times in the NT and refer to imperial decrees (Lk 2:1; Acts 17:7) or legal doctrines (Eph 2:15; Col 2:14, 20) that must be overcome by the gospel. Only once are they used to refer to Christian discourse — the resolution of social conflicts proposed by the Jerusalem apostolic council in Acts 16:4 (Kittel, 1964:230ff).

8. Deconstructionism is currently ascendant in the professional guild of North American theologians and biblical scholars. For many the preoccupation with discourse shrugs off the matter of practice (except, of course, "discursive practice"). While such attitudes no doubt reflect the social location of the university, I agree with Robert Weimann's warning about the "refusal of the latest avant-garde to serve in any re-presentative function":

> There is no point in ignoring the disruption suffered by the liberal imagination and the forlorn stand of the traditional humanistic education vis-à-vis the anonymity of the powers that be (not to mention the threats to the survival of human life, which are, literally, unspeakable). The urgency of the issues raised by the antirepresentationalist directions of post-structuralist thought must not be underestimated, especially when so many forms of interpretation and representation (including their political correlatives) can be shown to constitute "a technique of power," a form of "reduction, repression, obliteration of fact." (1984:291f)

9. Quakers and "Friends" (under the influence of Jn 15:15) are synonymous. This nonconformist movement was founded by George Fox (1624–1691) in Stuart England during the mid- and late seventeenth century, and quickly spread to North America, where William Penn attempted to found a colony on the socio-political ideals of the movement (see E. Russell, 1979). "Unprogrammed" Friends refer to their silent worship services as "meetings," and their polity is organized by local monthly meetings and regional yearly meetings. Today they are outnumbered by "programmed" Friends, whose churches and theology tends to resemble the independent baptist-type traditions more than those of the silent meetings.

10. Mainstream Christian reliance on the traditional just war ethic has rarely functioned to empower church members to critique, much less noncooperate, with authority when the demands of war violate the limits of principle (see Yoder, 1984). For example, many U.S. Catholics discovered that they did not know how to implement their bishops' 1983 Peace Pastoral at the parish or parochial school level, since there were few institutional precedents for moral formation on political issues (cf Myers, 1982; below, 8,D).

Peter Droege, *The Catholic Agitator,* June 1991

Los Angeles Catholic Workers demonstrate as Desert Storm victory parade
passes Blessed Sacrament Church in Hollywood, Pentecost Sunday, 1991.

Part Two

Denial

Do you have eyes, and fail to see?
Do you have ears, and fail to hear?
And do you not remember?
Mk 8:18

Biblical theology begins its work not with an otherworldly vision or a set of ideals, but with the concrete realities of human existence, the historical predicament of a people. The journey toward liberation begins in actual political space: captivity in Egypt, disenfranchisement in exile, or, in our case, Denial in the Palace Courtyard. Doctrinal theology understands such issues in terms of sin, depravity, or the Fall. Mark, however, rarely refers to "sin"; he prefers the metaphorical language of "eyes that do not see," "ears that do not hear," and "sclerosis of the heart."

Part Two examines these archetypal *dis-abilities,* patterns of objective, subjective, and historical Denial forming a deadly "triangle of fire" that keeps us firmly domesticated in the Palace Courtyard. We are *blinded* to our privilege and the oppression of others by our illiteracy (Chapter Three). We are *silenced* by our internalization of imperial illusions (Chapter Four). And our hearts are *hardened* by our disconnection from our own collective past (Chapter Five). I suggest "political" interpretations of traditional church disciplines that can help us begin to heal our eyes, ears, and hearts: Bible study as *literacy,* prayer as *dis-illusionment,* and liturgy as *revision.*

Thoreau's prayer at Walden fits for our task of facing Denial: "Let us... work and wedge our feet downward through the mud and slush of opinion, and prejudice, and traditions, and delusion, and appearance...till we come to hard bottom...which we call reality...and set a lamp post safely."

3

"Have You Never Read...?"

Literacy

The spectacle is the nightmare of imprisoned modern society which ultimately expresses nothing more than its desire to sleep. The spectacle is the guardian of sleep.

Guy Debord, *Society of the Spectacle*

The reformation of consciousness lies solely *in the awakening of the world...from its dreams about itself.*

Karl Marx

Mark's Jesus is sitting with his disciples by the Sea of Galilee, evaluating their first campaign in Capernaum. Things are not looking too good for their little movement. Everywhere they have gone there has been conflict, and if it is not bad enough that Jesus has broken with his natural family, now he is under investigation by authorities from the capital city (3:21ff). It is, then, a good moment for reflection. Jesus can see the doubt on their faces. They obviously did not anticipate so much opposition when they joined up and are probably not ready to hear that it will get worse. Yet it is time for them to deepen their understanding of reality.

"... **So that they may look but not perceive and listen but not understand, so that they may not turn again and be forgiven**" (4:12b). Jesus cites the commissioning of the great prophet Isaiah as a case in point. No sooner had Isaiah volunteered his services as Yahweh's emissary than he was informed that his message would be rejected (Is 6:8ff). That's just how the truth fares, says Jesus. And it's that way because otherwise good people have a profound capacity to refuse to see what they do not wish to confront—in themselves and in the world. Our job is to begin the healing by diagnosing the blindness—

and nobody will like us for that. But unless true "vision" is restored, he says, reminding them of the proverbial wisdom, we *will* perish (Prov 29:18).

The metaphor of impaired perception is introduced by Mark in the context of parabolic discourse. Blindness, deafness, and hardness of heart are *spiritual* disabilities, which characterize not just a few individuals but the human condition itself. To paraphrase Mark paraphrasing Isaiah, we *see* the contradictions in our way of life but learn to live with them, and *hear* the cries of the oppressed but refuse to *understand* why the system keeps crushing them. Why? Because if we comprehended the truth of our history, we would have to "turn," which is to say *change our lives completely*. We know this pathology today as Denial.

"**...That I might see again!**" Blind Bartimaeus, Mark's archetypal disciple, is willing to give up everything in order to see, and thereby heals *himself* (10:51f). Mark's Jesus thus redefines faith as the determination to shed denial and face the world as it is, in order to struggle for what could be. But remaining clear-eyed is a constant struggle. That is why the imperatival form of the verb "to see" (*blepein, blepete*) has a crucial discursive function in Mark. It can be translated any of the following ways:[1]

Beware!	4:24
Be/aware!	8:15
Be wary!	12:38
Watch out!	13:5, 9
Be vigilant!	13:33

The last such exhortation is further linked to "staying awake" (13:34ff), because Jesus is deeply cognizant of society's "desire to sleep," in Guy Debord's words. The tragic story of Peter is again illustrative. His denial in the palace courtyard is predicated upon his inability to resist temptation in Gethsemane, and so he succumbs to, as Marx said, the world's "dreams about itself" (14:34–38).

We First World Christians are far more like Peter in the garden than we are like the beggar at Jericho's gate. We see and hear more information about more things than any people in history, we are the most educated, economically powerful, and socially mobile people in the world, yet most of us experience a profound sense of confusion and paralysis when it comes to how power is distributed in the real world. This is the most crucial contradiction of imperial culture: The more U.S. hegemony is unrestrained, the more its citizens feel impotent to change the world. Instead of staying awake to structures of racism at home or displays of militarism abroad, our eyes grow heavy, sedated by the mediated reality of the Dream Factories. Our credulity nurtures a willful ignorance of the complexities of modern capitalism, a benumbed apathy, a preoccupation with the trivial, and a fascination with spectacle. This vicious spiral of dependence, delusion, and denial has led to a near-complete loss of vision: We see the world neither the way it is nor the way it could be (below, 12,B).

"**Haven't you ever read...?**" (2:25) Jesus' charge of "illiteracy" is another metaphor for blindness.

How then is it written...? (9:12)
Is it not written...? (11:17)
Have you not read this scripture...?" (12:10)

Jesus further understands that public texts and discourses usually function to cover rather than reveal social reality. We must learn to demystify them and to analyze how the actual relations of power are structured, how they were constructed, and how they can be deconstructed. In order to "see" and "comprehend," therefore, we must learn to "read."

A. THE LOS ANGELES UPRISING, 1992: APOCALYPSE MYSTIFIED

How does the "text" of the Los Angeles uprising, and the struggle over its interpretation, help us understand the ideological mechanisms of mystification in the locus imperii?

The Los Angeles uprising of late April and early May 1992 left in disarray not only the physical terrain of my city but the popular perception of the current state of urban America as a whole.[2] The meaning we give to these dramatic events, however, depends in large part on how critically we interpret the "texts" that narrated them (see Gooding-Williams, 1993).

1. The Moment Revealed

For those of us who experienced its violence firsthand, the uprising was first and foremost an existential text. I will not soon forget the smell and sight of an afternoon sky darkened by the smoke of the hundreds of fires burning throughout the county. I remember both the visceral rage of people in poor neighborhoods who took over the streets and the equally palpable fear of people in middle-class neighborhoods who cowered in their homes. I recall the furtive forays after curfew, the helplessness of watching stores being looted, and the depressing sight of soldiers on our streetcorners. My own emotions rollercoastered wildly as we at AFSC labored alongside other community groups to keep the peace in volatile Northwest Pasadena, where Rodney King was from (Myers, 1992b).

I suppose the fact that I was so unprepared for how painful it would be to watch one's own city burning indicates just how insulated we North Americans are from the direct experience of war. I was born in this place, once a beautiful coastal basin where the sage met the sea, now a sprawling urban jungle of poverty and opulence and facade. Keenly aware of its massive contradictions but weary of those who caricature it, I have learned to love Los Angeles and to appreciate the promise of its unparalleled cultural diversity. But this war on my doorstep revealed the depth of those contradictions and the extent to which that promise remains a "dream deferred." This time the fires of rebellion spawned by the New World Order raged through *my* house; the chaos ransacked *my* heart; the blindness of a white jury laid bare *my* culpability; the uprising welled in *my* spirit.

More important than such deeply felt individual texts, however, is the uprising as a historical text. At the time few would have disputed that the events were apocalyptic. But how this was understood diverged sharply between those who interpreted these events as *revelation* and those who "covered" them as *spectacle.*

Biblically speaking, *apokalyptō* means to "reveal" or "lay bare." There can be no question but that Los Angeles was unmasked by this uprising, and not for the first time. The city's structural marginalization of the poor and people of color has been a dark but unsuppressable truth, roaring out from the shadows in East Los Angeles in 1943 and again in Watts in 1965. After the urban uprisings that spread across the country in the late 1960s, two black psychologists issued the following warning:

> If existing oppressions and humiliating disenfranchisements are to be lifted, they will have to be lifted most speedily, or catastrophe will follow. For there are no more psychological tricks blacks can play upon themselves to make it possible to exist in dreadful circumstances. No more lies can they tell themselves. No more dreams to fix on. No more opiates to dull the pain. No more patience. No more thought. No more reason. Only a welling tide risen out of all those terrible years of grief, now a tidal wave of fury and rage, and all black, black as night. (Grier and Cobbs, 1980:179)

Apocalyptic words indeed, yet since they were penned conditions have steadily worsened for most African Americans in the U.S. and along with them other members of a growing underclass. The beating of Rodney King pushed African Americans to the limit of their normally Joblike patience with a relentless history of racism, the truth of decades of police violence laid bare in a few seconds of amateur videotape. The match that finally lit the fuse of combustion was the stunning Simi Valley acquittal of the four Los Angeles police officers accused of beating King.

The immediate cause of all the mayhem was a *verdict* — from the Latin *verum dictum,* "a word truly spoken." But this acquittal surely did not "speak truly" — neither about King's case nor about police abuse in general. The jury seemed blind to what the whole world "saw" on that infamous videotape. Was this trial then just another Hollywood fiction in a city uniquely constructed on illusion? Or did it unwittingly reveal a deeper truth? A local theological reflection group I work with concluded the latter, stating in a "confession" issued shortly after the uprising:

> The Simi Valley verdict revealed the truth. Not the truth about what happened to Rodney King, but the truth about us. Sadly, history has yet again

demonstrated that the dominant culture remains blind to race and class oppression and deaf to the cries of the disenfranchised unless and until there is a riot.... We feel profoundly saddened by the recent violence, particularly the loss of life and jobs and hope. But we must recognize that we too bear responsibility for it. Indeed, as long as violence remains the language by which the dominant culture maintains its power, the unheard will be forced to use violence to reach us with their demands for justice. (Lejeune et al, 1992:102)

In this sense, then, the apocalyptic moment of uprising represented a *kairos* in the Palace Courtyard, one in which the hard truth about ourselves would be either faced or denied.

Predictably, the politicians chose Denial; Republicans wasted no time in blaming the violence on "Great Society" welfare programs, while Democrats indicted the Bush administration's "lack of leadership." But the very fact that notables of both parties were suddenly rushing to South Central Los Angeles for photo opportunities and huddling with their advisers to make pronouncements on urban policy merely confirmed the truth they refused to face: *Violence works.* The uprising succeeded in capturing the attention, however shortlived, of the elite. Certainly many African American leaders saw it this way. "If we would have only had a verdict and not an uprising," said Charles Hamilton, professor of government at Columbia University, "would issues of urban poverty have rocketed to the top of the national agenda?" "We know," fumed local congresswoman Maxine Waters, one of the few politicians who refused to denounce the violence during and after the uprising, "that poor women caught looting ten dollars' worth of Pampers would do more jail time than white-collar males caught looting millions from the savings and loans — but it always takes events like these to get people to pay attention to the realities of life in South Central."

Horace Williams of the Martin Luther King Coalition in Northwest Pasadena pointed out that the trial and its aftermath revealed stark differences in points of view on either side of the huge gulf between rich and poor in the U.S. The Simi Valley jury, representing the point of view of the dominant culture, looked at King's beating "from above," intuitively empathetic with the police while fearing the black man on the ground and characterizing his actions as those of an "animal." Those who took to the streets after the verdict, on the other hand, represented the point of view of oppressed minorities. They looked at the same event "from below," intuitively empathetic with King because they fear the police on a nightly basis. Local alternative journalist Rubém Martínez made the same point about media coverage of the uprising. "White suburban LA watches from above," he wrote, referring to the "God's eye" aerial views of looting and burning from network TV helicopters. "The black and brown are down below," scolded by pious news anchors as "thugs and hooligans" (1992:24).

With the gulf so starkly revealed, the guns took over. By the second day it seemed every inner-city shopowner was brandishing automatic weapons. The National Guard was next, taking up streetcorner positions replete with Desert

Storm-issue camouflage uniforms and equipment. Then President Bush, having decided to make Los Angeles an object lesson, ordered federal troops (including a Light Infantry Division trained in urban warfare) and other law enforcement personnel (including Border Patrol and FBI agents) to join the military occupation of the city. By that time, of course, it was too late; communities had already restored their own peace. This was a purely political show of force. Then, on Friday afternoon, forty-eight hours after the lightning of apocalyptic judgment touched down at the corner of Florence and Normandie, Rodney King delivered his moving little homily about "getting along" — as poignant as any ever delivered by Martin. His was the first public expression of grief, one commentator noted, since the violence had begun.

The uprising revealed a Los Angeles not unlike John's vision of Babylon burning: "The merchants of the earth weep and mourn for her, since business has come to a halt.... They who gained wealth from her stand far off, in fear of her torment. ... They cried out as they saw the smoke of her burning, 'In one hour she has been laid waste!' But you saints and apostles and prophets, rejoice over her, for God has given you judgment against her" (Rev 18:11, 15, 18–20). That same dissonant clash of mourning and celebration describes perfectly the grim reactions of the city fathers and commercial classes to the uprising on the one hand and the exultation of looters reveling in the streets on the other.

To the dominant news media, however, through which the rest of the world perceived the events, the uprising was apocalyptic only in the sense of sheer horrific spectacle. It was dark, surreal, socially liminal — the stuff of *Apocalypse Now*. They churned out images engineered to convey maximum fear and chaos: unattended fires, unchallenged pillaging, everywhere the wail of sirens but nowhere a sign of police (Newhagen, 1992). There were grim analogies — Saigon, 1975; Beirut, 1983; Kuwait City, 1991. (A senior editor of the *Los Angeles Times* later characterized his feelings as those of "a worried Roman in front of a television set, watching Goths at their sack"; Miles, 1992:42). And as so often before, television became the primary instrument of reality mediation. The suburbs, the rest of the nation, and the world became voyeurs to our pain, fascinated with the spectacle. *Fascination*: Deriving from the Latin *fascinum*, "evil eye," it originally meant "to bewitch or cast under a spell."

2. The Moment Covered

"The revolution will *not* be televised," warned Gil Scott Heron in his famous proto-rap anthem a few years after Watts. But by the second Los Angeles uprising his prophecy had been swallowed whole by the omnivorous, omniscient eye-in-the-sky of the six o'clock news.

The tenor of news coverage during the uprising both reflected and fueled the anxieties of the dominant culture it serves. Live coverage of the looting and burning was handled mostly from the safety of helicopters. The few reporters on the ground, filing nervous talk-and-run dispatches, were clearly unfamiliar with the street realities of South Central, and after several scrapes with violence they stuck close to police command posts (Bender, 1992; O'Neill, 1992). Predominantly white television journalists freely editorialized, moralizing that the affected communities were "only hurting themselves" — a patronizing tone clearly playing to the suburban market. *Times* columnist Peter King captured the we-they discourse in a Simi Valley lunch-counter conversation: " 'Look at them,' said one, 'they're just burning out their own.' 'I heard,' countered another, 'they're coming over the hill to burn us.' " Press attitudes changed, however, once the uprising spread north; like a wildfire it jumped the Santa Monica freeway (a traditional boundary of the "ghetto"), set the Salvadoran district of Pico-Union ablaze, then Koreatown, and finally up into Hollywood. Though it was also moving south to Long Beach, news media focus suddenly spun away to fixate on Hollywood. This was, after all, *their* neighborhood; the burning buildings now had meaning, and "them" had become "us."

On the other hand, press coverage of the militia's deployment and conduct was almost exclusively positive. The papers were full of reassuring photographs of area residents offering food and drink to their "liberators," while ignoring the suppression of civil liberties during the curfew and the mass arraignments and railroading of those arrested for looting. Again, this bias was playing to the powerful middle-class fear of losing home and property. Objective reporting could have shown that this dread was unfounded; the looting and burning, though widespread around the county, was in almost every case directed at commercial districts, not residences. While the pattern did not strictly support the claim that only establishments owned by interests from outside the community were targeted, the uprising did have a distinct overall design, however unconscious: Its rage was focused on market symbols of an economic system that was simply not working for the urban poor. But the news media wasn't looking for socio-economic explanation, they were milking the spectacle. As a result the only conclusion drawn from the events by the audience was the need for greater control over the "forces of chaos," a perception exploited by reactionary political forces, as evidenced in millionaire Richard Riordan's successful law-and-order campaign for mayor of Los Angeles a year after the uprising.

The most telling example of the news media's dominant culture perspective was its attempts to frame the uprising predominantly in terms of race. The immediate spin portrayed this as yet another "black riot," instigated by gangs and other social deviants. (*Newsweek*'s May 11, 1992, cover was typical, featuring an angry African American youth silhouetted against a raging fire — a classic icon disinterred from the white subconscious dating to Watts. Inside, a spread showing a police car being flipped was captioned: "Frustration turned into fury. Justice was beyond their reach, many blacks believed — but revenge could be taken nearer at hand." In the picture, however, all but one of the persons was Latino.) In fact this was the most multicultural uprising in U.S. history, the ethnic mix of the participants closely matching the demographics of the city. Once this reality could no longer be denied, the focus of official racism shifted from blacks to Latinos. On the third day of the uprising LAPD Chief Daryl Gates made the absurd but widely covered announcement that the majority of the looters were "illegal aliens." Official racism was mirrored by television; a news anchor at one point asked a helicopter cameraman filming a mini-mall being looted: "Can you see if they are illegals?" In contrast, when federal immigration agents dispatched to Los Angeles cynically used the opportunity to conduct random deportation sweeps in the Latino barrios, the press ignored it — until the immigrants rights community screamed loudly enough.

The race-baiting was most lurid in regard to interethnic violence. One of the most dramatic media images, immediately picked up around the country, was that of armed Koreans perched on the rooftops of their stores. Years of painstaking work by the County Human Relations Commission's Black-Korean Alliance was unraveled within minutes, once the news media decided to fixate on this conflict, though without ever asking *why* local Korean grocers had become surrogate targets for legitimate economic rage. In the months following the uprising, the *Los Angeles Times* continued this trend, giving disproportionate attention to the simmering tensions between blacks and Latinos, blacks and Asians, and internecine debates within each of these embattled communities (Myers, 1992a). This led the largest black-owned newspaper in Los Angeles, *The Sentinel,* to editorialize that the "slanted media coverage of the Uprising is disgraceful...it has once again given the media, especially the visual media, an opportunity to reveal its true colors" (1992:A6). Meanwhile reporters of color working in the industry have spoken out about how its institutional racism was unmasked in the vortex of the breaking events of the uprising (see LaBrecque, 1992; Baird, 1992).

In the subsequent struggle to interpret the meaning of the uprising, the news media has arguably done as much to *cover over* what was laid bare as it has to investigate the causes of the violence. Its almost exclusive postmortem focus on the symptoms of victimization precluded analysis of structural or historical antecedents. For example, black anger over black poverty was acknowledged as a "cause" of the uprising. But what were the causes of black poverty? Here the news media demurred, occasionally canvassing a spectrum of opinion from right-wing laments over the "deterioration of the black family" to liberal admission of "unacceptable" income disparities. What was never mentioned was the systematic deindustrialization of South Central Los Angeles over the past two decades, which has destroyed the economic base of the working class. The corporate interests that for the sake of profit have exported tens of thousands of jobs from Los Angeles to the Third World have contributed more to the devastation of South Central than all the arsonists of 1965 and 1992 combined.

Similarly, economic and social tensions attributed to the massive influx of immigrants to Los Angeles over the last decade were identified as a "cause" of the spring violence (Miles, 1992). But again, little attention was given to the structural shifts — specifically the human displacement resulting from the global migration of capital and the long-term effects of U.S. military intervention — that are so rapidly transforming the face of Los Angeles (for example, most traditionally black neighborhoods are now at least 50 percent Latino; see below, 10,B). Los Angeles is a living laboratory where these social and demographic trends can and should be analyzed.[3] The problem is, the transnational interests for whom Los Angeles is just another international center for commodities management are not easily visible. Their gleaming corporate offices — where decisions are made that dictate the movement of capital, resources, labor, and therefore the fate of whole neighborhoods — were unscathed by the violence here. But the news media does not try to make these "invisible" forces manifest because they are *owned by them*. It is easier for the press, like the blue ribbon commissions it covers, to focus attention on the "pathologies of the black underclass" and the "plight of the welfare system."

Not only did the news media fail to provide analysis, it also ignored hopeful stories of community responses to the uprising by focusing on centrist initiatives, such as the largely symbolic "Rebuild LA" commission. The spontaneous volunteer cleanup brigades that fanned out around the city even as the fires still burned, the relief aid facilitated by hundreds of unheralded local churches and synagogues, the struggles by people in the most affected neighborhoods to organize — these stories went largely untold, aside from occasional anecdotes. The most dramatic "oversight" was the remarkable Bloods-Crips gang truce, which has deeply impacted the lives of African Americans in the city's toughest public housing projects. Not only have gang-related killings fallen off in South Central, but truce leaders have offered practical suggestions for reconstruction based on the principle of self-determination for poor neighborhoods (see Rodriguez, Sloan, and Scott, 1992; Cockburn, 1992; Myers, 1992a). Yet all this has earned them only police harassment and sporadic and skeptical media coverage. But this is typical, according to journalist Carol Shirley: "Sure, the press steps in when there is a riot or a shooting. Many a Pulitzer has been won by covering the woes of the inner city. But no one is there day to day to cover the issues that are standard in the coverage of any white middle-class area. While zoning and planning may not be a reporter's dream subjects, they provide the infrastructure of a community" (1992:26). The explanation for this, she points out, is the market: "Bad demographics" deter "good advertisers" (see also Shashaty, 1992). Fortunately grassroots efforts do not depend upon media coverage. Thus, for example, the gang truce still holds as of this writing and may spread, thanks to a national summit of gang leaders held in Kansas City on the first anniversary of the uprising (see Monroe, 1993).

The press, in hot pursuit of spectacle and good advertising demographics, did not unmask the truth of the Los Angeles uprising but covered it over. Indeed the attention span for spectacle is short. Exactly four months after the fires of the uprising seared their way through our consciousness, the *Los Angeles Times* reported that "normalcy" had apparently returned: "Sharply contradicting the popular assumption that the 1992 riots were a 'wake-up call' for Los Angeles, a UCLA survey has found that the cataclysmic events of this spring did very little to alter residents' attitudes about economic, ethnic, political and social life.... The survey found county residents had no renewed commitment to addressing poverty, racial inequality or prejudice" (Wallace, 1992:B1). National news media fixation had long since moved on to other spectacles of 1992, such as the situation in Somalia and presidential election year politicking. It is true that some news media, including the *Times,* have subsequently made an effort to broaden the range of voices commenting on the uprising and even ventured into some mild self-criticism of the way coverage was handled (Shaw, 1992a, 1992b). But there has been no public admission of major errors in omission or commission, and judging by the April 1993 federal civil rights trial of the four LAPD officers accused of beating King, it would appear that little was learned. For once again Los Angeles had to endure the same kind of media distortion, with its fixation on dire predictions of a second round of violent reaction and the proliferation of arms in the city, and its ignorance of the impressive and widespread community organizing to keep the peace (Newton, 1993). Meanwhile, we have learned that it is up to us to preserve the stories of community solidarity and compassion, to press the hard questions concerning police brutality and race and class justice, and, most of all, to confront the real verdict about ourselves and our system.

B. "WHY DO THE SCRIBES SAY...?" MEDIATING CREDULITY

Why do media saturation and the information "revolution" leave us so ignorant about the things that actually shape our lives?

Every society has sectors that seek to dispense "official" versions of reality: cultic oracles, chiefly councils, diplomatic spokespersons, propagandists. In Mark's story this sector is supremely represented by the scribal class, whose "authority" Jesus therefore seeks to challenge from the outset (1:22, 27). Not only does he repeatedly and publicly contradict the scribal party line, he also asserts an alternative authority in order to create "ideological space" for people to see things differently (2:6ff). In a particularly revealing moment, his disciples, having just witnessed an apocalyptic vision of the Human One (9:2ff), set about trying to correlate it with the six o'clock news: "Why do the scribes say...?" (9:11) It is no accident that immediately following this episode we find the disciples unable to prevail in an argument — with the scribes — over their inability to exorcise a demon of "silencing" (9:14ff; below, Chapter Four). The dominant culture rules ultimately by our internalization of its imperatives; those who are "all ears" to the official "voice" become "deaf" to alternative ones. To get the "mute" to find their own voice, Jesus' must turn this question back on them: "How is it the scribes can say...?" (12:35ff).

The more highly differentiated and complex the society, the more its members become dependent upon sectors of specialized knowledge. Technocratic capitalism socializes us to give greater credence to experts and "authorities" than we give to our own personal or community experience, insight, and tradition. Although its sophisticated technologies and divisions of labor claim to emancipate us from the drudgeries of life, they have in fact rendered us more rather than less dependent upon institutions of mediation. We are hostage to either too much or too little knowledge. On the one hand, public discourses (mainly through the media) overexpose us to the world, assaulting us with a surplus of unanalyzed and uncontextualized "facts." I am an educated person, but I cannot hope to understand in any meaningful depth the stories to which I am exposed in one late-1992 edition of the *Los Angeles Times:* the violence of underworld Mexican/Colombian drug cartels; political appointments concerning the administration of the Los Angeles Harbor; the violence between Muslims and Hindus in India; reductions in L.A. County supplements to AFDC welfare payments; U.N. negotiations around establishing "no-fly" zones over Bosnia; or the impact of six years of drought on metropolitan water supplies in California! This is why it has become an axiom of modern social psychology that in order to defend ourselves against being overwhelmed by information about the world, we inevitably become numb to it. On the other hand, the average urban dweller has too little practical local knowledge. We rarely build or maintain our own dwellings or produce what we consume. Do we have alternative technologies if the sewer line breaks or the electric power goes out? Do we know how to fix our watch or our computer or our automobile? Do we collaborate on projects with our neighbors or know whether there are natural food resources within a mile radius of our house? In most cases, probably not; instead our expertise lies in the use of intermediate systems — we know who to call to purchase or fix or service the things we depend on. Because there is too much technical knowledge to master, we necessarily rely on experts, from plumbers to political analysts. But these experts notoriously give us too little information, offering us a diet of overdigested, neatly packaged solutions to our problems, which perpetuate our dependence upon their services.

Whether too much or too little knowledge, the result is the same: increasing disempowerment and subjection to institutions that mediate reality. Mark's metaphor of "blindness" is truly apt for our dilemma: We see more than ever before, and understand less. It seems wise, therefore, to reflect a bit more broadly on those brokers and shapers of information we have come to refer to (in reified fashion!) as the "media." Though the media is only one mechanism of mystification in the *locus imperii,* I focus on it because it is arguably the strongest discursive force in our everyday life. Laurien Alexandre gives five indexes by which we can measure its influence:

1) The high rate of media consumption and the saturation of our society by the media;
2) The media's influence on shaping the perceptions, beliefs and attitudes of our people;
3) The growth in media industries and the importance of information in our society;
4) The importance of media in our central democratic processes; and
5) The increasing importance of visual communication and information. (1990:6)

As our own capacity to manage knowledge wanes, that of the media waxes, making it arguably the most powerful sector in modern society. It makes or breaks politicians and determines the vicissitudes of fame; it sells dreams and transforms mundane products into magical icons; it determines which issues will be the stuff of history and which places will be publicly invisible. We "apprehend" events, local or global, through the newspaper or television; we "experience" culture (music, theater, visual arts, storytelling) through movies and videos; we "know" about products and "learn" about consumer choices through commercials and advertisements. Let us take a brief look at the three major strata of media and how each persuades us to be credulous consumers of their discourse. Here I revisit the *history*-referent, or news media; in the next section, the *story*-referent, or "entertainment" media, and the *product*-referent, or commercial media.

My discussion of the form and content of the news media's coverage of the Los Angeles uprising is simply a dramatic example of a daily reality. The problem is not that reality is *edited* by the news media — that is the very nature of delimited coverage of life through stories — but that journalistic institutions perpetuate the myth of neutrality and objectivity. The genius of this myth is that it generates "notions and images that so fit into the dominant political culture's field of established images that they appear not as arguments and biased manipulations but as 'the nature of things' " (Parenti, 1986:xi).

It is conventional wisdom among social critics that "freedom of the press" in democratic societies belongs primarily to those who own the presses. Media conglomerates (publishing houses, newspaper chains, radio and television networks) dominate public discourse through their brokering of the information market. "One of the most profitable commodities in the modern world is human attention," writes media critic Ben Bagdikian; "Whoever can harvest it in wholesale quantities can make money in kind" (1989:819). The increasing centralization of the media reflects their control by big capital. Soon "five to ten corporate giants will control most of the world's important newspapers, magazines, books, broadcast stations, movies, recordings and videocassettes" (ibid:805). This ensures that independent media remain marginalized, exceptions that only prove the rule. Unable to compete economically or technologically with the networks, alternative media (even the liberal middle of public radio and television) are constantly embattled financially and/or ideologically. Small local newspapers are disappearing at a rate similar to family farms; those that survive are strictly provincial in influence and dependent upon the wire services for bigger stories. Independent television networks endure only by parroting the Big Three, and the advent of cable has brought little of the promised programming diversity.

The ideological conformity of the U.S. news media is seen in how little variance exists among competitors concerning which stories are covered and how. Let us take, as does *Manufacturing Consent*, a recent documentary featuring Noam Chomsky, an example so obvious it is easy to overlook. The brutal invasion of tiny Kuwait by its large neighbor Iraq in August 1990 was immediately accredited virtually cosmic significance by the news media. The U.S. military "response" to U.N. resolutions calling for Iraqi withdrawal dominated the news for almost a year; after the withdrawal of U.S. forces, coverage of Kuwait returned to its previous sporadic and incidental character (see Marchik, 1992). In contrast, the brutal invasion of tiny East Timor by its large neighbor Indonesia in December 1975 was scarcely noted by the U.S. news media. Despite U.N. resolutions calling for Indonesian withdrawal, the U.S. did nothing (indeed continued to arm its client state Indonesia); the ensuing genocidal Indonesian occupation and the heroic Timorese resistance have been ignored by Western media for almost two decades (Ramos-Horta, 1987).

Instances of such political reality-brokering, small and large, can be found every day in the *locus imperii* (see, e.g., Oreskes' analysis of the "war on drugs," 1990). But the way the press magnifies the presidential "bully pulpit" is always best observed during wartime, and recent U.S. military interventions in Lebanon, Grenada, Libya, and Panama were no exception. In each case the public found out about our inauguration of hostilities through highly dramatic reportage. Even the most rudimentary questions about these policies were not raised by the self-censoring news media until it was clear that U.S. forces had prevailed. The new, stricter guidelines for information control and press access to the battlefront, developed by the Pentagon during this period, only formalized the unofficial collaboration (Marchik, 1992:13f; see Winter, 1992). The absurd but logical extension of this military-media choreography was exhibited during the "landing" of Marines in Somalia in early December 1992. Having been "tipped off" about this "secret" night operation, the press corps packed the beach, while camouflaged soldiers in full assault gear crawled up the sand under the glare of media lights through a field of microphones and cameras (Fineman, 1992).

The more existentially powerful the narrative forms used by the news media, the more credulous our consumption of them. CNN live during the bombing of Baghdad or helicopter footage of looting in Los Angeles overwhelm us with dramatics, while the day-after statistics, carefully designed to read like baseball box scores, reassure us that the apocalypse is under control (see H. Smith, 1992). Guy Debord comments: "In societies where modern conditions of production prevail, all of life presents itself as an immense accumulation of spectacles.... The specialization of images of the world is completed in the world of the autonomous image, where the liar has lied to himself.... The spectacle is the existing order's uninterrupted discourse about itself, its laudatory monologue" (Martin, 1992:3). Television news is clearly influenced by the increasingly sophisticated special effects of current cinematography, with which it has to compete.[4] Thus we see the steady drift toward "infotainment," a discourse clearly designed to soothe or distract the viewer's perplexity about the world by replacing ambiguity and analysis with "mediagenic" soundbytes, EZ graphics, and "star-based" news personalities. Meanwhile coming to meet this drift from the other direction are the so-called "reality-based" entertainment shows ("America's Most Wanted," etc.). It is no wonder that an August 1989

Times Mirror survey concluded that Americans are becoming increasingly confused about which television programs are news and which are entertainment (Rosentiel, 1989).

The fourth estate has become another principality alongside those it claims to scrutinize; I am simply stating the case, not arguing it. Readers interested in studying the matter more are strongly encouraged to consult resources such as Parenti's *Inventing Reality: The Politics of the Mass Media* (1986); Chomsky's *Manufacturing Consent: The Political Economy of the Mass Media* (1988), or Bagdikian's *The Media Monopoly* (1990). My point here is that we should both seek alternative news sources and exercise the "hermeneutics of suspicion" on mainstream ones.[5] In short, we must learn to become "journalists of the dominant journalism," asking the classic questions about *what* is reported; *who* determines it and *why;* and *when* and *how* it is covered. We must exercise these critical muscles despite the fact that we are discouraged from doing so by the gloss and self-referentiality of the media forms themselves. In the *locus imperii,* we dare not read the morning newspaper without reading between the lines; we dare not watch the evening news without watching out!

C. "WHY DOES THIS GENERATION SEEK A SIGN?"
THE RULE OF IMAGE AND THE WAR OF MYTHS

How do the engineered images of the entertainment and commercial media encode deeper subtexts about the culture of capitalism?

The media in the U.S. is much more than the purveyor of information about world events. For example, a cursory glance at any supermarket magazine rack will confirm that we are inundated with the most astonishing variety of magazines specializing in "leisure" culture: our hobbies, our special interests, and our insatiable appetites for "self-improvement." But still reigning supreme in popular leisure culture are movies and television, probably because they are the major surviving forms of storytelling and cabaret that are so basic to human social existence. Unlike traditional societies, however, our dance, music, storytelling, and ritual traditions are largely produced and consumed as forms of "entertainment" (recall the warning of Silko's elder!), alienated — or at least highly differentiated — from "real" life. This also means that the entertainment and arts industries represent a discrete and powerful sector in the overall political economy.

A particularly troubling characteristic of the "narrative media" today is its tendency to offer the dangerous combination of spectacular settings, shallow characters, and facile plots (see Christie's analysis of the same tendency in Weimar Germany, 1993). Lack of complexity and depth contributes to the slow but steady atrophy of our "native competence" in storytelling and interpretation (Funk, 1988:5f). The triumph of form over content (lavish settings, "star" presence and power, special effects) ever more firmly shuts out the audience from imaginative interaction. We feel alienated from the story worlds of modern cinema, with their technically impressive verisimilitude, precisely because we do not have to employ our imagination. It is difficult to identify with characters if we can never escape from their star personas or to remain engaged when the plot turns are obvious; what often remains is only the power of bigger-than-life scenes of violence or sexuality. The function of this discourse keeps us firmly distanced as passive consumers of images that may indeed overwhelm us in the moment but that quickly fade because they have no real point of contact with our lives. Their staying power is rather in our subconscious, where the lingering images of idealized settings, persons, and/or happy endings nurture not struggle in the public world but dissatisfaction with our private existence. To take an obvious example, ideals of female beauty or male strength — the ubiquity of "cheesecake" and "beefcake" in the movies — has done little to inspire men or women to overturn patriarchy and much to engender social stereotypes and sexual alienation. Laurence Goldstein writes: "The fantasy body, the body offered as sexual fetish, becomes more and more inescapable, and the occasions for self-doubt and anxiety more and more frequent. Those who profit by preying on such anxieties rob us of our well-being, our sense of having a body sufficient for the pleasures of everyday experience. How to resist their blandishments becomes a cultural question as important as any in our time" (1993:M5). To combat these discourses of alienation and passivity, we would do well to learn from Augusto Boal's "Theater of the Oppressed," which teaches audiences how to move from being spectators to "spect-actors" by taking over roles and transforming the texts of performance to confront problems of exploitation and power (Boal, 1992; Salvorsen, 1993).

Much has been written about the advent of home television as a powerful force of social conformity — there is no need for Big Brother to watch us because we are watching Big Brother. Obviously in such a situation the entertainment media has enormous power to legitimate the dominant culture and to shape perceptions and values — however much it claims simply to respond to market demand. When popular television dramas or comedies disproportionately reflect the world of law enforcement and criminal justice, we are socialized to see those sectors as disproportionately important. When protagonists routinely employ brute force to overcome personal or social complications, it feeds our appetite for gratuitous violence in the service of self-justifying chauvinism. If the social setting of white middle-class life rules, such that other contexts are hailed as exceptional, this reinforces the dominant culture's comforting fantasy that it represents what is "normal." White baby boomers might remember how confused we were by the families without problems portrayed on 1950s- and 1960s-era television, such as "Father Knows Best." We can only imagine the havoc caused by the same entertainment menu projected across class, race, and cultural lines, however. A big part of the oppression of minorities in the U.S. is the difficulty of maintaining self-image when one is constantly bombarded with images of someone else's class or ethnic reality while rarely encountering one's own (and only then in a way that conforms tightly to the dominant culture's stereotype).

Ariel Dorfman reminds us in his important book *The Empire's Old Clothes: What the Lone Ranger, Babar, and Other Innocent Heroes Do to Our Minds* that no cultural product, no matter how allegedly innocuous, is ideologically neutral:

> Industrially produced fiction has become one of the primary shapers of our emotions and our intellect in the twentieth century. Although these stories are supposed to merely entertain us, they constantly give us a secret education. We are not only taught certain styles of violence, the latest fashions, and sex roles by TV, movies, magazines, and comic strips; we are also taught how to succeed, how to love, how to buy, how to conquer, how to forget the past and suppress the future. We are taught, more than anything else, how not to rebel. (1983:ix)

And what about the export of American popular entertainment culture abroad? Many who have traveled to the Third World have had experiences like mine during a visit to a remote village in Melanesia in 1983. I saw dozens of indigenous men and women gathered around a television, absorbed in an episode of "Gilligan's Island." The absurd socio-cultural gestalt of that moment — the very same show that trivialized "South Sea" island life to North Americans was trivializing North American comic culture to them — suggests the potentially demonic power of exported media.

This is not to imply that all U.S. cultural exports are categorically harmful. It can be delightful to see one of the many vital and even subversive pop-cultural expressions being encountered and integrated in another context. I think of watching teenagers in the Marshall Islands mixing rap music and break dancing with traditional material, for example. It is not necessarily a bad thing that Michael Jackson or Mickey Mouse are hugely popular in Asia or Latin America. Highly fabricated though these icons may be in their present form, they have roots in genuinely redemptive American cultural soil — rhythm and blues and early Disney animation (below, 10,D). But it seems that these commercial cultural exports are far outstripped by the inane or the insidious. Rambo and slasher-type horror films, for example — bad enough when consumed in our context — are aggressively marketed abroad, especially in the Third World; who can calculate their impact outside the cultural framework that produced them? Some of this has recently been acknowledged with satisfaction by the Right. Columnist Benjamin Stein, for example, calls television the ultimate American weapon:

> When the federal government's TV Marti began its much-heralded broadcast invasion of Fidel Castro's Cuba this week, its programming was not a stirring reading of the Constitution ... [or] "the Wealth of Nations" ... [or] a documentary about the right to vote or freedom of worship. Nope, TV Marti began its life programming an episode of the hit sitcom "Kate and Allie," some popular videos from MTV and a selection of World Series excerpts.... The fact is that American ... commercial TV has become a

major battering ram knocking down the walls of dictatorships everywhere. The sitcoms, game shows, cop shows...are an overwhelmingly powerful weapon for exposing just how good American life is, and how terrible life is in a gray, repressive Marxist dictatorship. (Stein, 1990)

This self-congratulatory cultural chauvinism was echoed by conservative commentators who attributed the demise of the Berlin Wall to the lure of the West as portrayed through television.

If First World Christians wish the role of entertainment media to be something other than projecting imperial illusions into hearts and minds here and around the globe, we must become more critical of their political and spiritual character. However wrongheaded their tactics of censorship may be, the Christian Right is not in principle wrong in their militant opposition to media violence and sex, for example. One of the most basic disciplines we can exercise is simply to discuss the popular entertainment we watch. If we are taking time to see a movie, let us take a bit more time to examine ways in which its narrative strategy and structure function to articulate social and political values: Is it subversive or supportive of the dominant culture? This is not to advocate turning all time and space for entertainment into dour discussions of deconstructive political correctness. What Frederic Jameson calls the "unmasking of cultural artifacts as socially symbolic acts" (1981:20) can be fun and can help us learn to better appreciate what we have seen. And sometimes we simply want to be distracted, and that is healthy — as long as we do not forget that every narrative encodes a social practice (*BSM:*14ff), and is thus part of the "war of myths" for our hearts and minds.

Even the briefest survey would not be complete without a "word from our sponsors." Advertising is omnipresent in the *locus imperii,* a relentless aural and visual onslaught upon our consciousness with objectified texts and seductive subtexts that we cannot help but absorb. Quite apart from the cacophony of radio jingles and thirty-second television skits, the maze of retail signing alone has profoundly transformed common space. Stuart Ewen has shown how twentieth-century visual discourse has come to be dominated by the graphic arts, which in turn have come to be dominated by commercial application.

This prevalence of graphic design is a historical outcome of social processes which gathered momentum during the 19th century, when the kinetic and confusing cultural terrain of urban and industrial life was suddenly suffused by the new and powerful instruments of mass reproduction. The dazzling variety of chromos and photographs, billboards and broadsides, packaging and publicity which pervaded and altered the nature of life by the end of the 19th century prompted the author Vachel Lindsay to declare America a "hieroglyphic civilization." By the 1920s the image was becoming a consciously managed element of modern marketing strategy: to move goods off shelves, to establish a prominent identity for corporations, to transform the consciousness of a proletariat into that of a consumeriat. Propelled by an increasing awareness of psychological motivation and of the powers of visual suggestion, businessmen increasingly looked toward graphic design (in advertising, packaging and public display) as an essential tool of what they termed "consumer engineering." (1990:69)

In the *locus imperii* we are surrounded by "a crazy quilt of graphic material shaping — in large part — the limits of perception." Take, for example, a billboard seen throughout southern California during the 1992 Christmas holidays. It read:

> ingle ells, ingle ells . . .
> What are the holidays without J & B?

This was an exceedingly sophisticated sign system, but one immediately intelligible to the average consumer. It was clever; it was cute; it could be read at sixty-five miles per hour; and it "worked." Afterward many thought of J & B scotch when singing Christmas carols — what little is left of European-American folk culture having been effectively commandeered into the service of capitalism.

An excellent study of the commodification of culture is Mark Miller's analysis of the expropriation of 1950s and 1960s rock and roll to sell products targeting the baby boomer market:

> Once too wild for television, rock and roll became, after 1981, a necessary adjunct to TV's all-pervasive ad. . . . A few years ago, advertisers started grabbing every serviceable oldie in the rock and roll canon, hoping that each vivid tag might jump-start the nostalgic yearning of the aging viewer. This was, and is, a deliberate project. "This music was once the most important thing in the lives of the people we're trying to sell cars to now," said a senior VP and "music director" at Young & Rubicam. . . . They see nothing wrong with revising an old love song so that it seems to woo a hatchback or a cheeseburger, a bowl of cereal or a chicken snack, as they have done, for example, by using "Ain't No Mountain High Enough" to pitch Fords, by redoing the Platters' "Only You" as "only Wendy's," by using the Turtles' "Happy Together" to sell General Mills Golden Grahams, and by using the Diamonds' "Little Darling" to push the Chicken Little sandwich for Kentucky Fried Chicken Corporation. (1988:39f)

Similarly, today few major rock, rap, or jazz concerts are held without corporate sponsorship.

With the proliferation of retail semiotics and commercial overdetermination of cultural discourses, argues Ewen, "an epistemological crisis has ensued: other ways of knowing, alternative ways of seeing have become increasingly scarce . . . encourag[ing] a comprehension of the world as a simulacrum of easily manipulated surfaces in which underlying meanings tend to vanish to all but the most critical eye" (1990:69). This is the rule of image, and we see it as much in industrial discourses as in those of fashion. For example, the July 27, 1990, *Los Angeles Times* carried a front-page article describing the Justice Department's recommendation that the Pentagon bar Northrop Corp. from future defense contracts because of the firm's conviction on criminal fraud charges (faking cruise missile tests). Never mind; a dramatic full-page ad in the business section heralded the results of Northrop's flight testing of the B-2 Stealth bomber. Image overwhelms fact. The marketing media overdetermines everything — even war. In his analysis of the commercial spin-offs from Desert Storm, Scott Shuger shows that twentieth-century advertising during wartime traditionally tried to portray the product in a way that "served the larger cause"; now "it's practically the other way around" (1991:20).

Regardless of our formal educational background, we are all extremely adept at deciphering the surface meanings of capitalist hieroglyphics. But while instantly suggestive images or sounds distract and even entertain us at the conscious level, at the deep-structural level of the subconscious they socialize us to be obedient consumers. By repeatedly absorbing the fictive jousting of rival car, deodorant, or television marketeers, we become more likely to believe their claims to offer us real choices and less likely to inquire about the real interests that lie behind these discourse games. Paul Wachtel, in *The Poverty of Affluence,* calls this the "Panglossian circle of mainstream economics, which defines our real preferences as revealed — conveniently — by precisely what we buy" (1989:32). As Marcuse put it, "People recognize themselves in their commodities": "Free choice among a wide variety of goods and services does not signify freedom if these goods and services sustain social controls over a life of toil and fear — that is, they sustain alienation. And the spontaneous reproduction of superimposed needs by the individual does not establish autonomy; it only testifies to the efficacy of the controls" (1964:8). We have fully internalized capitalism when the opportunity to choose between thirty varieties of toothpaste becomes the working definition of human liberty, and when we no longer experience cognitive dissonance when Budweiser does spots on "responsible drinking," or when Philip Morris makes grants to minority health fairs, or when Georgia-Pacific trumpets its commitment to the environment. All relationships have then been "consum-mated"; that is, our appetites are completely transformed, and we are consumed with what we consume. (For further exploration see Kavanaugh's *Following Christ in a Consumer Society — Still: The Spirituality of Cultural Resistance,* 1992:21ff; below, 6,D.)

"Why does this generation seek a sign?" asks Jesus. But in late capitalism we no longer need to supplicate the gods for signs; they surround us, direct us, consume us. A popular current beer commercial offers the perfect mantra for a credulous consumeriat: "Why ask why?" Ours is a passive-aggressive existence in the *locus imperii:* We are passive consumers of mediated reality through aggressive discourses that seek to form us socially and spiritually. In such a world the disciplines of critical literacy are indispensable in our struggle against de-

nial. If we are not "asking why," then, as Jacques Ellul wrote in his classic study
Propaganda, we assume the "mentality of the propagandee," wherein our "confused thoughts are crystalized" by the media. In this case, Ellul put it grimly,
"the reader himself offers his throat to the knife of the propaganda he chooses"
(1965:104).

D. "DO YOU SEE ANYTHING YET?"
POPULAR EDUCATION IN A FIRST WORLD CONTEXT

How can critical literacy help break the "culture of silence" and political
passivity into which capitalism socializes us?

"Do you see anything yet?" (Mk 8:23). Jesus' question to the blind man at
Bethsaida is Mark's most crucial query to disciple-readers. Is Chevy the heartbeat of America? It seems a silly, even antisocial, question to ask out loud as
one is enjoying a televised baseball game with friends. Everybody knows this
is "only" an advertising slogan, albeit backed up by seductive images of happy,
good-looking young models and fantasies of off-road invincibility. But if so,
why and by whom and for what purpose are we being force-fed such a grand
myth just to sell a car? Are Marines in Somalia "doing God's work"? Does Los
Angeles explode because of "thugs and hooligans"? Are California jobs being
taken by "illegal aliens"? "Have we never read" these texts, asks Jesus the Interlocutor — which is to say, *interrogated* them? To ask such "silly" questions
then is to take up the long journey toward becoming active, critical subjects,
not passive and credulous objects, of the discourses that swirl around us. It is
to "stay awake" to the spin the media puts on reality, because "spectacle is the
guardian of sleep" (below, 12,B). This is the work of literacy.

1. Liberating Pedagogy

It was in teaching the poor to read that Brazilian educator Paulo Freire developed the notion of "the adult literacy process as cultural action for freedom,"
known today around the world as the work of "conscientization" (1992:101).
Freire identified two problems confronting his students. On the one hand, their
technical illiteracy guaranteed their captivity to what he called the "culture
of silence" — their disempowerment and marginalization in a society dominated by the discourses of "literate" culture (paper transactions, contract law,
print media, etc.). These were people who believed their world was not important, a reflection of the fact that they did not have ownership of their work.
On the other hand, Freire recognized that traditional education — including
government-sponsored basic literacy programs — was the primary mechanism
by which people internalized their oppression. It taught them to mimic the dominant culture and dismiss their own experiences, reinforcing their feelings of
inferiority and powerlessness. Freire asserted that pedagogy should have a vision of transformation rather than simply socializing students into the existing

order: "When education is no longer utopian, i.e. when it no longer embodies the dramatic unity of denunciation and annunciation, it is either because the future has no more meaning...[or people] are afraid to risk living the future as creative overcoming of the present" (1971:269). For pedagogy to be liberating, however, its practices, not just its content, had to be changed.

Freire challenged what he called the "digestive, nutritional concept of knowledge," in which words, facts, and concepts determined by "expert" educators are deposited into and "nourish" the learner (ibid:252f). He advocated that learners should be seen as actively participating subjects in the discovery of reality, not passive objects in the transfer of knowledge.

> In the first hypothesis, interpreting illiterates as [people] marginal to society, the literacy process reinforces the mythification of reality by keeping it opaque and by dulling the "empty consciousness" of the learner with innumerable alienating words and phrases. By contrast, in the second hypothesis — interpreting illiterates as [people] oppressed within the system — ...the learner assumes the role of knowing subject in dialogue with the educator. For this very reason, it is courageous endeavor to demythologize reality, a process through which [people] who had previously been submerged in reality begin to emerge in order to re-insert themselves into it with critical awareness. (Ibid: 256)

Freire insisted that the illiterate learn to read using texts from their own lives ("the difficult apprenticeship in naming the world"), not a vocabulary supplied by and drawn from the dominant order ("memorizing an alienated world"). The role of the educator was to facilitate and to pose questions. This process has two steps. First, a group's experience (in which it normally would be unreflectively caught up) is "projected" as a kind of "text," which it then stands back from and reflects upon critically. Naming this text is what Freire called "codification." Second, the group seeks to analyze this text, breaking it into its constituent parts and their interrelationships (the "deep structure"), which are then placed in the wider context of other facts in order to discover relationships previously unperceived. This is "decodification." Through this process the group moves from "ad-miration" of the world (viewing it as an immutable reality) to a critical understanding of how it works, so that it can be engaged through "cultural action." Conscientization is an ongoing dialectic of critical reflection (literacy) and liberative practice (cultural action), since "myths remain after the infrastructure is transformed, even by revolution" (1971:263).

Many of Freire's ideas are used in contemporary literacy campaigns, though his pedagogy by no means has prevailed in the field.[6] Among thousands of base communities and sectorial groups throughout the Third World, however, Freirean-inspired popular education has animated critical reflection and social struggle. As with liberation theology, the methods of popular education have trickled up to North America. For example, women from Dolores Mission parish in an East Los Angeles barrio are using it (Vilchis, 1991), as are Central

American and Filipino immigrants in other parts of the city (Hernandez, 1991). My colleagues in AFSC's Nationwide Women's Program, in collaboration with the Religious Network for Equality for Women, promote "economic literacy" workshops for women of color, doing structural analysis in the context of the workplace (Lacey, 1990). The Highlander Center in Tennessee and the Center for Ethics and Economic Policy in northern California produce educational resources for community-based economic development. The Center of Concern has helped popularize the method by distributing Anne Hope and Sally Timmel's classic *Training for Transformation: A Handbook for Community Workers* (1984), as well as other resources (Holland and Henriot, 1984; Henriot, 1991).

There seems to be considerable question, however, about the degree to which methods developed by and for poor and oppressed groups can be adapted for dominant culture groups wishing to become critically literate. The problem is basically this: The "cultures of silence" are analogous, but the pathologies are inverse. The technically illiterate poor lack access to educational resources and suffer from social invisibility. The entitled are technically literate and have access to education but tend to be uncritical of what we read and learn. In fact we are *overeducated* — our knowledge is too specialized and our pedagogy too elitist, the result being that we are overly reliant on the authoritarian culture of expertise and meritocracy. At the same time, as I noted above (B), we have too little practical knowledge; our tendency to intellectualize constantly gets in the way of reflecting on our own concrete experiences, which our education has taught us to mistrust. We are socially visible, but only in the objectified or idealized reproductions of the media, which trivializes our life-experience just as it dismisses that of the poor, effectively alienating both of us from our own texts. But when we middle-class people do analyze our life-texts, we find them already overdetermined by gender, race, and class delusions, so that we have to struggle to distinguish our true selves from mystified and alienated images of ourselves. If the poor are underidentified in the dominant culture, we are overidentified. Thus the poor have to spend more time codifying, and we decodifying. It is my belief that First World people are every bit as much in need of a popular pedagogy of critical literacy as oppressed groups; but methods that have proven their vitality among the latter must be adapted to our context, not simply aped.

2. Demystifying Economics

The difficulties First World people typically face in this process are best illustrated by considering the question of economics. Now, capitalism is all about economics, but for most of us, nothing is more opaque. We feel disengaged from the complex, interdependent economic systems (international currency markets, Federal Reserve monetary controls) to which we are inextricably tied. The big issues that dictate how millions live and die (the debt crisis, free trade agreements) seem incomprehensible and remote. These feelings are reinforced by the economic discourse of the media:

When we hear about the ups and downs of the stock market, or the tugs of war in trade with other industrialized nations, we are meant to experience the same sense of facing "uncontrollable factors" as when we listen to weather forecasts. If even the experts appear to be so shaky in their predictions and explanatory powers, it is not surprising that the word economics scares most of us, especially women, keeping us from exploring it further. Such an attitude is encouraged by capitalism's orthodox advocates, who see the system as doing better without critics, as having its own built in checks and balances of power. (Lacey, 1990:4)

With the public economic discourse limited to the arcane numbers game of Dow Jones averages and daily interest rates, whose determinations are inscrutable to the common person, it is no wonder we feel mystified. The "analysis" found in the business press — what experts think about current trends and policy debates between rival capitalists — is further designed to disempower the laity.

Let us say a First World social justice group decides to meet to study economics. Invariably they will employ some secondary text of economic analysis pitched at a level several steps removed from their own experience. The discussion quickly becomes abstract or perhaps ideologically polarized between those "attacking" and "defending" a capitalist system they don't really understand. Meanwhile those who do not feel as though they have enough "expertise" quickly stop participating, assuming a passive "educate me" attitude — if they do not drop out altogether. (Needless to say, these dynamics would be different if the group's topic was fashion, baseball, or movies.) What is overlooked by this study group is the concrete texts of their own economic lives. We all participate in the same economic system, we all have positive or negative experiences with it — indeed it is the one thing each member of the group has in common. Is not this month's price fluctuations at the gas pump a text about the political economy of oil? Does not the experience of talking with landlords when searching for an apartment to rent, or of encountering the expensive maze of paper-handling middlepeople when buying a house, represent texts about the housing market — and homelessness? Yet we are dissuaded from talking about our real lives by a double taboo. First, we feel that our daily transactions are too trivial for a "serious" discussion of economics. Second, we are reluctant to disclose too much of our actual economic circumstances, fearing embarrassment about being too affluent or not middle class enough; this is our cultural tendency toward privatization.

Obviously there is a place for secondary texts and outside resources in learning about economic issues. Basic concepts and models are indeed crucial to critical perception — that is the great contribution of Marx, and why his ideas will stay relevant as long as there is capitalism. Lucid and readable analyses and organizational resources are readily available; that is not the problem in the *locus imperii*.[7] The problem is our sense of alienation and detachment from our actual economic existence. So the best texts to begin with are our own, because they reveal just how much we do know as well as what we need to learn. What if our group were to begin instead with the "text" of a simple purchase one of them made that day — let's say a carton of milk — and try to "map" the economy from there?[8] Any group of consumers can easily name the five generic "sites" of the economic production and correlate them to actual geography in their world:

Generic "site"	Concrete "geography"
(i) Consumption	home
(ii) Distribution/marketing	supermarket/advertisement
(iii) Production	dairy
(iv) Resource extraction	cows in a field
(v) Capital	bank/corporate office

As consumers we obviously know best what and how we consume (i); in this case, we drink the milk at home. We are also very sophisticated in how and why we purchased the product (ii), knowing how to "read" the commercial media (above, C); perhaps we are loyal to a brand of milk or saw it on sale somewhere. For most of us, however, our knowledge diminishes sharply once we go below the dotted line I have drawn. We tend to have far less experience with where and how a commodity was produced (iii); perhaps as a schoolchild we visited a commercial dairy, but do we know where *this* carton of milk came from? We know next to nothing about what a commodity is made of and where its material elements came from (iv); many of us still know that milk comes from a cow, but do we know what that cow is fed or what is added to the milk? The last site — who profits, and how, and how much (v) — is almost entirely invisible to the average consumer; do we have any clue about the horizontal or vertical diversification of the corporation that owns the dairy, or how the Milk Board lobbies, or what the profit margin is on a carton of milk? More important, do we even care?

Consumers are socialized to be preoccupied exclusively with what is above the dotted line: getting the "best" product at the "best" price in the most "convenient" manner possible. These are at the top of our economic agenda, and we are very adept at them. It does not matter to us that they are in fact at the bottom of the actual chain of production — the raw material has been extracted, the industrial processing accomplished, and the major profit realized long before we see the product. But we are content to live above the line, which represents a kind of wall of mystification past which we can rarely go with the kind of practical knowledge we employed so well above the line. What is more, we are not likely to get help from either side of the line. Consumer labels on a product (i) might tell us where it was manufactured but will certainly not inform us about the working conditions there or who owned the machines or what the workers were paid. Retail signing and pricing of items at the store (ii) might tell us a product's content but nothing about how its raw materials were extracted and who owned the rights to them or the environmental impact of extraction. Consumers do of course ultimately pay the social cost of problems occurring below the line — industrial pollution, for example. But this is passed on to us indirectly (i.e., not figured in to consumer pricing) and so seems even more obscure to us.

This exercise may seem discouraging, since it seems to reveal how much we do not know. But if we start interrogating reality in the consumer space we know so well and if we use our sophistication at that level, we can generate critical momentum that can empower us to venture below the line. Here is a list of three basic questions we might ask of each of the generic economic sites:

(i) **Consumption**
> Can we afford the product, and why or why not?
> Is its consumption good for us, or for the bioregion?
> Why do we want it or "need" it?

(ii) **Distribution/marketing**
> How is the product imaged and packaged, and why?
> Who takes a cut in the distribution? For what service?
> To whom is the marketing targeted, and why?

- -

(iii) **Production**
> What are labor relations at the point(s) of production?
> What are working conditions?
> How does supply influence demand?

(iv) **Resource extraction**
> Who "owns" the resources from which the materials come?
> Who does the extracting? Under what conditions?
> Are these resources exhaustible? How are they managed?

(v) **Capital**
> By whom has capital been invested in this venture, and why?
> How was this capital "created," managed, and controlled?
> What is the profit margin for the owners of the means of production?

Many other questions could be asked, and finding answers below the line may take some time and research. But this is just the point; the modest task of tracing the genealogy of one common product can open our eyes to both the complexity and the obfuscation of the "real" economic world.

The strength of the wall of mystification lies at the heart of the culture of silence for people in the *locus imperii*, which is why I believe First World literacy must focus on penetrating the discourses of the media to deconstruct the rule of image. Take the example of the *Guess?* clothing line, "known" to the consumer largely through its upscale advertising. The line was started by a couple of Beverly Hills fashion designers who decided to try to create a "high end market" for jeans, traditionally positioned in the blue collar/leisure clothing market (Schachter, 1990:D1ff). They began an aggressive promotional campaign whose wordless, quasi-abstract print ads set the industry standard for sexual seduction and postmodern design. The venture gambled on the power of sheer image — since the product itself was not extraordinarily different — and won, becoming southern California's largest apparel company. *Guess?*'s huge profitability, with $750 million in annual revenues, was chronicled in admiring business press profiles. What did not appear, and what could never be extrapolated from those trendy ads, was the company's rampant labor law violations. Its local contractors were paying sweatshop workers well under the minimum wage, refusing overtime, and employing child labor. Labor Department officials called *Guess?* the area's "most abusive employer," and it took the threat of a lawsuit to force the company to comply with federal standards, after which a company spokesperson said that *Guess?* planned to "stay American," but added that it was "conceivable some companies will shift production out of the country to hold their costs down" (Silverstein and Efron, 1992:A15). Pushing below the line to site (iii) opens up not only questions of the exploitation of immigrant labor in the apparel industry but also the larger trend toward a global "open shop" (see Kamel, 1990).

Finally, an example of how tools of basic economic literacy can facilitate cultural action for liberation is the recent Folgers boycott campaign. Shortly after the murder of the six Jesuit human rights activists and their two women companions in San Salvador in November 1990, a boycott of Salvadoran coffee — based on an analysis of site (iv) — was organized by Neighbor to Neighbor to pressure the government to prosecute the crime. On the West Coast the International Longshoremans Workers Union refused to unload ships carrying Salvadoran coffee beans in Los Angeles, San Francisco and Seattle. In Boston a television ad was produced that linked Salvadoran death squads to plantations producing beans for Folgers. But when the CBS affiliate WHDH-TV ran the ad, Proctor and Gamble, Folgers' parent company, was outraged and pulled their $1 million per year account, scaring off other stations from running the ad (Ramírez, 1990; Palmer, 1990). While only partially "successful," this campaign broke through the culture of silence by showing the power of economic engagement and resistance at site (ii), and in so doing contributed to the unmasking of how the system really works.

The ultimate critical task in a capitalist society, Marx pointed out, is to demystify capital (v). In the New World Order it has never been more urgent, for with the unraveling of state socialism — however problematic that model was — capital is being newly deified. Those looking for structural change under the Clinton administration should consider the dictum of Wall Street consultant Charles Morris: "One of the major political transformations of the past decade has been the recognition by the mainstream of both parties that capital markets impose absolute — and apolitical — limits on the freedom of action of the federal economic machinery" (1992:M1). *Politics transformed by the absolute rule of capital* — this is the capitalist dream, and the nightmare of its victims. But to those who believe there is a God greater than capital, and who dream of capital transformed by politics — that is, by "cultural action for liberation" — it is an invitation to the struggle for literacy. "No society," writes Jameson, "has ever been quite so mystified in quite so many ways as our own, saturated as it is with messages and information" (1981:60). But he adds that we can demystify these discourses only by way of "the stronger language of a more fundamental interpretive code." What alternative narrative do we use?

E. DISCIPLINES OF SEEING:
BIBLE STUDY AND LITERACY

Can the church, with its alternative texts of liberation, be a site where critical literacy is learned and practiced?

Christians have a unique responsibility to decipher the hieroglyphics of capitalist culture, or as José Comblin put it, to "provide some sort of discernment so that the church can shift its concern from surface appearances to the underlying reality, from abstract, rhetorical verbal charity to charity that is truly lived" (1979:68). Sadly, however, far from being a site where critical literacy is learned, practiced, and promoted, the First World church has more often helped throw divine canopies of legitimation and mystification over the dominant order. Nevertheless Third World base communities have demonstrated that the church can indeed be a host to popular education and empowerment (see Mesters, 1989; Gaspar, 1988). Can we do this in the *locus imperii?*

Many church-based peace and justice groups in the First World have attempted to bring Freirean insights into grassroots congregational life. Results, however, have been tentative, not only for the reasons just mentioned (above, D), but also because of our cultural resistance to doing social, economic, and political analysis in church. This is exacerbated when those promoting popular education make little or no effort to connect the process with traditional discourses of the church. The solution, however, is right in front of our noses: the Bibles that can be found in every church.

"Is this not why you are wrong — that you know neither the scriptures nor the power of God?" (Mk 12:24). As noted at the outset of this chapter, a central criticism of Mark's Jesus was the biblical illiteracy of his listeners. He understood that literacy in the texts of scripture can facilitate literacy in the texts of our world. He took the "revered" visions of Moses and the prophets off the dusty shelves and threw them like a Molotov cocktail into the middle of the power struggles of his time. The stories of how Jeremiah or Ezekiel unmasked oppression, "decontextualized" by the scribes, were "recontextualized" by Jesus, kick-starting the narrative of biblical radicalism back to life in the minds and hearts of his listeners. By undomesticating these texts, he wrested them from the grip of the powerful and put them into the hands of the poor; they became the fundamental interpretive code used to delegitimize discourses of domination (11:17) and legitimize radical practice (2:25). Mark the Evangelist does the same thing with Jesus — he recontextualizes his practice for another historical moment (*BSM*:92ff; 324ff). Our task, in turn, is to do the same with Mark; hence my political reading in *BSM*.

Popular Bible study has become a subversive act among Third World base communities because it is assumed that those stories lead us into our own life-texts and thus to liberative practice. Though *BSM* did not use that method, I use it in my work with groups, which I can note only briefly here.[9] The key is to get groups to commit to a synoptic reading of several "textual worlds":

(a) Texts from our culture
(b) Life-texts related to (a) (location)
(c) Texts from Mark
(d) Life-texts related to (c) (dis-location)

We then move back and forth among these texts or, as I prefer to say, within the circle of Story, using our imaginations to make correlations between them, allowing each to open up the other to new meanings. Once we become used to the method, we can start anywhere and get everywhere.

For example, I often begin with an analysis of a political cartoon (a). This cartoon, by Paul Conrad (from the *Los Angeles Times,* August 27, 1992), caricatures the famous Emanuel Leutze painting of Washington crossing the Delaware, but with a twist. Everyone in the boat is fishing; the caption reads: "Washington vacationing while crossing the Delaware." For most of us this is an immediately intelligible text, but we take the time to bring to consciousness how we interpreted its discourse. First we analyze its narrative form and content, then its ideological form and content. We consider the "graphic" subtext, a mid-nineteenth-century painting that legitimated the federal project of Manifest Destiny (below, 5,B). We probe why this image is so firmly lodged in our political unconscious (b). Then we look at Conrad's narrative transformation of the image, the conventions of caricature, and so on. Next we analyze the historical subtext. It alludes to the early weeks of the Gulf crisis, when President Bush assured the nation that while he was ordering troops to the Persian Gulf, he was not going to cancel his vacation in Maine. We discuss how we felt about that episode and analyze presidential posturing as a way of "managing" public perception through the press (b). Finally we look at how and why the mythic subtext (the Washington patriarchal hero myth) is recontextualized in terms of the historical one. We now understand that the discourse of the cartoon subverts Bush's presidential leadership — "George Bush is no George Washington." This opens space for us to talk about related issues.

This exercise (often referred to as deconstruction) allows us to imagine how similar narrative strategies of allusion, parody, or ironic twists might be going on in the gospel text, which comes from a historical and cultural context not as immediately intelligible to us (c). Thus we might take Mark's boat journey (a nice symmetry) and see how he is recycling biblical stories — the great flood, deliverance through the Red Sea, Ps. 107:23ff, Jonah — to make his ideological point about crossing social boundaries (*BSM:*194ff; Myers, 1991a). We reflect on how the Markan text illuminates our experiences (d): How are we afraid to cross the boundaries that were the cause of the "storm" of the Los Angeles uprising? Jo Milgrom has done excellent work at this level, using what she calls "hand-made midrash" (1989). Finally we come back around the circle to ask how this *faith* life-text dislocates us from the *enculturated* life-text, and what does that mean for our practice?

The method is dialectical and interactive and can move in any direction around or across the circle. The momentum created by analyzing a sophisticated but familiar text (we *are* literate!) helps us overcome our remoteness from the symbolic world of those unfamiliar Bible texts. Conversely, seeing how a text we were socialized to believe was purely religious functions politically empowers us to overcome our paralysis before the sacred texts of capitalism. This method encourages us to explore how symbols function politically and how politics functions symbolically.[10] The life-texts keep the discussion firmly rooted in our own historical context and experience. All this is of course helped by the fact that this work is fun as well as engaging, which helps overcome the alienation that is the legacy of boring, irrelevant, academic, or just plain bad Bible study.

My experience with synoptic and political readings of Word, World, and Self has convinced me that Bible study is the best way to engage in literacy work in the church. I am not suggesting the Bible is the only alternative narrative with which to deconstruct the dominant discourses; clearly others are needed, including tools of narrative and social analysis. Nor am I unaware that there are problematic elements in the biblical tradition that themselves must be critically decoded in relation to the core narrative of liberation (see Phyllis Trible's *Texts of Terror,* 1984). Nor am I being mercenary, using Bible study simply as a tactic to "organize the churches" — the unfortunate attitude of some religious activists. I believe the narrative of biblical radicalism represents for the church what Jameson calls the "stronger language of a more fundamental interpretive code" (Jameson, on the other hand, finds this in Marxism and the "historical narrative" of class struggle; *BSM:*36f). I maintain the protestant belief that the church can be renewed only by a fresh encounter with her own Story. But the theology of liberation was a new method before it was a new message.

We too need to reorient our disciplines of Bible study around appropriately adapted practices of popular education. This challenge stretches from the seminary, where critical thought needs to deprofessionalize (H. Clark, 1981), to the Sunday school class, where laypeople need to take critical reflection more seriously. The church should be promoting more intermediate and accessible forms of education that refuse the either/or dichotomy of reflection and practice. These are not new questions for the church, but very old ones. I like to think of each Bible as a stick of dynamite sitting in the basement of every church in the *locus imperii,* waiting for those with "eyes to see" to light the fuse. With the tools of literacy, the power of the dominant culture's dreams about itself can be broken, and the power of the Story to awaken us from our sleep broken open.

NOTES

1. *Blepein* is also used in both prophetic warnings in Mark (4:12=Is 6:9; 8:18=Jer 5:21). The *TDNT* contends that *blepein* "denotes seeing processes in the world of empirical phenomena as distinct from religious certainty, which has to do with things invisible" (1967:V/344). This metaphor should not be spiritualized; it concerns critical perception of concrete reality. Mark's strategy of bracketing his "discipleship catechism" with the two blind man stories — the first a tentative healing, the second a decisive one — confirms their essential relationship to the discourse of critical literacy (*BSM*:238ff; 281f; below, 12B).

2. To dispense with the semantic issue at the outset — riot? rebellion? civil disturbance? insurrection? — let me cite local social critic Mike Davis:

> LA was a hybrid social revolt with three major dimensions. It was a revolutionary democratic protest characteristic of African-American history when demands for equal rights have been thwarted by the major institutions. It was also a major post-modern bread rebellion — an uprising of not just poor people but particularly of those strata of poor in southern California who've been most savagely affected by the recession. Thirdly, it was an inter-ethnic conflict — particularly the systematic destroying and uprooting of Korean stores in the black community. So it was all of those things at once and issues of rage, class and race cannot be separated out. (1992b:12)

While *riot*, the dominant culture's preferred term, does not necessarily connote an absence of socio-political motive, its usage by the media and politicians does. Not only is *uprising* preferred by most Third World interpreters of the events, it also is plainly descriptive — the suppressed contradictions of the Metropolis did indeed erupt (see Gooding-Williams, 1993).

3. An excellent analysis of the structural contradictions that characterize post-industrial Los Angeles, and suggestions of socio-economic alternatives, was published on the one-year anniversary of the uprising by the Labor/Community Strategy Center, entitled *Reconstructing Los Angeles from the Bottom Up* (Mann, et al, 1993). See also Madhubuti (1993), and for further background Gaughey (1976), Didion (1993), and Sonenshein (1993).

4. Unfortunately this preoccupation with the "spectacular" infects alternative media as well. Erica Munk points out that images her team brought back from Baghdad after the Gulf War did not, because of the "surgical" nature of the bombing, reflect wholesale destruction, thus illiciting some "disappointment" from opposition groups: "A bombing whose toll is long-term and still invisible isn't useful for mobilizing anti-war sentiment. . . . The shots that 'work' are a child standing in rubble, a veiled mother holding her kerosene-burned baby, a building blown down to its skeleton. . . . But a photograph of untreated sewage pouring into a river from which people draw drinking water is just a picture of water flowing into water. A damaged electrical substation isn't emotionally useful, however profound its implication" (1991:585).

5. Fairness and Accuracy in Reporting and the Center for Media and Values in Los Angeles both conducted critical studies of media coverage of the Los Angeles uprising, for example. The *Sentinel, Korea Times,* and *La Opinión* — respectively the largest black, Korean, and Spanish-language newspapers in the West — offered significantly different perspectives on the uprising. A good resource for alternative media is the *Alternative Press Index* (Baltimore, MD). *Third World Resources* (Oakland, CA) is a monthly review and listing of critical resources with a Third World perspective. On

media literacy see Herman (1992), and Alexandre (1985, 1990). An example of local press monitoring is Bill Ramsey's analysis of the *St. Louis Post-Dispatch*'s post–Gulf War coverage (1992); see also Cummings (1992).

6. Alexandre reviews current definitional debates among literacy educators, particularly between "vocationalized" and "liberative" approaches (1990). UNESCO's literacy work has adopted some of Freire's method, as has Laubach Literacy Action in the U.S. Danielle Fauteux's *Palabras de Lucha y Alegría* teaches basic Spanish literacy using "themes such as education, food, child care and festivals drawn from the experience of those to whom the text is directed." More explicitly Freirean are Auerbach and Wallerstein (1987) and Shor (1987). See also the Center for Global Education's *Crossing Borders, Challenging Boundaries* (1988).

7. I would commend three primers on economics: Owensby (1988); Kamel (1990); and S. Rose (1986). For an excellent interpretation of Marx see McGovern (1981). There are many organizations in the U.S. that can provide further resources for use in socio-economic analysis. To name some is to risk leaving others out, but deserving mention are the Center for Popular Economics (Amherst, MA), the Center of Budget and Policy Priorities (Washington, DC), the Debt Crisis Network (Washington, DC), the Center for Global Education (Minneapolis, MN), Witness for Peace (Washington, DC), and the Center of Concern (Washington, DC).

8. This is precisely what John Cavanaugh does in a brilliant little study entitled "The Journey of the Blouse: A Global Assembly Line" (1985). He traces the production process of a "typical 35 percent cotton/65 percent polyester blouse" from the cotton plantations of El Salvador and oil rigs off the coast of Venezuela, to spinning mills in South Carolina and refineries in Trinidad and Tobago and petrochemical plants in New Jersey, to the blending of the cotton fiber and polyester filament into fabric at a textile factory in North Carolina, to sweatshops in Haiti for assembly, and finally to packaging in New York for distribution to wholesalers and retailers. At each point of this journey he offers a brief synopsis of social and economic issues related to that step in the chain. This article was developed into a group exercise module by the Religious Network for Equality for Women (1988).

9. This method was developed by a collective in order to promote social analysis around the Quincentenary (Taylor, Myers et al, 1991). Happily, the same collective is working on a shorter version of *BSM* based on a popular education style that we hope will aid groups in using Mark for this kind of Bible study. This volume will include further examples of what I am alluding to here. For another approach to popular Bible study see Wink (1980).

10. One can just as easily do a political reading of a nonovertly "political" text. For example, I compare the Conrad cartoon with a University of Phoenix Business School ad from a 1990 issue of *Time* magazine, which also caricatures the Washington painting, this time portraying everyone in the boat in three-piece suits and briefcases, with the caption: "The Art of Management: Master It." Same subtext, different argument: Corporate leaders are the true revolutionaries, leading heroically into the future; or, perhaps, business leadership has replaced political leadership. We explore why a business school would be appealing to the Washington myth. The point is, we can do this kind of work with any text, small or large — the sports page or the Constitution, a contract or a Dylan folksong, a daytime soap opera or a church bulletin.

4

"Why Could We Not Cast It Out?"

Dis-illusionment

> Grandiosity is the counterpart of depression within the narcissistic distur-
> bance.
>
> Alice Miller,
Prisoners of Childhood

> Neither Prometheus nor Narcissus will lead us out of our present predica-
> ment. Brothers under the skin, they will only lead us further down the road
> on which we have already travelled much too far.
>
> Christopher Lasch,
The Minimal Self

"**Teacher, I brought you my son; he has a spirit that has silenced him
...and I asked your disciples to cast it out — but they were not strong
enough!**" (Mk 9:17f). Here is another Markan episode that resounds deeply and
painfully in our readerly hearts. It exhibits fearless honesty about the experience
of impotence among disciples who would struggle against Denial. The scene
opens with the disciples locked in argument with the scribes (9:14f). Despite
having just been instructed by the divine voice on the mount of Transfiguration
to "Listen!" to Jesus (9:7), the disciples apparently are still captive to the internalized voice of scribal authority. "Why then do the scribes say ... ?" (9:11).
"Why are you bothering to argue with them?" Jesus queries (9:16).

Then comes the crowd's damning indictment: The very practice of exorcism
to which the disciples have been expressly commissioned (3:15; 6:7) they cannot accomplish. *They were not strong enough!* What a chilling disclosure! With
its mixture of disappointment and mockery, this complaint resounds through

church history, the refrain of supplicants and skeptics alike. We Christians are haunted by the truth of it.

"*How long* must I bear with you? *How long* has he been this way?" (9:19, 21). A weary Jesus here echoes the ancient lament of the Exodus God against a people who refuse to abide in the divine liberation (Num 14:27). But then Jesus beholds for himself the vicious power of this pathology that locks up the powers of speech, this demon that hurls its victims into fire and water (9:20, 22). To combat this malignancy, Jesus once again appeals for *faith* (9:23; cf 1:15; 4:40; 5:36; 11:22f).

"I believe! Help me in my unbelief!" (9:24). From the lips of the distraught father whose son's lips are demonically sealed comes this stunning — and utterly transparent — confession. Its honesty stands in stark contrast to Peter's grandiose triumphalism in the preceding episode (8:29). Jesus can work with *this* confession. As once before, his restoration of the victim truly seems like "raising the dead" (9:26; cf 5:35–41).

"Why could we not cast it out?" (9:28). A brief epilogue to the story revisits the embarrassing matter of the disciples' impotence. Instead of celebrating the deaf-mute's liberation, they withdraw, depressed and fixated on their own humiliation. The disciples, of course, are the real subjects of this episode. We know from the story that they are struggling to believe (4:40), and that they have been accused of "having ears that cannot hear" (8:17f). But what is the relationship between faith, silencing, and impotence?

"This kind can be exorcized only through prayer" (9:29). What an extraordinary conclusion for Jesus to draw from this episode! Has he not just announced that discipleship must engage politics and power (8:27ff)? Is not the narrative gathering momentum for the long march toward the Jerusalem showdown? Why then would Mark suddenly bring everything to a screeching halt with this counsel to prayer? Perhaps it is because he understands that *we cannot exorcize that by which we are ourselves still possessed.* Or, as Freud put it in somewhat different terms two millennia later, "What is unconscious is bound to be repeated."

A. THE GULF WAR, 1991: NATIONAL MANIC-DEPRESSION

How did the Gulf War and its aftermath express a national mood swing from self-aggrandizement to self-doubt — and how are we activists captive to this pendulum of denial?

In the midst of the horror of Operation Desert Storm, I was impressed at how many Christian peace and justice activists turned, quite independently of each other, to the strange gospel story above. From that first chilling moment on January 16, 1991, when it was announced that the bombing of Baghdad had begun, we sat helpless, forced to watch the media's grand production of the technological wasting of Iraq. As we witnessed a manic display of national solidarity with murder, the disciples' anguished cry grew within us like a terrible mantra, beating like a sledgehammer on our hearts. *Why* — after all our organizing and consciousness raising and demonstrating, our coalitions and conferences and church declarations and actions — *why* had we been so utterly unable to cast this demon of imperial militarism out of the hearts and minds of our people?

The following reflections on the Gulf War do not attempt to tell the story of the war itself or its geopolitics or its effects on the people of the Gulf region. Such analysis is by now readily available.[1] My focus is on what this war did to and meant for *us*, the citizenry of the country that sponsored the butchery. If the mystifying discourses of capitalist culture seek to make us *blind* to concrete practices of power and privilege (above, Chapter Three), our internalization of them renders us also *deaf and mute*. Behind the "silent majority" in the U.S. — the passive masses of whom we activists are often so contemptuous — lies a deeper psycho-cultural truth. So many feel so impotent to change the world because they have been silenced, not so much by external mechanisms of political repression as by a profound inner disconnection from their true humanity. Any analysis that does not take this phenomenon seriously is doomed to irrelevance in the North American context. It is one thing to "de-code" *objective* systems and ideologies of oppression through critical literacy. It is quite another to diagnose and confront *subjective* systems of repression that reinforce and reproduce domination at the level of what Frederic Jameson calls the "political unconscious."

1. The "Silenced Majority"

No less than four times in this episode Mark describes the viciousness of the demon of silencing. It throws the boy down, paralyzes his speech, and makes him rigid (9:18); unable to speak, he can only writhe in agony (9:20); it drowns him out and burns him out and, above all, *means to destroy* him (9:22, 26). What better description of what those of us who labor for peace and justice endured, politically and psychologically, during Desert Storm?

The Gulf War was a symphony of silence, performed by a chorus of muted voices to an audience of deaf ears, masterfully orchestrated by the conductors of sound in the *locus imperii*. Throughout the 1970s Iranian exiles struggled to bring to the attention of the U.S. public the brutal human rights crimes of the Shah of Iran, but as a U.S. client regime it could not to be overly exposed by the media, for it provided "stability" in the region. The announcement of the Carter Doctrine in 1980, explicitly stating that the U.S. would go to war to protect its oil interests in the Gulf region, hardly caused a stir. Attention was focused instead on the Iranian revolution, and then the spectacle of the hostage crisis; but when it ended in debacle, our interest again faded.[2] The ensuing eight years of bloody holocaust that was the Iran-Iraq War was a media nonevent even as U.S. officials brokered feverishly with both sides behind the scenes. Meanwhile billions of well-hidden U.S. tax dollars were secretly allocated for building military infrastructure in Saudi Arabia to support the Carter Doctrine, while almost a billion more was funneled into Iraqi weapons programs through "redirected" agricultural credits. Yet even after the Pentagon tipped its hand in 1987 and overtly intervened in the war by reflagging Kuwaiti oil tankers in the Gulf and bombing Iranian oil platforms, and even after the Iran-Contra scandal broke, the U.S. peace movement, with few exceptions, couldn't be bothered. And the majority of the public remained spellbound under President Reagan's good-natured paternalism and Teflon spin-doctoring. He got out; Ollie North got off.

And then this silent symphony swelled, as the U.S. nudged Iraq to force oil prices up, then nudged Kuwait to violate OPEC production quotas and antagonize its border agreements with Iraq, then looked away demurely as Iraq breathed threats of retaliation. The stage set, the imperial media suddenly riveted on this previously obscure scenario. The invasion was world news, outrage and disgust were trumpeted, the Pentagon's voice was broadcast loudly, and war fever was seeded. The silence now changed to the key of half-truth, as Iraqi military strength was exaggerated into the specter of a new Reich while strenuous efforts by Arab states to mediate the crisis were dismissed. The media fawned over the magnificent edifice of U.N. common cause, while off camera the U.S. patched together a coalition and bought regional acquiescence by holding a fire sale on economic assistance, debt forgiveness, loans, and military aid. Strutting the stage, the U.S. drew its line in the sand, gave its ultimatum, and started counting. The peace movement geared up for a countervigil. Scrambling to understand this latest geography of U.S. intervention, we organized teach-ins and demonstrations. Polls indicated that more than half the populace opposed war.

But then came that terrible moment when the bombing began. *That apocalyptic moment of war — live on CNN.* At AFSC our phones lit up like a Christmas tree; my spirit went numb and my stomach churned as I felt the whirlwind coming. I remember a defining scene as I was fielding calls, trying to help direct the confusion and rage and fear. Standing next to me on another phone, being interviewed by a local radio station, was Vicki Tamoush, a committed young Christian Arab American woman who had just returned from the Fellowship of Reconciliation's peace delegation to Iraq. During a lull I turned on the radio. Suddenly in one ear I was hearing Bush's official announcement that we had commenced bombing Baghdad, terse and carefully euphemistic. In the other was Vicki's trembling voice, describing how beautiful Baghdad had seemed, how friendly its people had been, as she struggled to hold back the tears. I felt sick, knowing which version of reality would be "heard" in this apocalyptic *anti-kairos,* when the Beast speaks with great authority while its victims cry to heaven in protest (Rev 6:1ff; 13:1ff), and when "signs and wonders lead astray even the elect" (Mk 13:21; below, Chapter Eight; Myers, 1991b).

Indeed, from that moment on, the public face of dissent was rendered virtually invisible in the U.S. The media in all its forms donned the yellow ribbon, consolidating the Bush administration's painstakingly manufactured "popular consent":

> During the first two weeks of the war only one peace activist was inter-
> viewed, while seven NFL football players were asked their opinions on
> the war. . . . CBS executives, concerned about raising ad profits, "offered
> advertisers assurances that war specials could be tailored to provide better
> lead-ins to commercials. One way would be to insert the commercials af-
> ter segments that were specially produced with upbeat images or messages
> about the war, like patriotic views from the homefront." At the same time,
> CNN network executives refused to allow the Military Families Support
> Network, a group which opposed the war, to purchase air time for an anti-
> war ad on the grounds that such views were not tastefully presented and
> already had been adequately covered. (Marchik, 1992:12)

All eyes were instead glued to television's celebration of "smart" bombs and
Patriots; all ears tuned into Schwarzkopf's brilliant "campaign." What we
witnessed, opined Daniel Ellsberg later, was a six-week commercial for the
Pentagon.[3]

When the noble slaughter was completed, months of manic victory parades
followed, culminating midyear with extravagant Independence Day finales.
Then the silence resumed, euphoric. We heard little about the 70 percent error rate of those Smart bombs, or U.S. casualties resulting from "friendly fire"
(a classic Pentagon oxymoron), or the "turkey shoot" during the last days of
the war, or the Iraqi corpses bulldozed into mass graves. We heard only about
suffering Kurds and the continuing "threat" of Iraqi nuclear weapons — not
about the environmental holocaust in the Gulf, or the devastated infrastructure
of Iraq and its horrific impact on children and families, or the continuing
struggle for democracy by the Kuwaiti opposition. The deaf and mute spirit
was summed up by General Colin Powell in an interview on public television on the first anniversary of the Gulf War cease-fire. *We will never know,*
he said, *how many Iraqis died in the conflict — nor is it important to know.*
The well-known liberal journalist accepted Powell's statement as self-evident
and didn't bother to cross-examine it. The media has *never* reported on how
its own reporting was so dramatically compromised throughout this entire
episode.

"Decayed social systems continue only as long as silenced people allow
them to last," wrote Marcus Raskin recently in reference to the political changes
in Eastern Europe but clearly with an eye to our own situation (1991:412). The
Gulf War presents us, yet again, with the genius of the cultural system of late
capitalism, a text in bold relief. Minority dissent is tolerated or marginalized or
squashed depending on the exigencies of the political moment. But the system
is predicated upon the creation and maintenance of a silenced majority. Yet it
is too easy to excoriate and scapegoat the silent majority for our national problems. My concern here is to understand, and to try to move toward a diagnosis
of, this phenomenon of silencing as a *collective condition* of empire. To do this,
I must also address the harder case, the apparent exception to this rule: the activists who do speak out, who do protest, who are critically conscious of U.S.

policies. Is it possible that we are impotent to exorcize this militaristic demon because we are part of this condition — or rather, it is part of us?

2. Postwar Depression

What if they held a war and everybody came? This play on its own slogan is the First World peace and justice community's worst nightmare, and we lived it in Desert Storm. I know few activists who were not utterly frustrated by the way in which dissent was steamrolled; some even began to doubt their own voice. In the aftermath of the war, as the rest of the country danced at the welcome-home parties, there was a widespread depression in our circles. The optimism of many liberals — who thought the world order had changed with the fall of the Berlin Wall — had withered in the face of this revelation of the unprecedented virility of global militarism. Morale was scarcely better among more radical activists who, understanding the North-South character of global economics and geopolitics, maintained perhaps fewer political illusions. The truth is, few were not to some degree surprised or overwhelmed by the viciousness of the imperial enterprise this time around.

Veteran Third World organizers, too, were demoralized, as they watched people of color yet again disproportionately put at military risk and saw domestic struggles for health care and welfare rights yet again sidetracked. Let us not forget that the LAPD thrashing of Rodney King happened just a few weeks after the cease-fire in Iraq, an incident that perfectly mirrored the overkill of Desert Storm — and eventually brought the war home to the streets of Los Angeles (above, 3,A). It left many wondering: Decades of civil rights, antiracism, and police monitoring work — for this? Overall, then, it was difficult for social change activists to draw any other conclusion from the first half of 1991 than the one trumpeted by our ideological opponents: "America kicked butt" indeed, at home and abroad.

Taking an interest in this epidemic of depression among us, I tried to pay attention to how we were dealing with our feelings. I noticed two contrasting trends, both of which attempted to anesthetize the pain: renewed activism or a retreat into apathy. The exhortation to redoubled organizing was captured in an editorial entitled "What Do We Do Now?" in a postwar special edition of *Nuclear Times:*

These are difficult times for those of us who believe in peace and the power of nonviolence. Antiwar groups that grew rapidly in December and January are now reeling in shock. The human suffering, the scale of destruction, the shift of opinion toward the war — at times it's been overwhelming. Despite our sadness and feelings of futility, we must not give in to resignation. The peace movement is needed now more than ever. We must rebound to face the enormous challenges ahead. (Cortright, 1991:11)

Now, it goes without saying that the work of peace and justice must continue —
the struggle stretches across generations. But was "rebounding" a healthy response? What was gained by reimmersing ourselves in the next set of crises or,
worse, returning to our single-issue campaigns so inconveniently interrupted by
the war? Shouldn't we have taken the time and created the space to reflect on
and learn from what we had just witnessed in order that we might proceed differently in light of it? Overall I was impressed (if not surprised) at the avoidance
of anything resembling introspection in the various movements' postmortem
critiques. Most simply hauled out the old explanations for the whirlwind and
resolved to be better prepared next time. Were we seeking refuge by intellec-
tualizing the experience through analysis? Did we think cynical retrospective
conspiracy theories — "We suspected all along that Big Oil and its minions had
planned this war for decades" — would heal our despair?

On the other hand, withdrawal was no better a solution to resolving trauma.
A-pathy after all means "not feeling." The temptation to abandon our small
piece of the struggle is an old and omnipresent nemesis in capitalist culture,
but especially after a good look at what we're up against. We might recall that
the civil rights/antiwar movement was followed, once it was clear the system
would not topple, by widespread defection from the wearisome work of organizing. To persevere in the long haul we need to be more deeply in touch with
our historical pain, not severed from it. The truth is, we had been confronted
sharply and rudely with our impotence in the face of imperial war fever — something my Vietnam-era generation had never before experienced to such a degree.
But rather than facing it and seeing it as an invitation to self-examination, we
activists sought relief from failure in one of these forms of Denial.

Yet as summer turned to fall, the victory parades mercifully over, activists
began to recover. Why? Was it because the national mood had begun to swing
back to depression? Indeed in the second half of 1991, the national euphoria
vanished almost as quickly as it had descended. The savings and loan bailout —
called by John Kenneth Galbraith (1991) "by far the greatest public scandal in
U.S. economic history" — had grown to such absurd proportions that the media
studiously refused to investigate its structural causes or political meaning (a silence maintained through the 1992 presidential elections; cf Shaw, 1992b, Risen,
1992). But the bad news of deepening economic recession was not entirely
suppressible. Its true indicators — unemployment, homelessness, discretionary
income decline, tight credit, and fading consumer confidence — were being concretely seen and felt now not only by poor and working-class people but by
almost every sector of the middle class. The dominant culture's sense of global
entitlement, internationally *projected* in a war tacitly understood to be about
control over natural resources half a world away, gave way to an equally pervasive sense of anxiety, domestically *introjected* in a variety of gender, race, and
class tensions throughout the country. The media-saturated Clarence Thomas
sexual harassment hearings and William Kennedy Smith rape trial became lightning rods for the rage of women feeling the pressure of what Susan Faludi calls
the "undeclared war against women" (1991). Even as Republican rhetoric in-

voked "family values," the erosion of state and federal welfare supplements dramatically accelerated the rate of poverty among women and children. As the Supreme Court continued to dismantle civil rights law, undocumented immigrants became the targets-of-preference for the hate crimes of resurgent white supremacist groups. David Duke launched his short-lived but high-profile campaign in Louisiana, which laid claim to the mantle of a "new populism" built on the myth of white victimization (below, 7,C). Finally came a new wave of anti-Japanese polemics; just as it was easier for us to reinvent Saddam Hussein as Hitler than to examine the historical duplicity of U.S. policy in the Gulf, it was easier to blame Japanese import/export policies for our economic woes than to acknowledge our own sellout to mercenary capital and industrial flight.

So, from an all-time high during Desert Storm, President Bush's popularity plummeted to an all-time low by December 1991, a fall from which he never recovered politically. On the first year anniversary of the start of the Gulf War, there were no parades and only scattered commentary. The thrill was clearly gone. Indeed the languor had spread to the entire capitalist world:

> The euphoria of the West's great victory over communism has been overwhelmed by a whole new set of problems that political leaders seem either unwilling or unable to confront and for which there seem to be few, if any, easy answers. The result: less than three years after Berliners danced on their wall to the applause of an elated free world, the globe's great industrial democracies find themselves stricken by a growing sense of disappointment, frustration and worry.... Four-fifths of all Americans, according to a Gallup Poll at the beginning of August [1992], declare themselves dissatisfied with the way things are going in their country. Such "malaise"...had not been seen since the very end of the Carter Administration. (T. Marshall, 1992:H1)

The demons of Vietnam Bush thought he had finally exorcized in Desert Storm came back to haunt him with a vengeance; he was soundly trounced in the November 1992 presidential elections.

How is it that the national mood could swing almost 180 degrees, from bellicose self-aggrandizement to distraught self-doubt, from triumph to turmoil, in barely a calendar year? This is a question of social psychology — for the political/economic system had not changed (some might say it was simply following its own logic). What was the true nature of this manic-depressive rollercoaster, and its relationship to the public's silence in the face of one of history's most horrific episodes of aerial bombing, and then again in the face of the massive public theft of the savings and loan bailout? And the harder question we must also ask is, Did we activists transcend this pendulum of grandiosity and depression, or simply ride it *on the opposite swing?* What do we make of the fact that so many of us were depressed during the postwar mania and recovered when the national mood plunged? Was this the reverse of the mid-1970s, when mainstream culture was depressed in the wake of the U.S. defeat in Vietnam while the antiwar movement celebrated? These painful queries bring those of us who do our work from a faith perspective back to the problem of trying to drive out demons by which we are possessed and to Jesus' startling invitation to "look within."

B. "HE INFLICTED HIMSELF": POSSESSION AND THE POLITICAL BODY

Can therapeutic models help us diagnose collective socio-political pathologies in the locus imperii?

The only other place Mark describes at length the ravages of possession on the body of the victim is in the story of the Gerasene demoniac. This vignette illustrates the profound connection between "internal" and "external" pathologies.

1. The "Two Bodies"

"There came to Jesus a man with an unclean spirit who lived among the dead... Night and day among the tombs and on the mountains he was always crying out, and inflicting wounds upon himself with stones" (Mk 5:2, 5). Only here in Mark does Jesus, the one who is "stronger-than" (1:7), extract the name of a demon: "My name is Legion, for we are many" (5:9). The singular/plural confusion of the subject suggests that he had fully internalized the spirit of empire, making him schizophrenic; he was so possessed by its pathological power that he could only live self-destructively.

It is interesting to note the correlations between this episode, the exorcism of the deaf-mute, and Jesus' master metaphor for exorcism, the binding of the strong man:

- no one can enter a *strong* man's house unless he first *binds* him (3:27);
- he had often been *bound*... but no one was *strong enough* to shackle him (5:4);
- they were not *strong enough* to cast it out (9:18).

In the symbolic discourse of Mark, the power of the "Strong Man" that keeps the "House" captive (3:27) also imprisons the bodies of those colonized by Legion (5:7). If we today do not recognize how this demonic force operates inwardly and outwardly, individually and collectively, we too will not be strong enough to cast it out. We must name the "Strong Man/Legion" through the "stronger language of a more fundamental interpretive code" (Jameson), which is for us the narrative of biblical radicalism (above, 3,E).

What Mark called possession Frantz Fanon called the "internalization of oppression" in his classic study "Colonial War and Mental Disorders" (1968:249ff). Fanon noted cases during the Algerian independence struggle in the late 1950s that indicated that the dominating pattern of colonial violence was being reproduced in the pathological behavior of those living under the system — both colonizers and colonized. For example, in one case, an Algerian survivor of a mass murder by French gendarmes is diagnosed with "undifferentiated homicidal impulsions" (he wanted to kill everybody around him); in another, a French police inspector in charge of interrogation and torture of political prisoners cannot stop abusing his own wife and children (ibid:254ff). His cases gave clinical credence to the notion that people can reproduce dysfunctional political practices in their own personalities. Sometimes this is manifested intrapsychically (through mental disorder), sometimes through self-destructive behavior (e.g., addiction), and sometimes interpsychically (in abusive relationships).

Cultural anthropologist Mary Douglas reflects on this same phenomenon more broadly in a seminal essay entitled "The Two Bodies" (1973:93ff). She writes:

> The physical body can have universal meaning only as a system which responds to the social system, expressing it as a system. What it symbolizes naturally is the relation of parts of an organism to the whole. Natural symbols can express the relation of an individual to his society at that general systemic level. The two bodies are the self and society. (ibid:112)

The "two bodies" always reflect each other. The *body politic* (the imperatives, symbols and hierarchies of the dominant socio-political order) is reproduced by how, where, and when we present our *political bodies* (what Douglas understands as the "socialized self," including the consciousness, physical body, personal habits, and socio-political practices of the individual).

> The social body constrains the way the physical body is perceived. The physical experience of the body, always modified by the social categories through which it is known, sustains a particular view of society. There is a continual exchange of meanings between the two kinds of bodily experience so that each reinforces the categories of the other. (ibid:93)

If we are socialized at home, school, and church to internalize the codes and boundaries of the body politic, we do not have to be regulated externally in our political bodies. We will conform our physical needs (economic, sexual), our social appearance and movement (where one does or does not "belong"), and our symbolic expression (religion, art) according to the conventions of the dominant ethos.

The notion of the political body as a mirror of the body politic is common to most traditional cultures, which do not make the radical distinctions between self and society that we do; it was certainly characteristic of first-century Palestine.[4] This explains why Mark's Jesus pays as much attention to healing and exorcizing individuals as he does to what *we* might recognize as "political" engagement (*BSM:*141ff). Jesus heals those who are physically impaired because they are also socially "dis-membered" according to the dominant Debt and Purity systems (1:41ff; 2:2ff). He enters into conflict because of how he places his body within the accepted/expected proprieties of social space, crossing boundaries of power and prestige. Thus the "politics" of Jesus are defined not only by his attack on the Temple marketplace but also by whom he sits at table with (2:15; 14:3), who comes in his house (7:24f), when and where his disciples eat (2:23f; 7:2ff) and whom he touches (5:30f). In Jesus' exorcisms, as with the Gerasene, the "possessed" political body symbolizes territorial struggles within the body politic. Through exorcism Jesus challenges the authoritative space of the scribes (1:24f); the political domain of the Powers (3:27); the military occupation of the Romans (5:10); and the sacred legitimacy of the Temple (11:15ff, cf 13:1f, 34f).

Though the political character of Jesus' symbolic action was intelligible within Mark's cultural context, it has been missed completely by a church which has alienated the political body from the body politic (above, 2,B,2). How does the biblical insistence upon their fundamental interrelationship help us interpret the "text" of Desert Storm? Surely the spirit of the *locus imperii* is aptly "named," then and now, by the military might of "Legion." Was our silencing during the Gulf War due in part to our internalization of the manic-depressive pendulum of the silenced majority? Fanon's analysis would seem to suggest that this could be a fruitful path of inquiry.

As a result of my own painful but liberating personal journey of psychotherapy I had pondered how psychological insights might help us diagnose, confront, and heal the oppression we internalize in our political bodies. But like other activists, I instinctively balked. We know that social and political injustices can be solved no more by "going into therapy" than by simply praying about them! We are rightly skeptical about psychotherapy's incessant interiority. As James Hillman complains:

> We're working on our relationships constantly, and our feelings and reflections, but...what's left out is a deteriorating world. So why hasn't therapy noticed that? Because psychotherapy is only working on that "inside" soul....Every time we try to deal with [problems in the world] by going to therapy with our rage and fear, we're depriving the political world of something. (Ventura, 1990:16f)

What if, Hillman asks, our anxieties or anger stem not from unresolved feelings about our fathers or mothers but from having to live in toxic environments or the situation of the homeless or war?

To Hillman's objections Christian activists could easily add others. We know that the psychological paradigm has replaced the religious one as the tradition of self-examination in secular modernity and is employed ubiquitously to both describe and prescribe our condition. Does not the bourgeois political economy of "mental health" exclude the poor even more than that of religion? Don't the pretensions of psychological professionals carry all the same liabilities of the old priestly system? And while we're at it, what about that spiritual stepchild of therapeutic culture, the New Age movement? Hasn't it simply revived the old heresy of nineteenth-century Protestant pietism — namely, that we can only "heal the planet" by doing our "personal inner work"? To be sure, the therapeutic establishment deserves the same kinds of suspicion and critique we radical Christians direct at the church. But that is precisely the point: Psychology has been thoroughly privatized in capitalist culture *just as religion was.* What is needed, then, is a therapeutic discourse analogous to liberation theology, a "politicization" of its legitimate insights. Rather than being solely preoccupied with existential angst and the maze of self-referentiality, therapy needs to embrace history — that is, social, political, and economic struggle.

2. Politicizing Therapy

Dominant culture psychology is only beginning to explore how the political body and the body politic are related. But it is becoming increasingly difficult to ignore the connections between epidemic substance abuse and chronic poverty, or between family violence and our culture of militarism. I suspect we will see increasing understanding of the structural relationship between individual, family, and social dysfunction over the next decade, if for no better reason than that the social psychology of the U.S. has become so patently pathological that it screams out for diagnosis. For example, though most mental health professionals during the Gulf War were busy comforting family members of deployed military personnel, there were a few indications of a new interest in employing therapeutic models to diagnose political demons. Two examples can suffice.

Robert Bly, the guru of the recent "men's movement" who has sustained his share of criticism for depoliticizing the struggle against patriarchy, spoke out very clearly against the war. In a March 1991 radio interview Bly applied the popular therapeutic model of addiction/codependence to the construction of "consensus" around U.S. Gulf policy. Was not President Bush, he asked, like the alcoholic father on a binge, drunk with the power of military superiority? Unable to deal with his own "household" (the various domestic social and economic crises), he instead picked on a weaker neighbor "ten blocks away." As in the alcoholic family, this had the predictable twofold effect. It diverted the household's attention from its own internal crisis of addiction (to oil, to militarism), and it rallied the deep-seated (and largely unconscious) power of familial loyalty — unity, so to speak, by yellow ribbon. Congress, Bly asserted, instead of "intervening" in the addictive cycle, exhibited classic codependent behavior. Divided and conquered, it immediately began apologizing for, then (once the binge had recommenced) defending, the addictive behavior. The response of these "elder siblings" was mirrored by the majority of the populace, whose own self-esteem was fused with that of their "father." The aftermath (or hangover) is equally predictable, Bly concluded. The family awakens to depression as we realize that yet again the addict has remained in control. And when the eventual damage incurred during the binge is realized, a deep sense of shame will follow. While hardly a detailed diagnosis, Bly's analogy certainly is descriptive of much of what we saw during and after the Gulf War.

Lloyd deMause (1991) offered a more elaborate analysis of America's war fever, using an approach he calls "psychohistoricizing." Positing an analogy between intrapsychic symbolic disorders and social ones, he likened recurring media images to "national dreams." DeMause asserted that before the war the media was preoccupied with representations of the "Terrifying Parent" and the "Hurt Child." Once Saddam Hussein was targeted as the national demon, he was portrayed as the archetypal child abuser. We saw this in the outraged media coverage of Saddam's "chat" with the children of his Western hostages; in the infamous cover of the *New Republic* with his photo subtly retouched to suggest Hitler; and in the widely circulated horror stories of babies being thrown out of hospital windows in Kuwait (later admitted to be fabrications — after they had served their purpose of catalyzing public outrage).

Such "intrusive images," deMause contended, could be understood as "flashbacks" of earlier traumas and thus indicative of post-traumatic stress disorder (PTSD): "The standard symptoms of PTSD characterized the nation's shared emotional life at that time: 1) emotional instability with extreme fluctuations of mood; 2) frequent panic attacks and exaggerated fears for the future; 3) frantic spending and borrowing; 4) drug abuse; 5) a constriction of affect and sympathy toward others; 6) hypervigilance toward imagined enemies; 7) feelings of unreality, detachment and estrangement" (ibid:304).

PTSD symptoms, moreover, portend punitive behavior. "Articles proliferated in the media claiming that America had been on an irresponsible binge during the previous years and that someone would soon have to pay for its excesses" (ibid). The *Washington Post* characterized the prewar national mood as "an ugly spasm of guilt, dread and nostalgia," ostensibly due to the excesses of "high living" during the Reagan years and apprehension that the U.S. was in economic decline. Our "sinful national fantasy" found the perfect scapegoat in Saddam Hussein to play out its need for retribution. Then, arguing from political anthropology, deMause noted some of the historical ways in which the symbolic need for national cleansing has been satisfied (ancient Babylon, the Aztecs, the War between the States), and noted that each exhibited one or more of the following dramatic enactments:

1) creating an enemy for ritual combat;
2) ritual humiliation of the leader;
3) staging the triumph of good over evil; and
4) the celebration of the rebirth of life.

Whatever one thinks of deMause's psychohistoricist method, the semblance of these ritual politics to what we witnessed in Desert Storm — from Saddam's demonization to Schwarzkopf's deification — is nothing less than chilling.

Obviously a comprehensive diagnosis of the political pathologies that manifested in Desert Storm cannot focus on psycho-social symbolics to the exclusion of other empirical factors. There are very real elite classes engaged in real struggle over control of real global resources. Still, these attempts to politicize the therapeutic paradigm are suggestive of a way forward. While relatively novel to First World practitioners, these connections have long been understood by Third World therapists. "There is no way for poor people to separate what is political from what is therapeutic," wrote Terry Kupers in his book *Public Therapy* (1981:235). I have mentioned the work of Frantz Fanon, which stands in the mid-twentieth-century European tradition of Marxist Freudianism (e.g., Wilhelm Reich, Eric Fromm) and Freudian Marxism (e.g., Herbert Marcuse, Norman Brown). This tradition has focused on "the extent to which the forms of class domination imposed on the masses by repressive society were related to a parallel process of psychological and above all sexual repression imposed on individuals during primary socialization within the context of the patriarchal family. Class society was seen as producing the authoritarian personality type it needed to ensure its survival" (B. Brown, 1973:24). The New Left found the parallel between sexual and political repression to provide the ideological underpinnings for the sexual revolution, though capitalist culture has subsequently proven its ability to absorb and objectify sexual license while becoming more repressive at other levels.

A more fruitful trajectory of New Left thought, following Marcuse, focused on the social psychosis of mass capitalist culture as it relates to Marx's theory of alienation. The commodification of life demonstrated the "irresistible tendency toward the universalization of alienation...turning all human subjects into passive spectators of their own alienated existence" (B. Brown, 1973:13f; above, 3,C). Michael Lerner (1991) calls this the "surplus powerlessness" of capitalist individualism. Christopher Lasch discusses this phenomenon in *The Culture of Narcissism* (1979) and *The Minimal Self* (1984), which I strongly commend to the reader interested in pursuing these issues. Lasch asserts that "modern technology had the same effect on culture that it has on production." By discouraging home production and making people dependent on the market, it effectively "resocialized them as consumers": "The conditions of everyday social intercourse, in societies based on mass production and mass consumption, encourages an unprecedented attention to superficial impressions and images, to the point where the self becomes almost indistinguishable from its surface.... The consumer lives surrounded not so much by things as by fantasies. He lives in a world that has no objective or independent existence and seems to exist only to gratify or thwart his desires" (1984:30). The alienation inherent in commercial culture generates what Lasch calls the narcissistic problematic, which is wrongly if commonly confused with selfish individualism: "The prevailing social conditions, especially the fantastic mass-produced images that shape our perceptions of the world, not only encourage a defensive contraction of the self but blur the boundaries between the self and its surroundings. As the Greek legend reminds us, it is this confusion of the self and the not-self — not 'egoism' — that distinguishes the plight of Narcissus" (ibid:19). The characteristic features of this narcissistic disorder include "our protective irony and emotional disengagement, our reluctance to make long-term emotional commitments, our sense of powerlessness and victimization, our fascination with extreme situations and with the possibility of applying their lessons to everyday life, our perception of large-scale organizations as systems of total control" (ibid:18f). Though critical of Lasch, Paul Wachtel's *Poverty of Affluence: A Psychological Portrait of the American Way of Life* (1989), agrees that our psychological disorders result from our internalization of capitalist economism. "Our society's preoccupation with goods and with material productivity is in large measure irrational and serves needs similar to those which motivate neurotic defense mechanisms in individuals.... Our excessive concern with economic goals has disrupted the psychological foundations of well-being" (1989:1).

This, then, is the "inner" world of the *locus imperii,* in which we are what we own and in which "Chevy is the heartbeat of America." Therapeutic confrontation with our narcissistic disorder which keeps us unable to distinguish our consumer self from our true self, with our internalization of empire which keeps us unconsciously reproducing the body politic's manic-depression in our own political bodies, with these demons that keep us silenced and captive to the world's "dreams about itself" (Marx) — this is hardly an abandonment of politics. Quite the contrary; unless we sustain struggle at the level of the political unconscious, we will have little hope of genuine transformation, personal or political.

C. "INTO THE FIRE AND WATER": SHAME AND THE IMPERIAL PENDULUM OF GRANDIOSITY AND DEPRESSION

How does family therapy's diagnosis of "shame-bound systems" illuminate our collective captivity to manic-depressive behavior?

I have alluded to my own therapeutic journey. It was during this most difficult season of my life that I was introduced to the work of Alice Miller, a Swiss psychotherapist-philosopher who has devoted her life to trying to uncover the roots of family and social violence. I was deeply impressed with her key arguments: about the "silent drama" of unresolved trauma that begins in childhood and ends in disconnection and destructive behavior; about how this condition is continually reproduced through repetition-compulsion; and about how these narcissistic disorders lead to the "true self's 'solitary confinement' within the prison of the false self" (1981:ix). But it was her assertion that "grandiosity is the counterpart of depression *within* the narcissistic disturbance" that I found most illuminating and challenging (ibid:56). In that mirror I recognized both myself and the dominant culture into which I was socialized. I had experienced the swing of that vicious pendulum between elation and despair, not only in regard to my personal aspirations but as historical shifts in the public mood. And I was being told that these emotional extremes — whether in my political body or the body politic — were twin poles of the *same denial*. I continue to explore this diagnosis in my personal life-text; my purpose here is to explore it in terms of political, social, and cultural texts of the *locus imperii*.

Diagnosing a narcissistic disorder is one thing; healing it is another. Finding the right tools for what we might call political therapy will entail sorting through the often bewildering maze of analytic theories used in contemporary psychology. Should we, for example, look to Anne Wilson Schaef's (1987, 1988) application of the addiction/codependence model to organizations and societies? Can the Twelve Step recovery strategy, with its emphasis on a covenant and community of resistance, be broadened to include socio-political pathologies (see Emeth, 1990; below, 6,B)? Can insights into the narcissistic disorder from the psychoanalytic tradition (Schwartz-Salant, 1982), or from the recent "mytho-poetic" movement (Moore and Gillette, 1990), be refocused on political symbolics? Probably, like most therapists today, we should work eclectically with a variety of techniques and frameworks. After all, no single paradigm — political, psychotherapeutic, theological, or otherwise — can exhaustively describe our complex cultural situation.

Of the major contemporary psychotherapeutic approaches used in North America today, the one already most inherently political is, I believe, family systems theory (for a summary see Kerr, 1988). In its critical analysis of relationships within kinship structures, family systems theory would seem to lend itself to being broadened to include economic and social systems. Indeed the founder of this approach, Murray Bowen, saw this early on: "Members of families replicate the same emotional patterns in society; family and societal emotional forces function in reciprocal equilibrium to each other" (1974:177). In other words, the family — primary site of socialization for the political body — reflects the imperatives of the body politic. Unfortunately most of those using family therapy today are not making these connections, though again Third World practitioners are demanding that social, cultural, and political contexts be taken into account (see Mirkin, 1990; Jackson, 1990; Ho, 1987). Still, I will pursue a recent contribution in this field that, in my opinion, deepens Miller's and Lasch's diagnosis of the narcissistic disorder.

In their pioneering work *Facing Shame* (1986), Merle Fossum and Marilyn Mason sketch a portrait of what they call the shame-bound system. They describe it as a "self-sustaining, multigenerational system of interaction with a cast of characters who are (or were in their lifetime) loyal to a set of rules and injunctions demanding control, perfectionism, blame and denial" (ibid:8). Like narcissism, the problem centers around loss of self, an inability to distinguish between healthy *guilt* and paralyzing *shame*. Because of pervasive feelings of despair and inadequacy, they cannot confront what they have done wrong because they feel that they *are themselves* wrong. Fossum and Mason contrast the main characteristics of the shame system with a healthy, "respectful" system; every family falls somewhere on a continuum between the two (ibid:21ff):

Respectful Systems	Shame-bound Systems
Violation of values leads to guilt	Violation of values leads to shame
Self separate, part of larger system	Self has vague personal boundaries
Rules require accountability	Rules require perfectionism
Relationship in dialogue	Relationship always in jeopardy
Reparation, resolution to conflict	Unresolved conflict
Deepening or modification of values over time	Increasing rigidity
Empathy	Alienation and distance

A major manifestation of this shame system, say Fossum and Mason, is what they call the control-release cycle: "The release phase, either by its chaotic nature or its violation of the control values, adds to the shame. The control phase feels like a refuge from shame, but is actually only a hiding place and covers the shame.... The coping responses within the system serve only to intensify the problem. Then the intensified problem serves to intensify the coping responses" (ibid:13). For example, in a shame-bound family, a father in the control phase might be rigid and disciplinarian, demanding and critical of his children. In his release phase, however, he boils over in anger, verbally or physically abusing them. But this only makes him feel more ashamed, and he tries to "fix" the problem by more control, which of course leads to greater frustration and worse abuse in the next release. Obviously we have here an analogue to Miller's thesis about grandiosity and depression.

The control phase, say Fossum and Mason, is typically marked by compulsive behavior and denial; the release phase by abusive behavior and self-indulgence (ibid:107):

Control Phase	Release Phase
Compulsive behavior	*Abusive behavior*
strict dieting	eating disorders
psychosomatic illness	alcohol/drugs
compulsive cleanliness	self-mutilation
helping/saving others	sexual/physical abuse
workaholism	money/consumption
Characteristics	*Characteristics*
hypercritical	self-indulgent
self-righteous	self-centered
pleasing, placating	unpredictable
rigid, blaming	lacking self-control

In reality it often seems as if both phases are coexisting. This is to be expected, say Fossum and Mason, because of the systemic imperatives of shame-bound systems: "These compulsions or addictions are found to cluster in the families of the shame-bound system and in some instances seem to be almost interchangeable with one another. As one of the behaviors is controlled or moves into the background, another may replace it. They are conditions which arise within the system and by their compelling nature act as central pillars to maintain the status quo within the system" (1986:10). In the popular jargon of psychologist John Bradshaw, the shame system is truly "toxic," poisoning all who are socialized into it (1988:25ff).

Most pregnant with political implications is Fossum and Mason's description of the ways in which those in the system adopt masks to hide their shame. Among these are

- adopting a fairy-tale identity;
- disconnecting or escaping from the family;
- assuming a "macho" or fatalistic attitude;
- presenting a veneer of niceness, *particularly religious piety.*

Having summarized some of Fossum and Mason's description of how shame works in the family system, let me suggest some possible social correlates.

Within our political bodies, shame typically expresses itself around sexuality. We are socialized in the family to be ashamed of our bodies — often because of suppressed secrets around sexual violations that were never resolved, such as rape, incest, or abortion. We cannot talk about desires openly in order to discern healthy erotic expression, so we live on a pendulum between torturous abstinence (control) or irresponsible license (release). In our social attitudes toward the body, we North Americans are known for our preoccupation with physical prowess, glorified in the bigger-than-life competition of professional athletes, or physical beauty, idealized in movies and magazines from high fashion to pornography. The quixotic quest after physical perfectionism (=control) lies behind our compulsion for sports, dieting, and working out, and certainly undergirds the huge cosmetics (and cosmetic surgery) industry. Yet at the same time, our culture is being ravaged by an epidemic of addictive and abusive behavior (=release) of every sort, from drugs to food disorders to incest. Are compulsive physical self-discipline and self-mutilation pendular responses to a culture that promotes a sense of shame about who we really are in our bodies? There is also a place in between the poles: ambivalence. The unresolved conflict between the extremes manifests in crazy-making double messages we give or get from our parents (e.g., "Sex is bad; save it for someone you love"). Double messages leave us stranded in ambivalence — unable to exercise any discipline or enjoy any pleasure.

Now let me suggest how our attitudes toward the body politic might be parallel. Historical guilt around racism, for example, has never been transacted by the dominant culture: Members of the dominant culture deny we are a part of the problem yet despair about race relations. Before the civil rights era, we managed the contradiction through segregation (control), which was broken by

periodic episodes of overt racist violence (release). Since the civil rights movement, the dominant culture has tried to manage its shame by exercising tolerance
of "minorities" through officially sanctioned paternalism (control). As soon as
genuine social power began to be redistributed through affirmative action, however, cries of "reverse racism" commenced, and with them, the current backlash
(release). The constant double messages about race keep us ambivalent about
addressing racism head-on. Indeed over many generations our guilt has become neurotic, generating what Fossum and Mason call meta-shame — feeling
bad about feeling bad. Individuals, they say, usually experience meta-shame as
waves of paralyzing depression after violating or being violated. This describes
well what the dominant culture experienced after the Los Angeles uprising and
what one encounters in a room of middle-class whites whenever a person of
color expresses his or her rage (below, 9,C).

The cultural heaving of our imperial ship of state between grandiosity and
depression was a pattern discernible well before 1991. Just over the course of
my own lifetime we have seen the "repressive" socio-political mood of the
1950s (control) swing to the "rebellious" 1960s (release), only to yield to the
"ambivalent" 1970s, which laid the groundwork for the resurgence of the authoritarian New Right in the 1980s. The pendulum could be seen in public
attitudes toward foreign policy. The Vietnam War era was a time of release
in terms of public criticism of U.S. military power to manage the cold war.
The cathartic impact of My Lai, Kent State, the Pentagon Papers, and Watergate
(not to mention losing the war) — all public traumas — resulted in a pervasive
sense of national shame. This persuaded the cold warriors to return to covert
operations (thus recovering control); what followed was a decade of secretive
low-intensity warfare around the globe. This new style of imperial conflict management slowly began to resurface midway through the Reagan years, until the
Pentagon was sure it could engineer its overt war making in a way that would
preclude criticism; in this sense, the Gulf War was far more a public relations
success than a military one. I was interested to discover that D. W. Winnicott,
one of the most influential psychoanalysts in the last several decades, made a
similar analysis in a 1969 essay about the Berlin Wall. Referring to the cold
war, he wrote, "One can see that there is an alternation between resolution
of the conflict, which means war or conquest, and toleration of the state of
strain, which means acceptance of a Berlin Wall or its equivalent. This is the
manic-depressive psychosis in terms of time and of sociology, which is the same
thing as the manic-depressive psychosis of alternating mood in the individual"
(1986:227). Thus, when Bush declared that Desert Storm had banished the Vietnam Syndrome, he was only confirming our utter captivity to this pathological
national pendulum.

The masks of shame observed by Fossum and Mason in the family system
are also recognizable in our social life, and in some cases are so ubiquitous
that they virtually define the dominant cultural ethos. Let us take *susceptibility
to mystification.* Shame-bound individuals typically romanticize their childhood,
the pain of which is buried in the unconscious. As a society, we idealize our

past (and present character) as a nation; the New Right simply combines romanticization of America's origins with a repressive discourse of "family values." Ronald Reagan sustained two terms in office on the power of his appeal to that heady mixture of fairy-tale identity and Ramboesque machismo. The efficacy of the blatantly propagandistic politics of the Gulf War is testimony to our passion for mystification. We are notorious as a people without a sense of history, cut off from our past; we cannot deal with events as recent as the invasion of Grenada, much less the profound legacies of genocide in the Americas (below, D; Chapter Five).

The *inability to maintain boundaries* is another symptom. In individuals it leads to failure to complete or process interpersonal transactions. Indeed today we see unprecedented transiency in friendship, sexual intimacy, and marriage. As individuals and as a society we prefer "mediated" communication to direct accountability and dialogue (above, 3,B). Rather than absorbing stress and adjusting to the rapidly changing world, we can only manipulate or react to events — "rapidly deploying" our military before there is time for public discussion. When persons (or groups) have a sense of identity, it allows them to be part of a larger, interrelated social universe; but our system promotes vague personal and group boundaries, resulting in constant but usually unacknowledged race and class tensions. Perhaps above all, instead of connectedness our society mirrors the profound lack of intimacy found in the shame-bound family: Relationships always feel in jeopardy, and we have resigned ourselves to feeling alone together. No wonder we are increasingly isolated from the world community in our imperialism, from the environment in our overdevelopment, and from each other in our steady drift toward technocratic individualism.

These characteristics describe the dominant culture. The harder task is to discover how we activists mask our shame. What about the ever-so-delicate matter of "liberal guilt" (that is, shame) among so-called progressives (below, 9,C)? Why are we who dissent from the dominant culture so divided and sectarian in our work, isolating ourselves by our differences rather than finding common ground in struggle (below, 7,F)? To what extent might our protest politics be a symbolic way of disconnecting from our society of origin? Are they public displays of religious piety — or political correctness? Or were our protests against the Gulf War merely a counterritual, the control-step to the dominant culture's release-step in a national codependent dance of shame?

In Mark's story the demon throws the boy into the fire and into the water, trying to destroy him (9:22). This is truly our profoundly dysfunctional national condition, impaled on the horns of grandiosity and depression. We had better understand it if we are to be healers of, and not merely participants in, the pathology. In the *locus imperii*, if we do not have the courage to face our true selves, we will be silenced and destroyed, just as surely as we have silenced and destroyed those who have dared to stand in the way of what our civilization calls, in its delusions of grandeur, Progress.

D. "HOW LONG?"
REPETITION-COMPULSION AND THE BODY POLITIC

"What is unconscious is bound to be reproduced"; what implications does Freud's conclusion have for the dominant political culture and our silencing within it?

In the midst of our gospel story, Jesus suddenly issues a sweeping indictment: "You unbelieving generation! How long must I be with you? How long must I put up with you?" (9:19). Today this apocalyptic lament of the martyrs is surely shared by the victims of our national policies (Rev 6:9f). It is echoed in the *Kairos* Documents (above 2,B), whose authors understand that the oppressed of the Third World will continue to suffer unless and until we who hold systemic power face our pathologies. And it is the fundamental question of modern therapy: *How long* will we remain codependent with dysfunctional and destructive systems? To face these painful queries is to seek the roots of our silencing.

"How long has he been this way?" asks Jesus to the possessed boy's father, now reframing the complaint as empathetic inquiry. The father replies, "Since childhood" (9:21). Ancient wisdom indeed! It is rearticulated in the modern psychological axiom that the seeds of adult pathologies are sown in early childhood trauma. To conclude the diagnosis of pathological narcissism in the *locus imperii,* therefore, I return to Alice Miller's thesis concerning the "silent drama" and the roots of human violence. Children, Miller argues, are utterly dependent on adult love and acceptance and therefore unable consciously to process anger resulting from experiences of violation or domination. Their sole means of survival is to internalize their sense of betrayal while rationalizing or idealizing the adult's "good intentions." The child must eventually repress the trauma, even to the point of "forgetting" altogether (that is, banishing it to the realm of the unconscious). It is only later, as an adult, that the true emotions associated with the trauma are discharged. This happens only indirectly, however, because of the "unconscious imperative" to "split off the disquieting parts of the inner self and project them onto an available object" (1981:67). When the pain and anger are *introjected,* the cost is intrapsychic, manifested through depression and various forms of despair. But when it is *projected,* the cost is social, taking the form of oppression of others, inevitably persons or groups who are vulnerable.

While the drama of reproduced trauma is most clearly played out in the family, the primary socializing system, Miller reminds us that its impact is socio-political as well. In the family the "vicious circle of contempt" usually targets the next generation of children, who become victims of adult-children who were victims. In society it often means projection of unresolved anger upon those already oppressed or disenfranchised. What else can explain our uncanny, vicious national habit of blaming the victims for social violence, regardless of whether it is rape, poverty, or insurrection (below, 7,C)? Miller cites as an example of socially split-off rage the "heroic willingness" of adolescents to fight the wars of older men, in which they can cathartically divert resentment from their family of origin to "a clear-cut enemy whom they are permitted to hate freely and with impunity" (1983:171). Another example is the political-cultural system of totalitarianism, in which adult citizens passively accept or actively promote ideologies and practices of State oppression. In the service of severe father-tyrants, "they allow their inmost selves to be completely dominated, as had been the case in their childhood" (ibid:66). Miller believes this helps explain how so many otherwise morally responsible German citizens could have so readily submitted to Hitler: "When a man comes along and talks like one's own father and acts like him, even adults will forget their democratic rights...allow themselves to be manipulated by him, and put their trust in him...without even being aware of their enslavement" (ibid:75). The 1991 Russian film *The Inner Circle* is a fascinating exploration of such internalized domination in Stalin's Soviet Union. This hypothesis surely also illuminates the widespread tolerance of the repressive paternalism of the Reagan personality cult.

Fossum and Mason essentially agree with Miller's model. They identify "three distinct elements of the origin and perpetuation of shame" (1986:39ff). The cycle begins with external shaming events. For the individual this is often sexual or emotional violations, but could include violent crime, exploitation, or war. "Post-traumatic syndromes are inherently shame-maintaining":

> Returnees from Vietnam...did not know where to take their recollections of some of the terror they faced there....The shame dynamic presented itself through the shutting down of feelings, a hardening to the pain of terror....One World War II survivor...had been the single survivor from his company; his memories of combat were returning and he was terrified. He held his jaw firmly as he stated, "I decided then never to care again." (Ibid:43f)

The next stage is "inherited generational shame, passed on to family members when the shaming events and the feelings they invoked were denied." Again, the sources can be personal or social, such as

> poverty resulting from bankruptcies, suicides, childhood deaths and accidents where the parents feel they were to blame (or were being punished), or secrets surrounding pregnancies, births, and adoptions. The rules of shame-based systems produce several generations of repressed affect. The family members often feel they individually have inherited some kind of "curse" and have anxiety and fears, even phobias, about breaking the powerful no-talk rule insulating the shame. (Ibid:44f)

Finally, once in place the system is maintained through shame-based behaviors and destructive relationships: "Shame seeks itself in others in its own magnetic field":

> With blurred boundaries, shame-bound people tend to fuse their entire
> selves with whatever the person or activity is and take all that is out-
> side them very personally by internalizing. . . . The pattern of self-defeating
> behaviors — self-hate, rejection, and self-alienation — metastasizes and
> gradually seems to fill up the whole self, becoming the person's identity.
> The individual feeds the downward spiral of the cycle of shame through
> these patterns. (Ibid:49f)

This explains why so many people today first get into and then cannot extricate
themselves from dysfunctional or abusive relationships.

Now we must ask: If our captivity to shame-based behavior at the level
of the political body is rooted in an intergenerational fabric of unresolved individual and family trauma, does it not follow that the pathologies of our
body politic are similarly rooted deep in the shadow side of our *collective*
past? Consider for a moment the psychic health of a people in whose past is
buried incalculable traumas — Indian massacres and witch burnings, the African
slave trade and Jim Crow, economic exploitation and environmental devastation,
Dresden and Hiroshima. Obviously the intergenerational impact of such "external shaming events" on the victims of historical oppression is different than
it is on those who have materially benefited from them (Pinderhughes, 1990).
Oppressed people, as Fanon showed, internalize a pathology of inferiority, expressed in self-contempt and introjected in self-destructive behavior. Oppressors,
conversely, exhibit a pathology of superiority, expressed, for example, in the
ideology of entitlement. But post-traumatic stress disorders, as the example of
Vietnam veterans suggests, afflict all survivors, both innocent victims (civilians)
and active participants (combatants). The task of a First World theology is to
take both seriously.

Historical honesty, if the dominant culture had the courage to practice it,
would compel us to admit that our "prosperity" is predicated upon a legacy
characterized as much by racism and greed as by liberty and democracy. But
we do not face the shadow side of our own story because we are shame-bound
and instead suppress historical contradictions while reciting vicious fictions such
as the European "discovery" of the Americas, thinking them essentially benign. The mystified heritage passed on in our high school American history
books replaces complicity with idealized portraits of our "founding fathers" and
grandiose myths of Progress and Manifest Destiny. But historian Rex Weyler
reminds us that this is not without cost:

> The great denial has crept into every cell of European blood. Lies lived
> too long put a crick in the back and a hobble in the step. The patient
> loses vitality. The alcoholic father, the videoholic mother, the drugged-
> out teenagers in malls: these are the sad and confused inheritors of the
> lie, the denial, and the projection. Because the dream of the Americas
> was a nightmare for the land and the beasts and the people on it, the

horror seeped like water into the foundations of the culture, condensed in unvented corridors of power, and saturated the dream. (1992:14)

This burden of silence has taken a huge, intergenerational psychic toll on the dominant culture too. I will discuss this aspect of denial in Chapter Five.

We are a people who cannot resolve our traumatic past because we do not know the truth of our own history. From these severed roots grow the weeds of our narcissistic disorder. The identity of our imperial self is blurred, so we seek pseudo-relationships, allow ourselves to be dominated and others to dominate, and fuse with what we produce and consume. Unable to respect boundaries, we project our unresolved trauma around the world. We find ourselves divided by gender, race, and class because we seek out only those with similar pathologies. The psychic substructure of our political unconscious is more effective in keeping us domesticated than any superstructure of law, state, or military. "The cops in our head," as Boal says, are ultimately responsible for why we essentially police ourselves (Boal, 1992; Darling, 1992). So we swing on the historical pendulum of grandiosity and depression; and when America is anxious, the poor at home and abroad had better look out — because we *will* find new victims to vilify and new enemies toward whom we may split off our insecure rage.

As Miller writes: "It is part of the tragic nature of the repetition-compulsion that someone who hopes eventually to find a better world than the one he or she experienced as a child in fact keeps creating instead the same undesired state of affairs" (1983:241). Surely this describes the frustration we feel as people committed to social transformation. There is so much suppressed trauma in the *locus imperii*, so many generations of silence, such complex overlapping patterns of domination reproduced by individuals, families, and social and political institutions and traditions. *What is unconscious is bound to be reproduced:* This is why economic and political contradictions are so studiously ignored in the *locus imperii*, why the process of social change is so difficult here, and why we as a people continue to consolidate and extend our national pathologies and then remain silent in the face of our crimes.

These reflections are obviously painted with a very broad brush; as a "diagnosis" it is hardly precise, and there are exceptions to every generalization. I have offered this synthesizing interpretation of various psychological schools of thought because I find their explanatory power so compelling. Once we understand the power of the political unconscious we who work for social change will look more critically at our methods. Does traditional organizing have the power to motivate silenced, shamed people? We know by now (or should) that paternalism — doing it "for" the masses, the politics of the vanguard — prevents people from becoming their own subjects and only reinforces their sense of powerlessness. But we are less clear about prophetic exhortation — "Just do it!" the politics of moral imperative. Miller tells why this does not work: "What is unconscious cannot be abolished by proclamation or prohibition" (1981:90). Political education and conscientization alone will not suffice: "Since one's use and abuse of power over others usually has the function of holding one's own feelings of helplessness in check — which means the exercise of power is often unconsciously motivated — rational arguments can do nothing to impede this process" (Miller, 1983:277). Miller insists that the victims of childhood trauma must move past the "absurd hope that the past can be corrected by remaining silent about it" (ibid:258). Do we have the patience, compassion and courage to engage ourselves and each other in a painstaking excavation of our political unconscious, in whose strata are hidden the roots of our silencing? Radical self-examination will mean more than inserting political rhetoric into psychological discourse, or vice versa. If we wish to exorcize this demon, we will need to engage disciplines that are at once profoundly personal and profoundly political. In the language of scripture, we must do "spiritual battle" with principalities and powers who are contesting for our hearts and minds.

E. DISCIPLINES OF LISTENING:
CONTEMPLATION AND DIS-ILLUSIONMENT

How can prayer be a way to confront the political unconscious, unmask our illusions, and heal our collective pathologies?

Just as members of the dominant culture in the U.S. think they are free because the national ideology says they are, we activists hold the illusion that we are liberated simply because we speak of, organize for, and care deeply about liberation. In the *locus imperii* it takes encounters with our impotence for us to reckon with ever-deeper levels of our own "possession." But the gospel, Douglass John Hall reminds us, "dares to pronounce that real hope can begin where illusions end, and real life where death is tasted" (1989:44). Strangely enough, psychologist Irvin Yalom (1989) contends that "dis-illusionment" is also the fundamental task of psychotherapy. This is a task also claimed by the contemplative traditions. So we must now return to the conclusion of Mark's story of the unsilencing of the deaf-mute: Jesus' exhortation to prayer.

"This demon can be cast out only through prayer!" (9:29). But what is prayer? It is certainly a *petitioning* of God, but too often this becomes the notorious discourse of the foxhole — the frantic appeal to be delivered from the consequences of our own actions. Indeed Desert Storm drove many of us to unusually fervent petitionary prayer; problem was, Bush and his court pastors were conspicuously seen to be doing the same. But neither the official invocations of the powerful who seek to control history nor the anxious pleas of those of us who simply feel overwhelmed by history capture Mark's understanding of the way Jesus prayed. Closer to the mark is centering prayer, which has been taken more seriously in recent years by those committed to a genuine (and not merely rhetorical) practice of "resistance and contemplation." Such prayer will always be necessary in the continuing struggle for sanity and clarity. In light of how sparingly Mark speaks of prayer in his gospel, however, we should not be too quick to assume we understand what he means. Jesus' prayer takes place in the wilderness (1:31; 6:46), in contrast to his opponents, who exploit the public glare (12:40). It is instructive that Jesus invites his disciples to prayer on just two occasions. One is after his dramatic repudiation of the Temple as a "house of prayer become a den of thieves" (11:17). There Jesus urges his disciples to envision a different world in which the exploitive Temple State is overthrown and replaced by the community practice of reconciliation (11:24f). The other instance occurs just before Jesus is about to be seized by that same State's security forces, where he summons his followers to prayer as a way of "staying awake" (14:32–42; below, 12,B). Markan prayer, then, is clearly more than a private exercise in piety or even meditation. It seems to be a way of engaging the Powers in the apocalyptic struggle over history; this is why prayer is the site of tested loyalty, from the wilderness temptations to Gethsemane.

Mark's Jesus correlated the discipline of prayer with the vocation of exorcism — the struggle with the Strong Man in the body politic and the Legion in the political body (above, B). I believe, therefore, I am on firm ground in interpreting such exorcizing prayer as the contemplative discipline of dis-illusionment, in which subjects of the *locus imperii* try to unravel their personal and communal possession and silencing at the level of the political unconscious, so we can continue with the work of conscientization and action. Prayer-as-dis-illusionment is the complementary discipline to literacy-as-demystification; with the former we hear the truth about ourselves and find our voice to speak; with the latter we see the truth of the world and find our hands to act. While I believe the discipline of dis-illusionment has vast implications for the work of empowerment, it is far from clear exactly what it might consist of, or how the process might be carried out in a popular fashion. The following thoughts are only suggestive of some basic components; it is my hope we will learn more about the process by experimenting with it in concrete circumstances.

1. "Listening the Silenced into Speech": An Archaeology of the Political Unconscious

I have heard feminist theologians speak about the therapeutic process as *listening the silenced into speech*. It strikes me as an appropriate description for the contemplative work of dis-illusionment. A metaphor for this patient process of unsilencing the self might well be the painstaking work of an archaeological excavation, in which we sift carefully through the compressed strata of our political unconscious to unearth and interpret the psychic artifacts, from which we will reconstruct the truth of the buried past — not for its own sake, but so that we can be liberated from repetition-compulsion. To begin with we must, like the archaeologist, know something about the surface terrain (our present lives) and the received history (however mystified) of that terrain. Otherwise we will not know where and how to begin digging. Then we must tenaciously lay bare the various layers of memory and consciousness. In order to identify the fragments we unearth, we must already have some sense of the basic attributes of the strata from which they come, which means the process occurs within a wider framework of historical-cultural analysis. This suggests that it is best done with trained and experienced facilitators.[5] Above all, because the excavation takes place on *inhabited* terrain, it must, like surgery on wounded flesh, be done with care and compassion. Once the re-collected data have, like fragile potsherds, been assembled, the excavator of the political unconscious lays them out for a "reading." As in both therapeutic and archaeological analysis, the fragments of the past form a complex puzzle, and interpretation is inductive, not linear. But whereas psychotherapy assumes the uniqueness of each person's symbolic "text" (the goal being individuation), political therapy also pays attention to the class, race, and gender matrices of commonality (the goal being liberation). We must reckon with both the texts of victimization and texts of entitlement within the oppressive system (the wounds and distortions of the latter may be more difficult to identify).

We can and should appropriate tools of traditional family therapy. Here I will give just one concrete example, the "genogram," in which one's family genealogy is mapped back several generations. Family therapists look to the genogram for evidence of system stressors such as alcoholism, suicide, and divorce in order to determine intergenerational patterns of inherited trauma. Political therapy would simply extend this map to include indicators of cultural tradition, political location, and social mobility. For example, how was the family system shaped over time by experiences of unemployment or elite work; war or revolution; poverty or affluence; educational opportunity or lack thereof; class discrimination or privilege; racial tensions or "invisibility"? These theoretical notions may seem overly abstract, so let me illustrate them with brief examples from a group I worked with in Washington, DC. A young professional woman from the South related how her upper-middle-class family never visited a particular aunt in Louisiana, for reasons that were not made clear. Finally as an adult she decided to go visit this aunt, who was in her eighties. Once she arrived, she immediately understood why this part of the family had been severed: The aunt was not only one of the rural poor, she was utterly uninterested in the upward social climbing that had characterized this woman's upbringing. This was a painful encounter, because for the first time she saw her nuclear family from the other side of the social and historical fence and because she found this aunt genuinely delightful. As she talked about these matters, she began putting together the fragments into a "text" that she could work with to "de-code." She encountered feelings of being "deprived" of the wisdom and humor that arose from the life-experience of this aunt, and she used that to reflect on issues of severance. She was able to name certain suppressed class anxieties she had always sensed growing up and could begin to identify how she had internalized those biases.

Another white woman spoke about how she came from a family of "mathematicians" — university professors, engineers, economic consultants — all men. The flip side of this legendary family character, passed on through her mother, was that "women can't do math." She had spent much of her adult life trying to overcome her own unconscious internalization of this message and then to deal with her family's disapproval when she completed college and became a professional. As a group we looked at this textual artifact — "women can't do math" — and examined how it reproduced the patriarchal division of labor within the family system, which in turn tried to produce women who fit in with the patriarchal division of labor. A middle-aged white man, progressive and "politically correct," described growing up in a blue-collar steel town in western Pennsylvania. He allowed that he didn't really know any people of color because they just didn't live around there, and that he couldn't recall any worker playing in the industrial league baseball team who wasn't physically scarred or crippled from the mills. We wrote on the board the words "They just don't live here" and examined that text as a mystification of complex but concrete social boundaries and codes that reinforced racism and economic discrimination. We also reflected on the memory of disfigured bodies as a text about work and class. Finally an elderly black woman told of growing up in Washington, DC, and of the tensions between her father, who came from rural Georgia, and her mother, an "educated" city girl who had finished high school. She had a painfully vivid memory of the KKK coming to town in the 1930s; her mother tried to persuade her father not to go to work because it would be too dangerous to walk the streets, but he told her not to worry, that he "knew how to act around these people." And her eyes filled with tears as she related how he died young, of an enlarged heart resulting from the strain of lifting large plates at the Government Printing Office — work at that time reserved for black men only. It was hard for the predominantly white group to listen to these two painful texts of racism, and it opened new space to get past the shame and look at those suppressed issues.

Such simple exercises take those of us socialized into the dominant culture beneath the masks of entitlement and its illusions to reveal how the structures of gender, race, and class privilege and oppression have intimately shaped our own families. We must press taboo questions on our own life-texts: Where did our family's wealth come from? How was miscegenation dealt with? Who was displaced where our ancestors settled? This helps us name and confront how we unconsciously carry the viruses of entitlement. It also is a revelation to hear stories of how the same historical processes have impacted unentitled people — oppression is no longer abstract. Sometimes simply by talking about what has been traditionally repressed opens new bridges across gender, race, and class gulfs. Organizers in Northwest Pasadena, for example, found that community-sponsored roundtable forums inviting people to share personal stories was a way to head off racial tensions in the weeks before the 1993 federal trial of the Los Angeles police officers who beat Rodney King.

A life-text from my own family system represents a typically ambiguous mixture of victimizing and victimization. For example, my idealized apprehension of my father was essentially heroic, as is typical in many middle-class families. Rising from Depression poverty to become the successful business executive I knew him as, so the myth went, required discipline, hard work, and self-sacrifice. Any possible shortcomings he may have exhibited as a parent were to be excused, since he had "provided" for us against difficult odds. Occasionally we heard that he had given up his own vocational aspirations in order to support his children — a text we effectively internalized into feelings that we were somehow responsible for our father's "deeper discontents." Rarely spoken of was my father's father, a shadowy but sympathetic figure whom I never knew except in terms of the same heroic narrative; he too was a hardworking tire salesman who brought his family through the Depression. Only obliquely alluded to was the fact that my father never really had a relationship with his dad, a matter wholly unresolved when the latter died of a heart attack when my father was twenty-seven. Before doing therapeutic work I had simply rationalized that my dad was trying to be to us what his father never was to him. I had to dis-illusion myself of the heroic myth in order to see how his severed relationship with his father unconsciously shaped his emotional absence from me and to get at my feelings of abandonment.

So far this is a traditional text for family therapy. But what about the *social* dimensions of my father's story, growing up half-*mexicano* in northern California in the 1930s? This context was only ever in the background of the myth, but I also carry it in my bones; it must similarly be reinterpreted to reveal the costs of the "heroic" journey (see below 11,E,1). How did the cultural-linguistic suppression (first involuntary and then internalized) of my father's "Chicano side" contribute to my own cultural ambivalence? How did his subsequent class alienation (trading his working-class ethnic roots for the WASP upper-middle-class ethos of his wife's family) instill in me an artificial class identity and loyalty? My father always qualified his otherwise rote patriotism with the admission that fighting two wars within a decade robbed him of his dreams to be a foreign diplomat; how did this influence my attitudes about politics and vocation? And how was the "provider" myth a mask for his addiction to work, a surrogate for intimacy that in the end killed him prematurely? Despite the fact that this life-text does not reflect some of the more dramatic aspects of deprivation, abuse, or addiction found in so many other families, these are nevertheless painful dis-illusionments because they are mine. By combing the psychic geography of my family past, I can identify dysfunctional patterns I have unconsciously reproduced and can begin to confront my own illusions. What are the myriad large and small ways in which I subvert the values I hold publicly as an activist or theological educator through my own narcissistic, sexist, or racist behavior?

Finally let us look at the life-text of a public figure. Irish singer Sinead O'Connor created a stir in the fall of 1992 when she tore up a picture of Pope John Paul II on national television in the U.S. Whatever we may think of this particular public ritual, her subsequent explanation represented, in my opinion, an extraordinary text:

> I am an Irish woman. And I am an abused child. The only reason I ever opened my mouth to sing was so that I could tell my story and have it heard. The cause of my abuse is the history of my people, whose identity and culture were taken away from them by the British with full permission from the "Holy" Roman Empire.... The only hope for me as an abused child was to look back into my childhood and face some very difficult

memories and some desperately painful feelings and a lot of very tricky conversations. I had to have it acknowledged what was done to me so that I could forgive and be free. So it has occurred to me that the only hope of recovery for my people is to look back into our history. Face some very difficult truths and some very frightening feelings. It must be acknowledged what was done to us so we can forgive and be free. If the truth remains hidden then the brutality under which I grew up will continue for thousands of Irish children. And I must by any means necessary *without* the use of violence prevent that happening because I am a Christian.... The story of my people is the story of the African people, the Jewish people, the Amer-Indian people, the South American people. My story is the story of countless millions of children whose families and nations were torn apart for money in the name of Jesus Christ. God *is* Truth. (Hochman, 1992:F10)

Here we see the political and theological power of dis-illusionment from someone who has reestablished the connection between her own life and the collective life and history of her people.

The dis-illusionment of family myths in their social context empowers us to take the next step: dis-illusionment of the body politic. Those in power trade heavily in mystifications concerning the nobility of our "national family" (Reagan's "America is back and walking tall," *BSM:*3ff). The political myth of Manifest Destiny is deeply embedded in our unconscious, as is the cultural myth of the melting pot, the economic myth of Horatio Alger stories, and the class myth that there are no real classes in the U.S. (below, 9,D). This mythic stock functions to obfuscate, suppress, and finally erase national experiences of contradiction, and it guarantees our history as repetition-compulsion. Dis-illusionment here requires what we might call (with some trepidation) "society of origin" work. We must help each other look deeply and critically at our roots, unsilencing the past and calling into question behavior so that we can face our real story as a people, both the "little traditions" of our respective subculture(s) and the "great tradition" of the dominant culture (below, 5,D). Breaking the negative power these unconscious texts have over us can be as searing as an exorcism. But by handling them gently and respectfully, I believe we can build a dis-illusioned community freed to explore ways to empathize with and redeem our past (below, 11,E).

2. *"Only through Prayer": From Mourning to Response-ability*

O'Connor's "confession" raises the matter of what we do once our excavation of the political unconscious has uncovered repressed trauma or historical contradiction. Here the old adage of labor activist Joe Hill — "Don't mourn, organize!" — becomes our most formidable opponent. Alice Miller contends that the healing journey must go through "indignation and rage, which can then give way to mourning and reconciliation" (1983:266). Without mourning what has been lost and can never be recovered, she insists, we cannot achieve "structural transformation" (ibid:270). I might be able to grasp intellectually how inter-generational dysfunction — say, my grandfather's paternalistic dismissal of my mother — might have affected me in my relationship with her and thus all other women. But this information, while illuminating, is not in itself healing; nec-essary, so to speak, but not sufficient. I might even feel rage about the way this psychic inheritance has deformed me, hurt me, and led me to hurt others. But anger is not mourning (cf H. Lerner, 1985). How do I, in any meaningful existential sense, mourn that which is past and cannot be changed? Politically speaking, how do we grieve a distant cultural past, in which our ancestors were slaves or slavetraders, land squatters or robber barons, exploited new immigrant laborers or dispossessed natives?

This is a formidable question, and we would do well to learn from a variety of therapeutic practices. Feminist therapy has learned to work with women to mourn the loss of their full humanity because of intergenerational patterns of patriarchy; indeed it has invited men to mourn the loss of their *anima* result-ing from macho myths of maleness (J. Miller, 1976; Eichenbaum and Orbach, 1983). The men's movement, in turn, is experimenting with rituals and spaces to help men grieve their father-wounds in the struggle to recover their "emo-tional bodies" (Bly, 1990; Keen, 1991). Beyond the gender struggle, however, analogues are scarcer. The analysis of psychic numbing in the nuclear age is certainly a prototype, since it tries to uncover and address the traumatic di-mensions of wider political realities; in this field, however, only Joanna Macy's "despair and empowerment" work went past diagnosis to "treatment" (1983). M. Scott Peck's analysis of the My Lai massacre as "pathological group narcis-sism" moves in the right direction (1983:212ff). And "unlearning racism" work and those doing therapy with torture survivors also deserve mention. Still, we have a great deal more to learn about how to mourn embedded socio-political trauma.[6]

Our journeys will be different, and Miller reminds us that therapeutic (or religious) techniques can often impede as well as help. She describes her path to recovery of her true self as a long and difficult one:

> How does one arrive somewhere when, without knowing it, one has always been there? How does it happen that confusion turns into clar-ity, fear of pain into freedom to experience feelings; that volumes of empty words turn into simple facts, the constant flight-from-self into being-with-oneself; that blindness turns into vision, deafness into hearing, indifference into empathy, ignorant crime into informed re-sponsibility, murderous lusts into calm, clenched despair into relaxation, self-destruction into self-protection, self-alienation into self-harmony? (1990: 147)

Here we can see how close we are to the ancient traditions of contemplative prayer. Mystics have long explored the journey into the heart of darkness, that place of emptiness and self-confrontation, and have much to teach us about prayer as dis-illusionment (Merton, 1971). The church's liturgical traditions of forgiveness and reconciliation can also aid our search for ways to mourn. Here, however, Miller adds an important caution: She is adamant that if forgiveness is required as proof of healing, it becomes instead merely another symptom of "pedagogic manipulation" (1990:181ff). Nor can those who have perpetrated the violence, the pain, and the illusions demand reconciliation; that is the role of "wounded healers" (Nouwen, 1972).

Mourning is not an end in itself; it animates "response-ability." We have a lot to learn here from the Twelve Step movement, which for all its idiosyncrasies remains arguably the most popular form of group transformative work in our contemporary cultural context, cutting across gender, race, and class lines (below 6,B). The process rightly begins with acknowledgment of captivity (step one), but also includes "confession" (step five) and reparation (steps eight and nine). To be sure, like various brands of religious conversionism, it can be criticized for its nonpolitical, personalist definition of "recovery." Indeed Wendy Kaminer's recent *I'm Dysfunctional, You're Dysfunctional* excoriates the recent proliferation of derivative groups — such as Sex Addicts Anonymous, Overeaters Anonymous, and the codependency movement — as spreading "victim mentality" and the "politics of powerlessness." In response, however, psychotherapist Ellen McGuire has rightly pointed out that Alcoholics Anonymous has remained clear about requiring addicts "to confront the damage they have caused, to accept the consequences of their addiction and to shoulder responsibility for all their actions; blame is strongly discouraged for the recovering alcoholic/addict both as a 'cop out' and as a likely route to relapse" (1992:822).[7] This is an important discussion for those of us trying to sort out the layers of victimizing and victimization in our life-texts. We must mourn ways in which we have been severed from our true selves and violated. But we must also take responsibility for the patterns of domination we reproduce. The oppressed will rightly be skeptical of our dis-illusionment if it issues only in the rhetoric of reconciliation and not participation in the struggle for justice (see below, 6,E). Political therapy, in other words, must lead to therapeutic politics. Intervention is a necessary part of the struggle against addictive systems. We need to be clear about this because in the Palace Courtyard, therapy, like religion, is notorious for getting stuck in the interior site. Our adage, then, must be: "Mourn, *and* organize!"

In proposing a "political" interpretation of the discipline of contemplation, I am not suggesting that there is no place for either traditional therapy or traditional prayer (Rohr and Ebert, 1990). Peace and justice activists, in particular, need to take both far more seriously. *Radical* introspection and self-criticism is not something we are strong in; shame-based behavior, however, is. We must be open to resources and insights from many directions for the practice of dis-illusionment, for it will require far greater clarity, empathy, patience, and fortitude than we usually demonstrate. And only grace, as Gerald May has shown so eloquently, can empower us to recover discernment, honesty, dignity, community, and simplicity (1988:162ff). For we struggle with the pathologies of the *locus imperii* from the inside out, never entirely free of Legion's claim on us. Like the demon-possessed boy's father, we can only cry: "We believe! Help us in our unbelief!" (Mk 9:23).

When confronted and named by Jesus, the thoroughly dis-illusioned one, the demon of silencing convulses our political bodies on its way out, such that it seems to those around us that we have died (9:26). Indeed the unsilenced are those who have died to the system, their true political bodies "resurrected" (9:27). No wonder the life of discipleship was understood by its earliest proponents to be a constant process of "dying to the old/enslaved self" and "rising to the new/liberated self" (e.g., Romans 6)! Perhaps we can yet rescue the therapeutic lexicon from its captivity to cultural narcissism and restore it to its rightful place at the center of messianic practice. After all, the verb used in the gospels for Jesus' ministry of healing is *therapeuein*, and the New Jerusalem envisioned as a garden for "the *therapeia* of the nations" (Rev 22:2). Dis-illusionment, like literacy, invites us to faith as political imagination, to belief that the world we see is not the only world possible (below, 12,B). The times call for no less — neither Prometheus nor Narcissus can save us from our repetitive, compulsive history. This is the kind of prayer Jesus commends to disciples who live in the shadow, externally and internally, of the "mountain" of empire (11:22f); such prayer is "strong enough" to cast that mountain, like Legion, into the sea.

NOTES

1. The literature is already voluminous. I recommend Clark (1992), Menos (1992), Bennis and Moushabeck (1991), Hiro (1992), Bresheeth and Yuval-Davis (1991), and especially Norris (1992).

2. Jeanie Wylie, editor of the *Witness* magazine, brought to my attention the incredible demonstration of press chauvinism/racism under the guise of "analysis" during the Iran hostage crisis. Consider, for example, these descriptions of the Ayatollah Khomeini's regime by Ray Mosely in an article syndicated by the Chicago Tribune Press Service:

> A nation has put its fate in the hands of men who, in many cases, are narrow and bigoted in outlook, have only limited education, and have no training in statecraft.... Tehran was, and is, one of the world's most brutally ugly capital cities... spoiled by tasteless, rampant development, utterly devoid of graceful architecture or coherent city planning.... People who consider dying to be an honor are, by definition, fanatics. Vengeful blood lust and a yearning for martyrdom seem especially pronounced among the Shia Moslems of Iran.... Iranian men, like the Palestinians, are innately macho. They obviously love the sense of power they derive from carrying weapons.... The mood on the streets of Tehran in the present crisis is a blend of paranoia, hysteria, and fantasizing. (1980:3f)

It is not difficult to see how such "analysis" set the tone for a new generation of enemy creation and scapegoating of Arab/Persian "terrorists." Many of these same themes echoed in journalistic "accounts" of Saddam Hussein's Iraq leading up to the Gulf War.

3. There was a taxonomy to the media's complicity, of course. Marchik gives an example to illustrate:

> Following modifications in the anti-trust laws during the Reagan era, General Electric, a major arms manufacturer and nuclear vendor, acquired NBC and its parent RCA in 1986.... Reportedly GE manufactured some $2 billion worth of military equipment, including components for the Patriot missile, which were deployed in the Gulf during the war. NBC produced a laudatory segment on the SCUD-busting Patriot missile (1/18/91), neglecting to mention GE's role in its production.... NBC reporters failed to inform viewers that the government of Kuwait reportedly owned some 2.1 percent of GE's stock and that the company expected to win hundreds of millions of dollars in contracts for the rebuilding of Kuwait. When NBC stringer Jon Alpert returned from Iraq with video footage of the effects of the allied bombing, NBC President Michael Gartner refused to allow the footage to be shown and subsequently dismissed Alpert from the network. (1992:11)

But not a word of this was heard *during* the war; what truth that has come out has been wrestled to light by the alternative media, long after the fact.

4. In traditional societies the human (or animal) body functions as the central social and political metaphor; we see this expressed not only in the totemistic liturgies of indigenous peoples but in the cult of biblical Israel as well. The political body of the priest (or of the sacrificial animal) was "representative" of the body politic — it purified (or bore the sins of) the people. Thus Levitical legislation moves back and forth seamlessly between purity codes meant to regulate the political body and debt codes meant to regulate the body politic. Even in Hellenistic antiquity the Roman imperial cult centered around the political body of Caesar, though in the "republican" tradition the Senate was the preferred symbol of the body politic. The apostle Paul was probably influenced by this latter tradition in his famous argument about the "body of Christ" and the church (1 Cor 12:12ff).

5. Clarissa Estes uses a similar metaphor, proposing "extensive 'psychic-archaeological' digs into the ruins of the female underworld" (1992:3). As to the question of whether this process is best done individually, in pairs, or in groups, my experience suggests that there is a time and a place for all three. And while we need to try to ensure the process is accessible and popular, I think there is a role for the trained therapist. I am not persuaded by the egalitarian approach of the "co-counseling" movement, though there is, no doubt, much to be learned from it. Some of the exercises I allude to here are similar to those developed in women's literacy work; as I noted, the two disciplines are mutually supportive (see Lacey, 1990).

6. For a family systems perspective on the men's movement see Erkel (1990); for a feminist critique see Hagan (1992). Physicians for Social Responsibility have helped revive earlier work in social psychology by Robert J. Lifton (1961; also Lifton and Erikson, 1982); a bibliography can be found in Nelson (1981); see also Mack (1981), M. Day (1981), and Sandman and Valenti (1986). The "unlearning racism" process was developed by the late Ricky Sherover-Marcuse and others, and is today being popularized by the People's Institute for Survival and Beyond in New Orleans and the National Coalition Building Institute. Psychologists working with torture survivors seek to recognize not only the physical trauma, but also the massive feelings of failure, depression, and loss of identity experienced by victims whose movements of political opposition were crushed by brutal military dictatorships. One of the best healing techniques for

political trauma they have discovered is simply for victims to tell their stories, thus resisting the temptation to fall into silence about such painful and costly experiences of political dissonance (Cienfuegos and Monelli, 1983; Stevenson, 1989, summarizes this field and provides an excellent bibliography).

7. Kaminer, 1992. See also the critiques of "addiction addiction" in the *Utne Reader* (November–December 1988). The valid points raised in this forum are however compromised by what I take to be a reactionary debate about whether there is any scientific basis for the diagnosis of addiction (cf Peele, 1989), as well as libertarian objections to anything that smacks of moralizing personal restraint. For a balanced discussion of the taxonomy of addiction see G. May (1988). Still, the Twelve Step movement's unwillingness to link its insights to social and political expressions of, or contributors to, addiction is problematic. Therapy of any kind that only empowers people to liberate themselves from individual addiction can be accused of serving as socializing therapy — that is, helping people feel better about themselves and function "well" in a pathological social system.

5

"Do You Not Remember?"

Revision

Nothing of the past five hundred years was inevitable. Every raised fist and brandished weapon was a choice someone made. The decision to become a nation of thieves and liars was a choice. The decision to censor the native truth was a choice. The decision to manipulate the knowledge of American history was a choice. My immediate choice is to celebrate or mourn. With my relations around me, I go into mourning — but I go angry, alive, listening, learning, remembering. I do not go quietly. I do not vanish. I do not forget. I will not let you forget.

Wendy Rose,
"For Some, It's a Time of Mourning"

History, despite its wrenching pain,
Cannot be unlived, but if faced
With courage, need not be lived again.
Maya Angelou,
"On the Pulse of Morning"

The spirit drove him out into the wilderness (Mk 1:12). At the outset of Mark's story, Jesus undertakes a mysterious but compelling call to wilderness solitude. Why? Because here, according to Mark's prologue, the Story of liberation can be renewed (Mk 1:2f). God's sovereignty breaks ground in this barren soil precisely because it is ignored by human sovereignties, because here the dominant culture is irrelevant. History is regenerated at the point where our historical projects are exhausted, where our explanations of the past that merely justify the present are silenced.

He was put to the test by Satan (1:13). The desert, says theologian-activist

111

Jim Corbett, is unconquered, undomesticated space, undefined and unfettered by the fictive constructs of "civilization." But he adds that "whoever leaves the world to wander alone in wildlands should be prepared to meet a devil or two, when busyness ceases to drown out the dream side" (1991:10). The desert monks of early Christianity understood this too; for them, wrote Thomas Merton, the wilderness was "the country of madness" and "the refuge of the devil," and anyone "who wanders into the desert to be himself must take care that he does not go mad and become the servant of the one who dwells there in a sterile paradise of emptiness and rage" (1956:17f). This stands to reason: Unbuttressed by the comforts, props, and fabrications of the dominant culture, one's socialized sanity is indeed tested. Thus the desert is the place of "temptation," a place where we journey to confront our true selves and end up wrestling with the demonic.

"A renewal of the Dreaming" — this is how elder Guboo Ted Thomas describes this journey, referred to among Australian Aborigines as "going walkabout" (1987:90ff). The Sioux call it *hanblechia,* vision seeking. Vision quest is a tradition found among native peoples the world over. Lost to modern urban cultures, it survives still in the wilderness. The popular account of a Lakota shaman *Lame Deer, Seeker of Visions* begins: "I sat there in the vision pit...all by myself, left on the hill-top for four days and nights without food or water.... If *Wakan Tanka,* the Great Spirit, would give me the vision and the power, I would become a medicine man and perform many ceremonies" (1972:11f). Vision quest is a ritual passage that combines what Joseph Campbell (1988) calls "initiation ceremony" and "hero-journey." "Out of love for their community," explains anthropologist Christopher Vecsey, and "with the help of guardian spirits," shamans undertake the passage "to the land of the dead in order to restore the lost or stolen or diseased souls" (1991:120f). Vision quest, then, is at once an outward adventure beyond the margins of society; an inward passage of purification and self-encounter; and a journey "in the spirit" through mythic time to find the identity and destiny of one's people. This surely describes Jesus' sojourn deep into the wilderness, confronting the Beast and supported by angels — apocalyptic symbolics suggesting the heart of darkness. But Jesus is not just dealing with "personal demons"; he is somehow interiorizing and reliving the experience of Israel.

For forty days.... This time span is clearly meant to invoke Israel's wanderings in the wilderness; but what exactly is the connection? Israel's extraordinary identity as God's people commenced when they were sprung from Pharaoh's imperial straitjacket: "I will bring *My people* out of Egypt" (Ex 3:10). Similarly, Jesus' extraordinary identity has just been confirmed at baptism: "You are *My child,* the Beloved" (Mk 1:11). Now he, like his ancestors, must struggle in the wilderness to discover what this vocation means. So this inward-outward journey is a "test of character." But is there more to it still? What if Jesus is going "walkabout" in order to *retrace the footsteps of Israel through story-time* in the hope of discovering where his people went wrong? A people's "myth of origins," writes Robert Bellah, defines who they are; therefore it is to the

Exodus wilderness that Jesus, "in the spirit world," must return. He is not rem-
iniscing; he is *revising* the wilderness test, facing again the dark forces that
lured his people into the historical dead ends of idolatry and oppression. To
forge a different future he must confront the past — especially the repressed
and denied past, the traumas that remain deep within the political unconscious.
This is a radical quest for the root causes of the present crisis of his people,
so that Jesus can "see again" — re-vision — their true vocation: the kingdom of
God (1:15f).

"Do you not remember?" (8:18). Dead center in Mark's story Jesus warns
his disciples that they cannot have eyes to see or ears to hear if they do not
remember. He is not referring to the Platonic notion of recollecting preexisting
ideas but to solidarity with one's own history: "Remember this day on which
you came out of Egypt, out of the house of slavery" (Ex 3:13). Not to remember, on the other hand, is to be seduced into idolatry (Dt 8:18f), lured from
exodus back to Egypt; in Mark this is understood as Pharaoh's disease: "Are
your hearts hardened?" (Mk 8:17). Mark's gospel is an attempt to remember
and revise the liberation Story. Its very first line echoes the creation (1:1 = Gen
1:1) and its very first character, John the Baptist, is portrayed as Elijah (1:6
= 2 Kgs 1:7f). In his mission, Mark's Jesus follows in the footsteps of David
on campaign (2:25f = 1 Kgs 21:1ff) and Moses in exodus (3:4 = Dt 30:15f).
Jesus revises Ezekiel's parables (4:26f = Ez 17), Elisha's feedings (6:33ff =
2 Kgs 4:38ff), Isaiah's prophecies (11:12ff = Is 28:4) — the list goes on. But
when Jesus ascends a mountain to "name" his disciples (3:13ff), he is revising two of the most revered traditions of Israel: God's covenant with Moses on
the mountain (Exodus 19:1f) and Moses' founding of the free tribal confederacy in the wilderness (Numbers 11:1f). It is also the moment in which Jesus,
who has taken the torch from the prophets of Israel, prepares to pass it on to
us, for here we are commissioned and renamed for the vocation of proclamation, healing, and exorcism (3:14f). That is, we are invited to join the vision
quest, to examine the choices of *our* ancestors and lay bare the roots of *our*
pathologies.

Do we have the courage to follow the way of revisionism in our time?

A. THE QUINCENTENARY: POLITICS OF MEMORY

*Why is the struggle over the interpretation of our past necessarily
enmeshed in the politics of the present?*

Thus far we have examined two ways in which the dominant culture lives
in Denial. At the *objective* level the actual structure and function of socio-
economic systems are mystified to us — unless we learn to "see" (disciplines
of literacy, Chapter Three). At the *subjective* level we internalize the dysfunctional shame culture of empire and its pathological pendulum of grandiosity and
depression — unless we learn to "listen" (disciplines of dis-illusionment, Chapter Four). We now turn to a third aspect of Denial: At the *historical* level we

are disconnected from our own past and thus unaccountable — unless we learn
to "unharden our hearts" (disciplines of revision).

Rex Weyler, in his excellent summary of the continuing history of genocide
against the Indian peoples of the Americas, confirms my thesis in Chapter Four
when he writes:

> Denial and projection work within the unwieldy collective egos of na-
> tions, as well as within individuals. There is no better case of myopic
> national denial than the story of the European occupation and colonization
> of the Western Hemisphere. The quincentenary celebration of Columbus'
> so-called "discovery of America," which began with the intention of hon-
> oring European history, has in fact flushed that long history of denial out
> into the open, and exposed the shadow behind certain European myths
> about honor, liberty, and democracy. (1992:13)

The much-ballyhooed 1992 Quincentenary represented an opportunity for all
the peoples of the Americas to face this denial; the focus on Columbus invited
us to look again at our "myths of origin" (below, B; on Columbus see Lyon,
1992; Sale, 1990). Because of this, the Quincentenary evoked a struggle over
the politics of memory, legacy, and identity (Uchitelle, 1990). This was to be
expected; as historian David Kennedy points out, "In memory the mythical and
the actual mysteriously commingle, making memory an often unreliable historical source, but an indispensable component of both individual and collective
identity" (1991:M1).

What, according to those questioning whether Columbus should be celebrated, was being denied? In the profoundly ambiguous project of European
civilization in the "New World," it was argued, the most suppressed historical
reality is genocide. A single statistic, presented not by a political activist but
by a Yale epidemiologist, suffices to make the point: "Approximately 56 million people died as a result of European exploration in the New World. In many
areas, this translated into a reduction of the population to 10 percent of its initial
size. Some died in combat and many as a result of social disruption, but most
died of introduced diseases" (Black, 1992:1739). This holocaust is often referred
to as the "great dying" (Wolf, 1982:133). So brutal and total was the massacre
of the Taino people of the Indies, where Columbus first landed, for example,
that Bartolomé de las Casas, one of the earliest Spanish critics of the genocide,
wrote: "Who of those born in future centuries will believe this? I myself who
am writing this and saw it and know most about it can hardly believe that such
was possible" (Reid, 1992:66).[1]

Carlos Fuentes, in his Quincentenary reflections, rightly insists that the
meaning is deeper than numbers:

> The reasons for this demographic catastrophe were complex, cumula-
> tive and brutal: European diseases, immunological breakdowns, forced

labor but also culture shock and sheer anguish. But numbers are not the most important fact about the European conquest of America. The violent deaths with which the Europeans — Spanish, Portuguese, English, French, Dutch — implanted their power in the New World is but the statistical index of a far larger occurrence: the irreparable death of great civilizations that possessed education systems, a separate moral and artistic universe, and forms of human relationship in constantly evolving creativity. (1992:M1)

The destruction of these communities, their traditions, and their wisdom represents an incalculable loss to the human family and without doubt jeopardizes our collective survival (on Native America before 1492 see MacLeish, 1992; *National Geographic,* 1991). "We know how to bless the world and make it flourish," said an elder from the Kogi people in the highlands of Colombia; "the Younger brother, all he thinks about is plunder...he is killing the heart of the world" (Ereira, 1992). As las Casas predicted, today we live in disbelief of this legacy and this loss. That is what is being denied.

The Quincentenary argument had begun at least a decade earlier, in 1982, when Spain proposed to the U.N. General Assembly that 1992 be celebrated officially as "The Meeting of Two Worlds." This provoked a walkout by African delegates, who took exception to the idea that a body set up for the purpose of decolonization should celebrate the beginning of modern colonialism, thus killing the proposal (Dunbar-Ortiz, 1990:16). Years of heated prolegomena followed. Some North Americans were inspired by the way Aborigines and their supporters were able to impact significantly the bicentennial of European arrival in Australia in 1988 (Mydans, 1988). When 1992 finally arrived, it took no time for the opening salvo. In nearby Pasadena the theme of the New Year's Day Rose Parade was "The Spirit of Discovery." A Spanish aristocrat purporting to be a direct descendant of Christopher Columbus was chosen as grand marshal, creating a firestorm of outrage among Native Americans and Chicanos. Hundreds of protesters turned out to pray for rain on the parade, though they were studiously ignored by the media — and the bands played on.

But as the year went on it became clear that there were more counter-commemorations and protest skirmishes than official celebrations. Most of the state-sponsored events were abandoned as too expensive or politically problematic. For once, Native Americans and supportive activists seemed to win the struggle to frame the debate. "These grand Quincentenary events toppled under their own weight," concluded local performance artist Guillermo Gomez-Peña, only slightly overstating the case; "After so much hoopla, Columbus is winding up a cheesy logo for friendly expansionism and a bad actor in a couple of films" (Breslauer, 1992:83).[2] For most of the citizens of the *locus imperii* it passed barely noticed, eclipsed by the more immediate economic anxieties of the deepening recession, by fears generated by the Los Angeles uprising, or by the quadrennial circus of presidential elections. And the pro-Columbus

galas never got off the ground. It makes one wonder whether those who stew-
ard the Columbian myth of origins simply backed off once it appeared that
all this might occasion a genuine debate about the "cosmic" issues of genocide. The dominant culture was content to forfeit a gratuitous celebration of
the European legacy to avoid grappling with the political implications of an
unsuppressed history. On the other hand, peace and justice groups could be accused, not entirely unfairly, of having responded to the Quincentenary merely as
"that year's fashion issue." After all, Columbus bashing was easy, while briefly
focusing on the plight of Native Americans was trendy. In retrospect, the Quincentenary was, in one sense, a nonevent that never lived up to its acrimonious
billing.

For some, however, the Quincentenary was a defining moment in the war of
myths. This was particularly true for native peoples, who for the most part were
less interested in ragging on the last five hundred years than in trying to build alliances to make the next five hundred different in the Americas. Fuentes reminds
us that "the Indian culture of the Americas, if it did not prevail, did not perish,
either. Rather, it became part of what one might term the counterconquest, that
is, the Indian response, followed by the black response, to the purely European
presence in the Americas" (1992:M1). Beginning in 1990 the first of several
historical gatherings of native peoples from all the Americas was convened in
Quito, Ecuador, to reassess and renew the determination of First Nations not
only to survive but to reclaim sovereignty (Warrior, 1990; Cayuqueo, 1991). The
representatives of some 120 Indian nations declared that "we have never abandoned our constant struggle against the conditions of oppression, discrimination
and exploitation which were imposed upon us as a result of the European invasion of our ancestral territories. . . . Our nations are basing our struggle on our
identity, which shall lead us to true liberation" (*Quito Declaration,* July 1990).

Fortunately there were also Christian groups throughout the Americas who
took this opportunity to wrestle with their identities. Some asked whether the
Quincentenary moment might be a *kairos* one — pregnant with the demands
of repentance and the hope of transformation (cf Wallis, 1991; above, 2,B).
Challenged by the *Kairos Central America Document* "to hold penitential celebrations of great prominence on the occasion of the 500th anniversary of Latin
American subjugation, committing themselves clearly before their governments
to its emancipation" (Brown, 1990:103), some of us did organize such events.
In so doing we realized that the Quincentenary was only the "first year of the
rest of our lives," demanding of us a commitment to a long-term process of self-
examination in order that we might understand how our national past remains
embedded in the present.

That the politics of memory would be contested fiercely is hardly surprising,
for it takes us to the heart of the struggle over our future. The Quincentenary debate was and is all about myth and history, recollection and amnesia,
responsibility and Denial. That is, it is all about which stories will be used
to construe our collective experience, to interpret where we as a people have
been, where we are, and where we are headed. Stories "aren't just entertain-

ment," says Leslie Silko's elder; "Don't be fooled" (above, Introduction). Will the ideologies of Progress and Manifest Destiny prevail for yet another generation? Or will we listen to and learn from the long-silenced voices, stories, and perspectives of marginalized peoples — Native Americans, women, people of color? "The principal stock in trade of historians is the retold story," writes David Kennedy (1991:M1), which means that history is determined by *how* it is narrated, and by *whom*. The past "sounds" different depending upon whose "voice" is telling the story. It stands to reason then, Calvin Martin asserts, that "historians are the new high priests of our collective consciousness, the keepers of the sacred memory" (1987:219; cf *BSM:*28ff). Or as Marshall Sahlins puts it, history represents the "dominant site of symbolic production" (Martin, 1987:13). *Who we are is who we think we were:* This is as true for us as it is for totemistic traditional societies. The query at the heart of the Quincentenary is this: Is not the past always embedded in the present, like an unsevered umbilical cord between the children of today and the parents of long ago? If so, Freud's psychological ultimatum concerning the unconscious is accurately restated by Santayana: "Those who do not remember history are doomed to repeat it."

Those who want to change the relations of power in the present, to break the cycle of violence, must deal with history; those content with the status quo must keep history remote, fragmented, and inaccessible. Thus the "official" historical narratives of the dominant culture in the *locus imperii* are both highly selective and highly mystified. Shameful episodes — the Trail of Tears or the Middle Passage or anti-Chinese immigration laws or the annexation of Hawai'i — have no place in our historical consciousness. What takes their place are heroic tales and high myth: Washington crossing the Delaware; Lincoln weeping at Gettysburg; the boys and the flag at Iwo Jima. Amnesia is the tool of denial. And when, as happened in my generation, we can no longer suppress traumatic events — the assassinations of King and the Kennedys, the fall of Saigon, Watts and Selma and the Chicago Democratic Convention — we find a way to dismiss history altogether and descend into sheer daydream; this was the power of Reagan's "morning in America." All this has earned us a reputation around the world as a people disconnected from history — our own and others'. This is why most North Americans were ambivalent about the Quincentenary debate: Why dredge up the ghosts of Columbus and Cortés, of Wounded Knee and Sand Creek, of the wartime internment of Japanese Americans and the peacetime lynching of African Americans? The past is past.

In the following two sections I will not try to deal with issues of political historiography; for this I recommend resources such as Martin's *The American Indian and the Problem of History* (1987). Instead I take a more practical look at two ways in which the dominant traditions of historical narrative in the *locus imperii* have mystified or obfuscated our story as a people: by *devising* it, and by *dismembering* it.

B. "WHAT WOULD THE LAST LIE LOOK LIKE?"
HISTORY DEVISED

Why are we as a people so disconnected from our history, and what are the consequences of such a mystified heritage?

Christina Pacosz, reflecting on her attempt once to find out what really happened at "Custer's last stand," writes:

> Crazy Horse, it says in my American Heritage, was "killed while resisting arrest." Lies can make you crazy faster than anything else. This is not the first lie I have discovered in the dictionary, but I wish it was the last. **What would the last lie look like?** How would it feel? Would we miss lies if we didn't have them? Living with lies is a shattering experience. The dictionary tells us the root for *craze* is *krasa,* Old Norse meaning to *shatter.* This is not a lie. (1985:95)

There are "too many lies in the world," she laments. "We must chase them to the sun, again and again, no matter how tired we think we are...until all the lies in the world are herded together and burned up" (ibid:96).

The entrenched, popular tale of the "martyrdom" of General George Armstrong Custer — Weyler calls it part of the "great myopic mantra of American history," and explains what really happened (1992:62ff) — is a classic example of how U.S. history is devised. To *devise,* according to Webster, is "to contrive, plan or elaborate; invent from existing principles or ideas." Indeed much of our official history is sheer invention — shrouded in elaboration, filtered through preconceived and self-justifying ideas, and interpreted according to mythic contrivances. One of its most common preconceptions concerns the "natural superiority" of European culture. For example, we assume that "civilization" — a slippery concept that is sometimes measured by technology, sometimes by art, and sometimes by social institutions — only went one way: from the Old World to the New. Jack Weatherford has exploded this vicious fiction in his brilliant book *Indian Givers: How the Indians of the Americas Transformed the World* (1988), showing how countless aspects of indigenous culture were adopted or adapted by Europeans, profoundly changing how the latter lived and thought. These included native foods (corn and the potato, see below), resources (silver and furs), technologies (polycultural farming and rubber production), and social institutions (egalitarian democracy, confederalism, and even urban planning). So who civilized whom? Yet Indian contributions are culturally invisible in the dominant narrative, while the genealogy of European traditions is carefully articulated.

"History consists wholly in its method" wrote Lévi-Strauss (Martin, 1987: 15). The dominant discourse still refers to the people who lived in the Americas before the arrival of the Europeans as "pre-historic" or "pre-Columbian." This continues despite the fact that anthropologists are finally recognizing what indigenous peoples have long known about themselves, namely, that their "memory" — articulated and passed on through songs and chants, rituals and sacred sites rather than in books and archives — is truly ancient, in some cases possibly preserving traditions of the migration from Asia. Indian people are far more connected to their story and their past than we are. Yet we refuse to acknowledge them as historical *subjects* because we have fashioned them into strictly historical *objects*. The notion of "pre-history" may be a chauvinistic, ethnocentric construction of time and the world, but for the European bias it is fundamental (ibid:192ff). "To retrench the traditional concept of Western history at this point would mean to invalidate the justifications for conquering the Western Hemisphere," says Vine Deloria (Churchill, 1992:17).

In truth, just as Indian peoples have history, we have myths. In his classic study of American civil religion, *The Broken Covenant,* sociologist Robert Bellah writes: "America's myth of origin is a strategic point of departure because the comparative study of religion has found that where a people conceives itself to have started reveals much about its most basic self-conceptions" (1975:3). The development of European American "mythography" (the term is Vecsey's, 1991:1ff) was in fact complex; Ronald Sanders charts it in his brilliant *Lost Tribes and Promised Lands: The Origins of American Racism* (1992). What is clear, however, is that most European immigrants tended to articulate their sense of purpose by invoking the biblical stories (see Bellah, 1974:21ff). Whether religious refugees, economic opportunists, or soldiers of fortune, they understood themselves to be on a Christian mission, from Spanish explorers claiming the land for Cross and Crown to Quakers pursuing a Holy Experiment for the Peaceable Kingdom. Yet two conflicting mythic traditions coexisted in the European consciousness. On the one hand, their journey to the New World was interpreted, as Columbus wrote in his log, as a "discovery of Paradise," a miraculous passage through the flaming swords of the Fall to the garden of delights. On the other hand, they understood their migration as an exodus flight from Old World oppression — an "errand in the wilderness," to use the phrase coined by Puritan preacher Samuel Danforth in 1670 (Miller, 1964:1). Upon the screen of America, Bellah says, the newcomers "projected certain fantasies, dreams, and nightmares long carried in the baggage of European tradition but seldom heretofore finding so vivid and concrete an objective correlative. Thus America came to be thought of as a paradise and a wilderness, with all of the rich association of these terms in the Christian and biblical traditions, or more simply . . . as both a heaven and a hell" (1975:6). The myth of paradise regained, which arose from European *idealism,* portrayed its native peoples as (passive) "noble savages" and legitimated exploitation and possession in terms of Adamic "dominion" of creation. The myth of the dangerous and dark wilderness, the product of European *anxiety,* saw indigenous peoples as uncivilized pagans and demanded that the land and its inhabitants be converted, domesticated, or destroyed. These archetypal polar projections correlate to my thesis concerning the pendulum of grandiosity and depression argued in the last chapter (above, 4,C). The European mind, whether fleeing from unresolved traumas in the Old World or projecting its imperial fantasies, could not face the truth about itself and thus could apprehend the cultural or geographic "other" only in either idealized or demonic terms.

Recall, however, that these were twin poles of the same Denial. Despite the difference between the myths, the historical practice was the same. The ideology of America as a promised land — regardless of whether it was understood as Eden or Sinai — justified a new conquest of Canaan. A classic expression is the famous 1630 sermon of Governor John Winthrop assuring his band of Massachusetts Bay colonists that "we shall find that the God of Israel is among us, when ten of us shall be able to resist a thousand of our enemies, when he shall make us a praise and glory, that men shall say of succeeding plantations: the Lord make it like that of New England: for we must consider that we shall be as a City upon a Hill, the eyes of all people are upon us" (W. Smith, 1969:70f). The genocide suggested obliquely in Winthrop's allusion to the Joshuaic conquest was indeed carried out on native peoples.

One can gaze directly at the canvas of European-American origin myths in the so-called frontier art produced in the nineteenth century, a genre recently analyzed in *The West as America: Reinterpreting Images of the Frontier, 1820–1920* (Truettner, 1991).[3] This was a defining period for nativist art; the U.S. was forging its continental empire, and origin myths were being pressed into the service of the new project of Manifest Destiny. Noting that "between 1870 and 1900 Americans settled more land than they had during the previous three centuries," Truettner points out that "myth and ideology intersect continuously in western images":

> The "myth of the frontier"...guaranteed progress without encumbering social and environmental debt....Ideology, however...serves to extol progress, "authorizing" westward expansion as a beneficial national undertaking....Much of this iconography...serves to endorse expansionist activities on the frontier: Columbus becomes Daniel Boone, gesturing toward new lands; ships crossing the ocean are replaced by covered wagons crossing the Great Plains; the founding of the colonies (models of civic order and religious toleration) anticipates the development of western frontier towns; ...religious symbols, stressing Christianity as the foundation of an enlightened government and social code, return in numerous images; and Europeans triumph over Indians in every New World encounter, setting the stage for later confrontations. (Ibid:40f)

Even as the myths were being recycled, however, the primal dialectic of grandiosity and depression persisted as a subtext. For example, in an 1855 painting entitled *The Departure of Columbus from Palos in 1492,* by immigrant German Emanuel Leutze (of *Washington Crossing the Delaware* fame), Columbus stands on the ship's bow above the crowd, pointing stoically westward, embracing destiny. But the ship's mast looming behind him faintly suggests a cross, while at the bottom right-hand corner, gazing up, is a pining, white-clad Mary

Magdalene figure, as if at the foot of Calvary. Here the "discoverer" is both hero and martyr.

Many of the frontier images from this school tended in the direction of either the idealized paradise or the threatening wilderness motif. Examples of the former would be Albert Bierstadt's *Giant Redwood Trees of California* (1874) or the Hudson River School: Romantic, softly backlit, almost dreamy landscapes suggest nature-as-Eden. In contrast is George Caleb Bingham's *Daniel Boone Escorting Settlers through the Cumberland Gap* (1851–52). Employing a thinly veiled Flight into Egypt motif (Boone as Joseph leading the Madonna on horseback), the intrepid pioneers are etched in chiaroscuro against a frightfully dark and threatening wasteland that seems to press in around them. The same poles appear in portraits of native people. John Stanley's *Osage Scalp Dance* (1845) is a typical depiction of savage, menacing Indians surrounding a captive European woman and child, who are gazing up to heaven in the center of the picture; the allusion would appear to be the stoning of Stephen the Martyr. Such anxiety-producing fictions were of obvious ideological utility while Indian wars were still raging. On the opposite side of the pendulum is Charles King's studio-contrived portrait of *Young Omahaw, War Eagle, Little Missouri and Pawnees* (1822), a classic depiction of the noble savage according to the conventions of European royal portraiture. The primal mythic struggle between the Indian and "Progress" was a dominant theme of this artistic school (see below, 12,A). We find the depressive end of the pendulum in Theodore Kauffman's *Westward the Star of Empire* (1867): A distant locomotive (universal icon of Progress during this period) heads straight toward the viewer from the sunrise, while in the foreground shrouded in darkness we see Indians crawling snakelike to put debris on the tracks. If the Indians weren't trying to derail Progress, on the other hand, they were run over by it, completely remade in its image, as in Charles Nahl's *Sacramento Indian with Dogs* (1867): The docile subject is dressed and groomed as a European, and around his feet are "domestic" animals! The Indian was caricatured as either noble and subservient or diabolical and resistant; and the land, either romanticized or feared. European-American ideological reproductions could not apprehend the "other" on any terms other than their own. They could not imagine a more complex and nuanced picture of the New World, with a full spectrum of light and darkness, because full of grandiose innocence, they could not see this spectrum in themselves.

It is instructive to note here the contrast between Native American and European-American origin myths. Indian creation stories, though as numerous and diverse as the First Nations themselves, all share a common discourse of *indigenous* origins, narrating birth-in-place: the People emerge from the earth-womb and are given the task of caring for that place (cf, e.g., Ortíz, 1991; Vecsey, 1991:34ff, 64ff). The European stories, on the other hand, are exclusively *exogenous,* narrating arrival: The heroic voyage of the *Santa Maria* or the *Mayflower* brought the people from afar to possess by divine right. Joshua Shaw's *Coming of the White Man* (1850) is a good case in point. Painted from the perspective of the shore, it portrays the appearance on the horizon of a distant tall ship with the rising sun as a virtual epiphany; the Indians in the foreground clutch their tomahawks, cower, and cover their eyes. Added for good measure to this religious legitimation, however, is a secular one: Above the whole scene geese fly south in formation, suggesting the "natural law" of migration — this was after all the nineteenth century! Today Indian creation stories are known only to tribal peoples and the few non-Indians who "study" them; the European American stories are taught in our schoolbooks — as history.

Through the myth of Chosen Peoplehood the newcomers granted themselves license to colonize and disinherit the native peoples of their land and way of life. Its secular successor, Manifest Destiny, extended the ideology of dominion west, south, and north, until the continental empire had been consolidated, and then to the Pacific basin and beyond (White, 1992). Leutze's 1862 *Westward the Course of Empire Takes Its Way (Westward Ho!)* was commissioned to decorate the Capitol, then under expansion; it is called by Patricia Hills "the most important expansionist mural painting of that era" (1991:117). The depiction of scores of pioneers perched atop a Rocky Mountain ridge, looking and gesturing into a sunset-golden west, inspired the following rave review from Nathaniel Hawthorne at the time: "It looked full of energy, hope, progress, irrepressible movement onward, all represented in the momentary pause of triumph; and it was most cheering to feel its good augury at this dismal time, when our country might seem to have arrived at such a deadly standstill" (ibid).[4] He was referring of course to the "dismal time" of the Civil War, when the nation was being forced to come to terms with its self-destructive contradictions. What better way to distract and restore "faith" in the historical illusion than by pumping up the vision of Manifest Destiny! Our manic-depressive pendulum has a long and distinguished history.

Reproductions of devised history are of course found at every level of cultural discourse. I strongly recommend Ward Churchill's *Fantasies of the Master Race: Literature, Cinema and the Colonization of American Indians* (1992) for his excellent critiques of literary fiction (from Puritan journals to Castaneda and Hillerman), historical and social analysis (liberal and Marxist), the movies (from the cowboy Western to *Dances with Wolves*), and even New Age ritual. Another fascinating study is Christopher Lyman's *Vanishing Race and Other Illusions: Photographs of Indians by Edward S. Curtis* (1982; also associated with a Smithsonian exhibit). He shows how Curtis's widely known and well-loved sepia-toned "documentary portraits" of Native Americans were not only contrived but subtly engineered to shape a new, tragic myth. At the turn of the century, with the "closing of the American frontier" and the subjugation of the last sovereign Indian nations, the dominant culture could now safely afford to "feel sorry" for this "defeated race," relegating them to the past and eventually to museums. This discourse is repeated in Henry Farny's painting *Morning of a New Day* (1907): A distant train heads through a mountain pass toward the "morning," while in the foreground, heading out of the picture, are the "mourning" Indians. They "labor through the wintery landscape, dragging their goods on travois. . . . Not only do figures travel in the opposite direction but a chasm separates them from the train, from the white world of progress" (Schimmel, 1991:172).

The myth of the vanishing race is an ingenuous invention by the dominant culture; if it can generate empathy for a "lost cause," it can effectively suppress the ongoing struggle of real Indian people for survival and preclude the possibility of whites practicing solidarity. The contemporary shape of this myth is the notion that the history of conquest is over. But Churchill reminds us that the colonization of North America continues; some four hundred native peoples still retain traditional land, representing "approximately 3 percent of the acreage in the 'lower 48' ":

> Moreover, these indigenous peoples — having never ceded it in any of the 371 ratified treaties by which the United States acquired deeds to the remainder — still retain unassailable legal title to about ten times the area now left them. Put another way, the United States lacks even a pretense of legitimate ownership over approximately one-third of its main continental land mass. In all of this vast and unceded area, the U.S. is an occupying power, pure and simple. (1992:5)

Today ideologies of "economic development" are used to legitimate the European American's continuing sense of entitlement. The same assumptions that in the nineteenth century drove the Seminole into the Florida Everglades, the Yaqui into the Sierra Madre, and the Chumash into the Santa Ynez Valley are at work today wherever Indian people are pressured by corporate interests to open reservations to outside commercial exploitation (see Weyler, 1992). But this war is not narrated in popular culture, nor does the image of Indian resistance survive. The Indian today is still either romantically caricatured or invisible (see the essays by Momaday, Whiteman, and Vizenor in Martin, 1987).

This brief discussion of devised narrative has focused on the domination of the European over Native America, yet it could be extended to every aspect of U.S. history. Sir Francis Drake was commissioned by Elizabeth I to be a pirate, but in our historical narrative he *must* be remembered as a noble explorer and British gentleman (W. Williams, 1980:19f; Sugden, 1991). General MacArthur *must* be enshrined as the savior, not subverter, of democracy in Korea and the Philippines (Thomson et al, 1981). And today, General Schwarzkopf *must* be the architect of victory, not slaughter, in Iraq. This is because Schwarzkopf, like his predecessors from MacArthur to Daniel Boone to Drake to Columbus, is an archetypal protagonist in the official story of the *locus imperii.* We would do well to recall that the ideological architects of the Third Reich, from artists to archaeologists, reached all the way back to neolithic Europe to devise Nazi history, portraying the German homeland as the cradle of civilization (Arnold, 1992). We shudder at such a notorious example of history-as-propaganda. But is it any more devised, or viciously racist, or consequential to its victims, than U.S. history according to Manifest Destiny?

To ask this question is to assault the most revered canons of the dominant culture. But it must be done. Devised history is an idol. As the prophet Habakkuk said,

> we have shaped this idol
> and it is a teacher of lies;
> we trust in it, but it cannot speak;
> it cannot wake up, for it has no spirit. (Hab 2:18f)

We must stop dancing around this golden calf, manufactured from the gold jewelry of our plunder (Ex 32:2ff). This history did not lead European immigrants out of Egypt; it lead us to reconstruct Egypt on American soil. We must chase the lies to the sun, again and again, writes Christina Pacosz, herd them together and burn them up — just like that golden calf. Then at last, tasting the ashes, we too will know their bitterness (Ex 32:20).

C. "I MARVEL THEY NEVER SPOKE OF THESE MATTERS": HISTORY DISMEMBERED

What voices have been silenced by the dominant historical narrative, and why?

In *devised* history, the protagonist is paramount and the voice heroic — in our case, it is the European-American patriarch. The antagonist, on the other hand, eventually disappears altogether — the vanishing race. Thus in popular culture, just as white minstrels wore black-face, Indians were played by white actors in the cowboy Westerns of early Hollywood. This is the cultural politics of total erasure and the control of memory and represents a fundamental mechanism in the ongoing process of colonization. The myths and symbols of the dominant culture's stories are everywhere given power and respect, reproduced in the discourses of education, the media, commerce, and religion. The stories (and even the languages) of the subjugated cultures are ignored or actively suppressed by the same social mechanisms. Thus silenced, the oppressed are effectively *dis-membered* from the body politic: They become second-class citizens with a second-class historical legacy, which justifies their continuing marginalization. And in turn, this dismembered body politic is mirrored back again in dismembered historical narrative. The official story is a fabric full of holes and broken threads and conspicuous patches, in which the subjugated are incidental at best, invisible at worst. If mentioned at all, they are pejoratively caricatured or spoken for. This is why we must speak in terms of "dominant" and "minority" cultures in the *locus imperii*.

1. Three Great Silenced Stories

There are three great narratives fundamental to our history that have been silenced, both contributing to and reflecting the dismemberment of three great sectors of our population from the body politic: Native Americans, African Americans, and women. It is no accident that each of these groups has had to struggle mightily simply to be seen as fully human in the U.S.

Native America. We know little of how the First Nations perceived their side of our common history, from the arrival of the Europeans through their eventual confinement on reservations (see Blackburn, 1979; Tinker, 1993). It is a fact that the first European immigrants absolutely depended upon the help of local native people during their initial years in America. Thanks to this hospitality, the colonists survived — but not the stories of their rescuers. What we get instead are a few mystified stories about the "Indian wars," which in most cases saw Indians fighting defensively under the constant threat of voracious European expansion, but which are always narrated with the European as protagonist.[5] It is inconceivable that the conquest of an entire continent — a project that involved fifteen generations or more, innumerable treaties and treaty violations, removals and incarcerations and massacres — could be so successfully suppressed in European-American consciousness. There is not a county in the U.S. today (including Alaska and Hawai'i) that does not have a chapter in this story. Yet very few citizens know that local history, or the pain behind it.

My home, California, is a good case in point. Indigenous peoples were as diverse and sophisticated as the bioregion would allow. But through what historian Carey McWilliams calls a "bizarre pattern of cultural miscegenation... in which the Indian influence was almost wholly obscured" (1946:23), generations of European caricature have instead established the "reputation" of California Indians as primitive, underdeveloped, and passive. Writes McWilliams in her dated but still classic regional history, "In effect, the Indians of California were ground to pieces between two invasions: the Spanish from the south up the coast, and the Anglos from the east and north across the mountains and over the desert" (ibid:41). The romanticized history of Junípero Serra and the Spanish mission era has smothered a legacy of oppression that again can be best characterized in one statistic: "From 1769 to 1833, 29,100 Indian births were recorded in the Missions of California, and 62,600 deaths" (ibid:32). As Edward Castillo (1991, 1992), a Cahuilla Indian, has shown, this devised history persists, particularly in the current campaign supporting Fray Serra's candidacy for canonization in the Catholic church. Yet as devastating as the missions were for California Indians, their secularization (beginning in 1834) during the Mexican period was worse. As mission lands were plundered and huge land grants were parceled out, neophyte Indians were either killed, driven away, or forced into peonage, while free Indians were kidnapped and sold as labor on the ranchos, despite slavery having been abolished in Mexico in 1829. But the brutal paternalism of Spanish/Mexican rule was benign compared with U.S. policies and practices — the third wave of colonization in the Southwest.

"The relative impact of Anglo settlement was about three times as severe," writes McWilliams, so that by 1880 the indigenous population of California had been reduced to 15,000:

> "Indian life," wrote Stephen Powers in a government report of 1877, "burst into air by the suddenness and fierceness of the attack.... Never before in history has a people been swept away with such terrible swiftness." American settlers came to California with two centuries of Indian warfare behind them. The Indian had no rights that the white man was bound to respect. If the Americans had a policy, it was to extirpate Indian culture, not to transform it. (1946:41f)

Yet the legacy of genocide in California is not only absent in state textbooks, it barely earns mention in discussions of the great Indian Wars of the continent.

These silenced stories are not necessarily distant in time or space from us. As a Quincentenary field trip, a group of us visited the little village of Pala in northern San Diego County for a feast day of the Cupeño Indians. We discovered that this was the site of one of the saddest stories of modern California history. A tiny mission Indian community, the Cupeño survived the first waves of Yankee settlement precisely because their desert home near Agua Caliente was considered to be of no value. In 1902, however, the land was sold from underneath them because of the real estate boom then underway throughout southern California. Charles Lummis recorded what a Cupeño woman elder told him upon hearing they would be relocated: "You see that graveyard out there? There are our fathers and grandfathers. You see that Eaglenest Mountain and that Rabbit-hole Mountain? When God made them, he gave us this place. We have always been here. We do not care for any other place.... If you [remove us] we will go into the mountains like quail and die there, the old people and the women and the children. Let the government be glad and proud. It can kill us. We do not fight" (Margolin, 1991:25). On the day of the removal, this woman did indeed disappear up into the mountains. Her wrenching words remind us that there was not one Trail of Tears or Long Walk but hundreds across this continent. So many voices — famous and eloquent like Black Elk or Chief Seattle, small and humble like the Cupeño grandmother — are still waiting to be heard.[6]

African America. A second great silenced narrative is the other terrible chapter of genocide: the Middle Passage. We do not hear that this story began when the first Africans arrived in Jamestown in 1619, a year *before* the Mayflower, as stolen "cargo" from a Spanish vessel on an English pirate ship that exchanged them for food. Who can say how many tens of millions were taken from Africa, and how many reached the Americas as slaves? Lerone Bennett estimates 40 million and 20 million respectively in his classic *Before the Mayflower: A History of Black America.*[7] But Bennett reminds us, as did Fuentes:

> The slave trade was not a statistic, however astronomical. The slave trade was...a black man who stepped out of his house for a breath of fresh

air and ended up, ten months later, in Georgia with bruises on his back and a brand on his chest. The slave trade was a black mother suffocating her newborn baby because she didn't want him to grow up a slave.... The slave trade was a greedy king raiding his own village to get slaves to buy brandy. The slave trade was a pious captain holding prayer services twice a day on his slave ship and writing later the famous hymn, "How Sweet the Name of Jesus Sounds." The slave trade was deserted villages, bleached bones on slave trails and people with no last name. (Bennett, 1982:29f)

How can a legacy of such staggering proportions be so ignored by the dominant culture? How is it that North Atlantic theology in the post-World War II era has been so impacted by the Nazi Holocaust, whereas only black writers raise the implications of the Middle Passage? We in the white peace movement wonder why most people are too "psychically numbed" to protest the madness of nuclear weapons; with such a hidden wound in our national soul, as Wendell Berry calls it (1989b), how could we possibly be otherwise?

Precious few of the positive stories of black America make it into mainstream historical consciousness, and those that do usually support the dominant narrative. We may be told that blacks fought heroically in the War of Independence (as in every U.S. war since) but not that "some twenty thousand blacks, four times as many as served in the American army, embarked with the British troops when they left American ports in 1782 and 1783" (Bennett, 1982:68). We hear of the occasional slave revolt, particularly the one led by Nat Turner in 1831 (W. Rose, 1976; Styron, 1970), but not of sophisticated alternative political institutions such as the Free African Society of Massachusetts, which was petitioning and organizing for an end to slavery prior to the Constitutional Convention (Bennett, 1982:55f). We know the story of Eli Whitney the inventor but not that of Joseph Cinquez, the leader of a slave-ship mutiny in 1839 (ibid:449). Few Californians know of the remarkable story of Allensworth, a cooperative colony of African American farmers founded near Tulare in 1908 to prove that black enterprise and culture could work if given a chance.

Let me situate this silencing in my own life-text. I am not atypical of someone educated in the institutional bosom of the dominant culture — and I was *never* exposed to black history. Secondary school: not a chance in a predominantly white suburb. College: not one required class, textbook, or lecture, never a whisper that there was a "cradle of civilization" debate (Njeri, 1991a) — and I was a humanities major! My first real taste was Eugene Genovese's *Roll Jordan Roll: The World the Slaves Made* (1974) — only because I scoured an optional reading list. Seminary: Elective courses on black church history and experience were offered only occasionally, usually under the sponsorship of the tiny Center for Urban and Black Studies(!), effectively ghettoizing the subject. Incredibly I find myself, a relatively widely read person, having only recently read so basic a text as *Before the Mayflower.*

Female America. A third great silenced narrative is that of women (see

Ruether and Keller, 1983; Cott, 1972). It is the most massive silencing of all, what Elizabeth Cady Stanton called the "injustice which had brooded for ages over the character and destiny of half the race" (Martin, 1972:42). Just as Anne Hutchinson was banished from the Massachusetts Bay Colony for engaging in critical reflection on the public ideology, women's voices have always been suspect (ibid:15ff). Since Mary Rowlandson became the first woman to write a published book in colonial America — "published anonymously in Cambridge...in 1682, with an editorial apology for bringing a woman into 'publick view'" — women have struggled for their stories to be heard (Read and Witlieb, 1992:381f). The voices and stories of the countless Indian and black women who were raped and enslaved still cry out from the earth for justice.

We are taught to memorize the Declaration of Independence but are never told of the "Declaration of Sentiments and Resolutions" of the Seneca Falls Convention of 1848, where early feminists such as Stanton and Lucretia Mott drew up a more inclusive version: "We hold these truths to be self-evident: that all men and women are created equal.... Such has been the patient sufferance of the women under this government, and such is now the necessity which constrains them to demand the equal station to which they are entitled" (Martin, 1972:43). We do not read of the slave woman who had the courage to change her name to Sojourner Truth and devote her life to preaching the same (ibid:101ff), or the struggle of the Grimke sisters in the Abolitionist movement (Lerner, 1973:152ff), or the story of Elizabeth Blackwell, the first woman trained as a physician, who was ostracized by the medical profession and operated a small clinic in the slums of New York in 1853 (Martin, 1972:208ff). The long struggle of women to gain what dignity and equality they have achieved is not taught as *fundamental* history (see Sochen, 1973). How much more silenced are the countless local stories that inhabit every corner of U.S. life, such as the poor "cotton mill girls" of the South (Byerly, 1986). Like black history, it was a major achievement simply to get a "month" in which to get the culture to focus on women's history (Rich, 1987).

It says something about the character of oppression in our history that these three great narratives of genocide are constantly crossing and overlapping. For example, it is well known that the majority of African Americans have some Indian blood, for the entirely logical reason that many escaped or freed slaves found native communities to be the far more hospitable environment. This alliance of necessity between two marginalized groups was, however, constantly antagonized by the government. When the U.S. government had removed the "five civilized nations" to Oklahoma, it urged them to accept black slavery — in part to appease the southern states, because so many African Americans were seeking freedom there. Then, after the Civil War, instead of keeping its Reconstruction promise of "forty acres and a mule," the U.S. turned around and cynically encouraged ex-slaves to homestead — in the Oklahoma territory! But these fascinating histories are explored only in the most specialized corners of the field (Katz, 1986, 1987). The narratives of African and Indian women are, of course, doubly silenced (Bataille and Sands, 1984).

2. Costs of Repression

The stories and perspectives of all minority cultures have met the same fate. The decades of discrimination against European immigrants in North America's industrial underclass, the brutal exploitation of Chinese labor to build the railroads, the generations of *bracero* farmworkers from Japan, the Philippines, the Caribbean, and Mexico (J. Jones, 1992) — these and so many other voices have been silenced. I marvel at how I know so little about the people who surround me in multicultural Los Angeles, yet I understand that this ignorance is due to the effectiveness of the ideological and social "architecture" of my dominant-culture socialization in this city (below, 7,B,C). So I must go in search of alternative history if I am ever to learn anything significant about the Gabrielino people, or the black *pobladores,* or Pio Pico, or Chinese farmworkers, or Llano del Rio, or the Central Avenue renaissance, or the Zoot Suit riots, or the meaning of Santa Anita to Japanese Americans, or Rubén Salazar, or Sweet Alice Harris — even though these stories are important not to some distant narrative but to that of my own place![8]

The best single popular source for some of these stories is still Howard Zinn's *A People's History of the U.S.* (1980). He makes it clear that not only have the voices of Indians, Africans, Asians, and Latinos been suppressed; so too has that of Europeans who, consciously or not, failed to fit the dominant narrative. Zinn notes, for example, that eighteenth-century English colonial authorities were worried at how many Europeans were leaving to go live with the Indians. A number of white children, captured during the French and Indian wars and later located by their parents, refused to leave their Indian homes to return to English society. This caused one French colonial observer to remark: "There must be in their social bond something singularly captivating, and far superior to anything to be boasted among us; for thousands of Europeans are Indians, and we have no examples of even one of those aborigines having from choice become Europeans" (Zinn, 1980:53f). What remarkable testimony; yet the voices of such "converts" have not been preserved.

Landed, privileged white men who spoke out against oppression and envisioned a truly just America, such as de las Casas or John Woolman (see below, E,2), are some of the most suppressed voices of all, since they gave the lie to the myth of European innocence. Take, for example, Roger Williams, founder of the Baptist movement in North America. Paula Womack writes:

No colonial leader had more influence among the Indians, was more trusted by them or understood them better. He befriended them, learning several Indian languages, and he mediated between them and the British to prevent war and bloodshed. ... In October 1635, while serving a Puritan Separatist congregation in Plymouth, Williams was brought before the Boston court. The first of the four charges against him was that he taught "that we have not our Land by Pattent [royal decree] from the King, but that the Natives are the true owners of it, and that we ought to repent of such a receiving of it by Pattent." He argued that the Indians were sovereign peoples and not subjects of the king of England. Williams insisted that if others wanted the land, they had to buy it from the Natives, a revolutionary human rights concept in his day. In the spring of 1636 he was exiled, in part for his championing of Native land rights. (1992:23)

After breaking his orders not to speak out on these matters, Williams fled into the wilderness to escape arrest and was there taken care of by the Indians. He began the first Baptist congregation in 1639. More than a century and a half later, in 1791, we find another story of Baptist conscience. Robert Carter III, one of the richest and most powerful men in colonial America, owner of sixteen plantations and some five hundred slaves, issued an unprecedented proclamation of manumission. "On July 28, 1991, in a twilight ceremony on a torch-lit clover field near the site of Nomini Hall, the people of Westmoreland County [Virginia], black and white, gathered to commemorate the 200th anniversary of Carter's momentous but little-known act of conscience — the first such act of any scale in American history and almost certainly the largest private emancipation ever recorded" (Ringle, 1992:8). This ceremony was an attempt to unsilence a story hidden for generations, even from local residents.

How many episodes of European-American conscience, great or small, have been lost — conspirators in the underground railroad, or experimental utopian communitarians, or war resisters, or labor organizers? Such stories abound, if we have eyes to look for them; they may even be as recent as last week and as close as next door — yet dismembered just the same. Detroit resident Jeanie Wylie (1991), editor of the alternative Episcopalian journal *The Witness,* is someone who listened to, and through documentation helped unsilence, the heroic and tragic voices of a nearby blue-collar Polish American community in its struggle — heroic if finally unsuccessful — to resist relocation by the construction of a new General Motors plant in the early 1980s. We are just as profoundly impoverished — and disempowered — by the suppression of stories of white resistance and goodness and compassion. As Wylie puts it, "We were bought: the price was our heritage" (1992:5).

Indeed the dominant culture socializes us to be uninterested in "minority reports," however well documented. The dismembered truth may be as fundamental as the fact that Vikings were the first Europeans to sail to the Americas ("Vinland") — and probably before them, Africans. These facts do not matter, for they do not fit the narrative of Manifest Destiny (after all, these explorers came, looked around, traded perhaps, and left!). So when a replica ship arrived in Canada to commemorate a thousand years since Leif Ericsson's voyage, the story earned barely four column inches on page six of the August 3, 1991, *Los Angeles Times.* The dismemberment may lie at the heart of the dominant culture's history, such as the fact that crucial concepts used in drafting the U.S. Constitution were borrowed from the Iroquois Confederacy. No matter; credit still goes to the Magna Carta, Jefferson, and Franklin (Weatherford, 1988:133ff). Or it may be on the edges of the official narrative, such as the

Great Mahele, which robbed Hawaiians of their land while they were still a sovereign nation (M. Kelly, 1992). The result is the same; we shrug, presuming all that was somehow "resolved" when Hawai'i became a state (see Trask, in Martin, 1987:171ff; Otaguro, 1992). "Let sleeping dogs lie," we think.

What is the cost of this devised and dismembered legacy? My discussion of repressed trauma and the political unconscious in the last chapter wondered what the impact of so many lies and secrets in our "family history" might be on our political unconscious. Obviously we have had to sever ourselves from it, just as adults who experienced or witnessed abuse as children suppress the memory in order to survive the trauma. But this severance simply reproduced more dismemberment! Moreover, the repressed (and hence unresolved) traumas from our collective memory keep resurfacing violently in our body politic in ways that seem mysterious to us. What else can explain our need to *project* violence onto a demonized foreign enemy and the epidemic of *introjected* social violence in our families and neighborhoods? The cost of repression is not only psychological and social but concretely political. As Bruce Schulman recently pointed out, the degree to which we forget the past is the degree to which we allow those in power to reinvent it to suit their interests.

> David Duke transforms himself from klan wizard to racial moderate and champion of the dispossessed as easily as Arnold Schwarzenegger's evil "Terminator" metamorphoses into a noble android in "Terminator II." The silver-spoon Ivy Leaguer George Bush reinvents himself first as a down-home Texas "wildcat oil man" and then as a "pork-rind munching outsider assailing...snobby Harvard liberals." (1991:M1)

This is what King et al. call our susceptibility to "false villains and false victims" (1988:152). Only a repressed and amnesiac people could have so enthusiastically and credulously embraced a B movie character-actor as its president for two terms!

We European Americans see our faces mirrored in official history, and for most of us that is comforting, that is enough. But if we become suspicious of the orthodox story line and scratch the surface of the memory, we will slowly begin to encounter this suppression in all its forms. Nathaniel Hawthorne's story of Young Goodman Brown narrates his encounter with the devil, who takes him on a walk deep into the forest:

> "Too far! too far!" exclaimed the goodman, unconsciously resuming his walk. "My father never went into the woods on such an errand, nor his father before him. We have been a race of honest men and good Christians since the days of the martyrs; and shall I be the first of the name of Brown that ever took this path and kept" —
>
> "Such company, thou wouldst say," observed the elder person, interpreting his pause. "Well said, Goodman Brown! I have been as well acquainted with your family as with ever a one among the Puritans; and

that's no trifle to say. I helped your grandfather, the constable, when he
lashed the Quaker woman so smartly through the streets of Salem; and
it was I that brought your father a pitch-pine knot, kindled at my own
hearth, to set fire to an Indian village in King Philip's war. They were my
good friends, both...."

"If it be as thou sayest," replied Goodman Brown, **"I marvel they
never spoke of these matters...."** (Hawthorne, 1902:92)

Like Goodman Brown, when we encounter the unmystified past, and realize that
our ancestors consorted with the devil, we will feel disoriented, depressed, and
despairing.[9]

This is why the vision quest takes courage. To confront duplicity is the
most painful human task. No one likes to be confronted with past lies; how
much more difficult will this be collectively. And if and when we become
dis-illusioned, we confront a new dilemma: If the fabulated and manipulative
historical voices of presidents and generals and captains of industry no longer
speak for us, what and who and where is our real voice? We will feel culturally
alienated and historically orphaned. But we must persevere, for we cannot be
genuine collaborators in the struggle for justice if we have no liberating story
of our own.

D. "A NATION OF ESAUS?" REMEMBERING

*How might naming our complicity and listening to the voices of our own
family histories help us to reconnect to the past and recover from our
sense of alienation?*

We of the dominant culture cannot pretend that we have not benefited from
devised and dismembered history and the arrangements of privilege it masks.
After all, it is not *our* teeth that were set on edge by the sour grapes of our
parents (Jer 31:29f). That is why we must first learn to listen to the voices
that have been silenced. As people of entitlement, we must walk with the devil
and face the history of empire, because our structural advantages are predicated upon the suppressed traumas of the past. We must dredge up the ghosts
of Columbus and Cortés, Custer and Calley, not because we can change *their*
historical behavior but because otherwise we cannot change *our own.* If we do
not, we will keep reproducing the illusions and violence of that history through
repetition-compulsion.

But it is also the case — both psychology and politics teach us this — that
we will simply be unable to hear the pain of others, or to build new alliances of
solidarity with them, if we are not in touch with our own pain. The truth is, we
also are deformed by these lies, for in most cases the stories of our ancestors
have been erased too. Jeanie Wylie suggests that we are "a nation of Esaus":

How many white Americans know their ancestry? How many can sing a song, say a prayer, bake the bread of their country/countries of origin? As important, how many know the positions their foreparents took in the struggles of their native land? Did they fight for or against the monarchy? Did they support or reject ecclesial authority? ... There is power in knowing these things. They offer a construct through which to consider the United States today. And most of us forfeited it. It was exchanged for employment at Ford Motor Company, or for admission to the elite schools of the nation, or for the appearance of upward mobility. Like Esau, we sold our inheritance for a mess of pottage. (1992:5)

Buried in our own legacies are both stories of collusion and collision with empire. But somewhere in there are stories of primal trauma. They are the most suppressed, but we know they are there because only they have the power to drive our unconscious historical repetition-compulsion.

Psychologist Chellis Glendinning calls this "Original Trauma" (1992:69). For a child it might be abuse or abandonment; for a culture, however, the causes are harder to trace, for they lie in the distant past. Donna Awatere (1984), in her devastating critique of the colonial legacy in Aotearoa (New Zealand), believes that for European immigrants, original trauma lay in the disconnection from their roots. Only a people severed from their own land and culture, she contends, could turn around and so systematically disinherit indigenous peoples from theirs. I think Awatere has given us a crucial clue. Are not dislocation and displacement universal in the historical experience of the dominant culture in the U.S. (see below, 11,A)? We must, in my opinion, inquire into these primal traumas and their relationship to the conquest of this continent if we want to break their power over us.

Countless victims of family violence and dysfunction have come to terms with the roots of their repetition-compulsion through three essential disciplines of recovery. First, that which has been repressed and denied must be recollected: The dismembered past must be *remembered.* Second, the devised meaning of this past must be critically *revised:* Literally, it must be "viewed again" with a new perspective that challenges the myths of "happy childhood" and the taboos of "good family." The last step is to make *reparation:* The recovering person must move from disconnection to responsibility and, if possible, reconciliation. Our vision quest must apply these same disciplines to our national experience and our place within it. Remembering for us means recovering stories of our own people that have been silenced as well as listening to the past and continuing pain of all who have suffered oppression and displacement (cf M. Taylor, 1990:17). We must then revise the meaning of this history, taking special care to demythologize our pretensions to innocence. Above all, we must embrace responsibility for past injustices that remain embedded in the institutions and entitlements of the present, since the trauma for the progeny of both victimizer and victim alike will continue until concrete reparation is made. As in the natural family, if we practice these disciplines, we will encounter fierce resistance from those who claim we are being disloyal to the national family. We must nevertheless insist, gently but firmly, that only the truth about ourselves can heal us as a nation. The next two sections will examine the disciplines of remembering and revising; the formidable task of reparation will be discussed at the conclusion of the next chapter (below, 6,E,2).

Oppressed people remember. At the recent centennial commemoration of the massacre at Wounded Knee hundreds of Lakota and other native people gathered in subzero December temperatures to honor the spirits of their ancestors. In interviews relatives of victims expressed the visceral pain they still feel concerning that event (Warrior, 1991). Every sermon I heard from black preachers during and after the Los Angeles uprising angrily mentioned the fact that African slaves were not included in the Declaration of Independence. Japanese Americans remember their World War II internment; Jewish Americans remember the Holocaust; Palestinian Americans remember their homelessness. Few European Americans, on the other hand, feel history so existentially (though some southerners still chafe at the mention of Sherman's march). The oppressed are dismembered; the oppressors are detached. But it is not up to minority people to teach us how to remember. To heal history, *we* must reconnect with it.

There are basically two practical ways to approach this task. The first is to do it through place. Take a locality — preferably one you are connected with — and trace its history. Will Campbell has demonstrated this in his brilliant new book *Providence* (1992). He recounts the story of a one-square-mile plot of land in Mississippi — history narrated from the point of view of the land — and ends up touching on virtually all the major forces of southern history. I reiterate: In every county in this country are dismembered stories, as well as evidence of the dominant narrative. These places all have local historians and archives; we would do well to learn the stories, the pain, and the promise of the place we live in (below, 11,E).

The other approach is to remember history through people, and this is best approached through family history work, which has close parallels with the "archaeology of the political unconscious" discussed earlier (above, 4,E,1). Here, however, the genogram exercise concentrates explicitly on plotting sociohistorical data; our "life-texts" are expanded into "family-line texts." This will seem awkward at first — precisely because we are so remote from our own ancestors. But this approach has the advantage of intimately engaging us as historical subjects. We simply cannot meaningfully deal with something as huge as genocide in the Americas; no matter how much data we know about this grand narrative, we will remain safely distanced from it. Ideologized or rhetorical renarration of it does little to heal the body politic. "Reading" history through family-line experiences, however, lets us discover how "we" ("I" being now understood as a historical product) have been complicit in dislocation and how we have been victimized by it, how we have been shaped by both the dominant and the minority narratives. This is the only way we will discover the original traumas that are embedded in our unconscious.

I have experimented with a relatively simple group process that invites European Americans into reconnection with history. I ask them to try to trace their genealogy, if possible, as far back as the immigrant generation(s) — a formidable but revealing task. In the framework of this basic family map, we begin looking for indications of socio-historical trauma, particularly dislocation, cultural erasure, and social mobility resulting from assimilation. To do this we explore the following kinds of questions: Under what circumstances did the European immigrant leave, and how voluntary was it? Whether in terms of land or work, who did they displace upon arrival? What discrimination was experienced, and what strategies of accommodation resulted? When and how was the native language or dialect suppressed? How did traditional family patterns erode and distinctive cultural practices atrophy? How many times did the direct family line move states or regions? What kind of ethnic mixing was there, and why or why not? How was land procured and wealth obtained and consolidated from generation to generation? What entitlements were passed on, and what rivalries resulted? How was the family fractured along class or race lines? In what ways did upward (or downward) social mobility occur, and how was status expressed? What kinds of opportunities were there for women? What wars affected your ancestors? What relationship was there to the institutions of slavery? Do you know the indigenous people who resided or still reside in the place you live now? What are the prominent family legends?

Participants are surprised at how this exercise provokes deep feelings of anxiety, confusion, or sadness — not only about what is known but also about what is not known. A woman from New Orleans began to weep as she remembered her Cajun grandfather reading to her from the prayer book in French. A priest grimaced as he told of the civil struggle in Ireland during the 1920s that resulted in his family's migration, and of the anti-Irish sentiment they encountered here. A friend from Nebraska was deeply troubled when, at his family centennial, he discovered that his great-great-grandfather had been given squatters rights on Indian land through the Homestead Act of 1862. A Canadian school teacher told about how his nineteenth-century Scottish ancestors were given cheap one-way tickets to the end of the train line in western Canada and seemed to understand that they were being used as a buffer class between the wilderness and the settled cities. In her own work on her heritage, Wylie has come to realize that southwestern Pennsylvania holds the bones of both the Lenape Indians and her immigrant Scottish Presbyterian ancestors, who in some cases stalked them and took their land: "There is blood, enmity and a common desire for life buried in that earth. It gave me life. I need to atone for some specific things.... While I learn things I do not like, I also come to respect the immigrant coal miners, farmers and school teachers who are my people.... [This] can help restore my birthright" (1992:5). Indeed it can, as another Pennsylvania story suggests. Robbie Diaz Brinton, an accomplished neuroscientist from a working-class background, for years sadly described herself as "a real American, from everywhere and nowhere." She knew dislocation: Her family had moved around constantly as her father could find work. Then she discovered that the first Brintons were English Quakers who had come to Penn's colony in the late seventeenth century to escape persecution, that the Lenape people had sheltered and fed them for the first year, and that these Quakers and Indians had then lived in peace for several generations (below, 8,D). The healing that came from discovering her roots was extraordinary, and she has since delved into the legacies of the Brintons *and* the Lenape.[10]

A small group I worked with in New Mexico provided interesting fragments that suggest repressed material. As they shared what they knew of their family histories, each person quite independently shared a "family joke" that alluded to "shady" circumstances in the immigrant generation. One woman spoke about her grandparents coming from France to Louisiana "on the lam"; another about her Italian grandfather's "Mafia" connections; a third referred to her ancestors as "Irish rogues"; and a fourth shared that his Swiss immigrant generation was laughingly called "cow thieves." As I listened I recalled how my father used to joke that his Mexican ancestors "should have stolen land instead of horses." These were all related as whimsical family lore, preserved in a humorous manner; yet the pattern is worth reflecting upon. Regardless of their truth, do they articulate an unconscious derogation of one's own immigrant roots? Might this subtle form of self-contempt be a way of distancing oneself from embarrassing class origins, or of coping with the pain of severance, or both? This may seem farfetched. Yet shortly after that gathering I had a strange emotional experience while attending a Quincentenary play produced locally by a multicultural alternative theater group. An Indian, a Chicana, and an Anglo actor were narrating the story of California through a series of vignettes. One scene portrayed a land court from the 1850s in which the Mexican *Californio* was told by the American judge that his land title would not be recognized and that he and the Indian "squatters" who lived on his land would be evicted. The defendant — speaking in broken English and completely frustrated that none of the conventions of measurement and title he knew and understood were accepted in this new Yankee real estate culture — finally in despair began cursing in Spanish at the judge and was dragged away. At that moment I found myself in tears coming from some unknown deep place within me — perhaps a reconnection with a family story long lost and empirically unrecoverable (on the history behind this see W. W. Robinson, 1948).

Excavating family texts helps unmask myth and reality in the "melting pot" experience, particularly concerning the ideology and practice of social mobility and displacement, and it reveals new information about the socio-historical matrix of inherited family patterns. These can be as shadowy as secrets concerning real or imagined miscegenation, as simple as why certain foods are enjoyed, or as fundamental as the tendency for one parent's cultural or class heritage to receive more emphasis than the other's. But I believe that beneath it all, for many of us, is the original trauma of displacement. Recently therapists working with minority peoples have begun to recognize and treat these traumas (Ho, 1987), showing that immigrant families as a rule trade their mental health (as embedded in cultural identity) for conformity in order to survive both racism and economic marginalization in the strange and new land. An indication of how detached dominant culture people feel from this trauma is the fact that we do not think of ourselves as immigrant people at all. But the persistent episodes of anti-immigrant sentiment and violence in the history of a nation of immigrants suggests there is something unresolved in our political unconscious (below, 10,B).

Again let me briefly illustrate this by summarizing my own family-line text. *Paternal grandmother's line:* Francisco Mendosa came from the Azores to California in 1848 via Veracruz, Mexico; he married a *Californiana* and (after going bust in the goldfields?) ended up a day laborer in the Sierra foothills. *Paternal grandfather's line:* All that is known is that Myers (English? German?) came west working for the railroads. *Maternal grandmother's line:* Jacobs — probably Jewish — emigrated from Bavaria to Louisiana to escape the emerging German empire and the Franco-German War in 1870. *Maternal grandfather's line:* King left the rural west country of England in the 1830s because of deteriorating economic conditions probably related to the early industrial revolution. My eldest brother, a historian, has analyzed some fascinating correspondence from these immigrant Kings that reveals that they almost immediately managed to homestead land in Wisconsin. This basic matrix is fairly typical. For example, it reflects two of the most common factors in European immigration: economic hardship and political pressures. The Hispanic who chased the dream of instant riches didn't "make it" (Mendosa); the Englishman who followed the dream of land did (King). It has been difficult to identify the primal traumas (or triumphs) represented in these four immigrant stories; as in most cases, the evidence is indirect in my family's heritage. The European cultures of origin were either soon lost to assimilation (cultural erasure) or unknown (historical erasure). One minority narrative survives, but ambiguously. Though I find it lamentable, I am able to understand in retrospect why my paternal grandmother, Ynez Guerena, a small-town, devoutly Catholic Latina, was marginalized in our family. As a dependent widow, she was an embarrassment both to my upwardly mobile father (who wanted nothing to do with the Roman church) and my Anglo, nominally Protestant mother. Little of my grandmother's *Californio* heritage was passed on to us — or any other cultural tradition, for that matter. Ours were the assimilated values of an urban middle-class family. Perhaps my grandfather Myers's legacy survives in my brother's passion for trains; but virtually no ethnically specific symbolic traditions did.

We are who we were, but most dominant culture Americans have no idea who their people were. It can be liberating, of course, to leave the past and the strictures of tradition behind. Schulman points out that we have lauded the immigrant habit of "altering their names, their stations and their destinies, inspiring in us tremendous faith in people's capacity to remake themselves" (1991:M1). Probably the emphasis on self-discovery in my family was a positive result of this "freedom." But Wallace Stegner (1992) reminds us that "the rootlessness that expresses energy and a thirst for the new and an aspiration toward freedom and personal fulfillment has just as often been a curse . . . our migratoriness has hindered us from becoming a people of communities and traditions." The steady atrophy of ethnic identity drives us to surrogates and pseudo-solidarity: our felt allegiances are to social clubs or football teams or pop stars or hobbies. But these innocuous loyalties in capitalist culture are easily manipulable and can be reproduced in order to invoke political allegiances. The media discourse during Desert Storm, for example, presented the war as if it were the Super Bowl (military charts looked like box scores); indeed, halftime at the Super Bowl was a pro-war extravaganza. The politico-military architects of the war were put forward as "genuine American heros" and received all the exposure warranted by the "star" system: interviews, book contracts, business and political opportunities. As Silko's elder warned, when our stories as a people are forgotten, we become defenseless against the devised, dismembered, and ultimately deadly narratives of the *locus imperii*.

Conversely, to remember — particularly when that process reconnects our own family texts with a historical context — is to rebuild those defenses by giving us an understanding of who we truly are. Remembered history is not a narrative by and about the elite but is from the perspective of regular folk — *like us*. We will assuredly get to know the main plot lines of the dominant history — in my case, a major European war and the California gold rush, the effects of the English industrial revolution, and the saga of the transcontinental railroad. But we also encounter the rich ethnic variations, hidden stories, and regional subplots: Wisconsin farmers, Bavarians in New Orleans, railroad towns in remote western Nevada, and "Greasers in the Diggings" (Pitt, 1966:48ff). As an antiwar activist I am suddenly interested in the Franco-Prussian War, because it made my ancestors either refugees or resisters or both. I am interested in the social history of early nineteenth-century England, because it pushed my ancestors out. And I yearn to know why a poor man would leave the Azores for the visionary gold of California (below, 11,E,1).

How different the teaching and learning of history in school would be if it proceeded on inductive lines, beginning with the reconstructed texts of each student's family story and allowing a portrait of bigger historical events and forces to emerge. Rather than committing disembodied dates and names to short-term memory, students would, I suspect, become interested in historical data that is linked to their families. Students of color might not feel quite so alienated, for they would have equal place to tell their stories and vent their feelings. Dominant culture students would learn that history is about open wounds, not a closed and irrelevant past. And everyone would find things to feel proud about as well as to mourn. For our history *also* includes settlers who lived at peace with the indigenous people, farmers who loved the land, communities that embodied values of solidarity, common folk who struggled for social justice. In short, such students would get to know the real America — one they would *want* to remember. As Christopher Vecsey, a professor of Native American studies at Colgate University, puts it, "In this way history can serve as cultural therapy, releasing for us and our students the repressed images of our full humanity" (1987:126f). By reconnecting with history and facing original traumas we engage in the practice of, as Vecsey puts it, "envisioning ourselves darkly," so that we can in turn "imagine ourselves richly."

E. "THAT THESE SEEDS MAY NOT RIPEN
TO THE RUIN OF OUR POSTERITY": REVISING

Can taking another look at our story help us forge an alternative narrative of the past, and from it a new vision for the future?

Not only is our task to remember the history that has been hidden or silenced; it is also to take a fresh look at the history we "know." David Kennedy defines revisionism thus: "A familiar event or person is cast in a new light, occasionally by adducing new evidence, but most often by adopting a new perspective or putting things in a new context — by looking at the Industrial Revolution from the point of view of women, for example, or rethinking the Civil War and Reconstruction in the moral climate of the post-civil-rights era" (1991:M1). Revisionism of course has long been a dirty word to the cultural Right, stewards of the Official Story. But Vine Deloria has cautioned that much of the allegedly revisionist history of white-Indian relations written by liberal European Americans is in fact "reversionist" (1987:84ff). Here I am simply suggesting we practice revisionism literally: "looking again" at the old story with new eyes. I am not talking about the moral outrage of hindsight. "History," Kirkpatrick Sale reminds us, "is what did happen, not what should have happened." Rather I am talking about reinterpreting history from the perspective of the liberation Story and of the poor. To break the power of devised narratives, we need an alternative narrative of both the past and the future. The task of revision is to give us a new vision of historical possibility; that is why it is a vision quest.

1. The Wilderness Temptations: "Empire as a Way of Life"?

Revisionist historians such as Howard Zinn and Eric Wolf have made monumental contributions to the task of rereading the past. But in my opinion it is William Appleman Williams who has provided the most liberating alternative narrative for our national story (Copelman and Smith, 1991). Williams argued that our entire historical project has been defined (and fatally contaminated) by the imperial urge, and he reexamined U.S. history to identify the crucial points at which we turned away from democracy and pluralism toward oligarchy and empire. He knew that only by understanding these past crossroads as *choices* — not as inevitabilities or accidents or divine plans — would we as a people be able to "say no to empire," now and in the future, and to reconstruct an alternative vision of community (1980:213). I often encourage groups to undertake a study of Williams's concise and highly readable *Empire as a Way of Life* in concert with political Bible study. They find this synoptic reading of Story/story to be extraordinarily powerful and transforming. Doing this myself I have discovered a nice correlation between Jesus' vision quest in the wilderness and Williams's revision of U.S. history.

As I have articulated elsewhere, the longer form of Jesus' temptation narrative (Q tradition, Lk 4:1–13 = Mt 4:1–11) identifies three archetypal crossroads faced by Israel and faced again by Jesus (Myers, 1993). They are

(1) *the temptation to economism* by "turning stones into bread," which in the history of Israel I take to be the archetypal seduction away from a political economy based on subsistence and distribution (Exodus 16) into one based on surplus extraction, accumulation, and control (roundly criticized by the prophets, Am 8:5f; Hos 2:5);

(2) *the temptation to political power* by "showing homage to the Prince of the World," which in the history of Israel I take to be the archetypal seduction away from decentralized "republican federalism" into centralized monarchy (1 Sam 8; below, 11,C,1);

(3) *the temptation to idolatry* symbolized by the devil's citation of Psalm 91, which in the history of Israel I take to be the archetypal seduction away from Yahweh's radical nonidentity (Exodus 3) into imperial theology symbolized by the Temple State (Jeremiah 7).

I believe these same archetypal crossroads have also haunted the story of the Europeans' America. I offer, then, a brief re-reading of the three temptations in the American wilderness.

The settled subsistence/pastoral nomadic peoples that the Europeans encountered in North America knew little of economic exploitation, political centralization, or empire. One need not romanticize the First Nations to acknowledge that with few exceptions their economies operated within the limits of the land's hospitality, their politics remained local, and their alliances limited in power. Kirkpatrick Sale (1990) rightly contends these were essentially bioregional cultures. The European exodus had a different agenda, however; it was about not subsistence but prosperity. The New World indeed represented new beginnings for those fleeing the contradictions of the overcrowded, impoverished, and oppressively oligarchic kingdoms of Europe. Yet the colonists understood those contradictions to represent not failed social, economic, and political practices, merely flawed ones. It did not occur to them to dialogue with the native peoples they encountered or to learn from their quite different social practices. Instead they drove indigenous communities off their lands and destroyed or expropriated the natural resources on which these cultures depended. Then our ancestors set about reproducing and re-creating the Old World in the New, a context which, their elite quickly perceived, offered fewer economic limitations and political constraints to their aspirations. They even re-created the old class system:

For the Puritan leader John Winthrop the "errand" was committed [to] the thesis that God had disposed mankind in a hierarchy of social classes, so that "in all times some must be rich, some poor, some highe and eminent in power and dignitie; others mean and in subjeccion." It is as though, preter-naturally sensing what the promise of America might come to signify for the rank and file, Winthrop took the precaution to drive out of their heads any notion that in the wilderness the poor and the mean were ever so to improve themselves as to mount above the rich. (P. Miller, 1964:5)

It was not long before the inherited (inherent?) contradictions of the European way began showing up. Howard Zinn describes at some length how economic stratification was built into the English colonial experiment from the beginning (1980:39ff). In 1770 the top 1 percent of Boston's property-owning taxpayers already controlled 44 percent of its wealth. By the time of the American revolution there had already been eighteen attempts to overturn colonial governments, six slave rebellions, and forty-odd riots, not to mention increasing numbers of Indian wars. Lamented William Berkeley, governor of Virginia at the time of Nathaniel Bacon's 1676 rebellion, "How miserable is the man that governs a people where six out of seven at least are poor, endebted, discontented, and armed" (ibid:40). William Penn, one of the gentry himself though a conscientious Quaker, had to admit in 1683 that "the low dispensation of the poor Indian out shines the lives of those Christians, that pretend an higher" (1970:45).

European economic and political prosperity in the "land of freedom and opportunity" was constructed upon twin pillars of stolen land and slave labor. From the colonial silver mines of Potosí and the fur trade of the old Northwest to the modern clear-cut logging of the Pacific Northwest and strip mining in the Southwest, freedom for the European American has been fundamentally associated with the right to exploit the land for profit. Our people have indeed turned wilderness stones into bread — and mountains into coal pits, forests into board-feet, rivers into interstate power grids, deserts into weapons test sites, and, ultimately, human life into just another commodity. "The love of possession is a disease with them," said Sitting Bull more than a century ago of the European pathology (Black Elk, 1982:144). Economic exploitation became economic domination became economic determinism, reaching now to every corner of the globe. This has been the story of "Progress" — *the first temptation* (below, 12,A).

Williams points out that there was a real debate among eighteenth-century colonial revolutionaries about the political destiny of the new nation. Virginian John Taylor, for example, envisioned a loose federation of republics and criticized centralized Federalism: "The executive power of the United States is infected...with a degree of accumulation and permanence of power, sufficient to excite evil moral qualities" (1980:49). It was the expansionist designs of Jefferson and Madison that prevailed, however, a spirit reflected in verse penned by friends of the latter:

> Shall we ask what empires yet must arise...
> when British sons shall spread
> Dominion to the north and south and west
> From th' Atlantic thru Pacific shores. (ibid:44)

European-American societies were adopting the imperial aspirations of the monarchies they had supposedly left behind. The nineteenth century saw the completion of the project of domesticating the entire continent and its native peoples, from the Louisiana Purchase to the war with Mexico to the closing of the frontiers. This spawned a new project: the consolidation and concentration of U.S. wealth and power. After the Civil War there was increasing urbanization and industrialization, the rise of robber barons and corporate capitalism. This was the era of Manifest Destiny — *the second temptation.*

But it was at the turn of this century, with the annexation of Hawai'i, Puerto Rico, and the Philippines, that the U.S. made its most decisive and fateful choices to become an imperial people. And with this came acquiescence to *the third temptation:* placing God at the service of our national designs. The spirit of imperial piety is perhaps best exemplified in President McKinley's comments to a Methodist church delegation in 1899 justifying U.S. colonization of the Philippines:

> I went down on my knees and prayed to Almighty God for light and guidance.... And one night it came to me this way: ... that we could not give [the Philippines] back to Spain, for that would be cowardly and dishonorable; that we could not turn them over to France and Germany, our commercial rivals in the Orient, for that would be bad business and discreditable; that we could not leave them to themselves, for they were unfit for self government.... There was nothing left for us to do but take them all and to educate the Filipinos and uplift and civilize and Christianize them.... Then I went to bed and slept soundly and the next morning sent for the chief engineers of the War Department. (In Gerlock, 1991:1)

The Philippines were duly taken in what was, according to historian Ralph Graves, a "much quicker, cheaper and more resounding battle" even than the recent Gulf War (1992:88). Such idolatrous piety has characterized the public face of U.S. foreign policy ever since.

How different is the historical voice — also invoking God and conscience! — of Hawaiian Queen Liliuokalani one year earlier:

> Oh, honest Americans, as Christians hear me for my down-trodden people! Their form of government is as dear to them as yours is precious to you. Quite as warmly as you love your country, so they love theirs. With all your goodly possessions, covering a territory so immense that there yet remain part unexplored ... do not covet the little vineyard of Naboth's so far from your shores, lest the punishment of Ahab fall upon you, if not in your day, then in that of your children; for "be not deceived, God is not mocked." The people to whom your fathers told of the living God ... and whom the sons now seek to despoil and destroy, are crying aloud to Him in their time of trouble; and He will keep His promise,

and will listen to the voices of His Hawaiian children lamenting for their homes. (1964:373f)

Liliuokalani made this appeal in the closing lines of her book *Hawaii's Story,* published in 1898 in protest of the U.S. annexation of her island nation five years earlier. Her testimony was not unrelated to McKinley's — Hawai'i was crucial to the projection of U.S. naval power in the Philippines. But his voice prevailed, hers was lost. Like that of chiefs Red Jacket of the Seneca, Joseph of the Nez Perce, and other "vanquished" indigenous leaders, it is part of our dismembered history.

Jesus' wilderness journey to the place of origins led him to place again the fundamental Deuteronomic choice before the leaders of his own day: "Do a Sabbath people," he queried them at a Galilean synagogue, "practice good or evil, save life or destroy it?" (Mk 3:4; see below, Chapter Nine). When they responded in stony silence, Jesus immediately diagnosed them with Pharaoh's disease (3:5). Unable to remember, they were unable to choose. Williams, in the closing query to *Empire as a Way of Life,* places the same choice before *us:* "What happens if we simply say 'no' to empire? Or do we have either the imagination or the courage to say 'no' to empire? It is now *our* responsibility. It has to do with how we live and how we die. We as a culture have run out of imperial games to play" (1980:213). Our choice is between the voices of McKinley and Liliuokalani, between the voices of George Bush and Rodney King (above, Chapter One), between *conquest* and *conscience.* We know where McKinley's voice leads us. It is time to listen to Liliuokalani, to remember Hawai'i's story and all the stories like it. What is devised can be overcome only through revision. The devil tempted our ancestors in the wilderness, and they followed him. We have become economically and politically dominated and dominating, truly the children of empire. We must journey back to the places of original trauma, we must face the devil again, and this time resist him, just as Jesus did. We owe this to the victims past and present and to the inheritors of the future, to this magnificent land and to our own weary souls.

2. Coronado and Woolman:
American Journeys of Conquest and Conscience

Exodus Israel encountered its vocation in the wilderness. Jesus renewed that vocation by undertaking a *revision* quest. The apostle Paul seems to have made a similar desert sojourn after his dramatic conversion (Gal 1:15–17), and so have desert monks and countless Christian radicals since. The following accounts of two European journeys in the American wilderness represent the two archetypal narrative traditions of *conquest* and *conscience,* or as Gutiérrez (1993) put it in his study of Las Casas, *Dios o el oro* ("God or gold"). These radically divergent vision quests in the past present us with choices that continue to shape the narrative of our future.

We first consider the quest after the mythical Seven Cities of Cíbola that took the sixteenth-century Spanish conquistador Francisco Vásquez de Coronado deep into the heart of the North American wilderness — the first of the *entradas,* beginning the Europeans' long history of exploitation and violence north of the Rio Grande. The story begins deep in the political unconscious of Catholic Iberia, in a medieval legend that told of seven Portuguese bishops who, fleeing the Moorish advance, had founded seven cities (islands?) of silver across the Atlantic. The Spanish brought the legend to the New World, and after the conquest of Tenochtitlán (Mexico City), imagined that the Seven Cities lay somewhere to the north and west. There were many violent forces pushing the Spanish exploration of the Americas.[11] Pulling the conquistadors, however, were dreams of gold, silver, and other riches, and myths of lost cities and fantasies of other Tenochtitláns. After Ponce de León failed to find the fountain of youth in Florida, another expedition set out seeking these "visions" under Pánfilo de Narváez in 1528: "Landing in Tampa Bay with a band of some four hundred men, including cavalry, he marched northward in pursuit of a fabulous realm of gold called *Cale* by the Indians. (Historians have often noted the understandable readiness of Indians in those days to locate the most delicious objects of the white man's desires over the most distant possible horizons)... In the long run, only four men survived to tell the tale" (Sanders, 1992:168). Of these four, two were notable: Alvar Núñez Cabeza de Vaca, descendant of both early conquistadors and heros of the *reconquista;* and Estévanico, a black North African slave. These survivors endured eight years in the wilderness, including extended captivity among various Indian tribes, before finally finding their way to Spanish settlements in frontier Mexico. Cabeza de Vaca's reports refueled visions of the Seven Cities of Cíbola, and two major expeditions were launched in 1539. Hernando de Soto followed Narváez's route from Cuba and went as far west as Oklahoma but saw no golden cities; he died at the Mississippi in 1542, with only half his party surviving the return. The more consequential journey was Coronado's — with none other than Estévanico employed as an advance guide (ibid:172ff).

Estévanico went ahead of the main scouting expedition, led by Fray Marcos de Niza, into New Mexico and sent back a glowing report that he had found the first of the Cíbolas, describing a multiple-storied city of stone and mortar that accurately described Pueblo settlements. The African — the first non-Indian in the Southwest — seems to have met his end (or disappeared?) at Zuni; the friar returned to Coronado with the report, not having seen the pueblos himself (Chávez, 1984:15f). Then came Coronado, changing the world of the Pueblo people forever:

> The expedition was a spectacular one consisting of several hundred mailed and armed horsemen accompanied by Mexican Indian servants. Coronado and his men established headquarters in the pueblo of Tiguex, near the present site of Bernalillo, New Mexico. For two years the expedition was supported by provisions supplied by Tiguex and neighboring pueblos.

From his central headquarters Coronado sent expeditions to nearby pueblos as well as to the western pueblos of Acoma, Zuni and Hopi. Initially, the relations between the Indians and Coronado's party were friendly, but as demands for provisions became more demanding the Indians staged a minor rebellion to force the Spaniards out of Tiguex. Coronado immediately put down the revolt and then "punished" the pueblos by executing several hundred of its inhabitants. This news spread rapidly throughout the Pueblo country and laid the foundations for the mistrust and antagonisms that thereafter characterized relations between the Pueblos and Spaniards. (Dozier, 1970:43f)

Disappointed by the Pueblo "Cíbolas," Coronado was persuaded by the Indians that rich kingdoms called *Quivira* lay in the plains to the north, and he set off.

Here again we see the emerging native strategy of resistance, indicating how quickly they came to understand the true values of the European: appeal to their avaricious visions in order to get them to move on.

Led on another futile search, Coronado trekked through vast sections of what we now know as Texas, Oklahoma, and Kansas, only to realize the Pueblo Indians had lied to him. A fabulously rich Quivira had probably never been part of the local Indians' conception of the plains area, but had been invented purely for the imaginations of the Spaniards. Since the Spanish had conquered and brutally occupied the Pueblo villages, the Indians most likely fabricated the urban wealth of Quivira in order to lure Coronado into a wilderness from which they hoped he would never return. They must have realized he would believe the tale because they doubtless understood only too well that the Spanish image of the region was of a land of great cities and valuable metals, a land the Spaniards expected to conquer and exploit. (Chávez, 1984:16)

The strategy worked, for a while. Coronado returned to Mexico bitterly disenchanted, and the Spanish did not return to the area for another fifty years (see Spicer, 1962:187ff). But it only postponed the inevitable, for the Spanish chased down their dreams. "Cíbola" did not pan out, but Potosí and Taxco and Durango did; billions of dollars in silver and gold were drained from Latin America to pay the debts of feudal Spain, and countless Indians perished in the mines (see Weatherford, 1988:1ff; Wolf, 1982:135ff).

In 1991, while doing a Quincentenary workshop with the Center for Action and Contemplation in Albuquerque, our group visited the site of Tiguex. Walking through the low adobe ruins, under the vast Southwest sky, as Sandia mountain began to glow in the late afternoon sun, I felt the burden of Coronado's *entrada*. In 1552 Las Casas had lamented, "As soon as they made the Indians' acquaintance the Spanish hurled themselves upon them like the most cruel wolves, tigers and lions, which had not eaten for many days. And for forty years from then until now they have done nothing but tear them to pieces, kill them, distress, afflict, torment and destroy them.... A hundred thousand victims died and disappeared because of the labours which they out of their lust for gold imposed upon them" (Dussel, 1979:55). It was this archetypal "vision quest" after gold, and the exploitation of land and people that necessarily resulted, that undeniably characterized the spirit of conquest, not only of the Spanish but every subsequent European "settlement" in the New World. That this was done in the name of Christianity is the central, blasphemous truth the church must face today in our quest to revision.

But the history of the Europeans in the Americas is not a seamless garment of genocide. Consider, in contrast, a very different journey that took the eighteenth-century Quaker John Woolman deep into the Pennsylvania wilderness to a painful encounter with the sin of Coronado's legacy (Whitney, 1943). Little known outside of Friends' circles, Woolman was an itinerant preacher who led the renewal of the peace testimony among colonial English Friends. At the onset of the French-Indian War in 1756, for example, he persuaded some Friends to refuse to pay the "defense" taxes imposed by the Pennsylvania Assembly (the first example of organized tax resistance in the New World). He also helped organize the "Friendly Association for Gaining and Preserving Peace with the Indians by Pacific Measures," which negotiated treaties and offered relief to native peoples ravaged by the war. In 1758 Woolman was instrumental in Philadelphia Yearly Meeting's decision to censure Friends who purchased slaves (Brock, 1968:115ff).

Our story begins in 1761, when Woolman met some Delaware Indians who were visiting in Philadelphia. As he tells it in his *Journal,* he was moved by compassion for the "natives of this land who dwell far back in the wilderness, whose ancestors were the owners and possessors of the land where we now dwell, and who, for a very small consideration assigned their inheritance to us" (1989:122). In 1763 Woolman undertook to try to visit this tribe at their village, called Wehaloosing in the upper Susquehanna, some two hundred miles from Philadelphia. His motivations were remarkable for a European of that or any other period: "Love was the first impulse, from which arose a concern to spend some time with the Indians, that I might feel and understand their life, and the spirit they live in. Indeed I might receive some instruction from them, or in turn they be to any degree helped forward by my following the leadings of truth among them. So it pleased the Lord to make a way for my journey at a time when the troubles of war were increasing" (ibid:127). After discernment with his Meeting, Woolman determined to make the dangerous trip, even after being warned, on the eve of his departure, that in a recent skirmish Indians "had taken a Fort from the English in the west, and had slain and scalped English persons in various places" (ibid:124).

Battling his own fears, Woolman set off; his journal reflections, penned during this difficult and physically arduous journey through the forested mountains, demonstrate his keen insight into the roots of the European-Indian conflict. For example, after meeting an Indian trader he wrote:

I perceived that many white people often sell rum to the Indians, which I believe is a great evil. . . . Their skins and furs, which they obtained through much hard work and travel in hunting in order to buy clothing, they often end up selling at a low rate for rum when they are intoxicated. Afterward, when they suffer for want of the necessities of life, they are angry with those who, for the sake of profit, took advantage of their weakness. Of this their Chiefs have often complained at their treaties with the English. . . . To sell to people that which we know does them harm and which often works for their ruin for the sake of profit demonstrates a hardened and corrupt heart, and is an evil, which demands the attention of all true lovers of virtue to suppress. (ibid:125)

Woolman was realizing the hard-heartedness of his own people; his conscience was encountering the narrative of conquest. Yet attentive to the deeper, structural roots of injustice, Woolman reminded himself that the perpetrators were often also themselves victims of oppression:

I also remembered that the people on the frontiers, among whom this evil is too common, are often poor; they venture to the margins of a colony in order that they may live more independently from the wealthy, who often set high rents on their land. I was thus in a new way confirmed in this belief: if all our inhabitants lived according to sound wisdom, working to promote universal love and justice, and if they ceased from the inordinate desire after wealth, and from all customs associated with greed, it would be easy for our inhabitants, even though much more numerous, to live comfortably on honest employment. They would not succumb to the temptation to be drawn into schemes to settle on lands which have not been purchased from the Indians. (ibid)

Woolman demonstrates an extraordinary grasp of the cycle of oppression that led to the expropriation of Indian lands: The frontier poor were exploited by the landed colonial gentry, who were in turn exploited by the distant Crown.

The farther he traveled on this journey, the clearer he became about the fundamental contradictions embedded in the European project. The following passage on "the alterations in the circumstances of the native people of the land since the arrival of the English" was perhaps inspired by the difficult terrain he had to traverse en route to Wehaloosing:

The lands near the sea are conveniently situated for fishing; the lands near the rivers, where the tides flow, and some above, are in many places fertile, and not mountainous; while the running of the tides makes passing up and down easy with any kind of traffic. Yet the native peoples have, in some places for trifling considerations sold their inheritance so favorably situated, while in other places have been driven back by superior force. Just as their way of clothing themselves is now altered from what it was, the Indians, being remote from us, now have to pass over mountains, swamps, and barren deserts, travelling being very difficult, just to bring their skins and furs to trade with us. Moreover, because of the extension of English settlements, and partly because of English hunters, the wild animals they chiefly depend upon for subsistence are not as plentiful as they were. (ibid:128)

Woolman had identified the most basic mechanism of Indian marginalization: colonists seized the best lands and relentlessly drove the Indians into the wilderness. So it was to the wilderness Woolman (in the spirit of Mark's gospel) had to return in order to rediscover the Way.

The vision quest truly revealed to him the extent of the oppression; in "nine hundred miles of English settlements along the coast... the favorable situation of the English and the difficulties attending the natives in many places, and the Negroes, were open before me." It was the integrity of the gospel that convinced him he must "attend to universal justice, as to give no cause of offence to the Gentiles, who do not profess Christianity, whether the Blacks from Africa, or the native inhabitants of this continent" (ibid:128f). Woolman's conclusion is poignant:

> And in this lonely journey... the affluence and greed, and the resulting oppression and other evils, greatly afflicted me, and I felt in that which is immutable that the seeds of great calamity and desolation are sown and growing fast on this continent. Nor do I have words sufficient to describe the longing I felt at that moment that we who are placed along these coasts and have tasted the love and goodness of God might arise in God's strength, and like faithful messengers work to check the growth of these seeds, **that they may not ripen to the ruin of our posterity.** (Ibid:129)

Ironically, when he finally arrived among the Delaware, Woolman's visit was apparently anticlimactic, causing him to question his efforts.[12] Clearly, however, this journey had laid bare the root causes of the moral crisis of his people, issues that few if any at the time saw. And it shows us that there is an alternative narrative in European-American history, one we can choose to carry on.

Five hundred years after Columbus, European churches ornately bedecked with American silver and gold still stand. My home, California — itself probably named after another Spanish mythic island of gold (below, 11,E,2) — is riddled with places bearing the memory of conquistadors: Balboa, Cabrillo, Cortés, Bodega y Cuadra, and, of course, Coronado (see Marinacci, 1980:28ff). Today the Delaware Indians are long gone from the Pennsylvania wilderness, having walked the Trail of Tears to Oklahoma with the Lenape, the Cherokee, the Shawnee, the Choctaw, the Seminole, and so many others. And sadly, John Woolman's vision of a community of faith that would "work to check the growth of these seeds" of destruction has all too rarely been realized, while the seeds have ripened "to the ruin of our posterity." But the choice between archetypal journeys still faces a church struggling to redeem its vocation in a revision quest. In the New World Order, will we choose the path of conscience or conquest?

F. DISCIPLINES OF THE HEART: LITURGY AND REVISION

How can ritualizing memory in liturgy empower us in the vocation of revisioning?

Israel's pastors and prophets understood how crucial memory was to the identity and character of the people (Dt 8:2). This is why Israelite liturgical and symbolic life centered around historical remembrance, preeminently represented by Passover. This remains true among Jews today and is the best explanation for their exemplary character as a people with a profound historical consciousness. At the heart of the earliest Jewish-Christian liturgy was a similar institutionalization of memory: the Lord's Supper. This ritual meal was revising the Passover tradition in terms of the messianic vision quest of Jesus (*BSM:*361f; on this see M. Barth, 1988:7ff). It ritualized the historical choices made by Jesus of Nazareth, preeminently the via crucis, placing them existentially before the community each time it gathered. When the early church diverged from Judaism, it lost many things, not least this notion of liturgy-as-memory. Christian worship, as it assimilated into the dominant culture of the Roman Empire, was increasingly influenced by the mystery cults and Platonic intellectualism, traditions that were more concerned with religious experience than with history. The ritual of Eucharist came to be understood more as a mystical experience of communion with the disembodied Christ and less as a communion with the history of liberation as embodied by Israel and Jesus. Today, as Markus Barth has shown, the Lord's Supper has become a sacramental cult that divides the church rather than a symbol of ethical practice that promotes solidarity with salvation history, with the Body of Christ and with the poor.

"Do this in remembrance [Gk *anamnēsis*] of me" — these were the words of "institution" (1 Cor 11:24f; Lk 22:19; see Jeremias, 1966). The noun could just as well be translated "a reminder" (as it is in Heb 10:3), with the verbal form suggesting "call to mind again" (cf *anamimnēskō* in Mk 11:21; 14:72). In terms of my discussion above, this is an invitation to reconnect with the history of Jesus. Interestingly, however, Mark does not use the words of institution in his account of the Last Supper, probably because he was concerned about reification in the tradition. Remarkably he has removed them to a different episode altogether: the woman who anoints Jesus "as for burial" (14:3ff; *BSM:*358f). Her ritual gesture — she alone in Mark affirms Jesus' practice of the via crucis — gets the commendation: "Wherever the gospel is proclaimed in the whole world what she has done will be told *in memory of her*" (14:9; Gk *eis mnēmosynon*)! Needless to say, the church has felt embarrassed, for reasons both political and patriarchal, of this revision of its own liturgy and so has utterly ignored Mark's instructions.

Evidently Mark wished not to memorialize Jesus but to remember discipleship practice.[13] This is also what is at issue in Jesus' complaint in the boat ("Do you not remember?" 8:18; Gk *mnēmoneuete*). What the disciples have "forgotten" is Jesus' practice, specifically his feeding of hungry people with bread in the wilderness, by which he reenacted the exodus manna tradition (6:34ff; 8:1ff; cf Exodus 16). Indeed the disciples first became infected with Pharaoh's disease when they were unable to comprehend this "mystery of the loaves" (6:51). Does this mean Mark's Lord's Supper is not a memorial meal then? No, the "memory" of Jesus' feedings of the masses and the "memory" of his anointing by the woman are both clearly connected to the meal. There, as he did among the wilderness poor (6:41), Jesus "blesses and breaks" the bread (14:22); but he identifies it as "my body," which the woman has already prepared to be the new symbolic center for the narrative (below, 8,E). The cup — "This is my blood of the covenant" (14:23f) — in the symbolic discourse of Mark invokes the past, present, and future of the narrative of biblical radicalism:

- *covenant* represents the past, the "agreement" between the exodus God and the exodus people (Exodus 24), which Jesus is here renewing;
- *my blood* represents the present, the via crucis Jesus is about to walk, thus renarrating the liberation story in his own flesh;
- *the cup* represents the future, for it alludes to Jesus' promise that disciples too will embrace the via crucis and keep the narrative going.

So Mark's eucharistic moment, even without the words of institution, is also about remembering and revisioning — not the mystical Christ but the practice of radical discipleship.

In other words, Christians do not have to go far to rediscover the vision quest. It is right at the heart of our liturgy, in both Word and Sacrament. We tell the story — "This is the gospel of the Lord" — and remember together Jesus' messianic practice. We break the bread — "This is the body of Christ" — and remember the via crucis. The point of the liturgy is not to memorialize but to reproduce the narrative of biblical radicalism in our own historical context. This is why Bill Kellermann and others have argued that where we locate liturgy becomes all important; we must take it into the public arena where we engage the *locus imperii* in the war of myths. I direct the reader to his excellent overview of experiments in liturgy as nonviolent direct action, which "comprise something of a liturgical renewal movement that has flourished at the margins of the church" (1991:103; below, 8,E).

I would like to close this chapter by relating an experience of liturgical vision quest in the desert. In the high church, the traditions of Lent have most closely approximated liturgy-as-memory. Beginning the Lenten journey with a reading of the wilderness temptations, we commence our journey with Jesus through the forty days of prayer and fasting. Then we reenact his entrance into Jerusalem in Palm Sunday processions. And of course we walk with him the via crucis on Good Friday and keep vigil until we "see again" that Christ is risen on Easter morning. In places where ethnic culture is more intact, these liturgies become an occasion also to remember the people's struggles. In New Mexico, for example, the *santos* are processed, tying the great tradition of Hispanic Catholicism to the local traditions of each village and its *santero*. Among the Yaqui Indians, who remain poor and marginalized in southern Arizona and northern Mexico, the annual Lenten-Easter ceremony combines Catholic and indigenous liturgy to publicly narrate the history of Spanish colonization. This liturgical struggle between good (the *Pascolas, Matachinis,* and *Angelitos*) and evil (the *Chapayekas*) has taken the place of armed resistance, which characterized the Yaqui through the time of the Mexican Revolution. But it keeps alive the memory of conquest and the hope of liberation from white domination (Spicer, 1962:502ff).

Lenten traditions may be politically domesticated in our First World churches, but they remain a rich source of both symbolic action and subversive memory. With this in mind I went to Las Vegas in 1990 to help lead a Holy Week retreat for the Nevada Desert Experience (NDE). Since 1981 NDE has invited people of faith to come to the desert to pray, reflect, and resist U.S. nuclear weapons testing at the Department of Energy Test Site, an hour north of Las Vegas. The heart of the campaign is Lent, during which different church groups from across the denominational spectrum each take a weekend to bring their witness to the test site. In 1990 there was again a large gathering on Palm Sunday, but for the first time NDE decided to follow this with a Holy Week retreat. Our theme — "When the Stones Cry Out: Holy Week/Holy Walk/Holy Wake" — reflected our process. For five days a community of some fifty persons lived a rhythm of three disciplines: Bible study, "walkabout," and liturgy. In the mornings we reflected together on a political reading of Mark's Passion narrative. In the afternoons we went out to join the small part of the community that was walking from Las Vegas to the test site entrance. As we walked we sought to be mindful of the desert's fragile beauty underfoot, meditating and listening. At the beginning and end of each day we sang, danced, and prayed.

Walking from Las Vegas to the test site, carrying a large rough-hewn cross, we reflected on Thomas Merton's prophetic words, written thirty-five years earlier:

> Look at the deserts today. What are they? The birthplace of a new and terrible creation, the testing-ground of power by which man seeks to uncreate what God has blessed.... He can build there his fantastic, protected cities of withdrawal and experimentation and vice. The glittering towns that spring up overnight in the desert are no longer images of the City of God.... They are brilliant and sordid smiles of the devil upon the face of the wilderness, cities of secrecy where each man spies on his brother, cities through whose veins money runs like artificial blood, and from whose womb will come the last and greatest instrument of destruction. (1956:19f)

For the first time I had an inkling of the power of a wilderness vision quest. Somehow this ritual journey to the test site was retracing the footsteps of my people, a nation seduced by the primal temptation to power.

At one point I stopped to listen to the silence of the mountains, gazing alternately at the splash of yucca blossoms around me, the delicate sand hieroglyphics of insect trails below me, and the great canvas of sky painted with clouds above me. A Navajo prayer chant from Janet LaFarge's *Laughing Boy* welled up in my heart:

> With the sorrow of great beauty I wander
> with the emptiness of great beauty I wander
> Never alone, never weeping, never empty,
> Now on the old age trail, now on the path of beauty
> I wander; *Ahalani*, beautiful!

Here surely is a songline for the discipleship way in "Aztlán" (below, 11,E,2).

As we walked we held prayer stones, and at the end of Holy Thursday's pilgrimage we stood in a circle in the desert while each person shared what they had "heard" from their prayer stones. Never have I so deeply felt the pain of the land as in that circle — and all we had done was to take the time to listen. That evening we entered into the liturgy of the Paschal Tridium, with a "dry" mass and a beautiful dance around the blessing of bread and wine, followed by a celebrative and eucharistic chili supper. Good Friday began at the federal courthouse in downtown Las Vegas, where two Franciscans were being sentenced for a previous felony, a public liturgy of prayer deep inside test site property. The ironic symmetry to the story we were remembering was lost on no one, including U.S. District Judge Lloyd George. As two hundred of us looked on in support, the brothers received two months, but were released on recognizance to join us for the final leg of the pilgrimage to the test site. In the last mile we began the stations of the cross, at each station gathering a stone, reading the story, crying out. At the final station we were met, as is customary, by Shoshone elders, who issued us permits to hold a ceremony on their land. This modest ritual in the war of myths reminds all concerned that the Western Shoshone people are the rightful custodians of the 24.3 million acres they call *Newe Sogobia,* extending across vast sections of Nevada, Utah, Idaho, and Wyoming. Though this claim was recognized in the Treaty of Ruby Valley in 1863, the U.S. has never honored it (Morris, 1991:3ff). The violation of Shoshone sovereignty and the destruction of their sacred land by underground nuclear explosions and radiation contamination is at the heart of the stones' cry I heard that week.

Finally we gathered in front of the entrance to the DOE facility, a simple guardhouse surrounded by outdoor pens that have been constructed over the years to hold protesters. We placed our stones at the foot of the cross, which was leaned up against the barbed wired fence. Then came a dance I shall never forget, a noiseless reenactment of the crucifixion by four barefooted dancers on the jagged ground, accompanied only by the wind and the silent cry of the stone-strewn desert. Then fifty-three of us turned and commenced the ritual of trespass, crossing over the fence, in the frail hope that as we face the devil again in the wilderness, we can make different choices this time.

• • •

> Do you not yet understand?
> Are your hearts hardened?
> Do you have eyes, and fail to see?
> Do you have ears, and fail to hear?
> And do you not remember?

These were, and are, the queries of Jesus, Interlocutor, to disciples stuck in Denial.

They were mysteriously echoed in another time and place, far removed from Galilee, but at the heart of our history in the *locus imperii.* George Morgan, an Indian agent for the Continental Congress, had been dispatched to seek peace treaties with the Delaware people to the west, as the colonists prepared for the inevitable war with England. On June 11, 1776, less than a month before the Declaration of Independence, Morgan gathered in the great longhouse of the Lenape capital at Coochocking for an audience with the chiefs of the Lenape nation. He was welcomed in traditional style — the peace pipe was smoked, sending prayers to the Great Manitou, and they sat in silence in order to clear their minds and spirits. Then the head sachem, Netawatwees, welcomed Morgan with these words: "Brother: We wipe your *eyes,* that you may see us all as brothers and find your way clear. . . . We remove all bad reports from your *heart* and open your *ears* to hear our good words" (Schaaf, 1990:115). The story of this land joins the good news of the gospel in inviting us to look, listen, and remember.

The only reason we will refuse this invitation, according to Isaiah, is because what we would see, hear, and feel would lead us to "turn around" (Mk 4:12). Thus my attention moves in Part Three to the work of repentance — that way of life that takes responsibility for our past, the present, and the future.

NOTES

1. Las Casas, a contemporary of Columbus, became so disgusted with the holocaust occurring in Hispaniola that he renounced his wealth and withdrew into the Dominican order, reemerging as the first European advocate for the abolition of Indian slavery. As bishop of Chiapas, Mexico, his first pronouncement was that no owner of Indians would be absolved in confession; today he is remembered throughout Latin America as the first liberation theologian. On Las Casas see Gutiérrez (1993); Dussel (1979); R. Brown (1992); and Sanderlin (1992). For statistics, sources, and historical narrative on the "great dying" see Thornton (1987), Wolf (1982:133ff), and Ronald Wright (1992).

2. Unfortunately not all the official projects so benignly faded away. Alastair Reid describes the obsession of Joaquín Balaguer, strongman president of the Dominican Republic, with the construction of the *Faro a Colón,* a huge lighthouse memorial to

Columbus outside Santo Domingo. Begun in 1986, some fifty thousand people were driven out of their shantytowns to make room for this Quincentenary project, which cost the hemisphere's poorest country unrevealed millions of dollars (Reid, 1992:72ff).

3. This Smithsonian-sponsored pre-Quincentenary exhibit was supposed to tour four U.S. cities, but it never left Washington, no doubt because of the excellent demystifying and contextualizing commentary by a variety of art critics that accompanies the images. The excellent four-hundred-page exhibit book referred to here also quickly went out of print. If the exhibit presented nineteenth-century political art, the handling of it just as surely represented the twentieth-century politics of art! I have used images from this collection with groups in popular education work to illustrate the role of origin myths in the American political unconscious.

4. The mural, which can still be seen today, is bordered on the bottom by a mini-portrait of the Golden Gate ("from sea to shining sea"). Patricia Hills describes the rest:

> Centered in the top border, a bald eagle holds an unfurling scroll on which is lettered "Westward the Course of Empire Takes its Way," while Indians seek to escape the scroll and the maze of winding plant tendrils. The sides include iconographical motifs drawn from classical and biblical literature, making up an imaginative typology for westward expansion — Hercules, the Argonauts, Moses, a raven with manna in its beak, a dove with a branch, Columbus, the spies of Escholl bearing the fruits from Canaan," and the Three Magi. The sides also contained medallion portraits of Daniel Boone and explorer William Clark. (1991:119)

Another compelling image that similarly exemplifies the ideology of Manifest Destiny is John Gast's *American Progress* (1872), an equally grand piece commissioned for a far more mundane setting: the cover of a western travel guide. Two characteristics stand out in Gast's work. One is the absence of any traditional religious symbolism; it has been replaced by the secular icons of Progress (telegraph wire, locomotive, school book). The other is the polemical portrait of the Indians fleeing into the western darkness before the march of settlers, stagecoaches, and the goddess figure of Progress. Wrote Gast, they "turn their despairing faces toward the setting sun, as they flee from the presence of the wondrous vision; the 'Star' is too much for them" (Hills, 1991:136). Tourist agencies used this propaganda piece to try to persuade easterners that the West was "safe" for relocation and real estate purchases. Gast's *American Progress* is reproduced with comment in the afterword of Aldridge and Myers (1990:188).

5. For example, the fact that most of the northeast Indian nations sided with the French in the so-called French and Indian wars and then with the British in the War of Independence is sometimes cited as evidence of their duplicity and warlike nature. The political realities of the period indicate otherwise. In the mid-eighteenth century the Indians controlled most of the land north and west of the British colonies. They had a relatively good relationship with the French, who were for the most part content to trade with them and rarely tried to expropriate land. In contrast, the indigenous nations had a long list of grievances against the English, who had repeatedly swindled them out of land (e.g., the infamous "Walking Purchase" of 1737; Russell, 1979:209) and broken treaties. When the European conflict known as the Seven Years' War between England and France globalized to America, it stood to reason that the Indians would ally themselves with the party less threatening to their interests. However, at the conclusion of that war the French, ignoring their alliance with the native people, ceded their claims west of the Appalachians to the English. This led to the so-called Pontiac conspiracy

in which Indians attacked English frontier forts. Here we encounter the first instance of the gruesome practice of providing native peoples with smallpox-ridden blankets. Still, the English were unable to pacify the Iroquois confederacy, which included the Covenant Chain of tribes down through the Ohio Valley; so the Crown drew up the Royal Proclamation of 1763, which established a line at the Appalachian Mountains, west of which whites would not settle or encroach upon Indian life. But this angered the colonists, who were rapidly coming to believe that they had rights to the entire continent (the original Virginia Charter, knowing nothing about the vastness of North America, had claimed land westward to the ocean). It is easy to see why a decade later Indian people would ally themselves with the English Crown, which had finally set limits on colonization, and against the American independentists. In this sense the outcome of the Revolutionary War was very bad news for the First Nations — like every war since.

6. For contemporary Indian voices I recommend R. Gonzalez (1992). Some of the hidden stories are not so dramatic, yet just as basic. Jack Weatherford has shown that the potato, which most of us probably assumed came from northern Europe, is an indigenous American plant that was domesticated by Indians four thousand years ago and eventually cultivated in some three thousand varieties (1988:59ff). Europe before Columbus, meanwhile, depended upon grain crops for staple diet, but these were vulnerable to bad weather and pestilence. He points out that with countries such as Russia, Scandinavia, England, and Germany facing periodic famines due to crop failures, this dependence upon grains guaranteed that the major European population and power centers remained in the warmer climes of the Mediterranean. When the potato arrived from the Americas, it was despised as an ugly, misshapen, tasteless tuber. It was Adam Smith who first saw the importance of this root plant that could withstand weather and pests and defended it as an excellent source of nourishment, particularly vitamin C. In the wake of the famines, epidemics, and wars of the eighteenth century, northern European monarchs began to force their peasantry to grow the potato — once they learned that a field of potatoes produces more food and nutrition (7.5 million calories per hectare) more reliably and with less labor than a field of wheat (4.2 million calories per hectare). It is not too much to say, claims Weatherford, that the potato was crucial in the rise of northern Europe societies to world power. And this was only the beginning of the story: The Americas gave the world three-fifths of the crops under cultivation today.

7. Jeane Sindab (1990) cites much higher numbers. On the slave trade and the Middle Passage, see Willie Rose (1976); O. Patterson (1982); Fogel and Engerman (1974); and Harding (1981).

8. For the record: The Gabrielinos — it is their "mission Indian" name — were the indigenous people of the Los Angeles basin (Eargle, 1986; Miller, 1991). It seems that almost half of the first colonizing party to settle the pueblo of Los Angeles were black or mulatto (Romo, 1983:17). Pio Pico was the Mexican governor who surrendered California to the U.S. (Pitt, 1966:1–47). Much of the work at the turn of the century in California fields was done by Asian contract laborers, who seeded their own culture in the Central Valley (see Kingston, 1976). Llano del Rio was an early twentieth-century socialist community in the high desert (M. Davis, 1990:3ff). Central Avenue was the heart of black Los Angeles and a legendary spot for music and culture in the 1940s and 1950s (C. Jones, 1992b). Riots occurred in East L.A. in June 1943 when white servicemen antagonized young Chicano *cholos* in a community already upset over the "Sleepy Lagoon" murder trial in 1942 (Romo, 1983:166f); the story is well narrated in Edward James Olmos's movie *Zoot Suit*. Japanese Americans from the San Gabriel Valley were

penned in the horse stables of the Santa Anita racetrack while waiting to be shipped out to the internment camps during the Second World War (see below, 6,E,2). Salazar was a journalist shot and killed by police during the chaos following the forced breakup of the Chicano Moratorium in East L.A., the largest minority rally against the Vietnam War (cf E. Martinez, 1991). Sweet Alice is a true local hero, renowned in South Central as an organizer and matriarch; I first met her at a twenty-fifth anniversary conference for the Watts uprising. On the history of people of color in California, see Daniels and Olin (1972).

9. After beholding the reality of evil in the "communion of your race" Goodman Brown becomes "a stern, a sad, a darkly meditative, a distrustful, if not a desperate man," who "shrank from the bosom of Faith"; "his dying hour was gloom" (1902:101). I am grateful to Anthony Manousos for introducing me to this short story and agree with him that it seems to articulate Hawthorne's own "psychological Pilgrim's Progress into the heart of darkness." Crews (1966:98) discusses how Hawthorne (1804–64) battled chronic depression and his anxieties over his own Puritan roots.

10. Interestingly enough, Daniel Brinton (1883) was one of the foremost experts on indigenous cultures of the eastern woodlands in the nineteenth century. On the Lenape and the Quakers, see Penn (1970); for the fate of the Lenape, see Kraft (1986:219ff). Another interesting example of families reconnecting with a hidden past is that of the so-called crypto-Jews of northern New Mexico. Not a few of the first Spanish settlers in the Americas were Jews and Moors fleeing *reconquista* or Inquisition or banishment. Many Jewish *conversos* preserved their own faith and culture secretly underneath their public Catholicism; after many generations, some no longer knew why they celebrated Mass on Saturday, or lit a menorah in front of the *Virgen,* or had a distinct vocabulary. Today some are remembering this painful, dismembered legacy of their medieval Sephardic roots (see Prinz, 1973; Plevin, 1991). My AFSC colleague Fred Vigil has been supportive of the slow "coming out" among these *conversos.* He sees it as an integral part of his community organizing to protect the traditional water rights of his people, which also go back to the Hispanic settlement of the area in the sixteenth and seventeenth centuries (Briggs and Van Ness, 1987).

11. Columbus's voyages and the entire Spanish project in the Americas was inextricably tied to the struggle over the Iberian peninsula (see Foote, 1991). The relative tolerance among Jews, Christians, and Moslems during the eleventh-twelfth century "golden age" under Moorish rule came to an end with the unification in 1469 of the feudal houses of Castile and Aragon. In 1478 they fired up the Inquisition that purged the remaining religious-cultural tolerance from Spain (the context is set well in Sanders, 1992). Meanwhile as Portuguese sailors were making their way around the horn of Africa, threatening to discover and control the much-coveted marine trade routes to the Orient, Columbus's venture represented the Castile-Aragon countergambit. Wolf writes: "From this time on, all struggle for dominance within Europe would take on a global character, as the European states sought to control the oceans and to oust their competitors from points of vantage gained in Asia, America, or Africa" (1982:129). The newly resurgent Catholic kingdom reinvigorated the *reconquista* and, in the year Columbus sailed, finally conquered Granada and drove out the Moors, then delivered the expulsion decree ordering what had once been a flourishing Jewish community to convert or leave Spain (see Sanders, 1992:82ff; Raphael, 1992:iiiff). Ironically, then, as pluralism collapsed in the Old World, it was being given another chance in the many Jewish and Moorish refugees who found their way to the Americas (above, n 10).

12. Woolman had been preceded to the village there by a Moravian missionary, who

had greater influence among the Indians. Woolman had only a few conversations with the Indians, often without an interpreter; he preached anyway, hoping that God would somehow enable the Indians to understand in their hearts his message. There were no converts to the Society. Woolman left after a stay of only four days at the insistence of the chief, who, concerned about Woolman's return journey because of the rains, arranged for him to accompany a party of canoes heading down the river toward Bethlehem (Woolman, 1989:132ff).

13. There is a similar refrain in the epistolary tradition; the early communities were exhorted to *remember*

- the practice of Jesus (Acts 20:35; 2 Tim 2:8);
- the practice of the apostles (Acts 20:31; Col 4:18; 1 Thes 2:9; 2 Thes 2:5; Heb 13:7);
- the poor (Gal 2:10);
- their *own* stories (Eph 2:11; Rev 2:5; 3:3).

This is a good digest of what liturgy-as-memory ought to be in the church: reconnecting to the practice of Jesus and of those who have reproduced his Way, remembering those who have been dismembered, and revising our own journeys as a people.

Members of Homeboy Industries, a jobs program for gang members in the Aliso projects operated by Dolores Mission in East Los Angeles.

Part Three

Deconstruction

"Why do your disciples do what is unlawful?"
Mk 2:24

When we face our denial and our vision is restored, we begin to see that the basic structures of sin — that which creates and maintains the conditions of entitlement and oppression — are economic disparity (Chapter Six), social stratification (Chapter Seven), and military domination (Chapter Eight). These are the historical constructions of power that we First World Christians must work to deconstruct. Deconstruction is a metaphor for what traditional theology calls the doctrine of conversion. As Mexican theologian Luis del Valle writes: "Theology both derives from and leads to conversion. Conversion is here understood as a real commitment to, and involvement in, society. Society must be changed to measure up to a faith that is both utopian and rooted in the present moment. Thus theology is critical of itself. In the light of faith it is also critical of the praxis of Christians" (1979:83).

This section insists that First World theology must recover both the gospel vision of the kingdom of God and the discourse of repentance that necessarily follows. It then examines three ways in which the contemporary radical discipleship movement in the U.S. has experimented with practical models of conversion: communities of *discontinuity, ap-proximation* among the poor, and *somatic* politics. I also look at how our changing political and historical context problematizes our efforts and compels us to deepen our practices of repentance, relocation, and resistance.

6

"Who Then Can Be Saved?"

Repentance

"Voluntary" servitude (voluntary inasmuch as it is introjected into the individuals), which justifies the benevolent masters, can be broken only through a political practice which reaches the roots of containment and contentment.... Such a practice involves a break with the familiar, the routine ways of seeing, hearing, feeling, understanding things so that the organism may become receptive to the potential forms of a nonaggressive, nonexploitive world.... No matter how great the distance between the middle-class revolt in the metropoles and the life-and-death struggle of the wretched of the earth — common to them is the depth of the Refusal.

Herbert Marcuse,
An Essay on Liberation

The great obstacle is simply this: the conviction that we cannot change because we are dependent upon what is wrong. But that is the addict's excuse, and we know that it will not do.

Wendell Berry,
"The Futility of Global Thinking"

As Jesus was setting out on the way... (10:17). The story of Jesus and the rich man (10:17–31) lies at the crossroads of Mark's narrative. From there "the way" will turn sharply toward Jerusalem, a destination of confrontation with the Powers that evoked dread and denial among Jesus' disciples (10:32) and still does today. But it is a crossroad in a deeper sense as well. In this episode the concrete demands of discipleship starkly confront that primal human impulse for religious security. Here at last (and only here) Mark narrates a straightforward, properly *religious* inquiry about salvation. This is the point where we would expect Jesus — who, as the text makes clear, "looked at the man and loved him" — to open his arms to all, affirming universal enfranchisement in the New Order of God. But this is not what happens. Instead Mark narrates a decisive discipleship-rejection story. Worse, Jesus appears to explain the outcome with the crudest of class polarizations.

A man ran up and knelt before him, saying, "Good Teacher, what must I do to inherit eternal life?" Let us imagine this story from a point of view alongside the disciples. From the outset we are impressed with this man's approach: he has given proper deference to Jesus, and his inquiry surely reflects the ultimate concern of the human spirit. Here, we think, is someone of stature and resources who is asking the right question. If we can get folk like him on board, it will be a big boost for our movement. We are finally starting to reach people who count, to influence the influential. We wait expectantly for Jesus' answer.

"You know the commandments..." (10:19). Jesus' response takes us by surprise. This is all? Any rabbi could have given him *that* answer! We cringe, disappointed. Jesus has blown the chance; we tune out. Perhaps, we sigh, the question was just too conventional to deserve other than a conventional answer; Jesus is like that. In the background we hear him droning on, reciting the "short list." We are oblivious to the fact that he is playing the game of repartee just long enough to unmask the illusions lurking behind this gentleman's facade — and ours.

"Teacher, I have *done* all these things since I was young" (10:20). The man's tone is slightly impatient. Yes, he *knows* the commandments. We stare at the ground, shuffling, imagining what might have been. It is a tense moment. Is the discussion over, a standoff, we wonder, or will they haggle? They eye each other carefully. Perhaps Jesus did not understand his question, we hope halfheartedly. Finally Jesus clears his throat to reply. As our spirits plummet, his heart swells with love — the kind of love that refuses to equivocate.

"You lack one thing..." (10:21). What follows is disastrous. Redistribute all your wealth, Jesus says, then come be a disciple. Nothing about eternal life, no loopholes. Stung, the man whirls and slinks away. Stunned, we stand there, our jaws dropped. Jesus watches the man disappear, shaking his head, then turns and looks at us, bemused at our incredulity. That's how it's gonna be, he says. We stare at him dumbly. There you are, he repeats, that's how *it is*. We are confused, and mad as hell. Here was a big-time player, a CEO, for God's sake. You don't go saying stuff like that to folk like that, not if you want to be taken seriously! Are we going to be taken seriously, or just keep marginalizing ourselves with ridiculous and unrealistic demands? But we choke on the words, and all that comes sputtering out is an anguished protest: *Who,* then, can be saved?" (10:26).

This story is all too familiar to Christendom yet has never seemed to be particularly haunting or troubling. Knowing that it is too fundamental to ignore, theologians have instead concentrated their intellectual energies on undermining its plain meaning. Thus it has occasioned countless homilies about how those who are blessed with wealth must take care not to let their affluence get in the way of their love for God and the church. This despite the fact that the piety of the rich is precisely what this text rejects out of hand, in favor of the call to radical discipleship.

A. THE KINGDOM OF GOD AS ECONOMIC JUSTICE

Why is the gospel invitation to embrace the kingdom of God fundamentally linked to repentance?

Before proceeding with the next major part of my argument — the gospel invitation to "deconstruction," or conversion — let us take a brief look at its rationale. To contend that we First World Christians are in denial — the argument of Part Two — assumes that there is some other reality than the one embodied (and fabulated) by the *locus imperii*. To seek to "negate" the discourses and practices of the dominant culture presumes that there is some other discursive and practical place to stand. Otherwise we are just aimlessly rearranging signs and significations, an exercise that literary and philosophical deconstructionists may find entertaining but that hardly changes the actual relations of power (Eagleton, 1983:142).

There are only two reasons why human beings actively challenge the way things are in the world, why they defect from inherited alliances and struggle to transform actual social relationships. One is that they are deviant or crazy — that is to say, they are outside the circle of socialized sanity. The other reason is that they have convictions regarding alternative possibilities for individual and collective living. Such convictions vary, of course. They may be based on a vision of the Blessed Virgin or a belief in the imminent return of a cargo cult savior; they may invoke the "self-evident" right to life, liberty, and the pursuit of happiness or the historical inevitability of a dictatorship of the proletariat; they may be animated by ideals of egalitarian community or black nationalism; they may cling to hopes of a better life in *el norte* or in heaven. For Jesus of Nazareth, a conviction about an alternative reality he called the kingdom of God (1:15) drove his struggle to change the way things were and underpinned his invitation to radical discipleship.

1. "Treasure in Heaven": The Kingdom and Social Reversal

How are we to understand the gospel concept of the kingdom of God? This question has engendered no small debate in New Testament theology (see Mack, 1988:69ff). But while the scholars have debated, as a utopian image it has repeatedly inspired social movements throughout history. Is the kingdom of God merely a nebulous, eschatological metaphor that can just as easily be attached to any variety of human idealism as ignored altogether? Or is it a "dangerous memory" to be recovered anew in each generation by the church?

Mark's use of the phrase is sparing and somewhat slippery. Sometimes the kingdom is portrayed in temporal terms: it is an imminent *kairos* (1:15), a powerful moment of revelation (9:1), a future "blessed hope" (14:25). Other times Mark suggests it is more spatial in character: It is a place or a "state of being" into which one *enters* (9:47) and/or which one *receives* (10:14f). The kingdom of God is *paradoxical:* For disciples it is a "mystery," for others it is a "parable" (4:11). Yet it is nevertheless *concrete:* When pressed for an analogy, Mark's Jesus chooses not some arcane symbol but the reality most familiar to poor and plain folk: the land itself (4:26, 30; below, 11,A). In short, Mark never really tells us definitively what the kingdom of God is. He does, however, at one point make it clear what it is not. Only in the epilogue to the story of the rich man does Mark present substantial delimitation of this alternative reality. So that the reader/listener will not forget — repetition being the key to pedagogy — Jesus offers a lyrical little verse:

> How *difficult* it will be for those with *riches*
>   *to enter the kingdom of God!*
> ...Children, how *difficult* it is
>   *to enter the kingdom of God!*
> It is easier for a camel to go through a needle's eye than
>   for a *rich person*
>   *to enter the kingdom of God!* (10:23–25)

For we who are by any index or measure rich, this is a truly terrifying triplet, its point sharpened with the razor's edge of absurdist humor. Yet it seems its clarity has somehow escaped the church through the ages, its edge dulled by a hundred reasons why it cannot mean what it says. This text is as dissonant to our ears today as it was to the disciples in the story, provoking the same kind of amazement and astonishment (10:23,26). Traditional moral theology has been so anxious that Jesus might have been making an exclusionary statement that it has missed the fact that these are not propositions about the rich at all. They concern, rather, the nature of the kingdom. These three reiterations — all in the indicative mood — insist that the kingdom of God is simply that time, that place in which *there are no rich and poor.* This being the case, the rich by definition cannot "enter" — not as long as they are rich, that is.

To understand this, let us take another look at the story, revising it from a perspective that is more suspicious of the rich man's intentions — say, the point of view of those indirectly introduced in 10:21: the poor. The man's bold, direct approach to Jesus reveals that he is socially powerful. He "wants" something and so is willing to "give" something in exchange (deference, a compliment, 10:17). His grandiose claim to innocence (10:20) exhibits the characteristics associated with the "false consciousness" of entitlement. And the religious concern reflected in his question to Jesus is not as genuine as it appears at first glance. It isn't that eternal life itself is an unseemly concern. The problem —

we missed it, just like all the commentaries — is that his question assumes he can *inherit* eternal life.[1]

This man could understand eternal life only as a "status" to be inherited; let us examine why. In his world, land was the basis of wealth, and we are told "he possessed many properties" (Gk *ktēmata*, 10:22). The fact that he is an aristocrat is enough to earn him the automatic admiration ("credulous wonder") of the disciples. Jesus, however, practicing disillusioned literacy, focuses on *how* he became so affluent. Jesus could safely assume that his wealth was the result of inheritance; the landed class of Jewish Palestine was tiny, and great care was taken to protect entitlement from generation to generation (May, 1990:141ff). As Jesus later suggests in a parable about the struggle over deeded land, the politics of inheritance was often a bloody business (Mk 12:1ff). How did estates grow? Sometimes holdings were consolidated through the joining of households in marital or political alliances; sometimes expropriated land was distributed through political patronage. But the primary mechanism of growth was debt default. Small agricultural landholders groaned under the burden of rent, tithes, taxes, tariffs, and operating expenses; inevitably falling behind, they survived by taking out loans, secured by their land. When unable to service these loans, the land was lost to the lenders, who were in most cases the large landowners, who in the absence of banking institutions made available and administered surplus capital (see Oakman, 1986:37ff). This is how socio-economic stratification was constructed in agrarian Palestine, a logic of wealth concentration against which Jesus warned his disciples (cf Mk 4:24f). It was almost certainly how the man in this story ended up with "many properties."

The beneficiaries of this system could envision religion only as a reproduction of their own socio-economic privilege: eternal life, like property, must be inherited (thus Marx's contention that "material life determines consciousness"). Here Mark has given us, in other words, a concise portrait of the ideology of entitlement (a parallel portrait of patriarchal assumptions about the afterlife is presented in Mk 12:18ff; *BSM:*314ff). This brings us to another overlooked piece of the story: Jesus' "short list" of the Decalogue (10:21). Jesus leaves out the first four "theological" commandments, but this is unremarkable, since their meaning was not a matter of debate among Jews. What is disturbing is that he *replaces* (reinterprets?) the last of the six "ethical" commands — "Do not covet what belongs to your neighbor" (Ex 20:17) — with the Levitical censure of fraud (Lev 19:13). The section of Torah to which this redaction points us concerns socio-economic conduct in the Sabbath community: how to deal with agricultural surplus (leave the gleanings for the poor); stealing; false witness; fair distribution of wages; fair treatment of the physically disabled; and justice and vengeance (Lev 19:9–18). With this deft bit of midrash Jesus suddenly snaps into focus the cycle of indebtedness just described. The clear implication is that the "propertied" create and maintain their surplus through "fraud." They may justify their affluence by ideologies of entitlement, but Jesus unmasks it as the result of illegitimate expropriation of their neighbor's land.

Now comes the hard truth that arises from love: "You lack [Gk *hysterei*] one thing" (10:21). The rich man does not know his true "poverty" (cf *hystereseos*, the "destitution" of the widow in 12:44). The imperatives that follow do not exhort him to change his attitude toward his wealth or to treat his servants better or to reform his personal life. They invite him rather to receive the kingdom as that "social state" of redistributive justice where the dominant relations of power are turned upside down. "Get up," pleads Jesus — this is a Markan healing verb. If the one who is structurally advantaged within the dominant system sells what he has and gives to the poor, his "earthly plunder" will become "heavenly treasure" (Gk *thesauron*, distinct from the other three words used to describe wealth in this episode). This is a dramatic case of apocalyptic social reversal.[2] "And come follow me"; here discipleship is concretely defined as the deconstruction of a fraudulent system by restoring to the poor what has been taken from them. The meaning of repentance for the rich is *reparation* (below, E).

We have arrived at the reason why kingdom of God discourse has circulated at such a low rate of exchange within modern Christianity: Redistributive justice is high heresy in capitalism. But in the narrative of biblical radicalism, economic justice is the fundamental social goal of the people of God. The ancient vision of the Jubilee Year — another part of Levitical Sabbath legislation (Leviticus 25) — was not offered as an unattainable ideal but as a practical hedge against the inevitability of the stratification of wealth and power within human societies. The social model for free tribal Israel thus was periodically (every forty-ninth year, a Sabbath's Sabbath) to deconstruct debt, land alienation, and bond servitude — the three stages of impoverishment resulting from indebtedness. "The Jubilee legislation is an assault upon any understanding of the commandment against stealing that tries to justify the aggrandizement of wealth in the hands of an elite few. ... Land was given to families and clans, and it would stay with them forever. It gave hope to the impoverished by offering a promise of return to their land and a place of equality in the community. It became an aid to prevent the breakdown of the family as a social element" (Gnuse, 1985:36). Precisely because they proscribe the concentration of wealth, the Jubilee traditions have been the subject of considerable skepticism in the hermeneutical sphere of capitalist religion. Theologians doubt whether such legislation was ever practiced in biblical Israel and argue over the extent to which the idea might have influenced Jesus' preaching. But Jubilee ideology is the only plausible background to the conviction of Mark's Jesus that wealth must be redistributed as a precondition of the kingdom of God.[3]

The narrative sequence of Mk 2:1–3:6 is a compelling midrash on Sabbath economics (*BSM:*154ff). It begins with Jesus' unilateral disposition of debt (2:5).[4] When the scribes, who in fact control the debt system, warn Jesus that "only God can forgive sin," they are placing redistributive justice beyond the pale of history (Mk 2:7). In contrast, Jesus asserts that "the Human One has authority on earth" to deconstruct the condition of indebtedness (Mk 2:10). The next episode then portrays debt collectors at table with "sinners" (that is, the indebted; 2:13–17). This is strange fellowship indeed — unless Levi and his colleagues were practicing Sabbath redistribution! Their repentant discipleship is contrasted with the empty penitence of ritual fasting in the next episode (2:18–22). This leads to an action in which the disciples commandeer food from a grainfield (2:23ff; recall the role of land in the cycle of debt). There Jesus asserts again the Human One's authority, specifically in relation to Sabbath economics as the practice of surplus redistribution (2:27). The sequence culminates in Jesus' Sabbath ultimatum to the synagogue leadership (3:4). Later Jesus will reiterate the Sabbath principle in his parable of the sower (4:2ff; *BSM:*174ff) and in his manna action in the wilderness (6:34–44; *BSM:*205ff). In both cases, the marginalized are envisioned as "having enough," against the determinations of the market.

We who have been socialized within the womb of capitalism dismiss such notions as utopian, of course. True and universal economic justice, if it is contemplated at all, is done so as an eschatological hope; a noble ideal, but impossible to realize. But this attitude is precisely what is at issue in the pedagogic conclusion to our story (10:27–30). What is altogether impossible within our historical constructions is altogether possible within the reconstructive purview of God (10:27). Mark now argues that the hundredfold harvest promised in Jesus' sower parable (4:8) was not the pipe dream of indebted peasants but the concrete result of redistributive practice by disciples (10:28). Surplus is created when the entitlements of *household* (basic productive economic unit), *family* (patrimonial inheritance), and *land* (basic unit of wealth) are "left" — which is to say, restructured as community assets (10:29f). "Whosoever" practices kingdom economics will *receive* (not inherit) the community's collective assets, persecution (the inevitable result of subversive practice), and "in the age to come eternal life." *That* is the straightforward answer to the rich man's question.

But he has not stuck around to hear it. He has chosen to retain control over his property, unpersuaded by this alternative vision and thus unwilling (or perhaps, as trustee of his estate, perceiving himself unable) to change his economic practice. This illustrates another point of Jesus' sower parable: People of that class "hear the word, but the anxieties of this age, the love of riches, and the lust for everything else choke the word, so that it proves unfruitful" (4:19).[5] Later in Mark's story we encounter two more confirming object lessons, in both cases concerning members of the elite who are sympathetic to "the word." A scribe announces his agreement with Jesus' *idea* of justice; but without accompanying practice he remains "not far from the kingdom of God" (12:34; *BSM*317f). Even more tragic is Josephus, a member of the Sanhedrin who, we are told, was "receptive to the kingdom of God" (15:43). But in the end the duties of his station compel him to do the bidding of those committed to Jesus' demise (*BSM:*394f). The privileged, then, can enter into the kingdom of God through neither "intellectual assent" nor "openness." And we who are entitled certainly cannot inherit it. *Reparation* — restoring to the poor what is rightfully theirs — is our only way in.

2. The "Great Economy"

Throughout Christian history the church has rightly sought contemporary analogues for the kingdom of God, and the search is no less vigorous in our time. I am sympathetic to those who feel that today the term *kingdom* is not only an anachronism but further suffers from the fact that within the discursive context of Western history and culture it has connoted patriarchal and autocratic rule. (Strangely, the *Scholars Bible* chose the even more problematic "God's imperial rule"; Schmidt, 1990:105.) Many attractive analogues have been proposed. Two Native American theologians, George Tinker and Sr. Marie Therese Archambault (1992), offer the Lakota expression *Mitakuyeoyasin* (All my relations), a customary benediction. Scandinavians propose the term *Thoranblott*, old Norse for "the coming of the light." Filipino Christians sometimes use *Balikbayan*, Tagalog for "return to one's home country." Certainly Martin Luther King's notion of the "Beloved Community" deserves consideration.[6] It has a nice resonance with Mark's vision of the reconstructed "family" (below, 9,A), as does the feminist suggestion that we simply speak of the "kin-dom" of God.

The challenge is to find a phrase that retains the subversive *and* reconstructive character that the term *kingdom* had in a world of real kingdoms. In my opinion, the best metaphor for our capitalist context is the one used by Kentucky philosopher-farmer Wendell Berry: "the Great Economy" (1987:56). The all-encompassing and integrated system of creation, he suggests, should be understood in terms of a functioning economy: "It includes principles and patterns by which values or powers or necessities are parceled out and exchanged" (ibid:57). Human systems are "little economies" that by necessity depend upon and operate within the Great Economy. The gospel calls us to "seek the kingdom of God first; that is it gives obviously necessary priority to the Great Economy over any little economy made within it" (ibid:58).[7]

Berry's thoughtful essay, entitled "Two Economies," reads like an exposition of our rich man story. The problem, according to Berry, is that "the industrial economy," with its penchant for control and its lack of limits, "does not see itself as a little economy; it sees itself as the *only* economy. It makes itself thus exclusive by the simple expedient of valuing only what it can use — that is, only what it can regard as 'raw material' to be transformed mechanically into something else. ... The industrial economy is based on invasion and pillage of the Great Economy" (ibid:64f). Berry specifically links this to the gospel story of the rich man whose "sin" was accumulation rather than long-term stability: "By laying up 'much goods' in the present — and in the process, using up such goods as topsoil, fossil fuel, and fossil water — we incur a debt to the future that we cannot repay. That is, we diminish the future by deeds that we call 'use' but that the future will call 'theft.' We may say, then, that we seek the kingdom of God, in part, by our economic behavior, and we fail to find it if that behavior is wrong" (ibid:59).

Berry is particularly critical of the supremacy of artificially created "value," since ultimately "value can originate only in the Great Economy." Moreover, because the system is based on what Marxists call "surplus extraction," "it must accept impoverishment as the inescapable condition of abundance. The invariable mode of its relation both to nature and to human culture is that of mining: withdrawal from a limited fund until that fund is exhausted" (ibid:68). Berry agrees with Marx that the result is the alienation of human beings from the land and their own labor. And he agrees with Jesus that fraud is inherent in the system: "Competitiveness, as a ruling principle and a virtue, imposes a logic that...explains why it is so difficult for us to draw a line between 'free enterprise' and crime. If our economic ideal is maximum profit with minimum responsibility, why should we be surprised to find our corporations so frequently in court and robbery on the increase?" (ibid:72). In contrast, the Great Economy demands responsibility and stewardship based upon a consciousness of our profound interdependence with each other and the whole natural order: "Then, because in the Great Economy *all* transactions count and the account is never closed, the ideal changes...the loser's losses finally afflict the winner. Now the ideal must be 'the maximum of well-being with the minimum of consumption,' which both defines and requires neighborly love" (ibid:72). Because "there is no 'outside' to the Great Economy," Berry concludes, "whatever we do counts; if we do not serve what coheres and endures, we serve what disintegrates and destroys" (ibid:74f).

In the rest of this book I will adopt the rhetoric of "the Great Economy" as a compelling metaphor for the kingdom of God. This vision empowers us to critique the dominant economic practices of the *locus imperii*. Berry's metaphor has a similar quality to Mark's: It does not spell out a blueprint for the ideal economy, but it is clear about what economic practices are precluded. Privately controlled wealth is the raison d'être of capitalism and is predicated upon the exploitation of natural resources and human labor. Profit maximization renders socio-economic stratification, objectification, and alienation inevitable (we have yet to see a capitalist system not characterized by all three). According to the gospel, those who are privileged within this system cannot enter the Great Economy because they epitomize wrong economic behavior. This is not good news for First World Christians, because we are the "inheritors" of the rich man's legacy.

Typically we mask our entitlement by the myth that our wealth has been earned, not inherited, through thrift and industry. Our immigrant ancestors broke from the grip of the old European aristocracies, so the devised narrative goes, to coax prosperity "from a barren land" and become a country of free farmers and small businesspeople. No old money here, just hard work! This myth is correct in one respect only: our ancestors did not inherit in any conventional sense the material basis of their created wealth. A revision of our history (above, 5,E) suggests rather that they *stole* it. The *land* was stolen, with "title of ownership" drawn up either by those very European aristocracies (through grants of conquest with the imprimatur of the tyrants they fled) or by the Diety itself through convenient theologies of divine election. It was self-evident to our ancestors that the New World land belonged not to those who happened to be living on it (theirs were merely squatters' rights) but to those who could exploit them for profit. So they proceeded also to steal the land's *resources:* Nature belonged to those who could bend her will to theirs, her bounty to those who would transform it into commodities. And to extract those "assets" they stole *labor:* When exploiting the Indians of the Americas and the poor of Europe soon proved insufficient for their purposes, they stole millions of African lives and developed history's most systemic slave-based society.

The work of our ancestors' hands was predicated upon the violent expropriation of the land, resources, and labor of others. But their descendants have inherited that wealth — the fruits of amassed and productive capital, exploited labor and political hegemony — passed on by the fathers of Manifest Destiny to the children of Progress. Every one of us who lives in relative material affluence and privilege today, and who enjoys the opportunity for upward mobility, does so by rights of gender, race, and/or class entitlement. From the moment European flags were first planted in American soil to the Gulf War in defense of U.S. oil interests, the dominant culture has proceeded on the firm conviction that we are entitled to the earth and its wealth, by any means necessary. So the gospel text of repentance is addressed to us. If we wish to enter the Great Economy, we must deconstruct this inheritance and redistribute our wealth to the poor — "impossible" as that may seem. That is what it means for *us* to follow Jesus.

B. "HOW DIFFICULT IT IS!"
ENTITLEMENT AS ADDICTION, CONVERSION AS RECOVERY

How can we recover a theology and practice of repentance for North America?

Repentance is at the heart of the gospel; take it away and you have something other than biblical faith. The problem is, repentance represents *discontinuity* with the established order. But for those entitled within the system, the greatest social value is *continuity.* From the perspective of the dominant culture, the system works: It has no fatal contradictions, it perpetuates itself, it even grows and spreads. The belief in continuity is particularly essential in the maintenance of an imperial order; *substantive* notions of repentance, therefore, are necessarily held in contempt (as opposed to *spiritualized* ones, which are always welcome). Consequently conversion — a theme once taken seriously by the theologies of Protestant immigrants — has become increasingly marginalized in the churches of the *locus imperii.*

What liberation theologians call the "consciousness of sin" has steadily waned among all three major tendencies of twentieth-century Protestant theology in the U.S. (a trend mirrored by the other "minority" Christian traditions). Liberals were seduced by "progressive" myths, an ideology of optimism best symbolized by the naming of their flagship journal the *Christian Century.* The rhetoric of repentance was embarrassing to the ethos of Positivism, and even the prophetically oriented social gospel tradition was decidedly reformist.[8] Neo-orthodox theologies made the opposite error; they recovered the discourse of sin but abandoned a historical vision of the Great Economy. Their "political realism" seems in retrospect to have been captive to imperial cold war assumptions: The "free world" was sinful, but not nearly as sinful as the Communists.[9] Protestant evangelicalism, meanwhile, remained mired in nineteenth-century religious privatism. While the discourse of repentance remained strong, it was understood to be personally engaging but socially irrelevant. Today, under the influence of imperial shame culture, upwardly mobile evangelicals are succumbing to the notion of sin as "feeling bad" about oneself; repentance, consequently, is seen increasingly in terms of repairing one's self-esteem (see Hunter, 1982).

In the Palace Courtyard twilight, then, we who cannot sing the emperor's tune, but whose patrimony remains entitlement within the emperor's system, find ourselves theologically orphaned. It is time to listen again to the tradition of biblical radicalism. For the classical prophets of Israel, repentance represented a negation of continuity in the historical project of Israel, with its illusions of a benign past and an equally benign future. But theirs was a message of solidarity with, not escape from, that history, with the hope of reclaiming and redeeming that project (Brueggemann, 1978:44ff). Standing firmly within this tradition was the late Second Temple prophet John the Baptist. According to the ancient historian Josephus, John was a flaming Jewish nationalist (*BSM:*214ff); according to the gospels, however, his preaching relentlessly attacked Jewish ideologies of entitlement.[10] Mark and the other evangelists make it clear that Jesus adopted John's theology of repentance, tying it to his annunciation of a Great Economy that was discontinuous with the established order (Mk 1:4, 15). This was not a moral exhortation to "be better" but a historical ultimatum to a project in which there were fatal contradictions.

Such a discourse enjoys no hospitality in the *locus imperii* because we are socialized to believe that we (that is, our leaders) are in control of history. And if that faith is shaken, we usually swing over to the other end of the pendulum, abandoning history altogether. This is the strategy of modern Dispensationalism, which looks for the Rapture to render all historical contradictions moot (for a critique see Jewett, 1979). These strategies are opposite poles of a sophisticated and powerful religious system of Denial (below, 12,A). But the truth of Desert Storm and the Los Angeles uprising is that we are indeed sowing the seeds of our own demise, facing self-destruction either by our guns or by the gulf between rich and poor (above, Chapter One). We face a new century in which our exploitation of the earth *will* result in cataclysmic ecological rebellion — drought, aquifer contamination, rain forest destruction, ozone depletion (below, 11,B). If we continue, as Bob Dylan put it, "a hard rain's gonna fall." The U.S. — postindustrial, postmodern, post-Christian, but hardly postimperial — swings madly on the pendulum of manic-depression (above, 4,C). "The steps we have taken to quell the anxiety have actually exacerbated our sense of insecurity and — by ironic logic familiar to the student of neuroses — have thereby called forth still more of the same kind of efforts and thus still more undermining of security and still further acceleration of a one-sided and self-defeating pattern" (Wachtel, 1989:60). We are, in other words, captive in the "land of the free," culpable for both our own dehumanization and that of others, unable to dream of exodus because our own utopian dreams have soured. Whether we have the courage to acknowledge it or not, the historical project of the *locus imperii* has arrived at a cul-de-sac. The future is closed unless we *turn around.*

That, of course, is precisely the meaning of John's discourse of repentance (Gk *metanoias*): "The noun denotes a deliberate turning, a coming to one's senses resulting in a change of conduct" (Taylor, 1963:154). But this challenge is directed to the people collectively, not only individuals. This is articulated by the way Mark's prologue narrates a spatial tension between center and periphery in the political geography of Jewish Palestine. The regenerative epiphany occurs in the wilderness instead of the Temple; people come *from* Jerusalem *to* the margins to be baptized (Mk 1:2–6; *BSM:*121ff). The direction of this movement utterly contradicts the historical ideology of entitlement assumed by what biblical scholar David Jobling calls Israel's Zion myth (1992:104ff). The biblical theology of repentance, then, gives people permission to acknowledge that they are captive to demons of self-destruction, that their historical project has arrived at a dead end, that their myths of entitlement are the problem, and that they can, and must, change directions in order to continue.

Unfortunately, as we have seen at great length in Part Two, we in the Palace Courtyard do not have "ears to hear" this invitation to repentance because we are so deeply entrenched in Denial. Wendell Berry puts the matter plainly: We have become dependent upon what we know is wrong. "We all live by robbing nature," he writes, "but our standard of living demands that the robbery shall continue" (1989a:19). "Empire," concurs William Appleman Williams, "is the child of an inability or an unwillingness to live within one's own means; empire as a way of life is predicated upon having more than one needs" (1980:31). We are, in other words, *addicted* to an entitlement that destroys the land, exhausts its resources, and alienates and exploits human labor. We have become so internally and externally reliant upon our illusions and excesses and appetites that we simply cannot imagine the world differently. So our response to Jesus' insistence that the Great Economy is discontinuous with our addiction is, like the disciples, to despair: "Who then can be saved?"

Wendell Berry, like John the Baptist, refuses to accept the addict's excuse. If entitlement is an addiction — and given the interlocking mechanisms of social formation, denial, and dependence in capitalist culture, this is a legitimate hypothesis — we cannot expect that people will change just because we tell them they must. It is all very well to exhort each other to "live simply, that others will simply live," or as F. E. Trainer says, to "Abandon Affluence!" (1985). But the experience of the last two decades suggests that exhortations do not animate most people to radical change, even when we argue that it is in their self-interest to do so (Wachtel, 1989:289).

Perhaps instead we should experiment with a theology that merges prophetic and pastoral insights: understanding repentance as a *strategy of intervention* and conversion as a *strategy of recovery.* Recent therapeutic work has shown that the journey of recovery cannot be an exclusively individual one because of the systemic nature of addiction within families. Similarly repentance must be more than a private religious experience because of the systemic character of our economic-political-cultural pathologies. We must develop collective and long-term disciplines of "turning around" that, as Marcuse put it, empower "a political practice which reaches the roots of containment and contentment" and that are "receptive to the potential forms of a nonaggressive, nonexploitive world." In other words, political therapy must become therapeutic politics.

I agree with those who see the genuinely popular and practical Twelve Step model of recovery as instructive. Whatever criticisms can be made of the Twelve Step movement (above, 4,E,2), it reflects three important insights from which we can learn. First, it is a "conversionist" model with real parallels to the biblical theology of repentance. Step one, as essential as it is uncomfortable, is the acknowledgment that the addictive system that controls me is destructive to me and all those around me. If I want to be liberated from the nihilistic logic of that system I must:

- appeal to an alternative reality (steps two and three);
- accept my culpability in that system and "confess" it to others (steps four and five);
- seek to "repent" of those practices (steps six and seven);
- make reparation to those I have wronged (steps eight and nine).

The Twelve Step process assumes that because the dysfunctional system cannot be reformed, it must be disengaged. It is "apocalyptic"; that is, it recognizes fundamental contradictions in the addictive system and concedes that the power to change must come from "outside." The Twelve Steps aim at nothing less than revolutionary transformation: As the recovering addict becomes stronger, he or she invites other family members (as well as other addicts) to join in the "insurrection" against dysfunctional behavior so that the family system as a whole may be transformed.

The second key insight of the Twelve Step method is that it begins with our *own* experience of pain, oppression, culpability, and responsibility. This approach insists that abstract analysis of the system is unacceptable; *we* are the subjects of the struggle for change. This is a crucial ingredient for liberation, as we have seen (above, 3,D). It is true that the focus on oneself risks degenerating into *subjectivism*. Therapeutic culture is awash with people so preoccupied with the labyrinth of personal alienation that they fail to realize how the web of complicity relates to systemic causes, and thus they never get around to political action. This has indeed been a problem with Twelve Step programs. But too often activists trying to avoid this error fall into the opposite trap. Our diagnosis of systemic pathology places structural problems so far from our actual lives that it either disempowers ("What can one person do?") or rationalizes ("Only the 'revolution' will resolve these issues"). Change can and must begin with regular people where they are (see below, C).

The third, and perhaps most important, aspect of the Twelve Step recovery process is its recognition that an ongoing community of accountability and support is vital in sustaining resistance to the addictive system. However great our internal resistance to the process of disengagement, the external resistances are much more formidable, because the status quo always attempts to constrain fundamental changes in the system. In the family system, those who hold power are invariably the ones who, while rhetorically affirming the addict's quest for recovery, refuse to acknowledge their own complicity. Such "conserve-atism" is often desperate to maintain the family ideal (how it views itself) and reputation (how it is viewed in the community). As the recovering addict tries to stand his or her ground while refusing to cooperate with old family patterns, the alternative community becomes crucial as a place of understanding and identity.

How much more difficult it is for those of us in the *locus imperii* to break with the national "family" and its myths. Loyalty to the State is demanded as fiercely as in a kinship system, and defection can carry a cost higher than ostracism! Because the social and ideological mechanisms of seduction are so powerful, and the mechanisms of repression so potentially vicious, a community of resistance becomes key to a strategy of recovery from the pathology of empire. If our diagnosis of the macro systems of addiction around us were clearer, our recovery support groups would necessarily become more politicized. Then we might be able to speak of an analogy between First World recovery groups and the Third World base communities. But we have a long way to go to realize that.

Let us return one more time to the story of the rich man, reading now from the perspective of repentance as therapeutic intervention. "Gazing at him Jesus loved him" (10:21). This is a pastoral response to someone who is addicted. Jesus invites him to join the community of recovery: "Come, follow me." But to begin the process he must deconstruct his entitlement. Why? Because just as the alcoholic must at some point stop drinking in order to start recovering, the entitled must give up economic control in order to experience the Great Economy (10:29f). "How difficult it is," remarks Jesus as the man slumps away, for those possessed by possession to "enter into" the sobriety of economic justice! To drive this point home Mark follows this episode with two stories that illustrate contrasting responses to the notion of discipleship as recovery. The first, a highly caricatured, tragicomic portrait of the inner discipleship circle, symbolizes their retreat from the via crucis (10:32–34) deeper into the illusions of entitlement (10:35–45; *BSM:*277ff). When Jesus tries to point out their addiction, they react with fierce denial (10:39). This vignette about codependent religion in a society captive to the pathologies of domination (10:42f) ought to make the church in the *locus imperii* shudder.

The second episode is a portrait of conversion as "the courage to change": the story of Bartimaeus (10:46–52; *BSM:*281ff). This blind beggar stands in piercing contrast to the rich man and the ambitious disciples at every point. He is poor, landless, and disabled—a victim of the system, not its beneficiary. He dares not approach Jesus directly as a social equal with his request, as did the rich man and the disciples. He inquires persistently, not after the mysteries of eternal life or the top posts in the new administration, but after mercy (10:47f). Because of his low station, the disciples, ever anxious to enforce propriety, try to impede him (they had, of course, no objection to the rich man's importunity). Yet Bartimaeus is willing to give up what little he has to achieve liberation; the beggar's cloak he casts off represents the tool of his panhandler's trade (10:49). Then comes an echo that is surely the sharpest arrow in Mark's quiver:

> Jesus said to the disciples, "What do you want me to do
>   for you?" They answered,
> "Grant us to sit on your right and left hand in glory!"
>   (10:36f)
> Jesus said to the blind man, "What do you want me to
>   do for you?" He answered,
> "Master, that I might *see again!*" (10:51)

This contrast brings us to the crux of the matter.

Jesus cannot answer the rich man's question because he will not deconstruct his entitlement. Jesus cannot grant the disciples' request because it is based on delusions of grandiosity. He cannot help these would-be followers because he is committed to breaking addiction, not feeding it. So the rich man slinks away and the covetous disciples are scolded by their envious colleagues (10:41). But Jesus can welcome Bartimaeus because Bartimaeus knows he is blind. He is willing to make a decisive break with the system, he is willing to risk revising everything: "Let me see again!" So this time Jesus' invitation to "Get up!" receives a different response. "He followed on the Way": Bartimaeus embraces the discipleship journey of recovery, which is his healing (10:52).

C. "IF YOUR EYE SCANDALIZES YOU": *DEFECT-IVE* POLITICAL BODIES

Why does commitment to the Great Economy demand severance from the dominant culture in our struggle to embrace both culpability and responsibility?

To begin a new journey, Bartimaeus had to dis-continue the old one. To sustain the new journey, he had to join a *community of discontinuity*. In this community disciples support one another in their struggle to resist the dominant culture and to practice alternatives. According to Mark's narrative, such maintenance work is indeed demanding — disciples are forever *reverting* rather than *converting!* Earlier in his "discipleship catechism" (the section of the gospel on which I have been drawing in this chapter, *BSM:*236ff) are other object lessons concerning conversion as recovery. We see the disciples paralyzed by their impotence: "Why could we not cast it out?" (9:14–29; above, Chapter Four).

Immediately after this they are shown mimicking the dominant culture's grandiosity ("Who is the greatest?" 9:33ff). This is then followed by an expression of
their obsessive-compulsive need for control ("But they were not following us!"
9:38ff). No wonder Jesus stresses this community's need for support: "Whoever
gives you the least bit of help will not lose their reward" (9:40f)!

It is understandable that the community of discontinuity would be protective
of those in recovery, issuing warnings against "causing one of these little ones
who believes in me to stumble" (9:42). Compared to the massive systems of
addiction we are up against, we are "little" indeed — and vulnerable. But here,
in the very middle of the discipleship catechism, Mark introduces a troubling
contradiction to his discourse of healing: "If your eye gets you into trouble [Gk
skandalizē], rip it out! It is better for you to enter God's domain one-eyed than to
be thrown into Gehenna with both eyes" (9:47, SV). Here the one who restored
an atrophied hand (3:3), empowered a paraplegic to walk (2:9), and, above all,
opened "eyes to see" (8:23; 10:51) invites us to self-mutilation! What sense can
we make of this strange exhortation?

A verse of Dan Berrigan's comes to mind:

> In the house where all cry out "I see!"
> and continue to do the works of darkness
> there is only one classic action open to the wise:
> strike yourself blind and explore that Kingdom.

Mark's vexing discourse of amputation suggests *deformity* as the necessary
countermeasure to pressures for *conformity* in a social order characterized by
"works of darkness." To deform, says Webster's, is "to mar the natural form
or shape; to disfigure." If imperial politics and culture thinks it "natural" to
disfigure human life, we must disfigure ourselves in relation to it. Amputation
thus symbolizes our struggle to alter our political bodies in order to live discontinuously with the internalized and external imperatives of the body politic.
This makes us *defect-ive:* We are trying to defect from a dysfunctional system. Hand, foot, and eye represent the vehicles by which our political bodies
are "scandalized" by the pathology — what we see, what we handle, where we
stand.[11] Infected organs *will*, Mark emphasizes in triple refrain, lead us to hell,
that place wherein we are consumed by "the worm that does not die" (9:48) —
a credible description of the addicted state. Kicking an addiction, on the other
hand, indeed feels like amputation.

If these Markan metaphors seem bizarre to us today — they are rarely uttered in our churches — it is because we are not engaged in defect-ive struggle.
For they accurately describe the painful practices of severance that must characterize a genuine community of discontinuity. Gerald May rightly describes
recovery in terms of the traditional notion of "resisting temptation": "Any struggle with addiction is a desert because it involves deprivation.... With major
addictions... the desert can grow to encompass all of life: every habit may be
exposed to the searing, purifying sun; every false prop is vulnerable to relin-

quishment; and one can be left truly dependent upon the grace of God for sustenance" (1988:135). This is the ancient way of asceticism: "The word comes from the Greek *askēo,* 'to exercise,' " May reminds us; "asceticism is our willingness to enter the deserts of our lives, to commit ourselves to struggle with attachment, to participate in a courtship with grace" (ibid:141).

Defect-ive living, then, is a metaphor for the via crucis: "What can it profit us to gain the whole world and forfeit our lives?" (8:36; *BSM:*247). For the fatally affluent First World, this warning has surely become a historical ultimatum. The illusions and appetites of entitlement have invaded and taken up residence in our political bodies like a cancer: We must cut them out. But our reaction to the prospect of "surgery" is either fear (it seems like self-mutilation or suicide) or avoidance (we imagine we can remove the infected parts through some painless procedure). Worse, given the "confusion of self" characteristic of our narcissistic disorder (above, 4,B), we are unable to distinguish between invaded and healthy tissue. We cannot engage in severance from the dominant order unless and until we acknowledge and understand how we are part of it and how it is part of us. We must recognize the power of the system over us (our addiction) in a way that does not concede powerlessness (the addict's excuse). To do this we must recover both our sense of culpability within the body politic and responsibility within our political bodies.

As individuals we are socialized to feel powerless to change the economic system, for example. The only "difference" we can make, we are led to believe, is as consumers choosing between products, not as political subjects struggling to live converted lives.[12] Unfortunately, there is considerable truth to this proposition, since few of us are from among the multinational corporate-political elite who set global prices and policies.

> When we consider where we experience some degree of freedom, we always find it exists within a broader framework over which we have no control. We are like the little child who is free to run away from home but not free to leave the block. The environment is a conspicuous example. We can recycle paper and other waste materials, but industrial America fouls the environment in ways we seem helpless to restrain. In large measure it is the nature and dynamic of the economic order that controls the framework within which we can make only rather inconsequential decisions. (King et al, 1988:150)

Regardless of the individual choices we make, the structural imperatives of capitalism define the relations of production and power in the world. We must concede that our political bodies are relatively powerless (though our disenfranchisement is hardly comparable to that of those more directly exploited in the global economy).

This presents us with two somewhat paradoxical challenges. On one hand, it means that the notion of "personal liberation" from this system is an illusion, which is why capitalist culture promotes it so vigorously. Just as credulous con-

sumers imagine that a racy sportscar will "set them free" (Wachtel, 1989:32ff),
so do disaffected individuals imagine they can disconnect from the dominant
culture by wearing different clothes or fleeing the city or protesting or "living
simply" — or writing books! *Private* definitions of change only strengthen a
system whose purpose is to privatize all of life. The more we think we can reduce our culpability through individual nonconformity, the more culpable we
are. In order to deprivatize our definition of culpability, we must insist that
individualistic repentance does not constitute defection.

On the other hand, this does not absolve us of responsibility within our political bodies. Because we cannot personally change a system does not mean
we have ceased to exist as moral and political agents. This is precisely the
erasure capitalism seeks: to convince us that social, economic, and political processes are so complex and remote that we, as isolated producers/consumers, are
absolved of all obligation to think critically or act discontinuously. A classic,
almost clichéd example of this can be seen in the design, manufacturing, and
deployment of sophisticated nuclear weaponry. This project has from its incep-
tion demanded a massive national mobilization and organization of resources
and human talent. Despite its impact on our economy — including our personal
tax obligations — those of us not directly involved in this project do not consider ourselves responsible. This feeling is reinforced by the military culture of
secrecy. Yet those who are directly involved feel no greater sense of agency —
not design engineers or those working the assembly line, in the military bureaucracy, in the missile silo, not even the policymakers. This is how *systemic
ir-responsibility* is transformed into *pandemic exoneration* — that is, total capit-
ulation to the structural imperatives of the system![13] In order to repoliticize our
definitions of responsibility, therefore, we must insist that *abdication of personal
responsibility does not constitute defection.*

Privatization and exoneration represent the warp and weft of the fabric into
which our entitlement is woven in capitalist culture. To embrace both culpability
and responsibility is to begin to pull the strand that can unravel the whole cloth.
We cannot privately disconnect from the system, but we can take steps within
our political bodies to begin defecting from the imperatives and expectations of
the body politic where we are. Communities of discontinuity can sustain our collective engagement with the system in the actual social, political, and economic
spaces of our lives and can nurture alternative practices.

D. "NO ONE WHO HAS LEFT HOUSE OR FAMILY...": EXPERIMENTS IN DISCONTINUITY

*How have intentional communities revised traditional spiritual disciplines
to facilitate defection from the dominant culture?*

The answer to the rich man's inquiry, and the key to understanding the "mystery" of the sower parable (4:11), is Jesus' promise that those who have left
house, family, and/or land will receive back these things a hundredfold "in this

time" (10:29f). The construction of this saying knits it tightly to Jesus' invitation to the rich man: "Leaving" means "selling and giving back" (10:21). The consequences of deconstructing entitlement are not destitution, however, but the surplus of the Great Economy restored in discipleship community.

Brazilian theologian Rubem Alves, in *Tomorrow's Child,* a stinging indictment of the culture of technocracy, argues that the "community of faith is the social form of imagination":

> What the biblical sociology of liberation tells us through the symbol of community is unequivocal: the creative event cuts its way through the social inertia by creating *counter culture.* In the Old Testament the community of Israel was a counter culture. Its lifestyle, values, and patterns of human interrelatedness were radically different from and opposed to the dominant cultural pattern of its environment. The early Christian community was . . . an underground counter culture. The reason it was so ruthlessly persecuted was because the dominant powers perceived it as a basically dysfunctional and subversive social reality. The values it wanted to realize and live out implied in the long run the abolition of the very foundations of the Roman Empire. (1972:202)

This biblical insight has inspired renewal movements in each era of Christendom to attempt to dis-establish the church and to defect from its Constantinian alliances. In our time it has spawned a base community movement that is transforming the face of the church throughout the Third World. It also animates a less widespread (but no less important) First World trend toward alternative and intentional communities.[14]

1. Discipleship Communities as Counterculture

Historically in the U.S. Christians have pursued a variety of forms of voluntarist community, for a variety of reasons. But these alternative movements have always encountered a basic problematic. Because of their necessarily oppositional, reactive impulse, they have tended to one of two extremes. One tendency was to seek refuge from the social and cultural alienation that characterizes modernity. These communities, such as the Amish or monastics, stood in the sectarian tradition of disengaging the world for reasons of piety or heightened religious intimacy. The other tendency was to pursue specific tasks of outreach and service to the world. These groups, such as Catholic missionary orders or the Salvation Army, stood in the activist tradition that sees community not as an end in itself but as a better means for ministry. On the whole, then, focus on communal discipline has tended to come at the expense of socio-political withdrawal, while socio-political activism has tended to sacrifice coherent community life.

In part due to the influence of the secular counterculture, partly in response to the challenges of liberation theology, the 1970s and 1980s saw a renaissance of experimental house churches, residential communities, and alternative lifestyles among North American Christians seeking to defect from the dominant culture. Almost immediately, however, these renewal movements began to exhibit the polarizing tendencies just mentioned. Elizabeth O'Connor (1969), a founder of Church of the Saviour, one of the most significant and sustained ecclesial alternatives in recent times, called these impulses the inward and outward journeys and rightly insisted that they must be held together. Countercultural movements, agreed Alves, have failed whenever they have lacked both "communal discipline" and "political practice"; the atrophy of either has rendered "creative insights sterile."

A number of communities, therefore, attempted self-consciously to embrace the tasks of both personal renewal and mission. Bartimaeus Community in Berkeley, California, was one such attempt. Because I consider it a representative example, I will use it to interpret the movement as a whole and leave the task of giving an account of greater breadth to others. Named after Mark's archetypal blind disciple (Myers, 1980b), a small group of European-Americans (numbering from ten to twenty children and adults) came together in 1976 to share a common life. None of us had experience in communal living; this was a thoroughly inductive experiment. Reacting against the institutional church, we knew more about what we did *not* want to be and looked to other (only slightly less inexperienced) communities for clues on what we might be. The power of our experimentation lay in the fact that we were struggling concretely with issues of defection. We did not allow our lack of theory or sophistication get in the way of our desire to discover a discipleship lifestyle.

We relocated (below, Chapter Seven) to a low-income neighborhood in west Berkeley, where an extended community of worship and service began to grow around us. We affiliated with no one denomination, preferring to relate to an informal, ecumenical circle of kindred communities. This circle included Catholic Worker houses (locally and around the country); resistance communities (from Jonah House in Baltimore to Ground Zero near Seattle); radical evangelical Protestants (e.g., Sojourners in Washington, DC, and Koinonia in Georgia); and Episcopal charismatics (e.g., Community of Celebration in Colorado Springs and Church of the Messiah in Detroit). Our fellowship embraced Catholics (New Jerusalem in Cincinnati), Reformed (Christ Community in Grand Rapids), and Anabaptists (Reba Place Fellowship near Chicago). Some of us gathered occasionally as a "community of communities" or in networks of resistance groups to share the questions of our common search (Wallis, 1980; Sabath, 1980). At Bartimaeus we maintained a special relationship with a parallel community movement in Australia, particularly the House of the Gentle Bunyip in Melbourne, House of the New World in Sydney, and House of Freedom in Brisbane.

Community was a vehicle for resocializing our lives, beginning at the most fundamental level of kinship. No matter how broadly we define the dysfunctional system in the *locus imperii,* our political bodies are formed primarily at the site of the natural family. In modernity, kinship systems remain the first locus of socialization and last line of defense in the enforcement of the dominant socio-political ethos, as Engels recognized (Bottomore, 1983:161f). After all, in the family entitlement is inherited, sexual division of labor learned, race and class identity and prejudice absorbed, strategic alliances of privilege forged and maintained, and defect-ive social practices constrained — as recent Republican "family values" discourse confirms. Thus our attempts to redefine "family" in Christian community were inherently subversive. While no doubt influenced by trends in the secular counterculture, we at Bartimaeus were more conscious of pursuing the lifestyle suggested by Mark's discipleship catechism: radical contemplation (9:14–29); inclusiveness (9:33ff); defect-ive social formation (9:42ff); gender equality (10:1ff); redistributive economics (10:17–32); and nondominating leadership (10:35–45). Though never fully realized, these commitments took shape in consensus decision making, extended households, a communal purse, inclusive worship, and work for peace and justice. I will be more specific below.

For eight years we managed to hold the poles of inward/outward journey in creative tension, and flourished. But in the end we, like so many other communities, impaled ourselves on the horns of that dilemma. There were many factors, both personal and political, that led us to disband, but certainly one was disagreement among us about whether to become more pastoral or more prophetic. There is no way to capture the pain of community unraveling — it is like dying (Sofield and Hammett, 1981). In the aftermath, we found ourselves asking, now what? This became the true test of the degree to which the process of defect-ive living had led to genuine conversion.

To be sure, we hurt each other and disappointed ourselves. Our community model was too restrictive and inflexible, and we were too impatient and immature. Those who became convinced that wounds from this experience had disfigured them severed themselves from radical discipleship altogether. Others of us found ourselves confused and uncertain but too deformed to reintegrate ourselves into the welcoming bosom of the dominant culture. We realized that however disaffected we might become with our support group, however resentful of the recovery process itself, the fact of our addiction does not go away. Unfortunately, there is no neutral ground to return to in capitalist culture. If we leave efforts to live discontinuously behind, how do we propose to counter the dominant culture's siege on our humanity? For it is our addictions — not the tribulations encountered trying to live soberly — that truly disfigure us.

So we continue to look for ways to reconstruct long-term communities of defection, though ones that hopefully will be wiser and more honest. We are still searching for balance between inward and outward journeys, for community that will facilitate the exercise of disciplines which expose the symptoms of addiction in our political bodies while also sustaining critical engagement with the body politic. But we did learn a great deal from our experiments. So let me focus more constructively on contributions our movement has made to the search for repentance in the *locus imperii.*

2. Revising the "Evangelical Disciplines"

Most of us in the recent community movement felt we needed to invent the structures of our collective life. In so doing we managed to make many mistakes, some of which we might have avoided had we looked to older traditions of intentional community and thereby discovered we were only reinventing these things. Thus some of us began to examine models such as the Rule of St. Benedict (490–543 C.E.) and recognized in them many of our own impulses. Consequently we began to think less about forging lifestyle blueprints and more about the notion of *spiritual disciplines*. For purposes of critical reflection, the following sketch reinterprets the practice of Bartimaeus (and similar communities) in terms of the three monastic "evangelical disciplines" — poverty, chastity, and obedience. I correlate these to the disciplines spoken of in Part Two: literacy, dis-illusionment, and revision.

Poverty. The early monks understood three key things about socio-economic existence. First, that "civilization" was built on the concentration of wealth and exploitation; if their communities were to disengage, they must become as self-sufficient as possible. Second, that the root of wealth concentration was private property; if they wanted to resist the "temptations of the world," they must renounce private ownership. Third, the exploitation of human labor was the root of all alienation (Marx later rediscovered this); if their communities were to restore human dignity, they must center around manual (that is, unalienated) labor. Monastic communities thus renounced private property and the market of goods and labor, often invoking the Lukan vision of "communism" (see Miranda, 1981; Gnuse, 1985; and especially Avila, 1983). The vow of "poverty" actually intended to construct a model that would eradicate poverty.

Today the ever-deepening gulf between rich and poor is a fundamental characteristic of the *locus imperii*. Staggering facts swirl around us: U.S. government figures show that in 1989 the richest 1 percent of the nation's households had a net worth greater than the bottom 90 percent. The world has 157 billionaires and over 100 million homeless. North Americans "spend $5 billion a year on special diets to lower their calorie consumption, while the world's poorest 400 million people are so undernourished they are likely to suffer stunted growth, mental retardation, or death" (Durning, 1990:22). Even mainstream publications are beginning to admit that our economic system is fundamentally flawed (see, e.g., Bartlett and Steele, 1992).

Tragically, however, such facts do not have the power to inspire the majority of First World folk, much less animate us to conspiracy for change. They are too vast, too remote, too abstract. To overcome this paralysis, First World Christians must rediscover the practical, monastic focus on our own socio-economic existence. This is why lifestyle issues are relevant for North Americans. While they should not be a substitute for political engagement with structural forces, they are probably a necessary precondition to it (below, E,1). I will not discuss here the downward mobility and simple living movement that emerged among Christians (and others) in the 1970s, since that ground has been well covered in the literature (see, e.g., Gollwitzer, 1970; Wallis, 1976; Neal, 1977; Finnerty, 1977; Sider, 1977; McGinnis, 1989; and especially Kavanaugh, 1992). I will simply note two aspects of our lifestyle in Bartimaeus and other communities that we came to see as "spiritual disciplines" specific to middle-class whites. One was economic sharing; the other was social relocation into poor neighborhoods.

Those joining Bartimaeus were expected to join our "common purse." They could either divest of their assets, contribute them to the community, or put them in "storage" (retaining ownership but not use). All economic decisions were adjudicated through consensus decision making. Unlike many religious communities, we insisted upon being economically self-supporting; everyone was expected to earn some income. Some of us began a small house-painting collective, while others held outside wage jobs. We produced some of our own food (backyard gardens, animal husbandry, baking) and services (car and house repairs). Like others, we quickly discovered that "simple lifestyle" was a misnomer. Consensual administration of the common purse took much longer; doing things ourselves demanded more time and energy. Yet in small ways we discovered the monastic truth: Because our work was less alienated and alienating, we regained a measure of wholeness. Our alternative vocational patterns mitigated the tyranny of the rat race, and collective household living recovered the traditional practices of extended family and hospitality that have atrophied in modern urban culture. This is what the Catholic Workers call "building a new world in the shell of the old."[15]

Bartimaeus was situated in a poorer urban neighborhood not in order to "help" but so that we middle-class folk could view the world from that space. Given the social divisions of the *locus imperii* (below, Chapter Seven), this step was as important as it was unheroic. It helped us avoid liberal abstractions about poverty and "the poor" and enabled us to build relationships with poor people. The longer we are rooted in such neighborhoods, the more the issues so familiar to these new friends become genuinely ours. Our social change work moves from aid to alliance, from sympathy to solidarity (below, 9,A). Of course, objections can be raised. For example, given the social mobility inherent in our class privilege, we can (and do) move out as easily as we moved into poor neighborhoods. Does this not disrupt, alienate, and even threaten those for whom this is *home?* Only the length of our commitment can resolve questions like these; but at least for us they are the *right* questions.

These two lifestyle disciplines no more make us poor than does the vow of an institutionalized monk today. Nor have any of our communities (or monasteries) achieved significant economic independence from the dominant order. But the disciplines did facilitate two things. First, they made us more inclined to practice literacy concerning the bigger structural issues, because our awareness of the dominant system heightened in direct proportion to our discontinuity with it. In Bartimaeus our practical struggles drove us to deeper social analysis and Bible study (this was the context out of which *Binding the Strong Man* emerged, for example). Our lifestyle was not a political solution to anything, yet it represented a political question to everything, moving our intentions to defect beyond the rhetorical to the concrete. Second, the sweat and tears of constructing a socio-economic alternative, however modest and partial, gave us glimpses of another world, a space of renewal from which we could work for systemic transformation. In deconstructing a lifestyle of "too much" we experienced the surplus of "enough" (J. Taylor, 1975). No one, for example, had to work full-time unless they wished to; this freed us for ministry because together our dollars stretched further than if we had been living separately. Similarly, in our social relocation we found community among the very folk against whom we had been insulated by our suburban upbringings. In short, experimenting with the vow of poverty brought us unexpected richness.

Chastity. Behind traditional vows of celibacy lay the early monks' profound appreciation of the fundamental connection between flesh and spirit. Our communities, for the most part, did not require celibacy; indeed our struggles with sexuality and fidelity were every bit as difficult and ambiguous as they are in any mainstream church. But the spiritual discipline of "chastity" had another meaning for us: It challenged how we relate to the dominant political economy. Economic practices, like sexuality, are not inherently evil; they are intrinsic to our humanity. But our appetites — economic and sexual — are exploited mercilessly by the highly sophisticated techniques of seduction in capitalist culture. We could argue that the dominant economic culture is predicated upon the "rape" of land, resources, and human labor. Our efforts to resist the culture of rape and domination thus constitute a modern practice of chastity. The struggle to resist these powerful temptations calls for the contemplative discipline of dis-illusionment.

Community practices of socio-economic defection quickly deflower our virgin idealism, as we encounter our own captivity and that of others. We middle-class people have been spiritually formed by the capitalist mode of production and are thus hostage to deeply ingrained assumptions about private ownership, freedom, and control. This extends not only to material things but also to use of time, space, vocational options, and, above all, decision making. Community challenges this at a visceral level because we actually (not hypothetically) give up control. Only then do we discover how deeply we are, like the rich man, possessed by our possessions. So while collectivist structures are maddeningly burdensome, they are perhaps the most effective means of revealing to us our addictions and facilitating our recovery. Still, the demons of internalized capitalism are not easily exorcized. We soon learned the truth of Jesus' parable about casting out one unclean spirit only to have "seven spirits more evil than itself return" (Lk 11:24f). The more seriously an alternative is pursued, the deeper the place from which our resistances come. Disciplines that were initially embraced joyfully are later resented. Community members have been astounded to discover that even after ten or fifteen years, the seductive power of the dominant culture has grown not weaker but stronger, that there are reservoirs of selfishness within us yet untapped. We thus came to think of defect-ive living in terms of peeling an onion: Each layer we remove brings more tears.

Another startling discovery was that the community itself inevitably became the lightning rod for the lingering personal anxieties and unresolved family issues of its members. Because communal living re-created patterns of kinship, we each quite unconsciously fell into old patterns of relating that were rooted in our own families of origin. Our community conflicts were often reenactments of individual traumas and family-system dynamics. Unfortunately our strategies of pastoral intervention focused too much on symptoms — strained relationships, fatigue, anger, dissatisfaction — and not enough on root causes. This was in part due to our own immaturity, but our resources were few. The popular psychological axioms of mainstream church and society were usually insufficient to deal with the kind of anguish dredged up by our "aberrant" practices.

Our pastoral sophistication and contemplative commitments must be deepened considerably if we expect to sustain defection in the long run. I believe that it is because of underdevelopment in this area that so few of our communities have been able to last more than a decade, much less intergenerationally. If they do survive, it is usually by taking refuge in either extreme of the inward/outward spectrum. Pastoral/contemplative communities protect their common life from the corrosive influence of the world through withdrawal. Communities of service and/or political struggle experience a high rate of turnover due to burnout. I have become convinced that community is doomed without an accompanying therapeutic process undertaken by each member. This is no doubt why modern Catholic religious communities rely increasingly on psychological testing in their novitiate discernment. Neither politics nor piety can substitute for this inward journey of dis-illusionment. The sheer cultural power of the strong man's system — its murderous apathy and numbing trivialization, its seductive narcissism and insatiable appetites — attests to our need to take the discipline of chastity far more seriously.

Obedience. The vow of obedience was understood by the monks to represent single-minded attentiveness to the will of God. Unfortunately this commitment has often been corrupted by authoritarian hierarchies, as is the case in so many contemporary religious communities. Our communities attempted to embrace inclusive and participative decision making, though this did not preclude the exercise of leadership. For us the commonsense, biblical approach of "gifted diversity" tended to prevail over ideological egalitarianism, in which each person must do everything equally. We understood the vow of obedience, then, more in terms of the struggle against the severe, internalized voice of imperial authority that keeps us politically domesticated. This has led us to disciplines of intervention in and resistance to the body politic.

The invitation to live in some measure of fidelity to the Great Economy is an invitation to noncooperation with the social, political, and economic imperatives of the dominant system. We must understand how "remote" decisions and mystified structures intersect with our lives in order to claim responsibility. For some of our communities the focus has been resistance to racism through practices of integration — Clarence Jordan's Koinonia Partners in Georgia and John Perkins's Voice of Calvary in Mississippi are two classic examples (see D. Lee, 1971; Perkins, 1976). For others it has been solidarity with the victims of U.S.

foreign policy, particularly communities involved in the Sanctuary movement (MacEoin, 1985). For others of us the focus has been resistance to militarism (Dear, 1990; Durland, 1989).

Our resistance to a body politic defined by war involves two fundamental disciplines for our political bodies. A basic "defensive" discipline is tax resistance. Taxes are the mechanism by which the political economy of militarism directly demands our conformity in the *locus imperii*. This is thus a logical point to take individual responsibility. Tax resistance is an act of citizenship many of us believe to be more meaningful than voting. Some noncooperate by living on less than a taxable income, others of us refuse to pay all or part of our tax obligation, funneling the money into alternative funds that support work for peace and justice. The basic "offensive" discipline tries to unmask the geography of militarism through public witness at military-industrial sites. I will have more to say about our experiments with nonviolent direct action later (below, 8,E). Phil Berrigan and Liz McAlister (1989) suggest that the vow of obedience must lead to civil disobedience; it is "the time's discipline."[16]

This brief sketch can hardly do justice to our community experiments in discontinuity, or to the many stories that range from the deeply redemptive to the downright ridiculous. But one thing is certain: We have consistently underestimated the difficulties of sustaining alternatives that attempt to counter the grain of the dominant culture at almost every point. So our experience has been repeatedly tempered by demise and failure (*BSM:*454ff). How often we have become disenchanted with the demands of recovery and with each other, how loudly the trumpets of the dominant culture have sounded, and how quickly the walls of our little communities have crumbled! The socialization of generations is not undone in a few years — nor in a lifetime. The story of Bartimaeus community is over, and we are a family in diaspora. But the story of our namesake remains as an invitation to discipleship. We must continue to revise the ancient spiritual disciplines of the church, for we have only begun to experiment with discontinuity in the *locus imperii*.

E. "YOU LACK ONE THING": FROM PENANCE TO REPARATION

How have First World communities remained captive to personalistic expressions of responsibility, and what are the more political dimensions of repentance?

Dorothee Soelle and others are right when they argue that communities of resistance are how we "who are members of the white bourgeoisie — those who normally participate in oppression and profit from exploitation — participate in liberation struggles" (1979:178). Yet there are serious criticisms of the movement I have just described. Let us look at the three of the most substantive objections.

1. Is Defection a Middle-Class Luxury?

The first objection arises from a psycho-cultural critique of our historical context. It contends that given the ever-intensifying alienation inherent in capitalist culture, communal living may be self-defeating. Variations of this concern have been voiced by several veterans of the Christian community movement, most succinctly by Richard Rohr, a pastoral leader at New Jerusalem in Cincinnati and now animator at the Center for Action and Contemplation in Albuquerque. Rohr believes that the unrealistic expectations of intimacy generated by our narcissistic culture are impossible for community to fulfill. Our communitarian reconstructions of extended family — inherently fragile for reasons already discussed — simply cannot bear the overwhelming intrapsychic and interpersonal needs that people bring because of the epidemic dysfunction and breakdown in postindustrial family life.

It is indeed the case that our experiments with large group households were qualified failures, and that our communities found themselves mired in pastoral maintenance work that seemed to grow exponentially. Rohr's diagnosis is too widely confirmed in our experience to be dismissed. Whether or not it is fatal to community is debatable, however. Perhaps we were just too ambitious and need to be more judicious in understanding the constraints of psychic and physical space. Should we concede, as the French sociologist Louis Damont put it, that Western *homo hierarchicus* is too alienated to recover *homo comunitas?* Or are there less problematic strategies to restore a modicum of collective life and intimacy in the twilight of empire?

A second objection contends that communities of discontinuity, far from being too difficult for middle-class folk, are too easy. This view sees downward mobility as simply another example of those with race and class privilege confusing the personal and the political. It was given systematic articulation by Jens Harms at a World Council of Churches consultation on the church, development issues, and lifestyle strategies in 1977. Harms, a Marxist, argued that the "new life style campaign" pursued by certain sectors of the First World ecumenical movement is "clothed in individualist, penitential garb" and does nothing to challenge the overdetermining relations of production in capitalism (1977:18). Let us consider briefly two of the major problems he raises.

First, Harms contends that efforts "to reduce the total amount consumed by society through individual self discipline and asceticism" are restricted to those "who have an assured place both in the social structure and in the incomes pyramid." These "can afford a new life style, a different way of handling money, time and their fellow human beings because of their secure position in the production process," whereas the economic lives of working-class and poor people are far too precarious to experiment (ibid:5f). This has certainly been borne out in our experience. Most First World alternative lifestyle groups and communities have been decidedly white and middle class. Moreover, most of our communities began in the relatively prosperous 1960s and 1970s; few have come together, while many have fallen apart, in the more economically precarious 1980s and 1990s. In our circles it was not necessarily the case that our lifestyle was enabled by "secure incomes" (no one in Bartimaeus held a white-collar, salaried job with benefits, for example). It is nevertheless very much the case that we always retain the option of returning to our "assured place" in the socio-economic structure (though admittedly the longer we remain defect-ive, the harder this becomes).

Ironically a similar dismissal comes from the Right, which charges that re-pentant strategies are merely expressions of middle-class guilt and do nothing to change anything but the participants' conscience. But these objections lose their force if we acknowledge that discontinuity is a spiritual discipline of repen-tance shaped specifically for the inheritors of First World entitlement. Artificial structures of economic sharing or extended family are hardly necessary among peoples in less industrialized social formations. Third World base communi-ties are not nearly so preoccupied with lifestyle issues. But such contextual disparities do not relieve us of the responsibility to find specific strategies of intervention appropriate to the pathologies of our dominant culture addictions and denial.

Harms goes on, however, to dismiss this tactic by employing the categorical imperative (judging the ethical character of an action on the basis of what would happen "if everyone behaved this way"). He paints a very dark picture of "the consequences a different consumer behavior would have for ourselves and for the people of the Third World whom [it] is also intended to help" (ibid:6). This is because widespread consumer change, "if the existing production conditions are maintained ... produces the crisis of underconsumption," which would result in an overall "reduction in the social product and therefore a lowering of the in-come of households" (ibid:7). Such structural economic contraction would both reduce the resources available for social causes and negatively affect those most socio-economically vulnerable. The State would inevitably intervene to protect the interests of capital, and worse, "history shows that economic crisis can rein-force reactionary political movements concerned to preserve ancient privileges and dominant institutions" (ibid:10). Thus, Harms concludes, the "campaign for a 'New Life Style' remains purely moralising in character, since it does not direct its attention to the sphere of production which is the decisive centre of capitalism" (ibid:8). Even if it were effective, it would create the opposite socio-political results it hopes for.

Again, however, these are the very arguments used by the Right to discour-age disruptive economic tactics such as boycotts. How often did we hear how boycotts directed against companies doing business with South Africa "only hurt those they try to help"? In fact Harms is merely reflecting orthodox Marxism's skepticism of any praxis other than class struggle. "The classic organization of the workers' movement still seems the best guarantee of helping the op-pressed — wherever they are found — to a worthier human existence" (ibid:18). One can hardly dispute that "the equalization of wages seems ... the most viable way of achieving greater justice in our economic system" (ibid:16), which is why class alliances remain key to any broad political movement for change in industrial capitalism (below, 9,D). But must this *preclude* strategies that seek to liberate immediate social space as part of the wider struggle? What about ethnic identity movements among Latino, African, and Asian Americans, for example, which are predicated upon cultural "withdrawal" and resistance? Ward Churchill and others (1983) have strongly criticized leftists who dismiss Native American sovereignty movements as regressive. In the context of a capitalist culture that aims to preclude any and all critical political practice by socializing us as consumers, Lakota traditionalism, black nationalism, and white communalism all have subversive power.

It is easy to be contemptuous of the contradiction-riddled efforts of middle-class people to change their mode of social existence. The fact remains that, as Marcuse put it, "no matter how great the distance between the middle-class revolt in the metropoles and the life-and-death struggle of the wretched of the earth — common to them is the depth of the Refusal." That Refusal must at some point take practical shape in our lives. True, no matter how much our lifestyles may defect from "normal" consumer habits, Harms is right that "social institutions are, to the individual, public property which cannot be controlled by any change in individual behaviour but only by the creation of a political will" (ibid:17). That is why we see repentant lifestyle as neither a political solution nor a substitute for structural redistribution of wealth. It is nothing more or less than a spiritual discipline, a "necessary but not sufficient" condition for the privileged if we are to sustain a more strategic engagement with the dominant system.

The third objection to our lifestyle practices of defection I take to be the most compelling. This is the accurate criticism that Christians have not understood the relationship between repentance and reparation. We peace and justice activists, for example, tend to have a good grasp of the current ordering of power but not its historical construction. Yet defecting from our immediate entitlements does little to deconstruct generations of inheritance upon which our privilege is based, nor does it repair that legacy of oppression. I might repudiate certain vocational, financial, or locational options. What I cannot lose is my unearned birthright status as a member of the managerial class, a patrimony constructed upon the business transactions, real estate deals, and capital accumulation of my ancestors. Thus my spiritual disciplines of discontinuity, while important for me, can hardly be expected to impress those who have inherited the other side of that same historical legacy: displacement, loss of sovereignty, disenfranchisement. We must ask, then: Are our communities attacking the roots of the system or only severing branches? Are we *repentant,* or merely *penitent?*

This brings us to the third of the disciplines discussed in Part Two. Critical literacy and dis-illusionment can empower us to live defectively; but only revision can begin to heal the historical narrative of exploitation that victims and victimizers alike have inherited. In conclusion to this chapter I thus return to the most demanding of the revisionist disciplines spoken of in the last chapter (above, 5,E): reparation. We simply cannot get around Jesus' discipleship instructions to the rich: We lack only one thing — to follow we must *give back.*

Reparation is the only practice that can convert hearts hardened from a long history of theft and domination and that can forge reconciliation.

2. "Salted with Fire": Redistributive Justice

It is significant that Mark's Jesus closes his strange discourse on amputation with an equally strange exhortation to healing. "Everyone will be salted with fire. Salt is good; but if it loses its saltiness, how will we season it? Maintain salt among yourselves and be at peace with each other" (9:49f). Salt and fire (perhaps references to ancient medicinal remedies for amputation; *BSM:*264) apparently allude to the painful business of reconciliation. Mark, like Isaiah, understood that the restoration of justice is a precondition to forgiveness (Mk 4:12).

Forgiveness is something we the inheritors of privilege can neither ask for nor expect from the inheritors of marginalization. We can only create the conditions for reconciliation, and we do this by practicing reparation as a good faith sign of our repentance. Thus Twelve Step practice stipulates that we must "make a list of all persons we have harmed, and become willing to make amends to them all; make direct amends wherever possible, except when to do so would injure them or others." Today in the *locus imperii* we must explore meaningful ways of redistributing wealth and power in conversation with those who have been defrauded in order to create justice in the present and to heal the injustices of the past. If then they initiate a process of reconciliation, it is their gift to us, since nothing can truly restore what they have lost through victimization and violence.

During Quincentenary commemorations at the Nevada test site (above, 5,F), a European American announced she had purchased land not far from where protests are held. Part of this property she was putting at the service of ongoing organizing; the rest she was returning to the Shoshone people. A dramatic healing service followed (Barfield, 1992). This personal gesture of reparation was exemplary; but the real task is political. In the *locus imperii* this will be difficult, since the politics of forgiveness are so contaminated. Here criminal acts in high places are officially pardoned in order to "clear up" historical guilt. This was recently demonstrated by President Bush's 1992 Christmas Eve grant of clemency to key figures in the Iran-Contra scandal (Schneider, 1993) and by U.S. silence while the right-wing Salvadoran government offered blanket amnesty to death squad murderers (Wilkinson, 1993). In such an environment, apologies can only be understood as conscience-acquitting rhetoric, and pleas for reconciliation as petitions for exoneration. Only concrete reparation will speak in a way that can be heard by the victimized. Sadly we First World Christians have scarcely begun to think about these matters. There are movements, however, that are pioneering reparative politics in the U.S. I will look briefly at two: the successful Japanese American advocacy of redress for wartime internment, and the struggle of various indigenous groups for treaty rights and sovereignty. Because in both cases they are initiatives by the victimized, they are all the more instructive to the entitled.

The U.S. peace movement has kept the pain of history alive by regularly remembering the anniversary of the dropping of atomic bombs on Hiroshima and Nagasaki and has even built bridges of solidarity to Japanese *hibakusha.* Organizing is already underway for major "remember and repent" pilgrimages around the fiftieth anniversary in 1995 (Alperovitz, 1992). I have been involved in many such public liturgies and have experienced the moving commemorations held each August in the cities of Hiroshima and Nagasaki. Our efforts have been appropriate. Why, then, at gatherings held throughout 1992, organized by Japanese Americans commemorating their internment in U.S. concentration camps during World War II, were peace activists nowhere to be seen? This was troubling to me but only confirmed that the story of internment is one of our truly hidden histories.

Even before World War II, U.S. Nikkei (citizens or permanent residents of Japanese descent) had been subject to social, political, and economic discrimination. In California, Japanese farmers were growing almost 90 percent of the commercial produce despite operating only 4 percent of the farmland. Anglo resentment led to segregation and anticitizenship legislation, beginning with the Asian Exclusion Immigration Act of 1924. This racism culminated on February 19, 1942, ten weeks after Imperial Japan's attack on Pearl Harbor, when President Roosevelt signed Executive Order 9066 authorizing the removal of all Nikkei from the West Coast. The internment process began in March, and by August more than 120,000 Nikkei had been removed to ten camps for "security" reasons, though no one was ever charged with sabotage or espionage. The homes and property they left behind were sold or confiscated; while en route they were corralled in inhumane conditions. In Los Angeles, for example, internees were forced to stay in horse stalls at the Santa Anita racetrack. They finally arrived in concentration camps with names that still strike terror and grief in the hearts of those who survived — Poston, Arizona; Heart Mountain, Wyoming; Topaz, Utah; Manzanar, California. There, behind guards and barbed wire, Japanese Americans lived in cramped and cold quarters for an average term of three and a half years. The last camp, at Tule Lake, where resisters were incarcerated, was not closed until March 1946. The whole project was what writer John Hersey called a "mistake of terrifically horrible proportions." Sadly, however, few churches resisted, a notable exception being Quakers.[17]

After the war the internment experience disappeared into the silence of dismembered history, too embarrassing for mainstream culture and too traumatic for survivors to talk about. Pain and shame weighed heavily on the Nikkei, until many of their children began to call for the legacy to be unsilenced during the Asian American consciousness movement of the late 1960s. The reparation movement began symbolically on a cold December day in 1969 with the first pilgrimage to the site of Manzanar, in the eastern Sierra foothills of California. A decade later the movement had begun to achieve critical mass; Seriguchi and Abe describe the moment:

Many Seattle Nikkei had lived by a promise never again to set foot in the fairgrounds, race tracks and exhibition halls that were once temporary detention camps. But on Thanksgiving weekend of 1978, more than two thousand Nikkei and their friends joined a four-mile car caravan for a Day of Remembrance at the Western Washington Fairgrounds. Nisei . . . who had never talked about camp to their Sansei children started talking. . . . "Camp Harmony," once home to 7,200 Seattleites, was the scene of a flag-raising by Nisei veterans of WWII, a community potluck dinner, and exhibits of camp artworks and photos. Charles Royer, mayor of Seattle, swept away the words of his predecessor [in 1942 Seattle's mayor publicly supported evacuation], saying, "It's time to hold this country's feet to the fires of the past. . . . " Out of the chemistry of that day the internment conferences were born. (1980:3)

Shattering the silence and revising this painful story gave birth to reparative politics.

As a Congressional Commission on Wartime Relocation and Internment of Civilians (CWRIC) held nationwide hearings in 1980, the National Coalition for Redress/Reparations (NCRR) was organized to begin waging the political struggle. In its December 1982 report the CWRIC recommended that Congress: (1) issue a formal apology to the 120,313 Japanese American internees for the unconstitutional violation of their civil liberties; (2) authorize redress payments of $20,000 each to surviving internees; (3) establish an educational foundation to support efforts aimed at prevention of recurrence of such violations; (4) establish a $5 million fund for Aleuts evacuated during the war; and (5) grant presidential pardons to Japanese Americans convicted of violating evacuation orders (Nakagawa, 1992:12). After years of intense lobbying and political advocacy by the NCRR and its allies, and with the help of related legal petitions by three internee resisters seeking annulment of criminal convictions, a reparation bill was signed into law in August of 1988.

The government's gesture of reparation does not undo the pain of this past. But when the children of error acknowledge responsibility, it helps clean the wound and facilitate healing. During the fiftieth anniversary commemorations I found myself deeply affected by the pain and power of revised history that leads to reparation. I witnessed the unashamed tears of a survivor relating her story in front of a huge audience; walked alone through the quiet back room of a small church where Japanese American congregants had displayed their personal mementos from the camps; listened to stories of resistance from Frank Emi, a noncooperator who spent time in federal prison. It caused me to realize that "Tom the gardener" — who lovingly tended my mother's roses when I was young — was one of the many interned Japanese American men who afterward could get work only in manual labor because of lingering racism and suspicion. Today the struggle over this legacy continues for Japanese Americans. Vigilance is required to ensure that reparation payments are made; annual pilgrimages are made to camp sites; educational work goes on. This is best seen in Bacon Sakatani's lonely campaign of revision.

Sakatani, a survivor of the Heart Mountain relocation camp, could not abide a memorial plaque at the site by the American Legion in 1963, because it devised the memory of what occurred there. It proclaimed, among other things, that the internees were "loosely confined" and lived under "modern" conditions with "first rate schooling." In response, Sakatani organized his fellow alumni of the Heart Mountain school's "class of 1947" to put up an alternative plaque in 1985, setting the record straight with *their* truth. But Sakatani's war of myths was not over, for the same local residents who had erected the original plaque were intending to build a museum on the site. As he prepared to do battle with them, Sakatani made a trip to Montana, where he had heard that Indian people were contesting the National Park Service over the Custer Battleground National Monument. There Sakatani saw the official glorifications of Custer's heroism as well as the alternative monument erected by native people in 1988. The latter read: "In honor of our Indian patriots who fought and defeated the U.S. Cavalry in order to save our women and children from mass-murder, and in doing so preserving rights to our homelands, treaties and sovereignty — June 25, 1988, G. Magpie, Cheyenne." Sakatani decided to go visit this Indian elder, and writes: "George Magpie gave me the inspiration to speak out at my Wyoming meeting and not be pushed around" (1992:6f).

Truly, as Grayce Uyehara writes, "Redress was not a Japanese American issue, but an American one" (Deming, 1992:29). The Japanese American struggle gave new impetus to the widely ignored African American demands for reparation, for example.[18] It is, as Edison Tomimaro Uno put it twenty years ago, a matter of repentance:

> America had sinned, had been sinning for nearly a century, and the wages of sin is spiritual death.... Racism, economic and political opportunism were the root causes of this crime that is now a part of our American heritage. This, our legacy, is a reminder to all Americans that it can happen again. The Japanese American heritage is no exception to the experience of all minorities and oppressed people who know the bitter sting and enduring stigma of hate, fear and despair in a land of abundance.... Justice was trampled upon, and it is a responsibility all Americans must share. (Conrat, 1992:15f)

Indeed what about reparation for even greater historical crimes, such as the dispossession of Native America?

In the U.S., 60 percent of all families on Indian reservations are living below the poverty level, with 80 percent unemployment, while urban Indians lead all categories of social deprivation. How do we begin to repair such massive historical injustice? Journalist Alastair Reid relates a suggestion advanced by Dominican economist and historian Bernardo Vega during the Quincentenary: "since the Club of Paris, an organization that keeps a supervisory eye on Third

World debt, was already excusing the debts of African countries, it should make the year 1992 memorable by wiping off the slate all the European debt accumulated by the countries of Latin America, as partial compensation for the wealth that had been extracted from that region, starting in 1492" (1992:67). Such debt forgiveness as structural adjustment would seem to capture both the theological and political character of our task (see Branford and Kucinski, 1988). This, in turn, suggests that North Americans should look seriously at the matter of returning lands stolen from the First Peoples. We could begin by supporting current United Nations efforts to catalog treaty violations against indigenous people by national governments worldwide (Herscher, 1991; Jaimes, 1992).

Given our role in the colonization, displacement, and dispossession of native peoples, churches have a particular responsibility. In this spirit, the National Council of Churches in a May 1990 resolution called for "the church to reflect on its role in that historical tragedy, to repent of its complicity and, in pursuing a healing process, to move forward in our witness for justice and peace." Yet despite a laundry list of recommendations for action, not one strategy for reparation was included. Denominations have preferred proclamations of penance. The General Council of the United Church of Canada, for example, requested forgiveness of a gathering of native elders in August 1986 but offered no concrete redress. The following year the Sixteenth General Synod of the United Church of Christ in the U.S. acknowledged that because of "its long involvement with Indian people [it] bears a heavy burden of responsibility — as part of the dominant culture — for the ongoing injustice and religious imperialism that have been so disruptive to the inherent values of Indian life and culture." Later that year an ecumenical group of church leaders offered apologies to "The Tribal Councils and Traditional Spiritual Leaders of the Indian and Eskimo Peoples of the Pacific Northwest." In both these cases, however, the only specific gesture was a promise to help in the struggle for Indian religious freedom (Fox, 1988:247ff).

Closer to the mark was a resolution at the UCC's Eighteenth General Synod supporting the right of "self-governance for native Hawaiians." It stated in part: "the United Church of Christ has yet to acknowledge that some of its missionary descendants were party to an illegal overthrow of the Hawaiian Monarchy in 1893. . . . With the coming hundredth anniversary of that sad historic event for Hawaiians, an honest appraisal and acknowledgement of the Congregational missionaries' descendants' role in it should be made, because our Church needs to bring that matter to some appropriate closure." But while invoking solidarity with the growing movement for Hawaiian sovereignty, the church remained conspicuously silent on the demand by many in that very movement to restore some of the considerable UCC lands and assets to Hawaiians. The 1993 centenary of the overthrow of Liliuokalani's monarchy has sharpened these questions dramatically.[19]

What represents appropriate closure to historical injustice can finally be determined only by the disinherited. Indigenous peoples may not want development aid, for example; they may simply wish to keep their land and be left alone (Verhelst, 1990:43ff). It is true that restorative gestures will necessarily be symbolic to some degree. Returning land to Native Hawaiians cannot mend the atrocities and betrayals of Great Mahele of the nineteenth century, just as belated cash payments cannot return what was lost by Japanese American internees. This does not mean, however, that gestures cannot be *substantive* — in fact, they must be. As therapists point out, in order for reparation to be therapeutic for the culpable party, it must be felt. And the entitled feel it most when the disinherited demand back "title" to our inheritance. Sooner or later, therefore, our churches will need to reckon with a reparation that turns over land and/or assets. Tragically, the attitudes of mainstream church leaders toward this prospect appear to be much the same as that of mainstream exegetes toward the biblical Jubilee — the idea lends a nice rhetorical flourish, but they just can't seem to imagine how it could actually happen. Yet if we Christians can't be "salted with fire" and have the courage to embody a practice of reparation, who in the *locus imperii* will?

"America is in deep trouble," writes anthropologist Marvin Harris in his fascinating survey of cultural deterioration in the U.S.; "but let no one suppose that our plight cannot get a whole lot worse" (1981:174). The seams of our multicultural society are continuously strained to the tearing point because, fearful and ashamed of the past, we do not have the courage to admit that the fabric was long ago torn asunder in order that we might set about repairing it. With reactionary politics again on the rise, we who are entitled will face an ever-starker choice between the path of protecting our privilege and the more demanding and difficult path of redistributive justice. Without it, our rhetoric of reconciliation will remain empty; the longer we opt for cheap grace, the more costly real forgiveness will become.[20] Reparation will not become any less of a heresy in *locus imperii*. But neither will it become any less of a condition for *our* discipleship.

NOTES

1. The root of inheritance (Gk *klēronomeō*) is *klēros*, a plot of land (see Kittel, III:758f), which in some Hellenistic literature is synonymous with *ktēma*, "property," which appears in Mk 10:22 (ibid:762). Writes Foerster: "In the papyri *klēronomos* denotes specifically the heir of real property or goods, whereas he who simply receives movable property is never called by that name...The term is lined with essential possession" (ibid:769). The insurgent tenants in Jesus' parable of the vineyard (12:1ff) thus try to kill the *klēronomos* in order to wrest the *klēronomis* from the absentee landlord.

2. Thus the refrain of Mark's discipleship catechism in which this episode appears is "the last will be first." The social dimensions of this reversal is illustrated in the preceding object lessons about women and children, the most marginalized classes in patriarchal society: "Whoever does not receive the kingdom of God like a child will not enter it" (10:15). The story of the rich man illustrates the economic dimensions of this reversal, and the episode that follows it, the political ones (10:38–44). Since kingship means the politics of domination, argues Jesus, there should be no kings among the people of God (10:43). In this sense, Jesus' proclamation of the kingdom even more fundamentally reasserted the ancient vision of the sole sovereignty of God — i.e., that

place where there are no kings (see below, 11,C). On apocalyptic as social reversal see below, 12,B.

3. For a brief overview of Sabbath/Jubilee see Gnuse (1985:32ff; also Sider, 1977:87ff); for a more thorough examination see Ringe (1985). Most of the debate about Jesus centers around the Lukan tradition of his inaugural sermon and its use of Second Isaiah (Lk 4:16ff). See Yoder for the most programmatic assertion that Jesus came to restore/renew Jubilee economics (1972:64ff); Massyngbaerde Ford (1984:53ff) and Pilgrim (1981:69ff) are more equivocal. Sloan offers a longer treatment (1977). For the Jubilee as background to the Lord's Prayer see Crosby (1977:136ff).

4. "Sin" (Gk *hamartia*) appears only in Mk 1:4f and 2:5–10. In correspondence theologian John Pairman Brown responded to *BSM:*154ff: "Since the vocabulary of debt (*opheilei*, etc.) does not appear in Mark readers will be puzzled. What you don't explain is that in the underlying Aramaic 'your sins are forgiven' (2:5) is 'your debts are cancelled.' ... Matthew [6:12] in his exegesis follows the Talmudic idea that sin is a debt we contract with God as creditor.... Aramaic 'debts' is a general term covering both the burdens of oppression and guilt. But the obvious meaning is the political class-based one that the church has ignored."

5. Note the contrast between the "anxieties of this age" (Gk *tou aiōnos*) and the promise of eternal life "in the age to come" (Gk *en tō aiōni tō erchomenō*, 10:30). The fundamental connection between the sower parable image and the rich man story was keenly understood in the early tradition. For example, the *Similitudes of the Shepherd of Hermes* makes it explicit, clearly reflecting class tensions within the late first–early second century church and even suggesting the politics of reparation:

> The thistles are the rich, and the thorns are those who are mixed up with various affairs of business. These then who are engaged in many and various businesses do not cleave to the servants of God, but are choked by their work and go astray. And the rich cleave with difficulty to the servants of God, fearing that they will be asked for something by them. Such then "will enter with difficulty the kingdom of God." For just as it is difficult to walk with naked feet among thistles, so it is also "difficult" for such people "to enter the kingdom of God." But for all these there is repentance, but it must be speedy, that they may now retrace their days and the omissions of former years, and do some good. (Crossan, 1986:149)

See the midrash on the rich man story attributed by Origen to the Gospel of the Nazoreans (*BSM:*289). Jas 4:1–3 appears to have been addressed to a wealthy community suffering from the ravages of addictive-compulsive behavior (Tamez, 1990; Maynard-Reid, 1987).

6. Smith and Zepp write: "Although the doctrine of the kingdom of God did not occupy an explicit place in King's writings, it was obviously implicit in everything he said and did. The explanation ... lies in the fact that the kingdom of God and the Beloved Community were synonymous in King's thought.... In the Judeo-Christian tradition the Messianic Era and the kingdom of God have included a concern for communal life, corporate faith, social justice, and a hope for a transformed society. King drew upon all of these themes in his description of the Beloved Community" (1987:129f). King's metaphor envisions a social space and time in which enemies are reconciled.

7. This notion finds biblical echo in the Pauline vision of Christ's "administration [Gk *oikonomia*] of unity of all things in heaven and earth when the *kairos* is full" (Eph 1:10). On this text and its parallels with Mk 1:15, see Myers (1980a:18).

8. The obvious representative is Walter Rauschenbusch, whose *Theology for the Social Gospel,* formulated during World War I, in many respects still endures today. He

attempted to reassert and broaden notions of sin (1945:31ff) and certainly took both evil (69ff) and the kingdom of God (131ff) seriously as historical forces. But anything smacking of apocalyptic dualism in the biblical tradition he dismissed out of hand: Jesus "was not at all of the same family type as those who wrote and re-wrote the apocalyptic literature" (158). The rhetoric of repentance and conversion, while mentioned by Rauschenbusch in both individual and collective terms (95ff), was understood in terms of "higher social consciousness" (108), enlightened "cooperation" (112f), and the embrace of "real democracy" (117). His idealistic, almost Wilsonian, optimism is reflected in his notion of the kingdom of God as a "vital and organizing energy now at work in humanity. Its capacity to save the social order depends on its pervasive presence within the social organism. Every institutional foothold gained gives a purchase for attacking the next vantage-point. Where a really Christian type of religious life is created, the intellect and its education are set free.... Where religion and the intellect combine, the foundation is laid for political democracy" (165). On parallels between the social gospel and liberation theology see Sanks, 1980.

9. Here the representative is Reinhold Niebuhr, whose impressive opus similarly endures today. His most programmatic work, *Moral Man and Immoral Society,* written in 1932, took direct aim at Rauschenbusch: "The demand of religious moralists that nations subject themselves to 'the law of Christ' is an unrealistic demand, and the hope that they will do so is a sentimental one" (1960:75). But his heightened sense of human sinfulness caused him to despair of substantive transformation; repentance was internalized again as "the self's encounter with God in which the pretensions and pride of the self are broken and it is set free of self and sin" (1961:22). The messianic practice of Jesus was dismissed as "a completely unprudential rigorism" (1956:47). Niebuhr's captivity to cold war dualism can be seen in his preface to the reissue of *An Interpretation of Christian Ethics:* "Our nation has grown into the most powerful nation of the free world and carries tremendous responsibility in the contest between freedom and communist tyranny. Every resource for the performance of our resistibilities must be made available to this nation. One such resource would be a relevant Christian faith which is not debilitated by either complacency or by irresponsible idealism which ... forgets that our immediate responsibility is to avoid catastrophe and to secure a tolerable peace in a world filled with acute tensions" (1956:10).

10. The more elaborate Q version portrays John's preaching as taking dead aim at those who enjoy inherited entitlement: "Who warned you of the anguish to come? Bear fruits that befit repentance! Do not begin to say to yourselves, 'We have Abraham as our ancestor,' for I tell you God is able from these stones to raise up children to Abraham. Even now the ax is laid to the root of the trees" (Lk 3:8f). There follows a call to concrete reparation: "Let the one with two coats share with the one who has none." (Lk 3:10–14). This Q tradition offers a *radical* analysis of the system — "laid to the *root*" — concluding that insofar as the system is "unfruitful" it must "be cut down and thrown into the fire." This is a call to have the courage to admit failure, to deconstruct what is not working, to repair what has been broken, and to reconstruct along more fundamentally sound lines. But in the *locus imperii* such discourse is dismissed as irresponsible, revolutionary ranting.

11. According to Markan narrative syntax, there are three main things that scandalize — that is, that cause us to "fall from the Way." One is persecution, or pressure from the State (4:17; 14:27). The second is pressure from the kinship system (6:3; cf 3:21–35). The third is denial (14:29). This is insightful; for throughout the history of

the church, socio-political oppression, family suppression, and intrapsychic repression indeed have driven Christians to apostasy.

12. Of course even this is an illusion. "In the competitive capitalist system the consumer is not the master he is made out to be in the paradigms of economic theory and in the ideology of day-to-day politics," writes Harms; "it is the producer who is sovereign, with the technological structure determining the production plans" (1977:12). Since we have only the fiction of choice anyway, to stop "choosing" becomes the only genuine choice (above, 3.C).

13. A recent example of this in the nuclear weapons industry was the halfhearted attempt by the government to prosecute environmental violations at the Department of Energy's Rocky Flats plant in Colorado. A federal grand jury was so infuriated by one branch of government's unwillingness to prosecute another, and by the refusal to determine responsibility, that they mutinied, issuing an independent report that created a storm of political controversy. This fascinating story is told by Barry Siegel (1993).

14. For a good historical survey see Rausch (1990). On the struggle to dis-establish the church see D. J. Hall (1975:128ff). For an interpretation of the Christian base community movement in Brazil see Barbé (1987); in Nicaragua, Anitua (1982). On communities of faith and resistance in the Asian context see Digan (1984). For an account of the alternative Christian community movement in Britain in the 1970s see D. Clark (1977); in Australia see Gill (1990). An analogous impulse has occasionally found significant secular expression in U.S. history, including in our generation the counterculture of the 1960s and 1970s. On the broader social philosophies and practices of utopian communitarianism see Richter (1971).

15. Those embracing communistic economics are a tiny minority today among Christians concerned with peace and justice. Two other examples of economic discipline are worth mentioning, therefore, which represent different ends of a spectrum. The Church of the Savior's Ministry of Money attempts to disciple affluent people in responsible stewardship and includes exposure tours to poor countries and suggestions for personal economic partnerships. This approach explicitly recognizes the problem of "wealth addiction" (see Slater, 1983). Its interventionary strategies, however, which do not require divestment or redistribution, may only be addressing symptoms. The Twomey Center for Peace through Justice in New Orleans, whose *Blueprint for Social Justice* is a valuable resource, believes Christians should focus on building and supporting alternative economic institutions, particularly credit unions. As Caroline Rioux puts it, "Like so many other things under capitalism, there are few institutions you can trust unless you create them yourselves" (1992:6). Such efforts, while still limited in scope, are important institutional complements to lifestyle strategies.

16. On the theory and practice of tax resistance see Durland (1982) and Hedeman (1986); the best resource organization is the Conscience and Military Tax Campaign (Seattle, WA). On civil disobedience at nuclear weapons sites see also Myers (1981); Wallis (1987); Laffin and Montgomery (1987); Douglass (1972); Kellermann (1991).

17. Two basic volumes I would commend to those unfamiliar with this story are Conrat (1992) and Armor and Wright (1989). The latter includes Hersey's narrative and long-suppressed photographs by Ansel Adams. On the "no-no boys" — those who refused to take the loyalty oath in the camps — see Nakagawa (1992) and Moffat (1993). On churches in the camps see Suzuki (1979); on Quaker aid to internees see the articles in Deming (1992).

18. There have been demands for compensation for the criminal legacy of slavery ever since the U.S. reneged on its Reconstruction promise of forty acres and a mule.

Currently the National Coalition of Blacks for Reparations in America (Washington, DC) has worked with congressmen John Conyers and Ron Dellums in building support for HR 1684, longstanding legislation concerning African American reparation. On parallels between the internal exile of Japanese Americans and Indians, see Drinnon (1987).

19. On the current state of the Hawaiian sovereignty movement see Ahuna-Ka'ai'ai et al (1993). On the debate within the UCC see the collection of articles that appeared in a special issue of the denominational journal, *New Conversations* (Roberts, 1993).

20. As I was completing this manuscript I received a copy of the "Birmingham Confession" of the 1992 Cooperative Baptist Fellowship. This statement apologized for the Southern Baptist Convention's failure to reach out to the Sixteenth Street Baptist Church in Birmingham, Alabama, after it was firebombed in September 1963, killing four young girls. The confession, being distributed by the Baptist Peace Fellowship for wider endorsement, provides a model for acknowledgment not only of historical culpability but continuing complicity in the sin of racism as well. Unfortunately it asks for forgiveness, then speaks of repentance and restoration. Moreover the only commitment it makes is "to sustaining the struggle against racism for all the days of our lives" — not very specific, and not very concrete. We have a long way to go.

7

"Do You See These Great Structures?"

Relocation

You hammer against the walls of your house. You tap the walls, lightly, everywhere... you know what to listen for. Some of the walls are bearing walls; they have to stay, or everything will fall down. Other walls can go with impunity; you can hear the difference. Unfortunately, it is often a bearing wall that has to go.... Knock it out. Duck. Courage utterly opposes the bold hope that this is such fine stuff that the work needs it, or the world.

Annie Dillard,
The Writing Life

The moral bankruptcy of contemporary American society is found, in part, in the vast chasm which separates the conditions of material well being, affluence, power and privilege of a small elite from the whole spectrum of America's communities. The evil in our world is politically and socially engineered, and its products are poverty, homelessness, illiteracy, political subservience, race discrimination and gender domination.... Paul Robeson reminds us that we must "take a stand," not simply dare to dream.

Manning Marable,
Black America

    "Look, what magnificent structures!" (Mk 13:1). The disciples cower, fascinated, before the Temple edifice. It was indeed a magnificent structure, bigger than life, architectural symbol of their social project. But Mark's Jesus refuses to be impressed, for he understands what they do not. This House would have to

200

be deconstructed in order to make possible a more human society more pleasing to the true "owner of the House" (13:35).

"If a house is divided against itself, that house cannot stand" (3:25). Jesus' master political metaphor to describe his messianic mission is the struggle over a "House divided." He introduces it in his very first parable, which narrates an act of breaking into and entering a "strong man's house" in order to "loot his goods" (3:25; *BSM:*164ff). Later in Mark's story, this "divided House" is revealed to be none other than the Jerusalem Temple itself. Intended as "a home for all peoples" (11:17a), the *House* had instead become a "den" where criminal authorities practiced exploitation (11:17b). Jesus there performs his most dramatic exorcism, symbolically "looting" those who have looted the people (11:15f; *BSM:*299ff). Shortly thereafter he predicts its dismantling.

"Do you see these great structures? There will be not one stone left on top of another which will not be overthrown!" (13:2). This call to overthrow (Gk *katalythē*) the system would be used to convict Jesus in court (14:58) and would earn the scorn of those who preside at his execution (15:29). Yet as Jesus expires on the cross, "the curtain of the Temple was torn in two, from top to bottom" (15:38). Sometimes bearing walls must go, says Annie Dillard.

Christ has made us one, having broken down the dividing wall of hostility (Eph 2:15f). The conviction that dividing walls had been torn down by Jesus lay at the heart of the earliest church. Mark's sign of the torn curtain at the apocalyptic moment of the cross was later reiterated by one of Paul's disciples: "Christ abolished in his flesh the law with its commands and ordinances in order that he might create in himself one new humanity from two, so making peace, reconciling both in one body to God through the cross, thereby killing the enmity" (Eph 2:16).[1] Indeed the apostle Paul himself, like Jesus, wagered his entire ministry on this double task of deconstructing the *divided House* and reconstructing it on a foundation of race, class, and gender equality: "There is no longer Jew or Greek, slave or free, male and female; all of you are one in Christ" (Gal 3:28).

"A house divided cannot stand." So said Abraham Lincoln, appropriating the ancient verdict of Jesus to describe the crisis of our own country that led to the War between the States. The image has haunted our political unconscious ever since. More than 130 years later, in our own time, it remains a historical ultimatum to our body politic, seared again on our consciousness by the Los Angeles uprising — the largest "domestic disturbance" since the Civil War. A house constructed upon social and economic division will either collapse of its internal structural contradictions or be burned down by those whose disenfranchisement gives them no reason to feel a stake in its maintenance. The popular slogan of the L.A. rebellion thus restated the verdict of Jesus: "No justice, no peace." If the gulf remains, the guns will rule.

When Annie Dillard wrote about the difficult business of tearing down the walls of one's own house, she was referring to the writer's labor. But her metaphor strikes me as descriptive of the task facing First World Christians today, for we live in a global civilization constructed upon horizontal and vertical partitions of gender, race, and class. The architecture of our entitlement prevents us from encountering what is on "the other side." Yet if we are ever to be motivated to join Jesus in the deconstructive struggle, it will be because we have seen and been moved by the human faces of those condemned by the *locus imperii* to live on the other side of those walls. This, then, necessitates the discipline of *relocation.*

A. "NO STONE UPON ANOTHER": TEARING DOWN THE WALLS OF OUR OWN HOUSE

What is the biggest barrier preventing First World people from living in solidarity with the oppressed?

Liberation theology, in its recovery of the biblical bias toward the marginalized, challenges us to take, in the now-classic expression of Gustavo Gutiérrez, the "evangelical" or "preferential option for the poor" (1983:125ff). It is "preferential" because it is a priority; it is "evangelical" because *we* are evangelized by the presence of Christ among the poor (Tamez, 1982; O'Brien, 1991). As Jon Sobrino puts it: "God's existence as an 'other' is not mediated through such realities as beauty and power; it is mediated through the 'otherness' of the oppressed" (1978:395). Only when we have gazed into the human face of the oppressed will we undertake the long journey toward genuine solidarity. Then will we learn that "the measure of civilization is not whether it puts a man on the moon, but rather how it treats its poor" (Herzog, 1980:93).

This challenge, however, presents First World Christians with profound dilemmas. Liberation theology contends that solidarity comes not from abstract analysis of class interests but from conversion to the Christ of the poor. But the architecture of our House determines that we live at great distances from the poor, distances that often seem insurmountable to us. Worse, political, economic, and cultural forces systematically conspire to render the "social other" invisible. For example, Itabari Njeri writes that "the systematic distortion of the black experience has made the notion of invisibility a mantra in African American culture (*Nobody Knows My Name; The Man Who Cried, 'I Am'; Invisible Man*)" (1992:E4). Robert Chambers (below, E) puts it straightforwardly: "The poor are little seen, and even less is the nature of their poverty understood" (1983:25).

The fact that in the *locus imperii* we are insulated from the poor represents the biggest barrier to the encounter from which conversion may arise. We may talk (or write!) about the poor, or invoke the rhetoric of solidarity with liberation movements, or join the Rainbow Coalition, or serve food at a soup kitchen — but the *structures of distance* remain. Nor will mere anguish about the tragic divisions in our House tell us how or why they exist. We need to understand them as the result of social and ideological imperatives, predicated upon assumptions and practices long characteristic of the dominant culture.

Today the population of our American House is as diverse as any in the world. In the wake of the Los Angeles uprising, Ron Wakabayashi, director of the Human Relations Commission, pleaded for southern Californians to recognize that their human diversity is every bit as indigenous as their beaches and mountains. Just as residents have learned to see those geographical barriers as natural resources, he argued, they must learn to see diversity as an asset instead of a liability. Social groups vary according to many factors — age, cultural or linguistic background, native intelligence, physical ability, sexual expression, religious belief, economic practice, and so on. But we must not confuse how they are different with what divides them. It is when differences are used by some to exercise domination over others that they become divisions. Thus before we can examine queries about solidarity (below, Chapter Nine) and diversity (below, Chapter Ten), we must address the factors that impede their realization. We must ask ourselves how *we* abide by, and benefit from, what I will call the social architecture of division. Then we must inquire how we might socially relocate our political bodies within that architecture as a concrete defect-ive strategy in the long-term struggle to tear down the walls of our own House.

In capitalist modernity, divisions are constructed according to gender, race, and/or class differences — usually by some combination of the three. Obviously other social groups — such as gays and lesbians, youth and the elderly, and mentally or physically disabled persons — have also suffered the injustices of discrimination and oppression. But gender, race, and class have been the historically overdetermining indexes of structural oppression in the U.S. (below, 9,B,C,D). These dividing walls have deep pilings, as we have seen, in the European colonization of the Americas (above 5,E,1). The blueprints of our House may have promised life, liberty, and the pursuit of happiness, but its foundation was poured in the ideological concrete of oligarchy, patriarchy, and white supremacy. These realities severely constrained the scope of the Enlightenment ideals of the Constitutional architects, who enfranchised neither women nor non-Europeans nor those without land. These basic restrictions of entitlement have been mitigated over two centuries but never eradicated. Consequently they remain embedded in the deep structure of our political unconscious. This explains the dominant culture's ambivalence about racial, sexual, and economic justice: We believe in the ideal of equality and justice for all yet routinely ignore the practical demands of realizing it. So we live with incongruity — and with the resulting anxieties about the instability of a House divided.

At every level of U.S. society today there are conventions and institutions that discriminate against women, people of color, and the poor: in health care, housing, education, employment, recreation, religion, commerce, politics, criminal justice. It is impossible to characterize concisely or adequately the oppression resulting from these "norms," because it is so multifaceted and comprehensive. We must speak of an overall *system* of oppression. The exceptions found within it — anomalies in the local distribution of power such as a black-owned bank, a women's health clinic, or a United Mine Workers local — only prove the rule. Individuals born and raised outside the sphere of entitlement must overcome extraordinary barriers and must work harder just to compete or to be accepted. They must at every point accommodate the dominant culture in order to survive or be nominally included within it, and thus they must endure incessant violations, small and large. Not to conform is to face further marginalization, scapegoating, and in many cases even criminalization. A host of intrapsychic and group disorders in addition to political, social, and economic disenfranchisement result: alienation from oneself, hostility toward one's own group, self-destructive behavior, and even physiological dysfunctions (Akbar, 1981; Grier and Cobbs, 1980; Fanon, 1968:249ff).

The walls of division are tangible to those who daily confront them in the classroom, at the store, or at a job interview. To members of the dominant culture, however, who tend to be material beneficiaries of these same social patterns and practices, the walls are largely invisible — unless and until brought to our attention by the victims. Separate social realities are the reification of the Denial I examined in Part Two. Michael Harrington, in his classic book *The Vast Majority: A Journey to the World's Poor,* called this "the cruel innocence which prevents us from even seeing the wrongs we perpetuate": "America has worked against the poor of the planet in a spirit of sincere compassion.... We are a decent people. But intricate economic mechanisms, whose very existence is a mystery to most citizens, subvert that innate generosity and perpetuate misery around the globe" (1977:13). It is, in other words, fundamental to the architecture of the *locus imperii* that the center be insulated from the periphery, at home and abroad.

In the absence of human subjects speaking for themselves, we tend to "see" the social other through caricature and abstraction. The information brokers who mediate the world to us do not help, since they tend to reinforce rather than reduce the divisions (above, 3,B). We "know" the poor more through statistics about income, housing, teen pregnancy, or recidivism than in terms of actual names and faces and families. The exercises so common among our social justice organizations prove the point. Many of us, for example, have participated in world hunger groups that attempt to illustrate the inequitable global distribution of resources by dramatizing it in a banquet where only a few people eat most of the food. We are familiar with the popular graphic of the human pyramid that portrays the superrich standing on the backs of the managerial class on the backs of the working class on the backs of the rural poor. But the point is, we have to *imagine* the reality of the oppressed through such contrivances because we are so structurally insulated from it. Even when we do observe the disenfranchised with our own eyes — on the street, in a soup line, at a welfare office — have we really *encountered* them as people?

Let me probe still deeper. Peace and justice people in the church rightly spend a great deal of time agonizing about the gulfs between the First World affluent and the poor in Africa, Asia, or Latin America. But we are as a rule much less cognizant of the same divisions in our own nation, state, region, and city. For example, the most severe pockets of poverty in the U.S. are rural — parts of Appalachia, the Mississippi Delta, and Native America, to mention just three. But these places and their problems rarely affect our consciousness. Why? Because, as Robert Chambers points out (below, E), they are out of the way of our urban-oriented patterns of travel, they are off the beaten track of the dominant urban-based journalism, and they are out of the loop of Centrist political perceptions and mechanisms. The inner-city poor are equally marginal to the suburban biases of the dominant culture — until the inherent violence of their lives spills beyond its "boundaries."

Starvation in Ethiopia, or war in Sri Lanka, or deforestation in the Amazon reflects the plight of the "absolute victims" of the New World Order, and we must not allow that reality to become more diminished than it already is within the insular Metropolis. Yet what does it mean that we see more on the news about famine in Africa than we do about the hard-core urban and rural poor in our own region? It is part of the insidious distortion of our entitlement that we too often recognize social divisions with a clarity directly proportionate to their distance from our own homes. There are more First World Christian groups in the U.S. working on solidarity with Central America than on factory closings or racism in their own communities. After the Los Angeles uprising churches and peace groups, not unlike the mainstream politicians, scrambled to dispatch "fact-finding" tours to Los Angeles rather than examining the very same conditions in their own cities. The closer the social divisions are to home, the harder we find them to bridge. That is why I here choose to focus on domestic gulfs rather than international ones (below, E,2).

The genius of this social architecture is its ability to keep the enfranchised and disenfranchised in such different social universes. And it is the invisible efficacy of these dividing walls that makes them so difficult to tear down. The key issue, then, is not so much our consciousness (or lack thereof) about the oppressed but our actual social location in relation to them. Until we overcome the gulf between us, we will not start tearing down the walls that divide us. Of course, few U.S. churches have understood their vocation to be one of demolition. Quite the contrary: They have endeavored to fill the House with a good spirit, rarely questioning its construction. And why not? After all, the church's own social architecture bears such close resemblance, mirroring the culture's stratification. Have not congregations usually formed along class lines? Have churches not been the last to integrate, so that Sunday morning is still the most segregated time and space in our society? Are not Catholics and Protestants alike continuing to polarize over the issue of the ordination and role of women?

All this is true. But again, because of the alternative discourse of the gospel, the churches remain one of the few places left in the U.S. with the potential to resist the current deterioration in gender, race, and class relations. We Christians must, therefore, learn to "hammer against the walls" of the church. If we heed the gospel, we will, as Dillard says, "know what to listen for." And when a bearing wall has to go, and our fears of collapse threaten to overwhelm us, we must recall Jesus' promise that "the stone the builders rejected has become the cornerstone" of a new structure (Mk 12:10). Social reconstruction in our own life can animate political imagination for other architectural possibilities for the American House (below, Part Four).

Obviously, to deconstruct the walls of division we must understand how they are constructed. The walls of the older California house I live in consist of lath and plaster. To extend the metaphor, then, let us say that the lath (the substructure, so to speak) represents a social architecture engineered to create and maintain social distance. The plaster (or superstructure) consists of ideologies that cover over the fact of the lath, providing cosmetic relief from the uncomfortable reality of the divide. The next two sections will deal with each in turn.

B. "WHO TOUCHED ME?": THE SOCIAL ARCHITECTURE OF INSULARITY

What prevents the entitled from encountering the reality of the disenfranchised?

Mark's Jesus was committed to overcoming social divisions through a twofold strategy. First, he defied the social architecture and its conventions, relocating instead to live proximate to the poor. Second, despite the clamor and press of the crowd, he remained attentive to human contact; he was compassionate, able to "feel with" them. This is best seen in his encounter with the woman with the flow of blood. "And Jesus, perceiving that power had gone forth from him, turned around in the crowd and said, 'Who touched me?'" (5:30). Because Jesus is concerned with the empowerment of those who have been exploited (5:25f), he wants to know who has reached out to him (5:34). The disciples, on the other hand, uneasy with this proximity to the poor, protest. "The crowd presses in upon you, yet you ask, 'Who touched me?'" (5:31). Their insulation from the poor is dependent upon not knowing and not inquiring. Out of sight, out of mind.

Insofar as we conform to the social architecture of insularity, we remain in denial. We see this in congregations who move from their old downtown church buildings to the suburbs once the changing urban demographics make things "uncomfortable." But once we begin to question it, we find that it is not the result of historical accident or necessity. Social architecture is an economic and political *production* (Soja, 1989). Here I will look at three basic building blocks of social division: the politics of "urban planning," economic policies, and cultural reproduction.

1. Social Space

Let us begin with the most evident expression of division, what Henri Lefebvre calls social space (1991:68ff). Today most cities in the U.S. (and increasingly, around the world) consist of three elements: (1) aging, deteriorating inner-city neighborhoods populated predominantly by poor persons of color;

(2) a ring of suburbs populated by predominantly white and exclusively middle-class homeowners; and (3) a downtown "business" district accessible to the latter and protected against the former. All three spaces coexist side by side but are kept separate by what one African American journalist called the "thin blue line" of police brutality and the "thick red line" of economic discrimination. How did this architecture evolve?

The first phase in the construction of twentieth-century urban geography was the forced relocation of the rural poor. Jacqueline Jones has discussed the pattern of economic imperatives toward urbanization at length in her recent book *The Dispossessed: America's Underclasses from the Civil War to the Present* (1992). The pattern began when changes in agricultural markets, farm technologies, and/or tax burdens drove tenant farmers and smallholders off the land. Having lost the basis of their self-sufficiency, and displaced by even more disenfranchised immigrant farm labor, these families usually migrated to the cities in the hope of finding work. There, with a minimum of skills, they became the lowest wage-labor class in the manufacturing or service sectors (see Steinberg, 1991). In U.S. history this pattern of rural-to-urban migration has transcended national boundaries. At the turn of the century the forces bringing Irish peasants and African American sharecroppers to northeastern industrial cities were basically similar (see Lemann, 1991). The same forces that attracted southern blacks to the industrial boom in post–World War II Los Angeles are today pulling Mexicans into the burgeoning underground service economy in postmodern Los Angeles (below, 10,B). Robert Chambers, an international development analyst, calls this the "self-reinforcing, centripetal" character of the Metropolis, which inexorably draws everything from periphery to center.[2]

The second phase of urban geography happened once the migrants came to the cities. Already separated from established and acculturated urban dwellers by class and race, they were kept geographically segregated in "ethnic" neighborhoods. In the first half of this century the primary mechanism for accomplishing this was the restrictive housing covenant, which excluded non-Caucasians and sometimes even non-Christians from home occupancy. When this was outlawed, economic redlining continued the pattern of de facto segregation. Because of lack of mobility and the design of public transportation, poor people were forced to live close to their workplaces, reinforcing their ghettoization. Constraints in language or education kept first-generation urban migrants marginalized. Their reality was either caricatured ("Okies," "hillbillies," racist slurs) or ignored by the dominant cultural forms. Politically they were rarely able to advocate for their own cause in a system that was both unfamiliar to them and overtly hostile to their interests.

Los Angeles, as one of the newest major metropolises in the U.S., has represented something of a laboratory for the construction of the urban architecture of segregation. In 1880 the population of this formerly *Mexicano* village was still only a little over eleven thousand. During the real estate boom over the next ten years, however, the first great migration of middle-class, white easterners spelled the end of the *Californio* era (Pitt, 1966:249ff). The population of the area then began to more than double almost every decade. By 1940 Los Angeles was more than three and a half million; its boosters bragged it was one of the "whitest" big cities in the country (McWilliams, 1946:13ff). With the manipulative appreciation of land values and the rise of the white political power structure, people of color (once a majority) were increasingly marginalized and severely restricted as to where they could live. As a rule Mexicanos were pushed east of the Los Angeles River, while blacks were restricted to a small portion south of downtown referred to as late as the 1950s as Darktown (Romo, 1983:61ff). California's unique anti-Asian biases, fueled by the internment of Japanese (above, 6,E,2), continued after the war as suburban communities posted signs at their borders warning "Orientals" they were not welcome (see Daniels and Olin, 1972).

Here, then, was the fundamental contradiction: Larger economic forces were bringing the poor into the cities, while the urban elite tried to keep them "contained." Containment strategies have been essentially two here, as elsewhere — discrimination and white flight. Mike Davis, in his impressive *City of Quartz,* describes the role of post–World War II developers and home owner associations in constructing a discriminatory "white wall" throughout Los Angeles County by establishing "the national legal precedent for zoning districts exclusively for upscale, single-family residences":

> The local real-estate industry, dominated by "highend" builders exploiting economies of scale, specialized in the creation of large planned subdivisions of the urban fringe. Together with exclusionary zoning and stringent subdivision regulation, deed restrictions that "both mandated and prohibited certain types of behavior on the part of the present and future property owner" constituted the main method by which community builders implemented their planning and design vision. Although deed restrictions also specified details of lot and home design, their overriding purpose was to ensure social and racial homogeneity. (1990:161)

Similar strategies characterized federally subsidized Federal Housing Authority and Veterans Administration programs for mortgage-loan guarantees in the post-war suburban building booms. "Between 1946 and 1959, less than 2 percent of all the housing financed with the assistance of federal mortgage insurance was made available to Blacks" (Judd, 1991:740). Though a 1948 Supreme Court ruling outlawed restrictive housing covenants, they persisted in practice throughout Los Angeles until violence broke out. "In November, 1964, two thirds of California's white electorate virtually voted for a race riot when they repealed the state's fair housing law," writes Davis; this led to "the Watts riot 10 months later — which one black leader aptly described as 'the hate that hate created'" (1992a:M6). By the time official segregation was overturned, however, a new counterstrategy was already well established that would guarantee its unofficial continuation.

White flight is a central characteristic of the modern city. Davis points out that suburbanism represented the dominant culture's first reaction to the "threat" of integration:

> If white homeowner resistance in Southcentral Los Angeles gradually dissipated after the Korean War, although continuing ferociously along the ghetto's western and eastern edges, it was largely because Southside whites were fleeing to the new suburbs in the San Fernando Valley and across the southeastern tier of LA County.... The growth of the suburban population outside the LA city limits (a majority of the County's population by 1950) offered a new terrain for homeowner separatism: this time with the aim of putting the more permanent barriers of independent incorporation and exclusive land-use zoning between themselves and the non-white, or non-homeowning, populations. The emergence of suburban Southern California as a "metrosea" of fragmented and insular local sovereignties — often depicted in urbanist literature as an "accident" of unplanned growth — was in fact the result of deliberate shaping. (1990:164)

But suburban insularity was predicated upon the construction of Southern California's infamous freeway system, which could bring managerial commuters from far-flung bedroom communities into a "fortress downtown" business district.

This led to the third phase of the construction of urban geography: urban redevelopment. The not-so-hidden agenda of the regional freeway grid was to enable suburbanites to avoid driving through the poor communities of East and South Central Los Angeles. The city's (indeed the country's) first freeway — which goes right through my own neighborhood — was built from downtown to affluent Pasadena. Like almost every freeway since, its construction bifurcated and destroyed poor and ethnic communities. Today no less than three freeways (servicing the satellite counties of Orange, San Bernardino, and Riverside) slice up the heart of predominantly Latino East Los Angeles. Another freeway neatly severs the poorest section of Pasadena from the rest of the city — although its planned extension through affluent and predominantly white South Pasadena has been staved off by home owners and business interests for thirty years! Three other freeways effectively boundaried the eastern, northern, and western edges of predominantly black South Central Los Angeles. The Century freeway currently under construction is plowing right through the most devastated sections of South Central (including Watts). This project, which will provide eastern access to the airport "over" these neighborhoods, has received generous financial and logistical support from the Community Redevelopment Agency (CRA).

The CRA has been, in fact, the major force behind redevelopment. Its first projects were to clear out "deteriorating" ethnic neighborhoods proximate to downtown. The old barrios of Chavez Ravine and Bunker Hill succumbed respectively to Dodger Stadium and a complex of high-rise, high-priced condominiums. The next part of the redevelopment strategy was to establish a new business center that would be hospitable to corporate and international capital and inhospitable to the city's increasingly heterogenous street population. Davis exposes the fortress character of downtown Los Angeles: the vertical and horizontal design of its "citadel" architecture and the destruction of pedestrian and public space, including "bum proof" benches. Dominating the landscape is

> the emerging Pacific Rim financial complex which cascades, in rows of skyscrapers, from Bunker Hill southward along the Figueroa corridor. Redeveloped with public tax increments under the aegis of the powerful and largely unaccountable Community Redevelopment Agency, the Downtown project is one of the largest postwar urban designs in North America. Site assemblage and clearing on a vast scale, with little mobilized opposition, have resurrected land values, upon which big developers and off-shore capital (increasingly Japanese) have planted a series of billion-dollar, block-square megastructures. (Ibid:228f)

Meanwhile the older business districts have been abandoned to burgeoning Latino and Asian entrepreneurs and markets. This spatial apartheid is designed "to make such heterogeneity virtually impossible; it is intended not just to 'kill the street' . . . but to 'kill the crowd,' to eliminate that democratic admixture on the pavements and in the parks that Olmsted believed was America's antidote to European class polarizations" (ibid:231).

Similar redevelopment strategies have been pursued in other metropolitan areas, perhaps most notoriously Detroit's Renaissance Center, where elevated transports shuttle people between high-rise and high-security hotels, office complexes, and shopping/entertainment centers. Davis calls this a "seamless continuum of middle-class work, consumption and recreation." Fortress architecture also now characterizes suburbs as well. Throughout Los Angeles, "gated" communities, elaborate electronic home-security systems, and private patrols maintain insulation from the gulf through the wielding of guns.

2. Economic and Cultural Space

But urban political geography is still only superstructural. What determines where people live within this architecture is "economic space." Much has been written about the international debt crisis, in which "austerity" programs imposed by First World capital managers on Third World economies have functioned to further marginalize the poor (above, 1,A; see Cavanaugh et al, 1986; Potter, 1988; Branford and Kucinski, 1988; Vallely, 1990). But similar "structural adjustments" have been applied to the U.S. economy as well, so that the gulf between the rich and poor is growing exponentially at home too. One can see this just by the index of personal incomes. Journalist Kathy Kristof writes that in 1992 "the 100 top executives at California's biggest companies earned a whopping $212.98 million. . . . The compensation of top U.S. corporate executives has grown nearly ninefold over the last three decades, climbing at almost double the rate of the typical American factory worker's pay" (1993:D1). But there are far more visible signs. Today, just as the familiar face of foreign poverty is the hollowed eyes of some starving child in some unheard-of corner of the world, the equally familiar face of domestic disenfranchisement is in the downcast shuffling of the homeless person just down the block.

The major mechanisms of economic polarization during the Reagan/Bush era were regressive taxation, deregulation, and industrial flight. Analyst Priscilla Enriquez summarizes:

> Saying that it would "free entrepreneurial energy," the Reagan administration pushed through a massive tax cut that benefited the rich and penalized the poor: the tax share of the top 1 percent fell by 14 percent while that of the bottom 10 percent rose by 28 percent. Not only did the wealth not trickle down, as Republican Party theory said it would, but entrepreneurial energy went not to enhancing America's productive capacity but to financing corporate takeovers, mergers, speculative activities, and investment in low-wage sites in Asia and Latin America. Under the slogan of defeating communism, the Reagan administration spent massively on defense, financing it not only through heavy borrowing (especially from the Japanese) but also by gutting government programs that formed the already shredded safety nets that stood between millions of Americans and hunger. This tradeoff resulted not only in greater poverty but in the severe erosion of the international economic position of the U.S., which switched from being the world's biggest creditor country to being the world's biggest debtor. (1992:5f)

More than a decade of Republican frontal attacks on "government spending" masked the fact that their criticisms were carefully selective, decrying expenditures on social welfare and services (most notably public assistance) while remaining silent about skyrocketing police, criminal justice, or national defense budgets. Still, they managed to shift political debate over economic policy and public responsibility significantly to the right. Thus we have seen the rise of "neoliberals," who join in blaming the excesses of Great Society programs for such imagined social pathologies as welfare-dependency or the destruction of the black family (see, e.g., Forman, 1991).

The middle-class "tax revolt" has been a key reflection of those who wish to entrench the social architecture of insulation. In California in the late 1970s suburban home owner associations, feeling the squeeze of inflation and the promise of rapidly appreciating property values, formed the backbone of the movement that passed Proposition 13. This "Big Bang," as Davis calls it, froze assessed property values at 1975 levels. The subsequent decrease in state property tax revenues has been a major factor in the deterioration of public health, housing, and welfare. But the constituency that advocated this regressive property tax is, of course, the social group that feels least and last the effects of shrinking state services. Indeed historically they have tended to oppose socialized health care and to support building more prisons, in order to maximize the distance between themselves and the poor. Davis points out that "Proposition 13's explicit promise to roll back assessments and let homeowners pocket their capital gains was accompanied, as well, by an implicit promise to halt the threatening encroachment of inner-city populations on suburbia" (1990:183). This is confirmed by the fact that the tax revolt coincided with a fierce campaign against court-mandated school busing in parts of Los Angeles. The long-term result of Proposition 13's "structural adjustment" has been the decline of the once-proud California public education system. Consequently over the last two decades the same home-owning tax revolters have been pulling their kids out of public schools and placing them in private ones and are now organizing to have the state subsidize that private education through a school voucher initiative.

All of this is, of course, entirely legal. Almost fifteen years after Proposition 13 was passed, the U.S. Supreme Court ruled that this "distasteful and unwise" tax structure was nevertheless constitutional. This the court did despite recognizing that "California's grand experiment appears to vest benefits in broad, powerful and entrenched segments of society," and that it "frustrates the 'American dream' of home ownership for many younger and poorer Californians" (Hall and Carlson, 1992). Meanwhile, triagelike budget cuts have been engineered by California Governor Pete Wilson in his campaign to "balance" the state budget through political blackmail. Once again the cuts disproportionately affect programs such as state supplements to AFDC, Headstart, and indigent health care. Such policies shift the burden of economic recession to those who are already least able to bear it but who are also the least politically powerful: poor women and children (see Lefkowitz and Withorn, 1986; Couture, 1992).

Structural adjustments resulting from economic policies and political budget battles have dramatically deepened social divisions in the U.S. Because this happens incrementally, however, it is rarely news — until those who feel its effects most rebel. Yet I have shown how during and after the Los Angeles uprising, social insulation continued to distort perceptions (above, 3,A,2). Journalists and politicians alike had little clue about the real situation of the scorched neighborhoods they visited nor an understanding of the rage that was expressed through arson and looting (Clifford et al, 1992). We heard laments about the "black-Korean conflict" but little acknowledgment of the economic forces that prevented blacks from developing small businesses in South Central because of the unavailability of capital and that drew new Korean immigrant entrepreneurs into the "economic buffer zone" (small markets, liquor stores, flea markets, pawn shops, etc.) necessitated by the absence of major commercial institutions in those neighborhoods. In the political culture of the *locus imperii,* public officials and the media must define riots as a social aberration in order to deflect responsibility and prop up myths that urban structures are basically sound. But they are not. A recent UCLA study found fewer stores, higher prices, and less overall availability of food in the inner city than in nearby suburbs; more troubling still, it "found that 27 percent of residents in one South-Central Los Angeles neighborhood said they do not have enough money to buy food, and that their families go hungry an average of five days a week" (Nazario, 1993).

Cultural forces also create and maintain social distance between classes and races. The educational system is a good example. It was one thing to integrate the public schools, after a long struggle; it has been quite another to diversify curricula to reflect accurately our heterogeneous society. The acceptance of multicultural learning materials is still an uphill battle in most public schools, one that promises to get steeper due to three trends. One is shrinking budgets for public schools, which result in inferior teachers and resources. A second is the creeping privatization of education, threatening to resegregate schools as "separate and unequal." A third is ideological backlash against multiculturalism's challenge to dominant versions of history and the arts. The dream of the public school as a place to both meet and learn about race, class, and gender diversity — one of the few historically effective counterbalances to social insularity in the U.S. — seems to be fast fading.

We can hardly rely on the media or the arts to mitigate against this socio-economic polarization, since they necessarily revolve around images and narratives of their target market: white suburban society. In commercial movies and television women, people of color, and the poor have traditionally been either invisible or stereotyped. If and when a minority person or group is the primary subject — a rare exception — their "character" is still filtered through the predominantly white male production hierarchy of the major studios. Thus the representation of a Native American tribe or a steel mill town or a gay couple is still interpreted by and shaped for the dominant cultural perspective. But black directors in the commercial mainstream such as Spike Lee or John Singleton must constantly justify their artistic choices and resist pigeonholing (Goldstein, 1992).

Music has been a more successful medium for exposing middle America to cultural traditions that originated in minority communities, such as the blues, Afro-Cuban jazz, and gospel. Unfortunately music industry management and marketing forces are forever trying to domesticate and control such forms — white working-class punk rock and black rap being two recent examples. Though artists who refuse to conform to the canons of commercial culture sometimes survive and even flourish, they too must work on the defensive and tolerate unceasing public scrutiny — rapper Ice Cube, for example (Hilburn, 1992). In the visual arts, minority exhibits are usually curated and critiqued by white-controlled institutions even when the art itself is self-conscious about issues of cultural representation (M. Wallace, 1990). Nor does dominant culture "consumption" of minority artistic expression necessarily reduce social distance. For many years, high-profile entertainers of color in the U.S. had more freedom on the stage than in the street. Today their increasing numbers gives an illusion of widespread racial inclusion in our society. If anything, however, the political economy of big-time entertainment, with its corporate sponsors, high-powered agents, and media huckstering, only increases the distance between fantasy and reality. To watch a basketball star such as Michael Jordan perform, for example, provides enjoyment for the fan. But it does nothing to bridge the gulf between the thousands of kids imitating Michael on inner-city playgrounds and those who can afford the inflated ticket prices to see Jordan play.

Culturally defined gender roles are learned in the home, where the social architecture of division targets women across the board. True, women are no longer necessarily segregated in the home as in the past; the labor force has opened up with remarkable rapidity because of both feminist challenges and economic pressures. But the constraints of gender-role expectations have largely remained, so that women who work outside the home more often than not find their "traditional" tasks of nurturing, child rearing, and domestic maintenance undiminished. "Liberation" in too many cases has meant that women must work twice as hard. They still earn on average 30 percent less for their wage labor — and still nothing at all for work inside the home. Female workers continue to be more expendable than their male counterparts in the commercial work force — not only "last hired and first fired," but also more vulnerable to workplace health and safety discrimination, including sexual harassment.[3] Yet women are severely underrepresented in organized labor circles, not to mention political and economic decision making. These patterns are, of course, intensified for single mothers, the working poor, welfare families, and women of color.

Nowhere is the reality gap greater for women that in their ubiquitous idealization and objectification in the visual media. The highly engineered standards of physical beauty in North American popular culture hold almost universal tyranny over the desire of men and the esteem of women. The peddling of the young-and-beautiful mirage represents a huge industry, yet invades and subverts attempts to achieve intimacy with a woman's reality. These images are so much at the heart of advertising's strategy of seduction that most of us have become thoroughly socialized to the gratuitous use of the female face, voice, or body as a marketing tool. The image makers exploit, and thereby perpetuate, both sides of the vicious patriarchal caricature: The domesticated housewife sells us soap and soup; the fantasized seductress sells us lingerie and liquor. Every person — indeed every relationship — in the *locus imperii* has paid an exacting price for this derogation and trivialization of the feminine. And objectification breeds exploitation; a notable recent case illustrates what is at stake. Female employees filed a suit in 1991 against the Stroh Brewing Co., charging that there was a connection between the company's exploitive use of bikini-clad models in its beer commercials and the recurrence of sexual harassment of women in its workplace. Noted an analyst at the Center for the Study of Commercialism: "When a single voice badgers or degrades women in the workplace because of their gender we call it sexual harassment. When that voice is amplified for millions of people by millions of dollars, we call it advertising. The former is a legal wrong, the latter a legal right.... Men get mixed messages. The law tells men at Stroh not to treat women as sex objects, while company ads tell them to revel in the thought" (Collins, 1991). This example is hardly isolated; the culture is awash with sexual double messages, legal ambivalence, and political duplicity around gender issues.

I have noted only a few of the social, economic, and cultural ways in which the distances between gender, race, and class groups are constructed and maintained. Those of us who are not the primary victims of such divisions must learn that they are the result not of arbitrary discrimination or ignorance but of systemic imperatives. Insofar as we live at peace with this social architecture of segregation, privilege, and insulation, we continue to reinforce its power in and over us.

C. "SEND THEM AWAY!"
THE IDEOLOGICAL ARCHITECTURE OF DIVISION

How do the entitled justify their distance from and ignorance about the marginalized?

In Mark's story the crowds are characterized as importunate and demanding, pressing in on Jesus and the spaces he is trying to liberate. The marginalized persistently scream for attention (10:47), lunge out for help (5:27), and if necessary tear down the house to get to his promise of healing (2:4). The disciples, on the other hand, are typically dismissive of them, be they poor (10:48), women (14:5), or children (10:13). When confronted by hungry masses, their reaction is blunt: "Send them away!" (6:36) Sadly this attitude is not uncharacteristic of First World churches today. We have a relatively secure place in society and make choices big and small to keep our distance from the anomie of the poor. For some this stems from a positive ideological commitment to patriarchy, white supremacy, and the divine entitlement of the rich — but this book is obviously not addressed to them. I am speaking about those of us who consider social division to be a problem and who are concerned with justice. I argued in Part Two that denial is how we resolve the contradictions between our ideals and realities: We *mystify* the objective conditions of gender, race, and class oppression in the body politic, *internalize* their subjective character in our political bodies, and *suppress* their historical character. Here I want to note four basic ways in which we ideologically legitimate the gulf.

Philosophical legitimation. The most pervasive (and effective) strategy by which the dominant culture avoids problems of systemic injustice is to reduce them to the realm of individual attitude. Theo Witvliet points out the personalist fallacy:

In bourgeois societies, people are inclined to concentrate on the attitude and the mentality of individuals and groups in society and to lose sight of the fact that racism is above all a problem of the complex relationship of economic, political and ideological power structures. . . . There is a stubborn refusal to see the hard core of racism as the ideological organization of exploitation and dependence. So it is still quite common today to find racism defined in terms of attitude, prejudice and behavior. However true it may also be that racial oppression is indissolubly bound up with prejudices, discriminatory behavior and ethnocentrism, in such definitions the material basis of racism is ignored. (1984:43, 44f)

Racism (this also holds true for sexism and classism) must therefore be defined as *prejudice plus power* (see below, 9,B). Any other definition suppresses the systemic breadth and depth of the problem.

When racism is defined as an individual attribute it is "reduced to something which takes place inside human heads, and the implicit presupposition here is that a change of attitude which will put an end to racial oppression can be brought about by dialogue, by an ethical appeal for a change of mentality" (ibid:43). In the First World shame culture this game often begins and ends with personal dissociation: *I* am not sexist, *I* don't think women are inferior. If one does "own" the problem, the solution is seen as a matter of personal conversion: *I'm going to be more sensitive to women; I'll try to change my chauvinist habits.* Institutional change is equated with the conversion of the powerful: *If the CEO of this corporation were not sexist, or if there were more women in management, its problems of gender discrimination would disappear.* Such strategies deal only with prejudice, not with structural sexism; they will not by themselves alter traditional divisions of labor or unequal pay scales. Overcoming personal prejudice can make life more human, but it cannot undo a system. For that, relations of power must be transformed.

Another personalizing tendency is the argument from exception. For example, persons from poor backgrounds who have become "successful" in the mainstream are lauded by the dominant culture as proof that class divisions are topical, not systemic. The implication is that disadvantages can and should be surmounted through individual hard work but not political organizing. Obviously the Horatio Alger fairy tale dovetails with the ideologies of individualism and the Protestant work ethic (see King et al, 1988:56ff). "Exceptional" persons are aggressively promoted by the dominant culture because they can be particularly effective in socializing oppressed communities not to ask structural questions. Business leaders, entertainment stars, and politicians are held up as exemplary role models. This they may or may not be, but they are in either case exceptions that which only prove the rule. The truth is, once such persons have "made it," they rarely stay in solidarity with their people — residentially, socially, or politically. Meanwhile, among the entitled, individual social conscience is typically channeled into volunteerism. The affluent are forever involved in charity causes, which though good, refuse to raise systemic issues to the public eye.[4]

A second philosophical legitimation of division is to universalize the problem. "Everyone is racist." Much is made these days of black "racism" against Koreans, or of black rapper Ice T's "racism" in his "Cop Killer" lyrics. It has now become fashionable for neoliberals to demand "evenhandedness" in the critique of injustice. The media constructs alleged symmetry between crimes: if the beating of black motorist Rodney King by four white LAPD officers was racist, the beating of white motorist Reginald Denny by four black men shortly after the Simi Valley verdict was equally racist. Instead of recognizing how institutionalized oppression engenders reactive rage (below, 8,A), the dominant culture appeals to a moralizing discourse that universalizes the social condition: There are "good" and "bad" people of all races. We saw this after the Los Angeles uprising, as the media and politicians scrambled to assess blame for the violence. They never tired of pointing out how the majority of those in the affected neighborhoods — the law-abiding citizens — had remained off the streets, obedient to the curfew and cooperative with the National Guard. The rioting, they argued, was the work of a small minority of "thugs and hooligans." This discourse — most citizens are good, a few are bad — functions to redeem our faith in the essential viability of the social contract while obscuring structural injustice. But assertions that every group must be held to the same standards of public propriety conveniently ignore the fact that there is not a level playing field for every group in society to begin with.[5]

There can be no question that women, people of color and the poor may be prejudicial toward gender, race, or class "others." Post-uprising Los Angeles has certainly revealed how much mutual suspicion exists between the Asian, black, and Latino communities, for example. In places where "minority" groups hold local control — take again the black-owned bank, the women's health clinic, and the UMW local — it is certainly possible for bias to translate into discrimination. This is not, however, "reverse" sexism, racism, or classism, because these social groups are not in power in the overdetermining system. As black rapper Sistah Souljah pointed out in her infamous squabble with candidate Bill Clinton during the 1992 presidential campaign, the most repressive black African dictator does not have the power to force Europeans everywhere to learn only African history in school. But white America during the Reagan-Bush era bought into the impossible concept of reverse discrimination with a vengeance. The result has been a vigorous backlash against the one structural adjustment the system has made: affirmative action (see Williams, 1991; Faludi, 1991).

Political legitimation. Hegemonic ideology always portrays social reality in terms of "natural theology" — *this is the way the world is.* The liberal tradition, however, acknowledges that there is room for social change. The condition is that change must come gradually, and only in ways essentially continuous with the system itself. The system works, so change agents should work within the system. Liberalism is predicated upon the essential soundness of U.S. democratic and economic traditions. The ideal of constitutional parity, for example, assures us that our political system needs no radical changes. Tensions of social diversity will be effectively managed through assimilation. And exceptional minorities persuade us that capitalism provides limitless opportunity. Liberalism believes in the notion that there is a place for (most) everyone in the body politic and that discrimination against minorities can be overcome through more rational social engineering. Those trying to "get in" must, in turn, agree to adjust to the dominant ethos in the workplace, commerce, and public service.

Stokely Carmichael long ago pointed out that these powerful liberal fictions

of inclusion prevent minorities from being able to define clearly the structures
of their oppression (1969:165ff). They blind us to the fact that disenfranchised
people have always had to contest the dominant culture for inclusion. What sexual, racial, and economic justice there is in the U.S. was forged only through
protracted social and political struggle, not handed down by those in power.
Child labor laws, unemployment benefits, health and safety standards, food and
drug regulations, fair housing statutes, nonharassment codes — all have been
the result of organizing pressure by exploited groups (see Harding, 1990). Liberalism has generally responded to such social protest with a mixed strategy
of compromise and cooptation. Activists are allowed some political space to
organize as long as their demands remain moderate and reformist.

One can see this pattern in the U.S. over three generations since World
War I; in each era, however, it was economic forces that opened the system
more than political will. New Deal liberalism countered the serious challenge
of Depression-era labor activism with massive federally subsidized work and
social programs. World War II and the subsequent cold war economic boom
then opened blue-collar sectors to women and racial minorities. Great Society
liberalism responded to civil rights activism by opening more educational and
vocational opportunities, desegregating housing and public education, and experimenting with affirmative action. The expanding economy enabled significant
penetration by people of color into the middle sector. Post-Vietnam liberalism
responded to feminist activism by tolerating limited participation by women in
managerial and government sectors. But this has been arrested by declining
economic growth.

Through these three eras, gains were made by women and people of color in
the middle strata of our economic and political institutions. But this newfound
access has limits, and a cost. Once "in" the system, they are still constrained
by glass ceilings and must endure a certain level of institutional sexism and
racism. The *presence* of minorities and women is tolerated in the "culture of
power," points out educator Lisa Delpit, but their distinct *perspectives* are excluded; she calls this a "silenced dialogue" (1988:280). One African American
therapist terms it a "climate of micro-aggression," which she likens to a "persistent acid rain." Relationships are tenuous between whites who acquiesce to
but do not welcome affirmative action, and minorities who are reserved and defensive. But the psychological burdens upon those doing the assimilating are
largely invisible to liberals preoccupied with their own nobility.

As "stagflation"[6] has deepened into full-blown recession in the U.S., the
liberal strategy of reform is being eclipsed by the conservative strategy, which
promotes polarization and the politics of self-interest. Liberalism's "inclusivist"
ideals have atrophied in the popular consciousness and were replaced during the
Reagan-Bush era with ideologies of "limited social good" (cf Reed and Bond,
1991). The notion that gains by women and people of color pose a threat to
white middle-class entitlement fed anxieties at a time when the latter had finally
begun to feel the economic squeeze. Tim Wise (1991) calls this "the politics
of white resentment," which has focused on opposition to affirmative action

policies. It revolves, he points out, around a "myth of white victimization," consisting of three complaints:

- affirmative action discriminates against qualified whites and violates the principle of meritocracy (hence the Bakke case and Republican denunciations of "quota systems");
- affirmative action is unjust "punishment" of whites for the racism of past generations;
- there is no need for continuing structural adjustments today because serious gender, race, and class discrimination are things of the past.

It is not difficult to see the characteristics of Denial here, but "white rage" is potent stuff, as David Duke's recent campaigns in Louisiana showed. Economic insecurity and class discontent traditionally have been used to stir up racial antagonism among poor whites in the South; this strategy is simply being projected onto a larger canvas now.

Economic hard times in the *locus imperii* have thus ushered in a stunning reversion to victim blaming. The dominant culture has a long and notorious history of projecting responsibility for problems on marginalized groups. In the eighteenth century Indians were not only savages unfit for civilization; their obstinacy hindered the domestication of the continent and the march of Progress. In the nineteenth century African slaves were not only unsuited for full participation in society; their unruly desire for freedom strained the federal covenant. In the twentieth century, women's demands for suffrage, equal access to the workplace, and equal representation have torn the social fabric of the family asunder. And immigrants have always been stealing jobs and contaminating American society with foreign languages and habits.

Today this discourse continues. The "welfare reform" movement laments that people are on government assistance because they are shiftless and dependent. Anti-immigrant groups along the U.S.-Mexico border attribute everything from flu epidemics to economic recession to the flow of undocumented Latinos. Republicans lay the erosion of "family values" at the feet of feminists and single parents. The tradition of vilifying "drunken Indians" and scapegoating "lazy Mexicans" continues today in caricatures of "welfare queens" and "illegal aliens." The creed that the system works if you work hard is just as current today as it was on the colonial frontier. But when it becomes clear the system isn't working, that creed is replaced now, as then, with victim blaming.

Philosophical and political strategies of legitimation have shaped white perceptions of issues of enfranchisement in the U.S. from the Indian Wars and slavery debates of the antebellum period to the struggle for women's, immigrant's, and welfare rights today. If we understand social divisions as a problem of personal or institutional ignorance, we will focus our response on reforming persons and "adjusting" institutions that are essentially "good." If, however, we understand division to be, as Witvliet puts it, "embedded in the economic, political-juridical and ideological structures of society, and deeply rooted in the collective unconsciousness associated with them" (1984:45), we will see that structural problems demand structural solutions. The distinction is crucial: It will distinguish between those who would merely redecorate the House and those who would renovate it entirely — bearing walls and all.

D. "FORCING THEM TO CROSS TO THE OTHER SIDE": EXPERIMENTS IN *AP-PROXIMATION*

How do we breach the walls of Fortress Metropolis that separate us from those "on the other side"?

In Mark's story world, Jesus' mission to eradicate division is supremely symbolized by the boat journeys across the Sea of Galilee (4:35ff; 6:45ff). "Let us go across *to the other side*," he tells his disciples (4:35). The other side of what? A mere traversal of the sea would not have been so daunting to these fishermen. No, there is something deeper, more archetypal here. These voyages represent a defiance of the most fundamental social divisions of Mark's time, the evangelical journey toward solidarity (*BSM:*194ff). On "the other side" — after barely surviving the seemingly cosmic opposition to the crossing — they encounter a man whose political body has thoroughly internalized the violence of the body politic (5:2ff; above, 4,B). What a bewildering journey! No wonder that the disciples are not inclined to undertake this journey again. Thus Mark tells us that the next time Jesus had to "*force* them to get into the boat and go ahead of him to the other side" (6:45). The implication is clear: The "crossing" of solidarity is as difficult as it is compulsory.

For First World Christians, given the social architecture of division, the preferential option for the poor indeed demands a laborious journey of social relocation. We find this perhaps embarrassing to speak frankly about. It is easier to invoke the rhetoric of solidarity than to face the ambiguities inherent in our attempts to overcome insularity. But for us, genuine solidarity requires honesty, not pretense. For this reason, I will call our quest the journey of *ap-proximation.* I use this term to be accurate, not clever. The suffix (*apo,* "toward") establishes solidarity as a journey of intention. The word itself keeps before us the fact that we can only ever be "proximate" to the oppressed; alongside them, perhaps, but never in their shoes. No matter how much we may seek to identify with the poor, we who are entitled can never be identified *as* poor. The most rigorous defect-ive practices of our communities of discontinuity do not change the facts of our structural privilege, such as education, social mobility, or the fact that we have *opted* for this lifestyle.

I will use my own life-text for this reflection, because I believe my on-going journey of ap-proximation is not untypical. I am a social product of the social architecture I have just discussed. I grew up in one of the oldest white, middle-class suburbs of Los Angeles, a small incorporated city with its own school district and city council and shopping area and two staunchly conservative newspapers. My neighbors were all home owners, most of whom commuted (by freeway) downtown for work and "culture." Though my favorite baseball players were black, the gardener Japanese, and the housecleaner Latina, my immediate world was white and privileged, with all the attendant double messages about gender, race, and class. The schools, playgrounds, stores, parks, and streets of my world were effectively insulated from the poorer black and Latino communities just a few miles away in three directions. Freeways took us over and past these other worlds; spoken and unspoken taboos kept us physically out of them; stereotypes kept us psychically apart from them. And, of course, our suburban police kept "them" away from us. It is no exaggeration to say that the poor of India were more familiar to us (if only through the objectified images of the media) than were these neighbors of color. Our collective racism was rarely explicit; I did not grow up around mean-spirited epithets or race baiting. It was simply structured implicitly into the social architecture of our lives, making the "other" invisible. Looking back, I am awed by the efficacy of suburban apartheid.

Today I live in a Latino barrio only a couple of miles west of my childhood home. The office where I work with the AFSC is in Northwest Pasadena, on North Fair Oaks Avenue. It is in the predominantly poor black and Latino neighborhood I mentioned earlier, which is boundaried from the rest of the City of Roses by two freeways. A few years ago it struck me that the site where I now collaborate with people of color in community organizing is *less than four miles* straight up the road from my old junior high school, on South Fair Oaks. But how long and hard it was for me to traverse those few miles! My journey of ap-proximation took me some twenty years and led me all over the world.

Perhaps it was an advantage coming of age during the late 1960s — one of those rare moments in U.S. history when questions about the *locus imperii* were in the air. The contradictions around the Indochina War had penetrated suburban insularity, and as a teenager I felt the alienation keenly. Yet my process of awakening turned decisively upon experiences outside the U.S. As is the case for so many North Americans, I had to get away from what was familiar to see it more clearly. As James Sanders (1969) put it once in an eloquent sermon, the biblical witness repeatedly testifies that we who reside in the Metropolis must forsake Jerusalem to encounter the God of Israel (Jer 38:2f), must go to meet Jesus "outside the gate" (Heb 13:13f). Because our world is constructed around Denial, the journey of solidarity is the long way home.

It was during a year in Scandinavia as a high school exchange student that my questions began to ferment. Norway was, in one sense, an equally insular First World society. Yet having to adjust to a foreign language and a dramatically different physical environment began to erode the underpinnings of my psychic security. Sharing life with a working-class family in a small industrial town and attending a vocational school was dissonant enough to engender doubts about my own class entitlement. But it was around political issues that this new, extrinsic vantage point was most potent. I was challenged to defend the Vietnam War, but with an older brother in Indochina, I was not remotely inclined to justify U.S. policies. My opposition to the war deepened through exposure to the somewhat less-filtered northern European press accounts of it. It was not an easy year. I dispatched angry letters to my bewildered parents; the memory of having to face my Norwegian friends after Nixon's bombing of Cambodia is still vivid.

The overall experience of distance from the *locus imperii* left me in a state of vertigo. This was, I believe in retrospect, a decisive factor in my conversion to Christianity upon return to the U.S. My innocence and social equilibrium had been shattered, and I needed a new place to stand. Although my Jesus-movement faith was initially a depoliticizing influence, undergraduate studies at U.C. Berkeley soon demanded a confrontation between my nascent vision of discipleship and the contradictions of the dominant order. Out of this grew my first experiments with communities of discontinuity (above, 6,D). Pilgrimages to Christian communities located in the ghettos of Baltimore and Washington, DC, then exposed me to the "other side" of my own country, as did a relationship with Catholic Workers in northern California. Challenged by the axiom that "the difference between liberals and radicals is what they see when they get up in the morning," our newly formed community relocated from a middle-class university area to a working-class black neighborhood in West Berkeley. Slowly we began to build relationships with our neighbors. Modest experiments in "somatic politics" (below, 8,E) led to brief jail stints, introducing us to more of the disenfranchised. We were beginning to ask new questions, to adopt a different perspective. Yet, as I have noted, old patterns are persistent (above, 6,E). It took yet another journey "outside the gates" to bring me to the next turning point.

The Pacific Life Community's campaign of nonviolent resistance to U.S. militarism in the late 1970s had brought us into contact with activists from around the Pacific basin. When I was selected to be a U.S. delegate to the third Nuclear Free and Independent Pacific (NFIP) conference in 1980 in Hawai'i, I began to learn about the imperial periphery directly. The NFIP campaign is a unique self-determination movement that has attempted to forge collaboration between indigenous activists of the Fourth World (Pacific islanders and internally colonized native peoples of Australia, New Zealand/Aotearoa, and North America) and First World peace movements in the Rim countries. The Pacific typifies the stark contradiction between centrist illusions and peripheral reality. Behind the "flower curtain" of Metropolitan tourist brochures is a bitter history of colonization: The peoples of Oceania have been exploited by a long list of North Atlantic and East Asian nations. This legacy continues today in the rule of French colons in New Caledonia and Polynesia, U.S. neocolonialism in Micronesia and the Philippines, and the U.S.-sanctioned Third World imperialism of Indonesia in East Timor and West Papua (Myers, 1986a, 1986b). Finally no region has been more directly victimized by modern militarism. The nuclear powers east and west deemed the ill-named Pacific remote enough to test atomic and hydrogen bombs and delivery systems. Today they use its far-flung island nations to project power through forward basing and to locate command, control, and communication systems, and its waters for low- and high-level nuclear waste disposal (Hayes et al, 1987; Bello, 1992b).

Through exposure to the lives and stories of native peoples I slowly began to see disarmament issues in a new light. Our preoccupation with the number-crunching games of the arms race and eschatological nuclear scenarios had made us blind to the fact that centrist militarism was devastating the peripheries even without a war being fought (Myers, 1983a). In contrast, indigenous peoples insist there can be no demilitarization without self-determination and question why we are expert in First World weapons systems but not First World institutions of racism. The key issue, around which there is constant struggle, is whether we Rim activists (with our greater access to resources) are willing to open our agendas to the priorities of the poor or whether "solidarity" is another mask for First World control (below, 9,A). More than conference debates, however, it was my own concrete exposure to Fourth World realities that were the most confronting and transforming. Of the many powerful experiences I have had in the Pacific, a few stand out as moments I most keenly felt the touch of the oppressed.

I remember their pain. I remember one February night in the Marshall Islands, listening to elders of the Rongelap community tell the story of their exposure to radiation from U.S. atmospheric testing in the 1950s, of their subsequent exile, and of their ongoing struggle to return home and pursue reparation (see G. Johnson, 1983). I knew these facts well yet was understanding the human reality for the first time from the victims themselves. I remember Holy Saturday evening in a tiny Palauan village, sitting with the late Alfonso Kabokal, the "stubborn old man" who symbolized in his flesh local resistance to U.S. militarism (Aldridge and Myers, 1990). I heard him tell how he lost an arm and a leg when his hoe struck an unexploded World War II shell in the 1950s, and how he had refused attempts by three generations of government officials and tourist developers to take his land from him. Such an extraordinary Easter vigil: As midnight approached, under the thin light of a single light bulb surrounded by the thick sounds of the jungle, the old man held me in his powerful gaze and called me to a deeper solidarity that burned a hole in my soul.

I remember their hope. I remember a weekend on the *marae* with Maori friends, finding myself overwhelmed by their fierce cultural pride as for two days and nights they orated, sang, and performed the *haka*. I was awestruck by their ability to celebrate in the teeth of racist oppression, and I was transfixed when they chanted the names of the generations of tribal ancestors since the landing of the Great Canoes (see Awatere, 1984). I remember feeling the same *mana*, the same visceral power, one afternoon when some Hawaiian sovereignty activists escorted us past their roadblocks to an ancient Polynesian *heiau* at Ka'u, the southernmost point of the islands. From here those same Great Canoes, according to tradition, had departed — I could see the ancient mooring holes still visible in the lava rock.

These and other memories multiply in the heart's eye. The squalor of tiny Ebeye, home to the Kwajalein people forcibly relocated from their islands so the U.S. military could use their atoll as a missile testing range (see G. Johnson, 1984). The despair of Redfern, the Aboriginal ghetto of Sydney, and the defiant resistance of Japanese farmers impeding the construction of Narita airport at Sanrizuka. The palpable joy of a Melanesian solidarity rally through the narrow streets of Port Vila, Vanuatu, and the palpable fear of a tense stand-off between Kanak independence activists and right-wing French counterdemonstrators in the central park of Noumea, New Caledonia. But one moment above all seems to best symbolize my journey of ap-proximation.

A small group of us was visiting a village on one of the Loyalty Islands of New Caledonia, touring "popular schools" developed by the Kanak self-determination movement (Myers, 1985a). A group of young men sought us out and invited us to a local home for a "discussion." Eager for the viewpoints of grassroots Kanaks, we went along and sat on mats drinking coffee while the conversation slowly unfolded through three and sometimes four languages. One teenager volunteered to answer my question about the root problems of Kanak oppression. He launched into an unrehearsed fifteen-minute overview, brilliant and concise, of the political economy of the nickel industry and French control of the means of production. I was stunned at the sophisticated analysis of this young, barefoot villager. But the punch line came at evening's end, when the same teenager addressed me earnestly. "We have described to you our struggle; what are people in the U.S. doing to support us?" In that moment the "cruelty of American innocence" (Harrington) felt like an unbearable weight. How could I explain to him that few in the U.S. would even be able to find New Caledonia on a map, that people with multiple degrees and high-paying jobs were far less literate than he, that North American teenagers could find a hundred reasons *not* to struggle for a better future? It was a moment of reckoning, but the challenge came not from the pulpit of a great church or from the pen of a great writer or from a university lecture. Instead I had encountered the truth of the Palace Courtyard "outside the camp," in a remote corner on the periphery. It came from an anonymous "native youth" of whom the *locus imperii* is ignorant but who had made it his business not to be ignorant of the *locus imperii*. How could I do any less?

Again, I believe my story is not untypical of those of us who, though raised in the dominant culture, are struggling for ap-proximity. I had to travel a long way to overcome four miles of distance. And in the course of my current AFSC work — each time I sit with the African American tenant union members from the nearby low-income housing project; each time I walk the U.S.-Mexican border with my colleague Roberto Martínez and listen to the stories of abused undocumented immigrants; each time I talk with my colleague Ho'oipo DeCambra about the frustration among Hawaiians working to regain their land and dignity — I realize how far I have yet to go in this journey. But this simply testifies to the power of our structural insulation. Our illusions about personal prosperity and political powerlessness remain intact among the fictions of middle-class culture, but they wilt before the anguished human faces of real victims and the insurgent hopes of those who believe they can change the world. That is why solidarity groups over the last decade have developed reality tours, which bring First World people into human contact with life on "the other side" of the gulf. I believe such strategies of exposure are necessary to the work of repentance and conversion in the First World.

Exposure trips have long been used as a tactic of conscientization. The 1960s, for example, saw "Freedom Rides" in the South, "socialist summers" working in Cuban canefields, and "urban plunges" onto the mean streets of our cities. After the Nicaraguan revolution of 1979, however, an unprecedented number of North American activists began traveling there to witness Sandinista society in the making. Then, through the 1980s, as the war in El Salvador and Guatemala deepened along with the Contra counterinsurgency, the circulation between Central America and U.S. solidarity groups increased. The Sanctuary movement brought the realities of life and death on the periphery to the doorsteps of ordinary suburban congregations in the lives of Central Americans refugees (MacEoin, 1985; Golden and McConnell, 1988). During this time, exposure trips were being organized to other places, such as the Soviet Union, South Africa, and the Philippines. But Central America's visibility in the news and proximity to the U.S. made it the destination of choice, and the solidarity movement deserves credit for developing exposure into an economically and politically viable component of First World social justice work (see Griffin-Nolan, 1991). Some longer-term partnerships have grown from bridges built by exposure, including sister-church and sister-city relationships.

Organizations such as the Center for Global Education and the Voluntarios Solidarios program of the Fellowship of Reconciliation and Resource Center for Nonviolence now specialize in this work. Over the last decade literally thousands of North Americans have been tutored in political reality and had their worldviews shattered by the despair and the hope they have encountered in the Third World. It can, of course, be objected that this is an elite strategy of conscientization, since international exposure takes time and money that many do not have. This is true; these *are* strategies for the middle-class. Yet they represent perhaps the most effective existential challenge to insulated people. The harder question is this: What does the journey of ap-proximation mean here at home? Does the long journey to the other side abroad impel us to make the short journey to the other side nearby, symbolized for me by those four miles up Fair Oaks Avenue? Or does it excuse us from doing so? If the latter, we have not yet taken on the most difficult task of all: tearing down the walls of *our own* house.

E. "YOU ARE NOT FAR...":
FROM EXOTIC POLITICS TO OPTION FOR THE POOR

What are the pitfalls of "movement tourism," and why do we more readily see the poor who are distant than those who are nearby?

"You are right, teacher," responded a scribe to Mark's Jesus when discussing the Great Commandment; "To love one's neighbor as oneself is indeed greater that all the burnt offerings and sacrifices put together" (12:32f). Like the scribe, we First World Christians know what is right, we know what the Story asks of us. But neither knowledge nor good intentions can deconstruct the architecture of division. Solidarity requires a journey, real experiments in social relocation. Even then we, as structurally entitled people, will only ever be ap-proximate to the oppressed. The fact is, our deepest illusions can remain untouched by exposure trips unless we have the courage to keep confronting them. Therefore, I want to acknowledge two problems we must face regarding our practices of ap-proximation.

1. Illusions of Proximity

"When Jesus saw that he had responded thoughtfully, he told him, 'You are not far from the Great Economy'" (12:34). This reply suggests that we ought to be circumspect about the degree to which we have bridged the gulf. Unfortunately this is not always the case. There are those who return from a month in Nicaragua instant experts, parroting solidarity slogans and acting as though the distance between themselves and the poor has evaporated. We must guard against the temptation to conclude that in our limited encounters we have met the oppressed and now understand their struggle. If we comprehend so lit-tle of the lives of the poorest members of our own society, does it not stand to reason that as cultural outsiders in a foreign setting we will comprehend even less? How will we discern which parts of the picture we are getting — or missing?

These issues have been addressed by Robert Chambers in his analysis of the difficulties of the exposure strategies used in international development work (1983:10f). While he affirms the importance of well-intentioned First World groups visiting the poor in the Third World, he is unflinchingly honest about the constraints and distortions inherent in "rural development tourism." Cham-bers begins by noting that those who participate in these kinds of trips "usually have three things in common: they come from urban areas; they want to find something out; and they are short of time" (ibid:11). He then describes a typical scenario of the exposure itself:

The visitor is encapsulated, first in a . . . Jeep or car and later in a moving entourage of officials and local notables — headmen, chairmen of village committees, village accountants, progressive farmers, traders, and the like. Whatever their private feelings (indifferent, suspicious, amused, anxious, irritated, or enthusiastic), the rural people put on their best face and re-ceive the visitor well. According to ecology, economy and culture, he is given goats, garlands, coconut milk, coca-cola, coffee, tea or milk. Speeches are made. Schoolchildren sing or clap. Photographs are taken. Buildings, machines, construction works, new crops, exotic animals, the clinic, the school, the new road, are all inspected. A self-conscious group (the self-help committee, the women's handicraft class), dressed in their best clothes, are seen and spoken to. There are tensions between the visitor's questions and curiosity, the officials' desire to select what is to be seen, and the mixed motives of different rural groups and individuals who have to live with the officials and with each other after the visitor has left. Time and an overloaded programme nevertheless are on the officials' side. As the day wears on and heats up, the visitor becomes less inquisitive, asks fewer questions, and is finally glad to retire, exhausted and bemused, to the circuit bungalow...the guest house, the host official's residence, or back to an urban home or hotel. (Ibid:12)

Those of us who have participated in exposure trips know how true this description rings.

Chambers identifies six "biases" built into the process that make it difficult for those from the Metropolis truly to perceive the most entrenched characteristics of poverty. The first are what he calls the *spatial biases* of tarmac and roadside. Obviously outsiders can only see what they are able or willing to get to. Flying to New Caledonia is one thing; how much I see there is quite another. Limitations of resources, time, and comfort level mean that only the more accessible places are visited. But these sites are accessible only because they are already tied to "developed spaces" by transportation (airports, roads) and communication (radio, telephone) apparatuses. Chambers notes that this "elite roadside ecology" deceives the visitor, who never sees the "hidden poverty" in out-of-the-way locations.

Related to this are *project biases*. When we visit Guatemala, chances are we'll be shown "popular" organizations that have a high degree of political sophistication: functioning clinics, active base communities, and progressive rural collectives. Such projects get the exposure and are written about back home, which attracts other visitors to them, which generates more exposure. This means that "contact and learning are then with tiny atypical islands of activity which attract repeated and mutually reinforcing attention" (ibid). This may be natural and understandable, but it provides only a limited, even privileged, perspective. Visitors rarely recognize that such groups may not be representative, that we are seeing "those who use the health clinic more than those who are too sick, too poor, or too distant to use it; those who come to market because they have goods to sell or money with which to buy, more than those who stay at home because they have neither" (ibid:19).

Person biases can be similarly deceiving. Because outsiders have no indigenous contacts, we rely on those locals who are used to dealing with "movement tourists," who tend to be educated, socially mobile, and influential people like ourselves. These "hosts" inevitably broker what is seen and how it is interpreted, often speaking "for" the poor. In most cases they are men, thus giving a male perspective. Those who are "seen" tend to be those connected to the host's projects or politics.

Then there are *environmental biases*. Chambers points to the fact that most visitation to tropical climate zones occurs during the dry season, despite the fact that the

most difficult time of the year is usually the wet season, especially before
the first harvest. Food is short, food prices are high, work is hard, and in-
fections are prevalent. Malnutrition, morbidity and mortality all rise, while
body weights decline. The poorer people, women and children are particularly vulnerable. Birth weights drop and infant mortality rises. Child
care is inadequate. Desperate people get indebted. This is both the hungry
season and the sick season. (Ibid:20)

Yet monsoon rains (or other extremes of weather, or natural disaster) make
it unlikely that outsiders will ever witness such conditions. Finally, Chambers
continues, there are *diplomatic and professional biases.*

Urban-based visitors are often deterred by combinations of politeness and
timidity from approaching, meeting and listening to and learning from the
poorer people. Poverty in any country can be a subject of indifference or
shame, something to be shut out, something polluting, something, in the
psychological sense, to be repressed. If honestly confronted, it can also be
profoundly disturbing. Those who make contact with it may offend those
who are influential, the notables who generously offer hospitality to the
visitor. (Ibid:22)

Cross-cultural factors are decisive in exposure programs, determining what and
how things are seen and heard; yet few facilitators give more than cursory attention to such issues. Indigenous professionals hosting the tour may have more
in common with the visitors than with the poor of their own country.

All of these biases distance us from the point of view of the rural poor themselves. "The prosperity after harvest of a male farmer on a project beside a main
road close to a capital city may colour the perceptions," warns Chambers, while
"the plight of a poor widow starving and sick in the wet season in a remote and
inaccessible area may never in any way impinge on the consciousness of anyone
outside her own community" (ibid:24). The point is not that these inevitable constraints render the exposure strategy useless or futile, or that in some cases with
experience they cannot be overcome. They simply reinforce my thesis about the
social architecture of distance and the difficulties in surmounting it (see Lipton,
1976). We need to acknowledge them as constraints in order to disabuse ourselves
of the illusion that in any given exposure we have witnessed the unmediated reality of the poor. The more we are involved in strategies of social relocation,
the more incumbent it is to keep reminding ourselves that we are only ever ap-
proximate to the poor. The journey of solidarity takes a lifetime, and the longer
we are on it, the more modest we will be about the distance we've covered!

2. Hypermetropic Solidarity

The second problem is again the most troubling one. We must return to the
question I raised at the outset of this chapter: Why do so many First World ac-

tivists tend to "see" the poor and their issues with a clarity and passion inversely proportionate to their geographic distance from where we live (see Recinos, 1992)? Is our solidarity "hypermetropic," defined by Webster as "a condition of the eye in which distant objects are seen more distinctly than near ones"?

I recall an afternoon not too long ago in which an African American organizer from inner-city Boston was addressing a room of mostly white Christian solidarity activists. In the middle of his recitation of the litany of the woes facing young black males in the U.S., he stopped, on the verge of tears, and slammed his fist down on the table. "But y'all wouldn't know or care about any of this," he said in a trembling voice, " 'cause y'all are too busy running off to Central America to save the goddamn Sandinistas." Now he may not have hit a note of noble international solidarity, but by the way my colleagues were squirming, I could tell he had nevertheless struck a deep chord. I winced in empathy for both parties, remembering a moment in which the same truth had been flung in my face some years earlier, at an international NFIP conference in Vanuatu. I was involved in a hallway policy argument with two other delegates, a Tongan and a Canadian Indian, when the latter suddenly interrupted me midsentence: "So what the hell are you doing here anyway? Why aren't you back home working for our land rights?" As I stood stunned, my Tongan friend jumped to my defense, arguing that Pacific islanders needed solidarity and advocacy just as much as Native Americans. The Indian just gave me a hard look and walked away.

It took a few years, but eventually I was able to stop being defensive long enough to start grappling with the truth in his challenge. I realized that I knew more about the Maori land wars of the late nineteenth century than the Indian Wars of my own country, was more aware of black Melanesian politics than black American politics, had more Third World friends and colleagues outside than inside California. Here again, my story is not untypical of other international solidarity activists. Ironically our work for justice abroad often increases the distance between ourselves and the oppressed who are our neighbors. When a small, dedicated group of us were doing advocacy on behalf of Pacific issues from our base in San Francisco, for example, we achieved only marginal contact with the tens of thousands of Chamorros, Samoans, Tongans, Hawaiians, and Micronesians living on the West Coast. This was not for lack of trying; it was because our international agenda was irrelevant to their daily struggle to survive. Similarly in Los Angeles during the 1980s I knew many Central American solidarity activists who had fully immersed themselves in Salvadoran, Nicaraguan, or Guatemalan culture. Few, however, had the faintest clue about Latino gangs in the city, despite the fact that the children of Central American refugees here are now becoming a new generation of *cholos*. There are still more white activists doing South Africa solidarity organizing in Los Angeles than working with the black community around issues of police brutality, even after the spring 1992 uprising. In contrast, one can find many African American organizers in Los Angeles who move back and forth constantly between issues relating to southern Africa and domestic issues of racism and police brutality (see Stewart, 1992).

We must ask ourselves why we find it easier to stand with struggles for dignity everywhere else but our own neighborhoods? Is it because we are drawn to the "exotic"—both in Webster's first sense ("introduced from abroad") and second sense ("strange, exciting, or glamorous")? We white activists enjoy working with Third World expatriates who welcome our support and depend upon our ability to advocate for their cause in the U.S. When we visit our *compañeros* abroad, we are often presented as exceptions to the stereotypical ugly American. All this feels pretty good. There is nothing wrong with it, unless our hidden (even unconscious) agenda is the control we have by assuming leadership positions, speaking "on behalf of" Third World movements, and gaining the prestige of association with liberation struggles. In contrast, the daily struggles of Third World people here at home for better health care, housing, and education are rarely exciting or glamorous. Moreover, their experience of white racism or class or gender oppression makes them suspicious of us and less solicitous of our "help." Because their goal is empowerment, they do not want or need *our* leadership; we will be expected to play supportive and probably uncredited roles. At the same time, they rightly expect us to deal with our own racism and sexism. Proximity now means we are more likely to be targets of rage and to have our motives questioned and our privileges pointed out. This does not feel nearly as good. In my example above, it is easier to have my solidarity defended by the appreciative Tongan than questioned by the unimpressed Indian. Is it possible, then, that working on the home front is simply not as *gratifying* for First World activists, or that it is too demanding? If so, what does this reveal about our entitlement, and our denial?

All of this may be painful to admit, but only because we are still trapped in the illusion of our own altruism and self-righteousness. If we are to be committed to the journey of ap-proximation at home as well as abroad, we must have the courage to confront the shadow side of our own work for justice. In emphasizing the necessity of the shorter but more difficult journey to the poor of our own neighborhoods, let me be clear, I am not advocating swinging to the other side of the pendulum—the opposite of hypermetropy being myopia. Provincialism is merely a different kind of insularity in the *locus imperii:* the luxury to be ignorant of and unconcerned with anything outside our own immediate sphere. Bridges must be built to sisters and brothers around the world, and the primary responsibility for initiating this indeed lies with us, given our access to resources and mobility. I am simply arguing that we must always measure our commitment to ap-proximation against the walls of our *own* house.

There is no reason why we can't reanimate domestic exposure strategies, applying what has been learned abroad. The last few years have seen some attempts to update the freedom rides concept of the civil rights movement, for example. But we must be clear that this will be more difficult, because oppressed communities in the U.S. are less willing to welcome movement tourists, for the reasons just cited. The real challenge is for us to exhibit commitments to relocation that can become long-term partnerships of solidarity. For example, a small Catholic parish in Newark began working with local low-income people

after the 1967 riots. It has since helped found the New Community Corporation, a nonprofit development corporation that has built housing and provided
jobs and health care (Wexler, 1991; Bardack, 1992). Proyecto Pastoral, a Jesuit-
facilitated organizing effort run out of Dolores Mission in East Los Angeles,
has integrated organizing among Central American refugees and undocumented
Mexican workers with work among low-income residents of the public housing
projects and local gang members (see Smolich, 1990; Boyle, 1990).

Crossing domestic divides runs into all the difficulties noted by Chambers.
Take the example of postuprising Los Angeles, when a wave of concern to
"reach out" to the people of South Central washed over suburban churches.
Many soon realized they knew few people in South Central and understood little about how things get done there. But there was one clue: During the uprising
the media had anointed one particular African Methodist Episcopal church —
an already powerful and influential middle-class congregation — as the "voice"
of the black community. Consequently that church was flooded with aid from
the suburbs wanting "access." They were quickly overwhelmed, while calls for
help by other South Central churches went unheard or unheeded. Some white
congregations never got beyond seeing this as just another canned food and
clothing drive, as if it were for African famine relief. For others the effort ended
as soon as the first roadblock or hint of ingratitude was encountered. Had they
continued, they would have learned how little distance had been covered just by
arriving at the door of First AME Church.

This scenario is typical of the difficulties of ap-proximation in our own
cities. We can extrapolate from it a simple social map that, if overly schematic,
serves to illustrate the problem:

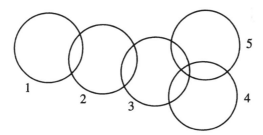

Sectoral access across urban divides

For purposes of this analysis, let us say that the five overlapping circles above
represent "sectors" of the stratified community, defined largely by class and/or
race. The three on the left symbolize sectors of the South Central black community (which whites usually misperceive as monolithic). The two on the right are
sectors of the dominant culture trying to "access" this community. The circle
on the far left (1) represents the most disenfranchised sector of the black community of South Central: gang members, housing project tenants, drug dealers,

the homeless, the unemployed, and so on. Next to it (2) is what we might call the black working-class sector; it is more stable but has both community and family ties with some of the disenfranchised (thus the overlap). The next sector to the right (3) is the "black bourgeoisie," upwardly mobile professionals who for the most part have moved out of the traditionally defined "ghetto" but who again have community, family, and professional contacts with the working-class sector (e.g., the First AME Church). On the right is what we might call the "liberal" white nongovernmental sector, such as concerned churches and peace and justice organizations (4). Finally there is the white economic-political power structure — politicians, government agencies, and professional and business interests (5).[7]

Generally speaking, each sector has some access to the sector next to it, but direct access across more than one sector is rare and requires mediation and translation. Thus working alliances grow more tenuous as they reach farther across this social map. To accommodate this, brokers and facilitators — with varying agendas of their own — arise in each sector. For example, an African American politician, who probably operates from sector 3, must rely on the street contacts of, say, a longtime Youth Gang Services worker (2) to establish contact and dialogue with the Blood and Crip leaders behind the gang truce (1). Given the complexities of negotiating across this social geography, the potential for carpetbagging is obvious, particularly when outside resources — government or private — begin to "target" the area's problems and compete for "clients." Mistranslations (or manipulation) result in misguided projects, while sectoral rivalries generate suspicion. Those best positioned to "direct traffic" at the left end of the map (those operating from 2) are notoriously underresourced. And by the time relationships and transactions have been mediated and filtered through so many sectors, little remains in the way of material or decision-making power for the poor. It is their plight that is used by all other sectors to justify involvement, but the disenfranchised often remain that way at the end of the process. Meanwhile both white sectors (4 and 5) gain access almost exclusively through the black persons and institutions closest to themselves in class character (3). If they have any interest in reaching farther across the social map, they will be constrained by the limited access of the black bourgeoisie they depend upon and even more constrained by their own double (race and class) outsider status. Thus the Bloods-Crips gang truce — one of the most significant political developments since Los Angeles burned — has seen almost zero involvement from white peace and justice groups (Myers, 1992a).

The analysis of this chapter may seem discouraging to the reader. It is not meant to be. I have focused on the architecture of distance because we are so inclined either to ignore or to underestimate it. Taking "the option for the poor" is easy to chant as a mantra, considerably more demanding to practice as a way of life. To go around or over walls in the journey of ap-proximation is important, but it is not the same as tearing them down. The walls of division are many and well built, and there are walls within walls. Above all, we must recognize that we are working on the house from the inside out, which is why perspective is so hard to get. Our communities of discontinuity are never free of the ideological or social architecture of the dominant culture, which we have internalized in our political bodies. A Turkish proverb puts it best: "When the axe came into the forest, the trees said: 'The handle is one of us' " (Chaliand, 1978:vii). Deconstruction is a lifetime vocation that goes on simultaneously with our attempts to reconstruct a "home for all peoples." Before turning to strategies for First World Christians working in solidarity across the gulfs (below, Chapter Nine), however, we must take a sober look at the guns.

NOTES

1. Remarkably, Ephesians 2, which commentators agree represents the "thesis" of the epistle, portrays social deconstruction/reconstruction as the essential meaning of Jesus' death as a "salvific" event. It goes so far as to assert that reconciliation with the social "other" is a precondition to reconciliation with God. The epistle understands the church as that community which abides by the "unilateral" messianic ceasefire (2:18–22) and goes on to reflect upon the internal and external challenges to such a social project (Myers, 1981). Paul's disciples are here testing this vision on the "worst-case" social division in Hellenistic antiquity: the thoroughgoing cultural, economic and political enmity between Jew and Gentile, what D. Smith (1973) has called the "proto-type of all human hostility" (see also Rader, 1978). As Markus Barth put it: "If Christ 'is peace,' then he is by nature a social, even a political event, which marks the overcoming and ending of barriers however deeply founded and highly constructed.... When this peace is deprived of its social, national or economic dimensions ... then Jesus Christ is being flatly denied" (1959:44f; see also Barth, 1974).

2. What Chambers writes about the centripetal character of the international system fits just as well for the domestic one:

At one end there coexist rich, urban, industrialized, high status cores, and at the other, poor, rural, agricultural and low status peripheries. In the cores there is a mutual attraction and reinforcement of power, prestige, resources, professionals, professional training and the capacity to generate and disseminate knowledge. Both internationally and within individual third world countries, centripetal forces draw resources and educated people away from the peripheries and in towards the cores. Within third world countries, skills migrate from rural to urban areas, and from smaller to larger urban centres, feeding in turn the international flows of the brain drain. The centripetal system is self-reinforcing. Staff and resources generate prestige and reward and attract yet more staff and resources. (1983:4f)

3. A recent survey conducted by the Los Angeles Commission on the Status of Women found that in city government female employees experienced a rate of sexual harassment higher than the nationwide average; 37 percent of the respondents said they had been harassed, with an even higher rate (almost half) among those working in public safety departments (DiRado and Becklund, 1992). In her study of women in the global economy, Rachel Kamel shows that blue-collar women are particularly vulnerable to layoffs, representing "at least 35 percent of the workers displaced by plant closings, according to a study by the federal Bureau of Labor Statistics that covered the years from 1979–83":

Women workers are heavily concentrated in labor-intensive manufacturing, especially the fiber industries.... Industries with a predominantly female workforce are often seen as marginal to the economy. However, the fiber industries still employ more workers than basic steel, auto assembly, and chemical refining combined. And this is true even though the fiber industries have lost some 800,000 jobs over the past twenty years. Labor-intensive industries with a predominantly female workforce — garment and textiles, electrical and electronics assembly, and others — were the first to be drawn into the global factory. (1990:6)

4. Private volunteerism is not restricted to the upper classes, but among them it does often tend to substitute for political action. The Reagan-Bush ideology that a "thousand points of light" should replace government social programs revealed the reactionary potential of the volunteerist approach. Yet one also finds such attitudes among the generation allegedly politicized by the 1960s. Take, for example, hipster guru Ram Dass's efforts to get yuppies involved in "volunteer outreach" to community groups as a way of dealing with their middle-class guilt or despair (Lattin, 1991). I do not wish to demean volunteerism or service work, for I consider it a crucial aspect of social change (see below, 9,E). I only mean to say that it can be, and is, domesticated in the *locus imperii*.

5. I recall a vivid exchange between church leaders during a WCC/NCC delegation visit to Los Angeles after the uprising. A prominent Korean businessman rose to assure the black clergy present that he knew that neither Rodney King nor the people in the streets during the rebellion "represented" the African American community as a whole. The hardworking, family-oriented black community, he suggested, should dissociate themselves from such aberrant behavior. After a strained silence an African Methodist Episcopal bishop stood up, fixed his eyes on the Korean, and said dramatically and simply, "I *am* Rodney King; I *am* those young brothers in the streets." He then went on to counter the politics of moralism with example after example of the systemic and historic oppression of *all* blacks. See Lynell George (1992) and J. Davidson (1993).

6. *Stagflation* is a term defined by Holly Sklar as "stagnant economic growth with associated widespread unemployment plus rampant inflation" (1980:7). It is used as analytical shorthand by leftist economists to describe the "deepening economic crisis of world capitalism" during the Vietnam War era, characterized by four major factors: growing trade rivalries between the trilateral powers (U.S., Japan, Western Europe); the transition in the U.S. balance of trade from surplus to deficit; the change in international monetary relations resulting from the weakening of the dollar against foreign currencies; and resulting U.S. protectionism and economic nationalism.

7. Obviously this is not meant to be a comprehensive model. It ignores the Latino sectors, who are half the population of South Central, as well as working-class white and Asian sectors. And there are persons and groups that are exceptions to the model. I use it only to illustrate the generic dynamics of negotiating social geography in a stratified city, dynamics that are in reality infinitely more complex and subtle.

8

"What Will Be the Sign?"

Resistance

[The] myth of redemptive violence undergirds American popular culture, civil religion, nationalism, and foreign policy... it lies coiled like an ancient serpent at the root of the system of domination that has characterized human existence since well before Babylon ruled supreme.

Walter Wink,
Engaging the Powers

This transforming coming of a new humanity, initiated by God in the Human Being, Jesus, has in its gospel roots the power to free the world from every kind of violence and injustice.

James Douglass,
The Nonviolent Coming of God

"Tell us, when will *these things* take place, and what will be the sign of their accomplishment?" (Mk 13:4). This is by all means an understandable question. We disciples/readers have just been informed by Jesus that we are supposed to tear down the walls of our own house, stone by stone (13:2). But this architectural symbol (the Temple State, the American way of life) defines our political consciousness: We both admire it and hold it in awe (13:1). So Jesus' proposition begs explanation: *When* is this likely to happen, we inquire skeptically — and, more to the point, *how?*

In the best of times it is asking a bit much of ordinary citizens to imagine a world no longer defined by what they fear and love the most. But the moment in which the voice of Jesus chooses to predict the demise of the dominant order is in fact the worst of times — it is *wartime* (*BSM*:324ff). Wartime: Danger is in the air, the State is under threat, our way of life is threatened. This is the moment we are expected to heed the voice of authority, not doubt it; the time to rally 'round the flag and exhibit a little loyalty to the body politic, not to question its legitimacy. Or, conversely, it is the moment for the people to rise up against the oppressor, not to remain patient; it is time for revolutionary solidarity, not refusal to fight. But Jesus isn't buying war hysteria. His response to our anxious query chants a singular warning, mantra-like: "Beware!" (13:5); "Be aware!" (13:9); "Be wary!" (13:23). And what are we to be wary of? *Deception* — specifically the claims of politico-military leadership, no matter which side (13:5f, 22f). Apparently Jesus shared Aeschylus's conviction that "in war, truth is the first casualty."

"When you hear of wars and rumors of war, don't be stirred up; ...because this isn't the end. Nation combatting nation...represents only the beginning of labor!" (13:7f). Rooted in the disciplines of literacy, disillusionment, and revision, Jesus anticipates the propaganda of the "defense department" or the "revolutionary council," flatly contradicting their interpretation of the historical moment. First, says Jesus, the war boosters will try to mobilize you ("get you riled up," Gk *throeisthe*) by claiming the justice of their cause. The bigger the war effort, the better the world will be as a result, they promise. It is our evil opponents who are the problem, and they must be rooted out: two-bit dictators or imperialist powers or communist tyranny. Be assured, they vow, our military intervention is just an extension of our rational politics (to paraphrase von Clausewitz), which will usher in a more stable and just international order.

Not so, counters Jesus: Despite its cataclysmic trappings, war changes nothing and is manifestly not a sign of world transformation. Parodying, he contends that war cannot "put an end" to political crimes; it can only commence a new cycle of suffering. The dominant order is in labor, all right, but it can give birth only to more of the same, or worse. Moreover, Jesus continues, the fantastic claims of the war State in a state of war are as predictable as they are idolatrous, and they should not come as a surprise or draw us into their vortex of lies (13:21–23). Ever the realist, Jesus does not fail to remind us at this point that resisting the call to arms will be a most unpopular stand: the press, the politicians, and the people (even our own families!) will vilify us. After all, in wartime there is no neutrality; to stand against the patriotic cause is to stand with the enemy. But to endure this rejection "to the end," with the Holy Spirit's companionship — that is the meaning of liberation (13:9–13, 17–20).

"But when you see the abominating desolation..., flee to the mountains" (13:14). If their cause doesn't persuade you, continues Jesus, his voice building in intensity, expect them at some point to pull out their trump card. Let's call this, in generic apocalyptic fashion, the "desolating sacrilege." *The reader will understand,* editorializes Mark, winking at us across the ages (13:14). In other words, here is the "most difficult case." In every war there is at least one great "abomination" attributed to the enemy that, all other arguments aside, clearly legitimizes our use of force. The allure of moral outrage obviates all opposition, which is why the blasphemy is often manufactured. During the Gulf War the Bush administration spun stories of Iraqi storm troopers allegedly yanking babies off incubators and throwing them out windows; Saddam, meanwhile, invoked the specter of infidel armies desecrating Mecca. These "abominations" represent the ultimate litmus test for those struggling to resist the deception of war propaganda.

For Palestinian Jews during the moment of wartime in which Mark writes, the "unthinkable" was the Roman siege of the Jerusalem Temple. Once it commenced, even those who doubted the wisdom of the revolt felt compelled to close ranks with the cause, while those who refused were indeed "hated by all" (13:13). Loyalty to the House: the sine qua non of the body politic. But Jesus is looking for the House to come down, so he tells his disciples to head in the *opposite* direction of those rallying to the Holy City to defend the Holy Place (13:14–18). How can this be? Is it not running away from responsibility, leaving to others the task of "protecting freedom"? Under the pressure of precisely such persuasion, the church has historically withered in every moment of war since.

But Mark's Jesus is counseling us neither to sell out nor to "get the hell out." His point is that we cannot topple the dominant order if we take up that most sacred tool of change, the gun. Revolution, but no violence. Go figure. The problem is that to "see" his strategy requires profound apocalyptic insight (below, 12,A). If we are fascinated with the abominations and persuaded by the logic of revenge, we will succumb to the gun. If, however, we "learn the parable of the fig tree," and watch for the true signs of transformation, then we will see that the "Human One is near" (13:24–33). This epiphany alone has the power to unravel the fabric of domination that canopies the world.[1]

A. "INEVITABLE, BUT NOT FINAL": REVOLUTIONARY STRUGGLE AND THE SPIRAL OF VIOLENCE

How can we urgently yet respectfully debate revolutionary strategy?

Sunday afternoon, January 17, 1993. Outside my window a watery torrent sheets down from the sky. It has been raining for two weeks. This somber, gray weekend seems fitting for the two-year anniversary of the beginning of the Gulf War, that apocalyptic moment of war that rudely awoke us to the cold light of the New World Order. But the steady drum of rain cannot drown out the voices of thin-lipped reporters and military spokespersons reporting that today we have bombed Baghdad again. It is the imperial president's parting shot. Suddenly the nightmare is happening again — the trumped up ultimatums, the U.N. mask of legitimacy, the night sky over Baghdad eerily lit up by surface-to-air missiles, live on CNN.

It is clear that this way of life and death will continue, a grim imperial mantra of wars and rumors of war. The missiles of two years ago ended nothing; they only made more missiles inevitable. I stare numbly out at the rain. The deluge has put Los Angeles under a state of emergency, so there is no chance of getting into the streets to protest. It is difficult to sit and write in this *anti-kairos*.

I feel Illich's "almost unbearable anguish...that only the word recovered from history should be left to us as the power for stemming disaster" (1973:119). But why write at all, except to try to make sense of *this* moment above all? Indeed according to Mark, this is precisely the time to resist the temptation to give in to this lie.

In the *locus imperii* the violence of the gulf between rich and poor can be maintained only through the violence of guns. The situation is primal, and it is ancient: According to the Genesis narrative, the division between Cain and Abel led inexorably to fratricide (Genesis 4). The gun is our deepest human addiction and presents the greatest challenge to the defect-ive community's journey of recovery. Walter Wink, in his important book *Engaging the Powers,* has provided an exhaustive analysis of the depth to which we are captive to "the Domination system" and its myths of redemptive violence (1992:9ff). Yet we, like the disciples in Mark's story, continue to live by its dictates: "As the authorities seized Jesus one of those standing with him drew a sword" (14:47; *BSM:*367f). Like them, we flee when Jesus repudiates those dictates, unable to imagine any other form of resistance (14:50).

Today as the gulf grows, the rule of the gun becomes increasingly absolute. How do we dismantle the Domination system? This is the central revolutionary question of our time, and it has resulted in different answers. Some Christians have answered it by taking up arms (or supporting those who do) against those who have killed or oppressed too many people too ruthlessly for too long. Such a response to protracted injustice is, as Nicaraguan priest Miguel D'Escoto puts it, "quite reasonable": "Violence is not wrong because it is unreasonable but because we are called to live according to another law....As I engage in this search to deepen my understanding of the cross, I try to share with my fellow countrypeople how we must express, with nonviolent, evangelical means, our disapproval of everything that separates rather than unites us" (1991:6). For the most part, the First World radical discipleship movement today has agreed with D'Escoto that we are called to nonviolent forms of struggle. But my purpose here is not to recapitulate the long-standing theoretical debate between "pacifism" and "principled use of armed force." There is more than enough literature available on that subject.[2] I am no longer convinced we can determine in the abstract which position is the more ethically coherent or politically powerful or biblically faithful. I am more interested here in Jesus' questions to our respective answers.

It does not trouble me that those committed to overturning oppression honestly differ on how this is to be done. What concerns me is that we do not seem to be *talking about our differences.* During the 1960s, when revolutionary sentiment waxed, there was vigorous dialogue about the merits and limitations of violent and nonviolent forms of engagement. Less than a quarter century later however — during which the *locus imperii* has only tightened its control — that dialogue seems to have atrophied into a nondebate that is captive to assumptions, caricatures, and platitudes.[3] For example, it is widely assumed that nonviolent tactics are more relevant to First World contexts, less so to Third

World ones. Armed struggle is accepted as necessary in Namibia or Peru or Afghanistan because oppression and violence are more concrete there. Nonviolence is considered appropriate to the U.S. because it is the only "practical" choice.

Under the sway of such reasoning, First World activists politely sidestep questions of tactics when in dialogue with Third World liberation movements. This is ostensibly in the interests of solidarity, or because "we cannot tell others what to do." This position was given early articulation in a thoughtful 1972 essay entitled "Nonviolence Not First for Export" by North American organizer James Bristol. He concluded:

> Instead of trying to devise nonviolent strategy and tactics for revolutionaries in other lands, we will bend every effort to defuse militarism in our own land and to secure the withdrawal of American economic investment in oppressive regimes in other parts of the world. For example, instead of trying to urge nonviolence upon the Guatemalan guerrillas, we will endeavor to keep the U.S. Marines at home.... I believe in nonviolent revolution but I also believe that it is neither humane nor practical to urge nonviolent revolution upon others whose situation is so totally different from our own. It is up to the Latin Americans and the Africans to decide how they will wage their struggle for freedom. We cannot decide for them. Certainly we dare not judge the morality of their choice. (1972:12)

This was, at the time, both a courageous and a necessary corrective to strident First World moralism, rightly pointing out that our first responsibility is to resist U.S. militarism. Today it has become conventional wisdom that revolutionary strategies should be discerned relative to their own socio-political contexts. But it hardly follows that there is no room for critical conversation. Polite silence is *not* the definition of solidarity (see H. Clark, 1986).

It seems to me that the question of what means are appropriate to truly deconstructive politics is becoming more, not less, urgent. Several of Bristol's key assumptions are no longer accurate, if they ever were. Geopolitical conflicts are even more internationalized now. To take his example, emissaries from the Guatemalan Guerilla Army of the Poor today make fund-raising trips to the U.S. and hold support workshops here, just as Peace Brigades International organizers travel to Guatemala to hold workshops on techniques of nonviolent resistance. We can hardly ignore each other in the name of solidarity. Neither do Bristol's distinctions between our respective situations serve us well. We forget that the tradition of active nonviolence in this century was forged by Third World people, not by the First World middle-class peace movement. Nonviolence is no less indigenous to revolutionary Third World contexts, where alongside and sometimes instead of armed struggle there are always popular forces utilizing nonviolent tactics (on this see McManus and Schlabach, 1991, and Gene Sharp, 1973). Indeed there are indications that today nonviolence is resurgent in some of the world's most difficult battlegrounds — Palestine and

China, the Philippines and South Africa, Myanmar and New Caledonia (Gibeau, 1990; Myers, 1985a). The inverse is also true: Violent resistance is just as common in First World contexts — and given the oppression, just as understandable. To assume that armed struggle is obviated in the industrialized nations simply ignores reality. In the U.S. one need only consider the Los Angeles uprising, urban gang culture, right-wing paramilitary groups, and left-wing terrorists. There are just too many guns on all sides of First World race/class divides to imagine that nonviolent opposition is the only viable choice.[4]

Few today deny that modern war is problematic. But there continue to be compelling arguments for and against both violence and nonviolence in the struggle for social change in *any* context. Why, then, is it so difficult to sustain conversation among those engaged in revolutionary practice? Part of the reason may be that we have too often been talking past each other. We tend to construe violence either too broadly or too narrowly.

Too broad. Pacifists often define violence so broadly that one does not know where to begin to address the problem. For some delicate souls, violence is anything that disrupts one's psychic equilibrium — a screaming infant or an angry motorist or a strident argument. For others, violence is whatever aims to coerce, which would rule out many of the classic tactics of nonviolent politics such as strikes, boycotts, and even fasts. I believe such diluted definitions actually contribute to the obfuscation of the Domination system. It goes without saying that Christians ought to "repudiate the entire continuum of violence from domestic violence to war," as a non-governmental working group put it to the 1992 United Nations Summit on the Environment and Development. But if one assumes (as I do) that we cannot resist, and therefore should not analyze, interpersonal and international expressions of violence in the same way, broad denunciations are not particularly helpful. Vocabulary that connotes so much that it denotes very little is of no help to those struggling to read a system with critical literacy.

Political scientist Joan Bondurant moved in the right direction when she delimited violence as "the willful application of force in such a way that it is intentionally injurious to the person or group against whom it is applied" (1958:9; see also Arendt, 1969). But it is just as violent to die from malnutrition or lack of medical care as it is to die from a bomb or a billy club. Thus the South Africa *Kairos* Document complained: "The State and the media have chosen to call violence what some people do in the townships as they struggle for their liberation, i.e. throwing stones, burning cars and buildings and sometimes killing collaborators. But this *excludes* the structural, institutional and unrepentant violence of the State and especially the oppressive and naked violence of the police and the army" (R. M. Brown, 1990:43). If we refuse to acknowledge *any* differentiation in levels or kinds of political violence, we make some rather dubious equations that serve only to obscure the actual relations of power in a given context. Are stones thrown by Palestinian school children just as violent as Israeli tanks, and the crude spears of West Papuan resistance fighters just as violent as the modern U.S. jet fighters of the Indonesian military?

Even when pacifist organizations such as the AFSC, with its long tradition of working alongside Third World liberation movements, try to be careful in stating their positions, moral absolutism tends to prevail: "Although we see the frequently gross disparity between violence of the powerful as against violence of those seeking to end their own oppression . . . we have not and will not formulate a theory of 'acceptable' revolutionary violence" (1981:3). This represents a "deontological" discourse: "Violence is *always* wrong regardless of the situation." This may be our conviction; but we should be aware that this categorical approach to ethics tends to antagonize those trying to confront injustice concretely and contextually, particularly when articulated from a privileged First World site.

Too narrow. Nonpacifists, on the other hand, run into difficulties as well when they seek to distinguish between levels of violence in a given context. For example, they may contend that guerrilla struggle in the Philippines should be understood in terms of "the people protecting themselves" against the greater structural violence of a feudal political economy. There may be justification for such a claim, but we should be clear that it appeals (consciously or not) to the moral logic of "just war." Self-defense is a legitimate reason in the principles of *jus ad bellum* (just cause for taking up arms). Similarly it may be contended that SWAPO or ANC guerrillas have been more restrained and discriminatory in their use of force than the South African government troops. This argument is employing notions of proportionality found in *jus in bello* (just conduct in warfare).

Christians who make such arguments — whether to justify armed struggle by the FMLN in El Salvador or U.S. military intervention in Bosnia — no doubt feel quite comfortable with just war doctrine. But this ethical tradition is no less problematic than the deontological one. Historically just war theory has proven itself largely unable to restrain actual military practice (see Yoder, 1984; Douglass, 1966:155ff). Michael Walzer has shown, for example, that the practice of guerrilla warfare is rife with dilemmas, not the least of which is its tendency to dissolve distinctions between combatants and noncombatants, which inevitably puts all civilians at risk.[5] But I know of no liberation theologian who has shown concretely *how* armed revolutionary struggle can remain accountable to the constraints of "principled conduct in war." Theological apologists on the Left, like those on the Right, are usually more concerned to legitimate military action than to offer practical suggestions concerning when, how, and by whom arms can reasonably be taken up, and for what ends (see Lehmann, 1975; Míguez Bonino, 1975). Are liberation theologians relying on the alleged leavening influence of the church's moral tradition, or perhaps the consciences of individual Christians? If so, they are reverting to the very bourgeois ethical tradition they so despise: theory with little relationship to practice. Some avoid this dilemma by forgoing any attempt at moral assessment of the tactics of struggle, only to end up sounding very much like their liberal counterparts by appealing to "tragic necessity" or "situational ethics."

The spiral of violence model. The conversation about violence and nonviolence is difficult not only for reasons of definition, then, but also because we are relying on discursive traditions that do not help us. We are unwittingly falling back upon either deontological pronouncements or just war casuistry. But *both* the moralistic, noncontextual discourse of pacifism and the theoretical, legitimating discourse of just war are bankrupt. This dilemma led Brazilian Archbishop Dom Helder Camara two decades ago to propose a more complex and dynamic "taxonomy" of political violence (1974). His "spiral of violence" model can be summarized as follows:

Violence 1: Actual Relations of Power. In a given situation the distribution of social, cultural, economic, legal, political, and military power is unequal. This results in many kinds of structural violence: racism and patterns of discrimination, poverty, denial of human or cultural rights, loss of land and economic deprivation, forfeiture of freedoms, and so forth. Oppression is thus the primary form of violence and can be combatted only through structural changes and the redistribution of power. Insofar as the dominant system is enforced through the security apparatuses of police or military, repression is part of violence 1.

Violence 2: Rebellion and Revolt. Inevitably a situation of oppression engenders some form of resistance by its victims. This can and does take many nonviolent forms, as well as spontaneous rebellions by small or large groups (Prague Spring, Tiananmen Square). Sometimes widespread disruptive tactics are organized into a full-scale revolt, with the aim of bringing down those in power (the Iranian revolution, the Palestinian Intifada, the 1986 "People Power" campaign in the Philippines). When armed struggle is sustained over time, revolutionary groups usually organize themselves and their strategy along military lines, pursuing the goal of political influence and/or hegemony (e.g., the FSLN, UNITA).

Violence 3: Reaction. Just as it is inevitable for the oppressed to resist, it is equally predictable that those in power will react by escalating repression. Those in power almost always use violence 2 as an excuse to reestablish or entrench the dominant relations of power (violence 1). "State security" is invoked to justify everything from economic austerity programs and martial law to strategic hamleting and low-intensity counterinsurgency. The examples of this are too ubiquitous to mention. Nuclear weapons, it might be argued, are the ultimate manifestation of violence 3.

How does this model help us break out of our discursive deadlock? It enables us speak about violence in a way that acknowledges, on the one hand, the actualities of power in a given context and that allows for some fundamental differentiations. On the other hand, it recognizes that each stage of violence is part of the overall process of escalation, so that none can be understood or critiqued apart from the other. The violence escalates in an endless upward spiral through the reactive relationship of numbers 2 and 3 against the backdrop of 1. The model is relevant to interpersonal, family, and social conflict as well as to the politico-military sphere.

The spiral of violence represents a system of which we are all a part (in the body politic) and which is part of each of us (in our political body). On this, it seems to me, advocates of revolutionary violence and revolutionary nonviolence should be able to agree. I suspect Mark's Jesus had in mind such a taxonomy of violence when he repudiated the myth of war as a transformative practice. In the Domination system, he argued, war is inevitable but can never be final: "It *is* necessary that this happen but it is not yet the end" (13:7; Gk *dei genesthai all' oupō to telos*). In other words, violence cannot put an end to itself; it can only spawn itself (13:8). The spiral itself must be broken.

B. "WARS AND RUMORS OF WAR":
THE POLITICAL ECONOMY OF MILITARISM

Given the political economy of militarism, can armed struggle overthrow the Domination system, or does it only end up strengthening it?

What if we who agree on ends, but not on means, provisionally laid aside our respective key assumptions in a search for discursive common ground? Now we can focus on the practical question of *where we intervene* to try to stop the spiral of violence. We must admit that we in the First World too often ignore violence 1 and focus on violence 2. Third World respondents rightly wonder why we wait to speak out against violence until the oppressed have taken up arms or torches. But it also must be said that advocates of armed struggle underestimate the way in which violence 2 feeds and legitimates violence 3. What would happen if those of us committed to nonviolence, rather than simply condemning violence 2, concentrated instead on building revolutionary alliances of common cause with our Third World colleagues against violence 1, the realities of which they have much to teach us? And what would happen if those not committed in principle to nonviolence, rather than simply citing violence 1 as justification for violence 2, concentrated instead on building revolutionary alliances with us against violence 3, the realities of which we, residents of the most militaristic society in the world, can help clarify?

Chapter Seven examined how we in the First World can deepen our alliances against violence 1. Here I wish to look at the prospects of common cause against violence 3. I am suggesting that regardless of our position on nonviolence, both First and Third World revolutionaries need to come to a deeper appreciation of the essential connection between violence 2 and 3. Moreover if we wish to be firmly contextual and structural in our analysis, it seems to me that we should acknowledge that opposition forces can never hope to match the empire's sophistication in guns and tactics. The romantic myth of the guerrilla fighter armed with only an AK-47 and a heart full of revolutionary love is just that — a romantic myth. And appeals to "successful" anticolonial wars of midcentury are anachronistic. The military technologies and policies of the New World Order are now adjusted to preclude them in the future — that is the meaning of Grenada, UNITA, and the Contras. As the Vietnamese, the Cubans, the Angolans, the Salvadoran FMLN, and the Filipino NPA have all discovered, liberating a village, a province, or even a whole country does little to break the power of global counterrevolutionary forces.

Even where political systems *have* been overturned through guerrilla struggle — for example, Indonesia, Mozambique, Afghanistan, and Ethiopia — the results have been profoundly ambiguous. The new regimes, with few exceptions, have still been fundamentally military in character, unable or unwilling to democratize and demobilize, at great internal social, political, and economic cost (Ball, 1981). It can even be argued that military regimes are the inevitable result of militarizing the political process of liberation.[6] Revolutionary societies usually justify their continuing military apparatus by the fact that they face the antagonism of hostile countries (e.g., isolation, destabilization, or externally supported internal opposition). This is true, but it only illustrates my point: violence 3 ultimately prevails in the spiral of violence. The empire cannot be defeated militarily — not, as the Sandinistas found out, by popular vanguards no matter how vigilant; and not, as the Soviet bloc learned, by protracted hegemonic competition or by a resource- and infrastructure-monopolizing arms race.

The true character of violence 3 is what analyst Michael Klare (1978) calls the "scourge of militarism" (for the statistics, see the SIPRI Yearbook, 1992). This global system creates and maintains dictators and supports counterinsurgency warfare around the world. And these are the rules of the game: In order to fight, military groups must contract into the political economy of the transnational weapons trade. Klare, for years a voice in the wilderness, has tried to show (1984) that the weaponry used by Third World guerrillas, the local authoritarian regimes they fight, and the First World counterinsurgency forces that intervene are all supplied through the sordid world of the international arms trade (see also Pierre, 1982). All who take up arms, regardless of their banner, are dependent upon this trade and are thus caught in its political Gordian knots. This was well demonstrated by the shady dealings of the Iran-Contragate scandal, the basic syntax of which was as follows:

(a) The U.S. purchased Communist bloc weapons, through the mediation of pro-U.S. Israel, in order to equip anti-Communist Contra guerrillas in anti-U.S. Nicaragua, whose army was equipped by Communist bloc countries;

(b) these purchases were made with the profits from arms sales to anti-U.S., anti-Israel Iran, which used the weapons to fight a war with Iraq and to equip terrorists to attack U.S. and Israeli interests.

(c) The U.S. and Israel were meanwhile also making arms deals with anti-U.S., anti-Israel Iraq, as well as with most other Arab countries in the Gulf region, which weapons later came back to haunt both countries in the 1991 Gulf War.

(d) In Nicaragua, U.S. gun runners caught in the act turned out to be veterans of similar operations in Indochina, Cuba, and Libya (their modus operandi: assassination, drug smuggling, and extortion).

(e) The justification used by Oliver North et al for their violations of the Constitution and lying to Congress was the need to support democratic movements.

This episode, which is typical of the trade, suggests that the only winners of the game are the thoroughly capitalist military hardware producers and their distributors. So we must inquire: Does not violence 2 serve only to strengthen the overall system? Another way to put the query: Is armed struggle "counterrevolutionary"?

Let us probe deeper. What little popular attention was paid to the arms race during the 1980s has faded in the wake of recent strategic weapons reductions and alleged U.S. military "downsizing." But as my AFSC colleague Harold Jordan has shown, restructuring only means that the Pentagon is honing its "assets" for its new mission of managing the New World Order through low-intensity conflict (1992). Post–cold war bilateral arms agreements, which are much too little and late, have spawned not wider disarmament but a fresh round of proliferation. Russian republics are dumping much of their leftover Soviet military hardware on whoever can pay hard currency, for example. Third World arms manufacturing and export, meanwhile, has been on the rise for years (see Husbands, 1990; Ross, 1990). Both developments are increasing market pressure on First World producers and the economic satellites that depend on them (see Healy et al, 1993). As one U.S. defense analyst put it: "Our defense industry is as nervous as can be about how to adjust to the budget cuts [and] how to transfer capabilities to serve other markets by designing simpler and cheaper versions of weapons they've been selling the Pentagon. . . . It is going to be hard to keep them out of the export business" (Toth, 1990). The proliferation of sophisticated weaponry throughout the Third World increasingly poses a problem for the security concerns of the *locus imperii* (see Klare, 1990). As the *Los Angeles Times* reported in 1990: "The battle to keep strategically sensitive technology safely in the hands of Western democracies is shifting — from Eastern Europe to the Third World" (Pine, 1990:A1).

This is, of course, a dilemma of our own making:

For thirty-five years, the major military suppliers — Britain, France, the former Soviet Union and the U.S. — have been providing their allies and clients in the Third World with billions of dollars worth of advanced weaponry every year. In the 1980s alone, total arms acquisitions by Third World countries amounted to $427 billion (in constant 1988 dollars), with the great bulk of this equipment going to the Middle East and South Asia. These acquisitions have stimulated local arms rivalries, fueled regional conflicts and fed the hegemonic aspirations of emerging powers like Iraq. (Klare, 1992:120)

According to an August 1991 Congressional Research Service study, the U.S. regained the lead from the Soviets in arms transfer agreements to the Third

World in 1990, reaching \$18.5 billion, 45 percent of the world total. In 1992 the *Ploughshares Monitor* reported that Asia accounted for over one-quarter of the world's current armed conflicts and more than a third of world arms imports. Between 1987 and 1990, three-quarters of U.S. arms transfers went to the Middle East; in August 1991 alone, almost \$7 billion in sales went to such developing countries as South Korea, Saudi Arabia, Oman, Egypt, Brazil, Turkey, Morocco, and Taiwan. And our legacy of arming and training brutal Third World military dictatorships is grim (Klare and Arnson, 1981). Nowhere is it more gruesome than in El Salvador, where atrocities by a military under leadership trained at the U.S. School of the Americas are still coming to light (see Santiago, 1990; Morley, 1992; A. Lewis, 1992).

The arms manufacturers will go wherever the business is, regardless of ideological commitments and alignments of their clientele.

> In the United States, the pressures to increase foreign military sales are coming primarily from arms manufacturers, who face a significant reduction in domestic demand for their products — a situation that could result in the closure of entire production lines unless new buyers can be found for these products.... Arguing that a "warm production base" is vital to national security, officials of these companies are putting immense pressure on Washington to approve foreign sale of these items. "Exports are no longer just the icing on the cake," observes Joel Johnson of the Aerospace Industries Association, an industry trade organization. "They *are* the cake." (Klare, 1992:124)

Does it not stand to reason, then, that the more purchases made by arms consumers, the stronger these producers grow? And do not these corporations always serve the interests of elitist hegemony?

We must never forget that nuclear weapons — representing the *fin de siècle* in the spiral of violence — remain the dark umbrella under which global militarism marches. Robert Aldridge (1983, 1989) has been arguing for two decades that improvements in all aspects of the U.S. strategic triad and its complementary command, control, and communications systems have belied their offensive posture. The line between nuclear and conventional war was long ago diffused by the increasing sophistication of tactical weaponry such as the cruise missile. And the increase in countries with nuclear warhead and delivery capability promises to spawn not only regional nuclear arms races but nuclear war fighting itself. No act of revolutionary violence can be isolated from this global system of nuclearized militarism; to do so is as naive and indulgent as any pacifist moralism. One need look no farther than South Africa, India, and Israel, all nuclear-armed states in regions of long-term structural instability (see Adeniji, 1985). In such situations, what is to stop opposition forces from using tactical nuclear weapons? It is widely agreed that such weapons will be available through the underground arms trade within the next decade. Given these realities, is it not true that all arms consumers — from urban gangs purchasing automatic weapons to guerrilla units purchasing antiaircraft missiles — only end up *strengthening* the very system they allegedly seek to repudiate?

This excursus on the political economy of militarism is not meant to be a thin veil for yet another sermonic scolding of violence 2. I take seriously the objections that we in the Palace Courtyard should restrict our tactical opinions to situations *we* face, and that we are hypocritical to suggest nonviolence to those in dangerous and difficult situations we have not ourselves experienced. Moral humility is indeed appropriate to those of us who by virtue of race, gender, or class entitlement are insulated from so much of violence 1. This is why I am trying to discuss militarism phenomenologically rather than ethically. The world today is ruled by the *locus imperii,* that in turn is ruled by a military-industrial-academic-bureaucratic complex. This system has spawned a virus that has reproduced itself rapidly from center to periphery, so that it is now almost impossible to find political space anywhere in the world that has not been thoroughly overdetermined by militarized national security statism. The grim statistics of this epidemic were noted by Ruth Sivard in 1985:

Of the developing countries covered in this survey, 22 out of the 78 which were independent in 1960 were under military-controlled governments. By 1985 the count had gone up to 57 military-controlled out of 114 independent states, an increase from 28 to 50 percent of the total. Almost half (27 in all) of the militarized governments are in Africa. Latin America and the Far East tie for second place with 10 each.... All of the military-controlled governments [surveyed] eliminated suffrage entirely or imposed major restrictions on it. All used forms of violence to control the citizenry.... Despite this record of terrorism, not one of the countries where repression was practiced failed to receive a substantial flow of arms from obliging supplier nations. (1985:25)

It is the realities of violence 3 — and the political economy that drives it — that empirically preclude the possibility that violence 2 can halt, reduce, or contain violence 1. To arm against the militarism system is like throwing water on an oil fire; even if it manages to temporarily dampen the flames in an immediate area, the fire will only burn hotter overall.

Strategies of liberation, therefore, once defined militarily, function to strengthen, not subvert, the self-reproducing power of this system. It will remain in control no matter who uses guns against it because its rule *is* the gun. Because we are all captive to the Domination system, an act of violence (or a refusal to confront violence) in one place affects those in another place. We are all impacted by each other's choices: Kurd resisters and Kuwaiti sheiks, East Timorese guerrillas and Khmer negotiators, Serbian irregulars and Somali bandits, U.N. peacekeeping forces and U.S. Marines, Amazon Indians and private oil company militias, Crip gangsters and LAPD cowboys, middle-class peace activists and aerospace engineers. This is why genuine solidarity requires that all who would seek to overturn this system must engage each other in deep and nonplatitudinous conversation that is both respectful *and* critical.

Christians cannot dictate to others what they should do. But it is our vocation to "watch" (be/aware) for signs of a truly revolutionary practice in a history sentenced to death by wars and rumors of war.

C. "THEN THEY WILL SEE THE HUMAN ONE COMING IN POWER": NONVIOLENCE AND POLITICAL ORTHODOXIES

How does nonviolence seek to defect from the political orthodoxies of the Domination system?

Perhaps it is gratuitous to speak of overthrowing the Domination system — its political economy, its institutionalized enmities, and its utter skepticism about alternatives to itself. In our hearts we silently despair: "Who is like the Beast, and who can fight against it?" (Rev 13:4). Yet this is precisely the "worship" the Beast would have us give in to (Kellermann, 1991:53ff). Alternatively Jesus equates faith with the belief that we can "move this mountain" (Mk 11:22f). But the truth is, the system awes us just as it did the disciples in the shadow of the House (Mk 13:1). Jesus' insistence that it *will be* deconstructed (13:2) only deepens our incredulity: "When will this be, and what will be the sign when these things are accomplished?" (13:4).

D'Escoto is right that "violence is quite reasonable" — *within* the Domination system this will always be the case. But the ideological, economic, political, and technological character of violence today has unwittingly exposed a deep paradox. Robert Gardiner wrote in his brilliant tract *The Cool Arm of Destruction,*

> Even to those who understand the implications and the dangers of their own finitude, there are deep satisfactions in the exercise of dominion. There is no clearer symbol of dominion than the weapon...the power to destroy....The striving for such power is a quest for the illusion of omnipotence....It is surely ironic, therefore, that the quest for omnipotence only succeeds in strengthening the limitation of finitude by making life even more fragile and dangerous. (1974:34f)

The escalating spiral of violence has unmasked the impotence of the gun to transform the Domination system. When Martin Luther King concluded that the choice facing us is between nonviolence or nonexistence, then, he was not presenting us with a moral ultimatum but a historical one (Washington, 1986:280).

The notion of a historical dead end in which we must turn around returns us to our theology of repentance. For Mark repentance, the subject of the first call to discipleship (1:15ff), is in the second call further clarified as the via crucis (8:34). Here the paradox of power is clearly articulated: to save life one must lose it (8:35–37). But the paradox concludes with a mysterious promise that "some of those standing here will not taste death until they see the Great Economy arrive with power" (9:1). This, we should note, speaks of a *realized* "arrival" (Gk *elēlythuian,* perfect tense), not an imagined or eschatological one. How then does the via crucis represent the definitive deconstruction of the Domination system and the actualization of the Great Economy?

It has often been pointed out that Mark's three "portents" of the Human One's political fate represent an intentional literary and theological structure (8:31; 9:31; 10:33f). Yet few have given attention to the fact that the epiphany of the Human One "in power and glory" is also promised three times in Mark. I have argued (*BSM:*390ff) that just as the portents of death are realized in the Passion narrative, so too the portents of this epiphany. It happens at the moment of Jesus' death on the cross:

"some of those standing here will...see" (9:1) =
 "bystanders" at Golgotha (15:35) and the female disciples watching
  "at a distance" (15:40);
"You [Sanhedrin] will see..." (14:62) =
 chief priests/scribes ridiculing Jesus on cross (15:31);
"the sun will be darkened...and the stars will fall from heaven...
  and then they will see..." (13:24–26) =
 midday darkness (15:33) and the curtain of the Temple tearing as
  Jesus expires (15:38).

In Mark's story the cross is neither a heroic nor a tragic moment. It is an *apocalyptic* one, the epiphany of a new power that "shakes the Powers in the heavens."[7]

In Jesus' apocalyptic sermon, Mark identifies this moment with the "parable of the fig tree" (13:28; *BSM:*350f). This is an allusion to Isaiah's vision of the end time: "All the powers of the heavens will melt, and the heavens will roll up like a scroll, and all the stars fall as leaves from a vine, and as leaves fall from a fig tree" (Is 34:4). Here, then, is Jesus' answer to the disciples' inquiry about times and signs: "When you see *these things* [Gk *tauta*] taking place, you know [the Human One] is near" (13:29). What things? We find the clue earlier in the story after Jesus' symbolic direct action regarding the fig tree and the Temple (11:13ff), which elicits this protest from the authorities: "By what authority do you do *these things?*" (11:28). The practice of the Human One attacks the "fig tree" at its roots (11:20). Mark's discourse suggests that when the central myths and institutions of centralized power are "exorcised," the Domination system is on notice; when the cross is "taken up," its omnipotence is broken. This is what the disciples ("learners," Gk *mathētai*) must *"learn* from the parable of the fig tree" (Gk *manthanō*). And it explains why the only "glory and power" Jesus can grant his disciples is that of the via crucis (10:37–40).

Jon Sobrino, following Jürgen Moltmann, has argued that Jesus' cross signifies the end of traditional theology: "It is here that we confront the real issue:

What sort of power is it that really and truly renders the deity present? Human beings automatically think of God as someone who possesses and wields power. Jesus forces people to consider whether that deeply rooted conviction is true or not" (1978:213). "The cross forces us to reformulate the whole problem of God," Sobrino continues; "God is to be recognized through what seems to be quite the opposite of divine, i.e. suffering" (ibid:222). But if this is the case, then does not the cross also signify the end of politics as traditionally understood? Does it not also force us to reformulate the whole problem of power and to adopt a radically new attitude toward revolutionary struggle? Oddly Sobrino, the Third World theologian, skirts this logic. Jim Douglass, the First World theologian, however, does not.

Over the course of two decades of practice and reflection — chronicled in four books, *The Nonviolent Cross* (1966), *Resistance and Contemplation* (1972), *Lightning East to West* (1980), and most recently *The Nonviolent Coming of God* (1991) — Douglass has argued that the apocalyptic politics of Jesus are best understood in terms of Gandhian nonviolence. He further contends that our own historical moment compels us to take both Jesus and Gandhi seriously. Douglass believes that Gandhi rediscovered Jesus' way of the cross, negating the revolutionary impotence of violence with the revolutionary power of nonviolence:

> The common factors in Jesus' and Gandhi's private and public experiments in reality is that all their experiments made them poor, increasingly poor in their very being. The voluntary poverty of the wilderness was completed by the state-enforced ... deeper poverty, realized in arrest, personal humiliation, and execution or assassination. An engagement with Reality at this depth is the spiritual constant analogous to the speed of light. ... The spiritual constant is self-emptying love for the sake of others, at an inconceivable depth in ourselves ... In that perspective the crucifixion of Jesus is the absolute opening and invitation into a new Reality. (1980:14)

Like Mark, Douglass holds the apocalyptic conviction that the end time was realized in the advent of the Human One on the cross, unleashing the only power that can liberate and transform a world captive to the Domination system (1991:36ff).

Ignatius Jesudasan, in his underappreciated *Gandhian Theology of Liberation* (1984), reminds us that Gandhi, like Jesus and people in the Third World today, faced a concrete historical situation of dependence: external colonial oppression, an indigenous order of rigid social stratification and intense racial rivalry, an agrarian political economy dominated by elite interests, and vast disparities between city and village. Gandhian nonviolence was much more than dramatic mass direct actions such as the famous salt campaign. He developed a theory and practice of *swaraj* (liberation) that advocated "revolution from below" (ibid:47ff). *Swaraj* was not limited to national liberation; it included the tasks of reconciliation between India's Hindus and Muslims and the eradication of the caste system. Gandhi took the option for the poor by insisting that social change must begin with the *harijan* (the lowest Indian caste) and advocated a comprehensive program of economic restructuring at the village level. Many of Gandhi's most successful campaigns were economic boycotts and employment alternatives, such as his advocacy of self-reliance through the spinning wheel. And in Gandhian political action suffering is the weapon not of the weak but of the strong. Suffering "in one's own person is...the essence of nonviolence and is the chosen substitute for violence to others" (ibid:96). Gandhi believed that through the power of *satyagraha* (truth-force or soul-force), "it is possible for a single individual to defy the whole might of an unjust empire" (ibid). But his movement was not individualist; at its center was the *ashram,* an alternative community of discipline and reflection.

The spiral of violence presents us with a structural problematic. Violence 2 can only be counterrevolutionary, given the political economy of militarism within the Domination system. Alone among modern political ideologies, nonviolence repudiates the orthodoxy of the gun. Gandhi was not a Christian (see Ellsberg, 1991). But, with Douglass and Jesudasan, I have contended (*BSM:*47, 257, 438, 452) that swaraj and satyagraha represent a kind of hermeneutic key to understanding Mark. The via crucis invites us to unswerving commitment to justice and compassion, to build community with the poor and marginalized, to refuse to take up arms against the enemy, and, above all, to believe in the power of the nonviolence to transform the world. This is the apocalyptic vigil over history that Jesus invites his disciples to keep (13:32ff; below, Chapter Twelve).

Needless to say, we First World Christians have not had "eyes to see the Human One coming in glory" on the cross. Those of us who are committed to nonviolence have a long way to go before our practice — which is partial, timid, and scarcely revolutionary — comes anywhere near our lofty theories. We have only begun to experiment with the truth of satyagraha as the via crucis.

D. "WHOSOEVER WOULD FOLLOW ME":
A CHURCH DISARMED AND MILITANT?

Why are both basic forms of nonviolent resistance crucial to the church as a community of discontinuity?

Mark's invitation to "take up the cross" (8:34) is the central characteristic of discontinuity with the Domination system. "*Whosoever* would" — this is one of Jesus' few universal prerequisites for discipleship. We must deny the self that is protected by the gun and its myths, and experiment with satyagraha. Some Christians in the *locus imperii* understand this in terms of a "vow" of nonviolent resistance as a way of life (Dear, 1987; Wink, 1992: 109ff). Resistance is how the community of discontinuity remains "sober" and how it "intervenes" in the dysfunctional and addictive system (above, 6,B). It is how we "defend" the political body against pathology and "offend" the pathological body politic.

These therefore represent the two basic trajectories of nonviolence: the struggle to remain "disarmed" on one hand and "militant" on the other. Both are equally necessary characteristics for a "peace church."

Disarmed. The "nonresistance" tradition (something of a misnomer) in the U.S. has roots in nineteenth-century religious pacifist movements (see Ballou, 1966). This tradition puts primary emphasis on personal and occasionally corporate noncooperation with the demands of officially sanctioned violence. In terms of recovery language, we try to prevent violence (as a dynamic system of addiction spiraling through human history) from feeding its frenzy on and in our political bodies. To do this, it is incumbent upon us to identify the concrete points where the social imperatives for violence intersect with our lives, and noncooperate *there.* In every U.S. war, for example, pacifists have refused conscription or other forms of military support and struggled for the right of "conscientious objection." But the nonresistant witness has also been expressed in other areas. Certain eighteenth-century Quakers, for example, freed their slaves and refused to purchase products they knew to be made by slave labor. As mentioned (above, 6,D), many of us believe that today federal income tax resistance is a basic place to resist the obligations of modern militarism (tax payment was also a litmus test of imperial loyalty in Mark's gospel; cf 12:13–17; *BSM:*310ff).

Ours is the most violent society in the world—even apart from our psychic domination by the prospect of nuclear war (Fein, 1981). We are saturated by violence at all levels of culture, as a recent media study shows: "In a single, random day (April 2, 1991) of television programming tracked in Washington for *TV Guide,* 1,846 individual acts of violence were observed.... Cartoons were the most violent category, with 471 violent scenes in just one day. 21 percent of all the violence — 389 scenes — involved a life-threatening assault; 362 scenes involved gunplay" (Disney, 1992). During 1992 there were more than 2,600 homicide deaths involving guns in Los Angeles County alone (see Hull, 1993). Similar grim statistics hold for assault, rape, and spouse and child abuse. No wonder one medical doctor has labeled violence as the primary public health threat in the U.S. today (Cavander, 1992).

The ideology that right can finally be secured only through might is reproduced in all the discourses of our culture, from education to religion. The myth of redemptive violence relies heavily, Wink points out (1992:17ff), upon primal hero narratives — from the historical-legendary (Joshua or Patton or Sandino) to the comical-fantastic (Rambo or Popeye or Teenage Mutant Ninja Turtles). As the young Jesse Jackson put it in the days of the black power movement: "The competition to nonviolence does not come from Stokely or Eldridge; it comes from America's traditions, it comes from little children seeing cowboys solving their moral problems by killing" (1971:147). In the *locus imperii,* therefore, commitment to nonviolence involves every aspect of daily life: how we consume, where we work, and how we raise our children. For many, purging violence from the political body includes personal disciplines such as fasting and vegetarianism.

Some pacifists have extended their commitment beyond their own unilateral disarmament. They seek also to mitigate the destructive effects of violence upon the body politic. Conflict mediation is another hallmark of this tradition at its best (etymologically *pacifism* comes from the Latin "to make peace"). Here the disarmed community offers itself as a buffer between warring parties, a vocation that the church has embraced at various times in its history. During the Middle Ages, for example, reform movements known as the Peace of God and the Truce of God attempted to extend spheres of immunity and cease-fire in the midst of the bloody wars of medieval Europe (see Bainton, 1960: 110ff). The notion of the church as arbitrator, combined with the humanist traditions of the Renaissance, gave rise to the modern just war theory and subsequently to international law (see Bailey, 1972:9ff). Unfortunately, as I have argued above (A), the church's use of moral codes for war has far more often led it into partisan support for one side than mediation and conflict reduction.

It may well have been a search for models of reconciling community that led John Woolman into the wilderness on his vision quest as the French-Indian War raged (above,5,E,2). He was seeking the counsel of the Delaware people, who, according to the nineteenth-century ethnographer Daniel Brinton, maintained extraordinarily peaceful relationships with the early Quaker settlers: "Their action toward the Society of Friends in Pennsylvania indicates a sense of honor and respect for pledges which we might not expect. They had learned and well understood that the Friends were non-combatants.... The fact that for more than forty years after the founding of Penn's colony there was not a single murder committed on a settlement by an Indian itself speaks volumes for their self-control and moral character" (1883:63). This represents an extraordinary exception to the otherwise virtually uninterrupted hostilities between Indians and Europeans during this period. The explanation probably lies in the fact that the Lenape tribe of the Delaware had a vocation not unlike that of the Quakers — they were recognized by other Indian nations in the region as peacemakers.

The Lenape peace chieftains "could neither go to war themselves nor send nor receive the war belt," wrote Brinton; "their proper badge was the *wampum* belt, with a diamond-shaped figure in the centre, worked in white beads, which was the symbol of the peaceful council fire, and was called by that name" (ibid:47).

A unique peculiarity of the political condition of the Lenape was that for a certain time they occupied a recognized position as non-combatants — as "women," as they were called by the Iroquois.... Among the Five Nations and Susquehannocks, certain grave matrons of the tribe had the right to sit in the councils, and, among other privileges, had that of proposing a cessation of hostilities in time of war. A proposition from them to drop the war club could be entertained without compromising the reputation of the tribe for bravery. There was an official orator and messenger, whose appointed duty it was to convey such a pacific message from the matrons, and to negotiate for peace.... There can be no question that the neutral position of the Delawares was something different from that of a conquered nation, and that it meant a great deal more. They undoubtedly were the acknowledged peacemakers over a wide area. (Ibid:109f)

It was from these people that the Quaker pacifist Woolman desired to learn about peacemaking. It is one of the truly remarkable hidden histories of the Americas.[8]

As the bloody twentieth century draws to a close, the post-Constantinian church is struggling to find a new political vocation. In a world riddled by local, regional, and global conflict, there has never been a greater need for unilaterally disarmed and actively peacemaking community (Yoder, 1971a; Myers, 1980a). Unfortunately the church has shrunk from such costly discipleship, leaving conflict mediation to the United Nations. While certainly First World Christians should support international peacekeeping efforts, it would seem we could do more. One problem is that much of the intellectual energy of the pacifist community has gotten mired in the liberal academic abstractions of the institutionalized "peace studies/conflict resolution" field. It is not that we have no need for disciplined and critical reflection on difficult issues of ethnic, racial, and economic enmities (see C. Stephenson, 1991). The problem is that the university site is removed from the actual situations of socio-political conflict, and peace studies departments have rarely included practical internships in their curricula. Peace Brigades International is a more engaged expression of what a peacemaking community might be — an organized and disciplined cadre of nonviolent mediators that is dispatched throughout the world to help mitigate hostilities and resolve conflicts. The AFSC has similarly tried to take Quaker skills of reconciling mediation into political hotspots around the world. Clearly, however, we are nowhere near realizing Gandhi's vision of "standing armies of *satyagrahis*," which are willing and able to wage peace in a world of wars and rumors of war.

Militant. The second characteristic of nonviolent resistance is the offensive task: placing our political bodies in direct conflict with the body politic. A tradition associated in this century with Gandhi and M. L. King, its main emphasis is to unmask the structural characteristics of oppression and violence by confronting them publicly.[9] Militant nonviolence does not wait until the State makes demands; instead, policies that undergird war and economic injustice are protested in order to provoke a moral and political crisis. The most common tactic in this tradition has been civil disobedience. But how does such nonviolent direct action, given its necessarily symbolic character (sitting in, or planting a tree next to a missile silo), function politically? Do such actions merely represent a strange form of social deviance — as is contended by prosecutors and judges — or, worse, rituals of private expiation for participants (below, F)?

Nonviolent direct action is indeed ritual, but public ritual can and does function politically, according to Bobby Alexander (1991). But to what end? Structural-functionalist sociology has long characterized protest rituals among oppressed groups — such as Melanesian cargo cults, Lakota ghost dancers, self-immolating Vietnamese Buddhist priests, or frenzied working-class Pentecostals — as basically conservative: " 'Ritual rebellion' reinforces the structural status quo by sublimating and thereby purging participants' antisocial sentiment.... It serves social differentiation by reinforcing the status distinctions on which social structure is based" (Alexander, 1991:2f). In other words, these groups were or are, just letting off steam without trying to change anything.

In direct contrast to this conventional wisdom anthropologist Victor Turner argued that

> ritual creates social conflict by relaxing or suspending some of the requirements of everyday social structure, making possible alternative social arrangements.... Ritual is essentially a means of transforming the fixed aspects of the everyday sociocultural world, making it serve communitarian ends.... Differentiation among social statuses and roles by nature creates "alienation," "distance and inequality," and "exploitation." The primary motivation behind ritual is the desire to break free of social structure temporarily in order to transcend its social and existential limitations and reconfigure it. (Ibid:1, 17)

It is not difficult to see these characteristics in many forms of nonviolent direct action (see Jordan, 1981). It carefully chooses where to confront the Domination system. The site for "ritual" struggle must be representative of wider (but often mystified) political realities: say, a salt factory in India, a lunch counter in the South, or a nuclear weapons factory. Refusing the salt tax and marching to the sea, demanding service in a segregated restaurant, or taking carpenter's hammers to missile nose cones are symbolic actions meant to provoke public debate about official policies and structures of oppression: respectively, the colonial economy of British India, Jim Crow laws, and U.S. militarism.

Turner suggests three elements that characterize subversive ritual (Alexander, 1991:27ff), each of which the tradition of militant resistance reflects. First, the "performance" creates "anti-structure." Nonviolent direct action is fashioned around resistance to oppressive laws or institutions. Legal and social orthodoxy are suspended and subverted; as Jim Douglass often says, the barbed wire fence around a military base, which represents a red light to the average citizen, should instead be seen as a green light to those trying to transform the world through nonviolence. Second, the performance provokes "liminality" among those who witness or participate in them. Civil disobedience is liminal behavior. Indeed for some it represents a kind of exorcism of the political body, "dis-possessing" the participant of the demon of silenced conformity even while resulting in incarceration. Third, the performance arises from alternative social space. Nonviolent direct action is both planned in and supported by communities of discontinuity, whether Gandhian ashrams, affinity groups, or Plowshares retreats. I will discuss experiments in nonviolent direct action more in the next section (below, E).

These two aspects of nonviolent resistance — disarmed noncooperation and militant direct action — are not mutually exclusive, though some view them that way. There are, for example, those on the Left who equate pacifism with "passivism," just as there are those on the Right who view civil disobedience as too "politicized" (e.g., Lewy, 1988). I believe both are essential, not only to a genuine "peace church" but also to a genuinely democratic political culture. One of the central problems in the *locus imperii* is that so much of the violence generated by our socio-economic system is either hidden or exported, victimizing those we cannot see. Our disempowerment is real because responsibility has become so remote or abstract (above, 6,C). Public discourse is strangled by obfuscation, marginalized by unaccountable political leadership, and silenced by our own denial. No matter how literate we are in the structures of oppression, or dis-illusioned of the dominant myths, or revisionist of our past, it is still difficult to know how and where to intervene in the Domination system.

That is why both defensive and offensive resistance is so crucial to the struggle for social justice in the U.S. Democracy is a good idea, insofar as it redistributes power on a regular basis. But its great vulnerability is that it demands an empowered citizenry, one that is constantly training itself to identify and resist concentrations of power. This is hardly the case in the *locus imperii* today. Regular citizens have steadily decreasing control over the steadily increasing centralization of State power, which electoral politics simply no longer has the power to change.[10] The steady decline in voter turnout indicates that popular political participation — and if the recent Ross Perot phenomenon is any barometer, populist politics as well — is atrophying rapidly, at least at the national level. Because electoral politics under capitalism is firmly under the rule of image, it is also under the sway of those who can afford to manufacture those images. Representation has degenerated into consumer choices between rabidly competing, but scarcely differing, political personality cults. Elitist decision making, structured advantages for big capital, two-party monopolizing, public mystification — these are the true enemies of democracy.

In such a context, the politics of nonviolent resistance is inherently empowering. Injustice is perpetuated by the passive assent of political bodies: To refuse to conform is to quickly identify the limits of dissent within systems of repressive tolerance. The more collective the defection, the more significant it is. Genuine democracy is the function of a citizenry able freely and responsibly to offer and to withdraw its consent to be governed. When we vote with our political bodies, we take our responsibilities seriously, refusing to shrug them off by electoral proxy. This at once challenges the alienation of our political bodies from the body politic. Resistance demands more of us — we are no longer passive consumers and must be clearer about what we think about the issues in order to put our lives on the line. But it also demands more of the political process: We become active participants who refuse to allow the press, congressional committees, or special interests to determine what is possible and what is important.

If human freedom and justice are to have a future, we can no longer hide behind the myth of redemptive violence or cower before the rule of the gun. Satyagraha demands that we take responsibility for speaking truth to power and embrace the consequences of our actions. The same is demanded by true and living democracy. In commending to disciples the via crucis, Jesus understood that to "save" the body politic, people had to be willing to "lose" their political bodies (8:35). Let us take a closer look at this paradox.

E. "THIS IS MY BODY": EXPERIMENTS IN SOMATIC POLITICS

Why are our bodies our most potent nonviolent tool?

On the eve of his showdown with the Domination system, Mark's Jesus said to his betrayal-bound companions: "Take: this is my body" (14:22). This phrase, which lies at the heart of the church's theology, should also lie at the center of our politics. In Mark's Passion narrative, the war of myths is stripped down to the fundamental struggle between Jesus' political body and the body politic as represented in the Jerusalem Temple. Those who testify against Jesus at his trial before the Sanhedrin claim, "We heard him say he will destroy this Temple made with hands and in three days build another not made with hands" (Mk 14:58). It is perjured testimony because Jesus nowhere actually says these words in the narrative; but it is not *wrong* (*BSM:*375f). Jesus did call for the Temple's demise (13:2ff), enacted it in a direct action in the Temple precinct (11:15ff), and invited his disciples to join him in the struggle to overthrow this system (11:23ff). But without this architectural symbol of the body politic, what is there around which to organize a new order? In the midst of a Temple-centered ritual meal of Passover, Jesus offers the alternative: his political body (*BSM:*361ff).

From beginning (14:3ff) to end (16:1ff) in Mark's Passion narrative, it is women who intuit the meaning of this new *somatic* politics. Mark rejects the ritual commemoration of Jesus' body: The "memorial words" ("Do this in remembrance of me," 1 Cor 11:24f; Lk 22:19) are not said during the Last Supper but rather in commendation of the discipleship practice of the "anointing" woman (Mk 14:9). Similarly at the end of the story Jesus' body is not there to solemnize: "He is gone: see the place where they put the body" (16:6). The women encounter instead an apocalyptic figure in white. When faced with a similarly transfigured body earlier, a fearful Peter had suggested building a "tabernacle" (9:5f). The women at the tomb are afraid too, for they have been informed that the practice of Jesus' political body is not over but continues (16:7). Mark thus leaves us with a choice: to return to the politics of tabernacle construction (an internalization of Temple State ideology) or to follow Jesus in practicing somatic politics.

Various traditions of militant nonviolence in the twentieth century have experimented with the truth of somatic politics. Gandhi believed that satyagraha was the best weapon of the poor because it relied on the only thing they had control over and could mobilize: their bodies. Dr. King believed that only by violating real social boundaries with real political bodies could the U.S. come to terms with the duplicity of its racist body politic. And Plowshares activists have pioneered resistance to imperial militarism by calling Christians to trespass into the most sacrosanct nuclear security areas. Common to each tradition is the conviction that *where* we place our political bodies in the body politic makes all the difference. Philip Berrigan, as is his way, expresses the thesis of somatic politics somewhat more bluntly: "Hope," he is fond of saying, "is where your ass is."

Civil disobedience attempts to unmask socio-political contradictions by representing them in public ritual, thus rendering the war of myths visible in real time and space. Such actions cannot be dismissed by the authorities as merely deranged opinion or antisocial behavior, because actual bodies must be dragged away, arrested, and jailed. At each point in the process the possibility of genuine political debate is opened up. To illustrate the alternative power of somatic politics, I will make brief mention of three examples drawn from the last several decades of nonviolent struggle in the U.S.[11]

When Rosa Parks refused to sit at the back of the bus in Montgomery, Alabama, on December 1, 1955, she was not the first to do so. But her solitary gesture triggered a bus boycott that launched a civil rights movement that changed the character of the whole society (Parks, 1992). By not standing, Rosa made a stand against a racist body politic in her own political body: "People always say that I didn't give up my seat because I was tired, but that isn't true. I was not tired physically, or no more tired than I usually was at the end of a working day. I was not old...I was forty-two. No, the only tired I was, was tired of giving in" (ibid: 116). Similarly when Joseph McNeill, Ezell Blair, Jr., Franklin McCain, and David Richmond, all freshmen at North Carolina Agricultural and Technical College in Greensboro, sat at a segregated department store lunch counter on February 1, 1960, their political bodies became a lightning rod that grounded the racist power of the Old South. Their strategic placement was more premeditated than Rosa's, but no less intentional and no less consequential. "By the end of the following September, over 70,000 students, both black and white, had participated in similar demonstrations across the country" (Washington, 1986:94; on King's similar 1963 campaign in Birmingham see ibid:534ff).

The civil rights movements of the late 1950s and 1960s could well be construed as "defensive" action, in which African Americans protected the integrity of their political bodies against the daily assault of Jim Crow. Yet the mass protests and pray-ins and sit-ins became also an "offensive" assault on the color line, which not only unmasked U.S. racism but eventually raised other fundamental contradictions of the *locus imperii*. As King put it after he publicly broke with U.S. policy in Vietnam:

A more tragic recognition of reality took place when it became clear to me that...we were taking the black young men who had been crippled by our society and sending them eight thousand miles away to guarantee liberties in Southeast Asia which they had not found in Southwest Georgia and east Harlem. And so we have been repeatedly faced with the cruel irony of watching Negro and white boys on TV screens as they kill and die together for a nation that has been unable to seat them together in the same schools. We watch them in brutal solidarity burning the huts of a poor village, but we realize that they would never live on the same block in Detroit. I could not be silent in the face of such cruel manipulation of the poor. (Washington, 1986:635)

The civil rights movement not only forged, for the first time, a politics of mass civil disobedience in the U.S. It is no exaggeration to assert that it was responsible for animating all of the subsequent social and political turmoil that followed, from black power and other ethnic identity movements to the white counterculture and antiwar movement.

When Bryan Willson, a Vietnam veteran, was run over by a train loaded with armaments bound for El Salvador at the Concord Naval Weapons Station on September 1, 1987, losing both legs, he offered the penultimate expression of somatic politics (Douglass, 1991:16ff). His sacrifice triggered a campaign of nonviolent resistance on those same tracks, still stained with Bryan's blood, for several years after. Such actions have become the hallmark of the militant wing of the peace movement in the U.S., born out of the legacy of antiwar protests such as the draft-file burning of the Catonsville Nine. In the early 1970s as the secular movement collapsed, this tradition reconsolidated in religious circles (Kellermann, 1991:103ff). These faith-based activists agree with James Bristol that their primary task in the First World is to resist imperial militarism (above, A); but the question of *how* we "keep the U.S. Marines at home" is difficult. Strategies that focus on shaping legislative and public opinion, though important, have become increasingly proscribed by the realities of both covert military operations and the speed of deployment in overt interventions. Given the abstract and secretive character of U.S. foreign and military policy, therefore, peace activists have tried to respond with actions that unmask its true character. The politics of trespass was thus reappropriated from the civil rights movement in order to reveal the actual geography of militarism — weapons factories, distribution depots, missile silos, research and development sites, forward deployments, secret communications installations, even training centers.[12]

The physical presence of resisters at these sites means to provoke what Jim Douglass calls a moral and political crisis. The tactics vary. Sometimes the aim is token impediment, disrupting business as usual for a few hours, as in the repeated "die-ins" in front of Pentagon entrances; the antiapartheid movement's blockading of corporate offices in financial districts; or actions to obstruct the nuclear "White Train" on its route around the country. On other occasions, the focus is on somatically violating the sacred space of the national security state, as in the case of active gestures of disarmament (hammer-wielding Plowshares actions) and presence (prayer pilgrimages to nuclear weapons sites; Myers,

1981). Bill Kellermann (1991) has shown how such resistance to the "gods of metal" reinterprets traditional liturgical practices by moving the geography of worship to spaces of contention.

When Jack Elder was arrested on April 13, 1984, for transporting three Salvadorans from Casa Romero, a hospitality house in San Benito, Texas, he was representing a third tradition of somatic politics (Corbett, 1991:156ff). Central America solidarity work through the 1980s developed several notable aspects of creative nonviolence. The Sanctuary movement sought to protect Central American refugees from immigration and political authorities, as well as from mercenary *coyotes* along the refugee trail. This was done first by working for safe passage through an "underground railway," and then through offering hospitality in churches and families. The political bodies of refugees made the distant realities of U.S.-sponsored war on the poor concrete to middle-class congregations in the Palace Courtyard (MacEoin, 1985; Golden and McConnell, 1988). A second aspect of somatic politics arose subsequently as refugees returning to their homes asked First World supporters for *acompañamiento*. This spawned the flip side of the nonviolent partnership, as North Americans relocated their political bodies to war zones, hoping to provide a deterrent to further violence aimed at the refugees. One of the most impressive expressions of both aspects of this solidarity was the work of Our Lady Queen of Angels parish in downtown Los Angeles. There refugees and undocumented immigrants found safe haven, while priests and other volunteers regularly traveled to Central America to accompany the poor in their resettlement (see M. Kennedy et al, 1990).

A related aspect of this tradition is the work of Witness for Peace, which trains nonviolent observers to place their political bodies in war zones between combatants, in an effort to deter fighting and human rights violations (see Griffin-Nolan, 1991). This faith-based strategy was conceived as a way to expose the covert U.S. war on the Sandinistas, and there is some reason to believe it was in fact a reason why the Reagan administration never launched a full-scale invasion of Nicaragua. On the home front, Witness also developed an emergency response network, which prepared teams to mobilize sit-ins at congressional offices at crucial moments in the struggle against U.S. policy. Witness for Peace is now experimenting with this model in such places as the Middle East, South Africa, and even inner-city areas in the U.S.

Christians from diverse traditions have been deeply involved with each of the three examples of militant nonviolence I have noted. And whether it was Dr. King, the black Baptist minister (Garrow, 1987), Jean Gump, the Catholic mother of twelve and a nuclear resister (Bearak, 1988), or Jim Corbett, the Quaker rancher and Arizona Sanctuary activist (1991:115ff), such Christians have repeatedly appealed to the "logic" of the cross to understand their practice of somatic politics. In a world in which the Domination system holds history hostage to ever-bigger guns and ever more fabulous myths of redemptive violence, the apocalyptic myth of the cross is the end of politics as usual. Perhaps *only* somatic politics — which invites us to drop all weapons from our hands and "take up" our political bodies — can rehabilitate the hope for justice, freedom, and democracy in our time and heal our body politic.[13]

F. "BUT THEY WERE NOT FOLLOWING US": FROM SECTARIAN WITNESS TO *SATYAGRAHA*

How has our practice of nonviolent resistance been unconsciously elitist, and how can we make it more inclusive and empowering?

In the middle of Mark's catechism on nonviolence comes a rather odd objection from the disciples: "We saw someone casting out demons in your name and we forbade him because he was not following us" (9:38). Against their attempt to franchise the liberative practice of exorcism, Jesus asserts the widest possible principle of inclusion: "Those who are not *against* us are *with* us" (9:40). This is a sharp reminder that powerful political practices can deteriorate into sectarian exclusivity. It is something that radical Christians must pay particular attention to. No matter how theologically and symbolically grounded our nonviolence may be, it must as a political discipline take into account issues of coherence, accessibility, and appropriateness.

Potential allies have raised serious questions about our practice of direct action in the First World. The most troubling ones, to my mind, have to do with whether we Christians are more concerned to protect the moral integrity of our personal witness than to build a movement that seeks to realize concrete social change. Religious witness is admirable, but it carries an inherent danger of being self-righteous — that is, elitist instead of populist. Insofar as this is the case, we are simply not practicing satyagraha. Let me address what I take to be three legitimate challenges to our practice of nonviolent direct action. Acknowledging these criticisms cannot help but broaden and deepen our efforts in the future.

Too symbolic. Some have voiced suspicions as to whether our symbolic actions are not sometimes a privileged discourse, by and for those who do not face the raw edge of the system. Many actions by First World Christians, for example, choose to employ liturgical and biblical symbols: from the primal elements of blood or ashes to Plowshares hammers. How intelligible is this symbolic discourse to the public conversation? For some activists this is simply not an important consideration — but if not, what is the purpose of acting publicly? Actions understood only by the actors is neither good theater nor good politics. To be sure, direct action may well involve elements of religious theater and private catharsis, but that is not its point. Its purpose is to engage the dominant order in a war of myths, which implies that actual communication is taking place. At the point at which our symbols and liturgy become esoteric or self-referential, they cease to be truly subversive. This is not to imply that symbols cannot be important tools, or that our actions must be immediately understood by the opponent (in confrontation they rarely are), or that we have failed if the opponent remains unconverted. Rather it means that whenever we take the initiative, we are responsible for interpreting our actions as best we can. It is not

enough to argue that "if enough people did what we are doing, we would fill the
jails and bring the system to its knees." Appealing to the politics of categorical
imperative merely begs the question of *how* more people can be persuaded to
practice these tactics.

It is worth noting that Gandhi's direct action and the civil rights movement
rarely relied on props. Their basic theater involved the unembellished political
body confronting strategic spaces. More important, although King was rooted in
the discursive world of the black church, he appealed consistently to the Constitutional tradition. He knew he had to find an inclusive discourse if he was to
build a movement broad enough to threaten white power in the U.S.; the Constitutional argument was the necessary hermeneutic for his message to the larger
society. The same concern has led some nuclear resisters to add to their gospel-
based rationale the secular hermeneutic of international law, which is used in
legal defense (see, e.g., Aldridge and Stark, 1986). We must think creatively
how to talk *with,* rather than merely at or past, our ideological opponents in the
body politic.

This touches on a long-running and important debate in religious peace and
justice circles between "moral witness" and "political efficacy." Mike Affleck,
in a thoughtful analysis of a decade of resistance at the Nevada Test Site, concludes: "When strategy is good, people of faith do not feel compromised. Good
strategy is empowering, inclusive, and bolsters hope.... Strategy needs faith.
Strategy is unhappy with clinical, sterile answers.... The union of faith and
strategy is imagination" (1991:21). I agree. "Faith" and "strategy" must be held
in dialectical tension. We must never allow one to erase the other completely,
for their respective truths can be found only in each other and in the crucible
of practice. It is true that satyagraha demands that means never be sacrificed to
ends; for Gandhi political goals were given up when nonviolent discipline collapsed. But he never construed this to mean that we sever the means from the
ends altogether. Gandhi insisted that we disabuse ourselves of results, *not* that
we isolate ourselves through a "politics of pure means," which is unconcerned
with historical goals or strategic engagement.[14]

Obviously if mere logical argument were sufficient to persuade our opponents, there would be no need for direct action. Thus those most adept at
symbolic direct action have rightly stressed that another key to its political in-
telligibility lies in persistence. The integrity of our symbolic actions will be
demonstrated only by their longevity; unfortunately such protracted campaigns
have been rare in the *locus imperii.* Nonviolent change is forged in the long
term; a given action is rarely decisive, but repeated engagement can wear down
the opponent and sustain the moral crisis. The more often we assert our alternative discourse, the greater chance it has of becoming part of the public
conversation. This is where Kellermann's suggestions seem particularly wise,
that Christian actions be linked to the traditional symbols and seasonal rhythms
of the church's liturgy (1991:103ff). Over the last decade, for example, in a
growing number of places around North America, Christian peace and justice
activists have organized public Holy Week liturgies that situated the Stations of

the Cross at weapons plants, financial districts, or neighborhood crack houses.[15] This moves symbolic action from the activist periphery to the worshiping heart of the church's life and helps parishioners discover a new geography of faith.

Too exclusive. A second disconcerting tendency is the way in which our attempts at somatic politics sometimes degenerate into an aberrant form of piety. As actions become more refined, the grounds for participation become more defined. While there is nothing inherently wrong with this focusing process, breadth is often sacrificed for depth, the result being ever smaller numbers of participants rather than a growing community of resistance. One wonders about the extent to which, particularly among religious activists, traditional codes of ascetic rigor or "faith by works" have led us into sectarianism. Hierarchies of value based on risk of arrest or length of jail time, which often creep into resistance consciousness despite ourselves, compromise the democratizing character of somatic politics. The problem with "heroic" action—in war and nonviolent struggle alike—is that it can engender heroism, an elitism just as disenfranchising as power-grabbing leadership. There is no *best* technique or *most* strategic space to place our bodies! Truly popular struggles have always affirmed that those who cook, clean up, make phone calls, and write press releases behind the scenes are just as important to the struggle as those who go into battle.

Building a satyagraha movement requires accessible entry points for newcomers, which is why there is always a role for low-risk somatic actions such as those sponsored by the Nevada Desert Experience (above, 5,E,2). While crossing the line at the test site has become highly choreographed and no longer results in jail time, it is an ideal place to "midwife" new resisters into the process and experience of civil disobedience. At the same time, high-risk witnesses that hazard significant jail time, such as the Plowshares actions, have challenged us all to push the boundaries of our courage. Because the cross stands before all of us as a question to our practice, there surely ought to be respectfulness toward each other on our journeys into resistance. Why then does our movement so often splinter along the lines of new orthodoxies? There are so few who take the truth of nonviolence seriously; should we not rather embrace the multiplicity of expressions and promote a maximum of unity? Or do we wish to mimic the revered tradition of Western leftism, infinitely subdividing according to our minute differences? The ruling class smiles; it need not lift a finger, for we marginalize and atomize ourselves.

We First World resisters should be more circumspect about our tentative experiments in somatic politics. There are a host of others—mostly the poor and people of color—who forged this tradition long before us and who continue to practice it, often in less contrived fashion. Many current struggles have little to do with our peace movement: Canadian Indians blocking logging roads in remote northern Saskatchewan; Guatemalan mothers keeping vigil outside government buildings for their disappeared sons and daughters; homeless activists breaking into abandoned buildings in Oakland; laid-off South Korean workers traveling to suburban New York to camp on the lawn of the factory owner's home. Every march, sit-in, vigil, picket line, or labor strike expresses somatic politics. It seems only sensible that we should be looking for opportunities to learn from others who approach nonviolent practice from very different directions (see below). Too often, however, we are simply not interested. Even worse, sometimes First World pacifists are overly cautious of being associated with those who don't share our nonviolent ideology — gang members, for example, or militant labor unions. By making nonviolence a litmus test, instead of a difficult query to all parties, we sink into measuring purity of principle rather than wrestling with principles in practice. We also guarantee our isolation from broader alliances.

Genuine satyagraha does not tolerate political abstractions and moral elitism: It insists that the truth can be found only in actual situations of conflict. Experience suggests that once pacifists enter into genuine collaboration with groups who hold different political philosophies, we are compelled to acknowledge the principles in their positions and the ambiguities in our own. This should not cause us to abandon our convictions regarding nonviolence, but to deepen them in light of other insights. Sadly, groups that do become so involved are often criticized by purists who charge that proximity to violence contaminates the pacifist witness — guilt by association, so to speak. Such accusations have been leveled at AFSC workers all over the world, from South Africa and the Middle East to U.S. inner cities (Lewy, 1988). It is alleged, for example, that when the AFSC "takes sides" in a struggle for social justice, it can no longer claim to be resolving conflict. But even when our role is mediation, we will never be equidistant from all parties in a conflict. If we support universal suffrage, or human rights, or a "fair day's pay," or self-determination, we will, in a concrete political situation, undoubtedly be labeled partisan. Satyagraha affirms that "everyone has a little bit of the truth," and that this includes the oppressor. But remaining open to conversation with all parties does not mean that one is uncommitted. Jesus, Gandhi, and King were hardly neutral.

Peacemaking without practical alliances is no more possible than community organizing without neighborhood participation. This is not to minimize the fact that coalition work is thorny. There is always pressure for *alliance* to become political *alignment*. The line between our intentions to make tactical common cause and the expectations of our partners for conformity is a shifting and tenuous one. Thus while satyagraha is not neutral, it must exercise critical discernment of the moral claims and political strategies of all parties. For example, guerrilla movements for national liberation can be just as gratuitous in their claims of popular support as the regime in power, and their administration of "revolutionary justice" just as lacking in due process. In the end, the hardest query for practitioners of militant nonviolence is also the oldest one: Do we really love our enemies? It is hard because, on one hand, capitalist piety forever urges politeness and reconciliation (i.e., we should have no class enemies). On the other hand, revolutionary fervor is always only a short step away from the lockstep of holy war (i.e., our class enemies are unredeemable). To remain equally committed to alliance building against oppression *and* to the ultimate goal of including the opponent in the "beloved community" — that is the formidable dialectic of satyagraha.[16]

Too captive to the dominant culture. The third and most telling objection is the charge (not unrelated to the first two) that First World practices of nonviolence are limited by our gender, race, and class biases, however unconscious. Let us take them in order. Women have long complained about the patriarchal attitudes that persist within our circles, particularly machismo. Included in their indictment are men's subtle assumptions that resistance to militarism or economic oppression takes obvious precedence over issues of domestic violence or rape. For Sharon Welch, nonviolent community means "women helping other women and children recover from the trauma of rape, incest, and wife-abuse, with men working against rape by identifying and challenging the equation of sexuality and violence in male socialization" (1985:90). Feminist nonviolence in the First World has developed a quite distinctive tone that takes preservation of the whole web of life more seriously and has led into the integrative insights of eco-feminism.[17] Even more impressive has been the resistance by women in some of the world's most vicious armed conflicts, such as the witness of Women in Black in the Yugoslav bloodbath (Zajovic, 1993).

Although satyagraha has been developed by people of color in this century, white activists in the U.S. have rarely been successful in building multiracial alliances. One reason for this is that nonviolence is still too much of a theoretical creed among First World practitioners, who are insulated from harder social realities. This makes our partnership of limited usefulness to poor people's movements facing street-level violence. But there are at least two more unsettling reasons why the movement is so segregated. Why are whites so unable or so unwilling to give up leadership? This question deserves closer attention, so I will deal with it in discussing solidarity (below 9,A). The other problem is more onerous. White peace activists have simply remained racist at some very basic but unexamined levels.

There are two typical expressions of our unconscious racism. One is our frequent (if ignorant) contention that people of color do not join our struggles against militarism because they are just not as interested in peace issues. "The conventional wisdom of both the U.S. government and the peace movement is that Afro-Americans are too busy trying to survive to be concerned with foreign policy," laments my AFSC colleague Michael Simmons. He points out that the black community has usually rejected the "liberal-conservative consensus" on militarism, recently reflected in its "overwhelming support for economic conversion and nuclear freeze referendums, opposition to the invasion of Grenada and the bombing of Libya, and Jesse Jackson's remarkable political success" (1987:56f).

The 1984 Free South Africa movement in the U.S. saw widespread black-led nonviolent direct action. Historians Beal and dePass write:

Observers unfamiliar with the contours of Afro-American history were surprised that the black community reached beyond its pressing domestic concerns and launched its first post-election protests around an issue of international concern. But a close study of the black community's past proves beyond a doubt that internationalist sentiment — particularly but hardly exclusively in relation to Africa — is a longstanding and deeply rooted feature of Afro-American life. As far back as 1848 Frederick Douglass condemned U.S. aggression against Mexico as "disgraceful, cruel and iniquitous"; Douglass' son Lewis spoke out 51 years later to deplore U.S. policy in regard to Cuba, the Philippines, Hawaii and Puerto Rico as "hypocrisy of the most sickening kind." Huge demonstrations of black protest greeted the Italian invasion of Ethiopia in 1935, and Martin Luther King Jr.'s public condemnation of the Vietnam war — against the "better judgment" of many white liberal supporters — was a watershed in the 1960s. (1986:2)

Scholar Robert Chrisman adds that W. E. B. Du Bois and Paul Robeson "were instrumental in founding the international peace movement that followed World War II" (1983:26). Third World people also, says Chrisman, have a different (e.g., anti-imperialist) but no less vigorous opposition to nuclear weaponry. Similar attitudes can be found among many Latinos (B. Richardson, 1985). Clearly, then, our self-congratulatory assumptions that peace is a white thing are false. As long as we hold onto them, however, we won't need to face our racism. The painful fact is, *our* organizing style, not *their* lack of interest, is what keeps people of color from joining our actions.

Our analysis and priorities are another expression of racism. Through my participation in the Nuclear Free and Independent Pacific Movement (above, 7,D), I was forced to acknowledge that nuclear militarism has been killing and colonizing people of color since the dawn of the atomic age — without a nuclear weapon ever being used (Myers, 1983a, 1985b). The nuclear cycle (from uranium mining to waste disposal), weapons testing, and forward basing have all had a disproportionate impact on the Fourth World (Bello, 1992b). Yet First World disarmament activists for the last two decades have been primarily concerned with what might happen if a bomb exploded over Chicago or London or Moscow (see Viereck, 1992). This blind spot is even more dramatic here at home, where, as African American activist Vincent Cobb puts it, "The U.S. peace community has committed a lot of time and effort in creating an ethos against weapons — everywhere but in the U.S."

When I look at the movement for disarmament I see two movements. I see the traditional efforts towards nuclear disarmament largely championed by a predominantly white peace community. I also see the little known and largely overlooked efforts at domestic disarmament led largely by people of color. When I join a protest at a nuclear test site the participants are almost exclusively white folks. When I see a candle light vigil in Chicago (or any other city) protesting the continuing handgun violence the participants are overwhelmingly people of color.... It's true that one nuclear weapon has the potential to destroy 100,000 people (or more) in an instant. But there are 30,000 actual deaths a year in the U.S. due to firearm violence. (1992:4f)

Cobb rightly wonders why white activists have *never* addressed our direct action to manufacturers of the automatic weapons used on our streets: "Only when we understand and stand against the relationship between General Electric (makers of ICBM component parts) and Colt industries (makers of multi-caliber handguns) will we begin to break free of the arms race" (ibid:5). To do this, however, we will also have to stand against our own racism (below, 9,C).

Finally ours is too often also a class-specific practice of nonviolence. Since the demise of the civil rights coalition, white activists have rarely participated in poor people's movements. When it comes to alliances with working-class struggles, we have rarely shown more than cosmetic concern for the workers at the sites where we protest, preferring to exhort them to quit their jobs. While our "witnessing" has had a role in a handful of dramatic individual conversions — I think immediately of Robert Aldridge (1983:13ff) — it has left untouched the harder task of systemic conversion to nonmilitary production while preserving jobs. Molly Rush, a longtime peace activist in Pittsburgh, told me how exciting it was when GE workers from a union local asked her to do nonviolence training for them during a labor dispute. Through that experience she began to realize how far she had drifted from her own blue-collar roots while organizing in the peace movement. Militant nonviolence, we must remind ourselves again and again, is the weapon of the socially disenfranchised and the poor; middle-class people working in isolation can only compromise its use.

We First World Christians need far more character and courage if we are to practice the somatic politics to which Jesus calls us and for which history waits. But we can learn from many quarters how to move beyond the political piety of sectarian witness to the world-transforming power of satyagraha. To do this is to follow Jesus in promoting "the nonviolent coming of God in a widening historical movement" (Douglass, 1991:53).

NOTES

1. Cf *BSM:*324ff. For a reading of this text against the apocalyptic moment of the 1991 Gulf War (above, 4,A), see Myers, 1991b.

2. Wink's work is the most recent theological treatment of the range of issues concerning violence and nonviolence. The best apologetic for Christian pacifism is still Yoder's (1970, 1971a, 1971b). For Catholic perspectives over the last three decades see Merton (1968), Shannon (1980; cf Myers, 1982), and Dear (1990). For those of mainline Protestantism see Marty and Peerman (1969), Childress (1978), and Johnson (1983). For Third World advocacy of nonviolence see Barbé (1989); for its rejection see Kuanda (1980). For the issue in church history see Hornus (1980), Bainton (1960), and Cadoux (1940). For an overview of contemporary peace views see Bello (1986); for a critique of war in the international system see Glossop (1983).

3. In 1982 the Humanitas Foundation and the Resource Center for Nonviolence convened a three-day dialogue in northern California between First and Third World activists, specifically to discuss issues of violence and nonviolence. Participants included opposition leaders from Ireland, India, Brazil, El Salvador, Chile, Mexico, and the U.S. The dialogue was frank, and all of us who were involved found it extremely fruitful. But such occasions are exceedingly rare. Elsewhere, meanwhile, questions about violent or nonviolent struggle have recently come quite alive. One is among former Soviet bloc nations now struggling to redefine themselves (see Hartsough, 1992). Another is in Myanmar and neighboring Thailand (Deats and Washington, 1992.)

4. David Apter offers a thoughtful discussion of the political logic behind violent resistance in both the Third and First World (1987:225ff). Whether nationalist terrorism by the PLO or the Irish Republican Army, peasant terrorism by the Shining Path in Peru, "religious" terrorists such as the Christian Phalangists or Muslim Hezbollah, or middle-class terrorism by Italy's Red Brigade or Germany's Baader-Meinhof Red Army faction, the common perception according to Apter is that "violence is the means of exploding false consciousness and, by ending it, bringing down the hegemony of the bourgeoisie and the state that pretends to stand above class interest" (265). Apter examines in detail the struggle against airport expansion at Sanrizuka in Japan — whose leaders I had the occasion to meet — a movement that he says "stands between terrorism ... and ordinary citizen protest" (256). Nonviolence, then, is not the only option in the First World, nor even the "natural" option for the bourgeoisie. "Especially in Germany and Japan, terrorists tend to come from middle-class families; a high proportion are the sons and daughters of professionals, teachers, and other respected representatives of the bourgeoisie" (273).

5. See Walzer's *Just and Unjust Wars* (1977:176f; also West, 1969). For a nonviolent critique of armed struggle see Deming (1968). For an overview of U.S. counterinsurgency involvement over the last half-century, see McClintock (1992).

6. This is the heart of Howard Clark's critique (1986) of armed struggle: the inherent militarization of politics by the process of the war of liberation itself. He points to three myths: that guerrilla combatants are simply representatives of "the people" (in fact they are a relatively exclusive and elitist vanguard); that this vanguard is "democratic" (its political organization is fundamentally hierarchical and militaristic, which if victorious inevitably carries over into the new regime); and that nonviolence is too slow (recent history suggests that armed struggle drags on just as long). Indeed many on the Left have begun to acknowledge some of these points and are taking more seriously that "constructive work around basic 'non-political' day-to-day matters such as health and education also becomes essential to the process of radical change" (ibid:5). For a sharp critique of the track record of Third World revolutionary movements, see Chaliand (1978). The question of the "efficacy" of violence vs. nonviolence, while a legitimate point of conversation, is inconclusive.

7. This was also the conviction of Paul (1 Cor 1:18–2:8) and his followers (Col 2:13–15; see Wink, 1984:40–45, 55–60). In 13:24f Mark is invoking high apocalyptic symbolics (*BSM:*343ff; cf Joel 2:10f; Amos 8:9f). In conservative Hellenistic thought, the "powers in the heavens" were a metaphor for the most immutable structures of law and order, upon which both the cosmos and society were built. Against this "establishment" ideology Mark pits the prophetic faith of the Isaian apocalypse: "The windows of heaven are opened and the foundations of the earth tremble. The earth is utterly broken.... On that day Yahweh will punish the host of heaven in heaven, and on earth the kings of the earth. They will be gathered together like prisoners in a pit.... Then

the moon will be abashed, and the sun ashamed; for the Lord of hosts will reign" (Is 24: 18–23). Mark's disappearing sun also alludes to Moses' war of myths with Pharaoh (Ex 10:21ff). As for the Temple veil, David Ulansey notes that the historian Josephus described the outer curtain, which hung in front of the doors at the Herodian Temple's entrance, as a "Babylonian tapestry [which] typified the universe.... Portrayed on this tapestry was a panorama of the entire heavens" (1991:124f). Ulansey rightly connects this piece of evidence with the "tearing of the heavens" in Mk 1:10 but oddly misses the correlation between its rending "from top to bottom" and the apocalyptic symbolics of "falling from heaven" in 13:25.

8. For general background on the Lenape see Kraft (1986); for their relationship to William Penn see Penn (1970); for their dealings with the U.S. government see Schaaf (1990). There are many other similarly fascinating but little-known traditions of nonviolence among indigenous peoples. The most compelling I have found is the militant nonviolence of the Maori prophet Te Whiti during New Zealand/Aotearoa's land wars (see D. Scott, 1975). Te Whiti's mass and sustained campaign included tactics of noncooperation, direct action, civil disobedience, and even alternative community — more than a generation before Gandhi! See also Paige and Gilliat (1991).

9. For a brief summary of Gandhian satyagraha see DeCelles (1983). The best primary source for Gandhi is *My Autobiography: The Story of My Experiments with Truth* (1957); see also *Nonviolent Resistance* (1961) and *All Men Are Brothers* (1980). The best secondary sources are still Bondurant (1958), Gene Sharp's *Gandhi as a Political Strategist* (1979), Iyer (1973), and Ramachandran and Mahadevan (1967).

10. To be sure, voter registration struggles among historically disenfranchised communities continue to be important, just as local electoral issues can still be substantive, as the election of millionaire Richard Riordan, one year after the Los Angeles uprising, makes clear. Some 85 percent of his votes came from whites (R. Simon, 1993). But the Riordan campaign also shows that while the right to vote may be a necessary condition for democracy, it is no longer sufficient. Diaz and Ohland (1993) analyze the "invention" of candidate Riordan by a high-powered marketing consultant and the role of Riordan's personal money in the campaign.

11. For general discussions of civil disobedience see Sibley (1970); Zinn (1968); and Zashin (1972). For specifically Christian perspectives see Stevick (1971) and Childress (1971). See also Corbett's discussion of "civil imperative" (1991:87ff); Daube's interesting historical study (1972); and my overview of biblical precedents (Myers, 1983b).

12. On the White Train campaign see Douglass (1991:1ff). Berrigan and McAllister offer a chronicle of twenty years of resistance at the Pentagon (1989:226ff). On the Plowshares movement see Laffin and Montgomery (1987) and D. Berrigan (1984). Civil disobedience at nuclear facilities has been covered for years by *The Nuclear Resister* (Tucson, AZ); see also Sam Day (1990). Nonviolent direct action has also been widely used by the U.S. antiapartheid movement (in Wallis, 1987:47ff) and Central American solidarity work (see Bourgeois, 1992).

I was closely involved with the campaign launched by Jim Douglass and former missile designer Robert Aldridge in the mid-1970s to resist the Trident submarine and strategic missile system. Pacific Life Community pursued actions at two sites: Lockheed Missiles and Space Corp. near San Jose, California (the designers and manufacturers of several generations of sea-launched ballistic missiles), and the Bangor Naval Base across the Puget Sound from Seattle, Washington. Over almost two decades, an extraordinary web of kindred organizing and action has emerged to engage the nationwide transport system of Trident components; related manufacturing sites from Missouri to Utah; the East Coast Trident base in King's Bay, Georgia; the Electric Boat works in Groton, Connecticut, where the submarines are built and commissioned; and the ELF communications system in the Upper Peninsula of Michigan. International resistance has been spawned as well. Trident forward bases around the Pacific Ocean have been located and U.S. warship visits protested and even blockaded by nonviolent flotillas in places such as Hawai'i, Fiji, Japan, New Zealand, and Australia. The British Trident system is actively resisted by a network throughout the United Kingdom. The Trident campaign is currently coordinated through the Trident Information Network (New Haven, CT), and broader international resistance to naval militarism by the *Disarm the Seas* network (San Diego, CA).

13. The rich tradition of somatic politics in the First World has been better chronicled elsewhere. Three good anthologies are Farren (1991); Shah (1992); and Wallis (1987). For a history of nonviolent action see Cooney and Michalowski (1984) and Lynd (1966). For women's resistance see McAllister (1990).

14. I am not alluding to, or taking sides in, the internecine debates within resistance circles over issues such as "purely symbolic" vs. property-destroying actions; or noncooperative vs. legal strategies; or "political" vs. "covenantal" sanctuary (see Dietrich and Huckaby, 1992; Corbett,1991:158ff). These matters are, in my opinion, usually more contextual than philosophical, to be carefully discerned according to the demands of nonviolent capacity and the historical moment. To splinter along such lines is absurd.

15. The Catholic Worker community here has organized Stations of the Cross for the last several years through downtown Los Angeles. It makes for a fascinating walk through the political geography of power and oppression in the city. I was interested to note the mixed reviews when the Worker organized such a via crucis for a visiting World and National Council of Churches delegation in the wake of the 1992 uprising. Several African American activists grumbled that the exercise was "too symbolic" and didn't really engage anybody—not an unreasonable objection from their point of view. Yet a prominent black pastor from Detroit and a ranking ANC officer from South Africa were both excited about its political and symbolic potential back home. Joe Agne's (1993) characterization of that event as "racist," therefore, is simply wrongheaded. A quite different example was a broad coalition campaign that nonviolently blockaded the federal building in downtown Los Angeles each Wednesday for months after the murder of the Jesuits and their female companions in El Salvador. This campaign was remarkably ordered, despite thousands of arrests, and involved a broad political cross section of participants. At the same time, more than once it degenerated into a media circus.

16. Hopefully this clarifies misunderstandings of my use of the term *"nonaligned radicalism"* in BSM (85f, 420f). By it I meant neither noncommitment, nonengagement, nor nonalliance. Just as Mark's Jesus allowed himself to be "perceived" as an armed insurgent (*BSM:*368, 387), so are accusations of alignment an inevitable consequence of modern practices of solidarity (below, 9,A). Obviously, given my argument that we live in a world defined by the spiral of violence, I believe it is a fantasy to think that one can practice nonviolence "purely."

17. On feminism and nonviolence see McAllister (1982, 1991) and Soelle (1991). On ecofeminism see Plant (1991) and Ruether (1992). It is from feminist nonviolence that we must approach the difficult question of abortion rather than from the moralism of the so-called pro-life movement. I share the anguish of those who believe the issues facing abortion and nonviolence are more complicated than often portrayed, and who

have not given up hope that there can be common ground between the principles of choice and the preservation of life (on this see Wylie and Heyward, 1992; Ennis, 1992). It is worth noting that militant antiabortion groups are exhibiting some of the most engaged nonviolent resistance in the U.S. today, whatever one thinks about blocking access to abortion clinics (obviously I do not include in this assessment the sporadic acts of terrorism).

C. Myers

Oak trees line the base of Eagle Rock in northeast Los Angeles.

Part Four

Reconstruction

"Is it not written, 'My House shall be called a house of prayer for all peoples'?"

Mk 11:17

"Knowledge breaks down," goes a Native American proverb; "Wisdom puts back together." Theology has traditionally understood the move from critical deconstruction to creative reconstruction in terms of redemption or sanctification. As Brazilian base community theologian Dominique Barbé puts it, "It is not enough to analyze the functioning of a given society; we must also lay out the means to arrive at another social structure" (1987:78).

The radical social message of Jesus was neither novel, idealistic, nor utopian; it was a revision of the roots of free exodus Israel. He called his people to reconsider "roads not taken" — Sabbath economics, decentralized tribal politics, a "house for all peoples." The theological work of reconstruction seeks to wed this vision of the Great Economy with the story of one's own people. The church should not assume it can persuade the body politic of its vision, as the liberal tradition imagines. Nor can the church reject the possibility that God will transform history, as the conservatives do. The biblical notion of redemption invites the church to commend that vision by modeling it in its own life and by vigorously engaging in the public debate about what America is and will be.

How can the church help in the reconstruction of a "house for all peoples"? First, we must move beyond paternalism and learn to form alliances (show that we are "reliable") with those seeking inclusion and justice (Chapter Nine). Second, we should follow Jesus in challenging all social boundaries that seek to exclude, and embrace the reality of pluralism so we can become an advocate of multiculturalism (Chapter Ten). Finally, we should investigate what can be reclaimed from our collective experience and common place. If we are to make a stand against technocratic monism, we must rediscover a love for the land, revision the possibility of local economic self-determination, and rediscover the radical political traditions of anarchism and bioregionalism (Chapter Eleven).

9

"Who Are My Kin?"

Solidarity

Will America, in a sudden gush of reason, good conscience and common sense reorder her priorities — revamp her institutions, clean up her racism so that blacks and Puerto Ricans and American Indians and Mexican Americans can be and will be fully and meaningfully included on an equal basis? Or will America, grown meaner and more desperate as she confronts the just demands of her clamorous outcasts, choose genocide? America, of course, is not an abstraction; America is people, America is you and me. America will choose in the final analysis as we choose: to build a world of racial and social justice for each and for all; or to try the fascist alternative — a deliberate policy on a mass scale, of practices she already knows too well.

Ossie Davis, "We Charge Genocide"

La solidaridad es mas que un derecho. Es un deber. Es el amor hecho público, colectivo, político. (Solidarity is more than a right. It is a duty. It is love made public, collective, political.)

Pedro Casaldáliga,
"Sigamos Haciendo Camino"

The air is warm and thick with tension inside the Capernaum synagogue this Sabbath. Jesus slowly walks to the front, turns and faces an antagonistic audience, and fixes his gaze on them. The city fathers clear their throats, smile thinly, their jaws set, waiting for him to go too far. Weighing the silence, Jesus nods to a disabled man to come up and join him. Taking his shriveled hand, Jesus' eyes sweep the gallery, narrowing. Then he begins his sermon. **"What are we as a Sabbath people all about? You tell me. Is it about doing good,**

or doing evil? Is it about saving life, or destroying it?" (3:4). Yet another mythic Markan moment. And it seems like we have been here before.

"I have put before you today life and prosperity, death and adversity" (Dt 30:15). Time suddenly collapses: We are not in Capernaum but gathered with exodus Israel on a mountain above the Jordan, overlooking the Promised Land. The ultimatum being laid before us comes not from the Jesus of Mark but from the Moses of Deuteronomy. Moses is exhorting us that to get where we are going, we must remember where we have been — the long journey from slavery, its pain and joy, its hard lessons. The liberation Story is not just a matter of the remote past: "No, the word is very near to you" (Dt 30:14). The Deuteronomist thus suspends us, in this parallel mythic moment, between "heaven and earth," between history and destiny, between ancestors and descendants. The future depends utterly upon this archetypal choice between life and death.

"So I say to you my friends that even though we must face the difficulties of today and tomorrow, I still have a dream." Just as suddenly we are standing before the Lincoln Memorial in Washington, DC, on August 28, 1963, among a hundred thousand civil rights supporters. We are listening to another sermon, by another prophet struggling to retell the Story and renew the vision. Martin Luther King is calling weary marchers to persevere in their quest for freedom, though it "has left you battered by the storms of persecution and staggered by the winds of police brutality." But he is also calling the country's leadership and citizenry to account before their own fundamental ideals, serving warning that "America has defaulted on this promissory note in so far as her citizens of color are concerned." This too is a mythic moment, indeed a defining one for the U.S. ("At that moment," Coretta King later wrote, "it seemed as if the Kingdom of God had appeared"; Washington, 1986:217). Dr. King set before us that ancient choice so that one day we might "be able to join hands and to sing in the words of the old Negro Spiritual, 'Free at last, free at last; thank God almighty, we are free at last' " (ibid:220).

These three moments of truth, each so carefully staged, mysteriously mingle. In them the people confront again the seductive Dream of empire and the liberative Promise of human solidarity.

... but they said nothing (Mk 3:4b). We are back in that Capernaum synagogue. Jesus is staring at his audience, trembling slightly. As the silence builds, stifling, deafening, a hot fury is kindled inside him. They have forgotten. His diagnosis is immediate: Their "hearts had hardened" — just like the old Story of Pharaoh, just like what happened in Memphis on April 4, 1968.

This is a strategic turning point in Mark's gospel. Jesus "chooses life" and sets about revisioning an exodus people. A powerful Galilean coalition of Pharisees and Herodians choose differently and set about plotting murder (3:6). From here on, Jesus will escalate his critique of the system, and the stewards of the system will escalate their counterattacks. Jesus declares his intention to retribalize Israel (3:13–19), commencing his reconstructive discourse. When the Jerusalem authorities come to investigate him, he declares his intention to deconstruct the *House* (3:22–27). And when his own family comes to take him into custody, Jesus declares his intention to revise the *house*. Thus, as the first campaign closes, he offers another query to his people: "Who are my mother and brothers? (3:33)

"God's allowed me to go up to the mountain. And I've looked over. And I've seen the promised land. I may not get there with you. But I want you to know that we, as a people, *will* get to the promised land" (ibid:286). So vouched Dr. King on the eve of his assassination. But King, like Moses, did not get to the Promised Land; like Jesus, he walked the via crucis instead. And what about us, in whose land the Promise has yet to be realized — will we "get there"? To do so we must defect from the imperial Dream and choose life. It is up to us, says Ossie Davis. America is you and me.

A. "WHOSOEVER DOES THE WILL OF GOD...": THE CHURCH RE(AL)LIANT

Can we move away from charity and paternalism in order to learn how to collaborate with oppressed groups in their struggles for justice?

"His relatives came to take charge of him, for people were saying he was out of his mind; but the scribes coming down from Jerusalem were saying he was under the control of Beelzebul" (Mk 3:21f). This twin counterattack represents a careful narrative construction of Mark's: Jesus' family and the scribal authorities seek to restrain him simultaneously. Why? Because Mark understood that in the dominant culture, the family and the State are supposed to reinforce each other. The ethos of the *house* (socializing site of the political body) is expected to reproduce the imperatives of the *House* (laws and conventions of the body politic).[1]

Jesus' query — "Who are my kin?" — is hardly rhetorical then. His answer is, in fact, shocking. "Whosoever does the will of God" implies that the practice of the Great Economy alone will determine the constituency of his new community. Jesus is beginning his reconstructive politics by calling for discontinuity with the conforming and socializing "natural family" (above, 6,D). The new kindred group will function instead to *de*socialize us from the obligations of the House and *re*socialize us to inclusive and just living. The messianic house will resist the dominant ethos rather than reproducing it, will support new social practices rather than suppressing them. The church is not, in other words, supposed to be an end in itself, catering to whosoever calls themselves Christian. Jesus' redefinition of kinship means the church is supposed to build alliances with whosoever is "practicing the will of God," because it is a community committed to realizing the Great Economy *in the world*.

This vision of the church has, needless to say, been marginalized in the history of Constantinian Christianity. But it has survived at the margins of church and society. Saint Francis is a great example of Christian reconstructive struggle. The call to "rebuild the church" led him to shed the clothes of his entitlement — literally — and embrace solidarity with the disenfranchised. Francis's way continues to commend itself to First World Christians today (Dennis et al, 1993). This chapter will explore prospects for a church in solidarity in the context of a society groaning under the weight of patriarchy, white supremacy, and poverty. How might Christians contribute to the wider struggle for liberty and justice for all in a country whose Promise has been strangled by the Dream of empire? Can we engage the public conversation by challenging the House to live up to its own best ideals, while also rediscovering the house as a place where all forms of "doing good and saving life" are supported?

1. Surrogates for Solidarity

I have discussed the problem of our insulation from the poor (above, Chapter Seven). Now we must look at the challenges facing us if and when we do approximate. Though in the *locus imperii* our churches have tended to be places where the dominant culture is legitimized and deviance discouraged, we cannot ignore their long tradition of service to the sick and compassion for the outcast. Today many First World Christians are involved in works of mercy and social action. Unfortunately our efforts have often been confused and compromised by a lack of understanding of what true solidarity demands. We do not understand why our programs do not bring us closer to the poor, or why they sometimes unwittingly promote further disenfranchisement. Let us look at three barriers to genuine solidarity in our attitudes and practices: charity, paternalism, and control. I call these barriers "surrogates" because, in the name of "Christian service," we allow ourselves to be satisfied with relationships with the poor that fall well short of real partnership. Does our rhetoric of solidarity prevent us from seeing how our socio-political work might be "codependent" with a dysfunctional and oppressive social system?

Charity. Charity is an institution in the piety of the church, from the "poor box" to "World Hunger Sunday" to "ethnic liturgies." It is easy for activists to dismiss this tradition as tokenistic. I believe, however, that "good works" can and do facilitate genuine relief and compassion. Making regular donations to a social agency, volunteering at a soup kitchen, or sponsoring a child in the Third World should be valued as nothing more or less than expressions of basic human kindness. At the same time, we should gently but firmly insist that charity does not constitute solidarity. This is because charity seeks to *mitigate* social problems without a clear commitment to or strategy for *eradicating* them.

The difference between giving to the poor and redistributing the wealth is all the difference in the world (above, 6,A; see also Mk 12:41ff; *BSM:*320f). Whenever we do not ask structural questions concerning *why* and *how* people are hurting or poor, we are failing to do them a service. Whenever we objectify those we serve by viewing them as recipients of largesse rather than as subjects in a process of empowerment, we are strengthening the dominant relations of power. "Giving to" and "doing for" the victim are social strategies designed by and for the entitled. They facilitate our good conscience but fail to challenge assumptions that gender, race, and class stratification is an "inevitable" socio-political condition.

For example, the marketing approaches of the largest hunger organizations in the U.S. concentrate on appeals to "save starving children." Though these agencies do engage in advocacy work — organizing urban squatters in India to demand better sanitation facilities, for example — these efforts are not highlighted in public relations promotion so as not to offend donors who might regard such work "too political." In contrast, development organizations that explicitly pursue organizing for structural change are experiencing steadily declining budgets. Indeed U.S. tax laws for charitable giving encourage depoliticization. Individual and corporate donations to nonprofit agencies are tax deductible, but those agencies are tightly restricted in how much political advocacy they can engage in. Thus massive amounts of charitable monies go to established nonprofit organizations that do not challenge the social order, while social change organizations and grassroots groups are small and notoriously underresourced. The ideology of charity was also at work during the Reagan-Bush era, when private, volunteer social initiatives ("a thousand points of light") were vigorously promoted while structural adjustments such as affirmative action were being dismantled.

Paternalism. Social service agencies such as homeless shelters, health clinics, and employment projects seek to move beyond charity by "solving" the problems of marginalized people. Another problem arises, however, when the service provider is so focused on "fixing" the situation that it fails to equip its "clients" to solve their own problems. When the service is institutionalized, the relationship between provider and user becomes codependent. Each facilitates the existence of the other, but the agency is in firm control, and the client still the "supplicant." It is not difficult to see why this happens. According to my little social map of "sectoral divides" (above, 7,E,2), service providers represent the primary brokers between the disenfranchised and the resources being directed "toward" them from outside sources. This funneling necessitates technically skilled fund-raisers, degreed administrators, and trained social service providers. These professionals, not the "clientele," define the terms of the engagement and control the decision-making. Social service agencies today, no less than churches in the past, are notorious for "knowing what is best" for those they purport to serve. This is the definition of paternalism.

A sad example of how difficult it is to operate outside of paternalistic control is a food distribution program that operated for years out of the back of our AFSC office in Northwest Pasadena. This all-volunteer effort was run by low-income people for low-income disabled people under the charismatic leadership of a spirited African American matriarch. By the standards of a social service bureaucracy, this program was disorganized and even chaotic, yet it managed to serve thousands of poor neighborhood families each year, with minimal overhead. Most of the food was begged from commercial food outlets or manufacturers or gleaned from farmers around the state. Volunteers would sometimes sell their own things at flea markets to raise money to pay rent.

But these grassroots folk never understood the need for administrative functions such as paperwork, accounting, or fund-raising. As a result, over time they alienated their institutional donors, from local charitable foundations to the City of Pasadena. It was not that the program was failing to provide a service; it was that it could not be administratively controlled by, and offered no benefit or prestige to, donor agencies. After our repeated attempts to find funding for the program's minimal overhead failed, the food program had to move its operations out to the street. The poor could not play the "human services" game.

This is a common story for those who work with low-income communities, where socio-economic problems of housing, health, and education are disproportionately concentrated because of social architecture (above, 7,B). Resources are perpetually inadequate to the felt needs of these neighborhoods. When government or private agencies do make funds available for "grassroots" development or organizing projects, the amounts are absurdly small, inviting the poor to compete for crumbs. By law, for example, 15 percent of the total federal Block Grant program to cities must be earmarked for "Human Services" — and this only because of the advocacy of civil rights and poor people's movements. Thus in Northwest Pasadena each year, the city makes a few hundred thousand dollars available (compare this to the millions in government grants to scientific research and development). Dozens of community groups must master a highly bureaucratic proposal process and survive intense competition and inside politicking in order to receive ten or fifteen thousand dollars. But this is scarcely enough to hire one staff person and get work off the ground before the next round of the funding scramble. AFSC's local community organizing program works in partnership with such groups: a black-consciousness tutoring program, a small landscaping business run by former gang members, a housing project tenants union, a minority AIDS education project. We try to help them in their pursuit of such resources or to learn to survive without them. But what we constantly encounter is how tired people are of having to contest for each public or private dollar, and how (rightly) suspicious they are of being "pimped" by outside agencies.

Control. "Progressive" European Americans who are committed to social justice advocacy and critical of paternalism are rarely more successful in building working alliances with people of color and the poor. The reason is that we, like the agencies just mentioned, have that dominant cultural need for control. How many times, for example, have we formed a coalition, worked out its principles and plans of action, and then invited people of color to join, hoping they will legitimize our project as a multicultural effort? But initiatives firmly under the direction of whites are hardly attractive to Third World activists; once it becomes clear that power will not be shared, they leave. The fact is, recent multiethnic social movements (such as the civil rights or farmworker movements) have been initiated by people of color, not whites. Yet white activists rarely remain in coalitions that they cannot lead or in which they must take a background role. When militant blacks in the South demanded that white northern civil rights supporters return home to work on racism in their own communities, most of the latter left the movement. Giving up control remains the most difficult thing to do for those socialized into entitlement, but it is the key to learning solidarity.

2. *Learning Collaboration*

Oppressed people look to us neither for handouts nor prescriptions nor leadership. They look for partnership. They need us to be reliable allies in their struggle for empowerment. To offer this, we who are entitled must become *really-able*. That is, we must be willing and able to defect from our "natural" gender, race, and class alliances in order to form new alliances with those who are marginalized. And to *re-ally* ourselves, we must change our view about what is *really* in our best interests (the words have common roots in Middle English). How can the church move beyond the traditions of charity, paternalism, and control and become more *re(al)liant?*

Albert Nolan, in an essay titled *The Service of the Poor and Spiritual Growth* (1985), reflects upon his own experiences as a Catholic priest in South African townships. He characterizes the journey from charity to genuine solidarity as a profoundly *spiritual* one for First World Christians and outlines four essential stages. The place most of us begin this journey is in service or relief work motivated by compassion, which has often been stimulated through an experience of exposure (1985:3f; above, 7,D). The second stage "begins with the gradual discovery that poverty is a *structural problem* ... [which] leads to feelings of *indignation* and anger" (ibid:4f). Here we begin to recognize the need to engage social institutions and policies: "Preventive action is political action" (ibid:6). In my experience these first two stages are where many of us get stuck: We are content either to "serve" the poor or to work politically "on behalf of" them.

The third stage thus becomes the most crucial. It centers on

the discovery that the poor must ... [and] will *save themselves* and that the poor don't really need you or me to save them. ... The realization that the poor know better than we do what needs to be done and how to do it ... [and] are not only perfectly capable of solving the structural and political problems that beset them but that they alone can do it, may shock and shake us. In spiritual terms this can amount to a real crisis for us and to a very deep conversion. Suddenly we are faced with the need to learn from the poor instead of teaching them. (Ibid:7)

Yet if we accept that we are not needed, we often slip into becoming needy, and so begin "romanticizing the poor or the working class or the Third World." Our *compañeros* can do no wrong, and we become totally compliant to their every demand, exercising no boundaries or discernment of our own. Nolan's fourth stage thus becomes the true test for the long-term journey of solidarity: "The crisis of *disillusionment* and *disappointment* with the poor" (ibid:8). He concludes: "Real solidarity begins when we recognise together the advantages and disadvantages of our different social backgrounds and present realities and the quite different roles that we shall therefore have to play while we commit ourselves together to the struggle against oppression" (ibid:9).

An extraordinary example of women of color empowering themselves, and then demanding collaboration from those wanting to "help" them, is the Wai'anae Cancer Research Project (WCRP) in Hawai'i. For years, nonnative public health professionals conducted studies of the abnormally high rates of cancer among native women in the predominantly low-income Hawaiian community of Wai'anae. The Wai'anae Coast Comprehensive Health Center, a community-based clinic, was hearing from local people that they felt like guinea pigs. They complained that the results and recommendations of these studies were never shared with the community, nor did programs to remedy the problems they identified seem to follow. The Health Center decided to challenge this objectifying and paternalistic approach. It initiated the WCRP in partnership with the Hawai'i Cancer Research Center and the National Cancer Institute.

The project developed six criteria for future research:

i) the community must participate in planning the research;
ii) there must be direct and immediate benefits for community residents and research participants;
iii) research participants must be active, not passive subjects, fully informed of the purposes of the work;
iv) projects targeting minority populations should insure their representation and inclusion at all levels;
v) data must be co-owned and decisionmaking shared about how it is used, including community-peer review;
vi) the community must share in resources and jobs coming from project funding. (DeCambra and Enos, 1991)

These criteria suggest a kind of "rules of engagement" for dominant cultural agencies who would collaborate with communities of low-income and minority people.

Putting them into practice, however, was not easy, according to my AFSC colleague Ho'oipo DeCambra, who works closely with the WCRP. At first, incoming professional researchers and administrators continued to ignore or to patronize Hawaiian women, imagining the criteria were merely rhetorical. But the relations of power slowly changed, as the community advisory committee helping to plan and implement the project became more assertive. Hawaiian residents demanded respect for their indigenous value of *kokua*, cooperation and sharing within extended family and community networks. As the project has matured, native women are insisting that additional aspects of their culture be integrated as well, such as traditional healing and spiritual practices. Ho'oipo has encouraged this kind of empowerment in other parts of her community by facilitating social analysis workshops designed specifically for Pacific Island women. In her gentle but firm style, Ho'oipo has taught me a great deal about the difference between role-specific partnership and controlling paternalism.

Solidarity for the entitled means being able and willing to take direction, to learn, and to accept our *specific roles* in a given struggle for justice. Sometimes this will mean we remain in the background while supporting the poor in their efforts to take charge of their own lives and not abandoning this process when it means diminishing prestige for ourselves. Sometimes it means being aware of how our presence can divide those we stand with, not because we wish to but because it is inherently problematic when the dynamics of dominant culture power and white privilege are inserted into an empowerment process already at work among the poor. Thus often solidarity will mean returning to our inherited social location in order to struggle with "our own" (below, 12,B,2). For example, if men take the initiative for challenging sexism, and whites for challenging racism, the energy of women and people of color will not always be monopolized by defensive action.

Whatever solidarity-as-collaboration might mean in various contexts, I agree with Nolan that we who are entitled will only embrace it over the long haul insofar as we are being transformed by a spirituality of repentance. Politically such a spirituality invites us to repudiate the notion that there is a limited economy of justice (above, 7,C) and to believe instead that inclusion empowers everyone (Snyder, 1992). Personally it invites us to the via crucis, for on this journey we will discover repeatedly just how we have internalized the dominant ethos in our own political bodies. Below I will look briefly at strategic points requiring our solidarity in the *locus imperii*. In each case I also offer examples from my own experience that illustrate what I consider to be collaborative work.

B. "LET HER ALONE!" GENDER

How can men forge partnerships with women to deconstruct both the patriarchal body politic and our daily practices of male privilege in our political bodies?

More than a half-century ago satirist James Thurber portrayed gender alienation in a cartoon narrative entitled "The War Between Men and Women" (1964:359ff). It is a whimsical yet deadly serious work. With considerable archetypal power it expresses the conflict through a parody of (the thoroughly patriarchal institution of) military combat. Thurber was clear that this "war" begins with an act of male aggression, victimizes everyone, and ends only in the surrender of embittered women.[2] Thurber's metaphor expresses my own sense of frustration, bewilderment, rage, and complicity in this battle.

The oppression of women by men is the most fundamental of human breaches, a wedge driven into the heart of our body politic and into each of our political bodies. Biological *differences* have been manipulated into male-dominant *divisions* throughout history. Thus feminists rightly speak of patriarchy as an almost universal phenomenon (Brock, 1988:1ff). This is not to legitimate it as "natural." Regardless of its cultural-historical form, patriarchy is a human construction. Rather it reminds us that by struggling to heal this rift, we are taking on primal sexual, social, and symbolic forces. I will not try to define or summarize patriarchal oppression or feminist struggles for liberation here; women's own analyses are widely available.[3] My concern is how we men can re-ally with, rather than being threatened by, women's efforts to tear down the walls of male privilege and to overturn the social acceptability of male domination and violence.

In some respects, feminism could be considered the most "successful" of the cultural revolts over the last thirty years in the *locus imperii*. Its challenges to traditional gender roles have spawned dramatic changes in the labor force, the marketplace, and the household (Sidel, 1990). But the deeper cultural task of transforming gender roles will be even more difficult, not least because of the deep inner confusions these recent changes have spawned in both men and women. For example, one of the women's movement's primary critical tasks has been to expose the social construction of the "feminine" that domesticates women and undergirds male privilege. However, many women have come to see that liberation is not found in merely "matching" male practices. Some "second stage" feminists (the term is Betty Friedan's, 1986) have therefore begun to reassert certain differences between the sexes. They contend that women are more inherently relational or less prone to violence than men. But Katha Pollitt (1992) cautions against the romanticism of this so-called "difference feminism," arguing that the goal of feminism should remain the principle of social *equality*.[4]

Men and women both are struggling to adjust to the shifting understandings of gender roles and expectations. But however confusing this period of redefinition may be, the fact remains that by any measurement, there is still a long way to go toward genuine gender equality. The 1993 United Nations "Human Development Index," for example, which measures combined health, education, and purchasing power, shows a 15 percent overall gap between men and women in the U.S., ranking us thirteenth in the world (Wright, 1993). Meanwhile reactionary forces of the cultural and Christian Right are scapegoating feminism for all our contemporary social ills, as recently documented in Susan Faludi's *Backlash* (1991). So the need for men's solidarity with women in deconstructing patriarchy is greater than ever. To do this, we must become more literate in how power is ordered along gender lines, and how women are marginalized in both the body politic and in their political bodies. Let us review a few of these basic ways.

In the body politic patriarchal legal and political entitlements persist. Women have suffered a number of recent political (the languishing of the ERA) and legal (the Kennedy Smith rape and Clarence Thomas sexual harassment trials) setbacks. Solidarity calls for supporting a variety of political struggles, from criminalizing domestic violence to protecting AFDC benefits. The absence of equal access and/or respect also continues at every level of society, including upper management, political decision making, tenured academic positions, entertainment, and sports. Solidarity calls for men to question every exclusively "male domain" remaining in public life. But the most basic dimension of gender oppression in the body politic is still the division of wage labor (see Bergman, 1986). For white women, the household as the exclusive site of female production, labor, and motherhood was a distinct social construction of bourgeois capitalism. It is rapidly atrophying in postindustrial society, though as much due to economic imperatives as social ones (Margolis, 1984; above, 7,B,2). Yet vocational opportunities for women continue to be attenuated, and the remunerative value of their labor inferior. According to the U.S. Department of Labor, the twenty lowest-paying job markets are still dominated by women, the twenty highest-paying by men. Two-thirds of minimum wage workers are women, and standard benefits, when available, tend to be inadequate for single mothers (on the feminization of poverty see Stallard et al, 1983). Women are the most exploited by the globalized open shop yet are still vastly underrepresented in the labor movement (see Epstein, 1987; Kamel, 1990; Needleman, 1988). These disparities are intensified among women of color (J. Jones, 1985; Asian Women United, 1989). Solidarity means support for women's struggles for equal pay and benefits, including such efforts as the recently introduced "Unremunerated Work Act" in Congress, which calls for the value of unpaid housework to be included as part of the nation's GNP.

The understanding and solidarity of men seems to come more slowly regarding how women are oppressed in their political bodies, however. When it comes to reproduction, men must give up attempting to control women and must instead increase our responsibility, from birth control to paternal accountability. On issues of sexual domination, solidarity means closing rather than breaking ranks with women in the struggle to fully delegitimize harassment and rape.[5] Another important issue is the persistent cultural mechanisms of objectification. The reigning ideals of beauty tyrannize the desires of men and, as Roberta Seid (1989) has shown, put women literally "at war with their own bodies" (endless dieting, cosmetic surgery, low self-esteem).

Male practices of repression, violation, and commodification of women's bodies can be legislatively constrained but not exhorted away, because gender socialization and the symbolics of patriarchy are rooted in our unconscious. The pendulum of grandiosity and depression (above, 4,C) has long distorted patriarchal perceptions of the feminine. On one hand, the lens of idealism (woman as virgin, mother, or helpmeet) leads to paternalism and possessiveness. On the other hand, the lens of misogyny (woman as whore, witch, or bitch) leads to violence and abandonment. These distorted perceptions, which alienate a man not only from respectful sexuality and relationships but from his own *anima* as well, are then mercilessly exploited by media discourses of seduction. Cultural critics, from "men's movement" founder Robert Bly (1990) to feminist Miram Miedzian, have traced the pathology more specifically to the "father-wound" that is so characteristic of the modern patriarchal family system. The absence of fathers in the home, attributable to the division of labor in industrial modernism, means that male children do not receive the proper nurturing and mentoring from adult males. This causes adolescent and adult men to place unrealistic expectations on their relationships with women, which when unfulfilled turn into rage and/or withdrawal. As a result, today we are seeing an epidemic erosion in male responsibility in the family (see Easton, 1992). "Male aggression poses the single greatest menace to society," writes Jerry Ortíz y Pino; "the antidote for this destructive tendency toward violence is to re-establish contact between men and their children" (1992:5; see further Sanford and Lough, 1988; R. Johnson, 1989; H. Lerner, 1985). In sum, we oppress women in their political bodies because of our own disfigured male selves. Solidarity with women begins, therefore, with a commitment to the work of dis-illusioning ourselves of the internalized lies of patriarchy (above, 4,E).

Finally, what about the struggle of women in the church? It is awkward for Christians to advocate solidarity with women when our churches cannot even keep up with secular culture where inclusive practices are concerned. Sadly, churches are among the last remaining social institutions in the *locus imperii* to bring down exclusive gender barriers. Cognizant of this contradiction, gender equality has been one of the most fundamental commitments of the radical discipleship movement. We prefer to work outside denominational structures if women are marginalized within them, supporting Catholic women who celebrate the Eucharist in defiance of canon law and Protestant women who experiment with alternative liturgies (see Russell, 1993; Schaper, 1993). Many of us agree with Rosemary Radford Ruether's call for a "feminist Exodus community":

> The Mother-face of God has fled from the high thrones of patriarchy and has gone into exodus with us. She is with us as we flee from the smoking altars where women's bodies are sacrificed, as we cover our ears to blot out the inhuman voice that comes forth from the idol of patriarchy.... We are not waiting for a call to return to the land of slavery to serve as altar girls in the temples of patriarchy.... We call our brothers to join us in exodus from the land of patriarchy, to join us in our common quest for that Promised Land where there will be no more war, no more burning children, no more violated women, no more discarded elderly, no more rape of the earth. (1985:172f)

Christian men must both offer solidarity to movements such as WomanChurch and continue to challenge male ecclesial leadership to repent of patriarchy.

Transformation will come only when the whole church acknowledges that the marginalization of women has radically impoverished Christianity — liturgically, pastorally, and prophetically. The institutional church simply *cannot* be renewed without the full enfranchisement of women, who are the vast majority of those sitting in its pews and carrying on its tireless service. Our message should be simple: Patriarchal clericalism must get out of the way and let women exercise their gifts! As the nineteenth-century American feminist Sarah Grimke put it: "All I ask of our brethren is that they will take their feet from off our necks, and permit us to stand upright on the ground which God has designed us to occupy" (Zinn, 1980:119). But this call is grounded still more deeply in the exhortation of Mark's Jesus, delivered to men who were indignant about the discipleship practice of women: "Let her alone; why do you make trouble for her?" (14:6).

Markan theology is an embarrassment to a patriarchal church that has long "made trouble" for women. Women are not only included in Mark's story, they are portrayed in the narrative as the true disciples — in the wake of the men's betrayal.[6] This is, no doubt, why Mark's voice has been so ignored by our churches. The story of the woman who anoints Jesus on the eve of his execution is a case in point. "So help me," Jesus announces, "wherever the good news is announced in all the world, what she has done will also be told in memory of her!" (14:9). This approbation, unparalleled in the early tradition, situates the struggle against patriarchy at the heart of the *kerygma* of the church. Jesus' unambiguous instruction has, however, gone unheeded in Christendom, past and present. Men must join women in insisting that we restore the "memory of her" to its central place in the church.

C. "YOUR FAITH HAS MADE YOU WELL": RACE

Can whites confront the "hidden wound" of racism in order to learn how to collaborate with people of color?

The most fundamental social principle in Mark's gospel is that those who have been "first" must learn from those who have been "last." This is clearly dramatized in the story of a synagogue leader and a social outcast (5:22–43; *BSM:*200ff). Jesus interrupts his mission to heal the family of privilege in order to attend to the needs of someone suffering from triple disenfranchisement: female in a patriarchal system, unclean according to the dominant purity code, and destitute because of the medical system's exploitation of her illness (5:25f). But it is this woman who takes initiative for liberation, and the text makes it very clear that upon contact power flowed *from Jesus to her* (5:30). This concrete symbol of her "empowerment" has been missed or dismissed by theologians. Yet Jesus commends her: "Daughter, *your* faith has made you well" (5:34). By welcoming her into the new kindred community, Jesus confirms his redefinition of family. In her restored political body, this nameless and outcast woman becomes the "daughter" at the center of the story.

But there is a consequence to the wider body politic, for this is not the end of the episode. The daughter of privilege has died; the narrative is ruptured and threatens to collapse in tragedy (5:35). Jesus instructs the synagogue leader, who though powerful needs healing, to *learn about faith from this woman,* who though disenfranchised has been healed through her empowerment (5:36). But the response of the synagogue leader's household — despair (5:35), grief (5:38), ridicule (5:40) — symbolizes the negative reaction of the entitled. They do not believe there is enough room for both "daughters" in the economy of social wholeness. Jesus, however, contends the synagogue daughter is only *asleep* — a symbol in Mark's narrative for incomprehension. His touch subsequently also restores *her* political body (5:41). The moral of the story: Only when everyone's political body is included can the ailing body politic be restored to health. But the "last" come first.[7]

This is a piercing parable for our racist body politic in the *locus imperii*. Because of the legacy of slavery, African Americans are unique historical victims of white racism, and their experience in many respects defines the pathology. Grier and Cobbs show how whites in the U.S.

> developed a way of life, an American ethos, a national life style which included the assumption that blacks are inferior and were born to hew wood and draw water. Newcomers to this land (if white) were immediately made to feel welcome and, among the bounty available, were given blacks to feel superior to. They were required to despise and depreciate them, abuse and exploit them, and one can only imagine how munificent this land must have seemed to the European — a land with built-in scapegoats. The hatred of blacks has been so deeply bound up with being an American that it has been one of the first things new Americans learn and one of the last things old Americans forget. Such feelings have been elevated to a position of national character, so that individuals now no longer feel personal guilt or responsibility for the oppression of black people. The nation has incorporated this oppression into itself in the form of folkways and storied traditions. (1980:171f)

The legacy of racism in California, on the other hand, because of its geopolitical relationship to both the east and the south — and hence its large Asian and Latin American population — includes but does not center upon black-white relations (see Daniels and Olin, 1972).

"This way of life is a heavy debt indeed," conclude Grier and Cobbs, "and one trembles for the debtor when payment comes due" (1980:172). Like the synagogue daughter, the project of white supremacy has taken us truly to "the verge of death." Yet the inheritors of white privilege are forever underestimating the pain of this legacy, downplaying its continuing violence, avoiding our complicity (see McIntosh, 1993). If we think about the legacy of racism at all, it is usually in order to talk our way around or out of it. Whites must heed Native American writer Vine Deloria's (1970) dictum: "*We* talk, *you* listen."

I recall an African American woman at a recent gathering of homeless activists who shared a particularly painful memory of growing up poor in Oakland, California.

> My parents were constantly instructing my brothers how not to offend or intimidate whites. They were big and dark-skinned you see, and so were warned to be careful not to be walking on the wrong street at the wrong time, and to always watch out for the police. It seemed to me at the time like these young men were being castrated. Well, my son is now 12, tall

for his age and his voice is deep. And the other day I found myself telling
him the same damn things.

Listening to her anguish, the weight of the racist legacy became almost too
heavy to bear. Such moments open our eyes and our hearts and put us on the
road to solidarity.

The first rule of collaboration is this: Only people of color have the right to
describe and analyze the realities of their oppression and the rage that results
from it.[8] Placing ourselves in venues where we must listen to people of color on
their terms is the opposite of inviting them to join our committees, our churches,
or our causes. As noted (above, A,1), whites often employ the latter tactic, re-
cruiting a select few black, Latino, Asian, or indigenous persons in order to
give multiracial legitimation to organizations we control. In contrast, if we join
their groups, we quickly discover how ambiguous and painful the dynamics of
"integration" are. Suddenly *we* are experiencing the host of small and large difficulties associated with being the "minority": what it feels like to be ignored
or invisible; to be talked "about" or caricatured; to be surrounded by cultural
discourses and practices that are not our own; to be treated with awkwardness
or hostility or reserve. While such experiences can never approximate the ordeal
of systemic racism, they can cause us to reflect on the suffering, patience, and
fortitude of those who live under this reality all the time.

But whites will truly be able to hear the truth of people of color only if and
when we have uncovered our own truth. We must come to see not only how
we have benefited from white privilege but also how we have been disfigured
by it. Wendell Berry, in a book entitled The *Hidden Wound,* states the matter
succinctly:

> If white people have suffered less obviously from racism than black
> people, they have nevertheless suffered greatly; the cost has been greater
> perhaps than we can yet know. If the white man has inflicted the wound of
> racism upon black men, the cost has been that he would receive the mirror
> image of that wound into himself. As the master, or as a member of the
> dominant race, he has felt little compulsion to acknowledge it or speak of
> it; the more painful it has grown the more deeply he has hidden it within
> himself. But the wound is there, and it is a profound disorder, as great a
> damage in his mind as it is in his society. (1989b:3f)

Only a recognition that we are all victims of racism, and a strong desire for
healing, will motivate us to undertake the journey of solidarity. "This wound is
in me, as complex and deep in my flesh as blood and nerves," writes Berry;
"I want to be free of the wound myself, and I do not want to pass it onto my
children" (ibid). Here again, then, solidarity must be rooted in our struggle for
liberation in our political bodies.

Racism, like sexism, is at the core of the shame culture in the *locus imperii.*
According to antiracism trainer Ardella Dailey (adapting the work of Kupers,

1981), there are five basic positions taken by whites toward people of color: (1) bigotry; (2) neutrality; (3) paternalism; (4) compliance; and 5) collaboration. The first four of these stances express different "masks" of shame (above, 4,C). It is not hard to see bigots masking their shame through macho behavior such as the paramilitary ethos of white supremacist groups. Purportedly *neutral* whites mask shame through a fairy-tale identity that assumes there are no fundamental racial problems in the U.S. Such color-blind innocence is, of course, the ideological product of social insulation from the harsh realities of race relations (above, 7,B). Liberals tend to mask their shame with polite and pious *paternalism*. They are eager to "help" people of color but insist that, while there may be racism in the U.S., it is not inherently a structural problem. Though they abhor the notion of legislated segregation, liberals often perpetuate a de facto system of separation through their own severely circumscribed and monocultural social interactions.

But what of those of us who fancy ourselves "conscientized" — social workers, peace activists, and community organizers? When people of color confront us with the realities of our white privilege, our reflexive response is invariably dissociation: "Well, the system may be racist, but *I* am not." This defensive reaction suggests we are masking shame through escape or disconnection, and it misses the point, which is that we cannot *not* be racist in a system of white privilege. But instead of facing the truth about ourselves, we often immerse ourselves in another culture — in the name of solidarity, of course. Then, if asked to articulate an ethnic tradition of our own, we exhibit feelings of self-contempt: "I so admire your connection with Africa; I don't feel like I have roots." This is the stance Dailey calls *compliance,* and it represents another mask for the dysfunctional white shame culture. In it whites will agree to almost any demand made by our "compañeros" of color and are easily "mau-maued" ("guilt-tripped"), as comically parodied by novelist Tom Wolfe during the days of the Black Power movement (1970).

In order to move to a stance of *collaboration,* whites must recognize our wound, unmask our shame, and face the pathology of racism in both our political bodies and our body politics. Our primary role in a partnership with people of color is to do this work aggressively with other members of the dominant culture. In any given context — around a meal table, at an organizing meeting, in a classroom, at a workplace — it is a betrayal of our responsibility to wait for the issue of racism to be raised by people of color or, worse, to consider it moot if there are no people of color there to raise it. We must take initiative yet without speaking "for" the oppressed. We must speak our own truth about how racism disfigures yet be able to take direction from people of color. This is a delicate dialectic; only experience can teach us when and how to speak or listen, and only over time can we earn the trust of those with whom we would collaborate. It is a matter of our will and our courage.

Recently mainstream U.S. denominations have offered prophetic denunciations of racism.[9] But real solidarity lies not in rhetoric but in individual and collective action. The Young Women's Christian Association, for example, has conducted "racism audits" to help organizations uncover and change hidden practices and assumptions that marginalize people of color. Resources for "undoing racism" work are widely available (see Barndt, 1991; J. Katz, 1978). Two basic approaches have emerged among those involved in anti-racism work. One approach, employed by the New Orleans–based People's Institute for Survival and Beyond, for example, uses a racially mixed leadership team to facilitate mixed groups, with opportunities for caucuses during the process. Another approach emphasizes whites working strictly with whites, although it invites people of color to sit in as "observers" with the right to intervene in the process at any time. I prefer the latter method, which I learned from the racism education program of the New Zealand Council of Churches. Each approach has strengths, and we probably ought to use both.

Unfortunately a third approach is emerging that is problematic. This approach, increasingly popular among government and corporate human relations programs and social service agencies, is "cultural diversity" training that never directly addresses the issue of white racism. To be sure, bias awareness work is crucial to our multicultural society — the Bridge Building Institute of Washington, DC, for example, is pioneering "prejudice reduction" workshops. But before whites can learn tolerance, or understand newer ethnic immigrants such as Cambodians or Armenians or Japanese Brazilians, we must confront the shadowed legacy of how people of color have been oppressed in our midst for centuries. The *first* responsibility for members of the dominant culture is to deal with white racism, and any approach in which this is played down or avoided only further strengthens the system of white privilege.

To live in discontinuity with racism, we must do more than overcome personal or group prejudice. We must also engage socio-political structures. Consider three examples, in each case local struggles against the racist political economy of substance abuse. The Reverend Michael Pfleger, a Roman Catholic priest in Chicago, was acquitted by a jury after being arrested in 1990 for defacing neighborhood billboards advertising alcohol and tobacco products. Pfleger had seen the ways in which substance abuse was ravaging the lives of so many in his predominantly black and Latino parish. Counting 118 such billboards within the ten-block radius of his church, in contrast to only three in a comparable area in a nearby white neighborhood, he decided to take direct action against these "twenty-four-hour pushers." In so doing he conscientized his parish to one of the concrete mechanisms of racial oppression in capitalism (McLory, 1991). Similar sentiments have coalesced into a wider political struggle in postuprising Los Angeles. Community sobriety groups and churches are organizing to prohibit the rebuilding of a disproportionate concentration of liquor stores in the low-income minority neighborhoods of South Central Los Angeles. Grassroots activists (often black) battle each permit sought by small grocers (often Korean) but understand they are ultimately fighting a white political establishment that has long been "under the influence" of the powerful alcohol lobby (on this see Lacey, 1992). Sadly, however, this effort has received minimal help from churches outside South Central. Finally, in Northwest Pasadena, I have had the

pleasure of collaborating with several African American organizers who are trying to draw the connections between drug and alcohol abuse and other forms of
violence and oppression in communities of color. We are developing workshops
to challenge social service providers to understand white privilege and black
disenfranchisement as flip sides of the same pathology that leads to substance
abuse in both communities. These are, it seems to me, the kind of practical
engagements Christians can and should be offering.

The overall task of eradicating racism from the body politic is, of course,
complex. For example, integrationist strategies of the past, Harold Cruse argues,
can no longer go unquestioned:

> American society, which is multiracial, multiethnic, and multicultural, has
> reached its internal limit, or saturation point, allowable for racial integra-
> tion as the NAACP once defined it. The United States is not anymore
> a simplistic black versus white encounter (in political, economic and cul-
> tural terms). In present-day America, what groups (whites, blacks, Indians,
> Japanese, Chinese, Latinos, immigrants, white ethnics) are going to in-
> tegrate with whom? And for what compelling reasons? ...Thus future
> black leadership options lie in the direction of black political, economic
> and cultural group consolidation — not for separatism, but for group plu-
> ral accommodation to the changing fact of racial and ethnic configurations
> taking place before our very eyes in America today. (1990:25)

This is an important departure from the politics of integration that characterized
older liberalism, and it has confused and distressed many whites whose thinking
was shaped during the civil rights era. They do not understand how the same
movement that struggled to overturn structures and discourses based on race
can now be insisting that we must pay attention to ethnic identity.

The problem is that integration was (and is) predicated upon assimilation-
ism, which is simply the flip side of the politics of segregation. Both are
expressions of the hegemony of the dominant culture. So "group plural accommodation" is an attempt to deconstruct the integrationist model in favor
of cultural pluralism (below, Chapter Ten). The struggle is still for freedom and
against white supremacy. This is precisely why the politico-cultural Right —
which never supported integration — is suddenly now a champion of assimilation and a vigorous opponent of multiculturalism, which it denounces as
incipient "Balkanism." The concern about how to construct common social
space and covenant in a world of group difference is, of course, a legitimate
one. The point is, it cannot be constructed in a space still overdetermined by
the dominant culture. Alternatively the diversity of group interests could con-
verge in the struggle for justice, by promoting the empowerment of marginalized
people and affirming the politics of self-determination (below, Chapter Eleven).
A new era of multicultural coalitions working in mutual solidarity could reignite
our political imagination for America.

I believe the legacy of racist oppression also calls First World Christians to recognize how much people of color have to teach us about the gospel itself. We have everything to learn from the black church and black theology about the struggle for freedom and justice in this country, for example. This is what makes it so tragic that our churches are still so segregated — more so than the culture in general. (Most congregations do not practice what small businesses by law must: basic affirmative action.) This is not to imply that the task is to integrate every congregation; that would contradict what I have argued above. Indeed ethnic churches have been crucial historically to the survival and sanity of minority communities. What we need to do is break down the walls between churches. I believe this could begin to take place if every predominantly white parish did three modest things: (1) conduct an internal racism audit and regular workshops with its membership; (2) commit itself to a functional partnership with a Third World congregation nearby; and (3) participate in one action each year that resisted local manifestations of a discriminatory political economy. Such a program could put the churches on the forefront of the wider movement against racism, and just as importantly, it could restore a modicum of solidarity within the body of Christ![10] In any case, a Deuteronomic choice between life and death remains before the white church. Either we collaborate fully in the empowerment of people of color at home and abroad or we ensure that race wars, large and small, will continue.

D. "THE POOR ARE ALWAYS WITH YOU": CLASS

Can we overcome the "invisibility" of class oppression in order to construct solidarity with working-class and poor people?

"The poor are always with you" (Mk 14:7a). How many times has this utterance been pressed into the service of ideologies that legitimate social division? Let us return to the story in which this phrase appears (above, B). Jesus, socially relocated among the marginalized at the house of a leper (14:3), is ministered to lavishly by a woman (probably a prostitute). Those who object that the oil she uses could have been "sold and the money given to the poor" (14:5) appear to be on solid ground, since these are precisely the instructions given by Jesus earlier to the rich man (10:21). But the context here is different. Jesus is not challenging the entitled to practice redistributive justice; he is sharing table fellowship with the outcast. Apparently his companions are so preoccupied with noble political strategies to help the poor that they cannot see the woman practicing solidarity right in front of them. Could it be their class prejudice? So Jesus reminds them — somewhat dryly, one imagines — that because they are a community committed to sharing life with the poor, they will have the opportunity to "do the right thing" (14:7b; Gk *eu poiēsai*). This is a statement about the *social location of the church*, not about the *social necessity of poverty*. Again, we have gotten Jesus backward because the site from which we read him is insulated from, rather than in solidarity with, the poor.

1. Class Dismissed

If gender and race are the most primal social divisions in the *locus imperii,* class is the most objectively persistent yet subjectively suppressed. The contributions of the "working class," like those of women and people of color, have been either erased or devised in our official historical narratives, and the voices of the socio-economically marginalized have been silenced (above, 5,B,C). Those who have attempted to name class realities have been fiercely repressed, none more than communists and the left wing of the labor movement, particularly during and after the Great Depression. The point of this suppression is to prop up the capitalist myth that there are no real classes in the U.S. and that social location is determined by personal, not economic or political, factors (above, 7,C).[11]

Benjamin DeMott, in his important work of cultural criticism *The Imperial Middle: Why Americans Can't Think Straight about Class,* contends that "the power of this icon of classlessness derives from history, the media, and the national experience of public education . . . enabling the state to behave as though episodes of state-administered injustice are accidents. . . . Social wrong is accepted in America partly because differences in knowledge about class help to obscure it, and the key to those differences is the degree of acceptance of the myth of classlessness" (1990:10f). This myth has been extraordinarily effective in rendering class stratification invisible in public political discourse. The genius of our class system, says Alan Wolfe, is that "liberal democracy made a sharp separation between the economy and the political system, one in which the formal equality promised within the latter ('one man, one vote') actually sustained a rampant inequality within the former. Working classes, in short, accepted political rights in return for a general sacrifice of economic ones" (1980:295). Precisely because they are not explicated, class realities overdetermine our electoral politics. The U.S. is the only industrialized nation without a class-based political organization (e.g., a labor party); the poor for the most part do not vote; and the U.S. Senate consists almost entirely of millionaires.[12]

There are, of course, social classes in the U.S., even if defining them is a complex task. We must begin, argues William Domhoff, by recognizing the class at the top.

> Dominant power in the United States is exercised by a power elite that is the leadership group of a property-based ruling class. Despite all the turmoil of the 1960s and 1970s, and the constant chatter about economic crisis that is ever with us, there continues to be a small upper class whose members own 20 to 25 percent of all privately held wealth and 45 to 50 percent of all privately held corporate stock. They sit in seats of formal power from the corporate community to the federal government, and they win much more often than they lose on issues ranging from the nature of the tax structure to the stifling of reform in such vital areas as consumer protection, environmental protection, and labor law. (1983:222f)

"To claim that there is an upper class with enough power to be considered a ruling class does not imply that other levels of society are totally powerless," Domhoff reminds us, however; "domination does not mean total control, but the ability to set the terms under which other groups and classes must operate" (ibid:1f). Analysis of the ruling class in the *locus imperii* is widely available (see Jaher, 1973; Bottomore, 1967; Gross, 1980). But because I believe it is far easier for middle-class people to criticize those "above" them than to forge solidarity with those "below" them, my focus here is on the latter.

King, Maynard, and Woodyard offer helpful reflections upon the "structural entrapment" of the middle class in U.S. society:

> General economic conditions leave us increasingly like the other segments of the laboring class, vulnerable to the bite of poverty; low-level participation in corporate decision making, however, leads to middle sector cooperation in the oppression of both the working fraction and the poor; finally, our structural powerlessness as employees and our individualism create a sense of isolation and meaninglessness, of being unable to change either our vulnerability to or our cooperation in that oppression. (1988:61)

Their solution is for the middle sector to recognize the increasing tenuousness of its economic position, and to realize that its interests lie with the blue-collar and poor sectors rather than with the elite. Through a new kind of class consciousness they call "social heroism," the middle sector can be motivated to build broad-based coalitions toward a "larger labor class movement." Their pragmatic strategy of building common cause on the basis of overlapping self-interest is analytically sound. But I fear they underestimate the barriers to cross-sector collaboration (above, 7,E,2).

To begin with, economic stratification is intensifying. The situation is summed up by the 1988 Commission on the Cities:

> Recessions, manufacturing moves and closings, the flight of jobs and the middle class to the suburbs, and a reduction in real wages ... hit the most vulnerable Americans hardest. There were determined efforts to cut social programs in education, housing, jobs, training, ... affirmative action and vigorous enforcement of the civil-rights laws.... Poverty is worse now than it was twenty years ago. More people are poor — both white and nonwhite. Those who are poor are poorer. Escape from poverty is harder. Overall unemployment in America is twice what it was twenty years ago. And unemployment for blacks is now twice what it is for whites. The Kerner Report is coming true: America is again becoming two societies, one black (and today we can add to that Hispanic), one white — separate and unequal. (Harris and Wilkins, 1988:xiif)

This means that the middle sector itself is also polarizing. It is now widely acknowledged that Reagan-era "tax breaks" served to benefit the upper middle class while everyone else began to experience "slippage." Katherine Newman's *Falling from Grace: The Experience of Downward Mobility in the American Middle Class* (1988) has demonstrated that because of persistent economic stagnation since Vietnam, assumptions about increasing intergenerational affluence, which have characterized the broad middle sector since World War I, are no longer viable. This new reality is shattering both conservative myths of endless private prosperity and liberal myths of public progress. It will undoubtedly change the face of U.S. politics and culture — but how?

Barbara Ehrenreich, in her thoughtful *Fear of Falling: The Inner Life of the Middle Class* (1989), suggests that insecurity and anxiety is not leading middle-class families toward greater class solidarity. Instead their home and work lifestyles are becoming increasingly defensive, indicating they are less likely to build alliances with those perceived to be a threat to their traditional entitlements. U.S. politics in this emerging context is not only returning to its long tradition of race baiting, as in Bush's 1988 "Willie Horton" campaign (Marable, 1992b). It seems also to be explicitly encouraging class enmity. A clear example is California Governor Wilson's 1992 budgetary politics of "welfare reform," which blames public assistance and health and education programs for the state's recessionary woes. Given the culture of selfishness promoted in capitalism, therefore, long-term class self-interests alone will probably not motivate a large number of middle-class people to solidarity with the poor. Christians will also have to look to the gospel as a motivator.

But again we must keep in mind the difficulties presented to the quest for social relocation by the social architecture of division (above, 7,B,C). The poor are "in our midst always," but if it is so difficult for us to "see" them, how are we to build alliances with them? For example, media-driven stereotypes conflate color and class to persuade suburban whites that the poor in the U.S. are urban, black, and on welfare. This racist stereotype effectively renders invisible not only the working poor and new immigrants (particularly the undocumented) but obscures the fact that

> the largest and perhaps least understood poverty group in California [is] the white poor. Largely dispersed in rural areas and small communities, they defy the public image of poverty as primarily a problem of blacks and Latinos in the inner cities. While that image was reinforced by the Los Angeles riots, the 1990 census tells a different story: 1,821,146 non-Hispanic whites, 1,598,213 Latinos and 437,201 blacks lived in poverty in California.... More Anglo families received financial aid, food stamps and other public assistance last year in California than any other racial or ethnic group. (Hurst, 1992:A1)

It surely says something about the power of class in our country that the greatest socially engineered distance of all is between rich and poor whites.

2. Solidarity in the New Economic Order

I would suggest three relatively modest steps to crossing the class divide in order to build solidarity. The first is simply to begin recognizing the diversity of class backgrounds *among those we already associate with each day*. Our middle-class assumptions hide the fact that not all of our co-workers, fellow church members, or friends come from the same socio-economic context we do. DeMott notes that the illusion of sameness accounts for violations small and large in daily interaction: "Calling the myth of classlessness larcenous is, indeed, no empty figure of speech. The myth blunts the feeling for the contradictoriness of experience, steals the capacity to suspend judgment and look before and after. Because of its oversimplifying power, pieces of the truth are constantly being mistaken for the whole, connections between each part and every other part are neglected, and immodesty and self-righteousness take command" (1990:192). Our challenge, then, is to recognize and take seriously "differences in people's actual physical, mental, imaginative activity as workers, differences in what people come to learn and master in the course of their general lives, differences in levels of self-respect, and differences in the visions of life possibility that attain vivid meaning for people as family members and as participants in larger communities" (ibid:53). Persons who on the surface seem similar may have dramatically contrasting class upbringing and thus divergent attitudes toward social mobility, family, culture, and so on. Many couples, for example, have discovered belatedly that such differences are at the root of many of their relationship struggles.

Sennett and Cobb's *Hidden Injuries of Class* (1973) offers a sensitive analysis of how dominant class assumptions oppress working people. The hierarchy of labor value, for example, "accords the world's best welder less respect than the most mediocre doctor." Education is another case in point. The traditional route to upward class mobility, it also fosters a sense of inferiority among those who have not had the opportunity. "Being educated" thus represents

> what psychologists call a "cover term"; that is, it stands for a whole range of experiences and feelings that may in fact have little to do with formal schooling. . . . Education meant to the people we interviewed getting certificates for social mobility and job choice, and they felt that American society parcels out the certificates very unequally and unfairly, so that middle-class people have more of a chance . . . than workers to escape from becoming creatures of circumstance, more chance to develop the defenses, the tools of personal, rational control that "education" gives. . . . And yet, if that class difference is a *fait accompli*, what has a man without education got inside himself to defend against this superior power? (1973:24f)

I have experienced how "using big words," or being known as an author, can impress or give immediate entree in some class settings, while in others it can alienate or make me suspect. Class collaboration begins, therefore, by simply acknowledging our own class socialization and learning to be more respectful toward those from different backgrounds.

An equally modest second step is to overcome the class divisions among our churches. For example, middle-class Protestants today — mainline and radical alike — have very little contact with low-church traditions (such as Pentecostals, Assemblies of God, and independent Baptists), which consist primarily of working-class or poor people. It is far easier for ecumenically-minded white peace and justice activists in Los Angeles to collaborate with one of the several prominent middle-class African Methodist Episcopal congregations than with one of the many small fundamentalist churches serving blue-collar whites. (Similarly, those black AME parishioners may have less difficulty relating to us than to members of Church of God in Christ storefront churches in their own neighborhood.) We may protest that the reasons for this are theological, but they are undoubtedly more related to class. After all, most low-income churches are profoundly concerned with both the Bible and the social welfare of their membership — so what is our problem? Is it not our class biases (particularly around education) that prevent us from exploring with them such potential common ground? Class gulfs in the church are no more acceptable than gender or race ones. We need to venture across town (or across the street) to listen to and learn from our economically poorer, but often spiritually richer, sisters and brothers.

A third step across the class divide will be more challenging for middle-class people. It is as obvious as it is rarely taken: to become more familiar with working-class institutions, notably labor unions. The last two decades have been very difficult for the labor movement as it has been relentlessly scapegoated, suppressed, or ignored by the forces of capital. Labor has been increasingly marginalized in the public consciousness because of capital's control of the media, which would persuade us that the struggle between workers and owners is simply no longer relevant to our modern, technocratic world. David Noble reminds us that however much these "corporate engineers"

> convinced themselves that they served the interests of society as a whole, they in reality served only the dominant class in society, that class which, in order to survive, must forever struggle to extract labor from, and thus to control the lives of, the class beneath it. No myth of classlessness, no "end of ideology" ideology, however comforting, however innocent, can ever obscure this fact. And it is precisely this fact, manifested in the myriad "problems" which must forever be analyzed, engineered, or administered away, which both underlies the evolving corporate design for America and defies it. (1977:324)

Los Angeles, for example, commonly thought to be the paragon of postindustrial cities, "still leads the nation in manufacturing employment," which accounts for one out of five jobs in the county (Peterson, 1991). There continue to be, in other words, compelling reasons for solidarity with blue-collar justice.

Most First World churches, unfortunately, continue in a legacy of ambivalence toward organized labor, which reflects the decidedly professional class location of much clerical leadership. To be sure, established unions, like churches, are a mixed bag. It has been pointed out that today

> organized labor and organized religion share a unique and difficult place in American society. The two must both function as "institutions" and "movements" at the same time.... We must both find ways to adapt the historical principles that define and guide us to the realities of the modern world without sacrificing the essential elements of those principles. We must both avoid succumbing to the temptation to reshape ourselves to fit the current fashion; but, at the same time, we must constantly work to make our traditional values vital to new generations. (AFL-CIO, 1991:iii)

I think this analogy is valid. It confirms that radical Christians have a great deal in common with the radical wings of the labor movement. Today some of the most committed activists in the U.S. continue to be union organizers in, for example, the garment, mining, and electronics industries (see Hollyday, 1989).

Many of us were midwifed into social justice work through the farmworker movements of the 1960s and 1970s. Indeed immigrant labor has always pioneered class solidarity in the U.S. Generations of Irish, Italian, and Polish workers brought their indigenous traditions of struggle to infuse new life into the U.S. labor movement at the turn of the century. More recently Mexicans and Central American immigrants have employed their Christian base-community experiences to organize in *maquiladoras* and sweatshops. It is worth noting two local examples in which newer Latino workers have broken new ground. The drywallers' strike of 1992 took on the notoriously conservative building trades in developer-dominated Orange County (T. Hernandez, 1992). Justice for Janitors has challenged the hotel and commercial office sector with remarkable boldness and nonviolent creativity, from public fasts to large direct action protests (Banks, 1992).

Threats to fairness and dignity in the workplace are only becoming more rampant in the globalizing economy. Cavanaugh and Clairmonte (1983) identify four major characteristics of this new era:

(1) the growth of international corporate conglomerates with huge capital resources who are able to manipulate prices and undermine national and foreign competitors;

(2) the shift in transnational ownership from primary commodity output to processing, marketing, and distribution and services — choosing to control world markets rather than the means of production;

(3) fragmentation of production processes through new technological advances, i.e., forming subsidiaries and subcontracting wherever possible in "free trade zones" in the Third World, thus locking developing countries more firmly into the world market;

(4) internationalization of finance through the growth in transnational banks.

The new internationalism consists of "a very close relationship at the production and marketing levels between Trans-National Banks, Trans-National Corporations, mega multi-commodity trading companies and certain segments of State power" (ibid:6f). It spells disaster, however, for the domestic workforce.

Citing the "rising costs of doing business," corporations seeking to maximize their profit margins are abandoning sites where labor is organized, wages fair, and environmental standards enforced, and moving production to the Third World. There they find huge tax and tariff breaks offered by indebted governments desperate for foreign investment; plentiful cheap and unorganized labor; lax or nonexistent environmental regulations; and minimal health and safety standards for the workplace. Even within the U.S., companies can force concessions from state or local governments by threatening to move operations to a "right to work" state. The result is an international "open shop," where capital is in control and labor held hostage to the blackmail of (often absentee) management. *Maquiladoras* ("twinplants") along the Mexican border represent the leading edge of this phenomenon. They are case studies in how workers lose in both places — abandoned in the U.S. and exploited in Mexico.[13]

The North American Free Trade Agreement (NAFTA) is a major step forward into this global economy, where capital and goods move freely while labor markets are undercut.[14] The result will be the atrophy of urban manufacturing centers, which means that U.S. cities will face a continuing rise in unemployment, deepening economic isolation, and the inevitably resulting social unrest. "There are 'quiet riots' in all of America's central cities: unemployment, poverty, social disorganization, segregation, family disintegration, housing and school deterioration, and crime are worse now. These 'quiet riots' are not as alarming as the violent riots of twenty years ago, or as noticeable to outsiders. But they are even more destructive of human life" (Harris and Wilkins, 1988:xiii). But these are social costs for which the departing firms bear no responsibility. In this new order of deindustrialization, mercenary capital, and global open shop, therefore, Christians must take new responsibility for standing with workers. In a 1991 letter to the U.S. trade representative, the U.S. Catholic Conference asserted that "the economic choices of our two nations should be guided by a priority concern for the poor in both lands and by a firm commitment to the dignity of work and the rights of workers.... We believe, as Pope Paul VI said in *Populorum Progressio,* that 'the rule of free trade, taken by itself, is no longer able to govern international relations.... Freedom of trade is fair only if it is subject to the demands of social justice'" (Lynch, 1991). Unfortunately the debate over the NAFTA has to date received very little sustained attention from most church-based peace and justice activists.

How do we practically stand in solidarity with the victims of the globalizing economy? An example of AFSC work illustrates local and national points for strategic involvement. The *Comité de Apoyo* based in Texas has helped support the development of a Mexican organizing project among maquiladora women in five border cities, called *Comité Fronterizo de Obreras* (CFO). The CFO trains *promotoras* who facilitate groups in the factories to address living and working

conditions. It also builds links with other workers and women's groups and ed-
ucates about injustices in the maquiladoras. On the national and international
level, AFSC has helped start the Coalition for Justice in the Maquiladoras.
This broad-based coalition has developed and is pressing for industry and government adoption of a "Maquiladora Standard of Conduct," which addresses
environmental, health and safety, fair employment, and community impact issues. The program also promotes communication among trade unionists in
Canada, the U.S., and Mexico on issues related to the NAFTA (Scott, 1991).

There is no lack of groups with whom Christians can collaborate, from
corporate responsibility advocates to plant closures networks to community organizing movements such as the Industrial Areas Foundation.[15] Avenues for
solidarity exist; it is our class-hardened hearts that must be opened to the victims of the new economic order. First World Christians must use critical literacy
to overcome our sense of impotence when it comes to complex issues such as
international trade. Through local collaboration with those struggling for dignity
in the workplace, we can come to see how global trends profoundly affect our
lives. To paraphrase Dr. King, justice denied to the farmworker, the *maquila*
worker, the janitor, and the housecleaner is justice denied to us all.

E. LIBERTY AND JUSTICE FOR ALL?
MINJUNG THEOLOGY FOR NORTH AMERICA

*How can the church's solidarity, including its special vocation to be pres-
ent to the "insignificant" outcast, help realize the Promise of America?*

There are a few other important aspects of solidarity that must be mentioned before concluding. The gospel calls us not only to venture into churches
we have never visited before; it also challenges Christians to move beyond our
traditional reluctance to work alongside non-Christians. There are many church-
based movements for justice we can join, but to collaborate only with them
gives us an unrealistic notion of the pluralistic context in which we live. It is
true that political alliances can result in strange bedfellows, but this should not
bother a community whose definition of kindredness is "*whosoever* does the
will of God." Obviously there is a need for discernment, which will at times
lead us to offer a distinctively Christian witness or even to withdraw from a
coalition. But given the power of the domination system, the church ought to
rejoice in Jesus' radically inclusive politics: "They who are not against us are
for us" (Mk 9:40; below, 10,A,2).

Nor should we limit our concern to those experiencing gender, race, and
class oppression. Selectivity concerning which of the oppressed we will stand
with can be merely another characteristic of imperial privilege. We are also invited to learn solidarity with social "others" who differ from us significantly in
their body politics or in their political bodies.

Those different in their body politics. Jacques Ellul has raised some troubling questions in an essay entitled "The Truly Poor and the End of the Left"

(1978:82ff). Some Third World liberation struggles, he argues, are well publicized and even celebrated in the Metropolitan media. On the other hand, the plights of those considered too politically insignificant by Western news editors, or too ideologically inconvenient for activists on the Left, are passed over. The causes of Palestinians, Eastern Europeans, or South Africans are well known to us, for example; the plights of Appalachian coal miners, Haitian farmworkers, Tibetan Buddhists, Brazilian Indians, or traditional Laplanders are not. Both the Left and the Right have a tendency to ignore cultural minorities (Gypsies, Japanese, Koreans) or refugee groups (Hmong, Kurds) who are unorganized politically, or who tout no national or ideological cause. A decade ago Jim Corbett protested that certain church-based networks were practicing a "selective sanctuary," which sponsored only Central American refugees willing to support the leftist causes back home (1991:160f). The church must be bigger than the "solidarity" politics of the day, open to the "truly poor" as well as to the well organized, never allowing tactical alliances to constrain the scope of compassion.

It is necessary to make practical decisions, of course — solidarity with the poor in general is solidarity with no one in particular. But Ellul's complaint is a sharp reminder that even as we build strategic alliances with those already engaged in the struggle for self-determination, we must not turn away from those who have little or no political capital to offer because they are small in number or geopolitically remote. Ignominy is always the fate of the poorest among us; the gospel calls us to stand with them especially when it is politically or vocationally inconvenient.

In North America this would apply preeminently to indigenous peoples, particularly those who are "out of sight" on reservations (see Jaimes, 1992; Weyler, 1992; Engelstad and Bird, 1992; Angus, 1991). True, Indian causes receive occasional celebrity because of a movie (e.g., *Dances with Wolves*) or a dramatic rebellion (Wounded Knee). But this distorted exposure generates only short-lived attention from the dominant culture. Because issues raised by Native Americans strike most deeply at our national denial (above, Chapter Five), we tend to become easily discouraged at the seeming intractable problems facing them — particularly if the funders, the press, and the politicians quickly lose interest in our solidarity work. Another problem is that "political progressives" have in the past been ambivalent about Indian demands for sovereignty (Churchill, 1983). We are often uncertain how to deal with their traditional gender-based divisions of labor or other cultural practices that do not conform to our own social ideals. Development analyst Thierry Verhelst insists that in order for our solidarity not to degenerate into another form of cultural imperialism, we must embrace a certain amount of "perplexity" and affirm indigenous peoples' "right to be different" (1990:79ff, 113ff). An exemplary approach is that of the Honor Our Neighbors' Origins and Rights coalition, based in Milwaukee. Here non-Indian groups work in role-specific alliance with tribes on issues of local concern, particularly treaty rights.

Those different in their political bodies. This leads to an arena of solidarity that was for centuries almost the exclusive domain of the church: the traditional "works of mercy" among the old, the sick, prisoners, the mentally and physically disabled, and the dying. Although today the medical and nursing professions do much of the care giving for society's infirm, the church rightly continues its pastoral work of offering comfort to those who are shut in, locked down, and cast out. Yet this work has, at times, been looked down upon by activists of both the Right and the Left. *The works of mercy should not be confused with charity* (above, A). Christians who criticize sheltered workshops as "Band-aid" programs are as unconscionable as those who scapegoat AIDS victims. I know firsthand the daily patience and compassion — always unsung and often unremunerated — demanded of persons who take the senile elderly on walks or help quadriplegics with their bowel movements or visit the children's cancer ward or give sandwiches to the homeless. Such accompaniment invites the messianic community into what we might call the politics of presence. In our being present to the refugee, the weak, and the dying, the presence of Christ is revealed to us (see D. Berrigan, 1989).

Moreover works of mercy are not without social or political implications. The church's care for the sick has often led it into the forefront of the struggle to destigmatize and even decriminalize certain illnesses, from Father Damien's leper colonies to Jean Vanier's L'Arche communities. Indeed many hospitals and hospices began by Christians (and others) simply sharing life with the "contaminated." If the reigning epidemiology is oppressive, as in the case of AIDS today, then the vocation of simple compassion demands political struggle. A good example is the struggle of disabled people for full rights in a society that discriminates against their bodies. Recently activists demanding that public space be made accessible for the disabled, and that resources be made available for "nondependent living," have employed powerful and poignant expressions of somatic politics (above, 8,E). The deaf community, similarly, has fought for recognition of its distinctive culture and signed language.

When we speak of the oppression of political bodies, the most notorious example is the struggle of sexual minorities for equal rights. From the Victorian era to the present, gay and lesbian people (as well as other sexual minorities) have been vilified as outsiders by the dominant culture, with the most vitriolic condemnations coming from the religious community. Today there are formidable forces organizing to reinforce this oppression by advocating the exclusion of gays and lesbians from full civil rights in society and full participation in the church. Predictably these trends are being accompanied by a rise in homophobic violence. The rationale used by Christian conservatives to marginalize sexual minorities — spurious arguments from nature, from the Bible, and from dominant cultural assumptions — are exactly parallel to those used in the nineteenth century to support slavery. They must be wholly repudiated. It remains important for churches to understand the biblical documents in the context of the sexual culture that produced them, as well as to discuss the real issues of sexual ethics. But there are simply no gospel grounds for creating new (or supporting old) categories of the outcast. All who have been oppressed in their political bodies by discriminative social boundaries deserve inclusion, equality, and justice in the body politic. The church must offer Christian solidarity *without exception.*[16]

Korean Christians, who know something about being a minority and about the history of oppression, have developed a concept that I think best clarifies the gospel demands of solidarity. Central to their understanding of biblical radicalism is the notion of *minjung,* a dynamic concept of the poor that takes into account the relations of power in a given context (see the Christian Conference of Asia anthology, 1981). Thus peasants are *minjung* in relation to landowners, women in relation to men, Koreans in relation to the Japanese, the disabled in relation to the nondisabled, homosexuals in relation to heterosexuals, and so on. The strength of this definition is that it calls us to identify in each new setting who dominates and who suffers. We dare not restrict our solidarity to just one group or place or time.

Why can't the church in North American embrace a minjung theology — and politics? Kim Yong-bok draws a crucial distinction between "political messianism" and "messianic politics." The former promises reform to the people, but institutes change from the top down, so that nothing really changes for the minjung:

> While political messianism attempts to make the *minjung* a historical nothing or an object of its messianic claims, the messianic politics of Jesus are the politics that will realize for the *minjung* their historical destiny. Fundamentally, messianic politics must be understood as that of the *minjung,* not that of the leader, especially not that of the ruling power.... To expose the reality of political messianism in the modern state, no matter however secular they claim to be, is one of the fundamental [tasks of] political hermeneutics of the Christian community today. (Ibid:191f)

The church in the *locus imperii* must heed Kim's challenge to "purge elements of political messianism from our Christian confession, proclamations, and theologies" and to embrace a practice of political change which works from the base (below, 11,C).

Finally we should recognize that the notion of inclusion is not entirely absent from dominant culture ideals in the U.S. "The Founding Fathers who wrote the Constitution in the 1780s embarked upon a great political experiment. But they also, without quite realizing it, began to engage in a great social experiment — whether a nation of immigrants, a multi-national, multi-cultural, multi-ethnic nation could long endure and endure in an atmosphere of mutual respect and toleration and equal rights and privileges for all" (Wollenberg, 1988:8). Inclusion and equality, however partially realized by those white, landed, patriarchal "founders," remains a subversive narrative in the U.S. I am not one who supports the ritual recitation of the pledge of allegiance in this country. But even there we find a remnant of the Promise, for the cant concludes by invoking "liberty and justice for all." That is a vision which Martin King offered to his people, one he lived and died for. It deserves our allegiance.

But in the end, it is the narrative of biblical radicalism that defines our vision of justice based on the eradication of socio-economic alienation. In Mark 4–8, two wilderness feedings stories and two crossings "to the other side" of the Sea of Galilee symbolically enact that vision of solidarity. In the last of these archetypal boat journeys Jesus, like Moses on the mountain, sharply reminds his followers of these wilderness lessons. But the disciples do not understand the "mystery of the one loaf" (6:52; 8:13ff; *BSM:*223ff). First World Christians continue this legacy of incomprehension today whenever we feign ignorance of the gender, race, and class divisions in our House or when we complain we do not know what to do about them. Do we understand? (8:21). The test of our literacy, dis-illusionment, and revisioning will be the degree to which we practice solidarity-as-collaboration.

NOTES

1. Jesus is forever moving between "public" (e.g., House-controlled) spaces, where conflict with the authorities is rife, and "liberated" spaces (e.g., the houses of followers), where alternative perspectives and practices are nurtured (1:29ff; 2:1ff; 7:24ff; 10:10; 14:3ff). In 3:19, however, the household space is also being contested, showing that the authorities understand the subversive nature of Jesus' program of resocialization. Mk 3:31–34 is tightly structured around a fivefold refrain of "mothers and brothers," beginning with Jesus' natural family and ending with the redefinition of kinship. "Whosoever does the will of God" is one of Mark's carefully chosen conditional relative clauses that articulate radical status-reversal throughout the gospel (*BSM:*283f).

2. The theme of mutual suspicion and misunderstanding between men and women was characteristic of Thurber's work. His male point of view is evident in his portraits of bewildered, henpecked men and angry, domineering women, as in his most famous short story, "The Secret Life of Walter Mitty," or the well-known cartoon images "House and Woman" and "Man in Tree" (1964:47ff, 348, 357). But the body of his work does not suggest he saw men as victims or even that he thought gender oppression was reciprocal. Two images from the "War" — the women's "Retreat" of the men's "Rout" — show that Thurber understood patriarchy to be the root of the problem. But they also reflect his pessimism that things would change.

3. Some of the recent major theological works are Young (1990); Welch (1989); Heine (1989); Christ and Plaskow (1991); Becher (1991); Erickson (1992); Deberg (1990); Brown and Bohn (1989); Buhrig (1992); Borrowdale (1992); Sewell (1991); Fischer (1988); Russell, Kwok, Cannon, and Isasi-Diaz (1988). Virginia Mollenkott, Letty Russell, Mary Daly, Rosemary Ruether, Dorothee Soelle, Delores Williams, Mercy Oduyoye, and Chung Hyun Kyung have published multiple works as well.

4. On the social construction of femininity see S. Miller (1984). An interesting, and highly consequential, discussion emerged during the 1980s as feminist scientists began to challenge the alleged biological bases for gender difference, showing how the dominant naturalist paradigms are themselves patriarchal constructions; see Bleier (1984), Keller (1985) and Hubbard (1990). For a socio-linguistic version of the "difference" argument see Tannen (1990).

5. The so-called sexual revolution of the 1960s and 1970s has been a mixed blessing for women and men both. The politics of desublimation has helped liberate women as sexual subjects and has thus challenged widely dysfunctional heterosexual patterns. It has also inspired movements for equal rights for sexual minorities, particularly gays and lesbians, whose cries for justice and inclusion in the church and in society deserve our full support (see 9,E). At the same time, increased license has escalated sexual expectations and thus also anxieties. This is quite apart from the AIDS plague; reflecting on the way in which the patriarchal ethos makes women vulnerable to sexually transmitted diseases, Dr. Jonathan Mann, director of the International AIDS Center at Harvard, concluded that "male-dominated societies are a threat to public health" (*New York Times,* July 21, 1992). Sexual license has certainly not encouraged male commitment to the family. We have also seen a dramatic growth in an underground economy based on the objectification and commodification of sex, from pornography to sexual slavery. Will the legacy of my generation's relatively unrestrained sexual ethos be a future era of restriction and repression? If so, what will have been achieved by the sexual "revolution"?

6. See *BSM:*280f, 396f, 407, 434f. Mark portrays women as having less resistance to the way of the cross and the practice of service (Gk *diakoneo*). I believe this represents a "feminist" insight into the differences between men and women concerning competition and the struggle for power. I will, however, take this opportunity to apologize for my misrepresentation of Winsome Munro's 1982 article on women in Mark (*BSM:*281,407), which she has pointed out to me in private correspondence (August 1, 1990). Munro does not contend that women are invisible in the gospel, as I implied; rather she points "to their relative invisibility in the first fourteen to fifteen chapters as compared with men" (1982:241). She and I continue to disagree on the meaning of Mark's narrative strategy, however. Working from the fundamentally different approach of historical-criticism, Munro contends that Mark narrates female discipleship only "evasively." Nevertheless she admits that his portrait "reveals, though with reluctance and ambiguity, that certain women exercised a key role in the primitive church" (ibid). Ironically, then, we concur that women were in fact in leadership roles in the discipleship community. On feminist biblical interpretation see Schüssler Fiorenza, 1983; Laffey, 1988.

7. Sleep is what disciples must fight off in order to stay awake to the Great Economy (13:36). The implication in 5:39 would seem to be that the dominant culture of synagogue Judaism must awaken to the object lesson Jesus is offering. The poor must come first if their social project (Israel is symbolized by the association of both daughters with the number twelve; 5:25, 42), which is "on the verge of death" (5:23), is to be "resurrected" (5:41f; "to rise" [Gk *egeiren*] and "ecstasy" [Gk *ekstasis*] appear in combination only here and in 16:6–8). It is ironic that the synagogue leader's daughter "eats" (5:43) after she has awakened from this "sleep," while the disciples eat with Jesus (14:22ff) only to fall asleep when the *kairos* arrives (14:37, 40f). Later in Mark, Jesus demonstrates in his own person the lesson he was pressing upon the synagogue leader: Jesus learns about inclusion from a Syro-Phoenician woman (7:24ff).

8. The literature by people of color on racism is voluminous. As a good basic analysis I recommend Cornel West's discussion of "the genealogy of modern racism" (1982:47ff). Marable (1992a) and San Juan (1992) are good recent overviews. On the social construction of race see Horsman (1981) as well as R. Sanders (1992). For a statistical summary of the social indicators concerning people of color in the U.S., see Foster et al (1990).

9. The 1984 "Policy Statement on Racial Justice" of the National Council of Churches, USA Governing Board, for example, begins by providing accurate definitions of the problem (see above, 7,C):

Prejudice is a personal attitude towards other people based on a categorical judgement about their physical characteristics, such as race or ethnic origin. *Racism* is racial prejudice plus power. Racism is the intentional or unintentional use of power to isolate, separate and exploit others. This use of power is based on a belief in superior racial origin, identity or supposed racial characteristics. Racism confers certain privileges on and defends the dominant group, which in turn sustains and perpetuates racism. Both consciously and unconsciously, racism is enforced and maintained by the legal, cultural, religious, education, economic, political and military institutions of societies. ... *Institutional racism* is one of the ways organizations and structures serve to preserve injustice. Intended or not, the mechanisms and function of these entities create a pattern of racial injustice. (1984:26.5–1)

If widely embraced by churches, this definition would go a long way to helping us think straight about these matters. See also Wallis and Hulteen (1992).

10. In the wake of the Los Angeles uprising, many churches tried to forge relationships across the race/class divides of the city, mostly through Sunday exchanges. But few of these efforts endured beyond a year. I would argue that this was because the "goodwill" gestures of white congregations never dared to go beyond paternalism in order to address the substantive issues of racism, social architecture, and economic partnership. Very few churches in the city have attempted internal racism work. Those that have conducted cultural diversity trainings have done so only because they found themselves with a separate Korean or Latino congregation using their facilities, which had given rise to tensions. A handful of Los Angeles churches have sustained "community dialogues" since the uprising, but most of these have dwindled. As for actions, the national ecumenical call for churches to make local witness against racism on the first anniversary of the Los Angeles uprising in 1993 was a good idea but not widely heeded.

11. For a basic analysis of class in modern capitalism see Bottomore (1966); on its suppression in U.S. political and cultural consciousness see Coleman and Rainwater (1978) and B. Eisler (1983). The absence of class-conscious history is being redressed through revisionist efforts such as the American Social History Project's *Who Built America?* (Levine et al, 1989; see also Katz, 1975). For a concise sketch of the Left and labor activism see Nakawatese (1989).

12. It is estimated that people earning over $75,000 per year give half of all private campaign contributions to candidates, are four times more likely to vote and six times more likely to protest. In the 1992 California Senate race, for example, the four major candidates received almost $30 million in campaign funds between them, with tens and sometimes hundreds of thousands of dollars coming from political action committees representing such industries as agriculture, defense, finance, energy, and real estate, as well as organized labor.

13. The AFSC's Maquiladora Program summarizes the situation thus:

The "Border Industrial Program" (BIP) was initiated by the Mexican government in 1965 as a substitute for the *bracero* program. Whereas the *bracero* program provided low cost labor from Mexico for sectors of economic activity within the United States, the BIP was to transport U.S. production centers to locations of low cost labor in Mexico. Under the BIP, Mexico granted licenses to foreign corporations to establish subsidiaries (in-bond assembly plants) and to import machinery, raw materials, and components duty free. After being assembled in Mexico into semi-final or final products they are subsequently exported. Most of the corporations are U.S.-based, and the duties leveled for export are based solely on the value added (Mexican labor costs). By early 1990 it was estimated that 470,000 workers labored in approximately 1,750 *maquiladoras* along the border from Texas, Arizona and California, producing car parts, television sets, semiconductors, paints, toys, etc. Between 80 and 85 percent of the workers are young Mexican women, many of them teenagers. Most have no more than an elementary school education and many have migrated to the border from rural areas in the interior of Mexico, where the economy, racked by a $107 billion international debt, has left many local populations impoverished. Few of these young women have any prior experience with factory work and almost all are unaware of their rights under Mexican Federal Labor Legislation, which is progressive in character but rarely enforced voluntarily. Their average daily wage is from $23 to $40 for a 48 hour workweek, while they are subject to a variety of abuses ranging from forced (and illegal) overtime to sexual harassment.

The best summary of maquiladoras and other Third World "free trade zones" can be found in Kamel (1990). Aside from labor rights, the most prominent problems are environmental, particularly toxic wastes (see Kochan, 1989; Althaus, 1988; and Beebe, 1987). On the effects of plant closings on U.S. workers and organizing in opposition to industrial flight see Moberg (1988).

14. The NAFTA is the latest in a series of bilateral trade agreements seeking economic integration between the U.S., Mexico, and Canada. The 1989 value of goods traded between the U.S. and Mexico (our third largest trading partner) was $51 billion; already over 70 percent of Mexico's exports come to the U.S., while 65 percent of Mexico's import market is controlled by the U.S. The NAFTA will formalize and accelerate the process of integration; broaden deregulation beyond tariff and nontariff trade barriers to include investment and financial markets; impact wages, labor mobility, environmental standards, land ownership, and agricultural production; influence the way in which the three countries conduct their foreign and economic policy; and probably increase the already huge economic disparity between the U.S. and Mexico. An AFSC statement in 1991 recognized that

the debate focuses on who will represent working people's interests, which social issues will be incorporated in the NAFTA, what procedures will be followed for their incorporation and how effective monitoring and enforcement will be guaranteed.... Signing of the NAFTA should be conditioned both on the direct incorporation into the NAFTA of labor mobility and labor and environmental standards, and on the signing of related agreements on issues such as debt relief for Mexico. Women and men representing social sectors and communities that would be affected by the NAFTA ought to be included in the talks as well as in the process established to monitor implementation and enforcement.

The literature abounds (see P. Rodriguez, 1993; Browne, 1992; Dawkins and Muffett, 1993; Barry, 1991).

15. To name a few: Asian Immigrant Women Advocates in Oakland, CA; the Center for Ethics and Social Policy in Berkeley, CA; The Asian Pacific American Labor Alliance in Los Angeles; Philippine Workers Support Committee in Honolulu; the Federation for Industrial Retention and Renewal in Chicago; Hometowns Against Shutdowns in Bricktown, NJ; Interfaith Center for Corporate Responsibility in New York;

International Labor Rights Working Group of Washington, DC; La Mujer Obrera in El Paso; Mujer a Mujer/Woman to Woman in San Antonio; and Southerners for Economic Justice in Durham, NC.

16. On the campaign of the religious Right to repeal gay and lesbian civil rights, particularly in the 1992 Colorado referendum on Amendment A, see Hardisty (1993). On the rise in gay bashing, see Cleaver and Myers (1993). On the changing scientific consensus about homosexuality as a genetic trait and its implications for church positions, see Stammer (1993). On sexual culture in the New Testament, see Countryman (1988). On homosexuality and the church in history, see Boswell (1980).

10

"Why Don't Your Disciples Live According to Tradition?"

Diversity

A true border, a true place of encounter, is by nature permeable; it is not like medieval armor, but rather like skin. Our skin does set a limit to where our body begins and where it ends... and even sets certain limits to our give-and-take with our environment.... But if we ever close up our skin, we die.

Justo Gonzalez,
"Where Frontiers End"

We may be able, handful that we are, to end the racial nightmare, and achieve our country and change the history of the world. If we do not now dare everything, the fulfillment of that prophecy, recreated from the Bible in song by a slave, is upon us: "God gave Noah the rainbow sign; no more water, the fire next time!"

James Baldwin,
The Fire Next Time

"Why don't your disciples live according to tradition?" (7:5). In Mark the Pharisees represent the guardians of social orthodoxy. They believe the boundaries of the body politic can best be policed through control of political bodies. Thus they seek to maintain gender, ethnic, and class divisions by stressing fidelity to their "traditions." At issue here were rules of table fellowship that functioned socially (maintaining Jewish group identity), politically (who you ate with reflected your status in the hierarchy), and economically (control over production, distribution, and consumption of food).

To be sure, all groups establish boundaries to determine who is in and who is out. Sometimes these are physical impediments — fences or moats. Other times they are symbolic — church altars or "colored only" entrances. Sometimes boundaries are merely customary, as in male-only sports or how one dresses for the beach as compared to for an art opening. In modern capitalist societies group boundaries tend to be defined and enforced either legally (protecting conventions of space or time, property or person by criminalizing violations of them) or economically (redlined neighborhoods, stratified consumer markets). Boundaries that are recognized and obeyed are effective in keeping people apart. This was the Pharisaic strategy. Now this can be a good thing, such as when recognized boundaries help protect weaker people from domination by stronger people. But while this "defensive" function is usually cited as justification by those who construct or maintain boundaries, more often the actual relations of power are the opposite: the boundaries function to protect the strong from the weak.

It is such boundaries — the kind that define and insulate the architecture of entitlement enjoyed by a dominant culture (above, 7,B) — that Jesus challenged in the name of solidarity with "outsiders." The Pharisees' accusation that his disciples weren't living "according to tradition" is thus a charge of group disloyalty. In defense Jesus accuses the Pharisees of rejecting the "commandments" of justice (7:8f). In attacking the ideological basis of the Pharisaic boundary making, he tries to show how their purity codes preempt biblical commitments to justice (7:10–13; *BSM*:217ff). Here, then, is a reenactment of the earlier Deuteronomic showdown in the synagogue (3:1–6). What will guide the people — the "commandments" of biblical radicalism or the "traditions" of the dominant culture?

"There is nothing which goes into a person that can defile her; only that which comes out of a person defiles her" (7:15). In his subsequent explanation of the issue, Jesus uses the political body as a parable of the body politic. He asserts that the social boundaries constructed by the purity code are powerless to protect the integrity of the community. Transgression or "contamination" can arise only from *within* the community. By "declaring all foods clean" Mark rejects all culturally exclusive and/or proprietary boundaries that protect the community from perceived external threats. The dispute over meal fellowship in this episode, in turn, "sets the table" for Jesus' welcoming of Gentile foreigners into the circle of renewal (7:24–37) and then his dramatic breaking of bread with "outsiders" (8:1–9). As a conclusion to these object lessons, Jesus warns his followers: "Be/aware of the leaven of the Pharisees and the leaven of the Herodians" (8:15; cf 12:13ff). Their leaven — symbolizing the "traditions" of social and political conformity, respectively — alone has the power to ruin the "one loaf" around which the church is called to gather.

Hidden at the heart of postmodern Los Angeles, surrounded by gleaming skyscrapers built by and for Big Capital, lies the *placita,* once the center of the old Mexican pueblo. Under a spreading oak tree, ignored by the teeming tourists and the new Latino immigrants who fill the plaza each day, is a plaque commemorating the founding of *El Pueblo de Nuestra Señora la Reina de Los*

Angeles sobre el río de la Porciúncula in November 1781. It notes that of the original twenty-two adult *pobladores* who came from northern Mexico to colonize Los Angeles, there were eight mulattos, eight Indians, two blacks, one mestizo, and only two Spaniards (Chávez, 1984:16f). In its first century Los Angeles was a sleepy Mexican and Indian village; in its second it grew into a world metropolis. But this plaque reminds us that from the very beginning the city has been a singularly *multicultural* project.

The same could be said of the Americas as a whole. "It is impossible to say to which human family we belong," said the Venezuelan nationalist Simón Bolívar to the Congress of Angostura in 1819; "Europeans have mixed with the Indians and the Negroes, and Negroes have mixed with the Indians; we were all born of one mother America, though our fathers had different origins." But El Libertador's vision stands in sharp contrast to French statesman Alexis de Tocqueville's observation in *Democracy in America* (1835): "The European is to the other races of mankind what man himself is to the lower animals: he makes them subservient to his use and when he cannot subdue them he destroys them." Indeed post-Columbian America has in some sense always been defined by the struggle between two realities: dominant culture ideologies and structures on one hand, and multicultural populations and practices (however marginalized) on the other. In order to take sides in this struggle today, therefore, the church must "hear and understand" Jesus' parable: "What goes into the body from the outside cannot contaminate."

A. "HE DECLARED ALL FOODS CLEAN": THE CHURCH ECUMENICAL

Can the church affirm a new social philosophy of pluralism in order to protect and promote the cultural diversity that characterizes America?

"Can we all get along?" asked Rodney King (above, 1,A). It is no overstatement to say that the future of North American society — indeed of the human experiment as a whole — depends upon our ability to live peaceably with diversity. The question this chapter will deal with is whether we can, in the church and in American society as a whole, forge models of coexistence-with-congruence rather than unity-by-uniformity.

1. "Only One Loaf": Diversity within the Church

Cultural diversity is a fact in the U.S. today. The 1990 census shows that "minorities" represent a quarter of the nation's estimated population of 250 million; almost 14 percent speak a language other than English at home (Usdansky, 1992). California leads this demographic curve:

"Ethnic minorities" account for 12.5 million residents — more than 40 percent of the population. By 2000, the Hispanic, Asian and black population will grow to 17.1 million people, almost 50 percent of the state's population.... In the Los Angeles-Orange County metropolitan area, Anglos compose 52 percent of the population; in Los Angeles County schools, Latinos, Asians, blacks, American Indians and Pacific Islanders account for 74 percent of the student population. (Njeri, 1991b:E8)

If such demographic trends seem foreboding to insular white suburbs, they merely reflect the actual texture of life today in urban Los Angeles. For example, Itabari Njeri relates a story not untypical of a day in our city:

Jerry Yoshitomi, director of the Japanese-American Community Center, Stanford-educated and married to an Irish-Catholic American, recalled a recent New Year's day in Los Angeles with their children. "We woke up in the morning and went to Mass at St. Brigid's, which has a black gospel choir...then we came to the center for the Japanese Oshogatsu New Year's program and saw Buddhist archers shoot arrows to ward off evil spirits for the year.... On the way home we stopped in Chinatown for a lunch at King Taco." (1991b:E1)

Similarly Jesús Treviño (1991) writes: "Within a mile radius of my Los Angeles home you can find a Buddhist church, a Roman Catholic private school, a Mexican bakery, an Armenian-owned gas station, a junior high school with a Hispanic woman principal and a prestigious college with an African American president; nearby restaurants feature Italian, Yucatecan, Russian, Thai, Bolivian, Chinese and Japanese food." Treviño's description fits my neighborhood perfectly — and many others.

Multicultural visions can, of course, be easily romanticized, as in dewy-eyed Hollywood jingles such as "We are the World." In fact the extraordinary diversity of Los Angeles is more often segregated or conflictive than benignly cosmopolitan, and it causes residents as much anxiety as enrichment (Kotkin, 1989; Schuck and Rieff, 1991). This is, after all, the city of the spring 1992 uprising, which has spawned renewed race, class, and cultural fragmentation and the politics of mutual suspicion. My point here is simply that diversity is our reality; the challenge is how to build a *just* society around it.

What role should the church play? We must begin by acknowledging that churches reflect all of the tensions of the society as a whole, for the same demographic and sociological reasons. For example, in Los Angeles many churches find their constituency changing with the neighborhood. A traditionally black Episcopal congregation in South Central wonders how to meet the linguistic and cultural challenges presented by growing numbers of Central American parishioners; a staid old Hollywood United Methodist church in the heart of the gay community tries to reflect this context in its ministry; a Lutheran church in Pico-Union struggles to include its older white members in the new Latino majority. Indeed if an urban church is not experiencing these changes, it is probably because it consists of suburban commuters and is largely disconnected from its own neighborhood. Frequently ethnic congregations — Korean Presbyterians, Filipino Methodists, Guatemalan Pentecostals — spring up separately. These newer, grassroots groups often use buildings belonging to older mainstream churches, which creates unique opportunities for multiethnic fellowship. Unfortunately these arrangements more often result in noninteraction, strained distance, and even mutual suspicion.

That multicultural tensions exist in our churches is natural, given our context. The challenge is for the church to be a place where these matters are worked through, thus providing a desperately needed example for the wider society. If, on the other hand, such tensions continue to be ignored or suppressed in our churches, and if monocultural congregations remain segregated from each other, the church obviously will lack credibility in advocating social diversity and tolerance. As with the issue of gender justice, Christians can hardly promote publicly what we do not practice internally. Reconstruction must begin, therefore, with a consideration of ecumenism. In a fragmented church, the challenge of overcoming division between the various Christian traditions in a way that respects diversity yet values communion could not be more relevant.

Among mainline Protestants worldwide the ecumenical vocation has become quite institutionalized in the various local, national, and international councils. Unfortunately the resources of the contemporary ecumenical movement continue to be monopolized by official denominational strategies of high-level conversations, in the apparent belief that if church leaders and bureaucrats are able to discover common ground this will trickle down to the pews. These efforts, however, have had remarkably little impact at the congregational level. More often it has been through the practice of grassroots ecumenism that Christians have rediscovered each other. Often this has been in practical collaborations — serving together at a soup kitchen, citywide meetings to address urban problems, or simply the economic necessity of sharing church facilities or unifying seminary resources.

An example of ecumenism at the base is *Sojourners* magazine, which started as an expression of the Protestant "evangelical Left" in the early 1970s yet today represents a fundamentally ecumenical movement whose constituency is almost half Roman Catholic. Like other radical Christian groups, *Sojourners* affirms dialogue with institutional churches and the histories they represent but long ago stopped waiting for ecclesial hierarchies to sanction such practices as liturgies conducted by laypeople, women in congregational leadership, and Catholic-Protestant intercommunion. Some in these circles choose to remain affiliated with mainline churches, others attempt to forge in their own ministries and communities a new ecumenical identity. But all are proceeding vigorously with "ecumenism from below," convinced that the future of the church lies in the unity of discipleship practice and at the same time the diversity of symbolic expression.

My experience is not unusual. An adult convert, I was not raised in a church. My "tradition" is the diaspora of radical discipleship communities around the country and in many parts of the world. Yet I do much of my teaching in denominational settings — Catholic and Protestant. Through my collaborations with different Christians I have been nurtured and challenged by the best in these various traditions. I have found refuge and fellowship among Australian Baptists and Midwest Mennonites, Presbyterians in New Mexico and Episcopalians in North Carolina, contemplative Benedictines and activist Franciscans, Native American Lutherans and African American Adventists, Northern Congregationalists and Southern Methodists. I have learned that each community holds part of the church's truth, and none holds it all.

I am a member of a joint Methodist-Presbyterian congregation in Los Angeles, I retreat at Trappist monasteries, and I feel at home in any community that wishes to take the Story seriously. Am I Catholic? Liturgical symbolism is important to me, and a *retablo* of Our Lady of Guadalupe is on our wall at home. Am I Protestant? Bible study is at the center of my life, and I value good preaching. Am I Anabaptist? I repudiate Constantinian Christianity and fail to understand infant baptism. Officially I am "part" of none of these great Western traditions, yet each is a part of me.

Steven Charleston, a Choctaw Indian and Episcopal bishop of Alaska, calls the struggle for cultural diversity within the church a Second Reformation:

> There will still be splinter groups. But there will be a whole community within the Church, stretching around the globe, that will be much more horizontal in its relationships. There will be more equal understanding of the role of men and women, of laity and clergy, of youth and elders. It will be a more tolerant and accepting community. Its ritual and worship life will be far more integrated with the sight, sounds and smells of its many different members. (Nunley, 1992:28)

This is the church of the future: a people of the *oikumene* and of the one loaf, a community of discipleship, a church that has overcome the deep divisions of the past, a "wounded healer." In my opinion, it is the only future the church has.

2. *"Those Not against Us": The Church and Pluralism*

An even bigger challenge to the church is interfaith work. Interfaith collaboration, when conducted respectfully and honestly, is not syncretistic but invites each of the participating communities to draw more deeply from the wells of their own traditions by learning about the living waters of others. I have experienced this dynamic often in the peace and justice movement: working with Buddhists and Native American religious practitioners at the Nevada test site, for example, or participating in the remarkable Jewish-Christian-Muslim coalition that arose in Los Angeles to oppose the Gulf War. I have also worked closely in common cause for humanization and justice alongside people whose attitudes toward Christianity range from the ambivalent to the antipathetic: black nationalists, Chicano immigrants rights lawyers, Korean human rights activists, radical environmentalists, lesbian feminists, and socialist labor organizers. I have found that I have a great deal to learn, and as much to offer — without either losing or imposing my identity. Are we secure enough to work with those hostile to our faith, humble enough to recognize that non-Christians have part of the truth, and nonimperial enough to collaborate without having to control? "Those not against us are for us," said Jesus (Mk 9:42).

Unfortunately many Christians find interfaith work both troubling and threatening. The reason for this is our theological resistance to the notion of pluralism. Pluralism is heretical wherever the church continues to be infected by Constantinian assumptions about its privilege and power within society. Historically Christendom has not been hospitable to those defined as cultural outsiders. They were dealt with defensively (e.g., wars with Moslem competitors) or offensively (evangelizing or conquering "heathens") but rarely fraternally. The church's collaboration with State oppression and repression of minorities is a haunting legacy, from the Inquisition to the Holocaust. (Establishment Christianity has not been alone in this; most dominant groups with strong ideologies have had difficulty being tolerant — communists and Moslems no less than Christians.) A theology of repentance must reject religious entitlement as a "Pharisaic tradition." A theology of reconstruction believes the church will be made stronger by its disestablishment (see Hall, 1975; Carroll and Roof, 1993). If we reject Christianity's identification with the dominant culture, we remove the barriers to interfaith collaboration.

The church must come to terms with the fact that our postmodern historical context is thoroughly post-Christian. Mark K. Taylor calls the challenge facing the church in this new context a trilemma. "Postmodernism's three traits each presents a demand that invites attention and development: to acknowledge tradition, to celebrate plurality, and to resist domination — all three together" (1990:40). I find this a useful conceptualization. It is both possible and necessary that the church rediscover its identity in the narrative tradition of radical discipleship; welcome postmodernism's celebration of plurality without endorsing its uncommitted relativism; and join in the deconstruction of dominant cultural conformism. For help we can look to older traditions of Christian dissidence, such as Franciscans and Anabaptists, who were advocates of discipleship and religious tolerance. We can also look to Asian Christians, who have shown that a minority church can still be a force for social justice (Digan, 1984:24ff; Song, 1984:20, 50ff). These three commitments — to a convictional tradition, to pluralism, and to justice — are not contradictory, though it is challenging to integrate them in practice, as Taylor recognizes. Solidarity, which can entail taking sides in social struggles, is not incompatible with pluralism, which entails acceptance of differing points of view. The church must understand that by embracing pluralism it is not giving up its convictions; it is simply refusing to exercise them from a position of domination. A commitment to social inclusion frees Christians to be critics of certain traditions even as we defend their right to coexist with full and equal rights.

Significantly we find this trialectic in the narrative of biblical radicalism itself. The Exodus God "calls and names" *certain* peoples, cares for *all* peoples, and takes the side of the *poor.* Contrary to Christendom's rejection of pluralism, the New Testament *assumes* it. Australian theologians Don Carrington and Chris Budden (1984) have pointed out three major indications of this: Jesus and his movement were influenced by the multicultural context of ancient Galilee; the early Jerusalem church accepted the distinct cultural needs of "Hellenists" and affirmed a ministry to Gentiles, though not without struggle (Acts 6 and 15); and Paul's notion of the "body of Christ" (1 Corinthians 12) and his own apostolic practice among various Mediterranean cultures reflect a commitment to diversity. Indeed Mark's declaration that "all foods are clean" was understood as a central argument for cultural diversity by the early church, as reflected in its later reiteration by Luke (Acts 10).

The strongest biblical argument for pluralism, however, is also the oldest: the ancient Hebrew story of the tower of Babel (Genesis 11). This tale was a thinly veiled criticism of the concentration of power represented by the Mesopotamian city-state and was later understood as an etiology of idolatry (Is 2:11–16; see Kaufmann 1972:294f). Biblical scholar Thomas Mann rightly notes that Babel culminates the rebellion theme in the primeval narrative cycle, that includes disobedience, fratricide, and abuse (1988:24ff). It portrays an imperial centralism (Gen 11:4) which resists the "scattering" of human diversity in explicit violation of God's instructions (9:1). The divine counterstrategy is to intervene in Babel's construction project, dispersing the nations and instituting cultural/linguistic diversity (11:7–9). The tower of Babel story suggests that cultural diversity is a hedge against dominating centralism. In the narrative of biblical radicalism, the redistribution and dispersal of social power is essential to the struggle against empire and for the Great Economy (below, 11,C).

First World Christians have both a prophetic and a pastoral obligation to embrace pluralism in the context of a dominant culture that will resist it at all costs. Having said this, however, there is an important caveat. The church can and should be a place where diversity and inclusion are practiced. But as a community of conviction it cannot pretend to be all things to all people. Discipleship communities, like other convictional groups, can support a greater degree of pluralism in society than they can absorb internally. This is not a contradiction but a definition of true pluralism. Equal openness to all beliefs, like thoroughgoing syncretism, actually negates pluralism, sacrificing distinctive identity to a cultural and/or convictional melange consisting of the lowest common denominator of each group. "Universal culture" is no more possible — or compelling — than universal language; one need only consider the utter failure of the great liberal idea of Esperanto. Nor does a commitment to tolerance preclude evangelism, as long as vigorous advocacy of one's views is not linked to practices of domination.

As communities of conviction in a world of diversity, we will have to completely rethink our social strategies and assumptions. We must resist the impulse to defensively ghettoize as well as the temptation to offensively impose our worldview. In this First World Christians have a great deal to learn from the African American church, which has not only survived but flourished without the props of dominant culture support. Above all, we must examine ways in which we reproduce the "traditions" of division in our own church bodies and hear again the radically inclusive discourse of Jesus: "All foods are clean."

B. "WHAT COMES FROM THE OUTSIDE CANNOT DEFILE": A NATION OF IMMIGRANTS?

Can nonindigenous North Americans rediscover their identity as immigrant peoples in order to stand in solidarity with those labeled as "outsiders"?

To this point I have concentrated on social, economic, and political boundaries that define the dominant gender, race, and class relations of power in our House. Yet from the beginning of the Europeans' America, one geographically defined (if politically shifting) boundary has been persistent: the inferior status of immigrants. To be sure, the immigrant experience in the U.S. has been liberative as well as oppressive. But attitudes toward immigrants have always profoundly conflicted. Saskia Sassen, in her important study of the political economy of immigration, writes:

> Immigration has traditionally aroused strong passions in the United States. Although Americans like to profess pride in their history as a "nation of immigrants," each group of arrivals, once established, has fought to keep newcomers out. Over the past two centuries, each new wave of immigrants has encountered strenuous opposition from earlier arrivals, who have insisted that the country was already filled to capacity. The single exception to this was the South's eagerness to import ever more slaves. (1989:811)

Whether we acknowledge it or not, this ambiguity defines our character as a people. European Americans have justified their domination of North America through myths that invoke the divine right of immigration even as they restrict or deny that right to new immigrants. The dominant culture has attempted to forge national coherence by insisting that immigrants lose their distinctive identities, while it defines itself primarily over against its foreign enemies of the day. We are, in short, an immigrant people who are ambivalent at best and contemptuous at worst toward immigrants. Not only is this yet another indicator of our denial, it suggests a deep insecurity.

Early expressions of the imperious character of older immigrants loathing newer ones can be found, not surprisingly, among the "founding fathers." Journalist William Langewiesche writes:

> As early as 1750, after German farmers settled in Pennsylvania, Benjamin Franklin worried about their "political immaturity and social incivility," and wrote that "those who come hither are generally the most stupid of

their own nation . . . not being used to liberty they know not how to make a modest use of it." In *Observations Concerning the Increase of Mankind,* published in 1751, he asked, "Why should the Palatine Boors be suffered to swarm into our settlements and, by herding together, establish their language and manners to the exclusion of ours? Why should Pennsylvania, founded by the English, become a colony of aliens who will shortly be so numerous as to Germanize us instead of our Anglifying them?" (1992:65)

This complaint, reflecting the ethnocentrism and xenophobia that form the backbone of antiimmigrant sentiment, has been heard in refrain countless times since.

Actual U.S. immigration policies, however, have been driven as much by political and economic forces as by ideological ones. During the era of Manifest Destiny and the early industrial revolution (1855–1930) the percentage of foreign-born residents in the U.S. hovered consistently between 12 and 15 percent, with northern and southern Europeans accounting for about 90 percent of new immigrants. In 1882 the first politically specific restriction was passed — convicts, polygamists, anarchists, and communists were banned. But the ebb and flow of immigration was above all economically determined (see Cabezas et al, 1992). During the 1870s boom, Chinese laborers were recruited; in 1883 the Chinese Exclusion law was passed. Later, American farmers demanded that those laws be repealed, but the depression of the 1890s brought instead new restrictions. After the turn of the century, immigration law enforcement was lax (though Japanese were restricted in 1907); during the depression of 1914 it was reinvigorated. Mexicans were recruited due to World War I labor shortage; one-half million were deported during the Great Depression of the 1930s. Mexican agricultural workers were again recruited during World War II through the *bracero* program, and again one million were deported in the late 1950s during Operation Wetback. During the cold war, ethnic quota systems were introduced, targeting nonnorthern Europeans. And after the Vietnam War, ideologically specific refugee and asylum laws continued to be passed, affecting Cubans and Southeast Asians positively, Chileans, Iranians, and Haitians negatively. Immigration and naturalization laws were overhauled in 1965 (abolishing quotas) and again in 1986 but still discriminate against Third World refugees and immigrants.

California now receives some 40 percent of all new immigrants:[1] "Population change has been swiftest in California, which has been called 'The World State' and 'The New Ellis Island' because virtually every racial and ethnic group is represented here. . . . The nation's predicted mid-21st-Century majority has already arrived in Los Angeles. Here, *minority* is a meaningless term: Latinos, blacks and Asian Americans make up about 59 percent of the population" (Njeri, 1991b:E8). But if "minority" is no longer an analytically accurate concept in California, it continues to be a politically loaded one. As the recessionary 1980s overtook the stagflationary 1970s, antiimmigrant sentiments reemerged with utter predictability, as the country moved into the "control phase" of its (manic-depressive?) immigration cycle (above, 4,C). As Mexican scholar Jorge Bustamante recently put it, "There is an unmistakable pattern to recession in the United States; when unemployment rises beyond politically acceptable levels, xenophobic sentiments go on the march" (1992). Indeed the vilification of immigrants reached fever pitch just as double-dip recession peaked in California, with a new rash of antiimmigrant bills now before the legislature (Bailey and Morain, 1993). We are also seeing a rise in hate crimes and reactionary nativist activism, such as the recent "Light up the Border" campaign in San Diego.[2]

African American labor built the wealth of the agricultural South and later the industrial North, only to be scapegoated after Reconstruction; the same narrative applies to Asian and especially Latino immigrant labor throughout the Southwest (Wollenberg, 1988). Certainly the agricultural wealth of California was (and still is) built on the backs of Mexican migrant workers, as is the emerging "underground economy" that supports the service sector and garment industries here. Despite these facts, recessionary paranoia has led to the criminalization of both undocumented immigrants and their work through the employer sanctions provisions of the Immigration Reform and Control Act of 1986 (IRCA). At the same time, the U.S.-Mexico border — the only place in the world where First and Third World stand adjacent — has been militarized and the Border Patrol unleashed. With this have come gross violations of the human rights of undocumented migrants, already the poorest of the poor, now further dehumanized as "illegal aliens" (see Jimenez, 1987; ILEMP, 1992).

If North Americans are to stand in solidarity with the immigrant poor, we must understand three basic issues. First, it is larger structural forces, not national attitudes, that drive immigration; migratory patterns do not react to nativist antipathy. Journalist Jack Miles rightly notes that "American discussion of immigration tends to focus on pull rather than on push — that is, on those aspects of American life which pull immigrants in rather than on those aspects of life in their native countries which push them out" (1992:68). Thus most critics today accuse Third World immigrants of simply trying to take advantage of social conditions (health, education, welfare) and economic opportunity in the U.S. While this is true for a minority, the vast majority of legal and undocumented immigrants have been pushed here by one or more of three forces: military, political, and economic. A decade of U.S.-sponsored counterinsurgency war in Central America drove thousands of Salvadoran, Nicaraguan, and Guatemalan refugees to *el norte,* who end up struggling as day laborers on the streets of our cities. A decade of Reaganomics, deregulation, and privatization saw economic deterioration and massive increase in foreign debt in Mexico, which has driven thousands of Mexicans into our fields and our poorest barrios. U.S. collaboration with national security states in Asia (Taiwan, South Korea, the Philippines, Indonesia) has spawned rapid industrialization, repression, and thus migration, which for many ends up in tiny sweatshops around my city. Solidarity with immigrants begins by shifting the focus from how *they* allegedly impact our society to how *our* national policies have disrupted their lives.

For example, during the five years before U.S. military intervention in the

Dominican Republic in 1965 some five thousand Dominicans emigrated to the U.S. In the five years following, the number increased to some sixty thousand. One can trace the increase in the immigration of Cubans, Koreans, Southeast Asians, Pacific Islanders, and Central Americans directly to the impact of U.S. politico-military policies toward those countries. A second cause is our foreign investment and economic policies. U.S. industrial flight to Mexico, the Philippines, and other "free export zones" has meant social disruption in the host country. As Sassen puts it, "The necessary labor supply for these new modes of production was obtained through the massive displacement of small landholders and subsistence farmers" (1989:819). She describes how the exodus of young women to the maquiladoras has uprooted village life, destroying its social fabric and intensifying rural poverty. "For men and women alike the disruption of traditional ways of earning a living and the ascendance of export-led development make entry into wage labor increasingly a one-way proposition" (ibid:822). A third and related cause is deindustrialization in the U.S. and the resulting transition to a service-oriented, low-wage, and even "underground" economy. The casualization of labor in southern California today — from migrant farmworkers to urban day laborers and domestics — not only attracts undocumented migrants, it depends upon them.

In other words, economic restructuring in the First World has led to social disruption in the Third World which in turn has led to social restructuring back in the First World.

> Paradoxically, the very measures commonly thought to deter immigration — foreign investment and the promotion of export-oriented growth in developing countries — seem to have had precisely the opposite effect. The clearest proof of this is the fact that several of the newly industrializing countries with the highest growth rates in the world are simultaneously becoming the most important suppliers of immigrants to the United States. (Ibid:814)

Those who wish to stem undocumented immigration, therefore, would do better to work to close the international open shop (above, 9,D,2) than to support the futile attempts to close our historically porous southern border.

A second requisite understanding for solidarity is to recognize that immigrants continue to contribute far more to our social and economic life than they "cost." Julian Simon, writing in the conservative *Wall Street Journal* (1990), has shown that virtually every one of the common reasons given to stem immigration is undermined by the facts. He notes that:

- immigrants do not cause native unemployment, even among low-paid and minority groups; in fact they are necessary replacements for our aging work force;
- immigrants do not rip off natives by overusing welfare services (in fact according to the National Immigration, Refugee and Citizenship Forum, im-

migrants over their lifetime pay $12,000 to $20,000 more in taxes than they receive in welfare benefits and are less likely than U.S.-born to use public assistance);

• immigrants are typically as well educated and skilled occupationally as natives and demonstrate "desirable economic traits" such as self-reliance and innovation;

• Asian and Latinos are the most rapidly growing immigrant populations, but the current foreign-born population is still less than a fifth of what it was at the turn of the century.

Simon concludes that "talented young immigrants help us advance every one of our national goals; they make us richer and not poorer, stronger and not weaker."[3] Those who would blame immigrants for our problems would do better to look to the dominant political economy itself.

Third and most important for solidarity, we must seek to know immigrants — particularly the poor and undocumented — not as statistics but as human beings who endure extraordinary hardship in the trauma of displacement. A dramatic testimony is found in *Where Destiny Takes Me: Story of a Salvadoran Exile,* a booklet published by AFSC's Immigration Law Enforcement Monitoring Program (ILEMP, 1991). As Aurora Camacho de Schmidt has argued at length (1991), such voices have the power to transform our biases and suspicions and lead us back to the biblical mandates to care for the stranger and sojourner in our midst. Solidarity has led AFSC and a handful of other immigrant rights groups to take a stance of noncooperation with the employer sanctions provisions of IRCA, in the conviction that criminalizing work is a cruel, as well as an ineffective, way to control immigration.[4]

Pastoral worker Charlie Lewis (1988) has outlined thirteen suggestions for ways churches can stand in solidarity with undocumented workers. Here in Los Angeles many Christians work tirelessly with refugees on political asylum and sanctuary cases; reach out to connect new immigrants with needed social services; or defend the rights of day laborers (Smolich, 1990). One who has committed his life to advocacy on behalf of the immigrant poor is my AFSC colleague Roberto Martínez. Roberto staffs an office in San Diego that documents Border Patrol abuses and provides immigrants with social and legal referrals. As one journalist put it, "In San Diego and Tijuana it is a matter of common knowledge that you have no recourse if you are beaten by the Mexican authorities; but if you are beaten by the Americans, or if your rights are trampled on, you can turn to Roberto Martínez" (Langewiesche, 1992:70). He sees hundreds of violations by immigration authorities each year, from the small (verbal abuse, illegal confiscation of documents, deportation of legal residents) to the large (maimings, rapes, and deaths in pursuit or custody). I have walked with Roberto along the border war zone where each day thousands of undocumented people try to evade the Border Patrol in their dash into the U.S.; I have walked with him into the canyons of northern San Diego County, where farmworkers live in caves and plastic tents just yards from affluent condominiums (Mydans, 1990). He is fiercely committed to asserting the human rights of these people, precisely because they are treated by U.S. agents as if they had no rights. In cooperation with AFSC's ILEMP network, Martínez has been able to expose immigration law enforcement abuses, to effect changes in policies and procedures, and, most important, to raise public consciousness about the undocumented as human persons.

Such work invites us to question why borders are so sacred to the modern nation-state. An AFSC working group, in a thoughtful assessment of some of the positive and negative functions of national borders, rightly notes that borders are sometimes necessary to defend a smaller people's self-determination (Shamleffer et al, 1989). For example, indigenous peoples around the world (and historically) have had their "boundaries" violated by Europeans, in part because they lacked reified borders. As I have noted, boundaries function most ethically when they are protecting the weak from the strong. But when borders represent an impediment to human solidarity, they must be questioned, crossed, and violated. Issues related to the continuing and often involuntary migration of peoples, and to the geopolitical definition of human communities, are complex in the modern world and deserve our careful reflection and deliberation. But they are finally theological issues, to which communities of faith must respond (see Bell et al, 1991). Just as Exodus Israel was warned that "you shall not wrong a stranger or oppress him, for you yourselves were once strangers in the land of Egypt" (Ex 22:21), so is it incumbent upon a nation of immigrants not to exclude outsiders or deny their human dignity. Undocumented immigrants are the most vulnerable in our midst, easy targets for politically driven xenophobia. Jesus, however, could not be clearer: "Nothing from the outside can defile us" (7:15). Whenever the church retreats from this truth, it is "without understanding" (7:18).

C. "DO NOT IMPEDE THEM":
MULTICULTURALISM AS *RECONQUISTA*

Will the gospel compel our churches to embrace multiculturalism, or will we be forced to come to terms with it by demographics alone?

In a refrain unique in the gospel, Mark's Jesus denounces two consecutive attempts by his disciples to exclude uninitiated outsiders and socially marginalized insiders:

"Do not impede him! ... for the one who is not against us is for us!"
(9:39f)
"Do not impede them! ... for to such belongs the Great Economy!"
(10:14)

Jesus is warning those "on the way" not to impede the way of others — or, as Mark also phrases it, to "cause little ones to stumble" (9:42).[5] These are exhortations to a community of faith to remain inclusive, to keep its group boundaries porous so as not to be inhospitable to the poor and the kindred spirited. Today the challenge to construct a "home for all peoples" confronts the church sharply in a world of growing diversity and pluralism.

Before Europeans arrived in the Americas, Great Turtle Island was a genuinely multicultural world. "Native America" was thousands of peoples, tribes, and nations coexisting throughout the continent. California alone

> had about 16% of the aboriginal population of the United States.... Even at the minimum estimate of 130,000 (the figure has been placed as high as 700,000), the density of Indian population in California was three or four times greater than for the nation as a whole.... The California Indians were a highly heterogenous lot. Some 22 linguistic systems and 138 different idioms have been recorded.... The Indians were scattered in small land-owning, politically autonomous groups. (McWilliams, 1946:25)

There was cultural and commercial interaction between the various indigenous groups, sometimes over vast distances. Moreover, attempts by stronger and larger tribes to unify disparate peoples or to assert military, economic, or cultural hegemony were never more than regional in scope. In other words, cultural diversity was the original social characteristic of this continent. This is important to acknowledge, because we who have been socialized into the dominant culture are tempted to believe that multiculturalism is a dubious historical *novum* to be feared.

The European took great pains to destroy the original social fabric of diversity in the Americas. Early Los Angeles, for example, was still a small town populated mostly by Mexican *Californios* and Indians as late as 1870. But then a massive migration of white easterners began, orchestrated by railroad and real estate interests, so that by 1940 the city fathers of this new metropolis of a million and a half people could boast that it was the most White Anglo-Saxon Protestant major city in the U.S. (McWilliams 1946:12ff, 57ff; W. Robinson, 1948). Yet at that point, the wheel of history began to turn again. Wollenberg writes:

> Since 1940 California's total population has quadrupled... but the two largest ethnic minorities, Latinos and blacks, have grown more than ten times during that same period. Since the immigration law reforms of the 1960s and the Indochinese refugee provisions of the 1970s, the Asian and Pacific Islander group is now the fastest growing segment of California's population.... By the early 21st century, California will become the first mainland state with a third world majority. Or a more accurate way of saying it is that by the year 2010 or even earlier, everyone in California will be members of one or another minority. (1988:3)

In the Southwest today, some Latinos speak of the "browning" of the region as a *reconquista*. They remember the multiethnic roots of this place. Los Angeles,

California, and the Southwest have already been transformed by demographic trends, regardless of whether or not we wish to be a multicultural society. And what is happening here represents the future of the U.S. as a whole. The question facing us is only how we will adjust to this new/old reality.

There are two kinds of multiculturalism—from above and from below. City officials, transnational corporations, and the Los Angeles tourist industry love to use rainbow rhetoric, but it is too often only a thin veneer for the same old dominant culture biases. Recently, for example, a half-million-dollar mural was unveiled in the lobby of the new seventy-three-story First Interstate World Center Building, the tallest skyscraper in the West. Entitled "Unity," the huge mural was hyped as an artistic paean to ethnic diversity in Los Angeles, and black, Latino, and Asian schoolchildren were invited to the gala opening. But they were stunned when the curtain fell away to reveal a piece dominated by *three white* angels (Pool, 1993). Genuine diversity—based upon social equality and mutual respect—cannot be engineered from above. Historically it has been the fruit of grassroots dynamics from below. Human migration transforms the social terrain in ways unpredicted by elite planners. A good example is the way "immigrant economics" have changed the face of Los Angeles. The poor Mexicanos who are being pushed north by transnational forces of economic disenfranchisement are bringing with them their traditions of grassroots entrepreneurship. One cannot go far in Los Angeles without encountering day laborers on the corners, cafeteria trucks (*loncherías*) doing brisk business at job sites, push-cart vendors selling tamales or ice cream bars on the sidewalks, or produce trucks winding through barrio allies, hawking the weekly specials by megaphone. Similarly, new Korean small businesses raise capital through family-based pyramid financing; Chinese shopkeepers become more fluent in Spanish than English; Salvadoran busboys work tables in Japanese restaurants and Filipino cooks make pizza; and Cambodians (many of them survivors of Pol Pot's killing fields) have captured a quintessentially American corner of the market—the urban doughnut shop. Such examples of immigrant ingenuity and economic diversity abound, despite the opposition of city regulators and the incomprehension of suburban shoppers.

Because of its immigrant history, America has always been multicultural from below. It is the dominant culture that has never known how to embody the nation's motto—*e pluribus unum*, "from many, one." Instead of valuing and nurturing cultural diversity, the ruling classes have pressured for assimilation. Still today minorities must live in a culturally defensive position, accommodating enough to survive in the dominant system while struggling to preserve their own traditions. Total acculturation is resisted by celebrating distinctiveness and difference, often through ritual, dress, music, or language. Yet these expressions of self-affirmation often must remain protected from too much public exposure. Hence African Americans celebrate life within the safe walls of the church, Filipinos use Tagalog only at home, and Native Americans hold ceremonies in private. "Keeping quiet" is the flip side of having one's story and voice silenced (above, 5,C).

The dominant culture is threatened by public expressions of "ethnicity." Severed from cultural roots of our own, we feel both attracted to and isolated from these minority traditions, which often makes us resentful or envious. Thus we demand that they be justified (the political battles over recognition of Black History month). Worse, we accept them only as "performance" (the commercialization of ethnic festivals), or through popular culture we attempt to expropriate or control their voices. This only intensifies the alienation and thus the defensive posture of minority peoples. Thus the recent "mainstreaming" of African American music, clothing, art, and even politics (e.g., Spike Lee's "selling" of Malcolm X), while understood by some blacks as signaling long overdue acceptance, is rejected by others as another chapter in white exploitation of black culture (C. Jones, 1992a).

The best example of these dynamics is the struggle over language. In 1989 a study found that almost 44 percent of the some 1.3 million students in public schools throughout Los Angeles County spoke a language other than English at home, with more than eighty languages represented. By the turn of the century, those who speak Spanish as a first language will be a majority in California. But resistance to linguistic diversity has taken place on a number of fronts, the most notorious being the 1986 proposition declaring English as the "official language" of California, which passed by 73 percent. English-only organizations have gotten twelve other states to pass similar symbolic measures (though in Arizona it was overturned as unconstitutional). They are also pressing for more substantive restrictions, such as dismantling multilingual state services and bilingual educational programs (see Henry, 1990). Employers have insisted that employees speak only English on the job, and suburban cities have passed laws dictating how much English must appear on commercial signs. This backlash comes not from pragmatism, as its supporters contend, but from ethnocentrism. Multilingual societies flourish around the world. There is no good reason why California cannot institutionalize what it is in fact and should be by historical rights: a bilingual society (see Lobdell, 1986). It is a matter of political will.

Cultural pluralism was one target of the ideological Right during the Reagan-Bush era (see Quigley and Bertlet, 1992). Conservative commentators regularly denounce efforts by racial and other minority groups to define themselves and/or assert their rights as "Balkanism" (Gabler, 1992). The liberal press has also chimed in. *Time* magazine's July 8, 1991, cover story entitled "Whose America?" fretted, "A growing emphasis on the nation's 'multicultural' heritage exalts racial and ethnic pride at the expense of social cohesion" (Gray, 1991). Such anxieties are ostensibly driven by fears that the social contract will unravel without the traditional "glue" provided by the dominant culture. Fragmentation is, of course, a real issue, as different groups compete for social space. Most of the inter-group tensions today, however, are the result of cultural oppression coming home to roost, but the critics of multiculturalism are not about to acknowledge this.

Let us consider this struggle as it is being played out in the five "fields of conflict" identified by James Hunter in his recent *Culture Wars* (1991): the family, education, media and the arts, law, and electoral politics. The *family* is becoming a notorious battleground, in which the political and religious Right vilifies any departure from its self-defined "traditional values." Yet changes in the shape of the family are due much more to forces in the political economy (e.g., both parents working, declining real wages, unemployment) than to lifestyle heterodoxy. Slowly, family psychology is being refashioned to address these new economic and cultural realities (Goleman, 1989; Ho, 1987; Mirkin, 1990). *Education* has seen the teaching of Eurocentric history and culture challenged. This is an issue of basic inclusiveness that conservatives have ingenuously redefined as one of "political correctness" (Berman, 1992). In Los Angeles the *media and arts* community is increasingly polarized by the demands of multiculturalism, as established artists and genres must now compete for funding and exposure with ethnically oriented ones (Breslauer, 1991; Christon and Benavidez, 1991). Though still one of the whitest professions, mainstream *legal* philosophies are being challenge by proponents of "critical race theory" (Goldberg, 1992). The lack of ethnic diversity among judges throughout the criminal justice system emerged as a key issue in trials relating to the Los Angeles uprising (Lindner, 1993). Finally, as Cornel West has discussed in *Race Matters* (1993), race and gender continue to play a volatile role in U.S. *electoral politics*. Obviously the struggle over diversity extends to other fields as well, but this suffices to indicate the turmoil being experienced at all levels.

It will be difficult for North American society to embrace its own cultural diversity, but the cost of not doing so will be great. In a thoughtful essay entitled "Pop Goes the World," Mitchell Stephens has sketched how local culture is being replaced by mass-marketed commodities and technologies both here and abroad:

> It is not just that National Basketball Assn. games are now televised in more than 100 different countries or that you can be listening to a Flemish radio station in Belgium and suddenly hear Cousin Brucie's "Cruisin' America" oldies show, exactly as it was broadcast on KCBS-FM in Los Angeles. It is not just that Paris today has about 70 Japanese restaurants, or that there are five Kentucky Fried Chicken outlets in Beijing, or that a small cafe on the road from Ceske Budejovic to Tabor in the Czech Republic offers a couple of Mexican specialties. It is not just that . . . you can quench your thirst with a Coke in 185 countries. (The United Nations only has 178 members). No, to understand the direction which we are going, we also have to examine the consequences of these dramatic developments: the growing sameness of products made in Japan, Portugal, Ecuador, Kenya and Kentucky; the decline of indigenous and unique athletic, musical, culinary and even linguistic traditions; the fading differences between the cultures of the United States, Belgium and China. (1993:24)

Stephens notes that while colonialism has long eroded local cultures, three factors make such processes more widespread and profound today. The first is the revolution in global communications, from satellite TV to Walkmen to computers, which "permit cultures to be trampled from a distance" (ibid:25). The second is the opening of trade barriers and the growth in multinational business and markets. The third is the cross-fertilization resulting from the mobility of world populations, from refugees to leisure travelers.

While there are aspects of this global mix that are surely liberative (below, D), many are troubling and some downright genocidal. We are losing cultural diversity as "ethnic" clothing gives way to Adidas shoes and baseball hats, traditional chants to Madonna, and regional dishes to McDonalds:

> Michael Krauss, the director of the Alaska Native Language Center reports that 6,000 languages, give or take 10 percent, are still being spoken today; but somewhere between 20 percent and 50 percent of those languages are no longer being spoken by children. "That doesn't mean they're endangered," Krauss explains. "It means they're doomed." Many more are at risk. Krauss estimates that only about 600 languages are "relatively safe...." The rest are falling victim to bulldozers, which are destroying the jungles that used to shelter them, to intolerant national governments and to the global forces of homogenization — as people are "catapulted...from the oxcart to a satellite dish that is picking up Ted Turner." (Ibid:26)

Here in the U.S. the same erosion is affecting regional folk culture, dialects, and musical traditions. Human variety — like biological and botanical diversity — is falling victim to global capitalism. More than any single factor this paves the way for what Nigel Calder (1970) called the "silent revolution of Technopolis."[6] The new melting pot is the banal homogeneity of global commercial culture; the new tower of Babel is transnational technocracy. It puts growing concentration of power in the hands of those Berry calls transnational corporate "vandals" and "mercenaries," who have no connection to, or respect for, place. The church must reassert the Genesis wisdom of a "scattered" human family by nurturing diversity (below, 11,C). Just as it is the church's vocation to critique each culture in light of the gospel, it is also her duty to defend each culture's rights, because each is a gift of creation as well as a result of the Fall.

As pressure to redistribute social power grows from below, dominant culture reaction will increase from above. The church must take sides in the struggle for cultural diversity. This is necessarily a struggle for cultural justice, since not all groups have equal access to social resources and space. It will require critical analysis of the actual relations of power and a commitment to building strategic coalitions across traditional group boundaries that are based on partnership and respect (above, 9,A). We must learn to preserve the differences among us while searching together for social cohesion, and, most important, we must teach our children a worldview predicated upon multiculturalism (see

Saville-Troike, 1978; Derman-Sparks, 1989). Unfortunately most white Christians share the dominant culture fear that as different groups assert their own ethnicity and identity, somehow the social fabric will be strained to the point of tearing. Tensions, competition, and even conflict will be inevitable, to be sure. But cultural diversity is far less a risk than conformity. Indeed multiculturalism is an asset to democracy, because it serves as a political guarantee against totalitarian tendencies, which are almost always ethnocentric in character. The most formidable barrier to democracy in the U.S. today is not our diversity but the monistic ideology of capitalist consumerism (above, 3,C). History, writes Asian theologian C. S. Song, "seems to suggest that a world community of peace and understanding cannot be built on a monolithic cultural foundation but rather on cultural pluralism" (1979:6).

But what will be the "common ground" on which diverse groups interact and cooperate, and how will inevitable conflicts be resolved? These are legitimate and important questions, and their answers are not simple. In the next chapter, however, I will suggest that a clue may lie in the land itself (11,D). The land — the title to which is legitimately held only by the Creator, not by market forces — is hospitable to all cultures. Yet it also necessarily shapes the character of its residents over time, requiring each social group to adjust to the opportunities and constraints of the environment. The land compels differing groups to resolve conflicts over how to adjudicate its assets and limits. If we build our social, economic, and political life around it instead of despite it, the land has the power to bind together all who live upon it, no matter how or why they came to it. Perhaps the ancient tradition of human stewardship of place will be rediscovered as the key to unity without uniformity.

D. VIGILING AT THE GOLDEN DOOR?
NUESTRA AMERICA

How does a celebration of diversity contribute to the promotion of democracy?

What might a contemporary strategy for multicultural advocacy look like? Let me address this to my own context in the Southwest.

1. Celebrating the Cultural Mix

I believe that reconstructive theology should take sides in support of the multicultural *reconquista*. This means learning respect for the multilayered cultural soil of the Southwest (below, 11,E). Because of the historical "cycles of conquest" there are three distinct strata: Indian, Hispano-Mexican, and "American" (see Spicer, 1962). California has the most indigenous people of any state, yet this population is virtually invisible to the dominant culture (Larsen, 1989; Eargle, 1986). We who have usurped Indian land should find ways to listen and to learn from them about it (Gomez, 1991; Margolin, 1981; a good resource is

News from Native California). Affirming Indian culture also means supporting their right to be different — respecting their ceremonies, helping them recover artifacts from our museums, and advocating for their religious freedom.

The second stratum — the history and legacy of Alta California — should mean more to residents here than Spanish place names and Mexican food. The demographic reconquista, if nothing else, is forcing those living in border states to acknowledge that the original European roots of this area are Hispanic (see Pitt, 1966; Romo, 1983). The Spanish language as well as Chicano history and culture should be accorded social space and respect rather than derogation and marginalization (Augenbraum and Stavans, 1993; Burciaga, 1993; E. Martínez, 1991). Just as African Americans hold a singular place in the continuing legacy of U.S. race relations, Latinos have a special stature in the past and future of the Southwest. Ironically, whites throughout this region will have to realize that it is in our self-interest to help establish the very bicultural justice we have for so long denied the soon-to-be-restored Latino majority.

The third cultural stratum consists of subsequent immigrant groups to California, a diversity we may justly call "American." Here our task is first to learn and to acknowledge the unique history of white racism in the Golden State (Daniels and Olin, 1972). It also entails looking past the dominant culture facades and caricatures of California life in order to acquaint ourselves with the myriad peoples who have sought to better their lives here. This includes the great migrations of Asian contract laborers, Mexican *braceros,* black southerners, and Dust Bowl refugees. It includes unique, culturally hybrid communities that resulted from this immigrant history, such as the Mexican-Hindus of the Central Valley (Pinsky, 1987). It includes more recent arrivals, from hidden micro-immigrant groups (Micronesians, Ethiopians) to newly growing refugee communities (Armenians, Haitians). And let us not forget the liberative episodes in white history as well, such as the socialist community of Llano del Rio, which though surviving in the high deserts of Los Angeles for a mere four years was, as Mike Davis correctly notes, symbolic of a future unrealized (1990:3ff).

Multiculturalism invites us not only to protect the fragile beauty of the world's multitudinous cultural traditions but also to celebrate the "upside" of global mixing. America — since the sixteenth century a cauldron of cultures great and small — is still the prime laboratory for hybridization and would remain so even if there were no pressure to assimilate. This is because culture can be porous as well as resistant, interactive as well as isolating. Cross-fertilization can be as wonderful in culture as it is in botany (see, e.g., Holloway, 1991). Baseball is a good example: a mix (mutation?) of English cricket and native ballsports, the *novum* attains a life of its own and becomes a defining feature of the new culture. Gay Talese speaks of this dynamic symbolized in the act of tossing a baseball to his immigrant Italian father: He had thrown him America, and his father could not catch it. The examples of such "synthetic" American cultural practices are literally innumerable, from Pentecostalist religion to what Benjamin DeMott calls the popular culture of "Talkback" (1990:211ff). They range from rodeos to surfing; Navajo jewelry to Shaker furniture; TexMex cuisine to soul food. But — if I may be allowed a gratuitous editorial — the true heartbeat of America (contrary to the inanity of Chevy ads) is to be found above all in our music. In America's music lies her redemption.

In American musical forms, African rhythms and Irish lilts and Indian chanting and Spanish guitars meet and mix and spawn, on equal terms and in peace. In its strains we can still detect the pain and Promise of America: the long-forgotten yearning of mountain folk in bluegrass gospel; the anger and sadness of slaves in the blues; the will to be free in jazz; the struggle to survive urban marginalization in Motown and hip hop. Listen to our music and hear the language of the people — not the elite, but regular folk who lived side by side and could not help but learn from one another. In the whitest cowboy music (say, the Texas swing of Bob Wills) is the unmistakable influence of Louis Armstrong and the blackest blues and jazz riffs. Black and white traditions have merged in ragtime and rock and zydeco; Elvis and Ray Charles are fruit from this same hybrid tree. African, mestizo, and Indian fervor fire Latin music from Cuban rhumbas to Brazilian jazzpop to Chicano salsa, each of which pulsate throughout the Southwest. The culture of strolling mariachis is as strong on the streets of Los Angeles today as it is in Mexico City. The gentle, rolling tones of Pacific island a cappella meet the strumming of the caballero's guitar in Hawaiian slack-key. Northern Mexican *ranchera* and *banda* music (and dance) owes as much to the German polka as to Spanish flamenco. Fiddlers from Cape Breton Island to Texan honky-tonks breathe new life into floating waltzes and brooding love songs and manic Irish jigs.

The tools of this trade themselves reflect the transformative passion of American musical lovemaking. "Classical" instruments such as the mandolin and piano were wrested from the elite into the hands of popular culture. The fiddle, banned as a tool of peasant resistance during the English colonization of the Scottish highlands, was brought to America by those fleeing the oppression and taken up by a new culture of highlanders from Appalachia to the Rockies. The banjo, Mexican harp, harmonica, scratchboard — these are all offspring of musical crossbreeding. And alongside it all have been similarly eclectic dances, poetry, and storytelling. America's children all play and sing and dance to each other's music, for it "belongs" to all of us. So whenever I witness someone getting lost in that passion, whenever I am lost there myself, I imagine we have come mystically close to realizing Bolívar's vision of a people "born of one mother America, though our fathers had different origins."

The churches in North America, Protestants in particular, have all too often frowned on the passions of popular culture — at least on those not identified with "classic" European traditions — typified by those who place dour bans on dancing and nonchurch music. But it is also the case that countless strands of folk music and other crafts have survived and even flourished in the churches of the poor, black and white alike. Christians would do well, therefore, to recall the vision of John of Patmos, who understood that only "a new song" could bring together from among "every tribe and language and people and nation" (Rev

5:9). This indeed is the Promise of America, which churches above all should be willing and able to embrace.

2. Posadas *Theology*

In a recent reflection on the future of multicultural Los Angeles, Victor Valle and Rudy Torres argued that we "must find the words to continue the dialogue of inclusion that writers such as José Martí started more than a century ago when he redefined Latin America as '*nuestra* America' " (1992:M6). Martí, a Cuban patriot, was a vigorous critic of U.S. imperialism, but he understood that there was Promise here: "In our America it is vital to know the truth about the United States. We should not exaggerate its faults purposely, out of a desire to deny it all virtue, nor should these faults be concealed or proclaimed as virtues" (1975:49). Martí thrilled at the dedication of the Statue of Liberty on the occasion of the first U.S. centenary precisely because it suggested a repudiation of imperial ethnocentrism in favor of those remarkable lines from Emma Lazarus. "Give me your tired, your poor, your huddled masses yearning to breathe free," says the statue; "Send those, the homeless, tempest-tossed to me; I lift my lamp beside the golden door" (ibid:133ff). A mongrel nation of *outcasts* — only here has this vision found any hospitality at all. As long as that statue stands, the "minority tradition" (the double entendre is intentional) it symbolizes will continue to haunt us.

The *locus imperii* faces increasing pressures from within and without: the worldwide refugee crisis; the spread of regional insurrection and "instability"; agitation by poor nations for a just economic order; domestic urban decay and revolt; rising expectations among the historically marginalized. These are all, as Malcolm X put it, "chickens coming home to roost," the inevitable result of our traditions of division and oppression. The "global village" is growing ever smaller, but as the Third and Fourth Worlds impinge, the entitled of the First World grow fearful, whispering about the "new barbarians" and alluding to socio-economic triage. They are demanding a Fortress America where the internal poor are strictly controlled and the external poor kept out by militarized borders. The church can see this only as a cruel parody of its call to be ecumenical. The leaven of the Pharisees and of Herod will ruin the one loaf we have been called to gather around. Fortress America is also an affront to the legacy of Emma Lazarus's "golden door." Christians, therefore, by living in fidelity to the narrative of biblical radicalism and its call to solidarity, can nurture the Promise of *nuestra* America. We can and should collaborate with all kindred spirits to *revise* the body politic of this nation of immigrants according to its own best ideals.

"He put his servants in charge, and commanded the doorkeeper to keep watch" (Mk 13:34). The last parable of Mark's Jesus imagines disciples watching the door of the "Lord's house." This house represents for Mark the reconstructed "house for all peoples" sought by Jesus when he exorcized the Temple House (11:17). I conclude this chapter with an American midrash on this parable. We, the inheritors of entitlement, the descendants of immigrants, stand at the "golden door." As our conquests around the globe continue to displace the poor, we would bar the door. We whose ancestors experienced hospitality from the native peoples of this Great Turtle Island refuse to extend it to others. We whose ancestors respected no boundaries — neither those of the indigenous people nor those of the land — have set up borders and militarized them. The disinherited and the marginalized, the poor immigrant and refugee, stand outside, seeking inclusion. The voice of Christ speaks in them: "Listen! I stand at the door, knocking; if you hear my voice and open the door, I will come in to you and we will share communion" (Rev 3:20).

The image sharpens. This vigil at the door is a reenactment of *posadas,* that old Mexican liturgy with Catholic and Aztec roots, that Advent ritual of remembrance in which the people accompany the Holy Family from house to house as it seeks shelter, waiting to be recognized and allowed in so that the Christ-child may be born.[7] Is not the history and the future of nuestra America a narrative of posadas? This "creation story" surely represents a more redemptive origin myth for us than the triumphal tales of "discoverers" and conquistadors. It reminds us that we who have found shelter must continually resist *nativism* and embrace *nativity.* It challenges us to keep the door open, to welcome those we have excluded.

The image sharpens further. The community of Dolores Mission in East Los Angeles is celebrating posadas. Their nighttime procession winds slowly through the tough Aliso housing projects, illuminated by candles and carols. The people petition for entrance at each door; those inside answer back that there is "no room" for Jesus. It is a fitting ritual, for the people of this parish know both sides of the "golden door." First- and second-generation Latinos, they are themselves poor. Yet led by the women, they have reached out to their own alienated youth, urging them to give up gangbanging, trying to create jobs for them. And they welcome new immigrants and refugees, sheltering and feeding them in their small church. The community of Dolores Mission, having become "re(al)liant," does not live according to Church traditions but according to the commandments of biblical justice. So does it embody the kind of inclusive house envisioned by Jesus, keeping the vigil of hospitality at the Golden Door.

Such practices might yet transform our American House into a home for all peoples.

NOTES

1. Between 1882 and 1924 some 12 million immigrants were processed through Ellis Island; the site has recently been restored as an Immigration Museum (see Turan, 1990). For varying interpretations of immigration statistics reflecting the 1990 census see Vobejda (1991) and Usdansky (1992). On Asian-Pacific people as the fastest-growing immigrant population see Tachibana (1986) and O'Hare and Felt (1991). For an in-depth analysis of Mexican immigration and the changing labor force see W. Cornelius (1988).

2. "Light up the Border" was a mean-spirited initiative by several antiimmigrant groups in which participants would park their cars at twilight along certain spots where undocumented persons commonly cross over into the U.S. and shine their headlights over onto the Mexican side, purportedly to help the border patrol apprehend people. The group reflects the anxieties and hostilities among newer, affluent Anglo arrivals to San Diego County. Prosperity in the area has traditionally been based on agriculture (and thus dependent upon migrant labor). Because it is one of the fastest growing counties in the country, however, much valuable farmland along the coastal strip has been lost to rapidly spreading new suburban housing developments, placing wealthy condominium owners and poor migrant farmworkers literally side by side (see Mydans, 1990). I witnessed a telling exchange between State Senator Art Torres and the main organizer of Light up the Border during a hearing on border violence in 1991. Torres, a Chicano, listened patiently as the Anglo woman from the well-to-do beach resort of La Jolla recited the standard litany of complaints about farmworkers (they spread disease, they urinate on our lawns, they threaten our children, etc). Then he asked her a series of questions that revealed that she was from the Midwest, had been in California only six years, and had no previous experience with Latinos. Torres then gently but firmly offered two responses. He reminded her that Latinos (including his ancestors) had been crossing back and forth between California and Mexico long before Anglos arrived to live there. Then he allowed that the streets, sewers, schools, and shopping malls built to support the new affluent bedroom community *she had migrated to* probably placed more strain on the infrastructure of the state than any migrant farmworker camp. He concluded by agreeing with her that perhaps the border should be more tightly controlled — not the southern border of the state, but the eastern one, so that fewer "socio-economic migrants" like herself would be allowed in with their heavy demands and intolerant attitudes.

3. Similar arguments have appeared in most of the major print media, such as the equally conservative *Business Week*, which agreed that immigrants are "helping to revitalize the U.S. economy" (Mandel et al, 1992; see also Passell, 1990; Shuit and McDonnell, 1992). For a good summary defense of immigrant contributions see Irwin (1992). On the impact of newer Latinos see Hinojosa-Ojeda et al (1991).

4. In 1986 IRCA stipulated that employers must verify the legal resident status of all employees through an "I-9 form," unless "a widespread pattern of discrimination" against legal immigrants was, upon review, found to exist. In March of 1990 the General Accounting Office issued the last of three congressionally mandated reports monitoring the impact of these sanctions. The GAO found a 19 percent level of discrimination directly attributable to the law, but the sanctions were not repealed. The AFSC filed suit against the INS to try to win exemption from the sanctions on grounds of religious conscience; when the suit was thrown out, AFSC remained in noncompliance with the law (see AFSC, 1989). Supporters of the law have suggested several further strategies to curb hiring of undocumented workers, ranging from national identity cards to increased employer education and improved protection against discrimination. These deal with the symptoms, however, not the causes of undocumented immigration to the U.S. and intensify the plight of poor immigrants by preventing them from supporting themselves.

5. The Greek verb in the refrain is *kōlyō*, "to hinder, forbid or keep back," the same meaning as the Latin *impedire*, literally "to snare the feet." Both warnings are immediately followed by the Markan solemn conditional subjunctive: "Truly I say whosoever..." (9:41, 10:15), which also is used in 9:42.

6. Kleinberg describes technocracy as "a new kind of 'value-neutral,' politically flexible 'technototalitarianism' (cloaking itself in the mantle of a meritocracy of techni-

cal knowledge that best understands the public interest), which may yet be distinctive to the post-industrial society" (1973:231f). For other critiques of technocracy see Noble (1977); Gendron (1977); Winner (1977); Gross (1980); and Hopper (1991). On the loss of linguistic diversity see Long and Meisler (1993).

7. *Posadas* (shelter) are celebrated throughout Mexican America during the last days before Christmas. Based on an Aztec tradition of nine days of dances honoring Huitzilopochtli, it was transformed into a Christian celebration by Catholic catechists. The procession, traditionally bearing figurines or statues of the Holy Family, ritually re-creates the story of "no room at the inn" until at last (usually at the church) the procession is let in for the final celebration on Christmas Eve.

11

"How Shall We Describe the Great Economy?"

Reclamation

Radical decisions in obedience are of course the stuff of biblical faith, but now it cannot be radical decisions in a private world without brothers and sisters, without pasts and futures, without turf to be managed and cherished as a partner in the decisions. The unit of decision-making is the community and that always with reference to the land.... The central [biblical] problem is not emancipation but rootage, *not meaning but* belonging, *not separation from community but* location *within it.*

Walter Brueggemann,
The Land

The usual focus of attention for most Americans is the human society itself with its problems and its successes, its icons and symbols. With the exception of most Native Americans and a few non-natives who have given their hearts to the place, the land we all live on is simply taken for granted — and proper relation to it is not taken as part of "citizenship." But after two centuries of national history, people are beginning to wake up and notice that the United States is located on a landscape with a severe, spectacular, spacey, wildly demanding, and ecstatic narrative to be learned. Its natural communities are each unique, and each of us, whether we like it or not — in the city or countryside — live in one of them. When enough people get that picture, our political life will begin to change, and it will be the beginning of the next phase of American life, coming to live on "Turtle Island."

Gary Snyder,
"Coming into the Watershed"

Jesus is sitting in a boat, pushed back a few yards off the shore of the Sea of Galilee (Mk 4:1f). He is gently rocking, his eyes closed, his face warmed pleasantly by the sun glancing off the water. He has come out here to get a little distance from the political heat of his Capernaum "campaign." The contours and consequences of his mission have become clear. He has tried arguing Torah with the stewards of the Story, Sabbath economics with the administrators of Debt, social boundaries with the adjudicators of Purity. But he has concluded that the literate cannot read (2:25), that the authorities cannot lead (3:4), and that the House cannot stand (3:25). Political polarization has begun, perhaps quicker than Jesus was prepared for. He needs to think things over, to consolidate his gains and cut his losses, to reflect with his followers upon what all this means.

Jesus has made it clear to all concerned that he is struggling against the dominant system. But what is he struggling *for?* The poor who are attracted to him, the outcasts who flock around him, the skeptical onlookers who carefully measure his words, even his own disciples — they all want to know what alternative Jesus intends to offer. Jesus stares out on a glassy sea, blinking back the glare, anguishing over what to say and how to say it. How can he speak intelligibly to these people about human possibilities so discontinuous with the arrangements of power and privilege they all know so well? What metaphor, what symbol can he employ to revise the ancient Yahwist vision of a Great Economy? What discourse can he use that has not already been co-opted by the dominant media? *What parable shall we use for the Great Economy?* The question burns within him.

Jesus turns back, watching the crowd muster at the water's edge. They are setting up a "camp meeting" in a lakeside field offered by a local farmer; most are already seated on the ground, waiting patiently to hear from him, the patience of those who have seen hope come and go too many times. They are peasants and plain folk, uneducated and "illiterate." This is not the place for elaborate scriptural arguments and legal debates. Popular pedagogy, the villager from Nazareth reminds himself as he studies the crowd, begins where the people are, starts with what they know. Then it comes to him: What we must stand for is what they already stand on. Reconstruction must build upon the most radical foundation, renewal must take up the oldest story: The land itself.

"Listen!" he begins. **"A sower went out to sow..."** (4:3).

A. "A LOVE SONG FOR THE VINEYARD": THE CHURCH REGROUNDED

How can rediscovering love for place help the church overcome the alienation resulting from our geographical and cultural displacement and restore a sense of identity from which we can struggle for reconstruction?

At several points in this book I have reiterated that those who would call for repentance must do so out of love for the people and the place to which their challenge is directed. The reminder is necessary because negation so easily deteriorates into nihilism, criticism into calumny, defection into disaffiliation. To concede that we are part of the problem is a crucial hedge against both self-righteousness and escapism. But it is not enough: We must also imagine how we can be part of the resolution, the healing and the reconstruction. Our communities of discontinuity (above, Chapter Six) need to promote alternative possibilities for our collective social existence. Redeeming or preserving the good among one's people is the task of reclamation, all the more crucial for theology in the Palace Courtyard because of our legacy of genocide and empire. But it is a task notoriously sidestepped by radical Christian critics of the dominant order, since it is so much easier to articulate what we are against than what we are for.

A theology of reclamation is about redemption — the healing of our individual, but more importantly our collective, humanity. It is thus, in the North American context, fundamentally concerned with the struggle to become a nonimperial people, neither grandiose nor ashamed. It is about practicing discernment, honesty, dignity, community, and simplicity — according to Gerald May, the hallmarks of "recovery" (1988:162ff). These characteristics are not entirely absent from our past and present as a people, but they are rapidly disappearing under the repressive onslaught of technocratic centralism (below, C). A theology of reclamation will assert that "empire as a way of life" is not our fate but a betrayal of the Promise seeded in the social experiment called America (above, 5,E,1). It will seek the "subversive memory" embedded in our myths and institutions, however flawed (above 10,D). It will unearth the liberative fragments of our dismembered story, for every stratum of U.S. history and culture contains the footprints of plain folk who believed in the virtues of the American vision and who refused to internalize its darkest illusions. A theology of reclamation will listen again for the minor keys that have competed dissonantly against the imperial symphony: tunes carried by abolitionists and anarchists, populists and dissidents of all stripes, Quakers and Methodist reformers, communitarians and labor leaders, and countless others, distinguished and indistinguishable, including those to be discovered in our own family histories (above 5,D). It will celebrate the rich and diverse veins of folk culture that have not been erased, commoditized, or controlled, including that of European Americans. But all of this must be predicated upon the most fundamental reclamation of all: restoring our sense of place on the land.

1. "Taking Root Downward": The Bible and the Land

Reclamative theology may be instructed by Isaiah, a prophet of repentance who loved his people. We should note that predicating God's call to Isaiah to speak truth to power — with its hard words about blindness and deafness (Is 6:1ff) — was a love song for a vineyard (5:1ff). This oracle begins with a reminder to a frustrated farmer about his tender feelings for the land: "Let me sing to my friend the song of his love for his vineyard" (5:1). It recalls his hard labor of clearing, his patience in cultivation, and his investment in the tools of harvest

(5:2), apparently to mitigate his despair over a ruined crop (5:4) and his bitterness at having to abandon land that will not yield (5:5f). Isaiah soon makes it clear that the "vineyard" is a metaphor:

> The vineyard of Yahweh Sabaoth is the house of Israel
> and the people of Judah God's chosen planting;
> God expected justice, but found bloodshed,
> integrity, but heard only a cry of distress. (5:7)

But it is not merely a metaphor, for it reflects the lived experience of the people to whom it is addressed. Palestinian farmers struggled to cultivate the land's rocky soil and often lost the battle for subsistence with the elements. More often, however, people were driven off their land by unnatural economic forces, specifically the concentration of agricultural holdings in the hands of a few. Thus Isaiah's love song turns into an angry indictment of rich landowners, who justify their vast *latifundia* by an ideology of entitlement that presumes "everywhere belongs to them" (5:8). This draws from the Deuteronomic tradition of the prophetic song as a "witness against the people" (Dt 31:19f; cf Rev 15:3ff).

Mark's Jesus reappropriates Isaiah's song, revising and repoliticizing it in his parable of the vineyard in order to renew the prophetic attack on the Judean absentee landlord class (Mk 12:1ff; *BSM:*308ff). The vineyard parable, moreover, is narratively and ideologically related to the earlier parable of the sower (Mk 4:3ff) — both reverse the relations of power in order to criticize them. The vineyard tale, told to and about the Jerusalem authorities, challenges actual landowners to imagine life from the perspective of rebellious tenants. The sower story, conversely, told to and about peasant sharecroppers, invites them to imagine a situation in which they controlled the surplus they extract through their labor. There is a further connection. The sower parable alludes to Isaiah's later apocalyptic version of his love song, which speaks of Yahweh's "declaration of war on the thorns" (Is 27:4 = Mk 4:18f?).[1] Both Isaiah's love songs and Jesus' parables, then, affirm the people's identification with the land while at the same time using the vineyard as a metaphor for an oppressive agrarian political economy. The Great Economy is envisioned not as some otherworldly place and time but as the reclamation of the very soil upon which Palestinian farmers toil (*BSM:*176f). The liberation of the people depends utterly upon the liberation of the land itself.

There is a certain constraining character to this discourse of the land. Jesus' sower parable strikes a tone very different from the "master metaphor" of deconstructing and reconstructing the House, introduced just a few verses earlier in the parable of binding the Strong Man (3:25–27). It is almost as if Mark anticipates the ways in which revolutionary commitment can become mired in the illusion that we can erase the past, raze the present, and build a new house from the ground up. The enthusiasm of would-be revolutionary architects is thus tempered by the image of cultivation: The Great Economy comes about through patient sowing, mysterious growth, and the wise farmer's ability to discern the time of harvest (4:26–29). Mark understands that while we can defect from the House, we can never finally defect from land, because it is the universal foundation of all human societies. This is presumed throughout the narrative of biblical radicalism. When in exodus, the people are promised a homeland; when in exile, a return (Is 40:1ff; 65:21ff). Indeed, the biblical story begins with the myth of a garden home on the land that is lost (Genesis 2–3) and concludes with the myth of that garden home's restoration (Rev 22:1f).

Only by "taking root downward," claims Isaiah, "can the surviving remnant ... again bear fruit upward" (Is 37:31). I believe that our recovery of the biblical song of the vineyard is crucial to the church's reconstructive theology. Unfortunately few modern theologians have recognized the importance of the land to biblical faith. An exception is Walter Brueggemann's study *The Land: Place as Gift, Promise and Challenge in Biblical Faith* (1977). "We can no longer settle for the antithesis of the God of history versus the gods of the land," contends Brueggemann (ibid:185). He is particularly critical of the way both the existentialist and historicist traditions of theology have stressed

> categories of event to the disregard of *structure,* of history to the denial of *nature,* act to the disregard of *abiding continuities,* distinct deliverances to unawareness of *enduring blessings....* Israel is to be discerned not as people waiting only for occasional intrusions but as living always with gifts that are entrusted and grasping that seduces. Such a notion of *placed history* may be an important affirmation about the character of human life, about the strange struggle of homelessness and home, about the God who both leads out and brings in, about the Messiah who has no place and yet who is the very one with authority to give place. (Ibid:188f)

His study shows that for both Israel and Jesus, "a history of risking homelessness ... yields the gift of home" (ibid:189). Brueggemann argues that recovering the biblical dialectic of the land as both "possession" and "gift" will aid contemporary theology in four ways. First, it will help the church to be more sensitive to struggles over land in our own history. Second, it will better ground Christianity in its dialogue with materialist traditions such as Marxism. Third, it reminds us of "Yahweh's alliance with the poor against the landed" (ibid:192); biblical rootedness *in* the land always makes a place for the dispossessed *of* that land. Finally, a theology of the land can help us resist total accommodation to the production-consumption values of urban technocracy.

World Council of Churches analyst Wes Granberg-Michaelson (1988) notes that traditional Protestant theology has begun to move from the notion of domination over the earth to stewardship of it. He argues, however, that we must go beyond this to a theology of interrelationship, which stresses the inherent value of creation over its utility value (1990:12ff). This is undoubtedly a necessary ideological shift; but what does it mean for Christian practice? Quaker theologian Jim Corbett (1991) takes a pragmatic approach. The best way to reestablish communion with the land, he contends, is to rediscover dependence upon it.

He does this by practicing a spiritual discipline he calls "goatwalking." In the rugged Sonora desert Corbett has learned to live for days off whatever the land offers, supplemented only by the milk of a few goat companions.

> To live peacefully as members of wildland communities, human beings who have been domesticated to live by possession must become untamed. This is the heart of errantry.... Learning to go *cimarrón* [an old Spanish term for going feral] opens an exodus. Learning to live by fitting into an ecological niche rather than by fitting into a dominance-submission hierarchy opens human awareness to another kind of society based on equal rights of creative agency for all. (1991:23–25)

By re-creating the exodus wilderness experience of communion, he continues, the church can begin to rediscover the politics of sabbatical covenant. For Corbett and his community, this has taken two primary forms. Their covenant with the poor is expressed through their Sanctuary work with borderlands refugees (ibid:158ff). Yet they also have covenanted with the land itself. In 1988 they formed the Saguaro-Juniper Association to acquire land in southeast Arizona. The covenant agrees to protect this land from erosive human activity and to ensure that its resources will "never be rented, sold, extracted, or exported as mere commodities" (ibid:213). Corbett's reclamation of the biblical land ethic anticipates the socio-economic and political themes of this chapter.

2. New Cosmology or Theology of **Re-place-ment?**

The dominant culture of urban modernity is fundamentally characterized by displacement and alienation. It has often been pointed out, for example, how mobility has been more important than roots for nonindigenous North Americans. Novelist Wallace Stegner writes:

> The initial act of emigration from Europe, an act of extreme, deliberate disaffiliation, was the beginning of a national habit.... But the rootlessness that expresses energy and a thirst for the new and an aspiration toward freedom and personal fulfillment has just as often been a curse. Migrants deprive themselves of the physical and spiritual bonds that develop within a place and a society.... American individualism, much celebrated and cherished, has developed without its essential corrective, which is belonging. (1992:30)

Maori sovereignty advocate Donna Awatere is considerably less charitable in her assessment of this phenomenon:

> This wrench from the land did not come easy, but once done, spirituality in white culture died. From the rural-urban shift, and the intra-urban shifts

demanded by industrialization, the...urban-colony step was easy. Separated from the land, separated from tribal and clan loin bonds, the now
individual person or family is free to disperse to the colonies. Rooted now
in mechanical materialism and convinced now of its superiority over land-
based living, the settler is ready to destroy "barbaric" savages to give them
the benefit of the "civilization"...that has disrupted their own spiritual
immersion in their homeland. White culture is thus critical for colonialism
because it is nomadic. (1984:62)

In short, Awatere contends, the "original trauma" of European displacement led
inexorably to the dispossession of other peoples from their land (above, 5,D).

The cost of this historical repetition-compulsion has been truly staggering,
not only for those we have displaced and for the land itself but for ourselves.
There are at least three fundamental phases of displacement most European-
American families have experienced over time. The first and most crucial phase
is that spoken of by Awatere. It was the displacement *from* European land and
culture, and displacement *of* Native American land and culture, that took place
during the seventeenth, eighteenth, and nineteenth centuries. Still, despite this
holocaust and their complicity in it, many European Americans developed their
own affection for the new land they worked. But this bond was in turn eroded
by the second traumatic phase, characteristic of the first half of the twentieth
century: The migration, for mostly economic reasons, from rural communities
to urban areas. The third phase of displacement has occurred with increasing
frequency in the second half of the twentieth century: The atrophy or disap-
pearance altogether of settled urban neighborhoods, in which a semblance of
community was still intact. Today a majority of city dwellers live an atomized
and isolated lifestyle (how many of us know our neighbors?). Without a relationship to culture, land, and community, is it any wonder the modern urban
family is in crisis? The family has been further dismantled by work patterns
demanded by twentieth-century capitalism, which have displaced first one and
now increasingly both parents from the rhythms of home life. This cumulative
alienation has had profound erosive impact upon our humanity, which we have
yet to comprehend.

As the social consequences of our First World way of life become increasingly impossible to suppress, however, we are being forced to come to terms
with its cost. International development analyst Thierry Verhelst, in his book *No
Life without Roots,* summarizes our plight:

The West has become culturally underdeveloped because it, too, is the
victim of the idea of progress and the model of development which it has
transmitted to the Third World and which it imposes on itself. People in
the West suffer from the "withering of consciousness...." Increasingly
detached from their fundamental cultural identity, Westerners, too, find
self-determination difficult to achieve. This is the meaning of the current
crisis whose economic, ecological, political and social features are only

the visible part of the iceberg, emerging from the deep, icy waters of cultural and spiritual alienation. It is an alienation amidst plenty at least as dehumanizing as alienation in poverty. (1990:69)

Sadly, Christian theology is only now beginning to address this alienation. Liberal theology has tended to celebrate the "secular city" and the freedom of mobility, while conservatives have sought refuge in interiority. But both trajectories are merely symptoms of the alienation itself, and of Denial.

Until very recently, prophetic advocacy on behalf of the land has been left to the environmental movement, a few rural organizers and writers, and Native Americans. It is no accident, therefore, that these movements have identified the church, indeed the Jewish and Christian traditions, as a root of the problem. It is also why many are turning to hybrid varieties of neopaganism, which have resuscitated the myth of "Gaia." These so-called new cosmologies — so-called because in fact they are quite ancient — present a genuine and necessary challenge to traditional Christian theology. The questions raised by proponents of creation spirituality such as Matthew Fox and Thomas Berry are in many ways the right ones, and they must be addressed.[2] Rosemary Ruether takes them up in her recent *"Gaia" and God: An Ecofeminist Theology of Earth Healing:*

> We need to transform our inner psyches and the way we symbolize the interrelations of men and women, humans and earth, humans and the divine, the divine and the earth. Ecological healing is a theological and pyschic-spiritual process. Needless to say, spirituality or new consciousness will not transform deeply materialized relations of domination by themselves.... Rather we must see the work of eco-justice and the work of spirituality as interrelated, the inner and outer aspects of one process of conversion and transformation. (1992:4)

Ruether thoughtfully and critically sifts through ecofeminism and the new cosmologies, affirming many of their insights while questioning some of their myths (below, 12,A).

Creation spirituality, which is rapidly gaining influence in both Catholic and liberal Protestant circles, exhibits two notable problems. One is its tendency to exploit — and in the case of some New Age gurus, commercialize — Native American religious traditions. Ward Churchill complains that such "culture vultures" represent merely a new form of the very old white pathology of colonialism (1992:187ff). Christians would do better to reappropriate their own biblical tradition's love song for the land than selectively to expropriate native traditions wrenched from their indigenous context. A second problem is the political and social location of this movement. If creation spirituality's attempts to recover earth symbols and earth spirit for the church also inspires concrete politico-economic struggle in a defense of Gaia, then it will become a major component of reclamative theology. Insofar as it animates a flight from the alienation of modern capitalism into nature mysticism, however, it will prove to be nothing more or less than the contemporary equivalent of nineteenth-century bourgeois transcendentalism.

Whatever else may be said about the new cosmologies, I am not persuaded that it is helpful — or even accurate — to blame the Jewish and Christian traditions for the present global crisis, as has become so fashionable. To be sure, modern Christianity reflects the displacement of European culture as a whole, because it long ago departed from its own roots in the land- and place-based culture of the Bible. This makes the church a legitimate target, if an easy one. But is it the right culprit? Is not the far more formidable enemy global capitalism itself? Capitalism demands the objectification and commodification of nature in ways that the precapitalist Jewish and Christian traditions simply never could have. Christianity may have been complicit in the ascendancy of capitalism, but it has also been one of its victims. I am not excusing the church but arguing that we should seek to attack causes, not symptoms, of alienation.

I find the writing of Kentucky farmer Wendell Berry more theologically compelling and politically cogent than that of new cosmologist Thomas Berry. Wendell's critique of the mercenary character of modern capitalism is trenchant, and his call to respect the Great Economy uncompromising (above, 6,A). In an essay entitled "Higher Education and Home Defense" he warns:

> A powerful class of itinerant professional vandals is now pillaging the country and laying it waste. Their vandalism is not called by that name because of its enormous profitability (to some) and the grandeur of its scale. If one wrecks a private home, that is vandalism, but if, to build a nuclear power plant, one destroys good farmland, disrupts local community, and jeopardizes lives, home and properties within an area of several thousand square miles, *that* is industrial progress. The members of this prestigious class of rampaging professionals are the purest sort of careerists — "upwardly mobile" transients who will permit no stay or place to interrupt their personal advance. They must have no local allegiances; they must not have a local point of view. In order to be able to desecrate, endanger, or destroy a *place,* after all, one must be able to leave it and to forget it. One must never think of any place as one's home; one must never think of any place as anyone else's home. (1987:50f)

How do we stand against such robbery, he asks, if we who have been displaced by it *have no place to stand?*

The new cosmology's discourse of "global consciousness" — employed by New Age religionists, urban environmentalists, and peace activists alike — may be a less-than-useful fiction in the struggle against capitalist technocracy. Wendell Berry admits that such a discourse rightly points "to the interdependence of places, and to the recognition, which is desirable and growing, that no place on the earth can be completely healthy until all places are. But the word *planetary* also refers to an abstract anxiety or an abstract passion that is desperate and useless exactly to the extent that it is abstract. How, after all, can anybody — any particular body—do anything to heal a planet?" (1989a:16). "The question that must be addressed," he contends, "is not how to care for the planet but how to care for each of the planet's millions of human and natural neighborhoods, each of its millions of small pieces and parcels of land, each one of which is in some precious way different from all the others" (ibid:18). Christopher Lasch agrees: "Many advocates of disarmament and environmental conservation, understandably eager to associate their cause with the survival of the planet as a whole, deplore the local associations and attachments that impede the development of a 'planetary consciousness' but also make it possible for people to think constructively about the future instead of lapsing into cosmic panic and futuristic desperation" (1984:17).

It may be, then, that the challenge for creation spirituality is not so much one of cosmology as of geography. We need a theology of *re-place-ment*. Wendell Berry describes the "demands of affection" with characteristic simplicity: "Make a home. Help to make a community. Be loyal to what you have made. Put the interest of your community first. Love your neighbors—not the neighbors you pick out, but the ones you have" (1989a:22). Where people have no relationship with the land, it is abandoned to the forces of vandalism; conversely, only those who are rooted in a place will defend it. That is the difference between Hispanic farmers in Tierra Amarilla, New Mexico, who battled resort developers trying to monopolize local water resources, and white suburbanites in south Orange County, California, who stood by and watched the systemic destruction of their hills and canyons and beaches, offering almost no opposition. It is the difference between the immigrant residents of Poletown in Detroit, who fiercely if unsuccessfully fought General Motors' plan to replace their blue-collar neighborhood with a new factory (Wylie, 1991), and the elitist redevelopment boards of most U.S. cities, which routinely authorize razing older districts to accommodate corporate capital. It is the difference between the protracted nonviolent resistance by native Hawaiians to the U.S. Navy's use of the island of Kaho'olawe as a bombing range, and the total disinterest of southern Californians in the navy's use of San Clemente island for the same thing. Only love for specific land— what Hawaiians call *aloha 'aina*—can motivate us to struggle on its behalf.

Re-place-ment is a marginal notion in mainstream political and theological discourse alike. Right and Left, liberation theologies of the Third World and liberal theologies of the First, have been equally captive to the ideological and conceptual frameworks of industrial modernity. But there are signs that this is beginning to change. World Bank economist Herman Daly and theologian John Cobb, for example, in their important study *For the Common Good: Redirecting the Economy Toward Community, the Environment and a Sustainable Future* (1989), have called for a major shift from anthropocentric to "biocentric" economic theory and practice. Similarly Montana politician Daniel Kemmis, in his equally groundbreaking little book *Community and the Politics of Place*, believes that place-centered practices could transform public life" (1990:81). Drawing off bioregional writers such as Gary Snyder and "civic republicans" such as Robert Bellah, Kemmis urges us to return to a "re-inhabitory politics" which rediscovers the power that arises "from the efforts of unlike people to live well in specific places" (ibid:82).

Meanwhile church activists are learning to listen to traditions that never gave up their rootedness. For example, the Quincentenary newsletter published by the Latin American Council of Churches reflects a new priority being given to issues of land distribution and respect for indigenous cultures: "Today, as in ancient Israel, the land is an essential element of *campesinos'* and native peoples' present and future" (May, 1992:6; see Wagua, 1992). First World solidarity activists are also learning about long-term fortitude from native peoples, such as Inuit resistance to economic and military displacement in Canada and the repatriation struggle of Guatemalan Indian campesinos in the refugee camps of southern Mexico. Nor should we forget that there are many geo-cultural pockets in the U.S. where the love song for place has not yet been lost: among black farmers and Chicano farmworkers, deep in mountain hollows and out on open ranchlands, alongside Southwest *acequias* and Northwest riverbeds. These voices and their traditions have been marginalized by the dominant culture, but they can and must be heard again.[3]

To be sure, it will be difficult to reconstruct a "politics of place" in the U.S., because the social forces of dis-placement are so advanced here. It will surely require as many generations to reclaim our land and sense of place as it did to destroy them. What is clear is that we have no alternative. In the following sections, I will investigate elements for a theology of re-place-ment in the American Southwest, and more specifically California and Los Angeles. Using the three seed parables of Mark's Jesus as metaphors, I will look at the possibilities latent in social, economic, and political traditions often considered new but in reality quite old: local control of development, anarchism, and bioregional self-determination. These traditions have been at best ignored by theology, at worst considered anathema; they are deemed heretical within the ideological field of modern capitalism. I believe, however, that they represent the best way forward for reconstructing a collective life beyond the *locus imperii.* I conclude this chapter with my own love song for the land that is my home.

B. "SEED SOWN IN GOOD SOIL": ECONOMICS WITHIN THE LIMITS OF THE LAND

Can an economics and environmentalism of place combat development based upon growth and "robbery"?

"And other seed fell into good soil and brought forth . . . a hundredfold!" (Mk 4:8) This is the happy conclusion to the famous parable of the sower, reminding us that good land, when taken care of, can yield a harvest that will ensure that everyone has enough (*BSM:*174ff). Human culture is dependent upon the hospitality of the land, which both constrains it and sustains it. But over the last two centuries, industrial capitalism has built a culture that defies the land and its limits. This defiance, Wendell Berry argues, robs the environment and ruins local communities, all at the behest of outside forces that think only in terms of global markets and maximized profits (above, 6,A). Instead, he asserts, we must construct our economic life upon the "demands of affection" for the land, cognizant of our place in the Great Economy. Let us look briefly at two movements that have emerged over the last few decades in resistance to capitalist vandalism and dis-placement: environmentalism and sustainable economics.

1. Repoliticizing Environmentalism

Capitalism promotes "exotic" lifestyles — literally, patterns of domestic life, work, and leisure that are "not native, naturalized or acclimatized" to the land on which they take place. Los Angeles is a perfect example of a metropolis founded upon this model (Nichols and Young, 1991). The atmosphere of this coastal desert basin cannot bear the pollutants of the millions of cars we use; virtually none of the land's indigenous natural resources are used in local economic production; and the water table could not support one-twentieth of our current population (see Hundley, 1992; Kneese and Brown, 1981). Instead ours is a city based on import (or theft) — of water, of deciduous plants, of human labor, of electrical power — the list goes on. But this is inevitable, for economic prosperity within capitalism assumes the exploitation of labor, the exhaustion of natural resources, and the degradation of the environment. Labor can organize and fight back. The land, however, cannot. Yet the consequences of mismanagement and depletion of the land have finally caught up with us, resulting in an environmental crisis that is both profoundly local and profoundly global (for a comprehensive overview see L. Brown et al's *State of the World, 1993: A Worldwatch Report on Progress Toward a Sustainable Society,* 1993).

Calvin DeWitt (1990) has identified seven major environmental problems facing us today:

- Land conversion/habitat destruction, including urban encroachment, deforestation, and overgrazing
- Species extinction (at a rate of some three per day)
- Land degradation, including topsoil loss or exhaustion
- Waste, including introduction of new synthetic chemicals, oil spills, planned obsolescence, by-products, and overall disruption of natural cycles
- Global toxification, particularly the poisoning of water systems and the atmosphere, which has left no corner of the earth untouched
- Ozone depletion/greenhouse effect, which is causing the atrophy of protective layers in the stratosphere and thus global warming
- Human and cultural degradation, the severance of cultures from the land, and loss of diversity.

"Under this arrogant assault on the fabric of the biosphere," DeWitt concludes, " 'the earth dries up and withers, ... the earth is defiled by its people' (Is 24:4f)."

The ecological alarm was first sounded internationally in the 1972 study entitled "The Limits to Growth." Since then, the environmental movement has grown steadily. Two decades later, however, its achievements are decidedly ambiguous. They can be measured by the recent 1992 United Nations Conference on Environment and Development (UNCED) in Rio de Janeiro (see Mazur, 1992). On one hand, the fact that an "Earth Summit" was convened at all — and in the Southern Hemisphere — indicates how widespread concern has become. On the other hand, the way in which northern nations stonewalled key initiatives suggests that environmental issues remain subordinate to the interests of big capital and superpower politics. The literature related to the environment and the struggle on its behalf is voluminous (Ehrlich, 1991; Berger, 1987). Here I will address only two issues facing green politics today that are relevant to a theology of re-place-ment.

The first issue is the co-optation and "depoliticization" of ecological consciousness by government and corporate capitalism. Environmentalist rhetoric has clearly found acceptance in popular culture. A good example is a recent (March 29, 1993) *Newsweek* special pull-out section for kids, entitled "Saving the Earth: You and Your Environment." It includes a list of the "ten biggest challenges to the environment," children's questions to Vice-President Al Gore, and a "Where's Waldo" picture page with tips on "ecological dos and don'ts." Analyst Anthony Ladd warns: "By inferring that the ecological crisis can be cured through recycling, double-pane insulation, tree-planting and 47 other 'simple' things that individuals can do to save the earth, an apolitical and reductionist consciousness is fostered amongst the public that only offers consumptive solutions to consumptive problems" (1993:5). This is not to imply that conducting one's life, work, and consumption in an ecologically responsible fashion is unimportant; such disciplines are constitutive of discontinuity (above, 6,D; see Levering and Urbanska, 1992). But lifestyle choices are not yet political — and frankly do little to mitigate corporate vandalism.

The problem is, conservation discourse is increasingly being shaped and sponsored by entities that are in fact enemies of the land. Thus, bracketing the *Newsweek* section are full-page ads by the American Plastics Council and the U.S. Council for Energy Awareness that promote nuclear power! Brian Lipsett (1993) calls this "greenwashing," and he identifies two major aspects. One is the "selling" of environmental rhetoric, best seen in the commercialization of Earth Day celebrations. The other is the "selling out" of the larger environmental organizations, best seen in the growing influence of corporate interests among the so-called Group of 10 national conservation groups (see Dowie, 1992). Meanwhile the same corporate forces that are greenwashing the environmental middle are "green-baiting" more radical environmental groups such as Greenpeace and Earth First!, vilifying them as "antibusiness" and "extremist." Of even greater concern is the institutional harassment of activists and whistle-blowers — the Karen Silkwood case being only the most notorious.

These are all characteristic trends of what Ladd terms the "environmental backlash." The Reagan-Bush administrations relentlessly offered "regulatory relief" to corporations; dismantled or refused to enforce existing environmental protection legislation; opened federal lands to renewed exploitation; and gutted funding for alternative energy research and development.

> The size, scope and effectiveness of ecological protection was decimated, few new federal regulations were issued, and existing ones were reinterpreted or revised to reduce their impact on industry and government.... The last two years also witnessed the Bush team backing industry's efforts to dismantle the nation's strip mining bill, weaken hazardous waste laws, oppose tighter controls on ozone-depleting CFCs, lobby against proposals for higher auto mileage standards and cleaner fuels, as well as continue the Reagan hard-energy policies at the expense of conservation and renewable technologies.... After waffling on whether or not he would even attend the Earth Summit, Bush then personally worked to water down the global warming pact, circumvent the proposals on population issues, and refused to sign the biodiversity treaty altogether. (Ladd, 1993:2f)

In 1990 "industry helped defeat California's 'Big Green' initiative, the most ambitious environmental measure ever offered to U.S. voters, by outspending supporters by more than a 2 to 1 margin" (ibid:3). The courts, the media, and universities for the most part have cooperated with this backlash.

Re-place-ment is a good antidote to efforts to domesticate popular environmentalism by individualizing its mandates. Efforts to defend specific local places through community organizing will tend to be more credible than proxy battles for distant wetlands or forests. The fact that we urban dwellers may have little relationship to the land apart from a recreational one makes it all the more important for our environmental struggles to begin in our own neighborhoods, cities, and regions. Protecting or restoring the ecological integrity of our own places will help reconstruct our relationship to them. It also can teach us and empower us for larger environmental struggles. Such an approach degenerates into the fragmented provincialism of NIMBY-ism ("not in my back yard") only if and when we ignore two basic realities: environmental interdependence and the divide-and-conquer tactics of corporate globalism. Local ecological defense groups must work in cooperation with one another not only because each part of the earth is related to overall planetary well-being, but also because the economic-political forces we resist already collaborate at a high level.[4]

This leads to a second issue facing the repoliticization of environmental struggle: the gender, class, and race dimensions of ecological degradation. Ecofeminists, for example, have begun to draw parallels between the abuse and exploitation of women's bodies and the rape of the land (see C. Adams, 1993). Similarly the mainstream environmental movement — still predominantly white and white collar — has been criticized for being more concerned about rare gnatcatchers and remote coral reefs than working-class victims of black lung and inner-city toxic waste dumps. It is blue-collar workers who have borne the brunt of environmentally unsound industries, from traditional coal and uranium miners to modern textile and semiconductor assembly-line workers. Charles Lee (1990) shows how hazardous waste landfills, disposal sites, and incinerators are disproportionately located in African American communities, both rural (Sumter County, Alabama) and urban (Chicago, Houston).

If environmental degradation due to industrial overdevelopment has victimized domestic Third World communities, it is infinitely worse internationally. Manifestations of environmental racism include:

- U.S. industry's marketing of atomic power plants in Asia;
- nuclear testing and radioactive waste dumping in the Pacific islands;
- clearcutting tropical forests in South Asia and the Amazon;
- lax environmental, health, and safety standards in Mexican maquiladoras and other "free export zones";
- "debt for nature" swaps, representing the international equivalent of domestic "national sacrifice areas."

Multinational corporations continue to take advantage of the economic vulnerability of poor nations by supplying quick fixes of capital and jobs in exchange for unrestrained rights of resource extraction (see, e.g., Emberson-Bain, 1993). In their quest to maximize profits, these companies seek to stay ahead of the growing international forces who would constrain them and demand environmental and economic responsibility.

The analysis of environmental (and environmental movement) racism and classism has led to new initiatives among people of color and working people in the U.S. (see Bullard, 1993). Notable has been the United Church of Christ Commission for Racial Justice, which in 1987 released a study entitled "Toxic Wastes and Race in the United States: A National Report on the Racial and Socio-economic Characteristics of Communities Surrounding Hazardous Waste Sites." The UCC also helped convene in 1991 the First National People of Color Environmental Leadership Summit in Washington, DC. Three local examples of such leadership in Los Angeles deserve mention. Concerned Citizens of South Los Angeles, a largely black and Latino group, successfully fought the city's attempts to put in a huge "waste-to-energy" incinerator in their neighborhood and have subsequently continued to organize around other community-related environmental issues. Mothers of East L.A. led Latinos in a similar struggle around a proposed incinerator and abandoned toxic waste sites, as well as a major jail facility. The Labor/Community Watchdog is a working-class organization that focuses on the problems of air pollution while trying to preserve manufacturing jobs in the city.

Internationally, a significant precursor to the U.N. Earth Summit was the 1991 "Morelia Declaration," issued in Mexico City by a gathering of native peoples' representatives, scientists, and environmentalists from twenty countries. Equating ecocide with ethnocide, and resource depletion with neocolonialism, this manifesto called for "an immediate end to the international traffic in toxic waste...and an end to the unprincipled export of banned pesticides and other chemicals to economically desperate countries of the Third World." Perhaps most important, it asserted that

> traditional societies are generally the best managers of biodiversity...
> Respecting the interests of indigenous peoples, both in the Americas and throughout the rest of the world, who have become exploited minorities in their own countries is crucial for the preservation of biological and cultural diversity. We deplore the cultural pollution and loss of tradition which have led to global rootlessness, leaving humans, through the intensity of mass-marketing, vulnerable to the pressures of economic and political totalitarianism and habits of mass-consumption and waste which imperil the earth. (Aridjis et al, 1991)

Traditional societies, precisely because of their geographic, social, and economic vulnerability, continue to be victimized by an industrial economy from which they do not benefit (see Grumbine, 1992; Durning, 1992).

In North America, Indian lands have been poisoned both by the front (uranium mining), middle (testing), and back ends (waste storage) of the nuclear cycle. They are now being targeted by the growing private and public trash-exporting industry, whose lucrative disposal deals are often difficult for capital- and job-starved tribal councils to resist. The Cree people are currently waging a dramatic struggle against Hydro-Quebec over the huge James Bay project, which, according to the Natural Resource Defense Council, "may well cause more ecological damage than any other single development project in North American history"! A theology of re-place-ment must insist that environmental organizing never be segregated from the demands of gender, race, and class solidarity (above, Chapter Nine). Shifting ecological burdens to the poor is a corporate strategy and must be utterly repudiated by those concerned with true justice.

2. Sustainability: Placeless Markets or Marketplaces?

In both First and Third Worlds, environmental issues are inevitably tied to thorny questions of economic development. Centuries of capitalism have resulted in both over- and underdevelopment. Thus if it is understandable that the children of overdevelopment should want to slow growth because of environmental degradation, it is equally understandable that the children of underdevelopment should insist upon their right to experience the material fruits of economic growth. This continues to be the basic quandary when it comes to balancing environmental and economic justice.

The problem is that since the late nineteenth century, capitalism has equated development with economic growth, predicated specifically upon industrialization. Marxism, though the major ideological competitor and critic of capitalism, did not question this basic assumption. Indeed, socialist countries followed the Western development model, with similar (or worse) environmental consequences; one need look no further than the Chernobyl disaster. According to development theorist Thierry Verhelst, this tradition — with its practices of exotic acculturation, economism, technological imposition, and political control — is attributable to the ideology of social Darwinism, which assumes that "superior" societies are those who progress technologically and that less developed countries must "catch up." But Progress has failed to deliver on its promises:

> At the present moment, there are no valid development models. Nowadays, everyone is ready to admit that attempts at global development, in its many guises, have ended in failure. They represent the "bankruptcy of the paradigm of development," for on four essential fronts the Third World has suffered setbacks: the equitable distribution of available goods and services; the creation of jobs; the increase in economic independence; and the social cost of investment. (1990:10)

Western-style, growth-oriented development, concludes Verhelst, was a "Trojan Horse" (ibid:52f). Postindustrial societies thus face a crossroads. The dominant tradition would lead us further down the path of technocracy, commodification, and alienation from land and roots — the consequences of which are increasingly clear. We need a "third revolution," argues Paul Harrison (1992), to succeed the agricultural and industrial revolutions: sustainability.

"We can't grow," contends Donella Meadows, coauthor of *Beyond the Limits* (1992), the sequel to *Limits to Growth,* "but we can go on developing indefinitely." To do this we must learn to make "distinctions between sustainable development and unsustainable growth":

> Smart development builds on a region's own skills, resources and local businesses. Dumb growth invites a big corporation in, surrenders control and profits to a distant headquarters, undercuts local manufacturers and risks layoffs without warning. Recession-resistant development produces things people need. Unsustainable growth churns out tinsel products that consumers have to be seduced into buying.... Sustainable development ensures that forests and fields continue to produce wood, paper and food, to recharge wells, to control floods, to harbor wildlife, to attract tourists and to please residents. Fly-by-night growth clear-cuts forests to keep loggers and sawmills going just a few more years until the trees run out. It waives environmental regulations, as long as the cleanup costs can be transferred to the public or into the future. (1992:M2f)

This approach is not "soft-headed or anti-economic," Meadows insists; rather, it is "practical and sane to look for an economy that doesn't delude itself with booms that create their own busts, or with drawing down and polluting the resources of the Earth, upon which all economic activity depends" (ibid).

The propaganda of global capitalism — particularly since the demise of the state socialism — insists there are no viable socio-economic alternatives to the "free market," of course. But Daly and Cobb have pointed out the tendency of this market "to destroy its own necessary social context," because of its inability to take into account such factors as public goods, community morality, and the social costs of development (1989:44ff). They show how classical economic theory has relied upon abstractions such as GNP measurements and the anthropology of *homo economicus* (the individual as insatiable consumer), while marginalizing the land itself as a factor (ibid:97ff). Their study discusses at some length the realistic prospects for a re-placed political economy in the U.S. Kemmis notes that today the old orthodoxy of nationally controlled and oriented economies is being challenged from two opposite points of view: "There is a growing chorus of commentators who argue that American businesses cannot regain their competitiveness until they recognize that they are operating not in a national, but in a global economy. At the same time, the primacy of the national economy is challenged from below by theories which argue that entities smaller than nations are the natural locus of economies" (1990:86). He calls this the struggle between "the placeless market and the market*place*." He advocates a notion he calls economic re-inhabitation: "Specific goods should be produced, not just for *the* market, but for *this* market, in *this* place" (ibid:88). Kemmis illustrates how this has worked with examples from his own state, Montana.

How might we reconstruct an economics of place? Minimally, writes Wendell Berry, it would be characterized by decentralized, diversified, and small-scale industries appropriate to the land, which would add value (and reinvest profits) locally and give human skills priority over technological complexity. Basing a local economy on the export of raw material and the import of exogenous consumer products is "ruinous," he argues. "The influence of a complex, aggressive national economy upon a simple, passive local economy will also be ruinous. In a varied and versatile countryside, fragile in its composition and extremely susceptible to abuse, requiring close human care and elaborate human skills, able to produce and needing to produce a great variety of products from its soils, what is needed, obviously, is a highly diversified local economy" (1990:112). Kemmis shows in particular how local economies can be reconstructed through import substitution and place-based production and regulation (1990:86ff).

Kirkpatrick Sale, in *Dwellers in the Land: The Bioregional Vision*, agrees that sustainable local economies depend upon "a *minimum* number of goods and the *minimum* amount of environmental disruption along with the *maximum* use of renewable resources and the *maximum* use of human labor and ingenuity" (1985:69). He lists several advantages of self-sufficiency (ibid:76ff):

(1) control over investment, production, sales, and development would promote economic stability and provide insulation from the boom-and-bust cycles of distant market forces;

(2) it would break dependence upon remote bureaucracies, transnational corporations, and the "vortex of world-wide trade";

(3) the trade balance would tend to be favorable because the economy would be geared to local "import-replacements" rather than more expensive imports;

(4) locally-controlled currency would provide quicker economic feedback and reinvestment and could discourage accumulation and capital flight;

(5) local production would enhance overall health of residents because of reduced consumption of toxic or nonnutritious industrially fabricated products.

Self-reliance liberates the community from "distant and impersonal market forces,... remote governments and bureaucracies, and unseen corporations dictating consumer choices" (ibid:47). Most important, the social and environmental costs of resource extraction and production would be managed locally because they would be felt locally.

We can also be helped to recover economic re-place-ment by listening to those who never stopped practicing it. Bioregional economics is an old notion, not a new one, having characterized indigenous cultures throughout the world, from Guatemalan and Philippine jungles to Canadian and Lapland tundra. "Such traditions, long considered mere 'obstacles to development,' might well constitute an ultimately beneficial force of resistance to a foreign model of society whose effects are undesirable. Furthermore, indigenous values and the religions which uphold them offer alternative social models as well as different forms of action to implement such models" (Verhelst, 1990:1). Verhelst gives numerous examples of sustainable development projects currently thriving throughout the Third World and calls for "reverse development," in which First World peoples learn from traditional cultures about the very socio-economic practices that market capitalism has done its best to destroy (1990:91ff). This approach is being promoted in the U.S. by groups such as Cultural Survival and Survival International.

We should also recognize that such practices are not unprecedented in our own context. Within the capitalist sphere one can find credit unions, consumer cooperatives, land trusts, and alternative trade syndicates functioning at the local and regional level. The notion that public services such as health, education, and transportation could be socialized to the benefit of the majority is now accepted almost everywhere but in the U.S. Nowhere today is there more interest in sustainable economic and social models than in the field of regional planning. Planned economies are heretical in free-market capitalism, but global planning is done all the time by the managers of big capital. It is a matter of who does the planning and in whose interests.[5]

Today the forces of the placeless market would sever and alienate all productive and consumptive processes from the site where resources are extracted and obliterate the market*place*. The North American Free Trade Agreement and other current U.S. free trade initiatives represent major structural steps toward a system under the absolute control of unaccountable capital (see Cavanaugh et al, 1992). The times could not be more critical or the choices more consequential (see Makhijani, 1992). I believe that the call to repentance not only challenges affluent First World Christians to find ways to redistribute wealth (above, Chapter Six); it also challenges us to repudiate the glorious future promised by the free traders as a fast-track to the hell of universal displacement. It challenges us to "turn around" and see what we have lost. If we are to have a human future, we must re-place economics within the limits of the land. "Our places are asking us questions, and we do not have the answers," writes Wendell Berry in "An Argument for Diversity" (1990:114). "Answers, if they are to come and if they are to work, must be developed in the presence of the user and the land."

C. "SCATTERED UPON THE EARTH": RETRIBALIZATION?

Is there a political model that promotes the dispersal rather than the concentration of power?

Immediately preceding the second of Jesus' seed parables is a warning against those who counsel resignation to the inevitability of stratified power:

Be/aware . . .
to the one who has, more will be given;
from the one who lacks, even what that one has will be
taken away. (4:25)

In explicit contrast to this "realism of the market," Jesus portrays the Great Economy as a system of gift and grace: "It is as if someone scatters seed upon the earth . . . which produces of itself" (4:26ff). The farmer puts in work, the land yields, the farmer receives but does not control (*BSM*:178ff). The people of Israel were invited to reproduce this natural order of reciprocity in their own social organization. Economic power, like manna, was to be constantly redistributed. Sabbath and Jubilee legislation sought regularly to deconstruct accumulated wealth in the community (Horsley, 1989:72ff). The same principle applied to political power. Like seed, it was to be "scattered" rather than concentrated.

1. The Biblical Vision of Decentralized Politics

Yahwism exhibited a profound antagonism to the centralized and centralizing political economies of the Babylonian, Egyptian, and Canaanite city-states, in whose midst the Israelites dwelled. This can be seen, for example, in the ancient folktale narrating the fall of the tower of Babel (Genesis 11; above, 10,A,2). Against the orthodoxies of such royal cosmopolitanism, argues Hebrew Bible scholar Norman Gottwald, "early Israel was a risky venture in 'retribalization' ":

> Israel burst into history as an ethnically and socioeconomically mixed coalition of pastoral nomads, mercenaries and freebooters, assorted craftsmen and renegade priests. These sectors of the indigenous population joined in a combined sociopolitical and religious revolution against the imperial and hierarchic tribute-imposing structures of Egyptian-dominated Canaan...The socioeconomic relations of Israelites were egalitarian in the sense that the entire populace was assured of approximately equal access to resources by means of their organization into extended families, protective associations of families...and tribes, federated in an intertribal community. (1985:284f)

Upon the foundation of this tribal confederacy the ethos of Yahwism was built.

Israel's experiment in decentralized politics failed, of course, eventually succumbing to a monarchy and then to a Temple State under David and Solomon. In just a few generations, however, this centralizing impulse led to civil war, disastrous external political alliances, and finally conquest and exile (ibid:319ff). Indeed even during the Israelite monarchy the suspicion of state authority survived in the narrative of biblical radicalism, and with it the subversive memory of retribalization. This is most visible in 1 Samuel 8, which describes the people's desire for a king as a rejection of Yahweh's sovereignty. The narrative concedes that the old tribal adjudicatory system of local judges had deteriorated due to corruption (8:3). But the request for a Canaanite-style king elicits from the old prophet Samuel a litany regarding the oppressive nature of State rule: militarism (8:11f), expropriation of resources and labor (13, 16), and taxes (14f). "You shall be his slaves. And in that day you will cry out because of your king, whom you have chosen for yourselves; but Yahweh will not answer you in that day" (8:17f). This text articulates the antagonism between Yahweh's claims to sovereignty and those of the royal court.

Jacques Ellul, in a seminal essay entitled "Anarchism and Christianity," claims we can find no other historiographic tradition, ancient or modern, that is as critical of State authority as is the Hebrew Bible:

> The books of Chronicles, as they describe the kings following Solomon in Israel and Judea, offer us a very strange assessment of political power. Systematically ...*all* those shown objectively to be "great" kings historically are represented as bad kings: idolatrous, unjust, tyrannical, murderous. These kings brought about better political organization, made conquests, and enriched their people. In other words, they exercised their power "normally." On the contrary, when it comes to historically weak kings, those who lost their wars, allowed their administration to unravel, and lost wealth, Chronicles considers as good kings. This observation

could mean that the only acceptable power in the long run is the weakest one. Or it could mean that if a political leader is faithful to God, he [or she] is necessarily a poor political leader, and vice versa. (1988:165f)

Alongside the skeptical historians, Ellul adds, were even more skeptical prophets: "For every king there was a prophet [who] was most often a severe critic of royal acts" (1991:51).

Mark's Jesus seeks to resuscitate this radical tradition of the sole sovereignty of Yahweh. At the outset of his ministry he announces that "the kingdom *of God* is at hand" (1:15f). He then names twelve disciples on a mountain, a symbolic political act of "retribalization" (3:13ff; cf Numbers 1; Josh 13f; *BSM:*163f). This is followed by a parable about overthrowing the House/Kingdom of the "Strong Man," because they are built upon division (3:23ff; above, 7,A). Next come Jesus' seed parables, which allude to Ezekiel's critique of imperialism (4:30ff; below, D). More symbolic action repudiates Roman hegemony in the exorcism of "Legion" (5:1ff; *BSM:*190ff). In the second half of Mark, Jesus makes this critique of centralized power still more explicit in a pointed little verse:

As you know
the supposed rulers of the nations lord it over them,
and their *great* ones tyrannize them.
But this is not so *among you!*
Whoever would be *great among you* must be your servant.
Whoever would be first *among you* must be slave of all. (10:42–44)

Perhaps the most important example of apocalyptic role-reversal in Mark (below, 12,B), this is a key text in Mark's narrative, because it establishes Jesus' alternative political model: Leaders are called to practice "service," and "slaves" rise to the top of the social hierarchy.

Servant leadership is such a subversive practice that even within the discipleship community Mark attributes it only to women (*BSM:*277ff). It is not, however, without precedent in the biblical tradition. In fact, it is a *restoration* of the original political vocation of Exodus Israel. Thomas Mann writes in his commentary on Exodus 19ff: "Israel is set apart from all the people of the earth to render priestly service to Yahweh, and, in the context of the Pentateuchal narrative, to act as priest to the world" (1988:100). Thus the Hebrew scriptures envisioned not only retribalization, but also the commissioning of a covenantal people to serve all other tribes. Israel's "chosenness" implies not privilege but a responsibility to model servant leadership in the world.

This is also the New Testament vision of the church. The very last parable of Mark's Jesus completes the circle of discourse opened by his first parable. The one who promised to plunder/exorcize a House captive to the Strong Man (3:27), and who indeed plundered/exorcized that House (11:15–17) and called for its deconstruction (13:2), closes his apocalyptic sermon by envisioning a house in which "authority is distributed to his slaves, each with their own task" (13:34ff; Gk *dous tois doulois autou tēn exousian*). This household is the cul-minating expression of Jesus' reconstructive politics, and it certainly confirms Ellul's thesis that the biblical narratives "manifest in an astounding way the con-stancy of an antiroyal if not an antistatist sentiment" (1991:52). We can safely say that modernists such as Gore Vidal (1992), who lament that monotheism is the root of all antidemocratic evil, simply have not understood the biblical tradition. But they can hardly be blamed, for neither has Christendom.

2. Reconsidering the Anarchist Heresy

Is it hopelessly naive to speak of "retribalization" in our time? In 1925 Lewis Mumford issued this extraordinary ultimatum:

> The technical means of achieving this new distribution of power are at hand. The question before us is whether...we can remold our institu-tions so as to promote a regional development — development that will eliminate our enormous economic wastes, give a new life to stable agri-culture, set down fresh communities planned on a human scale, and above all, restore a little happiness and freedom in places where these things have been pretty well wrung out. This is a question that cuts diametrically across a large part of our current political and social problems; some of these it places in a new light, and some of them it makes meaningless. Regionalism or super-congestion? (Sale, 1985:142f)

As the century draws to a close and our body politic faces a historical cross-roads, Mumford's query remains. Will we repent from our imperial mistake, and redistribute decision-making authority regionally, so recovering a democ-racy that returns power to the people? Or will we continue our drift toward the de facto totalitarianism of global technocracy (Gross, 1980)?

There is no doubt that human societies everywhere are losing ground each year to the forces of politico-economic centralization. Yet several observers have pointed out that there is a simultaneous historical current moving in the opposite direction: the demand among smaller national and ethnic groups for self-determination. A "third world war" — this is how the *Utne Reader* de-scribed this trend in a series of articles that appeared, significantly, before the collapse of the Eastern bloc. Analyst Thomas Martin calls it "devolution," a political phenomenon that pits nationalist tendencies against statist regimes in places as disparate as Sri Lanka, Scotland, Zaire, and Puerto Rico. "When people cease to be passive subjects and begin to participate in government, they invariably reject artificial political boundaries and seek to regroup into more natural ethnic, linguistic, religious, or cultural domains" (1988:78). Martin's analysis has been borne out by both the recent breakup of the Soviet republics and the terrible war that currently rages in former Yugoslavia. But one can also see it in the protracted conflicts between Somalia and Ethiopia, among Basque and Quebecois separatists, and in the indigenous sovereignty movements in New Zealand/Aotearoa and Hawai'i (Gurr, 1993; Awatere, 1984).

Journalist Bernard Nietschmann points out that *de*colonization in the Third World has merely seen the rise of a new statism, which has meant *re*colonization for the Fourth World. He defines the Fourth World as "nations without a state," which may be "surrounded, divided or dismembered by one or more international states":

> More than 95 percent of the world's 168 states are multinational, that is, composed of many nations, some unconsenting. These 168 states assert sovereignty over the world's 3,000 to 5,000 nations and peoples, all of the continents, 40 percent of the oceans. . . . The Fourth World encompasses most of the world's nations, about a third of the world's population, and approximately 50 percent of the land area. Nation peoples may be industrialized (Latvians, Estonians, Catalans), or live from hunting and marketing (Inuits), herding (Samis), agriculture (Shan), ranching (Western Shoshone), or commercial and subsistence fishing (Haida). Nation peoples may not recognize a state's assertion of sovereignty. Many Irish do not consider themselves part of Great Britain; . . . Mayans of Guatemala; Tamils of Sri Lanka; Pathans of Pakistan or Afghanistan; Kurds of Syria, Turkey, Iran, Iraq; . . . Miskitos of Nicaragua or Honduras; Tigrayans and Oromo of Ethiopia; . . . the peoples of South Moluccas, East Timor and West Papua of Indonesia. . . . Out of 120 [current military] conflicts, 98 percent (118) are in the Third World and 75 percent (90) are between Third World states and Fourth World nations. (1988:85ff)

Such movements, declares Kirkpatrick Sale, represent the "centrifugal force of contemporary politics" (1988:95).

First World citizens and their rulers believe, of course, that devolutionary geopolitics represents a dangerous trend. It is referred to darkly as "Balkanization" or, worse, global anarchy (D. Morris, 1988). This pejorative perception comes in part from the fact that "nearly all media and academia are anchored in the world's centralized states" (ibid:84) and in part from the official need to legitimize a new era of U.S. military intervention in such places as Somalia and Yugoslavia. From a Christian point of view, the appalling bloodshed involved in tribal wars and "ethnic cleansings" is always terrible. But this hardly means that political fragmentation is in itself bad. Quite the contrary. If the greatest threat to justice and democracy today is the "super-congestion" of political power, then movements for self-determination are signs of hope:

> Of course no single small nation or small community movement can transform the huge global monoculture all alone. Yet when the numerous nations pressing their claims of sovereignty against imperialist states is added to the people in the West involved in ecological and bioregional activism, there is hope for the planet. Devolutionary, indigenous, and

reinhabitory groups taken together represent a "shadow movement" to eclipse late industrial society before it eclipses the earth's future. (Berg, 1988:82)

In order to appreciate the promise of devolutionary politics, however, we in the *locus imperii* need to understand how the myth of our individual political enfranchisement is undermined by the fact of our system of democratic centralism.

The illusion of choice in civic and consumer affairs mystifies our socialization into utter State dependency. Thomas Goodwyn, in his study of nineteenth-century American populism, notes:

Increasingly, the modern condition of "the people" is illustrated by their general acquiescence in their own political inability to affect their governments in substantive ways. Collective political resignation is a constant of public life in the technological societies of the twentieth century.... Older aspirations — dreams of achieving a civic culture grounded in generous social relations and in a celebration of the vitality of human cooperation and the diversity of human aspiration itself — have come to seem so out of place in the twentieth century societies of progress that the mere recitation of such longings, however authentic they have always been, now constitutes a social embarrassment. (In Kemmis, 1990:31)

The dominant forms of religion, education, and leisure culture in the U.S. tutor us in the art of political spectating. They function to persuade us that leaders lead, that experts will tell us information on a need-to-know basis, that authority trickles down, and that the credibility of institutions is directly proportionate to their size and complexity.

Sale notes that the political system itself has evolved in a way that discourages local participation:

By now effective power has been almost totally drained from regions, states, cities, and towns, leaving them fewer and fewer decisions of meaning while more and more matters of substance (especially of taxation, finance, regulation, defense, and planning) are concentrated in the legislatures and bureaucracies of the capitals. A measure of the efficiency of this process is that even in such an open and free-wheeling nation as America... the very simplest expression of political responsibility — voting — is undertaken by not much more than half the eligible voters, and in the case of local elections, since the purpose seems to them so trivial, by not much more than a fifth. (1985:102f)

Everything in the *locus imperii,* in other words, functions to persuade us to believe that change comes from above, not below. Our political culture is inherently disempowering at the base and "super-congestive" at the top. Moreover any practice that seeks to break our dependency upon centralized institutions will be caricatured as either utopian idealism or heresy. No ideology is more demonized by the State than one that dares to question the necessity of the State.

Common sense and empirical observation, however, tell us that social processes and covenants are truly enfranchising only to the degree they are locally meaningful. Theorists from E. F. Schumacher to Kirkpatrick Sale call this the political economy of scale. It is also the case that power is rarely dispersed voluntarily by those who have it; they must be sufficiently pressured by social forces from "below." Social change from the bottom up, therefore, represents not utopian but practical politics. Any community organizer can attest to the truth of this approach. We can see it in the example of three recent struggles in southern California around the issue of education:

- At a high school in Monterey Park, inter-ethnic tensions were not dealt with adequately by the administration until students and parents organized independently and began pressuring for change.
- Only weeklong protests by Latino students reopened the administration's proposal for gutting the Chicano studies program at UCLA.
- Top-down proposals to break up the huge Los Angeles Unified School District (currently covering 700 miles and 640,000 students with a budget of $3.8 billion), fruitless since 1968, are now being eclipsed by a grassroots organization advocating school-based management (Banks, 1993).

The common thread in each of these cases is that change results from pressure by empowered groups at the base, organizing around their local interests. And so it goes: Police brutality remains intact until citizens' review panels are set up to demand accountability; city zoning decisions favor the rich unless neighborhood political action committees are organized in poor areas; growers refuse to change oppressive labor practices until farmworkers strike; corporations keep objectionable products on the market unless embarrassed by consumer groups or pressured by boycotts (for examples of current grassroots movements around the world see Ekins, 1992).

The structural solution to overconcentrated power, then, is to train citizens how to organize and advocate for their concerns, the goal being to decentralize political decision making. Sale reminds us that there are ubiquitous precedents for localizing authority in our system:

Those who doubt that government is most effectively transmitted through smaller units might reflect on these figures: while there are 51 governments in the U.S. ostensibly set up to solve the people's problems, the actual business of providing services in America (transportation, housing, fire protection, water, power, etc.) is in the hands of more than 28,733 (in 1982) special-district governments at regional and local levels — *more than 500 times more small governments than large.* And even the national government, when it actually gets down to caring for its citizens' needs and desires, divides itself into some 1,460 general- and special-purpose organizations, and their number increases every year. (1985:97)

Today a variety of community-based organizations in the U.S., such as the Institute for Cultural Affairs and the National Association for the Southern Poor, are moving beyond the "town hall" rhetoric of professional politicians and experimenting with bottom-up politics, such as "community congresses" and citizen participation programs.[6]

Indeed state and federal devolutionism should by no means be ruled out; as Kemmis puts it, "This kind of politics implies at one and the same time a rejection of both of the fundamental federalist premises which underlay the U.S. Constitution" (1990:123). Movements to split California into smaller units, for example, have been around since statehood and continue to be advocated seriously today by some local government officials (Warren, 1991). The debate over Hawaiian sovereignty, with its secessionist implications, has moved from the periphery to the center of political debate in that state (Ahuna-Ka'ai'ai, 1993). These currents are operating even at the municipal level. The aftermath of the spring 1992 uprisings has brought calls to decentralize Los Angeles, for example. Journalist David Glidden asserts that Los Angeles should learn from the devolution of the former Soviet republics that "the more diverse ethnic and neighborhood interests are, the less likely that one large city government can adequately serve them":

> The real evil of Balkanization is not subdivision. Rather, it is anti-democratic sentiments leading to one group subjugating another.... The dream that generated Los Angeles has, in time, become a nightmare. ...Incorporation destroyed the sense of neighborhood that areas like Highland Park and Echo Park once enjoyed and made them thrive. As subdivisions of a sprawling megalopolis, the pocket cities that compose it now are more easily ignored in favor of lobbyists and special interests who spend their time downtown.... Los Angeles should be down-sized into the dozens of communities from which it was originally constituted, just as the Soviet Union has recently been reorganized into a commonwealth. (1992:M6)

In a similar vein Mike Davis advocates a "parliament of neighborhood councils," which, because it would reflect the diversity of the city, would be "more likely to encourage interethnic unity and negotiation of common interests than our current feudal City Council" (1992a:M1).

In their classical statist expressions, liberal capitalism and communism both have utterly discouraged the politics of local empowerment. For modern precedent we must look instead to the nineteenth-century nonstatist revolutionary movements of cooperative socialism and anarchism (see M. Miller, 1970). Political scientist Tom Bottomore summarizes this tradition:

Classical anarchism as an integral, albeit contentious, part of the wider socialist movement was originally inspired by the mutualist and federalist ideas of [the Frenchman Pierre-Joseph] Proudhon. Proudhon adopted an essentially cooperative approach to socialism, but he insisted that the power of capital and the power of the state were synonymous and that the proletariat could not emancipate itself through the use of state power. The latter ideas were vigorously propagated by [the Russian Michael] Bakunin under whose leadership anarchism developed in the late 1860s as the most serious rival of Marxist socialism at the international level. Unlike Proudhon, however, Bakunin advocated the violent and revolutionary expropriation of capitalist and landed property, leading to a form of collectivism. Bakunin's successor, Peter Kropotkin (1842–1921), emphasized the importance of mutual aid as a factor in social evolution; he was mainly responsible for developing the theory of anarchist communism, according to which "everything belongs to everyone" and distribution is based exclusively on needs. (1983:18)

Though anarchism was a serious political force mainly in the period between the Paris Commune of 1871 and the Spanish Civil War, its legacy has not disappeared: "There was a notable revival of anarchist ideas and tendencies (not always recognized as such) in the New Left movements of the 1960s. Currently, anarcho-pacifism, drawing on a tradition of Christian anarchism but inspired more by the nonviolent direct action techniques popularized by M. K. Gandhi, is a significant tendency within Western peace movements" (ibid:19). Today two of the most significant critics of technocratic centralism — Noam Chomsky and Jacques Ellul — are advocates of essentially anarchist politics.

It has been argued, rightly in my view, that anarchism is to Marxism-Leninism what Anabaptism was to the magisterial Reformation: a revolutionary movement predicated upon negating, rather than seizing control of, state power (Eller, 1987). Just as the Anabaptists were scorned by Protestants and Catholics alike, anarchism has been dismissed by Left and Right in modernity. But in our age of political bankruptcy, this is perhaps the best endorsement of all. I agree with Ellul that anarchism deserves to be reconsidered by postmodern liberation theory, particularly by Christians (1991:21). It coheres with the critical, interrogatory, and apocalyptic (below, 12,A) theological perspectives argued in this book. And it provides a constructive alternative to those who feel that postmodern politics can only be about deconstructing discourse or cynicism and withdrawal (on this see Rosenau, 1992).

Keeping in mind that anarchist theory represents an orientation, not a blueprint, for retribalizing politics, one significant problem must be addressed. If we affirm the maximum dispersal of power, on what basis can we imagine self-determining human groups voluntarily associating? How can a social fabric of peaceful coexistence and cooperation be forged among competing interests? Here the classic question of liberalism — What are the limits of freedom? — is redefined by postmodern politics: What are the limits of pluralism? Nineteenth-

century anarchist theory assumed that economic interests would provide the
common ground among groups, while twentieth-century dissident social movements such as communism and Islam have looked for unity in ideology. But the
centrifugal forces of devolutionism are defying both statist and ideological solutions. Indeed modern history provides few examples of politically uncompelled
federation but ubiquitous examples of interethnic conflict (see Stavenhagen,
1990). These are difficult problems, with no easy alleviations. This is where
I believe the insights of bioregionalism represent a crucial but complementary corrective to anarchism. Again, the insight is a biblical one: retribalization
requires people to live in covenant with the land.

D. "ALL THE BIRDS OF THE AIR":
BIOREGIONAL SELF-DETERMINATION

How can loyalty to the land shape regionalized economics and politics?

In the third and last of his seed parables, Mark's Jesus, ever one to affirm
apparent paradoxes, points out that the smallest seed can grow to be the biggest
shrub (Mk 4:30–32; *BSM:*179f). But there is more to this image than simple
folk wisdom. It alludes to Ezekiel's thoroughly political parable about "the trees
of the field" (cf also Daniel 4). Here the tall trees of empire are cut down, while
a simple sprig is raised up as "a noble cedar":

> Under it every kind of bird will live;
> In the shade of its branches will nest
> winged creatures of every kind.
> All the trees of the field shall know that I am the Lord.
> I bring low the high tree,
> I make the high tree low. (Ez 17:23f)

This image not only suggests a radical transformation of the relations of power
"from the bottom up" but also implies the politics of inclusion — "every kind
of bird" will find hospitality. Diversity in the branches of a tree that is rooted in
the earth. It is a nice metaphor for bioregionalism — politics predicated upon the
land, not upon human constructs of ideology, economics, or ethnicity. The land
alone is big enough to foster pluralism, but also limited enough to constrain it.

Kirkpatrick Sale defines bioregionalism as follows: "*bio* is from the Greek
word for forms of life... and *region* is from the Latin *regere,* territory to be
ruled.... They convey together: a life-territory, a place defined by its life forms,
its topography and its biota, rather than by human dictates; a region governed by
nature, not legislature. And if the concept initially strikes us as strange, that may
perhaps only be a measure of how distant we have become from the wisdom it
conveys" (1985:53). What prevents *homo industrialus* from seeing this logic is
our need to control nature, which is related to our fear of it and our need to live
outside its limits, which is a product of our alienation from the land.

In the natural order, "nothing is more striking than the absence of any centralized control, any interspeciate domination," Sale points out; "there are none of the patterns of ruler-and-ruled that are taken as inevitable in human governance" (ibid:91). There is territoriality, defense, and predation. "But this is not governance, it is not rule or dominance, it is not even aggression of an organized political or military kind... or control, or the establishment of power or sovereignty" (ibid:93). Nature's tendency to diffuse power is mirrored in traditional human social organization. History is characterized by the "urge toward separatism, independence, and local autonomy rather than agglomeration and concentration," argues Sale; "in the tribal councils, the folkmotes, the ecclesia, the village assemblies, the town meetings, we find the human institution proven through time to have shown the scope and competence for the most basic kind of self-rule" (ibid:94). This economy of scale, known to "preliterate peoples all over the globe," is precisely what we moderns must rediscover:

> The primary location of decisionmaking, therefore, and of political and economic control, should be the community, the more-or-less intimate grouping either at the close-knit village scale of 1,000 people or so, or probably more often at the extended community scale of 5,000 to 10,000 so often found as the fundamental political unit whether formal or informal. Here, where people know one another and the essentials of the environment they share, where at least the most basic information for problem-solving is known or readily available, here is where governance should begin. (Ibid:95)

Deconstructing "super-congested" decision making and reclaiming the power of place-based institutions is what Daniel Kemmis terms "the politics of reinhabitation" (1990:109ff).

Activist-poet Gary Snyder has suggested "watershed councils" as the locus of authority for bioregional governance (1992:68). Kemmis, on the other hand, calls for a revitalization of the old notion of the city-state:

> It may be that the boundaries which humans draw across landscapes create artificial and inefficient units both in economic and in political terms. If cities, in relation to their hinterlands, have the capacity to define working economies, then it makes sense that the same city regions which constitute economies should also be "city-states" — the manageable households within which the task of willing a common world takes place.... At least part of the reason the *polis* has this enduring paradigmatic power is because of the way it focuses our attention on the shared enterprise of inhabitation. The *polis* is, first of all, the place which a certain group of people recognize that they inhabit in common.... Given that fact, politics emerges as the set of practices which enables these people to dwell together in this place. (1990:121f)

Whatever the model, bioregional politics would resist the atomizing tendency of retribalization because inhabitants of the land "share the same configurations of life, the same social and economic constraints, roughly the same environmental problems and opportunities, and so there is every reason to expect contact and cooperation among them" (Sale, 1985:95).

This is, literally, the ground on which America's promise of multicultural diversity can be realized (above, 10,C). "Such a non-nationalistic idea of community, in which commitment to pure place is paramount, cannot be ethnic or racist," asserts Snyder.

> Anyone of any race, language, religion or origin is welcome, as long as they live well on the land. The Great Central Valley region [of California] does not prefer English over Spanish or Japanese or Hmong. If it had any preferences at all, it might best like the languages it heard for thousands of years such as Maidu or Miwok. Mythically speaking the region will welcome whoever chooses to observe the etiquette, express the gratitude, grasp the tools, and learn the songs that it takes to live there. (1992:70)

Re-placing the primary economic forces of the land under local knowledge and control (above, B) would further promote cooperation among groups, since all producers and consumers would be dependent upon local resource stewardship. Socio-economic diversity would arise naturally within the bioregion, following the ecological principle of "hetarchy" — a plurality of distinctive practices without hierarchy.

Finally, the absence of a dominating centrist governmental authority does not mean a return to political provincialism and the prospect of endless inter-tribal skirmishing over turf. Bioregional governance assumes the confederation of local entities for cooperation, planning, trade, adjudication, and mediation. Cobb and Daly go so far as to explore the prospects for a "community of communities," in which local sovereignty is constrained by larger representative and covenantal bodies, all the way to the world level (1989:176ff). Admittedly the immediate prospects of realizing such radically .different models seem remote within the *locus imperii*. But the truth is, from the beginnings of our national body politic there has been a struggle between centralism and decentralism. A significant force in "the democratic movement in the American revolution," historian Straughton Lynd reminds us, was the "insistence that the best of legislatures be continually checked and guided by 'the people out of doors,' acting through new institutions of their own devising. Theirs was a demand not simply for an end to conventional bicameralism, but for what might perhaps be termed bicameralism from below" (1968:171). Federalism prevailed in the nineteenth century, of course, first in continental expansion and wars of acquisition, then in the northern victory in the War between the States, and finally in the turn-of-the-century defeat of the Populist movement. Indeed Kemmis claims that the defeat of the predominantly rural-backed Populist platform in the presidential elections of 1896 represented a death knell for true Jeffersonian democracy in America (1990:28ff). Nevertheless, regionalist movements pepper our history, the white counterpart to resistance movements among oppressed minorities. One thinks of the struggle of Dakota farmers to retain their land through rural cooperatives, or Upton Sinclair's socialist campaign for governor of California in 1934, or the old Long Beach, California, "Spit and Argue" club.[7]

One could argue that regionalism is, ironically, every bit as American as imperialism (see Garreau, 1981; Markusen, 1987). The notion of regional self-determination has kept erupting in the public conversation, Sale notes (1985:137). He cites as an example the remarkable conclusion of a 1935 study by the federal government's National Resources Committee entitled *Regional Factors in National Planning and Development:* "Regional differentiation... may turn out to be the true expression of American life and culture... [reflecting] American ideals, needs, and view points far more adequately than does State consciousness and loyalty" (ibid:146). This was, Sale remarks, "for Washington quite a confession." Before we assume bioregional self-determination is too marginal a tradition to guide serious political struggle here, therefore, we would do well to remember the wisdom of Schopenhauer, the nineteenth-century German philosopher. He reminds us that revolutionary social ideas always go through three stages: first they are ridiculed, then violently resisted, and finally accepted as self-evident. We can see this borne out in U.S. history in the movements for independence, the abolition of slavery, and women's suffrage.

Whether we call it anarcho-syndicalism, cooperative socialism, or simply (like the Anabaptists) "mutual aid," the politics of bioregional self-determination can help Christians rediscover the biblical vision of the tree that when planted firmly in the ground, provides hospitality and justice for all. It is deeply rooted in the soil of the two main traditions from which reclamative theology in North America must draw. On one hand, it represents the best of our democratic legacy:

> The intellectual origins of the American radical tradition were rooted in men's effort to make a way of life at once free and communal. What held together these dissenters from the capitalist consensus was more than ideology: it was also the daily practice of libertarian and fraternal attitudes in institution of their own making. The clubs, the unorthodox congregations, the fledgling trade-unions were the tangible means, in theological language the "works," by which revolutionaries kept alive their faith that men could live together in a radically different way. (Lynd, 1968:173)

On the other hand, it is a compelling analogue to the politics of land-based retribalization advocated in the narrative of biblical radicalism. Can we Christians rediscover "mustard seed faith" and its new/old wisdom, in order to help reconstruct a human future for Great Turtle Island?

E. THE TREE AT THE CENTER OF THE WORLD?
SONGLINES OF *AZTLÁN*

How might we re-place our Christian symbols in the soil of a land we love?

Second Isaiah, a prophet of exile who knew the pain of displacement, beckoned his people to join the hymn of Yahweh's sovereignty to the ancient love song of the vineyard:

> Sing to Yahweh a new song of praise
> from the ends of the earth!
> Let the sea roar and all that fills it,
> the coastlands and all their inhabitants.
> Let the desert and its towns lift up their voice.
>   (Is 42:10f)

This biblical intimation that the land sings its own song may be more than poetic. Bruce Chatwin (1988) has written about how traditional Aborigines find their way across the vast distances of the Australian outback by learning its "songlines" — chants associated with sacred sites and other distinctive characteristics of the land.[8] Is it possible that such songlines exist in every place? If so, we the dis-placed — ever trying to control and contain the land with topographical maps, surveyors sticks, and ideologies of ownership — have not had ears to hear them. Similarly Chief Sealth Suquamish once warned that European Americans would forever be haunted by the spirits of those who dwelt here before us on Great Turtle Island: "At night, when the streets of your cities and villages are silent and deserted, they will throng with the host that once filled, and still love, this land; the white man will never be alone" (in Churchill, 1983:77). Is it possible that such spirits do indeed dwell here? If so, we whose past has been devised and dismembered have not had eyes to see them. I am convinced not only that these beliefs at the heart of traditional culture speak the truth of Great Turtle Island but that they represent an ultimatum to Christians. Will we continue to ignore the songlines and to excommunicate the spirits of the land in which we dwell? Or can we learn to hear the songlines as essential verses in the earthsong of God's praise and to see the spirits as part of the great "cloud of witnesses" spoken of in scripture (Heb 12:1)?

What follows is an attempt to listen and look in the Southwest, "the coastland and the desert" that I inhabit. Now, I am no John Muir nature-mystic. I have lived most of my life in cities, rarely work in the garden, and know the streets and buildings of southern California far better than its arroyos and foothills. I am, in other words, a social product of all the forces of urban alienation I have written about in this book. Nevertheless the love *in* this land has summoned in me a love *for* it. This love was buried in my soul like the smallest of seeds, placed there by ancestors I never knew. The nights and days of my life have passed and the seed has grown, "I know not how" (Mk 4:27). The more that seed comes to flower, the more I believe that a truly contextual theology must pay attention not only to history and to social location, but to the song-lines of the land. It was, after all, the land from which and for which we were created (Gen 1:26; 2:7). The task of re-placed theology is to reclaim symbols of redemption that are indigenous to the bioregion in which the church dwells, to remember the stories of the peoples of the land, and to sing anew its old songs. These can then be woven together with the symbols, stories, and songs of biblical radicalism. This will necessarily be a local, even personal exercise. My reflections below, therefore, may or may not speak to readers from other regions. I would simply invite them to learn and to re-claim the songlines of their own place.

1. Reemplazo: *Mendosa's Journey*

Francisco Mendosa, *mi abuelo!* What does it mean that you left the Azores, those remote Atlantic islands that in antiquity had inspired Edenic dreaming of *Insulae Fortunatae*, only to end up in California, another place that once fired mythic island dreaming?[9] Was it Cortés's dream of gold that drew you away into the frenzy of 1848? Or was yours a flight from oppression, or perhaps conscription? Or was your journey one of neither conquest nor conscience but simply of restlessness? What stories would that old leather chest in my mother's living room tell of your trip up from Veracruz, Mexico, to the little California boomtown of Sonora? What did you see, and what did you feel, when you arrived in a land on the cusp of an Indo-Hispanic past and a federal future? I will never know the answer to these questions, Francisco. I know only that you did not find *Cíbola* here, ending up just another poor *inmigrante* doing day labor in the gardens of those who did strike it rich. And that you married Ynez Nuñez, a *Californiana,* and that little of the *mestizaje* of your descendants survives. The only gold you found, abuelo, and all that remains to me more than a century later, is in the brilliant shine of golden poppies in the spring and in the dry summer grass of those western Sierra foothills where you are buried. It is enough. For in them are the true riches of Aztlán.

Aztlán was the ancient, mythic name by which Indians throughout Mexico referred to

the Edenic place of origin of the *Mexica* (the Aztecs). Aztlán, mean-ing either 'land of the herons' or 'land of whiteness' was an old name by Cortés' arrival. According to their own histories, the Aztecs had left that homeland, located somewhere in the north, in 1168 and journeyed to the lakes where in 1325 they founded Tenochtitlán. After the Spanish conquest Indian, mestizo and Spanish chroniclers, relying on native infor-mants, recorded the legend of Aztlán ... [and] influenced by the myth of the golden north, placed Aztlán in the Southwest. (Chávez, 1984:8)

John Chávez notes that although this geographical attribution was probably inaccurate, "this error would later lead Chicanos to refer to the Southwest as Aztlán, an application of the name that would, nevertheless, be paradoxically appropriate." It was appropriate because the notion of Aztec descendants "returning" to the Southwest inspired many Mexican-American activists in the 1960s to celebrate, rather than lament, their *mestizaje* (half-breed Indian and Hispanic roots). *Reconquista.*

But it is neither historical nor geographical precision that makes Aztlán an important symbol for reclamative theology; it is the richness of its geo-cultural texture. Writer Francisco Alarcón has suggested that "awareness of our Mesoamerican past should be projected into our present and our future in radically new ways": "I have called this praxis *mesticismo,* which purposely combines *Mestizo* and *misticismo* ('mysticism'), in order to differentiate it from *mestizaje. Mesticismo* comes out of the experiences that the dominant cultures have confined to the realm of 'other' and the 'marginal,' those condemned to live dangerously in psychological and cultural borderlands" (1992:36). He is echoed by Gloria Anzaldúa, who calls the U.S.-Mexico border an open wound, *"una herida abierta* where the Third World grates against the first and bleeds. And before a scab forms it hemorrhages again, the lifeblood of two worlds merging to form a third country — a border culture. . . . A borderland is a vague and undetermined place created by the emotional residue of an unnatural boundary" (1987:3). I realize now that the descendants of Mendosa too dwelled in this psychological and cultural borderland. My father, Mendosa's only great-grandson, was half-Californio.[10] He grew up speaking Spanish with his abuela Guerena, with whom he shared a room. But he was at the same time surrounded in San Francisco by the gringo's dream of middle-class prosperity. In the end he crossed over, trading away all but fragments of his *raza* in order to assimilate into the upwardly mobile world of business. My upbringing affirmed scarcely more *mestizaje* than a love for mariachis and chiles rellenos (above, 5,D). A fifth-generation Californian, but hardly Chicano, I inherited the "vague and undetermined" character of a borderland that is now fully colonized by the dominant culture. But *mesticismo* survived in my bones.

Abuelo, yo continúo su viaje. When I was ten years old we took, along with several other families from our neighborhood, the first of several annual camping trips to the Hollister ranch. This land, north of Santa Barbara and immediately south of Point Conception, was strictly private; for a few precious years we had access because of our parents' business contacts. It was there, among the pristine beaches and coastal hills, that I first recall awakening to mesticismo. The profound connection I felt to those ranchlands could be accounted for by the fact that they reflect the matchless beauty of central California the way it was, before it was overrun with development. It was also unquestionably due to the fact that this coastline was home to the best waves in the state — and as a teenager, surfing was my passion, baptizing me in the spirit of the coastlands. Yet my connection to this place somehow went deeper. It took me twenty years to discover how and why.

While in New Zealand/Aotearoa doing Nuclear Free and Independent Pacific work in 1985, some Maori colleagues invited me to join them on a trip to Cape Reinga. We traveled to the tip of the North Island, a hundred kilometers on dirt roads beyond the northernmost town of Kaitaia. At the cape I stood in silence, listening to my friends recite Maori chants, staring out beyond the windswept bluffs at the huge watery seam stretching to the horizon, as the Pacific met the Tasman Sea. It was explained to me how a certain tree below us was the place where the spirits of the Maori departed jump off to begin the great undersea journey to the spiritworld of *Havaiki.* I could sense palpably the *mana* (power) of this sacred land. I felt safe here. But there was also a certain sense of déjà vu. Slowly but surely it dawned on me: This place looked — and felt — exactly like Point Conception. *Refugio.*

I learned later that those Santa Barbara ranchlands I so love had been named by Spanish settlers after Nuestra Señora del Refugio, "Our Lady of Refuge."[11] And before them, local Chumash named their villages along this coast Shisholop and Lisil (Librado, 1981). To them, Point Conception was the "Western Gate," a sacred site where the departed traveled on to the spirit world.

> My heart goes to the other world;
> my heart goes to the ocean foam. (Margolin, 1981:67)

This verse from an old Cupeño Indian funeral dirge articulates what I felt at Cape Reinga, and before it at Point Conception. I was beginning to learn an ancient songline. *Mesticismo.*

That moment was a quiet turning point in my life, though I did not yet know how or why. I had fled to the Pacific as an exile, my world and my discipleship a shambles in the wake of a broken community and failed marriage. My island friends had offered me hospitality, and I was surrounded by the ocean I love, but I had not been able to shake my depression. Yet when I returned to California immediately after that day at Cape Reinga, I was feeling hope for the first time in several years. The months that followed were spent preparing to go back to Australia for a longer stint, but two events portended otherwise. I spent my thirty-first birthday in Baja California with my father, drinking tequila and playing cards and eating *pulpo en su tinta* at La Bufadora. It was the last true communion I would have with him. A week later I was on a flight from San Francisco to Los Angeles and found myself gazing down from the window, intently searching the coastline below for a glimpse of Point Conception. I wrote:

> Western Gate!
> I have not stood with you enough,
> wept for you too much.
> What have they done to you? And me.
> My memories, like your hills, are being bulldozed.
> We risked hospitality. We were pillaged.

From this height you are so beautiful!
The distances hide our blemishes.
Those who came later will never know how we were.

But the life you give from the Four Directions —
     swept in by swell and storm,
     from the north in winter and from the south in
        summer,
     shining in the sunrise when desert winds blow,
     and in the sunset after spring squalls,
     those reminders of the old Freedom,
     which alone can erode the high walls of Civilization
     that colonized your shores and my mind,
     brutalized us and left us for dead —
I feel it still.
And on any other shore I will be a guest,
ausente de mi propio país.

A few months later I was sitting on a beach in Sydney, Australia, staring east across the ocean. I realized my heart would not abide. I abruptly abandoned my new job and returned to Los Angeles, from whence I had fled two decades earlier. *Reemplazo.*

The feeling of my homecoming is best captured in the song "On Your Shore" by the Irish balladeer Enya:

And so, this is where I should be now
Days and nights falling by me.
I know of a dream I should be holding
Days and nights falling by me.
Soft blue horizons
reach far into my childhood days
as you are rising
to bring me my forgotten ways.
Strange how I falter
to find I'm standing in deep water
Strange how my heart beats
to find I'm standing on your shore.

Since returning to Los Angeles I have, with increasing intentionality, re-placed myself in this soil. Over the past six years I have worked on excavating the buried layers of culture and history in this land and in myself, to understand my connection to, and severance from, Aztlán. I have stood on the mesas of Acoma and Hovenweep, walked amid the red rock of Canyon de Chelly and Zion, sat by the running waters of the Rio Chama and Snowmass creek — and felt the same mesticismo, learned more songlines. And though I have only just begun this journey, it has brought me to the place where I can sit beneath the oak tree and reclaim the ceremony (above, Prologue; below, Epilogue).

2. Teología de los Robles

"The ultimate irony of today," writes Alarcón, "is that five hundred years after the first landing of Columbus, America remains as mysterious as ever and a huge *terra incognita* for many who act and live as if they had just jumped ashore." He queries: "Why not envision a new eco-poetics grounded in a heritage thousands of years old that upholds that everything in the universe is sacred? Ancient Native paradigms could possibly offer some viable alternatives to modern dilemmas. Old keys could open new doors" (1992:37). If we Christians ignore the songlines and spirits of the places where we dwell, we will perpetuate a *teología extranjera* (alien, out of place) whose roots lie in the imperial tradition of *conquista*. The challenge for the church is to re-place our theological discourse, to create symbolic space for us to imagine and work for re-placed societies, economies, and politics. That, suggests Gary Snyder, is the true task of reconstructive citizenship on Turtle Island.

I close this chapter, then, by suggesting a few possible characteristics of a theology specific to the Pacific Southwest, using the three concentric "spheres" of a bioregional map suggested by Sale.[12] I intend this only as a beginning attempt to name the promise and the pain within each sphere: the wounds (*heridas*), the discipleship communities of refuge (*refugios*), and the "angels" of place.

Aztlán. As I am (somewhat playfully) defining it, Aztlán is boundaried as follows: by the Colorado Plateau, Great Basin and Trinity Alps to the north, the Rocky and Sangre de Cristo mountains to the east, the Pacific ocean to the west and the great Sonora desert to the south. As an "ecoregion" it is characterized predominantly by desert climes and high tablelands punctuated by scattered river valleys and dramatic mountain ranges. Politically it corresponds roughly to the "Southwest" territories ceded to the U.S. by Mexico in the 1848 Treaty of Guadalupe-Hidalgo (New Mexico, Colorado, Arizona, and California). Yet within this conquered region are many Indian peoples and nations who have survived the Spanish and American invasion, from the vast Navajo reservation to the scattered Shoshone clans. At the geo-symbolic heart of Aztlán lie the four sacred mountains of the Dineh.

So many *heridas* fester in this land of enchantment: Los Alamos Weapons Laboratory, where the bomb was conceived; the Trinity site, where it was born; the Nevada test site, where it still spawns; and countless military-industrial installations, each surrounded by webs of economic dependence. The blight of strip-mining, uranium tailings, and huge dams is everywhere evident, monuments to theft and Promethean dreams. The oppression of Indian and mestizo peoples continues in every corner of Aztlán. Yet despite the impact of a century and a half of brutal resource extraction, massive water projects, and multiplying urban sprawls, despite four centuries of colonization, the Southwest remains a hard land that is still relatively undomesticated. Much of its terrain is "undeveloped," and its human population, though richly diverse, is still comparatively sparse. *In order to live at peace, find a place that no one else wants, and make your home there.* This was the philosophy that brought the Hopi to their mesas, and it represents perhaps the oldest human wisdom on this continent.

The promise of Aztlán, as I have suggested above (10,C,D), is embodied in the persistence and strength of this Indo-Hispanic legacy. Here the mix of human colors mirrors the brown and red of the land, and its songlines are preserved in the culture of *acequias* and *santos,* of *pueblos* and *kachinas.* And along the long stretches of road in the Southwest one finds discipleship *refugios* that offer hospitality and conspiracy:

- St. Benedict's monastery in the valley of Mt. Sopris, on the high western slopes of the Colorado Rockies, a place of refuge for brother Ladon and his friends;
- the Center for Action and Contemplation in the South Valley of Albuquerque, a place where inward and outward journeys of faith are nurtured;
- the good people of the Saguaro Juniper covenant in Tucson, goatwalkers and keepers of the land;
- the radical Franciscans and others who tend the fires of witness against the bomb at the Nevada Desert Experience in Las Vegas.

Watching over all this pain and promise is the angel of Aztlán, who surely is Nuestra Señora de Guadalupe. Though for some Latinos, Guadalupe is an ambiguous symbol of an oppressive church, I agree with those who "read" her as a symbol of the church in solidarity with the poor. Just as Cortés sowed the seeds of *conquista* in the New World, so did Guadalupe appear to Juan Diego sowing the seeds of *conscience.*[13]

California. Here is where my own deepest bioregional loyalties lie. California is where Aztlán meets the sea, a diverse coastal georegion west of the Sierra Nevada range and the Mojave desert, stretching north and south from Cape Mendocino to Cabo San Lucas. Gary Snyder points out that this is a diverse place, hosting all ten of the world's major soils, hundreds of natural communities and thousands of flora types, and more plant diversity than all of the central and northeastern parts of U.S. and Canada combined. He also reminds us that the state includes at least six distinct morphoregions: "If a relationship to place is like a marriage, then the Yankee establishment of a jurisdiction called California was like a shotgun wedding with six sisters taken as one wife" (1992:67).

To describe the promise and pain of this place would take another book. The assaults upon her songlines and insults to her spirits are too numerous to catalog; two examples must suffice. One is Vandenburg Air Force Base, the front end of the Pacific Missile Testing Range, a profound violation to the Western Gate it lies just north of. Instead of sending spirits on to rest, Vandenburg test-launches ICBMs far out into the Pacific. These messengers of death land in

Kwajalein lagoon in the northern Marshall Islands, and there too the U.S. military has driven indigenous people from their beloved land (G. Johnson, 1984). I have seen firsthand the pain of both ends of this dis-placement, an unconscionable sacrifice to the gods of metal. The other example is even closer to home — the Laguna hills of south Orange County. In my teenage years I loved to walk among the coastal canyons of this area and surf in front of its gentle bluffs. These peaceful rolling foothills were first the southernmost habitat of the Gabrielino peoples (B. Miller, 1991), then the domain of the old San Joaquin and Niguel land grants, and finally of the Irvine Ranch. Now they are buried beneath endless rows of high-priced homes and condominiums. Thanks to the ruthless alchemy of real estate profiteers, their golden beauty has been transformed into the obscene, gated suburban ghetto of Mission Viejo and the bourgeois "Riviera" of greater Laguna. The rape of Vandenburg and Laguna are *heridas* that provoke in me particular sadness, rage, and shame, because neither has sustained the attention of organized resistance. Indeed I often question why my own work for justice has always focused elsewhere, why I have not fought more directly for land that I love.

Yet my work around the state has woven me into the fabric of friendship among the *refugios* of hope:

- the Trappistine women at Redwoods Monastery in the Sinkyone wilderness of northern California, where they help lead the struggle to save the "Lost Coast";
- small discipleship communities and Catholic Worker houses that have arisen and folded around the San Francisco Bay area, among which my own, Bartimaeus, was one;
- friends at the Resource Center for Nonviolence in Santa Cruz, who continue to teach and experiment with the truth of satyagraha;
- my AFSC colleague Roberto Martínez, who daily struggles to mitigate the violence of the border patrol at the San Diego border war zone in his work to defend the rights of undocumented immigrants (above, 9,E).

Above all, the land itself offers refuge and renewal, ever offering its love, waiting for us to return it.

As for the angel of California, I do not know her name. I believe, however, that it is written on the wall of a cave in the mountains not far from the Western Gate, a Chumash holy site tucked away in the shady high recesses of an oak-studded canyon. We cannot decipher its idiom because our ancestors destroyed the *antap* culture that drew the magnificent pictographs in Painted Cave.[14] But Georgiana Sanchez reminds us in her poem "Chumash Man" that the mesticismo remains:

"Shoo-mash," he says / and when he says it
I think of ancient sea lion hunts
and salt spray windswept across my face

They tell him / his people are dead / "Terminated"
It's official / U.S. rubber-stamped official
CHUMASH: *Terminated*
a People who died / they say
a case for anthropologists
Ah, but this old one / this old one whose face is
ancient prayers come to rest
this old one knows / who he is
"Shoo-mash," he says
and somewhere sea lions still gather
along the California coast
and salt spray / rises / rainbow mist
above the constant breaking / of the waves.

                                        (Clinton et al, 1989:42)

My deepest desire is to relearn the forgotten songlines of this place and to defend what is left.

Los Angeles. Finally, a word about the city in which I live and work, nestled in the morphoregion south of the Tehachapi Mountains that is the southern California basin (McWilliams, 1946:3ff). It *can* be a place of desert radiance — when the Santa Anas blow, revealing the majestic San Gabriels; when the soft afternoon air of the east valleys are unchoked by smog; when the western beaches north of Malibu are unchoked by tourists. I have already written a great deal about the *heridas* of my city (above, 3,A; 7,B). Rather than reiterating, let me simply refer again to Fair Oaks Avenue, the symbol of my own journey from the pleasant but insular suburban enclave where I grew up to the poor neighborhoods of Northwest Pasadena where I work today (above, 7,D). The social architecture that keeps those two communities apart is still intact along the four miles up Fair Oaks, strengthened now by the barrier of a freeway and by pricey urban redevelopment in Old Town Pasadena. There are few oak trees left along the avenue, and the once-wild Arroyo Seco it parallels is now fully paved over.

Yet each day on my way to work I pass Eagle Rock, a sacred site to the Gabrielino. I cross old Red Car right-of-ways that remind me Los Angeles used to have the best urban transit system in the country instead of the worst (see W. Myers, 1976). And I see in my neighborhood the multicultural promise of nuestra America (above, 10,D). I am grateful to be able to share the promise and pain of this city with sisters and brothers at refugios such as the Catholic Worker, Dolores Mission, United University Church, and many other unheralded communities of faith committed to discipleship in this place. I am equally grateful for all those of diverse conviction in Los Angeles whom I have had the privilege of collaborating with in the work of resistance, humanization, advocacy, and reconstruction.

Who is the angel of the City of Angels? I believe it just might be the spirit of Luis Olivares, who passed on this spring. A Mexican-American priest from

San Antonio, Luis embodied the promise of Aztlán. His conversion to the God of the poor came while working with the United Farm Workers movement in the 1960s. In the 1970s he spearheaded community organizing throughout East Los Angeles, and in the 1980s he became the pastor of our Lady Queen of Angels parish in the downtown *placita,* which he turned into a refugio for thousands of Central American and Mexican immigrants. Luis was a vigorous critic of U.S. policy in Central America and a practitioner of *acompañamiento* while under threat by death squads — both there and here. I remember the Sunday Luis said his final mass, a fine June morning three years ago as I write. The old church was packed and suffocatingly hot, and Luis, beginning at last to succumb to his battle with AIDS, looked old and haggard in his wheelchair next to the altar. During mass everyone was crying, and it seemed as if all the tears of Aztlán's poor — Central Americans and Mexicans, Chicanos and immigrant rights supporters — were mingling in a lament of heartbreak. Yet no sooner had the mass ended than a huge fiesta commenced in the patio, as the hope Padre Olivares had brought was celebrated in true Latin style. Afterward, wrung out by emotion, we went across the street to the *placita* to rest under the huge oak tree. Presently a Chicano Aztec dance troupe in full costume began dancing, choosing to perform right in front of a bronze statue of Carlos III, the Spanish king who ordered the colonization of America del norte. Looking back now on that morning, I realize I had witnessed the war of myths at the heart of Aztlán. Luis Olivares, *¡presente!*

Christian theology in the Southwest has much to learn from such heridas and refugios. But the songlines of the land and the ancient traditions that preceded us here should also shape our discourse. "Christ and Quetzalcoatl are not opposing spiritual figures," writes novelist Rudolfo Anaya; "*los santos* of the Catholic church... merge with and share the sacred space of the Kachinas of the Indian pueblos" (1992:26). Affirming Quetzalcoatl is not to abandon Christian tradition for trendy neopaganism, nor do Protestants forsake their legacy by honoring Nuestra Señora de Guadalupe. It is a matter of *reemplazo.* Christian theology in pursuit of a universalist discourse has become not only idealist and abstract but docetic. It must be regrounded in incarnational faith: Immanuel, God among us in this place. The icons of New Mexican artist Robert Lentz (1992) express beautifully the rich potential for resymbolizing Christianity in the Southwest.

But what about the cross, which must remain at the center of a theology of radical discipleship? Anaya has an interesting suggestion: "The tree, or the tree of life, is also a dominant symbol of the Americas, and its syncretic image combines the tree of Quetzalcoatl and the cross of Christ. My ancestors nourished the tree of life; now it is up to me to care for all it symbolizes" (1992:27). It is a compelling analogy. Just as the cross keeps Christian faith rooted in the practice of discipleship and solidarity with the poor, so can the tree of life keep us rooted in the soil of real and beloved places. Just as the cross takes differing forms in varying contexts, so will the tree of life differ from georegion to georegion. In Arizona it might be the saguaro cactus, in northern California, the redwood, and in Baja, the yucca. But in central and southern California, the tree of life is most assuredly the oak tree.

California is home to nine species of oak trees (*genus Quercus*): "They occur from the Oregon border to Baja California and are found on offshore islands, along the coast, over most of the foothills, and throughout the valleys and high mountains of the state's interior" (Pavlik et al, 1991:9). The noble Coast Live Oak (*Quercus agrifolia*), with its magnificent gnarled and spreading architecture, is the species I know and love best, since it is the most widespread from the coastal plains and protected bluffs to the inland arroyos and foothills of central and southern California (ibid:25f). To "read" the oak is to understand the land and people of this place; it is thus a theological text. In conclusion, therefore, I propose a *teología de los robles*.

No matter how far one digs through the cultural-historical strata of this place, the oak is always there. "The human history of California began in the shade of her native oaks. Acorn foods sustained many diverse Indian cultures that evolved and thrived among the woodlands for centuries.... It is not surprising that oaks were revered by native Californians, held sacred in elaborate acorn ceremonies, and depicted as symbols of fertility, strength, and oneness with the earth" (ibid:95). Acorns, much more nutritious than basic European foodstuffs, represented the staple of the Indian diet in most places, where economic life centered around gathering and storing them. "Acorns were second only to salt among the food items most frequently traded among native Californians" (ibid:97), and they were used as well for medicine, dyes, toys, and music. Acorns represented to some tribes the *ikxareyavs* (spirit people) and were present in ritual life from birth (some tribes tied an infant's umbilical cord to the branches of an oak) to death (mourners were purified by the smoke of oak boughs and painted with acorn ash; ibid:101f).

What was here for the Indian was here for the Spaniard. When Sebastián Vizcaíno, the mariner who surveyed Alta California in 1602, landed at Monterey in December, his party held the first mass in this place under the shade of a huge oak.[15] "A large, deep cross was cut into the tree's trunk, which in effect became the Pacific coast equivalent of Plymouth Rock" (ibid:103). This same tree was visited again in 1770 by Junípero Serra, who again celebrated mass under it. Two years ago I visited Mission San Antonio, the third of the twenty-one missions established by Serra; he called it San Antonio de la Cañada de los Robles and hung its bell from the branches of an oak (Barton, 1980:61ff). Today the site is surrounded by a military base, yet its several acres have remained relatively untouched since the time of the Franciscans. One can still see the irrigation beds that piped down water from the hills and can still walk quietly among adobe ruins. I remember that the valley was carpeted with flowers that day and that we took refuge from the hot midday sun under an old spreading oak. Songlines.

And the oaks were here for the Yankees too. Not too far from where I live now is a plaque commemorating a tree that no longer stands. Under the so-called Oak of Peace, it reads, General Andres Pico surrendered to Colonel John

Fremont, ending the U.S. war with Mexico in 1847 and beginning the era of federal occupation. I grew up in an oak forest — that is, what was once an oak forest, before it was turned, early in the century, into a suburban neighborhood. But many of the trees were preserved; homes and even streets were built around them, streets with names like Los Robles and Oak Knoll and Edgewood. The house of my childhood was surrounded by extraordinarily beautiful oaks; my mother tended them lovingly. I spent many hours gazing up at them, and dreaming. But my neighborhood was, as I have said, a privileged exception. Because whatever else statehood has meant for California, it has brought a holocaust upon the native oaks. The golden hills and dry valleys were stripped of these wonderful trees first for firewood, then for construction materials, then for farming and grazing, and finally for housing developments. "Since the 1940s, California has lost more than one million acres of oak woodland as a result of rangeland clearing and agricultural conversion. Projections indicate that population growth — and the inevitable suburbanization that accompanies it — may claim another quarter million oak-covered acres by the year 2010" (Pavlik et al, 1991:121). For every tree that is ripped out, we who live on this land become increasingly uprooted. The native oak is now an endangered species. If we lose this tree of life, the songlines will cease, and the land will die.

The sacred tree at the center of the world. This is what Bruce Bartón called the cross planted by Serra in the oak-studded hills above San Diego in 1769 (1980:40). There is something deeply attractive about correlating the Indian tree of life with the cross. I imagine the oak as the new symbolic center for a re-placed church in California. But for this to be a redemptive, not merely a rhetorical, symbolic transformation, we Christians will need to go on a vision quest back to that first communion under the Monterey oak. For there is still *conquista* in our bones and not enough *conscience* at hand.

Hanging in my study is a photograph of an old Live Oak taken back in Tajiguas Canyon north of Santa Barbara, another place my family used to camp. Called by locals the Indian tree, one can still make out in its trunk two carved figures, thought to be a rendering of a Chumash neophyte receiving communion from a Spanish padre. Perhaps if Fray Serra and his descendants had understood and practiced a fundamental identification between cross and tree, rather than between cross and sword, the history of California would have been different. Perhaps those Indians would not have had to give back the Bible to Pope John Paul II, because the cross would have been a sign of solidarity rather than a symbol "which attacked the Indian soul" (above, Introduction, B). But that is not how it happened. And today, the *locus imperii* is no more hospitable to *Quercus agrifolia* than it is to the via crucis.

In this land of the Western Gate, therefore, "whoever would follow Jesus must take up" the tree of life as well. Ours must be also a *via roble*. For the Great Economy is like an acorn that, though small, when pressed into the earth grows up and puts forth large branches. *El roble sagrado al centro del mundo.* By it we can practice mesticismo, and in its great canopy "all the birds of the air can find a nest."

NOTES

1. Mary Ann Tolbert points out that "the two parables in Mark present in concise, summary form the Gospel's view of Jesus: he is the Sower of the Word and the Heir of the Vineyard.... Together they make up the Gospel's basic narrative Christology" (1989:122). Similarly Joseph Blenkinsopp writes that "the poem about the pleasant vineyard in the 'Isaian apocalypse' (27:2–5)... is clearly related to the song of the vineyard in the first part of the book (5:1–7), and is related as commentary to text" (1983:264). The text reads:

> On that day, sing of the pleasant vineyard!
> I Yahweh am its keeper;
> every moment I water it for fear its leaves should fall;
> Night and day I watch over it. I am angry no longer.
> If thorns and briars come I will declare war on them,
> I will burn them all.
> But if they would shelter under my protection,
> let them make their peace with me. (Is 27:2–5)

Do the "choking thorns" of the sower parable (Mk 4:7) allude to this song (cf Is 34:13)? In favor of this connection would be the fact that Mk 4:19 identifies the thorns with the anxieties of affluence — thus reiterating the song's critique of the rich. This connection is made even more explicit in a parallel early Christian text, the *Similitudes of Hermes* (ca 100 C.E.): "And from the third mountain, which has thorns and thistles, are such believers as these. Of them are those who are rich and are mixed up with many affairs of business, for the thistles are the rich, and the thorns are those who are mixed up with various affairs of business." (See above, Chapter Six, n. 5.)

2. Fox's (1988) and Berry's work (1988, 1991, 1992) have engendered quite a conversation. Some good appreciations and critiques of Berry by Christian theologians can be found in Lonergan and Richards (1987). See also Moltmann (1985) and D. J. Hall (1986).

3. There have been some attempts to reground North America theological reflection. The Commission on Religion in Appalachia in Knoxville promotes grassroots regional theology, for example, and the work of several generations of Southern Christian writers, from Flannery O'Conner to Will Campbell, is gaining a wider audience. The most systematic recent effort at re-place-ment is Robert Schreiter's *Constructing Local Theologies* (1985), which I strongly commend for those interested in questions of methodology. A different approach is Bill Kellermann's proposal that churches should be discerning the "spirits and powers" at work in their respective urban contexts; his own exposition of the "angel of Detroit" is exemplary (1989a) and has influenced my own attempts (E,2).

4. The AFSC now publishes the *NIMBY Report* to help promote interaction and critique provincialism. But local environmental action remains the most crucial, because the most committed defenders of the land are always people who live on or near it. For example, in northern California an important statewide coalition has fought for years to try to keep logging interests from clear-cutting the last coastal groves of virgin Redwoods in the Sinkyone wilderness area. While in some urban environmental circles this struggle became a cause célèbre, it has been local residents who have led the struggle; though distant from the state capital and corporate offices, they coordinated every step of the campaign, from direct action to lobbying. Prominent among these are the Trappistine sisters at Redwoods Monastery in tiny rural Whitethorn. Living on

the edge of the "Lost Coast" area, they closely monitor developments, and their deep love for the place has led them more than once to put their political bodies in front of bulldozers.

5. For a basic bibliography on economic alternatives see Sale, 1985:197ff. An engaging and practical journal is *In Context: A Quarterly of Humane Sustainable Culture* (Bainbridge Is, WA). On regional planning see Branch (1988), Friedmann and Alonso (1975), Newmann (1991), Southgate and Disinger (1987), Meredith (1992), Altieri (1987) and Larrick (1991). On sustainable development and the environment see Ahmad et al (1989), Krutilla and Fisher (1985), McHarg (1992), Steiner (1991) and Redclift (1987). For an example of local small-scale, community-based economic development in Los Angeles, see Sheine (1992).

6. The Institute for Cultural Affairs (1981) works with Citizens Participation strategies in rural Mississippi and urban Chicago. The National Association for the Southern Poor has promoted the building of grassroots Community Congresses based on a matrix of representative units no larger than fifty persons. For a primer on citizen advocacy at the various levels of government within the federal system, see Armstrong (1992). It is worth noting that many of these same grassroots political strategies are emerging in Third World contexts, such as Brazil, where oppositional movements are turning away from the macro-strategies of Marxism toward more locally determined organizing (Barbé, 1987:78ff).

7. The story of the Dakota farmers is movingly recounted in the classic film *Northern Lights*. Sinclair's candidacy, defeated only after a concerted effort by the state's ruling elite, is analyzed in Mitchell (1992). The "Spit and Argue" club was an outdoor gathering begun in 1918 by retired, mostly Iowan, farmers. Folk were invited to discuss freely the issues of the day, and it grew into such a tradition that the city had to make official space for it and rename it the "University by the Sea." For some fifty years this local exercise in democratic conversation generated "a lot of jawboning" and at least one consequential brainstorm: "Long Beach physician Francis Townsend's idea of a national pension plan of $200 a month for citizens older than 60 got its start at one of the club meetings. In 1934, Townsend's plans spawned a political movement that spurred the creation of the Social Security Act" (Rasmussen, 1993:B3).

8. Chatwin describes "the labyrinth of invisible pathways which meander all over Australia and are known to Europeans as 'Dreaming-tracks' or 'Songlines'" thus:

Aboriginal Creation myths tell of the legendary totemic beings who had wandered over the continent in the Dreamtime, singing out the name of everything that crossed their path — birds, animals, plants, rocks, waterholes — and so singing the world into existence.... Each totemic ancestor, while travelling through the country, was thought to have scattered a trail of words and musical notes along the line of his footprints, and these Dreaming-tracks lay over the land as "ways" of communication between the most far-flung tribes.... In theory, at least, the whole of Australia could be read as a musical score. There was hardly a rock or creek in the country that could not or had not been sung. (1988:2,13)

9. Early fifteenth-century Catalan maps identified Atlantic islands far to the west as the *Insulae Fortunatae* spoken of by Pliny, called by Plutarch the site of terrestrial paradise (Sanders, 1992:32ff). Sanders contends that the myth may have obliquely been referring to the Azores, or even "some dim notion of the Americas," and believes this "highly suggestive convergence of promised lands in the middle of the vast Ocean Sea" fired the imaginations of mariners. In any case, along with the Canary and Madeira

islands, the Azores were found by the Portuguese in 1432 and became, ironically, the first victims of the European colonization of the "New World."

California is a name that is contrived, like so much of the exotic culture that has taken residence here. It comes from an early sixteenth-century Iberian novel by Garci de Montalvo, which described an island "on the right hand of the Indies, called California, very close to the region of the terrestrial paradise." This mythical island is populated by dark-skinned, Amazonlike women warriors who fight with Turkish infidels against the Christian heros of Montalvo's tale; Queen Calafia, however, converts to Christianity after her defeat (Sanders, 1992:139f). Here there is at least poetic justice, for the conquistador Hernán Cortés, unsatisfied with the looting of Mexico City, shortly thereafter set sail from the Pacific side to find Calafia. He found instead the Baja peninsula, and there Cortés's dreams of gold, like Coronado's, were broken by desert disappointments.

10. *Californio* is the term given to Hispano-Mexican Californians before and after U.S. occupation. For the best narratives concerning this legacy see Pitt (1966), Rios-Bustamante and Castillo (1986), and Starr (1973).

11. Much of coastal central and southern California was allocated to private ranchos through 813 land grants given by the Mexican government after the secularization of the missions in the 1830s. After U.S. occupation in 1848, many Mexican land claims were dismantled through courts established by the Land Act of 1851; because of the different legal, cultural, and economic notions of land measurement, ownership, and use, many Mexicans were disinherited (Beck and Haase, 1974:24). Nuestra Señora del Refugio was one of 25 grazing concessions and was granted to the soldier José Francisco Ortega, a member of the Portolá expedition of 1769 who is considered the first European to see San Francisco Bay (Marinacci, 1980:112).

12. Sale distinguishes three spheres: an *ecoregion* has the broadest circumference, "taking its character from the broadest distribution of native vegetation and soil types"; within this are *georegions,* which share "physiographic features such as river basins, valleys and mountain ranges, and often some special floral and faunal traits" and which are often defined by watersheds; and again within these are *morphoregions,* such as a river basin (1985:56ff). I am taking poetic license by correlating the three spheres of Aztlán, California, and Los Angeles to Sale's rubrics, since they are considerably larger than his definitions and do not technically fit them. For reasons ecoregional and cultural (and perhaps also subjective and provincial), I am excluding Texas and including Baja California, southern Utah, Nevada, and northern California in my definition of Aztlán. On the post-Columbian history of the Southwest see Spicer (1962) and Chávez (1984).

13. "The Virgin of Spanish Catholicism and the Aztec Tonantzin culminate in the powerful and all-loving Virgen de Guadalupe" (Anaya, 1992:26). On Guadalupe in Mexican and Chicano popular religion see Guerrero (1987) and Romero (1991). For a Quincentenary reading of the *Virgen* see McKenzie's "¡Viva La Guadalupana!" (1992). For a recent attempt to integrate broadly Catholic and Native American traditions see S. Hall (1992).

14. This unassuming site off an old county road north of Santa Barbara is considered perhaps the most spectacular pictograph site in North America (see Hudson, 1982). The *antap* were shamans; for popular works on the Chumash see B. Miller (1988), Gibson (1991), and Eargle (1986).

15. The Spaniards were taken with the California oaks, reflected in many place names. Was it a primal natural symbol for them? Hugh Thomas writes of Spain: "Politically, from the early Middle Ages at least, assemblies composed of representatives of all men over 21 would meet every two years under an oak tree at Guernica, in Vizcaya.

There, the Monarch, or more usually his representative, would swear to respect Basque rights. An executive council would then be elected by lot to rule for the next two years. Both the oak tree and the city of Guernica acquired a sanctity for the Basques, suggesting a transference to political life of an ancient worship of the oak" (1961:54).

In *The Rembrant Bible*, edited by Oswald Goetz, NY: Greystone Press, 1941

"The Agony in the Garden" by Rembrant van Rijn. Pen drawing ca. 1658. Kunsthalle, Hamburg.

Part Five

Reflection

"Do you not care that we are perishing?"
Mk 4:38

Reconstruction is the work of generations. With our world balanced on the scales, will history allow radical change, or will the explosive power inherent in our social contradictions cause us to self-destruct? Part Five offers closing reflections on what traditional theology calls eschatological hope and divine grace.

Chapter Twelve asks what it means to hope for historical redemption without the delusions of Progress, the unifying principle of modernity. We are called to "stay awake" to the realities of history and the vision of the Great Economy; we can do this only by practicing the "bifocal vision" of apocalyptic faith. The discipleship journey will take us deep into the storms of history, but it is there, not in the safe confines of religion, that we encounter Jesus. Chapter Thirteen concludes, like Mark's gospel, with a meditation on the final quandary before Jesus' tomb–that moment in which we are terrified that the narrative of radical discipleship cannot be reopened yet uncertain whether we really want it to continue. Apocalyptic faith invites us to "look again and see that the stone is rolled away" and to rediscover that the Jesus we abandoned in the Palace Courtyard is our companion on the Way of radical discipleship.

12

"Are You Not Strong Enough to Stay Awake?"

Insomniac Theology

There is a picture by Klee called "Angelus Novus." An angel is presented in it who looks as if he were about to move away from something at which he is staring. His eyes are wide open, his mouth agape, his wings are spread. The angel of history must look like that. His face is turned toward the past. Where a chain of events appears to us, he sees one single catastrophe which relentlessly piles wreckage upon wreckage, and hurls them before his feet. The angel would like to stay, awaken the dead, and make whole that which has been smashed. But a storm is blowing from Paradise; it has gotten caught in his wings, and it is so strong that the angel can no longer close them. The storm drives him irresistibly into the future to which his back is turned, while the pile of debris before him grows toward the sky. That which we name progress is this storm.

> Walter Benjamin,
> *Zur Kritik der Gewalt*

No one can pick up the cord that is plugged into the New Testament gospel of expectation without becoming shocked into a quarrel with himself and his own people.

> Carl Braaten,
> "And Now — Apocalyptic!"

An image from Desert Storm lingers. Shortly after the bombing of Iraq ceased, the Islamic Center here in Los Angeles circulated an amateur videotape, obtained through a contact in Jordan, that surveyed the civilian devastation.

387

Soundless, the tape moved jerkily from close-ups of mutilated women and children to unsteady panning of ruined mosques, schools, and homes. It confirmed what we had feared; as usual, the truth was difficult to look at. But I was particularly moved by one brief, silent moment in which an elderly Iraqi woman appeared, swathed in black, standing alone atop a small mountain of concrete rubble. Alternately she would bend down, pick up a piece of debris, and heave it aimlessly away, as if she knew her salvage efforts were futile but would not be deterred from this rite of grieving, this terrible labor of love. Then she would bend her head back and raise her arms toward the heavens in noiseless wailing. As if asking: "Do you not care if we perish?" (Mk 4:38).

The attention of imperial culture has long since moved on to other spectacles. But this anguished madonna has hung like an icon on the bare walls of my conscience, staring at me with her wordless lament. I see her as the angel of history, sorting halfheartedly through the ruins of Progress, trying to "awaken the dead," weeping and petitioning heaven, sifting through the debris in the hope that a human cry might yet be heard from underneath the wreckage of empire. Jesus too knows something about this lonely vigil.

"Are you asleep? Were you not *strong enough* to stay awake? Watch and pray that you do not go the way of temptation" (14:37f). Of all the queries posed by Jesus the Interlocutor to his disciples, this is the most unsettling. Peter, having just vowed he will never take refuge in Denial (14:31), is invited to keep vigil with Jesus alongside the angel of history. His task is to resist the imperial coma by remembering the wilderness testing and to practice prayer as dis-illusionment in order to face the via crucis. But this is such a difficult vigil to keep; the desire of our spirits so rarely seems a match for the fragility of our flesh. Indeed Mark's portrait in Gethsemane makes clear that Jesus himself is no aloof demigod, serenely reflecting on the mystery of human pathos. Quite the contrary, he is profoundly distressed that it has all come to this (14:33). Jesus does not want to face the music — "He prayed that the hour might pass" (14:35). He hopes desperately that there is some other way to change the world — "Please remove this cup" (14:36). But he remains awake, while the disciples fall asleep, no doubt dreaming of better times. So, when the Powers come, all the disciples can think to do is fight or flee, both of which merely strengthen the hand of the authorities (14:47, 50). Only Jesus embraces the via crucis.

"What I say to you I say to all: *Stay awake!*" (13:37). For the church, history is long and hard and lonely, as the last of Jesus' parables articulates empathetically. We have been placed in service of this "house for all peoples" — but it is not easy trying to maintain it against the storms of Progress. It often feels as if the architect of the house has simply gone away and left us to our own devices (13:34f). We don't have answers for all the world's questions, and we don't know when, or how, or if the architect will return and put an end to the suffering. All we have been told is to keep vigil at the door with the angel of history, to stay awake with Jesus in a world become Gethsemane. This invitation to insomniac theology is strange and difficult. To "progressive" activists it surely sounds like yet another religious rationalization for doing nothing to try to change anything. Does Christian faith, then, contrary to the argument of this book, finally call us to abandon the struggle *within* history for some blessed hope that will rescue us *from* it?

A. "WATCH!"
IS THERE HISTORY AFTER PROGRESS?

Is there a "nonprogressive" basis for revolutionary politics?

I began this book by acknowledging that we face a crisis of political imagination in the *locus imperii* on the eve of the twenty-first century, and that this crisis may well determine the future of the entire human project (Chapter One). I have attempted to sketch the outlines of a theology and a practice that confront this historical crisis honestly, that do not back away from the diagnosis that we need radical collective change, yet that also refuse to abandon the belief that we can reconstruct human societies. But sober assessment of our situation suggests that the realistic prospects for reclamation are dim; Lasch may be right that Prometheus and Narcissus have already led us much too far down the road of historical domination and manic-depression (above, Chapter Four). It seems appropriate therefore to conclude with a brief reflection on Mark's theological basis for hope. I am no philosopher of history, but it seems to me that Mark's apocalyptic faith, properly understood, represents a way to remain committed to historical transformation that yields neither to the Scylla of depressed pessimism nor the Charybdis of grandiose optimism.

How do we "read" our historical *kairos?* George Bush, in his 1992 State of the Union address, best expressed the point of view of those today who cannot envision a future without empire. The cold war did not just end, he argued; America *won* it. His conclusion was striking; the vindication of U.S. hegemony means that "history has resumed." On the other hand, a January 1993 essay by journalist Michael Ventura entitled "The World Riots" articulates the perspective of those who cannot envision a future *with* empire.

> We are at a unique moment in God's seemingly endless temper tantrum (sometimes called "History"): every paradigm on earth is falling apart at the same time.... Both in the human and the non-human or "natural" world, nothing is working, nothing is proving strong enough to withstand the onslaught of this historical moment. Rain forests and cities; tigers and street kids; belief in the sacred and belief in reason; democracy and totalitarianism; money and poverty are in an equal state of panic as the demise of one feeds on the demise of the other. (1993:8)

Ventura views the Los Angeles uprising as symptomatic of wider global chaos, and he cites more than two hundred cases of ecological or social upheaval that occurred around the world during 1992 to prove his point.

Ironically the very thing that divides these two perspectives also unites them. They agree that the dramatic events we are witnessing (what I have called the apocalyptic moments of Desert Storm and the Los Angeles uprising) represent a historical turning point; they simply disagree about the direction. Ventura fears that history is unraveling into a global riot. Bush triumphantly announces that the locomotive of history — temporarily stalled by Soviet-sponsored opposition to U.S. aims — is back on track. What they both assume, however, is that history should be an ascent. This unquestioned and unquestionable assumption is, of course, attributable to the ideology of Progress — the central and inviolable dogma of modernity. There simply is no history without Progress.

Christopher Lasch's *True and Only Heaven* offers an excellent critique of the ideology of Progress, which, underpinned by the capitalist drive for accumulation, gave "the promise of steady improvement with no foreseeable ending at all" (1991:47).

By Lasch's account, one of the key texts of modernity is Adam Smith's argument in *The Wealth of Nations* that the creation and satisfaction of new needs in the course of economic development is a process potentially without limit. From this claim flows nearly every belief and value at the core of the modern outlook: the primacy of efficiency and economic growth, the perception of nature as resource, the ethical priority of individual welfare, the definition of the good life in terms of leisure and abundance, and most important, the image of history as continuous moral and material progress. This is the worldview of the Enlightenment, Marx's no less than Adam Smith's. (Scialabba, 1991:29)

But Lasch argues that the West — where the consequences of industrialization, militarization, economic stratification, and, above all, environmental limits are finally catching up — must finally abandon the dream of ever-expanding (and trickling-down) wealth.

The belated discovery that the earth's ecology will no longer sustain an indefinite expansion of productive forces deals the final blow to the belief in progress. A more equitable distribution of wealth, it is now clear, requires at the same time a drastic reduction in the standard of living enjoyed by the rich nations and the privileged classes. Western nations can no longer hold up their standard of living and the enlightened, critical, and progressive culture that is entangled with it as an example for the rest of the world. (1991:529)

We now face the undesirable choice between socio-economic polarization at the cost of protracted political upheaval or more equitable distribution of wealth at the cost of less affluence. History, in other words, does not appear to be following either Adam Smith's script or Marx's. Hence the optimistic creed of

Progress has fallen on hard times in our generation. I will mention three traditions of disillusionment with Progress; significantly, all three focus on the failure of Marxism to provide a workable alternative to capitalism.

Melvin Lasky, an old liberal, argues in his voluminous *Utopia and Revolution* that Western liberalism, which invented Progress by overturning the political absolutism of royalist oligarchies, has been betrayed by the very revolutionary impulse it generated. "Where history has taken, I feel, a profound tragic turn is in the triple error: utopia conceived as a sterile monolithic harmony; revolution as a dogmatic commitment to total change and violent reconstruction; principles of hope and belief transmogrified into an orthodoxy incompatible with heretical dissent or critical opposition" (1976:xii). Lasky believes that revolutionary radicalism is the problem and that Enlightenment rationalism purged of utopian absolutism is the solution.

The criticism of Marxism from the Left agrees with Lasky's assessment that the track record of revolution has been dismal but disagrees that there can be Progress without it. During and after the Stalinist era, a whole generation of socialists lost faith in the "Old Left" because of Communism's betrayal of human freedom (expressed eloquently in Ignazio Silone's *Bread and Wine,* 1946). Then, just when apologists for technocracy such as Daniel Bell were announcing the "end of ideology," the New Left rehabilitated Marxist criticism (Marcuse, 1964). Yet in the wake of revolutions in the Third World, another generation became disenchanted by the fact that wherever state power had been seized through revolutionary violence, the old politics of militarist elitism were being reproduced by the new regimes (above, 8,B). This recent tradition of disaffection is reflected in the work of two French intellectuals, Gérard Chaliand's *Revolution in the Third World* (1978) and Bernard-Henri Lévy's *Barbarism with a Human Face* (1979). Lévy's dark and cynical lament articulates his sense of resignation:

> A gloomy and frozen wind sweeps the world and turns it to stone. A wind from the East or a wind from the West? I have no idea, after all, for I have lost my compass and my charts. Socialism or capitalism? The question no longer means very much when the worst is possible.... When the wheels of history have been blocked and the promise has become a whisper, it remains for rats like us to find a corner in the ruins and wait there in peace. How sweet to live before the new barbarism! (1979:191)

Just as "history has resumed" for Bush, it has ended for Lévy. With Marxism and liberalism equally bankrupt, he proclaims, "We must proclaim ourselves *anti-progressive*" (ibid:130). But he sees no future, only anomie.

A third tradition, represented, for instance, by Native American philosopher Vine Deloria, rejects Marxism not because of its excesses but because its critique of capitalism did not go far enough:

> Western thinkers are greatly agitated with the insights of Marxism and with good reason. If applied primarily to an analysis of the effects of in-

dustrialism, the segregation of wealth and power by a miniscule group of our species and their subsequent inhuman treatment of the rest of us, Marxism gives us significant insights into our condition.... [But] from the perspective of American Indians, I would argue, Marxism offers yet another group of cowboys riding around the same old rock. It is Western religion dressed in economist clothing, and shabby clothing it is. It accepts uncritically and ahistorically the worldview generated by some ancient Western trauma that our species is alienated from nature and then offers but another version of Messianism. (1983:135)

The problem with Marxism, contends Deloria, is that it never questioned the capitalist assumption that human society had to be "saved" from the limits of the land — what Lasch calls the "technological conquest of scarcity and the collective control over nature that seemed to be inherent in the productive machinery of modern societies" (on technology and Progress see Hopper, 1991). Both capitalist transnationalism and Marxist internationalism are anthropologically economist, historically positivist, and have expressed the progressive compulsion to control through domination.

Of the three traditions of disillusionment, I find Deloria's the most compelling. He correctly defines the problem as the absolutism of history-as-Progress, which neither capitalism nor Marxism fundamentally questions. Each "system" represented a materialist monism, believing it would be vindicated by historical necessity, which would relegate the other to the dustbin. There could be no other historical possibility than their own. Sure enough, in the wake of Communism's collapse, liberalism has been "vindicated" as the orthodox expression of Progress. It is no accident that everywhere around the industrialized and industrializing world political discourse is now firmly in the control of liberal social democrats. Surviving socialist regimes are being either inexorably swallowed by global capitalism or, like Cuba, ostracized and left to wither on the vine. And all nonprogressive movements for historical change are rejected out of hand. For example, "devolutionary" nationalists and minority groups (whether Fourth or First World) that aspire to withdraw or noncooperate with global capitalism are accused of being disruptive and/or escapist (above, 11,C). Any radically different social vision (e.g., bioregionalism, above, 11,D) is dismissed as utopian dreaming and historically irrelevant. This is the ultimate put-down by the ideology of Progress — for "u-topia" is a place that does not exist. Many have coped with this severe judgment by internalizing it, holding onto humane ideals only by abandoning the prospect of realizing them in history. This is most notably the case among nonliberal churches, for whom the kingdom of God is a strictly otherworldly, ahistorical alternative.

Political imagination today is thus profoundly hostage to a Progress that precludes the possibility of history apart from itself. Thierry Verhelst sums up the situation:

The West is currently being shaken to its very foundations by formidable doubts raised by the question of "progress." People in the West remember how, according to the classical myth, Prometheus ended up enchained by the gods, his liver devoured by a bird of prey, for having stolen from them the sacred fire of knowledge and technology. They wonder about the future and worry that we might have entered the Age of the Vulture, the age of stress, pollution and the nuclear threat. The age also of a certain despair, symbolized by the punk slogan which covers the walls of the cities of the North: "No Future!" (1990:52)

Indeed that despair, like Ventura's grim picture of history unraveling into a riot, expresses the depressive politics of Decline (Cole, 1981).

Recently another oppositional ideology has emerged: history as "Regress." The notion of humanity's descent from a primordial golden age was of course common in antiquity, but today we see it being resurrected by two otherwise radically divergent social movements: New Age and New Right adherents. Disgusted with Progress for different reasons, both simply posit its antithesis. The myth of a preindustrial, prepatriarchal paradise lost is promoted, for example, in Riane Eisler's remarkably successful *The Chalice and the Blade: Our History, Our Future* (1987), which popularizes the work of feminist anthropologist Marija Gimbutas on "egalitarian" neolithic societies. Rosemary Ruether correctly calls this a revision of the "fall story" and offers a thoughtful critique of neopaganism and the new cosmology (1992:143ff). The New Right, in contrast, posits a more recent fall from the golden age: Liberal humanism is to blame for America's departure from the ideals of the founding fathers and the "traditional family values" of (presumably) rural Protestant farmers. These traditions of Regress are critical of the present and romantic about the past yet offer little more than the politics of nostalgia.

But what if we make a decisive theological break with Progress as a dysfunctional, addictive, and totalitarian system? What if history-as-Progress is a massive narrative of denial, a socio-historical expression of a narcissistic disorder, a shame system writ large? In such a view, true believers in Progress such as Bush are captive to the grandiose illusion that history is a triumphant march up the evolutionary escalator. On the other hand, apostates such as Lévy who prophesy an end to history are merely expressing the depressive end of the pendulum. And those embracing the counternarrative of Regress are only inverting the pendulum, imagining they can escape the system by becoming its antithesis. Each of these ideological narratives can be plotted schematically on the shame system grid as shown on the following page.

PROGRESS narrates an ascent from an undeveloped state of nature to a "paradise" of technological and economic fulfillment; its prescription for historical contradiction is "just a little more development." REGRESS narrates an entropic descent from a "paradise" of lost innocence to a hell of alienation; its lament is, "If only we could get back." DECLINE narrates the optimistic premise of Progress but the pessimistic conclusion of Regress and despairs.

GRANDIOSE

Golden Age   Technological Age
Nature benevolent   Nature controlled
Human communion   Humans conscious

REGRESS

PROGRESS   *DECLINE*

Primitive Age   Age of Sin
Nature uncontrolled   Nature hostile
Humans preconscious   Human alienation

DEPRESSIVE

Our break would be theological because we would begin by rejecting the monistic claim that redemption lies within progressive history. Verhelst understands that "Western modernity is in pursuit of a 'false infinite,' that is to say a quantitative in-finite according to which one constantly produces, consumes and 'progresses' more and more. Today, the consequences of this Faustian undertaking are devastating. As Raimundo Pannikkar has said, 'Western modernity produces a substitute for transcendence'" (1990:70). It was Critical Theory (above, 2,D) that first broke with history-as-Progress in this century. It rejected each of the conservative, liberal, and Marxist traditions of modern progressive social thought:

> Against the conservative hope in restoring some semblance of balancing contradictions after the fashion of the eighteenth century's *ancien régime,* critical theory hopefully despairs. Against the liberal hope of engineering contradictions after the fashion of nineteenth-century industrialization and urbanization, critical theory hopefully despairs. Against the radical hope of exploiting contradictions for the sake of revolutionary resolutions after the fashion of twentieth-century state socialisms, critical theory hopefully despairs. (Lamb, 1980:187)

Critical Theory was less clear, however, about what historical practice corresponded to "hopeful despair." Marxist critics therefore alleged that the politics of negation had no concrete alternative to offer and merely counseled passivity (cf Sartre's critique of Camus in Lasky, 1976:602). Is this so? Does placing redemption outside the history of Progress mean we must return to those religious systems (and there are many) that posit redemption exclusively beyond the bounds of history, replacing progressive monism with religious dualism? But this would give us no reason to struggle for or within history, which is why religion is politically domesticated under the system of Progress. Fortunately there is another possibility: the much-maligned and misunderstood historical ideology of biblical apocalyptic.

It is interesting to recall that many in the Frankfurt School were deeply attracted to Judeo-Christian eschatology, because "its teaching of a radical disjunction between history and redemption serves to illuminate the 'metahistorical' ground of human existence and destiny":

On a deeper level, Critical Theory was a quest for transcendence that was conceived not in metaphysical but in metachronic terms. Truth . . . is not in heaven but in the future. This conception of the truth endowed the Frankfurt School, according to Horkheimer, with "the hope that the earthly horror does not possess the last word." This hope, in turn, permits one to utter a confident No to the existent order. Or, as Adorno asserted in terms self-consciously theological, "the only philosophy which can be responsibly practiced in the face of despair is the attempt to regard all things as the way they would present themselves from the standpoint of redemption." (Mendes-Flohr, 1983:635)

Unfortunately Critical Theory did not get much help from the theological community. The liberals had abandoned the texts of biblical apocalyptic as too embarrassing, while conservatives trivialized them through gratuitous and literalistic readings. "There is no doubt," complained theologian Carl Braaten in 1971 in what surely was an understatement, "that the old apocalyptic currencies have been negotiated by the various versions of modern theology at a very low rate of exchange" (1971:482).

However, the same revolutionary turmoil of the 1960s that caused the New Left to reread Critical Theory also led theologians to rediscover apocalyptic (Koch, 1970). The liberal consensus about Progress was challenged in such studies as Braaten's *Christ and Counter-Christ: Apocalyptic Themes in Theology and Culture,* which contrasted two notions of the historical future:

The one could be described as evolutionary monism (Teilhard de Chardin); the other could be called a revolutionary dualism. The former thinks of eschatology as the extrapolation from the present to the future; its key concept is development. The latter think of eschatology as the power of the future entering the present through creative negation; its key concept is liberation. . . . In Jesus' preaching, God is the power of the future contradicting all history which wishes to build the future out of its present. That is history turned in upon itself; its vision of the future is only a far-off version of the present. There are two Latin words for future: *futurum* and *adventus. Futurum* . . . is the future actualization of potentialities within things. *Adventus* is the appearance of something new that is not yet within things.... Christian eschatology is not metaphysical finalism but apocalyptic adventism. (1972a:10–12)

Soon William Beardslee was complaining that "the struggle with apocalyptic has been the principal source of radical dislocation of vision in modern New Testament theology" (1971:419).[1]

Meanwhile the old orthodoxy in biblical studies continued to insist that the dualities of biblical apocalyptic were essentially cosmological and thus religious, not political. According to Hebrew Bible scholar Paul Hanson, "Prophetic eschatology is transformed into apocalyptic at the point where the task of translating the cosmic vision into the categories of mundane reality is abdicated" (1971:476). Such pejorative readings have found their correlate in the sociological study of millennial sects (about which I complained in *BSM:*415f). They continue, unfortunately, to prevail, despite studies by John and Adela Yarbro Collins (1977) and Elisabeth Schüssler Fiorenza (1985) that demonstrated how apocalyptic functioned as a discourse of political resistance in antiquity. The philosophical and anthropological categories of modern liberalism are simply inappropriate to the social world of ancient apocalyptic (see Batstone, 1992). The theological appropriation of apocalyptic still languishes, then, for lack of an adequate political hermeneutic. It may be that "apocalyptic is the mother of all Christian theology," in Ernst Käsemann's famous phrase, but if so, her children all left home a long time ago.

But what if we have been reading apocalyptic all wrong because we have forced it to comply with terms established by the ideology of Progress? What if apocalyptic narrative is not primarily about historical consummation at all? What if the theologians have been wrong and the Critical Theorist Adorno right — that apocalyptic discourse articulates nothing more and nothing less than the struggle "to regard all things as the way they would present themselves from the standpoint of redemption"? What if we are supposed to be "watching" not for the end *of* history but for an end to domination *in* history?

B. "LET ME SEE AGAIN!"
APOCALYPTIC FAITH AS BIFOCAL VISION

How can "re-vision" keep us engaged yet patient in the struggle for the Great Economy?

He said, "What do you see, Amos?" (Am 8:2)
And the angel ... awakened me as from sleep, and said to me, "What do you see?" (Zech 4:2)
Jesus laid his hands upon him and asked, "Do you see anything yet?" (Mk 8:23)

Immediately after challenging his disciples about the adequacy of their vision (8:18), Jesus encounters a blind man at Bethsaida (8:22ff). His query to him repeats the divine question to the prophets Amos and Zechariah (LXX *ti su blepeis*). Jesus restores this man's vision but sends him away. Mark then immediately launches into the "discipleship catechism" (8:27ff; *BSM*:235ff). At the close of this section, Jesus encounters another blind man, at Jericho, whose vision is restored and who "follows him on the Way" (10:52). The narrative strategy of this compositional structure was the earliest discovery of redaction criticism: True discipleship is contingent upon having "eyes to see." This is the central metaphor in the Markan drama. These two healings, which represent the two "stages" by which disciples have their vision restored, can help us understand Mark's discourse of apocalyptic faith and can serve to help me summarize the argument of this book.

1. From Vision to Re-vision

The first stage, Bethsaida, is associated with the Greek verb *blepein*. This story suggests that our blindness makes us unable to recognize what is truly human in ourselves or others: "I see [*blepō*] people but they look like trees walking" (8:24). The challenge of sight here is to examine *what seems to be* in light of *what actually is* — that is, to confront our Denial. As I argued in Part Two, this is the threefold task of:

- unmasking the mystifications about the world — "being/wary" of assertions about reality by those who practice domination. I have called this the discipline of *literacy* (above, Chapter Three);
- exposing our illusions about ourselves — "staying awake" to the way we internalize the world's dreams of itself. I have called this the discipline of *dis-illusionment* (above, Chapter Four); and
- remembering and revising the narrative of our collective past — "being/ aware" of how it has been dismembered and devised. I have called this the discipline of *revision* (above, Chapter Five).

Though the blind man at Bethsaida has his vision restored, Jesus sends him away, because like Peter in the very next episode (8:27ff), he does not yet understand the via crucis. Seeing reality — decoding the structures of our entitlement, acknowledging the power of our addictions, and realizing that the imperial fire that warms us also burns us — is not the end but only the beginning of the journey from Denial to discipleship in the *locus imperii*.

It is the discipleship catechism that lays the groundwork for the second stage of restored vision, as I shall show below. This stage is associated with the verb "to look up" or "to see again" (*anablepein*):

Jesus said to him, "What do you want me to do for you?"
And the blind man said to him, "Rabbi, that I might *see again* [*anablepsō*]."

> And Jesus said to him, "Get up, your faith has made you well." And immediately he *saw again* [*aneblepsen*] and followed him on the way. (10:51f)

We might translate *anablepein* literally as "to re-vision." Earlier I discussed revision as "taking another look" at our own story as a people (above, 5,E). Here I am speaking about re-visioning as the apocalyptic challenge to *reconsider what really is in light of the Great Economy*. In the literature of biblical apocalyptic, the night visions of Daniel provide a good example of this discourse and how it functions. Daniel's first vision reveals that world history is indeed firmly under the domination of the "beasts," a.k.a. the imperial rulers of the author's time (Dan 7:1–8). His second vision, however, reveals a quite different scene — the beasts are convicted in the court of the Ancient of Days (7:9–14). In the vision, the saints are being persecuted; in the re-vision, the beasts are being prosecuted and the saints vindicated (7:21–27). This is apocalyptic "bifurcation" of reality, but it takes "bifocal vision" to see it.

Much attention has been given to the alleged dualism in apocalyptic language, particularly the sharp distinctions made between the "old world" / "this age" and the "new creation" / "the age to come." The historicist bias of modernity has assumed that this language must be understood in terms of *chronological* succession. Among literalists and adventists this has spawned great speculation about when, where, and how the "new creation" will be ushered in. Liberal theology, on the other hand, in its captivity to the notion of Progress as endless improvement and history-as-redemption, dismissed apocalyptic eschatology altogether as unfortunate first-century mythology. More recently theologians of hope (following Critical Theory) rebelled against progressive optimism by asserting that redemption was mediated only from the future; thus all historical projects were "eschatologically relativized" (Richardson, 1974; Obayashi, 1975). Liberation theologians, in turn, wondered whether this was not simply a historicist way of placing redemption beyond history. They wanted to know if this future would ever arrive and considered eschatological "reserve" to be too equivocal to empower historical struggle (Segundo, 1979).

Again, the problem has not been apocalyptic language but the historicizing straitjacket of modern thought, which assumed that redemption could occur only exclusively within or exclusively outside history. In contrast, look at the apocalyptic discourse of Mark's Jesus:

> Truly, I say to you, this generation will not pass away before all these things take place. (13:30)
> But of that day or that hour no one knows. (13:32)
> Be/aware! Watch! For you do not know when the *kairos* will come (13:33).

Now, these conflicting signals — creating the expectation of temporal imminence and then immediately turning around and discouraging temporal speculation — could suggest that Mark, or Jesus, is hopelessly confused. Or they could provide the key to how to "read" apocalyptic discourse. The first assertion stipulates that redemption will be realized in history, because biblical faith knows no other place where it can be realized. The second assertion warns us that we cannot control the history of redemption — that is the mistake the Powers make. In the language of another, classically apocalyptic, New Testament image, redemption breaks into history like a "thief in the night" (1 Thes 5:1–8; cf Mk 3:27).

This apparent dualism is, in fact, a bifurcation of the one temporal reality. The "two ages" compete for sovereignty over the one history, which is why apocalyptic faith is all about conversion from one to the other. Paul Minear, in his studies of Revelation (1966, 1968) was one of the first modern exegetes to rediscover this. He argued that the symbolic dualities there were typological and ontological (I would say archetypal). The author of Revelation, with its central duality between the "two cities," Babylon and the New Jerusalem, "detected a profound antithesis between the ultimate status of one and the deceptive penultimate status of the other. He experienced the compresence of both cities in his own exile on Patmos and in the tribulation confronting the churches in Asia. His vocation as prophet included the clarification of those communal choices by which the churches of Asia could represent the city of God in its warfare with Babylon" (1966:100). The social function of apocalyptic prophecy, therefore, is not to predict the temporal appearance of the New Jerusalem but to exhort believers to live as citizens of the New Jerusalem in the midst of Babylon.

In Mark's story, one of the central archetypal bifurcations is between the inbreaking of the Great Economy (Mk 1:15) and the outbreak of war (Mk 13:5ff; *BSM:*338ff). Both represented crises of the historical "moment" that challenged Mark's audience with their respective exigencies. The war demanded their partisanship; the Great Economy demanded their discipleship. Both narratives were understood to be historical. The dualism represented not consecutive epochs (now and later) or segregated domains (worldly and otherworldly) but coexisting realities (what Minear calls compresences), which compete for the hearts and minds of Mark's readership. Mark exhorted his readers not to be confused, for only one "time" was the *kairos* — the other only pretended to be. To discern which was which required the community of faith to "watch" (13:9, 23, 33).

Apocalyptic bifurcation posits a "parallel universe" alongside the one we "see," which judges history not by the canons of Progress but by the "ultimate reality" of divine love and justice. Mark, like most apocalyptic writers, calls this other reality heaven (13:27, 31). Thus, for example, the "voice from heaven" provides legitimation of Jesus' radically discontinuous practice (1:10f), which is why twice, at critical junctures in his mission, Jesus stops and *looks up to heaven* (Gk *anablepein,* 6:41; 7:34). Conversely heaven is the reality that delegitimizes the dominating practices of the ruling class (11:25ff; 12:25), which is why the Pharisees should not look there for signs (8:11). Heaven is not a remote place to be reckoned with only after death; quite the contrary, it is that place and time in which the Great Economy is realized here and now through repentance and reparation (10:21; above, 6,A). The *kairos* of the Great Economy reasserts the sole sovereignty of God (already realized in "heaven") and commences a struggle for its realization in history (1:15). Heaven is realized on earth when the *via roble* "takes up" the tree of life (4:32), and when the via crucis "takes down" the Powers (13:25; 14:62).

Mark's narrative strategy does differ from "classic" apocalyptic (Daniel, Revelation, and the extracanonical apocalypses) in one important respect. The site of re-visioning is not the prophet's ecstatic journey into the mythic space/ time of heaven, nor is there any angelic interpreter to decode visions. Bifocal re-vision is proposed by Mark as a daily practice of discipleship. Let us return to the discipleship catechism that the healings of the blind men bracket. After Bethsaida comes the "confessional crisis" at Caesarea Philippi, where Mark reintroduces the essential duality. Jesus identifies Peter's invocation of messianic triumphalism (8:29) with the demonic attempt to control history: "Get back *behind me,* Satan! You are not on the side of God, but of Progress!" (8:33).[2] This unmasks the two competing narratives: the "divine" (revealed as the apocalyptic practice of the Human One) versus the "human" (understood by Peter as the conventional political practice of domination). Jesus then issues the second call to discipleship: "Whosoever would follow *behind me* must take up the cross" (8:34). "The cross" is immediately defined by another series of dualities:

"human" narrative	"divine" narrative
save life	lose life for my sake (8:35)
profit, gain world	forfeit life (8:36f)
ashamed of Jesus in this	shamed by Human One
adulterous generation	in glory (8:38)

I have contended that the discursive context adopted here by Jesus is the "heavenly courtroom" scene from Daniel's night visions; this context makes sense, since he has just stipulated that trial and conviction is the "route" the Human One will take to the cross (8:31; *BSM:*247f). Mark is beginning here the argument of the second half of the gospel: To persuade the disciple/reader that the via crucis is the way to transformation of self and world. But it takes bi-focal re-vision to see the Human One's cross as the "realized power of the Great Economy." This is why the Transfiguration scene (Jesus as vindicated martyr) is narrated next (9:2ff), which is as close as Mark gets to a traditional apocalyptic "vision."

The dualities, however, don't end there; the ensuing catechism narrates an almost continuous string of social, economic, and political oppositions. Below is a list of both major and minor narrative oppositions that occur in this section, correlated under the two competing narratives, which I have renamed as two compresent archetypal spaces:

"Hell" (9:44)

Why do scribes say? 9:11
Help me in my unbelief!
greatest (Gk *meizon*), 9:34
first/adults, 9:35
tried to stop them, 9:38
thrown into the sea, 9:42
entitled men, 10:2
hardness of heart, 10:5
humans tear apart
they rebuked them, 10:13
Good teacher, 10:17
inherit eternal life, 10:17
I have observed all these, 10:20
had much property, 10:23
human impossibility
did not sell/follow, 10:23
with persecutions
first is last
chief priests/scribes/Gentiles,
sit in glory, 10:37
domination among Gentiles, 9:42
great, 10:43

"Great Economy" (9:1, 47; 10:15, 23ff)

How is it written? 9:12
I believe! 9:23
little ones (*mikrōn*), 9:42
last/children, 9:36
Do not stop them! 9:39
salted with fire, 9:49f
responsible women, 10:12
beginning of creation, 10:6
God puts together, 10:9
Do not hinder them! 10:14
none good but God, 10:18
receive eternal life, 10:30
You lack one thing, 10:21
treasure in heaven, 10:22
divine possibility, 10:27
sold/followed, 10:28ff
receive hundredfold, 10:30
last is first, 10:31
Human One, 10:33
baptism and cup, 10:39f
Not among you! 9:43f
servants, 10:43

The catechism culminates with a blind beggar who is sitting *beside* the Way (10:46) but whose desire to re-vision allows him to "see again" and follow *on* the Way (10:51f).

This list gives considerable substance to each of the two coexisting "worlds" that were competing to form the character of Mark's community. As hortatory discourse, this catechism tells us a great deal about the conflicts between the ethos of Mark's community and the dominant culture of his time. Apocalyptic transformation in Mark is thus conceived primarily not as temporal rupture but as social reversal. David Batstone points out that hierarchical networks of kinship and group power were far more determinative to the social construction of reality in Mediterranean antiquity than abstract notions of history; their subversion therefore constitutes a far more consequential shattering of their world (1992).

Apocalyptic discourse bifurcates each historical moment because it acknowledges the deep conflict between what is and what should be. This functions to undermine pseudodualisms — such as Jew and Gentile, Christian and pagan, capitalist and communist — and refocuses our attention on the true struggle. The two worlds are indeed at war (hence the "combat myth," 1:12f; 13:24–27), but the battle is, as the Pauline disciple put it, no longer with the "flesh and blood" enemies of the State but with "principalities and powers, the rulers of this present darkness" (Eph 6:12). This struggle is not for individual salvation or religious success or national honor or even group survival, but for a practice of conversion. Thus, as I argued in Part Three of this book:

- vision tells us we are addicted; re-vision empowers us to live discontinuously with that addiction (above, Chapter Six);
- vision reveals that social boundaries that are supposed to protect us actually divide us; re-vision empowers us to cross those boundaries (above, Chapter Seven);
- vision unmasks the violence of the Domination System; re-vision persuades us that the revolutionary practice of the cross can overthrow the rule of the gun (above, Chapter Eight).

Conversion is the only practice that can transform history. Progress is the road to hell. We must "turn around."

2. "Return to Your Own": The Apocalyptic Mission

This brings us to the third stage of apocalyptic faith — *proclaiming what could be in the midst of what is.* There is only one other person in Mark's story besides Bartimaeus who responds to Jesus' healing in a way that implies discipleship. It is the Gerasene demoniac (5:1ff). The Gerasene, I have suggested, represents those who have internalized the pathology of empire in their political bodies (above, 4,B). Once possessed by the spirit of "Legion," a.k.a the Domination system, we as a people become caught in a cycle of self-destruction and the spiral of historical violence, inflicting hell upon ourselves and the good creation (above, 8,A). Indeed our possession is so complete we resist with all our colonized selves when confronted with Jesus' bifurcation of reality: "What has *your* world to do with *mine?!* ...Do not torture us!" (5:7). Jesus' vision of the Great Economy "tortures" us by presenting an alternative to the monism of Legion and Progress.

Now comes an interesting series of petitions "begging Jesus" for something. The demon, speaking for the occupying Powers, understands the situation perfectly: Jesus, the "stronger one" (1:7), who has named the demon "no one was strong enough to bind" (5:4), represents a direct threat to their colonizing control. In the symbolic discourse of exorcism, they try to negotiate a retreat:

And they insistently *begged* him [Gk *parakalei*] not to send them out of the country. (5:10)
They *begged* him saying "Send us into the swine; let us enter them." (5:12)

But Jesus, no doubt remembering the story of Moses and Pharaoh, knows better than to cut deals with imperial power. He dispatches the Legion into a herd of swine, which then meets the same fate as old Pharaoh's armies (5:13).

The question now is, What do the people "see" in this exorcism — promise or threat? Ironically those who lost the most, the pig-herders, become "evangelists" (Gk *apēngeilan*): "The herders fled and told the good news in the city and the countryside. And people came to see what had happened; and they saw the

one who had been possessed sitting with Jesus, clothed and in his right mind —
the one who had been occupied by Legion!! . . . And they began to *beg* Jesus
to leave their region" (5:14–16). Here the body politic is presented with the
concrete evidence of Legion's political body, which has "crossed over" from
one world to another, from self-destructive imperial schizophrenia to mental
health. Do the people celebrate? No, they plead with Jesus to get out of Dodge;
like all colonized people, they know the cost of defecting to "the other side"
(*BSM:*190ff).

A third petition comes from the healed demoniac. "And the one who had
been possessed *begged* Jesus to be with him" (5:18). This recovering imperial
addict, worn out from self-destructive repetition-compulsion, simply wants "to
be with Jesus." It is a poignant moment. Don't all of us who are weary from
the battle wish to escape and dwell in the healing Presence? "But Jesus refused,
saying, 'Go home to your own and tell them the good news concerning what
the Lord has done for you and how he showed mercy' " (5:19). Jesus dispatches
him back to the very "land of the dead" from which he just emerged (5:3) in
order that he might evangelize his own people. Jesus is not unaware that this is
asking the hardest thing of all; from his own experience he knows all too well
that "a prophet is not without honor except in his own country" (6:4). We don't
like this poor fellow's chances, but he complies, and his "proclamation" (Gk
kērussein, 5:20) opens the way for the disciples themselves to commence their
mission of proclamation, healing, and exorcism (6:7, 30).

Conversion, in other words, has nothing to do with withdrawal or sectarian
self-righteousness. It invites us to the work of reconstruction as I have argued
in Part Four:

- to practice true solidarity with the poor and the dismembered and to struggle
  alongside them for their rightful place in the body politic (above, Chapter
  Nine);
- to embrace the magnificent diversity of the human family and to stand with
  those who are labeled "impure" and to advocate for their right to dignity
  (above, Chapter Ten); and
- to re-place ourselves on the land, to re-vision an economics and politics of
  human scale, and to take up the *via roble* (above, Chapter Eleven).

Apocalyptic faith insists that those who have experienced the mercy of God in
their deliverance from addiction and Legion, and who have seen a glimpse of
the Great Economy, must return to the heart of the imperial beast to re-vision
what is possible and good while remaining awake to what is evil and terminal.
Who else will?

To summarize: Apocalyptic faith makes a decisive theological break with
Progress. Modernists and postmodernists alike ought to think again before
dismissing as antiquated and irrelevant the troubling mythic dualities of apocalyptic; after all, Progress isn't working out according to plan. The apocalyptic
narrative of history is one of neither ascent nor descent; it understands human

existence as ever wavering between two conflicting magnetic fields: "Is it lawful on the Sabbath to do good or evil?" (3:4). We are neither more nor less
"advanced" today than we were twenty, or two hundred, or two thousand years
ago. Individuals and societies are always caught in the conflict between practices of liberation and oppression within the material relations of power in a
given context.

If these archetypal "force fields" were absolutely equal, and our suspension
between them unresolvable, this would be an ideology of historical *dual-ism.*
Dualism is the depressive swing of historicism, which resigns itself to the "necessity" of oppression in the name of political "realism." But we are not doomed
to endless, cyclical futility — except insofar as we are captive to our own historical repetition-compulsion! Apocalyptic re-vision refuses to accept addiction
or oppression as fated; it affirms the possibility both of practices of liberation
within and divine intervention from *outside* history. Against pessimism, apocalyptic faith animates struggle for the redemption of history (the Great Economy)
based upon the conviction that ultimate reality (heaven) empowers conversion.[3]
It sends the liberated Gerasene back to the *locus imperii* to practice the via
roble.

When justice is done, or human life humanized — whether that is the abolition of slavery or the invention of penicillin — that represents a *kairos* of
the Great Economy, a "fulfillment" of the purpose of history. But this is not
Progress, the historical ideology of monism. Monism is the grandiose swing of
historicism, which seeks to deny its own duplicity and minimize human suffering in the name of political triumphalism. We are not doomed to stay captive to
our imperial illusions. Apocalyptic re-vision refuses to accept gnosticism (hear
no evil, see no evil) about what is; it affirms the possibility of real betrayal.
Against progressive optimism, apocalyptic faith animates struggle against oppression and injustice based upon the conviction that ultimate reality will settle
for nothing less than the Great Economy "on earth as it is in heaven." It sends
the blind man, who now sees, on to Jerusalem to practice the via crucis.

C. "WHO THEN IS THIS?"
FINDING JESUS IN THE STORM

Where is the presence of Jesus most reliably encountered in the world?

"That which we name progress is this storm," said Benjamin. Indeed the
ravaged hills of California testify to the fact that Progress is the (un)natural
enemy of the tree of life (above, 11,E,2). The "pile of debris" growing before
the angel of history includes countless oak trees uprooted by the profiteers of
Progress, just as it includes countless human victims buried beneath the rubble of Desert Storms blowing from the Strong Man's paradise. Just when the
children of Progress had abandoned the notion of the "end of the world" as
eschatological judgment from outside history, the very prospect has welled up
from within our history. It is hard to practice apocalyptic re-visioning in a cul-

ture that contemplates Armageddon in terms so coldly rational and technological as ours. Our language and our senses have failed us; "psychic numbing" has robbed us of our ability to be horrified, leaving us in a crisis of response-ability unparalleled in human history. So, while Jesus and the angel of history stay awake, practicing insomniac theology, most of us are fast asleep and thus unable to exercise political imagination at a moment in desperate need of creative thinking about human options.

Yes, history is long and lonely. This is why in the *locus imperii* people are forever trying either to control history or to escape from it, while institutionalized religion merely counsels us to stay warm by the Courtyard fire. Is it any wonder then that, when the storms of our own historical making break upon us, we ask, "Where is Jesus in all of this?" Where was Jesus when my city burned like Babylon, while all the merchants of the world wept from afar, shedding crocodile tears for the ravages of runaway development, open shop, and mercenary capital? Where was Jesus when my country inflicted the fires of hell upon Iraq, as it intends to do again to anyone who steps in our imperial path? Mark's gospel attempts to address this ancient human quandary with a stirring apocalyptic parable about crossing the sea in a storm (*BSM:*194ff).

In the first of two parallel episodes (4:35–41), Jesus accompanies the disciples on their inaugural journey to "the other side" of the Sea of Galilee, the master metaphor for boundary crossing in the first half of Mark. But a storm — the ancient Hebrew symbol of opposition and chaos — blows up. The little boat — the ancient Christian symbol of the church — begins to take on water. The disciples, among whom we may presume were experienced boatmen, realize they are going down. They panic while Jesus sleeps(!). Mark chooses this desperate moment to place on their lips the disciples' very first query in the story, screamed into the teeth of the howling gale: "Teacher! Do you not care if we perish?!" (4:38) This is such a compassionate vignette! How often have we felt like this, terrified that we will be overwhelmed by all that threatens us, uncertain whether Jesus cares? Yet there is something odd about this tale; the disciples are more unnerved after Jesus silences the storm than they were in the midst of it!

Mark tells us they were paralyzed by their "fear of great fear" (Gk *aphobēsthēsan phobon megan,* 4:41). Is this due to their awe before a nature theophany, as the standard commentaries assume, or is it due to their dread of liberation (as in the case of the people of Gerasa)? Interestingly Mark's language here echoes Jesus' inaugural exorcism in the synagogue (the only two appearances of the verb *hypakouein*):

What *is* this? A new teaching with authority! He commands even the
　unclean spirits and they *obey him!* (1:27)
Who then *is* this that even the wind and the sea *obey him?*

The incredulity arises from this: If Jesus opens new space with his alternative authority, we can no longer take refuge in the excuse that we cannot reasonably be expected to live differently. Lovers of normalcy, we are uncertain whether we want radical change; as on the Sea of Galilee, the storms of history are rough, but at least they are predictable.

In light of this resistance it is understandable that in the second boat episode Jesus must force the disciples to cross to the other side (6:45). Here now is a development that intimates Gethsemane to come: In the first crossing Jesus slept while the disciples fought with the storm; here Jesus prays and sends them off on their own (6:46). We find the hapless disciples alone upon a raging sea in the dead of night, straining pitiably against what must have felt like the roaring headwinds of hell (6:47f). Mark says literally they were "tortured at the oars" (Gk *basanizomenous en tō alaunein*, 6:48; cf 5:7!). Yet they were still losing ground. I can think of no more poignant portrait of the struggle of discipleship in a world dominated by the Powers: Like the angel of history, our efforts to realize the Great Economy are blown backward by the storms of Progress. And once again Mark chooses this moment — precisely when everything seems hopeless, when we are ready to give up the apparently futile task of rowing against the wind — to escalate his apocalyptic narrative.

Through a play on words he implies that Jesus' walk on the sea is a moment of revelation the disciples miss; they think he is a "ghost" (6:48f; Gk *phantasma*, from *phantazomai*, to "show oneself"). When they realize it is Jesus, they are profoundly agitated (Gk *etarachthēsan*) — another wordplay to indicate that the storm now rages inside them as well. At last comes the response to their query that concluded the first boat trip ("Who *is* this?"). Again challenging their captivity to fear ("Take heart ... do not be afraid"), Jesus identifies himself as the "I AM" (Gk *egō eimi*, 6:50), an extraordinary invocation of the exodus God (Ex 3:4). But the disciples don't get it; they are "beside themselves" (6:51), because in their hard imperial hearts they don't yet understand the purpose of the crossing, that is, the "mystery of the loaves" (6:52, cf 8:17ff). This explains why Jesus must later reframe this revelation as a question: "Who do *you* say I AM?" (8:22–29).

These boat stories are, of course, archetypal. They allude to some of the most primal symbolic narratives in the Hebrew tradition: the ark of Noah; the crossing of the Red Sea; the Psalmic odes to storms and the ships of Tarshish. But above all they draw on the story of Jonah, the prophet who resisted the call to "cross to the other side." Jonah's mission was to preach repentance to the imperial city-state of Nineveh, but he cared far more for his personal agenda than for the fate of the "hundred and twenty thousand" under Ninevite oppression (Jon 4:11). Because he would not go to the "great city," Jonah too was caught up in a "great storm" (1:2–4). But he was thrown overboard and swallowed by a "great fish" (1:17; see Gottwald, 1985:558ff). This story is surely relevant to a church today, stuck in the "bowels of the monster" (Martí), which would rather carve out private contentment than challenge the imperial Metropolis to repent. But the tale of Jonah has another connection to Mark's story, which brings the argument of this chapter full circle. Jonah's protest is specifically echoed in Mark's description of Jesus' vigil in Gethsemane!

"My soul is anguished enough to die." (Gk *perilypos ... heōs thanatou*, Mk 14:34)

God said to Jonah, "Is it right for you to be so anguished about [the destruction of] the bush?" Jonah replied, "Yes, extremely anguished, enough to die!" (LXX *sphodra lelypēmai egō heōs thanatou*; 4:9f)

The prayer of Jesus in Gethsemane inquired after "Abba's will" (14:36). But the response of Jonah's God to the "anguish" had not changed: "Should I not be concerned about Nineveh?" God's will is that we offer hope to those who "do not know right from left" and awaken all who are "asleep." That is the task of insomniac theology.

But the journey from denial to discipleship is costly in imperial history. John the Seer, a practitioner of apocalyptic faith at the end of the first century C.E., understood this well. If I may indulge in a little fiction here for the sake of the argument, let me suggest that John, in his former life, was the Gerasene demoniac (this is not a historical assertion, it is a poetic one). John knew the imperial sickness, literally, from the inside out. After Jesus had named his condition and started him on the journey of liberation, he had indeed gone back to proclaim the Great Economy in the *locus imperii*. For his troubles, many years later, he ended up a political prisoner on the lonely penal colony of Patmos. There, however, John persisted in his apocalyptic truthtelling. In letters to churches, no doubt smuggled out, he kept insisting to those on the "outside" that the imperial Dream was a nightmare and kept insisting that the vision of the New Jerusalem was not a fantasy. He tried to warn his readers that the chariot of State had broken and harnessed the four horses of hell in the politics of conquest and militarism and the socio-economics of scarcity and death (Rev 6:1–8); and he tried to urge them to realize the reconstructive Promise of a city in which God dwelled in solidarity with people who dwell in solidarity with each other (Revelation 21). Above all, John exhorted the churches under his care — specific communities in specific places — to ignore the *chronos* and to keep vigil with Jesus and the angel of history: "How long, O Lord, until justice is realized on earth?" (6:9f). For John knew that this is not a vigil in which one does nothing; it is the politics of apocalyptic patience, practiced by those willing, like the young man at Jesus' tomb (Mk 16:5), to put on the white robe (Rev 6:11).

"Be/aware among yourselves," Mark's Jesus warns his disciples, as much as guaranteeing that practice of the Great Economy will sooner or later land us before the Powers (Mk 13:9ff). This is precisely when we need apocalyptic faith the most, because it is that moment in which we are most powerless, most vulnerable, most fearful. And yet Mark's narrative insists that it is here, on the *via crucis*, the only practice powerful enough to defeat the Powers, that we most assuredly and intimately encounter the triune God. For when we stand before the Powers, challenging their claim to sovereignty in and over history, we must rely upon the *Holy Spirit's* advocacy (13:11), we must reckon with contempt "for *Jesus'* sake" (13:13), and we must endure all the tribulations visited upon the

Creator's world (13:19). Here we join the *perichorastic* dance of the Trinity, which offers history its only hope.[4]

Anyone who has ever stood before a hostile judge looking at serious time, or faced threats from death squads, or been pulled from their beds at midnight by security forces can testify that such moments are filled not with triumph and certainty but with trepidation and anomie. But contrary to the claims of religious tradition — mysticism, liturgy, and theology alike — it is in these moments, *in this storm,* that Jesus is most assuredly with us. To prove the point, Mark has Jesus invoke the I AM only one other time after that moment in the storm on the sea: As he stands before the high priest on trial for his life in the palace courtroom (14:62). That episode is the prelude to the cross, the eye of the storm of history, which apocalyptic faith re-visions as the opposite of what it appears to be: not defeat, but the Human One coming in glory (above, 8,C).

There is one more episode in Mark's story that attempts to persuade us of this strange and unlikely practice of apocalyptic faith. It comes after the world has supposedly ended on Jesus' cross. When the smoke clears, the world is still standing and Jesus is dead. What remains is the voice of the Roman soldier filing his report, and the silence of God (Mk 15:39ff). What the few remaining women "see" is Jesus' corpse thrown into a cave (15:47). Its entrance is sealed with a stone, and with that, the story slams shut, with the stupefying crunch of a steel cell door in a prison called history without hope. Now comes the ultimate test of re-visioning — and a tale of women who *look again* (*anablepsasai,* 16:4).

NOTES

1. The ensuing renaissance in the study of biblical apocalyptic spawned countless theological essays and monographs, of which I can mention only a few notables: Altizer (1971); D. Russell (1978); Minear (1981); and J. Collins (1984). Meanwhile the various schools of conservative dispensationalism continue their incessant attempts to correlate apocalyptic symbolics with modern historical events. But before we ridicule such an approach, we should acknowledge that apocalyptic discourse lends itself to such readings, given the plurivalent character of such euphemistic metaphors as "desolating sacrilege," "tribulation," and "in those days." Indeed apocalyptic is designed for reappropriation into differing historical circumstances; Mark, for example, reappropriates the symbolics of the anti-Seleucid Daniel (ca 170–160 B.C.E.) for his own situation during the Jewish Revolt. The problem with modern "Bible prophecy" then is not *that* it wants to rehistoricize these metaphors, but *how.*

2. I have exercised some poetic license — but the paraphrase is coherent with the point of the text. The phrase "get back behind me" (Gk *hypage opisō mou,* 8:33) combines a term normally associated in Mark with healing (*hypage;* 1:44; 2:11; 5:19, 34; 7:29; 10:52) with one that connotes discipleship (*opisō*). We are summoned to go "behind" Jesus in the first call to discipleship (1:17, 20) and now again in the second: "Whosoever would follow after me . . ." (Gk *opisō mou akolouthein,* 8:34). Similarly in the third call to discipleship we are told that Jesus "goes before us" (Gk *proagei hymas,* 16:7; cf 10:32; 14:48). Conversely, the demons attempt to control Jesus by "naming" him according to some orthodox formula (1:24; 3:11; 5:7), which is precisely what Peter has done in his "confession." Satan knows that when humans "name" the unnameable

God (Ex 3:6), they domesticate the one force capable of breaking the Powers' grip over history. The ideology of Progress, I have argued, did just that by identifying redemption with the history of capitalism.

3. This view obviates the classic debate between "cyclical" and "linear" philosophies of history. Empirically human history can be said to broadly repeat certain cycles. Yet temporal succession (which is not the same as chronology) is also a matter of fact; today is not yesterday, regardless of whether we perceive yesterday in terms of "past history" or "present memory" (see Nabokov, 1987). I find the circle of story a useful metaphor for history. One could imagine the narrative of Creation as a sphere whose field of gravity (Grace) holds everything in harmonious orbit around it. The "Fall" introduces another force, a competing field of gravity (sin), which draws human (individual and collective) history out of the "created orbit." History now orbits elliptically, and the closer it gets to the displacing force, the more powerful its influence. The prospect of being completely captured into its orbit represents destruction/self-destruction by sin (or addiction; it does not matter for purposes of the model whether this is an intrinsic or an extrinsic phenomenon). The historical orbit would be doomed by the exponentially growing force of sin were it not for the initiative of redemption/liberation, which has the re-placing power to draw history back into its created orbit. But again, within these orbits (cycles of history) is direction and consequence. After all, the biblical narrative "begins" with the myth of a garden lost (Genesis 1f) and "ends" with the myth of a garden reclaimed (Revelation 22).

4. The Reverend Patricia Farris introduced me to this notion of the Trinity as a circle dance. Barbara Zikmund explains: "John of Damascus, an eighth-century theologian, describes this way of understanding God by proposing that there is an exchange of energy between the persons of the Trinity by virtue of their eternal love.... [He] uses the Greek word 'perichoresis' to describe what is going on within Godself. 'Perichoresis' comes from the same root as the word 'choreography.' It suggests that there is a circulatory character within the eternal divine life" (1987:356). *Choreography* is indeed a nice image for what I am trying to describe here—if its political geography is maintained. No doubt this dance guided the steps of the three young men in Daniel's story, who in the midst of Nebuchadnezzar's fiery furnace encountered a "fourth with the appearance of a god" (Dan 3:25).

13

Closing Meditation

"Who Will Roll Away the Stone?"

*Happy are they who have reached the end of the road we seek to tread,
who are astonished to discover the by no means self-evident truth that
grace is costly just because it is the grace of God in Jesus Christ....
Happy are they who know that discipleship simply means the life which
springs from grace, and that grace simply means discipleship.*

Dietrich Bonhoeffer,
The Cost of Discipleship

*...there is life here
for the people.
And in the belly of this story
the rituals and the ceremony
are still growing.*
Leslie Marmon Silko,
Ceremony

**Very early on the first day of the week, when the sun had risen, they
went to the tomb** (Mk 16:2). Sooner or later those of us who have tried to
follow Jesus find ourselves on our way to bury him. It is the morning we awake
to that inconsolable emptiness that comes only from hope crushed. Like the
Galilean women, we arise wearily, aching with grief. Trudging to the tomb,
crimson streaks the eastern sky, but we feel only the night's lingering chill. This
dawn brings not a new day, only the numb duty of last respects.

It is a terrible moment, this "end of the road we seek to tread." But we
know it as surely as we did the *kairos* that once launched us on our discipleship
adventure. ("Come follow me and we'll catch some big fish!" he'd said; "We'll

plunder the Strong Man's House!" he'd said; "The Great Economy will be like a miraculous harvest!" he'd said; "These great edifices of domination will be dismantled stone by stone!" he'd said. It seems so long ago now, and that's just not how it turned out.) Let the record show that Jesus was summarily executed in the interests of empire, with an assist from his own confused companions. His dreams of a new human order of justice and love have been deferred, perhaps indefinitely, by the Powers that were, that are, and it appears ever will be.

Yes, we recognize this story line. Do we not have our own experiences of betrayal and tragedy, of apathy and overwhelming odds, of oppression and senseless suffering? And does not the weight of all of this finally force us to concede that the world cannot after all be transformed? Have not the storms of Progress blown us into a tenebrous future, while the visionary horizons of the Great Economy have receded so far into the distances of our cynical history we cannot even make them out anymore? So do we join those Galilean women for the last, bitter leg of the journey, which ends at the cemetery of hope.

They were saying to one another, "Who will roll this stone away for us from the door of the tomb?" (16:3). What remains is the duty of proper burial. We bring flowers, come prepared to offer last rites as we try to salvage some dignity before we go back and rejoin history-as-usual. Yet cruelly even this is denied us; the entrance to Jesus' makeshift tomb is sealed shut by a huge boulder (adorned, as Bill Kellermann has imagined, with yellow police tape: *Do not cross this line*). We stop in our tracks, pulled up short; we stand dumbly before it, orphaned and bereft. All that is left of our interrogatory faith, which in better times dared to query every arrangement of privilege and power, is one halfhearted question, uttered in both anguish and resignation: "Who will roll away this stone?" Is there not here an echo of Sisyphean tragedy?

This stone is our final ignominy. Put there by the authorities to certify Jesus' defeat, it serves also to ensure our separation from him. We are not even granted the presence of his corpse to comfort us in our therapeutic ritual of mourning. We cannot weep over his casket and muster brave eulogies to convince ourselves we were not crazy to have followed him. This stone blocking our way terminates, without explanation, the journey of discipleship upon which we had staked (to some extent at least) our lives. What an abrupt closure to this story: a stone that we cannot go around and cannot move.

But when they looked again, they saw that the stone, which was very large, had been rolled away (16:4). There is, however, one more *kairos,* and upon it hinges the possibility of the Christian church. It occurs when, with the Galilean women, we "look again" and see that the stone is *gone.* This aperture of hope against hope suggests there might be a future for this story after all; like the tomb, it has been reopened. Tentatively we move forward — but only to find that our noble mission of reburial is no longer needed. Peering around in the dim light of the cave, we make out the figure of a young man sitting alone, dressed in a white robe. (*Who is this stranger dressed in martyrs' clothes? Wait . . . haven't we seen him before?*) He is speaking to us.

"Don't be incredulous. You're looking for Jesus of Nazareth, I pre-

sume. Yes, *they* killed him; *they* put him in here. But he's gone on. See for yourself" (16:6). We look around frantically, our heads swimming, our hearts grinding to a halt. Don't be incredulous! Incredulity does not begin to describe our confusion at this inconceivable news, this absurd contention. Is it possible that neither the Executioner's deathgrip nor its imperial seal could put an end to the journey? We are too overwhelmed to think, too paralyzed to run. Then, as we gasp for air, comes one last word from this mysterious messenger (*where have we seen him?*).

"He's gone on ahead of you" (16:7). He is very matter-of-fact. Our knees buckle. Here is a possibility we never considered, a prospect too terrible to contemplate. An invitation to follow Jesus — *again*. To resume the Way, the consequences of which we now know all too well. Suddenly, from deep within us, from that unexplored space underneath our profoundest hopes and fears, roars a tidal wave of trauma, ecstasy, and terror all at once (16:8). We race out of that tomb as if we had just seen a ghost. And so we have: In Jesus' empty tomb there is nothing but the ghost of our discipleship past and our discipleship future.

A. BEGINNING OR END?
FACING DISCIPLESHIP IN EASTER'S FIRST LIGHT

In the Palace Courtyard twilight we are invited to face our Denial. In Easter's first light at the empty tomb, Mark's story ends as it began, inviting us to face discipleship. In the circle of biblical narrative, in the circle of our Christian lives, this *kairos* presents us with the most dangerous of memories, a *living* one; the most subversive of stories, a *never-ending* one (*BSM:*448ff).

But for us, standing between end and new beginning, is a stone. It is "exceedingly great" (Gk *megas sphodra,* 16:4), a boulder as hard as our hearts and a landslide of collapsed dreams. It is a demonic roadblock "we are not strong enough" to get around (9:29) and a mountain of collective addiction we cannot move (11:23). It is the debris of Progress, piling up to the sky before the angel of history.

This stone symbolizes everything that impedes the church from continuing the narrative of biblical radicalism. It represents our paralysis whenever we conclude that the discipleship journey is a dead end, that Jesus' vision of love and justice is, for all practical purposes, a well-meaning delusion. As we near the end of history's bloodiest century in the throes of the world's richest, most powerful, and most dangerous country, this is an attractive conclusion indeed, buttressed by the fact that the "Old World Order" has just been thoroughly renewed. Today it has never been easier to be credulous about the *locus imperii* and never more difficult to overcome our incredulity about the Great Economy. In short, the impediments to faith in the Jesus who calls us to radical discipleship are truly staggering.

Mark's gospel, a discourse of both trenchant realism and stubborn hope, does not flinch. It invites us to confront these impediments honestly, to expose our facades, to reveal our impotence, to test our convictions. But the First World church, like the culture in general, is for the most part in the business of avoiding the pain of this moment of truth. Rather than being, as the early apostolic tradition put it, "unashamed of the gospel" (Rom 1:16; 2 Tim 1:8), we remain profoundly captive to the imperial shame culture (above, 4,C). So we change the story to make it conform to our pendulum of depression and grandiosity.

On one hand, we cut the story short, applauding a Jesus who said and did many fine things but who nevertheless (let us be honest!) ended up entombed. Make no mistake, there is both rational and political evidence compelling us to opt for such a reading. After all, not only do we have the testimony of science to rule out the notion of corpse resuscitation, we also have the authority of the imperial autopsy (15:44–46). Why not take the official word? However reluctantly we may accept the hegemony of the Powers, there is a certain comfort in it, since the world as we know it may continue. Moreover we avoid the anguish of having to petition for the stone to be rolled away and are spared the disruption of having to struggle with "the meaning of resurrection" (9:10).

This is the church's narrative strategy whenever it has conceded the right of the State to determine the horizons of political imagination and human possibility; in the second half of this century it has been commended as "Christian realism." To be sure it allows for the noble tragedy of the cross, which makes for compelling religion. But such a reading merely places the church alongside all the others at Golgotha. Perhaps we agree with those who ridicule the via crucis as political futility, wagging our heads at the regrettable but iron law of history: Those who dare struggle to bind the Strong Man always end up bound by him (15:29f). Perhaps we join those demanding a religion without suffering, arguing with the fools on the via crucis that salvation is really about self-preservation (15:31f). Perhaps we stand with those who observe the via crucis from a safe distance, mired in magnificent regret (15:40). And whenever those in the service of empire express appreciation for Jesus' heroic martyrdom, we rush to canonize it as "confession" (15:39). So does the church join the politicians in erecting monuments — or declaring holidays — to dead prophets, lauding them as exceptions that only prove the rule.

The christology of Jesus entombed is ultimately rooted in despair and its host of related depressive conditions, as embodied by the Gerasene demoniac, the archetype of those who have internalized empire as a way of life (above, 12,C). If we accede to the imperial verdict, we will necessarily identify ourselves with those occupying forces of spiritual and military domination and become possessed by the rule of death. The stone blocking our path in this case is that of compulsive self-destruction: addictions, family violence, urban decay, ecocide. In the end our internalized oppression becomes so great that our greatest fear becomes liberation itself (5:2–10).

On the other end of the pathological pendulum, we push beyond the bounds of Mark's story, believing in Jesus enthroned. Our apocryphal "happy endings" narrate Jesus' ascent to heaven in order to avoid the pain of self-confrontation by an injection of the amphetamine of triumphalism (Mk 16:9ff; *BSM:*401ff). Are not such readings hugely marketable here in North America, where all manner of personal and social contradictions are suppressed by preachers hawking individual happiness and politicians promising national prosperity? If Christian narcissism sells, says the logic of capitalism, surely it must be theologically acceptable.

This is the church's strategy whenever it has confused Christus Victor with the conquests of the *locus imperii* — Desert Storm being the most recent case in point. But the church's direct identification with the State was more Kierkegaard's dilemma than ours (1968). In secular Protestant America our problem is that Jesus' sovereignty is restricted to "our hearts," an exclusive cloister that provides us (and Jesus?) an escape from a history we can no longer control. We may not be able to change the world, but at least we can find inner peace. But regardless of whether our christology enthrones Jesus or incarcerates him in our hearts, it is symptomatic of imperial grandiosity, a religion of public conformity and private narcissism that tilts at windmills and toes the line. This pathology is illustrated by Mark in his portrait of the disciples cowering in awe before the edifices of the Temple State: "Look at those wonderful buildings!" (13:1). The stone of impediment here is the architecture of domination, which we dare not challenge yet constantly reproduce in our own lives (cf 10:38, 42).

In the Palace Courtyard, if we remain in denial of our true humanity, individually and collectively, we will be condemned to swing on this vicious pendulum between resigned pessimism and manic optimism. In utter contrast, Mark's story faces our condition squarely, refuses to rescue us from the moment of truth before the stone. "Who will roll away this stone for us?" This last of the disciples' queries echoes their very first: "Do you not care if we perish?" (4:38; above, 12,C). Both articulate the primal anguish and anxiety at the core of human existence — as potent as our fear of death — over the prospects of realizing our deepest longings for love, security, and justice. In our world of spectacle and artifice, Mark's empathy for our condition, his solidarity with our frailty, is surely welcome. But if that were all his story had to offer, it could hardly be called *good news*. Which is why it does not end at the stone of impediment.

We can endure this moment of truth only through apocalyptic faith: to "look again" (Gk *anablepsasai*, 16:4) to see that this very stone *has been rolled away*. But how? Not by our muscle, nor by our technology, nor by any Promethean scheme. It has been moved by an ulterior leverage, a force from beyond the bounds of story and history with the power to regenerate both. The verb here (Gk *apokekylistai*) expresses the perfect tense and the passive voice — the grammar of divine action. It is a miraculous gift from the Presence outside the constraints of natural or civic law and order, from the one who is unobligated to the State and its cosmologies, nonidentified and unnameable, radically free yet bound in passion to us.

Theology has often called this grace. Mark would surely agree with Paul, Augustine, Luther, and all those who have carried on the biblical argument with Sisyphus and Prometheus: Nothing we can do could move this stone. It has *already* been rolled away for us. All we need is the bifocal vision of apocalyptic faith to see that the tomb is open and empty.

But where has the risen Jesus gone?

B. "HE GOES BEFORE YOU":
JESUS, *ACOMPAÑANTE*

Jesus "is not here" (16:6). Nor is he "up in heaven" (16:9). Nor does the young man suggest to the women that they look inward to find him. There is only one place we can "see" the risen Jesus: "He is *going before you* to Galilee" (16:7, Gk *proagei humas*). So the circle turns, and the story begins afresh: "Behold, I send my messenger *before you* who will reconstruct the Way" (1:2). *Their evil is mighty but it can't stand up to our Story.*

Mark's gospel, for all its sober realism, is not finally tragedy, but good news — even and especially for us. "Get up, go tell the disciples, *and Peter*" (16:7). The Palace Courtyard is not the end of the line — *if* we come to the end of our illusions and face our Denial in the *locus imperii.* There is no wayward journey that cannot be redeemed by the grace of new beginnings; there is always another invitation to the sacred circle of Story. But whenever the church imagines that Easter introduces a new and different story that cancels out the previous one, it makes its most fatal mistake. Whoever would follow Jesus must still take up the cross (8:34), because this is still the only practice powerful enough to deconstruct and reconstruct the world. When Christians deny the via crucis, Jesus is again *abandonado* (above, 1,B), not because he has abandoned us, but because we have abandoned him. We abandon Jesus whenever we forget that he is encountered not in calm waters or churchly confessions of the Christ but in the storms of history and courtroom confessions of the Human One (above, 12,C). Conversely, whenever we respond to the invitation to discipleship, we join Jesus where he already is: on the Way. This is Jesus, *acompañante* — the one who accompanies us.

Easter celebrates the restoration of the narrative of biblical radicalism, which like Jesus, goes on before us. Whenever the church abandons this story for some other Jesus and some other story, it worships an idol. Now idols, the prophet Habakkuk reminds us, are deaf and dumb (Hab 2:18f); they cannot hear our brokenhearted cries before the stone of impediment, and they have nothing to say to us in our historical *kairos.* Churches of the entombed Jesus can only parrot the rationalizing Realpolitik of his executioners. Churches of the enthroned Jesus revere his Way in fresco and stained glass in the sanctuary and then do as they please in the world. And churches that preach Jesus as Lord-of-our-hearts incarcerate the gospel in a subjective house of mirrors; who is to say that the interior voice we claim to hear is not simply our own self-referential whisperings?

Only the Nazarene-who-was-executed-but-who-now-goes-on can both hear us and speak to us. Jesus the Interlocutor questions and troubles us; silences our wrong-headed confessions (8:30) and liberates us from demons that silence us (9:25f); and calls us to discipleship as many times as it takes. This is the one who reasserted the sovereignty of the exodus God and set about revising the narrative of biblical radicalism: telling the truth and crossing boundaries, retribalizing the community and walking with the poor, healing political bodies and challenging the body politic, and, above all, embracing the apocalyptic vocation of the Human One. Only this Jesus can topple our idols, shatter our illusions, show us the way through denial, and transform our dance with death into a tango with the Trinity.

Jesus goes on ahead of the church, undomesticated by our christologies. We can encounter Jesus only by following him: "Discipleship," wrote the great Markan scholar Eduard Schweizer, "is the only form in which faith in Jesus can exist." But it is significant that Mark's epilogue stipulates a specific geography for this journey. The geography of Easter is not indeterminate or otherworldly (that is, dis-placed). No, it is back in Galilee, where we were first called from denial to discontinuity. The third call to discipleship invites us to re-place-ment among our own story, land, and people.

The world in which we struggle for reconstruction is the same world dominated by the systems of addiction from which we struggle to defect. This is precisely why discipleship is entirely a matter of grace. Bonhoeffer was right: The church desperately needs "to recover a true understanding of the mutual relation between grace and discipleship" (1959:60). Mark understood this clearly. The only times the verb "to have mercy" (Gk *eleein*) occurs in Mark are the two cases noted in the last chapter in which someone healed by Jesus responds in discipleship (above, 12,C). "Go back to your own," said Jesus to the Gerasene liberated from Legion, "and tell them what the Lord has done and how he showed mercy to you" (5:18). "Have mercy on me!" cried Bartimaeus the blind beggar, not once but twice (10:47f). Today in the *locus imperii,* given the dominating systems of addiction and the addictive system of Domination, it is indeed a miracle of grace that we attempt discipleship at all. Like Bartimaeus, we First World Christians will be healed of our blindness only by desiring to see again above all else. And like the Gerasene, our mission is to proclaim liberation among our own, insisting that we who have internalized the demons of empire can be restored, by grace, to our right minds. *Kyrie eleison!*

"Let us then head for the road and travel into the future . . . a journey full of hope, for us and all humanity!" It was with the assurance of grace that these words were written by theologian-activist-pastor Athol Gill, just a few years before he passed on to join the cloud of witnesses (1989:21). Athol, a faithful Markan reader-disciple, was simply reiterating the invitation of that strange young man at the empty tomb, whose clothes represented a conversion to apocalyptic faith, the faith of Bartimaeus and the Gerasene. "There you will see Jesus, *el acompañante*" (16:7).

C. EPILOGUE:
"I WILL BE WITH YOU ON THIS WAY"

I close this circle of Story where it opened, with a story about the stone of revisioning (above, Prologue). Sitting beside the San Gabriel River, I am thinking of Jacob's dream of angels. Like Mark's Easter narrative, this ancient Hebrew tale concerns an early morning moment of truth before a stone, the fear of encounter, and the assurance of *acompañamiento*.[1]

Jacob came to a certain place and stayed there for the night, because the sun had set. Taking one of the stones of the place, he put it under his head and lay down in that place. And he dreamed that there was a ladder set up on earth, the top of it reaching to heaven; and the angels of God were ascending and descending on it.

And the Lord stood beside him and said, "I AM [LXX *egō eimi*] the Lord, the God of Abraham, and the God of Isaac; the land on which you lie I will give to you and to your offspring; and your offspring shall be like the dust of the earth, and you shall spread abroad to the west and the east and the north and the south; and all the families of the earth shall be blessed in you and in your offspring. Know that I am with you and will keep you wherever you go, and will bring you back to this land; for I will not leave you until I have done what I have promised you."

Then Jacob woke from his sleep and said, "Surely the Lord is in this place — and I didn't know it!" And he was afraid, and said, "How awesome is this place! This is none other than the house of God, and this is the gate of heaven." So Jacob rose early in the morning, and he took the stone that he had put under his head and set it up for a pillar and poured oil on top of it.... Then Jacob made a vow, saying, "If God will be with me, and will keep me in this way [LXX *en tē hodō*] that I go, and will give me bread to eat and clothing to wear, so that I come again to my father's house in peace, then the Lord shall be my God, and this stone, which I have set up for a pillar, shall be God's house. (Gen 28:11–28a)

This is a story about continuing the narrative of biblical radicalism, represented by the passing on of the Abrahamic promise. It is also, as Thomas Mann points out, a story of conversion:

The place on which he stands, or lies, is a threshold of a different order; it is "the gate of heaven" (vs 17). Yahweh is here in this "awesome place." Bethel is both literally and figuratively an intersection of divine and human paths. Jacob is standing at a strange door which opens in three directions: behind is his past of failure and alienation; ahead is his future of both hope and uncertainty; and over above, coming down to meet him, is the presence of God. (1985:55)

Jacob's conversion is made possible by an apocalyptic faith that "sees" heaven and "hears" Yahweh's promise of *acompañamiento:* "Behold, I AM with you and will preserve you always on the way you go" (28:15). The next morning Jacob uses his "dreaming stone" to construct an altar and offer a vow of loyalty: "This stone will be God's house" (28:22).

The old story of Jacob's stone and Mark's new story of the stone rolled away both affirm that it is the Promise that transforms the stone of impediment into a "house for all peoples" (Mk 11:21). To be sure, Mark's narrative of Peter warns us to be wary of our own vows (14:29) and of building altars to heavenly visions (9:5). Yet there is a place for ceremony on this Way. After all, the chant of Leslie Silko's elder reminds us that the story continues and the ceremonies are still growing.

So we are keeping the ceremony at a small stone altar, underneath grandmother oak, beside the rushing San Gabriel. This is indeed an awesome place, the house of God. Here, deep in this canyon under the starry sky of Aztlán, hidden from the voracious eyes of civilization, Gabriel and the angels (Guadalupe! Padre Olivares!) surely ascend and descend from the gate of heaven.

Know that I am with you on this Way and will bring you back to this place (Gen 28:15). We give thanks, for the Promise that awakens us to discipleship and for the songlines of this land. I close my eyes and listen to the steady drum of the cascading river, my hand resting on the arroyo stone, cool and smooth, alive with *mesticismo.*

"Behold this stone, which rejected the builders of empire," I hear someone whisper. *"Upon it we can rebuild the church."*

I open my eyes and turn toward the voice but see only the great and gnarled *roble santo. "Have you never read this story?"* continues the voice, ancient and familiar. *"The very stone which the builders of empire rejected has become the cornerstone. This was the Lord's doing, and it is marvelous in our eyes."*

I look again. It is our *acompañante. ¡Adelante!*

NOTES

1. The Jacob cycle represents the third crucial link in the patriarchal narrative of Israel. Gottwald attributes much of this episode to the Elohist tradition (1985:150ff). Mann, however, contends that "the Bethel story is to the Jacob cycle what the charge to Abram was to the Abraham cycle (Gen 12:1–3); it provides the foundation for the redactional unity of the narrative" (1988:55). Whatever we might think of the thoroughly patriarchal character of these narratives, Mann reminds us that "the selection of Jacob represents the freedom of Yahweh, which has a revolutionary and creative dimension. As Northrop Frye suggests, 'the deliberate choice of a younger son represents a divine intervention in human affairs, a vertical descent into the continuity [of normal succession] that breaks its pattern, but gives human life a new dimension by doing so' " (ibid:56). In any case, the episode that immediately follows Jacob's dream — his journey east and encounter with Laban (Genesis 29) — has interesting resonance with Mark's epilogue. Jacob observes a well in the middle of three flocks of sheep; in order to water them, the local shepherds must "roll away" (LXX, *apekathistōn*) a "great stone" (*lithos de ēn megas*) from the mouth of the well (29:2f). This would appear at the level of symbolic discourse to "open up" the Jacob cycle in a new direction after the revelation of the dream. Mark may not have intended a midrash on this vignette, but I do!

References

Abayasekera, Anna, et al.
   1975   "Faith and Ideologies." *SE/84* (World Council of Churches Study Encounter, Geneva), 11:4, pp 1ff.

Abbey, Edward.
   1988   *One Life at a Time, Please.* New York: Henry Holt & Co.

Abraham, K. C., ed.
   1990   *Third World Theologies: Commonalities and Divergences.* Maryknoll, NY: Orbis.

Adams, Carol.
   1993   *Ecofeminism and the Sacred.* New York: Crossroad.

Adeniji, Oluyemi.
   1985   "The Concept of Disarmament in the African Context." Paper given at the Conference on Security, Disarmament and Development in Africa, August 1985. New York: United Nations Department for Disarmament Affairs Coordination, pp 21ff.

Affleck, Michael.
   1991   *Notes on Faith and Strategy.* Las Vegas: Nevada Desert Experience.

AFL-CIO et al.
   1991   *On the Condition of Workers in 1991.* Proceedings from a Continuation of the Dialogue between the Religious Community and Organized Labor, June 10, 1991. Washington, DC: AFL-CIO.

Agne, Joe.
   1993   "The Widow and the Judge: Is Liberal Racism an Oxymoron?" *Sojourners,* May, 16ff.

Agne, Joe, et al.
   1991   "1992/Kairos USA: A Call to the Work of Repentance." *Sojourners,* October, 27.

Ahmad, Yusuf, Salah El Sarafy, and Ernst Lutz.
   1989   *Environmental Accounting for Sustainable Development.* Washington, DC: World Bank.

Ahuna-Ka'ai'ai, Joyce, et al, eds.
   1993   *He Alo a He Alo: Face to Face. Hawaiian Voices on Sovereignty.* Honolulu: American Friends Service Committee.

Akbar, Na'im (Luther X. Weems).
   1981   "Mental Disorders Among African-Americans." *Black Books Bulletin* 7:2: 18–25.

Alarcón, Francisco.
1992   "Reclaiming Ourselves, Reclaiming America." In *Without Discovery: A Native Response to Columbus,* edited by R. Gonzalez. Seattle: Broken Moon Press, pp 29ff.

Aldridge, Robert.
1989   *Nuclear Empire.* Vancouver, Canada: New Star Books.
1983   *First Strike! The Pentagon's Strategy for Nuclear War.* Boston: South End Press.

Aldridge, Robert, and Ched Myers.
1990   *Resisting the Serpent: Palau's Struggle for Self-Determination.* Baltimore: Fortkamp.

Aldridge, Robert, and Virginia Stark.
1986   "Nuclear War, Citizen Intervention and the Necessity Defense." *Santa Clara Law Review,* 26:2 (Spring): 299ff.

Alexander, Bobby.
1991   *Victor Turner Revisited: Ritual as Social Change.* American Academy of Religion Series no. 74. Atlanta: Scholars Press.

Alexandre, Laurien.
1990   "Global Literacy: Basic Skills and Great Debates" and "Media Literacy for a Technological Age." *Global Pages Educator's Quarterly* (Immaculate Heart College Center, Los Angeles), Summer-Fall.
1985   "Global Communication: A One Way Flow" and "Foreign News: U.S. Style." *Global Pages Educator's Quarterly,* June–July.

Alperovitz, Gar.
1992   "To Drop the Atom Bomb: After 50 Years, Moral Reassessment of a Fateful Decision." *Christianity and Crisis,* February 3, pp 13ff.

Althaus, Dudley.
1988   "Toxic Waste Threatens Border Water: Lauded U.S.-Mexican Plants Pose Hazard." *Dallas Times Herald,* February 1.

Altieri, Miguel.
1987   *Agroecology: The Scientific Basis of Alternative Agriculture.* Boulder: Westview.

Altizer, Thomas.
1971   "The Dialectic of Ancient and Modern Apocalypticism." *Journal of the American Academy of Religion,* 39: 3 (September): 312ff.

Alves, Rubem.
1972   *Tomorrow's Child.* New York: Harper & Row.

American Friends Service Committee.
1989   *AFSC Perspectives on the Employer Sanctions Provisions of the Immigration Reform and Control Act of 1986.* Philadelphia: AFSC.
1981   *Perspectives on Nonviolence in Relation to Groups Struggling for Social Justice.* Philadelphia: AFSC.

Anaya, Rudolfo.
1992   "The New World Man." In *Without Discovery: A Native Response to Columbus,* edited by R. Gonzalez. Seattle: Broken Moon Press, pp 19ff.

Angelou, Maya.
1993   *On the Pulse of Morning.* The Inaugural Poem, January 20, 1993. New York: Random House.

Angus, Murray.
1991   "...And the Last Shall Be First": Native Policy in an Era of Cutbacks. Toronto: New Canada Press.
Anitua, Santiago.
1982   "Basic Church Communities: Delineating the Concept." Translated by T. de Johnson. Social Justice Review, January/February, pp 23f, and March/April, pp 60f.
Anzaldúa, Gloria.
1987   Borderlands/La Frontera: The New Mestiza. San Francisco: Aunt Lute Books.
Apter, David.
1987   Rethinking Development: Modernization, Dependency, and Postmodern Politics. London: Sage Publications.
Arendt, Hannah.
1969   On Violence. New York: Harcourt, Brace & World.
Aridjis, Homero, et al.
1991   "The Morelia Declaration." New York Times. National edition. November 8.
Armor, John and Peter Wright.
1989   Manzanar. New York: Vintage Books.
Armstrong, Bonnie.
1992   Making Government Work for Your City's Kids. Washington, DC: National League of Cities.
Arnold, Bettina.
1992   "The Past as Propaganda: How Hitler's Archaeologists Distorted European Prehistory to Justify Racist and Territorial Goals." Archaeology, 45: 4 (July/August): 30ff.
Asian Women United of California.
1989   Making Waves: An Anthology of Writings by and about Asian American Women. Boston: Beacon Press.
Auerbach, Elsa Roberts, and Nina Wallerstein.
1987   ESL for Action: Problem Posing at Work. English for the Workplace Series, Reading, MA: Addison-Wesley.
Auerbach, Eric.
1968   Mimesis: The Representation of Reality in Western Literature. Princeton, NJ: Princeton University Press.
Augenbraum, Harold and Ilan Stavans, eds.
1993   Growing up Latino: Memoirs and Stories. Boston: Houghton Mifflin.
Avila, Charles.
1983   Ownership: Early Christian Teachings. Maryknoll, NY: Orbis.
Awatere, Donna.
1984   Maori Sovereignty. Auckland: Broadsheet Magazine.
Bagdikian, Ben.
1990   The Media Monopoly. 3d ed. Boston: Beacon Press.
1989   "The Lords of the Global Village: Cornering Hearts and Minds." The Nation, June 12, pp 805ff.
Bailey, Eric, and Dan Morain.
1993   "Anti-Immigration Bills Flood Legislature." Los Angeles Times, May 3, pp A3f.

Bailey, S. D.
   1972   *Prohibition and Restraints in War.* London: Oxford University Press.
Bainton, Roland H.
   1960   *Christian Attitudes toward War and Peace.* New York: Abingdon Press.
Baird, Lisa.
   1992   "That Special Perspective They Say They Want." *Columbia Journalism Review,* July/August, p 27.
Ball, Nicole.
   1981   *The Military in the Development Process: A Guide to Issues.* Claremont, CA: Regina Books.
Ballou, Adin.
   1966   "Christian Non-resistance." In *Nonviolence in America: A Documentary History,* edited by S. Lynd. Indianapolis: Bobbs-Merrill Company, pp 31ff.
Bancroft, Nancy.
   1982   "Some U.S. Christian Views of Marxism: Continuity and Change Since 1975." *Religious Studies Review* 8:4 (October): 324ff.
Banks, Andy.
   1992   "The Power and the Promise of Community Unionism." *Labor Research Review* no 18: 17ff.
Banks, Sandy.
   1993   "Dissatisfaction Fuels Drive to Dismantle L.A. Unified." *Los Angeles Times,* May 17, 1993, pp A1f.
Barbé, Dominique.
   1989   *A Theology of Conflict and Other Writings on Nonviolence.* Maryknoll, NY: Orbis.
   1987   *Grace and Power: Base Communities and Nonviolence in Brazil.* Translated by J. P. Brown. Maryknoll, NY: Orbis.
Bardack, Paul.
   1992   "New Hope for Urban America." *USA Today,* July, pp 16f.
Barfield, Ellen.
   1992   "Healing Global Wounds." *The Nuclear Resister* 87, December 23, pp 1ff.
Bartlett, Donald, and James Steele.
   1992   *America: What Went Wrong?* Kansas City: Andrews & McMeel.
Barndt, Joseph.
   1991   *Dismantling Racism: The Continuing Challenge to White America.* Minneapolis: Augsburg Publishing House, 1991.
Barry, Tom, ed.
   1991   *Mexico: A Country Guide: The Essential Source on Mexican Society, Economy and Politics.* Albuquerque, NM: The Resource Center.
Barth, Markus.
   1988   *Rediscovering the Lord's Supper: Communion with Israel, with Christ, and among the Guests.* Atlanta: John Knox Press.
   1974   *Ephesians.* The Anchor Bible. 2 vols. Garden City: Doubleday & Co.
   1959   *The Broken Wall: Studies in Ephesians.* Philadelphia: Judson Press.
Barthes, Roland.
   1972   *Mythologies.* Translated by A. Lavers. New York: Hill & Wang.
Barton, Bruce.
   1980   *The Tree at the Center of the World: A Story of the California Missions.* Santa Barbara, CA: Ross-Erikson Publishers.

Bataille, Adrienne, and Kathleen Sands.

1984   *American Indian Women: Telling Their Lives.* Lincoln: University of
          Nebraska Press.

Batstone, David.

1992   "Jesus, Apocalyptic, and World Transformation." *Theology Today,* October,
          pp 383ff.

Beal, Frances, and Ty dePass.

1986   "The Historical Black Presence in the Struggle for Peace." *The Black
          Scholar,* January/February, pp 2ff.

Bearak, Barry.

1988   "Faith Leads Mother of Twelve into Prison"; "A Nuclear-Age Martyr
          Takes a Leap of Faith"; "Into Action after a Life of Good Intentions."
          Three-part series, *Los Angeles Times,* December 4–6, pp A1ff.

Beardslee, William.

1971   "New Testament Apocalyptic in Recent Interpretation." *Interpretation* 25,
          pp 419ff.

Becher, Jeanne, ed.

1991   *Women, Religion and Sexuality.* Philadelphia: Trinity Press.

Beck, Warren, and Ynez Haase.

1974   *Historical Atlas of California.* Norman: University of Oklahoma Press.

Beebe, Michael.

1987   "Mexico, the Border Industry: Mallory Plant Is Long Gone: Some Say It
          Left Grim Legacy." *Buffalo News,* March 11.

Bell, Peggy, et al.

1991   *A Nation of Immigrants? Religious Perspectives on Employer Sanctions.*
          Philadelphia: AFSC.

Bellah, Robert.

1975   *The Broken Covenant: American Civil Religion in Time of Trial.* New
          York: Seabury.

1974   "Civil Religion in America." In *American Civil Religion,* edited by
          R. Richey and D. Jones. New York: Harper & Row, pp 21ff.

Bello, Walden.

1993   "Population and the Environment." *Food First News,* Winter.

1992a   "Global Economic Counterrevolution: In the North-South Confrontation,
          It's Apocalypse or Solidarity." *Christianity and Crisis,* February 17,
          pp 36ff.

1992b   *People and Power in the Pacific: The Struggle for the Post Cold War
          Order.* San Francisco: Food First and Pluto Press.

1986   *Visions of a Warless World: Perspectives on Peace from Divergent
          Traditions.* Washington, DC: Friends Committee on National Legislation.

Bender, Harold.

1950   "The Anabaptist Theology of Discipleship." *Mennonite Quarterly Review*
          24: 1 (January): 25ff.

Bender, Penny.

1992   "Reporters on the Firing Line: How Much Do You Risk for the Big
          Story?" *Washington Journalism Review,* July/August, pp 29ff.

Benjamin, Walter.
1989   "N [Re the Theory of Knowledge, Theory of Progress]." In *Benjamin: Philosophy, History, Aesthetics,* edited by G. Smith. Chicago: University of Chicago Press, pp 43ff.

Bennett, Lerone, Jr.
1982   *Before the Mayflower: A History of Black America.* 5th ed. New York: Penguin.

Bennis, Phyllis, and Michel Moushabeck, eds.
1991   *Beyond the Storm: A Gulf Crisis Reader.* New York: Olive Branch Press.

Berg, Peter.
1988   "The Ecology Movement's Close Link with Regional Movements." *Utne Reader,* November/December, p 82.

Berger, John.
1987   *Restoring the Earth: How Americans Are Working to Renew Our Damaged Environment.* New York: Doubleday & Co.

Bergman, Barbara.
1986   *The Economic Emergence of Women.* New York: Basic Books.

Berman, Paul, ed.
1992   *Debating P.C.: The Controversy over Political Correctness on College Campuses.* New York: Laurel-Dell.

Berrigan, Daniel.
1989   *Sorrow Built a Bridge: Friendship and AIDS.* Baltimore, MD: Fortkamp.

Berrigan, Daniel, ed.
1984   *For Swords into Plowshares, the Hammer Has to Fall.* Piscataway, NJ: Plowshares Press.

Berrigan, Philip.
1978   *Of Beasts and Beastly Images: Essays under the BOMB.* Portland, OR: Sunburst Press.

Berrigan, Philip, and Elizabeth McAlister.
1989   *The Time's Discipline: The Beatitudes and Nuclear Resistance.* Baltimore: Fortkamp.

Berry, Thomas.
1988   *The Dream of the Earth.* San Francisco: Sierra Club Books.

Berry, Thomas, and Brian Swimme.
1992   *The Universe Story.* San Francisco: Harper San Francisco.

Berry, Thomas, and Thomas Clarke.
1991   *Befriending the Earth: A Theology of Reconciliation between Humans and the Earth.* Mystic, CT: Twenty-third Publications.

Berry, Wendell.
1990   *What are People For?* San Francisco: Northpoint Press.
1989a   "The Futility of Global Thinking." *Harper's,* September, pp 16ff.
1989b   *The Hidden Wound.* San Francisco: Northpoint Press.
1987   *Home Economics.* San Francisco: Northpoint Press.

Black, Francis.
1992   "Why Did They Die?" *Science,* 258 (December 11): 1739f.

Blackburn, Julia.
1979   *The White Men: The First Response of Aboriginal Peoples to the White Man.* London: Orbis Publishing.

Black Elk, Frank.
  1982   "Observations on Marxism and Lakota Tradition." In *Marxism and Native Americans,* edited by W. Churchill. Boston: South End Press.
Bleier, Ruth.
  1984   *Science and Gender: A Critique of Biology and Its Theories on Women.* New York: Pergamon Press.
Blenkinsopp, Joseph.
  1983   *A History of Prophecy in Israel: From the Settlement in the Land to the Hellenistic Period.* Philadelphia: Westminster.
Bly, Robert.
  1990   *Iron John: A Book about Men.* New York: Addison-Wesley.
Boal, Augusto.
  1992   *Games for Actors and Non-Actors.* Translated by A. Jackson. New York: Routledge.
Bondurant, Joan.
  1958   *The Conquest of Violence: The Gandhian Philosophy of Conflict.* Princeton, NJ: Princeton University Press.
Borrowdale, Anne.
  1992   *Distorted Images: Misunderstandings between Men and Women.* Louisville, KY: Westminster/John Knox.
Bonhoeffer, Dietrich.
  1959   *The Cost of Discipleship.* Revised ed. Translated by R. Fuller. New York: Macmillan.
Bosenbaum, Ron.
  1978   "The Subterranean World of the Bomb." *Harper's,* March, pp 85ff.
Boswell, John.
  1980   *Christianity, Social Tolerance and Homosexuality: Gay People in Western Europe from the Beginning of the Christian Era to the Fourteenth Century.* Chicago: University of Chicago Press.
Bottomore, Tom, ed.
  1983   *A Dictionary of Marxist Thought.* Cambridge, MA: Harvard University Press.
  1967   *Elites and Society.* London: Penguin.
  1966   *Classes in Modern Society.* New York: Pantheon.
Bourgeois, Roy.
  1992   "Thoughts from an Imprisoned Priest." *The Miami Herald,* June 6.
Bowden, Charles.
  1991   "Ken Kesey: Prophet in His Own Country." *Los Angeles Times,* November 3, p K1.
Bowen, Murray.
  1974   "Cultural Myths and Realities of Problem Solving." *Ekistics 220,* March, pp 173ff.
Boyle, Gregory.
  1990   "A Gangster's Future? It's a Wall of Despair." *Desde la Base* (Los Angeles, CA), Fall, pp 6ff.
Braaten, Carl.
  1972a   *Christ and Counter-Christ: Apocalyptic Themes in Theology and Culture.* Philadelphia: Fortress Press.
  1972b   "And Now — Apocalyptic!" *Dialog* 11 (Winter): 22ff.

1971   "The Significance of Apocalypticism for Systematic Theology." *Interpretation* 25, pp 480ff.

Bradshaw, John.

1988   *Healing the Shame that Binds You.* Deerfield Beach, FL: Health Communications.

Branch, Melville.

1988   *Regional Planning.* New York: Praeger.

Branford, Sue, and Bernardo Kucinski.

1988   *The Debt Squads: The U.S., the Banks, and Latin America.* London: Zed.

Bresheeth, Haim, and Nira Yuval-Davis.

1991   *The Gulf War and the New World Order.* London: Zed.

Breslauer, Jan.

1992   "Happy Quincentennial, Christopher Columbus! You Should Have Stayed Home, Cristobal Colon!" *Los Angeles Times,* Calendar, October 11, pp 5ff.

1991   "Fear of the M Word: Multiculturalism is Sweeping the Arts Community of LA." *Los Angeles Times,* Calendar, June 2, pp 6ff.

Briggs, Charles, and John Van Ness, eds.

1987   *Land, Water, and Culture: New Perspectives on Hispanic Land Grants.* Albuquerque: University of New Mexico Press.

Brinton, Daniel.

[1884] 1969 *The Lenape and Their Legends.* Brinton's Library of Aboriginal American Literature, no. 5. Reprint. New York: AMS Press.

Bristol, James.

1972   "Nonviolence Not First for Export." *Gandhi Marg,* October, pp 1ff.

Brock, Peter.

1968   *Pioneers of the Peaceable Kingdom: The Quaker Peace Testimony from the Colonial Era to the First World War.* Princeton, NJ: Princeton University Press.

Brock, Rita Nakashima.

1988   *Journeys by Heart: A Christology of Erotic Power.* New York: Crossroad.

Brown, Bruce.

1973   *Marx, Freud, and the Critique of Everyday Life: Toward a Permanent Cultural Revolution.* New York: Monthly Review Press.

Brown, Joanne, and Carole Bohn, eds.

1989   *Christianity, Patriarchy and Abuse: A Feminist Critique.* New York: Pilgrim Press.

Brown, Lester, et al.

1993   *State of the World, 1993: A Worldwatch Report on Progress Toward a Sustainable Society.* New York: W. W. Norton & Co.

Brown, Robert McAfee.

1993   *Liberation Theology: An Introductory Guide.* Louisville, KY: Westminster/ John Knox Press.

1992   "1492: Another Legacy. Bartolomé de las Casas — God over Gold in the Indies." *Christianity and Crisis,* January 13, pp 413ff.

1990   *Kairos: Three Prophetic Challenges to the Church.* Grand Rapids, MI: William B. Eerdmans.

1979   *Theology in a New Key.* Philadelphia: Westminster.

Browne, Harry.
1992   "Rethinking the Economics of Free Trade." *Resource Center Bulletin* (Albuquerque, NM), no. 27, Spring, pp 1ff.
Brueggemann, Walter.
1978   *The Prophetic Imagination.* Philadelphia: Fortress Press.
1977   *The Land: Place as Gift, Promise and Challenge in Biblical Faith.* Overtures to Biblical Theology. Philadelphia: Fortress Press.
Buhrig, Marga.
1992   *Woman Invisible: A Personal Odyssey in Christian Feminism.* Philadelphia: Trinity Press.
Bullard, Robert, ed.
1993   *Confronting Environmental Racism: Voices from the Grassroots.* Boston: South End Press.
Burciaga, José Antonio.
1993   *Drink Cultura: Chicanismo.* New York: Joshua Odell Editions/Capra Press.
Bustamante, Jorge.
1992   "If There's a Recession in America, It Must Be Time to Pick on Mexico." *Los Angeles Times,* February 16, p M2.
Byerly, Victoria.
1986   *Hard Times, Cotton Mill Girls: Personal Histories of Womanhood and Poverty in the South.* Ithaca, NY: ILR Press.
Cabezas, Amalia, Philip Chang, Lisa Magana, and Arturo Madrid.
1992   *Immigrants and the California Economy: Dispelling the Myths.* Claremont, CA: Tomas Rivera Center.
Cadoux, C. J.
1940   *The Early Christian Attitude to War: A Contribution to the History of Christian Ethics.* London: George Allen & Unwin.
Calder, Nigel.
1970   *Technopolis: Social Control of the Uses of Science.* New York: Simon & Schuster.
Camacho de Schmidt, Aurora.
1991   *In Their Presence: Reflections on the Transforming Power of Undocumented Immigrants in the United States.* Philadelphia: AFSC.
Camara, Helder.
1974   *The Desert Is Fertile.* Maryknoll, NY: Orbis.
Campbell, Joseph, and Bill Moyers.
1988   *The Power of Myth.* New York: Doubleday & Co.
Campbell, Will D.
1992   *Providence.* Atlanta: Longstreet Press.
Carmichael, Stokely.
1969   *Stokely Speaks.* New York: Bantam.
Carrington, Don, and Chris Budden.
1984   *Towards a Multicultural Church: Four Bible Studies.* Darwin: Board of Church and Community, Northern Synod of the Uniting Church in Australia.
Carroll, Jackson, and Wade Roof, eds.
1993   *Beyond Establishment: Protestant Identity in a Post-Protestant Age.* Louisville, KY: Westminster/John Knox Press.

Casaldáliga, Pedro.
1988   "Sigamos Haciendo Camino." *Nueva Utopia* (Madrid), December.
Cassidy, Sheila.
1991   *Good Friday People.* Maryknoll, NY: Orbis.
Castillo, Edward.
1992   "The Other Side of the 'Christian Curtain': California Indians and the
          Missionaries." *The Californians,* September–October, pp 9ff.
1991   "Mission Studies and the Columbian Quincentennial." *News From Native
          California,* May–July, pp 12f.
Cavanaugh, John.
1985   "The Journey of the Blouse: A Global Assembly Line." *Response*
          (Program Journal of United Methodist Women) 17: 11 (November): 10ff.
Cavanaugh, John, et al, eds.
1992   *Trading Freedom: How Free Trade Affects Our Lives, Work and Environ-
          ment.* San Francisco: Institute for Food and Development Policy.
Cavanaugh, John, Fantu Cheru, Carole Collins, Cameron Duncan, and Dominic Ntube.
1986   *From Debt to Development: Alternatives to the International Debt Crisis.*
          Washington, DC: Institute for Policy Studies.
Cavanaugh, John, and F. Clairmonte.
1983   *The Transnational Economy: Transnational Corporations and Global
          Markets.* Washington, DC: Institute for Policy Studies.
Cavander, Sasha.
1992   "Doctor Seeks to Cure Violence by Battling It Like Any Disease." *Los
          Angeles Times,* June 24.
Cayuqueo, Nilo.
1991   "Linking Indian Peoples of the Americas." *South and MesoAmerican
          Indian Information Center Newsletter* 6: 1 & 2 (Spring/Summer): 3.
Center for Global Education.
1988   *Crossing Borders, Challenging Boundaries.* Minneapolis: Center for
          Global Education.
Chadwick, Owen.
1964   *The Reformation.* The Pelican History of the Church no. 3. London:
          Penguin.
Chaliand, Gérard.
1978   *Revolution in the Third World.* Translated by D. Johnstone. New York:
          Penguin.
Chambers, Robert.
1983   *Rural Development: Putting the Last First.* London: Longman Scientific
          & Technical.
Chatwin, Bruce.
1988   *The Songlines.* New York: Penguin.   .
Chávez, John.
1984   *The Lost Land: The Chicano Image of the Southwest.* Albuquerque:
          University of New Mexico Press.
Childress, James.
1978   "Just War Theories: The Bases, Interrelations, Priorities and Functions of
          Their Criteria." *Theological Studies* 39:3 (September): 427ff.
1971   *Civil Disobedience and Political Obligation: A Study in Christian Social
          Ethics.* New Haven, CT: Yale University Press.

Chomsky, Noam.
1988   *Manufacturing Consent: The Political Economy of the Mass Media.* New York: Pantheon.

Chrisman, Robert.
1983   "Nuclear Policy, Social Justice, and the Third World." *The Black Scholar,* November–December, pp 26ff.

Christ, Judith, and Carol Plaskow.
1991   *Womanspirit Rising: A Feminist Reader in Religion.* San Francisco: Harper San Francisco.

Christian Conference of Asia Commission on Theological Concerns.
1981   *Minjung Theology: People as the Subjects of History.* Maryknoll, NY: Orbis.

Christie, Tom.
1993   "The Image in Our Cultural Mirror: Weimar Germany." *Los Angeles Times,* January 3, pp M1f.

Christon, Lawrence.
1992   "Going Her Way: Atallah Shabazz." *Los Angeles Times,* Calendar, March 1, pp 5ff.

Christon, Lawrence and Max Benavidez.
1991   "A Battle of Wills: Fear of the M Word." *Los Angeles Times,* Calendar, June 9, pp 6ff.

Churchill, Ward.
1992   *Fantasies of the Master Race: Literature, Cinema and the Colonization of American Indians.* Edited by M. A. Jaimes. Monroe, ME: Common Courage Press.

Churchill, Ward, ed.
1983   *Marxism and Native Americans.* Boston: South End Press.

Cienfuegos, Ana Julia, and Cristina Monelli
1983   "The Testimony of Political Repression as a Therapeutic Instrument." *American Journal of Orthopsychiatry,* 53: 1 (January): 43ff.

Clark, David.
1977   *Basic Communities: Towards an Alternative Society.* London: SPCK.

Clark, Henry.
1981   "The Ideology of Professionalism." *The Quarterly Review,* Fall, pp 92ff.

Clark, Howard.
1986   "Western Pacifists and Wars of Liberation." *The Nonviolent Activist,* July–August, pp 3ff.

Clark, Ramsey.
1992   *The Fire This Time: U.S. War Crimes in the Gulf.* New York: Thunder's Mouth Press.

Clayton, Janet.
1993   "Cornel West: Seeking to Expand America's 'Public' Conversation." *Los Angeles Times,* May 9, p M3.

Cleaver, Richard, and Patricia Myers.
1993   *A Certain Terror: Heterosexism, Militarism, Violence and Change.* Ann Arbor, MI: AFSC.

Clifford, Frank, Rich Connell, Stephen Braun, and Andrea Ford.
1992   "L.A.'s Leaders Lose Feel for City." *Los Angeles Times,* August 30, pp A1ff.

Clinton, Michelle, Sesshu Foster, and Naomi Quinonez, eds.
    1989   *Invocation L.A.: Urban Multicultural Poetry.* Albuquerque, NM: West End
               Press.
Cobb, Vincent.
    1992   "Disarmament's New Front: Bringing the Struggle Home." *Fellowship,*
               October–November, pp 4f.
Cockburn, Alexander.
    1992   "First the Truce, Now a Real Building Plan." *Los Angeles Times,* June 17,
               p B5.
Cole, Charles.
    1981   "The Rise of Decline and Fall." *The Christian Century,* November 18,
               pp 1197ff.
Coleman, Richard, and Lee Rainwater.
    1978   *Social Standing in America: New Dimensions of Class.* New York: Basic
               Books.
Collins, Adela Yarbro.
    1977   "The Political Perspective of the Revelation to John." *Journal of Biblical
               Literature* 96, pp 241ff.
Collins, John.
    1984   *The Apocalyptic Imagination: An Introduction to the Jewish Matrix of
               Christianity.* New York: Crossroad.
    1977   *The Apocalyptic Vision of the Book of Daniel.* Missoula, MT: Scholars
               Press.
Collins, Ronald.
    1991   "Bikini Team: Sexism for the Many." *Los Angeles Times,* November 20,
               p M5.
Comblin, José.
    1979   "What Sort of Service Might Theology Render?" In *Frontiers of Theology
               in Latin America,* edited by R. Gibellini. Maryknoll, NY: Orbis, pp 58ff.
Conrat, Richard and Maisie.
    1992   *Executive Order 9066: The Internment of 110,000 Japanese Americans.*
               Los Angeles: University of California Los Angeles Asian American
               Studies Center.
Cooney, Robert, and Helen Michalowski.
    1984   *The Power of the People: Active Nonviolence in the U.S.* Philadelphia:
               New Society Publishers.
Copelman, Dina, and Barbara Smith, eds.
    1991   "Excerpts from a Conference to Honor William Appleman Williams."
               Radical History Review 50 (Spring): 39ff.
Corbett, Jim.
    1991   *Goatwalking: A Guide to Wildland Living, A Quest for the Peaceable
               Kingdom.* New York: Viking.
Cornelius, Wayne.
    1988   *"Los Migrantes de la Crisis:* The Changing Profile of Mexican Labor
               Migration to California in the 1980s." Unpublished paper. Center for
               U.S.-Mexican Studies, University of California, San Diego.
Cortright, David.
    1991   "What Do We Do Now?" *Nuclear Times* 9:2 (Summer): 11f.

Cott, Nancy, ed.

1972   *Root of Bitterness: Documents of the Social History of American Women.* New York: E. P. Dutton.

Countryman, William.

1988   *Dirt, Greed and Sex: Sexual Ethics in the New Testament and Their Implications for Today.* Philadelphia: Fortress Press.

Couture, Pamela.

1992   *Blessed Are the Poor? Women's Poverty, Family Policy, and Practical Theology.* Nashville: Abingdon.

Crews, Frederick.

1966   *The Sins of the Fathers: Hawthorne's Psychological Themes.* New York: Oxford University Press.

Crosby, Michael.

1977   *Thy Will Be Done: Praying the Our Father as Subversive Activity.* Maryknoll, NY: Orbis.

Crossan John Dominic, ed.

1986   *Sayings Parallels: A Workbook for the Jesus Tradition.* Philadelphia: Fortress Press.

Cruse, Harold.

1990   "Stalled out History: The Past and Future of Integration." *Sojourners,* August–September, pp 23ff.

Cummings, Bruce.

1992   *War and Television.* London: Verso.

Daly, Herman, and John Cobb.

1989   *For the Common Good: Redirecting the Economy Toward Community, the Environment and a Sustainable Future.* Boston: Beacon Press.

Daly, Mary.

1968   *The Church and the Second Sex.* New York: Harper & Row.

Daniels, Roger, and Spencer Olin, eds.

1972   *Racism in California: A Reader in the History of Oppression.* New York: Macmillan Co.

Darling, Sara.

1992   "Listening to the Cops in Your Head." *Yukon News* (Canada), September 18, p 12.

Daube, David.

1972   *Civil Disobedience in Antiquity.* Edinburgh: Edinburgh University Press.

Davidson Joe.

1993   "Have Police Declared War on Blacks? *Emerge,* May, pp 27ff.

Davis, Mike.

1992a   "For a City Adrift, Look to Community Government." *Los Angeles Times,* October 4, pp M1f.

1992b   "LA: The Fire This Time." *CovertAction,* 41 (Summer): 12ff.

1992c   "When Demand for Justice is Apocalyptic." *Los Angeles Times,* May 3, pp M1f.

1990   *City of Quartz: Excavating the Future in Los Angeles.* London: Verso.

Dawkins, Kristin, and William Muffett.

1993   "Free Trade Sell-Out." *The Progressive,* January.

Day, Mark.
  1981   "U.S. Psychologists View Sanity of Nuke Activists." *National Catholic Reporter,* September 11, pp 1ff.
Day, Sam.
  1990   *Crossing the Line: From Editor to Activist to Inmate, A Writer's Journey.* Baltimore, MD: Fortkamp.
Dear, John.
  1990   *Our God is Nonviolent: Witnesses in the Struggle for Peace and Justice.* New York: Pilgrim Press.
  1987   *Disarming the Heart: Toward a Vow of Nonviolence.* Mahwah, NJ: Paulist Press.
Deats, Richard, and Robin Washington.
  1992   "A Conversation with Sulak Sivaraksa." *Fellowship* 58: 9 (September): 19ff.
Deberg, Betty.
  1990   *Ungodly Women: Gender and the First Wave of American Fundamentalism.* Minneapolis: Fortress Press.
DeCambra, Ho'oipo, and Rachelle Enos.
  1991   "Principles and Criteria of Participatory Research." Paper presented to Hawai'i Public Health Association Conference, Honolulu, May 24.
DeCelles, Charles.
  1983   "Holding Steadfastly onto Truth: Gandhi's *Satyagraha* Philosophy." *Social Justice Review,* May–June, pp 67ff.
Delegates of the Word.
  1990   "Giving Reason for Our Hope: A Word of Encouragement to Our People." Declaration signed by 148 religious and 233 coordinators of Christian communities in Nicaragua, November 16. Unpublished.
Deloria, Vine.
  1987   "Revision and Reversion." In *The American Indian and the Problem of History,* edited by C. Martin. New York: Oxford University Press, pp 84ff.
  1983   "Circling the Same Old Rock." In *Marxism and Native Americans,* edited by W. Churchill. Boston: South End Press, pp 113f.
  1970   *We Talk — You Listen.* New York: Dell Publishing Co.
Delpit, Lisa.
  1988   "The Silenced Dialogue: Power and Pedagogy in Educating Other People's Children." *Harvard Educational Review,* 58:3 (August): 280ff.
del Valle, Luis G.
  1979   "Toward a Theological Outlook Starting from Concrete Events." In *Frontiers of Theology in Latin America,* edited by R. Gibellini. Maryknoll, NY: Orbis, pp 79ff.
deMause, Lloyd.
  1991   "America on the Couch: The Gulf War as Mental Disorder." *The Nation,* March 11, 302ff.
Deming, Barbara.
  1968   "Revolution and Equilibrium." *Liberation* 12 (February): 10ff.
Deming, Vinton, ed.
  1992   "Japanese American Internment: A Retrospective." Special issue, *Friends Journal* 38:11 (November).

DeMott, Benjamin.
1990   *The Imperial Middle: Why Americans Can't Think Straight About Class.* New York: William Morrow.

Dennis, Marie, Joseph Nangle, Cynthia Moe-Lobeda, and Stuart Taylor.
1993   *St. Francis and the Foolishness of God.* Maryknoll, NY: Orbis.

Derman-Sparks, Louise.
1989   *Anti-Bias Curriculum: Tools for Empowering Young Children.* New York: National Association for Child Education.

D'Escoto, Miguel.
1991   "Foreign Ministry to Community." *Faith and Resistance* (Eerie, PA) 4:3 (November–December): 6.

DeWitt, Calvin.
1990   "Assaulting the Gallery of God: Human Degradation of Creation." *Sojourners,* February–March, pp 19ff.

Díaz, David, and Gloria Ohland.
1993   "The Consultant's Creation." *L.A. Weekly,* May 21–27, pp 24f.

Didion, Joan.
1993   "Trouble in Lakewood." *New Yorker,* July 26, pp 46ff.

Dietrich, Jeff, and Sandi Huckaby, eds.
1992   "Symbolic or Effective Action: A Plowshares Symposium." Special issue, *Catholic Agitator,* 22:9 (November).

Digan, Parig.
1984   *Churches in Contestation: Asian Christian Social Protest.* Maryknoll, NY: Orbis.

Dillard, Annie.
1989   *The Writing Life.* New York: Harper Collins.

DiRado, Alicia, and Laurie Becklund.
1992   "37% of Women in City Jobs Cite Sex Harassment." *Los Angeles Times,* September 23, p A1.

Disney, Anthea.
1992   "In One Day in One City, 1,846 Acts of TV Violence: That's Entertainment?" *Los Angeles Times,* September 10.

Domhoff, G. William.
1983   *Who Rules America Now?* New York: Englewood Cliffs, NJ: Prentice-Hall, Inc.

Dorfman, Ariel.
1983   *The Empire's Old Clothes: What the Lone Ranger, Babar, and Other Innocent Heroes Do to Our Minds.* New York: Pantheon.

Douglas, Mary.
1973   *Natural Symbols: Explorations in Cosmology.* New York: Vintage Books.

Douglass, James W.
1991   *The Nonviolent Coming of God.* Maryknoll, NY: Orbis.

1980   *Lightning East to West.* Portland, OR: Sunburst Press.

1972   *Resistance and Contemplation.* Garden City, NY: Doubleday & Co.

1966   *The Nonviolent Cross: A Theology of Revolution and Peace.* New York: Macmillan Co.

Dowie, Mark.
1992   "American Environmentalism: A Movement Courting Irrelevance." *World Policy Journal,* Winter.

Dozier, Edward.
    1970   *The Pueblo Indians of North America.* Case Studies in Cultural Anthro-
              pology. New York: Holt, Rinehart & Winston.
Drinnon, Richard.
    1987   *Keeper of Concentration Camps: Dillon S. Myer and American Racism.*
              Berkeley: University of California Press.
Dunbar-Ortiz, Roxanne.
    1990   "Christopher Columbus and 'The Stink Hiding the Sun': An Interview
              with Joy Harjo." *Crossroads,* October, pp 16ff.
Durland, William.
    1989   *God or the Nations: Radical Theology for the Religious Peace Movement.*
              Baltimore: Fortkamp.
    1982   *People Pay for Peace: A Military Tax Refusal Guide for Radical Reli-
              gious Pacifists and People of Conscience.* Colorado Springs: Center Peace
              Publishers.
Durning, Alan.
    1992   *Guardians of the Land: Indigenous People and the Health of the Earth.*
              Worldwatch Paper no. 112. Washington, DC: Worldwatch Institute.
    1990   "Life on the Brink: The World's Poor Became Poorer and More Numerous
              During the 1980s." *Absolute Poverty,* March–April, pp 22ff.
Dussel, Enrique.
    1985   *The Liberation of Philosophy.* Maryknoll, NY: Orbis.
    1979   "Modern Christianity in the Face of the 'Other': From the 'Rude' Indian to
              the 'Noble' Savage." In *The Dignity of the Despised of the Earth.* Edited
              by J. Phier and D. Mieth. New York: Seabury, pp 49ff.
Eagleton, Terry.
    1983   *Literary Theory: An Introduction.* Minneapolis: University of Minnesota
              Press.
    1981   *Walter Benjamin: Or Towards a Revolutionary Criticism.* London: Verso.
Eargle, Dolan.
    1986   *The Earth in Our Mother: A Guide to the Indians of California, Their
              Locales and Historic Sites.* San Francisco: Trees Company Press.
Easton, Nina.
    1992   "Life Without Father: As More American Men Disconnect from Family
              Life, Society Suffers the Consequences." *Los Angeles Times Magazine,*
              June 14, pp 15ff.
Ehrenreich, Barbara.
    1989   *Fear of Falling: The Inner Life of the Middle Class.* New York: Pantheon.
Ehrlich, Paul and Anne.
    1991   *Healing the Planet: Strategies for Resolving the Environmental Crisis.*
              New York: Addison-Wesley.
Eichenbaum, Luise, and Susie Orbach.
    1983   *What Do Women Want?* New York: Coward McCann.
Eisler, Benita.
    1983   *Class Act: America's Last Dirty Secret.* New York: Franklin Watts.
Eisler, Riane.
    1987   *The Chalice and the Blade: Our History, Our Future.* San Francisco:
              Harper & Row.

Ekins, Paul.
1992   *A New World Order: Grassroots Movements for Global Change.* London: Routledge.

Eliot, C. W., ed.
1910   *Marlowe and Goethe.* The Harvard Classics. Vol 19. Collier and Son.

Eller, Vernard.
1987   *Christian Anarchy.* Grand Rapids, MI: William B. Eerdmans.

Ellsberg, Robert, ed.
1991   *Gandhi on Christianity.* Maryknoll, NY: Orbis.

Ellul, Jacques.
1991   *Anarchy and Christianity.* Translated by G. Bromiley. Grand Rapids, MI: William B. Eerdmans.

1988   *Jesus and Marx: From Gospel to Ideology.* Translated by J. Hanks. Grand Rapids, MI: William B. Eerdmans.

1978   *The Betrayal of the West.* Translated by M. O'Connell. New York: Seabury.

1965   *Propaganda: The Formation of Men's Attitudes.* Translated by K. Kellen and J. Lerner. New York: Random House.

Emberson-Bain, Atu.
1993   "Sustaining the Unsustainable? Assessing the Impact of Mining in the Pacific." *Tok Blong SPPF* (South Pacific Peoples Foundation, Victoria, British Columbia) no. 42 (February): 11ff.

Emeth, Elaine.
1990   "Recovery and the Christian: A Bibliographic Essay on Addiction." *Sojourners,* December, pp 40ff.

Engelstad, Diane, and John Bird, eds.
1992   *Nation to Nation: Aboriginal Sovereignty and the Future of Canada.* Concord, Ontario: Anansi.

Ennis, Ann.
1992   "Toward Reconciliation Through Respect: Solving the Abortion Dilemma." *Radical Grace* (Albuquerque, NM) 6:4 (August–September): 1ff.

Enriquez, Priscilla.
1992   "An Un-American Tragedy: Hunger and Economic Policy in the Reagan-Bush Era." *Food First News and Views* (Institute for Food and Development Policy) 14:47 (Summer): 5ff.

Epstein, Rachel.
1987   "Micro-Chip Technology: Its Impact on Women Workers." *Voices Rising,* May–June, pp 11ff.

Ereira, Alan.
1992   *The Elder Brothers: A Lost South American People and their Message about the Fate of the Earth.* New York: Alfred A. Knopf.

Erickson, Victoria.
1992   *Where Silence Speaks: Feminism, Social Theory and Religion.* Minneapolis: Fortress Press.

Erkel, Todd.
1990   "The Birth of a Movement." Special issue on "Men Nurturing Men." *The Family Therapy Networker,* May–June, 1990.

Esquivel, Julia.
1993   *The Certainty of Spring: Poems by a Guatemalan in Exile.* Washington, DC: Ecumenical Program on Central America and the Caribbean.

Estes, Clarissa.
1992   *Women Who Run with the Wolves: Myths and Stories of the Wild Woman Archetype.* New York: Ballantine.

Ewen, Stuart.
1990   "Living by Design." *Art in America,* June, pp 69ff.

Faludi, Susan.
1991   *Backlash: The Undeclared War against American Women.* New York: Doubleday & Co.

Fanon, Frantz.
1968   *The Wretched of the Earth.* New York: Grove Press.

Farren, Pat, ed.
1991   *Peacework: Twenty Years of Nonviolent Social Change.* Philadelphia: AFSC.

Fein, Elihu.
1981   "The Sacred Weapons." *Bulletin of the Atomic Scientists,* August–September, pp 52ff.

Ferm, Deane William, ed.
1986a   *Third World Liberation Theologies: A Reader.* Maryknoll, NY: Orbis.
1986b   *Third World Liberation Theologies: An Introductory Survey.* Maryknoll, NY: Orbis.

Fineman, Mark.
1992   "Storming the Beach — and Meeting the Press." *Los Angeles Times,* December 15.

Finnerty, Adam Daniel.
1977   *No More Plastic Jesus: Global Justice and Christian Lifestyle.* New York: E. P. Dutton.

Fischer, Kathleen.
1988   *Women at the Well: Feminist Perspectives on Spiritual Direction.* New York: Paulist Press.

Fogel, Robert, and Stanley Engerman.
1974   *Time on the Cross: The Economics of American Negro Slavery.* Boston: Little, Brown & Co.

Foote, Timothy.
1991   "Where Columbus Was Coming From: Violent Europe, ca. 1492." *Smithsonian Magazine,* December, pp 28ff.

Ford, J. Massyngbaerde.
1984   *My Enemy Is My Guest: Jesus and Violence in Luke.* Maryknoll, NY: Orbis.

Forman, James, Jr.
1991   "Saving Affirmative Action." *The Nation,* December 9, pp 746–48.

Fossum, Merle, and Marilyn Mason.
1986   *Facing Shame: Families in Recovery.* New York: Norton.

Foster, Carol, Alison Landes, and Shari Binford, eds.
1990   *Minorities: A Changing Role in American Society.* The Information Series on Current Topics. Wylie, TX: Information Plus.

Fowl, Stephen, and Gregory Jones.
1991   *Reading in Communion: Scripture and Ethics in Christian Life.* Grand
        Rapids, MI: William B. Eerdmans.
Fox, Matthew.
1988   *The Coming of the Cosmic Christ: The Healing of Mother Earth and the
        Birth of a Global Renaissance.* San Francisco: Harper & Row.
Freire, Paulo.
[1970] 1992 *Pedagogy of the Oppressed.* Translated by M. Ramos. Reprint. New
        York: Continuum.
1971   "The Adult Literacy Process as Cultural Action for Freedom." In *World
        Development: An Introductory Reader,* edited by H. Castel. New York:
        Macmillan, pp 248ff.
Friedan, Betty.
1986   *The Second Stage.* Rev. ed. New York: Summit Books.
Friedmann, John, and William Alonso, eds.
1975   *Regional Policy.* Cambridge, MA: MIT Press.
Fuentes, Carlos.
1992   "The Birth of the Hispano-Indian Civilizations of the New World." *Los
        Angeles Times,* October 11, pp M1f.
Funk, Robert.
1988   *The Poetics of Biblical Narrative.* Sonoma, CA: Poleridge.
Furnish, V. P.
1968   *Theology and Ethics in Paul.* Nashville: Abingdon.
Gabler, Neal.
1992   "Moral Relativism? 'You Don't Get It'." *Los Angeles Times,* June 14,
        pp M1f.
Galbraith, John Kenneth.
1991   "The Price of Comfort." *Los Angeles Times,* January 9, p M1.
Gandhi, Mohandas K.
1980   *All Men Are Brothers.* Compiled and edited by K. Kripalani. New York:
        Continuum.
1961   *Nonviolent Resistance: Satyagraha.* New York: Schocken Books.
1957   *My Autobiography: The Story of My Experiments with Truth.* Boston:
        Beacon Press.
Gardiner, Robert.
1974   *The Cool Arm of Destruction: Modern Weapons and Moral Insensitivity.*
        Philadelphia: Westminster.
Garreau, Joel.
1981   *The Nine Nations of North America.* Boston: Houghton Mifflin.
Garrow, David.
1987   "Martin Luther King, Jr. and the Cross of Leadership." *Peace and Change*
        12:1–2, pp 1ff.
Gaspar, Karl.
1988   "Doing Theology (in a Situation) of Struggle." *BCC-CO Notes* (Philip-
        pines) 6: 1.
Gaughey, John and LaRee, eds.
1976   *Los Angeles: Biography of a City.* Berkeley: University of California Press.
Gendron, Bernard.
1977   *Technology and the Human Condition.* New York: St. Martin's Press.

George, Lynell.
1992   *No Crystal Stair: African Americans in the City of Angels.* London: Verso.
Gerlock, Ed.
1991   "Philippine National Dignity." *Catholic Worker* 58:7 (October–November): 1ff.
Gibeau, Dawn.
1990   "Nonviolence as Political Power Seen Contagious: Spreads from Eastern Europe to South Africa." *National Catholic Reporter,* March 2, pp 3ff.
Gibson, Robert.
1991   *The Chumash.* Indians of North America Series. New York: Chelsea House.
Gill, Athol.
1990   "Unity at the Center: Lessons on Diversity in Community." Interview. *Sojourners,* June, pp 21ff.
1989   *Life on the Road: The Gospel Basis for a Messianic Lifestyle.* Homebush West, Australia: Anzea Publishers.
Glendinning, Chellis.
1992   "Dreaming for the Earth: Soul, Addiction, and Technology." *Woman of Power* 20, pp 69f.
Glidden, David.
1992   The Days of Los Angeles Are Numbered — And They Ought to Be." *Los Angeles Times,* August 9, p M6.
Glossop, Ronald.
1983   *Confronting War: An Examination of Humanity's Most Pressing Problem.* Jefferson, NC: McFarland.
Gnuse, Robert.
1985   *You Shall Not Steal: Community and Property in the Biblical Tradition.* Maryknoll, NY: Orbis.
Goldberg, Carey.
1993   "May Day March Takes Violent Turn in Moscow." *Los Angeles Times,* May 2, pp A1f.
Goldberg, Stephanie.
1992   "The Law, A New Theory Holds, Has a White Voice." *New York Times.* National edition. July 17.
Golden, Renny, and Michael McConnell.
1988   *Sanctuary: The New Underground Railroad.* Maryknoll, NY: Orbis.
Goldstein, Laurence.
1993   "Perspective on the Body: It's Not Just an Underwear Ad." *Los Angeles Times,* July 4, p M5.
Goldstein, Patrick.
1992   "The Mission Beyond Hollywood: John Singleton." *Los Angeles Times,* Calendar, May 31, pp 5ff.
Goleman, Daniel.
1989   "From Tokyo to Tampa, Different Ideas of Self." *New York Times.* National edition. March 7.
Gollwitzer, Helmut.
1970   *The Rich Christian and Poor Lazarus.* New York: Macmillan.

Gomez, David.
1991   "A Sense of Place: The Urban Indians Who Have Always Been Here."
        San Jose Mercury News, West Magazine, September 1, pp 12ff.
Gonzalez, Justo.
1990   "Where Frontiers End . . . And Borders Begin." *Basta!* (National Journal of
        the Chicago Religious Task Force on Central America), February, pp 19ff.
Gonzalez, Ray, ed.
1992   *Without Discovery: A Native Response to Columbus.* Seattle: Broken Moon
        Press.
Gooding-Williams, Robert, ed.
1993   *Reading Rodney King, Reading Urban Uprising.* New York: Routledge.
Gottwald, Norman.
1985   *The Hebrew Bible: A Socio-Literary Introduction.* Philadelphia: Fortress
        Press.
Gramm, Phil.
1992   "Excerpts from Keynote Address to the Republican Convention." *New
        York Times,* August 19, p A16.
Granberg-Michaelson, Wesley.
1990   "Renewing the Whole Creation: Constructing a Theology of Relationship."
        Sojourners, February–March, pp 10ff.
1988   *Ecology and Life: Accepting Our Environmental Responsibility.* Waco, TX:
        Word.
Graves, Ralph.
1992   "When Victory *Really* Gave Us a New World Order: The Battle of Manila
        Bay, 1898." *Smithsonian,* March, pp 88ff.
Gray, Paul.
1991   "Whose America?" *Time,* July 8, pp 12ff.
Grier, William, and Price Cobbs.
1980   *Black Rage.* New York: Basic Books.
Griffin-Nolan, Ed.
1991   *Witness for Peace: A Story of Resistance.* Louisville, KY: Westminster/
        John Knox.
Gross, Bertram.
1980   *Friendly Fascism: The New Face of Power in America.* Boston: South End
        Press.
Grumbine, R. Edward.
1992   *Ghost Bears: Exploring the Biodiversity Crisis.* Washington, DC: Island
        Press.
Guerrero, Andres.
1987   *A Chicano Theology.* Maryknoll, NY: Orbis.
Gurr, Ted.
1993   *Minorities at Risk: A Global View of Ethno-Political Conflicts.* Arlington,
        VA: U.S. Institute for Peace.
Gutiérrez, Gustavo.
1993   *Las Casas: In Search of the Poor of Jesus Christ.* Maryknoll, NY: Orbis.
1983   *The Power of the Poor in History.* Maryknoll, NY: Orbis.
1973   *A Theology of Liberation: History, Politics and Salvation.* Translated by
        C. Inda and J. Eagleson. Maryknoll, NY: Orbis.

Hagan, Kay Leigh, ed.
1992   *Women Respond to the Men's Movement: A Feminist Collection.* San Francisco: Harper San Francisco.

Hall, Carlyle, and Ann Carlson.
1992   "Make 'Strangers' Truly Welcome." *Los Angeles Times,* June 19, p B11.

Hall, Douglass John.
1989   *Thinking the Faith: Christian Theology in a North American Context.* Minneapolis: Augsburg Publishing House.
1986   *Imaging God: Dominion as Stewardship.* Grand Rapids, MI: William B. Eerdmans.
1976   "Towards an Indigenous Theology of the Cross." *Interpretation* 30, pp 153ff.
1975   *The Reality of the Gospel and the Unreality of the Churches.* Philadelphia: Westminster.

Hall, Suzanne, ed.
1992   *The People: Reflections of Native Peoples on the Catholic Experience in North America.* Washington, DC: National Catholic Educational Ass.

Hamilton, Neill.
1981   *Recovery of the Protestant Adventure.* New York: Seabury Press.

Hanson, Paul.
1971   "Old Testament Apocalyptic Re-examined." *Interpretation* 25, pp 469ff.

Harding, Vincent.
1990   *Hope and History: Why We Must Share the Story of the Movement.* Maryknoll, NY: Orbis.
1981   *There is a River: The Black Struggle for Freedom in America.* New York: Harcourt Brace Jovanovich.

Hardisty, Jean.
1993   "Constructing Homophobia: Colorado's Right-wing Attack on Homosexuals." *The Public Eye,* March, pp 1ff.

Harms, Jens.
1977   "Bourgeois Idealism and Capitalist Production: Changes in Consumer Behaviour — The Way to a Human Society?" Paper presented to Commission on the Churches' Participation in Development, World Council of Churches, Geneva, August.

Harrington, Michael.
1977   *The Vast Majority: A Journey to the World's Poor.* New York: Simon & Schuster.

Harris, Fred, and Roger Wilkins, eds.
1988   *Quiet Riots: Race and Poverty in the U.S. (The Kerner Report Twenty Years Later).* New York: Pantheon.

Harris, Marvin.
1981   *America Now: The Anthropology of a Changing Culture.* New York: Simon & Schuster.

Harrison, Paul.
1992   *Third Revolution: Environment, Population and a Sustainable World.* London: I. B. Taurus & Co.

Hartsough, David.
1992   "From Desperation to Democracy? Amidst the Chaos of the Former Soviet Union, Seeds of Hope Abound." *Sojourners,* May, pp 20ff.

Hauerwas, Stanley.
1981   *Community of Character.* South Bend, IN: University of Notre Dame Press.

Hawthorne, Nathaniel.
1902   "Young Goodman Brown." In *Mosses from an Old Manse.* New York: Houghton, Mifflin & Co., pp 89ff.

Hayes, Peter, Lyuba Zarsky, and Walden Bello.
1987   *American Lake: Nuclear Peril in the Pacific.* London: Penguin.

Healy, Melissa, Glenn Bunting, and Dwight Morris.
1993   "Big Guns Aren't Sole Casualties." *Los Angeles Times,* May 23, pp A1ff.

Hedeman, Ed, ed.
1986   *Guide to War Tax Resistance.* 3d ed. New York: War Resisters League.

Heine, Susanne.
1989   *Matriarchs, Goddesses, and Images of God: A Critique of Feminist Theology.* Minneapolis: Augsburg Publishing House.

Hennelly, Alfred, ed.
1990   *Liberation Theology: A Documentary History.* Maryknoll, NY: Orbis.

Henriot, Peter.
1991   *Opting for the Poor: The Task for North Americans.* Washington, DC: Center of Concern.

Henry, Sarah.
1990   "Fighting Words: Can America Be a One-Language Country?" *Los Angeles Times Magazine,* June 10, pp 10ff.

Herman, Edward.
1992   *Beyond Hypocrisy: Decoding the News in an Age of Propaganda.* Boston: South End Press.

Hernandez, Martin.
1991   "Base Communities: The Church in Movement." *Desde la Base* (Newsletter of Proyecto Pastoral, Los Angeles), Winter, pp 2ff.

Hernandez, Tony.
1992   "Drywallers Break Through Construction Industry." *Beyond Borders,* Winter, pp 5f.

Herscher, Elaine.
1991   "U.N. to List Broken Treaties with Indians." *San Francisco Chronicle,* April 24.

Herzog, Fredrick.
1980   *Justice Church.* Maryknoll, NY: Orbis.

Hilburn, Robert.
1992   "The Rap Is Justice." *Los Angeles Times,* Calendar, May 31, pp 4ff.

Hills, Patricia.
1991   "Picturing Progress in the Era of Westward Expansion." In *The West as America: Reinterpreting Images of the Frontier, 1820–1920,* edited by W. Truettner. Washington, DC: Smithsonian Institution Press, pp 97ff.

Hinojosa-Ojeda, Raul, Martin Carnoy and Hugh Daley.
1991   "An Even Greater 'U-Turn': Latinos and the New Inequality." In *Hispanics in the Labor Force,* edited by E. Melendez et al. New York: Plenum Press.

Hiro, Dilip.
1992   *Desert Shield to Desert Storm: The Second Gulf War.* New York: Routledge.

Ho, Man Keung.
1987   *Family Therapy with Ethnic Minorities.* Newbury Park, CA: Sage Publications.

Hochman, Steve.
1992   "Sinead's Defense: She Says She Seeks Truth." *Los Angeles Times,* October 24, pp F1f.

Holland, Joe, and Peter Henriot.
1984   *Social Analysis: Linking Faith and Justice.* Rev. ed. Maryknoll, NY: Orbis.

Holloway, Joseph.
1991   *Africanisms in American Culture.* Bloomington: Indiana University Press.

Hollyday, Joyce.
1989   "Amazing Grace: Making History in the Appalachian Coal Fields." *Sojourners,* July, pp 13ff.

Hope, Anne, and Sally Timmel.
1984   *Training for Transformation: A Handbook for Community Workers.* 3 vols. Harare, Zimbabwe: Mambo Press.

Hopkins, Dwight, and George Cummings.
1991   *Cut Loose Your Stammering Tongue: Black Theology in the Slave Narratives.* Maryknoll, NY: Orbis.

Hopper, David.
1991   *Technology and the Idea of Progress.* Louisville, KY: Westminster/John Knox.

Hornus, Jean-Michel.
1980   *It is Not Lawful for Me to Fight: Early Christian Attitudes Toward War, Violence and the State.* Rev. ed. Translated by A. Kreider and O. Coburn. Scottdale, PA: Herald Press.

Horsley, Richard.
1989   *Sociology and the Jesus Movement.* New York: Crossroad.

Horsman, R.
1981   *Race and Manifest Destiny: The Origins of American Racial Anglo-Saxonism.* Cambridge, MA: Harvard University Press.

Hubbard, Ruth.
1990   *The Politics of Women's Biology.* New Brunswick, NJ: Rutgers University Press.

Hubler, Shawn.
1992   "Tears, No Love, for Inner City." *Los Angeles Times,* August 9, pp A1ff.

Hudson, Travis.
1982   *Guide to Painted Cave.* Santa Barbara, CA: McNally & Loftin.

Hull, Jon.
1993   "A Boy and His Gun." *Time,* August 2, pp 20ff.

Hundley, Norris.
1992   *Californians and Water: The Great Transformation, 1770s–1990s.* Berkeley: University of California Press.

1975   *Water and the West.* Berkeley: University of California Press.

Hunter, James.
1991   *Culture Wars.* New York: Basic Books.

Hunter, J.
1982   "Subjectivization and the New Evangelical Theodicy." *Journal for the Scientific Study of Religion* 21: 2, pp 39ff.

Hurst, John.
1992   "Invisible Poor — Whites: Anglos Are the Largest and Least-Understood Impoverished Group in California." *Los Angeles Times,* July 11, A1ff.

Hurston, Zora Neale.
1984   *Moses, Man of the Mountain.* Chicago: University of Illinois Press.

Husbands, Jo.
1990   "A Buyer's Market for Arms." *The Bulletin of the Atomic Scientists* 46:4 (May): 14ff.

Illich, Ivan.
1973   *Tools for Conviviality.* New York: Harper & Row.

Immigration Law Enforcement Monitoring Project.
1992   *Sealing Our Borders: The Human Toll.* Third ILEMP report. Philadelphia: AFSC.
1991   *Where Destiny Takes Me: Story of a Salvadoran Exile.* Philadelphia: AFSC.

Institute for Cultural Affairs.
1981   "The Human Factor in Local Development." *Image: A Journal on the Human Factor* 11:4.

Irwin, Richard.
1992   *The Newest North Americans: Why We Need to Help Them.* Paper published by the National Immigration Law Center. Los Angeles: Legal Aid Foundation.

Iyer, Raghavan.
1973   *The Moral and Political Thought of Mahatma Gandhi.* London: Oxford University Press.

Jackson, Anna.
1990   "Evolution of Ethnocultural Psychotherapy." *Psychotherapy* 27:3 (Fall): 428ff.

Jackson, Jesse.
1971   *"Playboy* Interview." In *World Development: An Introductory Reader,* edited by H. Castel. New York: Macmillan, pp 140ff.

Jaher, Frederic, ed.
1973   *The Rich, the Wellborn, and the Powerful: Elites and Upper Classes in History.* Secaucus, NJ: Citadel Press.

Jaimes, M. Annette.
1992   *The State of Native America: Genocide, Colonization and Resistance.* Boston: South End Press.

Jameson, Frederic.
1981   *The Political Unconscious: Narrative as a Socially Symbolic Act.* Ithaca, NY: Cornell University Press.

Jeremias, Joachim.
1966   *The Eucharistic Words of Jesus.* London: SCM Press.

Jesudasan, Ignatius.
1984   *A Gandhian Theology of Liberation.* Maryknoll, NY: Orbis.

Jewett, Robert.
    1979   *Jesus against the Rapture: Seven Unexpected Prophecies.* Philadelphia: Westminster.

Jimenez, Maria.
    1987   "Border Militarization: The History, the Effect, the Response." *Immigration Newsletter* (National Immigration Project of the National Lawyers Guild) 16:4 (July–August): 1ff.

Jobling, David.
    1992   "Deconstruction and the Political Analysis of Biblical Texts: A Jamesonian Reading of Psalm 72." *Semeia* 59, pp 95ff.

Johnson, Giff.
    1984   *Collision Course at Kwajalein: Marshall Islanders in the Shadow of the Bomb.* Honolulu: Pacific Concerns Resource Center.
    1983   *Marshall Islands: A Chronology, 1944–1983.* Honolulu: Micronesia Support Committee.

Johnson, James T.
    1983   *Can Modern War Be Just?* New Haven, CT: Yale University Press.

Johnson, Robert.
    1989   *He: Understanding Male Psychology.* New York: Harper & Row.

Jones, Charisse.
    1992a   "When Culture Crosses Over." *Los Angeles Times,* December 13, pp E1f.
    1992b   "Old Memories Confront New Realities in South L.A." *Los Angeles Times,* February 17, pp A1ff.

Jones, Jacqueline.
    1992   *The Dispossessed: America's Underclasses from the Civil War to the Present.* New York: Harper Collins.
    1985   *Labor of Love, Labor of Sorrow: Black Women, Work and the Family from Slavery to the Present.* New York: Basic Books.

Jones, T. Canby.
    1988   "Testimonies, Queries and Advices in Historical Perspective." In *Friends Consultation on Testimonies, Queries and Advices.* Proceedings of conference held December 8–11, 1988. Richmond, IN: Quaker Hill Conference Center, pp 1–15.

Jordan, Harold.
    1992   "Making Sense of the Military Cutbacks." *On Watch* (Newsletter of the National Lawyers Guild Military Law Task Force) 15:3 (October).

Jordan, Trevor.
    1981   "Religious Paradigms and Nonviolent Action: Continuities in Social and Religious Processes." Master's thesis, University of Queensland, Brisbane, Australia.

Judd, Dennis.
    1991   "Segregation Forever?" *The Nation,* December 9, pp 740–44.

Kamel, Rachael.
    1990   *The Global Factory: Analysis and Action for a New Economic Era.* Philadelphia: AFSC.

Kaminer, Wendy.
    1992   *I'm Dysfunctional, You're Dysfunctional: The Recovery Movement and Other Self-Help Fashions.* New York: Addison-Wesley.

Katz, Judy.
1978   *White Awareness: Handbook for Anti-Racism Training.* Norman: University of Oklahoma Press.

Katz, William Loren.
1987   *The Black West: A Pictorial History.* 3d ed. Seattle: Open Hand Press.
1986   *Black Indians: A Hidden Heritage.* New York: Atheneum.

Katz, William and Jacqueline, eds.
1975   *Making Our Own Way: America at the turn of the Century in the Words of the Poor and Powerless.* New York: Dial Press.

Kaufmann, Yehezkel.
1972   *The Religion of Israel: From Its Beginnings to the Babylonian Exile.* Translated and abridged by M. Greenberg. New York: Schocken Books.

Kavanaugh, John.
1992   *Following Christ in a Consumer Society — Still: The Spirituality of Cultural Resistance.* 2d ed. Maryknoll, NY: Orbis.

Keen, Sam.
1991   *Fire in the Belly: On Being a Man.* New York: Bantam.

Keller, Evelyn.
1985   *Reflections on Gender and Science.* New Haven, CT: Yale University Press.

Kellermann, Bill.
1991   *Seasons of Faith and Conscience: Kairos, Confession, Liturgy.* Maryknoll, NY: Orbis.
1989a   "Discerning the Angel of Detroit: The Spirits and Powers at Work in One City." *Sojourners,* October, pp 16ff.
1989b   "A Confessing Church in America? A Time of Discernment in the Community of Faith." *Sojourners,* August–September, pp 18ff.

Kelly, Marion.
1992   "The 1848 Mahele (Land Grab)." *Ka Leo O Hawai'i* (University of Hawaii at Manoa), January 17, pp 9ff.

Kelly, Tom.
1992   "New Worlds, Old Orders." *Christianity and Crisis,* January 13, p 403.

Kemmis, Daniel.
1990   *Community and the Politics of Place.* Norman: University of Oklahoma Press.

Kennedy, David.
1991   "Kennedy Assassination: Bonding a Generation." *Los Angeles Times,* December 12, pp M1f.

Kennedy, Michael, Gregory Boyle, and Luis Olivares.
1990   "Refugee Rights: The Cry of the Refugee; To Walk in the Shoes of Another." In *Yearning to Breathe Free: Liberation Theologies in the U.S.,* edited by Peter-Raoul et al. Maryknoll, NY: Orbis, pp 170ff.

Kenworthy, Leonard.
1981   *Quaker Quotations on Faith and Practice.* Pamphlet. Kennett Square, PA: Quaker Publications.

Kerr, Michael.
1988   "Chronic Anxiety and Defining a Self: An Introduction to Murray Bowen's Theory of Human Emotional Functioning." *The Atlantic,* September, pp 35ff.

Kierkegaard, Søren.
1968   *Attack upon "Christendom," 1854–1855.* Translated by W. Lowrie. Prince-
        ton, NJ: Princeton University Press.
Kim, Yong-bok.
1981   "Messiah and Minjung: Discerning Messianic Politics over against Politi-
        cal Messianism." In *Minjung Theology: People as the Subjects of History,*
        Christian Conference of Asia Commission on Theological Concerns.
        Maryknoll, NY: Orbis.
King, Paul, Kent Maynard, and David Woodyard.
1988   *Risking Liberation: Middle Class Powerlessness and Social Heroism.*
        Philadelphia: John Knox Press.
Kingston, Maxine Hong.
1976   *The Woman Warrior.* New York: Alfred A. Knopf.
Kittel, Gerhard.
1964   "Dogma, Dogmatizō." In *Theological Dictionary of the New Testament,*
        vol 2, edited by G. Kittel. Grand Rapids, MI: William B. Eerdmans,
        pp 230ff.
Klaassen, Walter.
1981   "The Anabaptist Critique of Constantinian Christendom." *Mennonite
        Quarterly Review* 55:3 (July): 218ff.
1971   "The Nature of the Anabaptist Protest." *Mennonite Quarterly Review* 45:4
        (October): 291ff.
Klare, Michael.
1992   "World Arms Market: It's Business as Usual." *The Nation,* February 3,
        pp 120ff.
1990   "The Arms Race Shifts to the Third World." *The Bulletin of the Atomic
        Scientists* 46:4 (May): 9ff.
1984   *American Arms Supermarket.* Austin: University of Texas Press.
1978   "The Scourge of Modern Militarism." *Worldview,* July–August, pp 37ff.
Klare, Michael, and Peter Kornbluh, eds.
1988   *Low Intensity Warfare: Counterinsurgency, Proinsurgency, and Antiterror-
        ism in the Eighties.* New York: Pantheon.
Klare, Michael, and Cynthia Arnson.
1981   *Supplying Repression: U.S. Support for Authoritarian Regimes Abroad.*
        Washington, DC: Institute for Policy Studies.
Kleinberg, Benjamin.
1973   *American Society in the Post-Industrial Age: Technocracy, Power and the
        End of Ideology.* New York: Merril.
Kneese, Allen, and F. Brown.
1981   *The Southwest under Stress: National Resource Development Issues in a
        Regional Setting.* Baltimore: Johns Hopkins University Press.
Koch, Klaus.
1970   *The Rediscovery of Apocalyptic.* Studies in Biblical Theology II, no 22.
        London: Allenson.
Kochan, Leslie.
1989   *The Maquiladoras and Toxics: The Hidden Costs of Production South of
        the Border.* Washington, DC: AFL-CIO.

Kotkin, Joel.
1989   "Fear and Reality in the Los Angeles Melting Pot." *Los Angeles Times Magazine*, November 5, pp 6ff.
Kraft, Herbert.
1986   *The Lenape: Archaeology, History and Ethnography*. Newark, NJ: New Jersey Historical Society.
Krauthammer, Charles.
1992   " 'Pentagon Paper 1992' is Right On." *Los Angeles Times*, March 15, p M5.
Kristof, Kathy.
1993   "Spotlight on the Top: Pay for California's Top Executives Continues to Climb." *Los Angeles Times*, May 23, pp D1ff.
Krutilla, John and Anthony Fisher.
1985   *The Economics of Natural Environments*. Rev. ed. Washington, DC: Resources for the Future.
Kuanda, Kenneth.
1980   *Kuanda on Violence*. Edited by C. Morris. London: Collins.
Kupers, Terry Allen, M.D.
1981   *Public Therapy: The Practice of Psychotherapy in the Public Mental Health Clinic*. New York: Free Press.
LaBrecque, Ron.
1992   "City of Anger: Reporting on a Riot" and "Racial Resentment Hits Home." *Washington Journalism Review*, July–August, pp 20ff.
Lacey, Marc.
1992   "Last Call for Liquor Outlets?" and "Liquor Industry Takes on Activists in Political Arena." Two-part series, *Los Angeles Times*, December 14–15, pp A1ff.
Lacey, Maria Ines, ed.
1990   *Women, Poverty and Economic Power: A Workshop Facilitator's Guide*. Philadelphia: AFSC.
Ladd, Anthony.
1993   "The Environmental Backlash and the Retreat of the State." *Blueprint for Social Justice* (New Orleans) 46:5 (January): 1ff.
Laffey, Alice.
1988   *An Introduction to the Old Testament: A Feminist Perspective*. Philadelphia: Fortress Press.
Laffin, Arthur, and Anne Montgomery, eds.
1987   *Swords into Plowshares: Nonviolent Direct Action for Disarmament*. San Francisco: Harper & Row.
Lamb, Matthew.
1982   *Solidarity with Victims: Toward a Theology of Social Transformation*. New York: Crossroad.
1980   "The Challenge of Critical Theory." In *Sociology and Human Destiny*, edited by G. Baum. New York: Seabury, pp 183–213.
Lame Deer, John (Fire), and Richard Erdoes.
1972   *Lame Deer, Seeker of Visions: The Life of a Sioux Medicine Man*. New York: Simon & Schuster.
Langewiesche, William.
1992   "The Border." *The Atlantic* 269:5 (May); 53ff.

Lape, Herb.
   1988   "Friends Testimonies, Queries and Advices in Revising Quaker Faith and
             Practice." In *Friends Consultation on Testimonies, Queries and Advices.*
             Proceedings of conference held December 8–11. Richmond, IN: Quaker
             Hill Conference Center, pp 17–30.

Larrick, Steve.
   1991   "Eco-Modeling: Principles for Planning Sustainable Communities." *The
             Western Planner,* November–December.

Larsen, David.
   1989   "The Invisible Minority: Often Unrecognized, Elderly American Indians
             Struggle to Maintain Tradition, Continuity in L.A.'s Melting Pot." *Los
             Angeles Times,* October 8, pp VI:1ff.

Lasch, Christopher.
   1991   *The True and Only Heaven: Progress and Its Critics.* New York: W. W.
             Norton.
   1984   *The Minimal Self: Psychic Survival in Troubled Times.* New York: W. W.
             Norton.
   1979   *The Culture of Narcissism.* New York: W. W. Norton.

Lasky, Melvin.
   1976   *Utopia and Revolution.* Chicago: University of Chicago Press.

Lattin, Don.
   1991   "The Problems and the Potential of Reaching Out." *Common Boundary,*
             September-October, pp 20ff.

Lee, Charles.
   1990   "The Integrity of Justice: Evidence of Environmental Racism." *Sojourners,*
             February–March, pp 22ff.

Lee, Dallas.
   1971   *The Cotton Patch Evidence.* New York: Association Press.

Lee, Martin, and Norman Solomon.
   1990   *Unreliable Sources: A Guide to Detecting Bias in News Media.* New York:
             Carol Publishing.

Lefebvre, Henri.
   1991   *The Production of Space.* Translated by D. Nicholson-Smith. London:
             Blackwell.

Lefkowitz, Rochelle, and Ann Withorn, eds.
   1986   *For Crying out Loud: Women and Poverty in the United States.* Cleveland:
             Pilgrim Press.

Lehmann, Paul.
   1975   *The Transfiguration of Politics.* New York: Harper & Row.

Lejeune, Sandy, et al (The East Los Angeles Theological Reflection Group).
   1992   "After the Simi Valley Verdict: A Christian Confession of Conscience." In
             *Dreams on Fire, Embers of Hope: From the Pulpits of Los Angeles After
             the Riots,* edited by I. Castuera. St Louis: Chalice Press, pp 101ff.

Lemann, Nicholas.
   1991   *The Promised Land: The Great Black Migration and How it Changed
             America.* New York: Alfred A. Knopf.

Lentz, Robert.
   1992   "Quetzalcoatl Christ." *Radical Grace* 5:5 (October–November): 1f.

Lerner, Gerda.
1973   "The Grimke Sisters: Women and the Abolition Movement." In *Our American Sisters: Women in American Life and Thought,* edited by J. Friedman and W. Shade. Boston: Allyn & Bacon.

Lerner, Harriet.
1985   *The Dance of Anger: A Woman's Guide to Changing the Patterns of Intimate Relationships.* New York: Harper & Row.

Lerner, Michael.
1991   *Surplus Powerlessness: The Psychodynamics of Everyday Life ... and the Psychology of Individual and Social Transformation.* Atlantic Highlands, NJ: Humanities Press International.

Levering, Frank and Wanda Urbanska.
1992   *Simple Living: One Couple's Search for a Better Life.* New York: Penguin.

Levine, Bruce, et al.
1989   *Who Built America? Working People and the Nation's Economy, Politics, Culture and Society. From Conquest and Colonization through Reconstruction and the Great Uprising of 1877.* Vol. 1. American Social History Project of City University of New York. New York: Pantheon.

Lévy, Bernard-Henri.
1979   *Barbarism with a Human Face.* Translated by G. Holoch. San Francisco: Harper & Row.

Lewis, Anthony.
1992   "When Truth was Buried in El Salvador." *San Jose Mercury News,* November 24.

Lewis, Charlie.
1988   "The Church's Mission of Solidarity with Migrant Workers in the United States." *Migration Today.* Current Issues and Christian Responsibility no. 40. Geneva: World Council of Churches.

Lewy, Guenter.
1988   *Peace and Revolution: The Moral Crisis of American Pacifism.* Grand Rapids, MI: William B. Eerdmans.

Librado, Fernando.
1981   *The Eye of the Flute: Chumash Traditional History and Ritual as Told by Fernando Librado to John Harrington.* Edited by T. Hudson et al. Santa Barbara: Santa Barbara Museum of Natural History.

Lifton, Robert Jay.
1961   *History and Human Survival: Essays on the Young and Old, Survivors and the Dead, Peace and War, and on Contemporary Psychohistory.* New York: Random House.

Lifton, Robert Jay, and Kai Erikson.
1982   "Nuclear War's Effect on the Mind." *New York Times,* March 15.

Liliuokalani.
1964   *Hawaii's Story by Hawaii's Queen.* Tokyo: Charles E. Tuttle Co.

Lindner, Charles.
1993   "Judicial L.A.: South Africa without the Formality." *Los Angeles Times,* March 14, pp M1f.

Lipsett, Brian
    1993   " 'Dirty' Money for Green Groups? The Corporate I nding Controversy."
              The Workbook (Southwest Research and Information Center, Albuquerque,
              NM) 18:1 (Spring): 2ff.

Lipton, M.
    1976   *Why Poor People Stay Poor: A Study of Urban Biases in World
              Development.* Cambridge, MA: Harvard University Press.

Lobdell, Terri.
    1986   "Immersing Our Children in a Second Language: New Elementary School
              Programs Can Make All Children Bilingual." *California Tomorrow* 1:2
              (Fall): 8ff.

Lohfink, Norbert.
    1987   *Option for the Poor: The Basic Principle of Liberation Theology in the
              Light of the Bible.* Berkeley, CA: BIBAL Press.

London Yearly Meeting.
    1964   *Advices and Queries.* London: London Yearly Meeting.

Lonergan, Anne, and Caroline Richards, eds.
    1987   *Thomas Berry and the New Cosmology.* Mystic, CT: Twenty-third Publi-
              cations.

Long, William, and Stanley Meisler.
    1993   "Languages on Brink of Extinction." *Los Angeles Times,* April 3, pp A1ff.

Los Angeles Sentinel.
    1992   "Slanted Media Coverage of Uprising is Disgraceful." Unsigr d editorial,
              June 25, p A6f.

Loukes, Harold.
    1968   *The Uncomfortable Queries.* Study in Fellowship no. 30. London: Friends
              Home Service Committee.

Lyman, Christopher.
    1982   *The Vanishing Race and Other Illusions: Photographs of Indians by
              Edward S. Curtis.* Washington, DC: Smithsonian Institution Press.

Lynch, Rev. Msgr. Robert.
    1991   Letter from the Office of the General Secretary of the U.S. Catholic Con-
              ference to the Hon. Carla Hills, U.S. Trade Representative. Washington,
              DC, June 4.

Lynd, Straughton.
    1968   *The Intellectual Origins of American Radicalism.* New York: Vintage/
              Random House.
    1966   *Nonviolence in America: A Documentary History.* New York: Bobbs-
              Merrill.

Lyon, Eugene.
    1992   "Search for Columbus." *National Geographic,* January, pp 2ff.

MacEoin, Gary, ed.
    1985   *Sanctuary: A Resource Guide for Understanding and Participating in the
              Central American Refugees' Struggle.* San Francisco: Harper & Row.

Mack, Burton.
    1988   *A Myth of Innocence: Mark and Christian Origins.* Philadelphia: Fortress
              Press.

Mack, John.
1981   "Psychosocial Effects of the Nuclear Arms Race." *The Bulletin of the Atomic Scientists,* April, pp 18ff.
MacLeish, William.
1992   "From Sea to Shining Sea: 1492." *Smithsonian,* January, pp 34ff.
Macy, Joanna Rogers.
1983   *Despair and Personal Power in the Nuclear Age.* Philadelphia: New Society Publishers.
Madhubuti, Haki, ed.
1993   *Why L.A. Happened: Implications of the '92 Los Angeles Rebellion.* Chicago: Third World Press.
Makhijani, Arjun.
1992   *From Global Capitalism to Economic Justice.* New York: Apex Press.
Malbon, Elizabeth Struthers.
1986   *Narrative Space and Mythic Meaning in Mark.* San Francisco: Harper & Row.
Mandel, Michael, et al.
1992   "The Immigrants: How They're Helping to Revitalize the U.S. Economy." *Business Week,* July 13, pp 114ff.
Mann, Eric, et al.
1993   *Reconstructing Los Angeles from the Bottom Up: A Long-Term Strategy for Workers, Low-Income People and People of Color to Create an Alternative Vision of Urban Development.* Los Angeles: Labor/Community Strategy Center.
Mann, Thomas W.
1988   *The Book of Torah: The Narrative Integrity of the Pentateuch.* Atlanta: John Knox Press.
Marable, Manning.
1992a   *The Crisis of Color and Democracy: Essays on Race, Class and Power.* Monroe, ME: Common Courage Press.
1992b   *Black America: Multicultural Democracy in the Age of Clarence Thomas, David Duke and the LA Uprisings.* Open Magazine Pamphlet Series no. 16. Rev. ed. Westfield, NJ: Open Magazine.
Marchik, Billie.
1992   "Rhetoric vs. Reality: The Media and the Gulf War." *Middle East Peace Notes* (AFSC, Denver, CO), March, pp 1ff.
Marcuse, Herbert.
1969   *An Essay on Liberation.* Boston: Beacon Press.
1964   *One Dimensional Man: Studies in the Ideology of Advanced Industrial Society.* Boston: Beacon Press.
Margolin, Malcolm.
1991   "The Cupeno Expulsion of 1903." *News from Native California.* May–July, pp 24ff.
1981   *The Way We Lived: California Indian Reminiscences, Stories and Songs.* Berkeley, CA: Heyday Books.
Margolis, Maxine.
1984   *Mothers and Such: Views of American Women and Why They Changed.* Berkeley: University of California Press.

Marinacci, Barbara and Rudy.
1980   *California's Place Names.* Palo Alto: Tioga Publishing.
Markusen, Ann.
1987   *Regions: The Economics and Politics of Territory.* Totowa, NJ: Rowman & Littlefield.
Marshall, Tyler.
1992   "Rich Nations Get the Blues." *Los Angeles Times,* September 1, pp H1ff.
Martí, José.
1975   *Inside the Monster: Writings on the United States and American Imperialism.* Edited by P. Foner. New York: Monthly Review Press.
Martin, Calvin, ed.
1987   *The American Indian and the Problem of History.* New York: Oxford University Press.
Martin, Thomas.
1988   "Devolutionism: The New Nationalist Movements Transforming the World." *Utne Reader,* November–December, pp 78ff.
Martin, Victoria.
1992   "Waging a War on Images." *Artweek* 23:24 (September 17): 3ff.
Martin, Wendy, ed.
1972   *The American Sisterhood: Writings of the Feminist Movement from Colonial Times to the Present.* New York: Harper & Row.
Martínez, Elizabeth, ed.
1991   *500 Años del Pueblo Chicano.* Albuquerque, NM: Southwest Organizing Project.
Martínez, Rubém.
1992   "Sentence of Fire: A City Judges Itself." *L.A. Weekly* 14:23 (May 8–14): 14ff.
Marty, Martin, and Dean Peerman, eds.
1969   *New Theology No. 6: On Revolution and Non-Revolution, Violence and Nonviolence, Peace and Power.* New York: Macmillan.
May, D.
1990   "Leaving and Receiving: A Social Scientific Exegesis of Mark 10:29–31." *Perspectives in Religious Studies* 17:2 (Summer): 141ff.
May, Gerald.
1988   *Addiction and Grace.* San Francisco: Harper & Row.
May, Roy.
1992   "Toward a Latin American Ministry of the Land." *500 Years* (Latin American Council of Churches, Quito, Ecuador) 5 (May): 6ff.
Maynard-Reid, Pedrito.
1987   *Poverty and Wealth in James.* Maryknoll, NY: Orbis.
Mazur, Laurie, ed.
1992   *Conversations about UNCED — Where We Go from Here.* New York: Environmental Grantmakers Ass.
McAllister, Pam.
1991   *This River of Courage: Generations of Women's Resistance and Action.* Philadelphia: New Society Publishers.
1990   *You Can't Kill the Spirit.* Philadelphia: New Society Publishers.
1982   *Reweaving the Web of Life: Feminism and Nonviolence.* Philadelphia: New Society Publishers.

McClendon, James W.
1986   *Systematic Theology: Ethics.* Nashville: Abingdon.
McClendon, James, and Nancey Murphy.
1989   "Distinguishing Modern and Postmodern Theologies." *Modern Theology* 5:3 (April): 191ff.
McClendon, James, and James Smith.
1975   *Understanding Religious Convictions.* South Bend, IN: University of Notre Dame Press.
McClintock, Michael.
1992   *Instruments of Statecraft: U.S. Guerilla Warfare, Counter-Insurgency and Counter-Terrorism, 1940–1990.* New York: Pantheon.
McGinnis, James.
1989   *Journey into Compassion: A Spirituality for the Long Haul.* Bloomington, IN: Meyer-Stone.
McGovern, Arthur.
1989   *Liberation Theology and Its Critics: Toward an Assessment.* Maryknoll, NY: Orbis.
1981   *Marxism: An American Christian Perspective.* Maryknoll, NY: Orbis.
McGuire, Ellen.
1992   "A Place Called Hope." *The Nation,* December 28, pp 818ff.
McHarg, Ian.
1992   *Design with Nature.* New York: John Wiley & Sons.
McIntosh, Peggy.
1989   "White Privilege: Unpacking the Invisible Knapsack." *Peace and Freedom,* July–August, pp 10ff. Reprinted in M. Anderson and P. Hill-Collins, eds. *Race, Class and Gender.* London: Wadsworth, 1993.
McKenzie, Sabra.
1992   "¡Viva La Guadalupana!" *Catholic Worker,* December, pp 1f.
McLory, Robert.
1991   "Jury Acquits Rebel Priest on 'Necessity' Defense." *National Catholic Reporter,* July 19.
McManus, Philip, and Gerald Schlabach, eds.
1991   *Relentless Persistence: Nonviolent Action in Latin America.* Philadelphia: New Society Publishers.
McWilliams, Carey.
1946   *Southern California: An Island on the Land.* Salt Lake City: Peregrine Smith Books.
Meadows, Donella.
1993   "Economic Growth Can't Continue But There Is No End to Development." *Los Angeles Times,* April 12, pp M2f.
Meadows, Donella, Dennis Meadows, and Jorgen Randers.
1992   *Beyond the Limits.* Post Hills, VT: Chelsea Green.
Mendes-Flohr, Paul.
1983   " 'To Brush History Against the Grain': The Eschatology of the Frankfurt School and Ernst Bloch." *Journal of the American Academy of Religion* 51:4 (December): 631ff.
Menos, Dennis.
1992   *Arms over Diplomacy: Reflections on the Persian Gulf War.* Westport, CT: Greenwood Publishing.

Meredith, Thomas.
1992   "Environmental Impact Assessment, Cultural Diversity, and Sustainable Rural Development." *Environmental Impact Assessment Review* 12.

Merton, Thomas.
1971   *Contemplative Prayer.* Garden City, NY: Doubleday Image.
1968   *Faith and Violence: Christian Teaching and Christian Practice.* South Bend, IN: University of Notre Dame Press.
1956   *Thoughts in Solitude.* Garden City, NY: Doubleday Image.

Mesters, Carlos.
1989   *Defenseless Flower: A New Reading of the Bible.* Translated by F. McDonagh. Maryknoll, NY: Orbis.

Michaelis, Wilhelm.
1967   "Horaō, eidon, ktl." In *Theological Dictionary of the New Testament,* vol 5, edited by G. Kittel. Grand Rapids, MI: William B. Eerdmans, pp 315ff.

Míguez Bonino, José.
1975   *Doing Theology in a Revolutionary Situation.* Philadelphia: Fortress Press.

Miles, Jack.
1992   "Blacks vs. Browns: The Struggle for the Bottom Rung." *Atlantic Monthly,* October, pp 41ff.

Milgrom, Jo and Duane Christiensen.
1989   "Encountering the Exodus Story through Handmade Midrash." In *Experiencing the Exodus from Egypt,* edited by D. Christiensen, Berkeley, CA: BIBAL Press.

Miller, Alice.
1990   *Banished Knowledge: Facing Childhood Injuries.* Translated by L. Vennewitz. New York: Doubleday Anchor.
1984   *Thou Shalt Not Be Aware: Society's Betrayal of the Child.* New York: Farrar, Straus & Giroux.
1983   *For Your Own Good: Hidden Cruelty in Child-Rearing and the Roots of Violence.* New York: Farrar, Straus & Giroux.
1981   *The Drama of the Gifted Child.* New York: Basic Books.

Miller, Bruce.
1991   *The Gabrielino.* Los Osos, CA: Sand River Press.
1988   *Chumash: A Picture of Their World.* Los Osos, CA: Sand River Press.

Miller, Jean Baker.
1976   *Toward a New Psychology of Women.* Boston: Beacon Press.

Miller, Mark Crispin.
1988   "Gonna Hawk around the Clock Tonight: How Television Stole the Soul of Rock and Roll." *Mother Jones,* November, 38ff.

Miller, Martin, ed.
1970   *P. A. Kropotkin: Selected Writings on Anarchism and Revolution.* Cambridge, MA: MIT Press.

Miller, Perry.
1964   *Errand into the Wilderness.* Cambridge, MA: Harvard University Press.

Miller, Susan Brown.
1984   *Femininity.* New York: Linden Press/Simon & Schuster.

Minear, Paul.
1981   *New Testament Apocalyptic.* Nashville: Abingdon.

1968   *I Saw a New Earth: An Introduction to the Visions of the Apocalypse.* Washington, DC: Corpus Books.

1966   "Ontology and Ecclesiology in the Apocalypse." *New Testament Studies* 12, pp 93ff.

Miranda, José Porfirio.

1981   *Communism in the Bible.* Translated by R. Barr. Maryknoll, NY: Orbis.

Mirkin, Marsha Pravder, ed.

1990   *The Social and Political Contexts of Family Therapy.* Boston: Allyn & Bacon.

Mitchell, Greg.

1992   *The Campaign of the Century: Upton Sinclair's Race for Governor of California and the Birth of Media Politics.* New York: Random House.

Moberg, David.

1988   "Keeping the Company in the Company Town." *In These Times* 12:24 (May 11–17).

Moffat, Susan.

1993   "Draft Rift Lingers 50 Years Later." *Los Angeles Times,* March 12, pp A1ff.

Moltmann, Jürgen.

1985   *God in Creation: A New Theology of Creation and the Spirit of God.* San Francisco: Harper & Row.

1976   "An Open Letter to José Míguez Bonino." *Christianity and Crisis,* March 29, pp 57ff.

Monroe, Sylvester.

1993   "Trading Colors for a Future." *Emerge,* July–August, pp 46ff.

Moore, Robert, and Douglas Gillette.

1990   *King, Warrior, Magician, Lover: Rediscovering the Archetypes of the Mature Masculine.* San Francisco: Harper San Francisco.

Morley, Jefferson.

1992   "When Reaganites Backed D'Aubuisson, They Unleashed a Political Assassin." *Los Angeles Times,* March 1, pp M1f.

Morris, Charles.

1992   "But What Do the Markets Think?" *Los Angeles Times,* December 13, p M1f.

Morris, David.

1988   "Planetary Corporations Thwart Devolutionism." *Utne Reader,* November–December, pp 98f.

Morris, Glen.

1991   "The Battle for New Sogobia." *Western Shoshone Nation Newsletter* (Duckwater, NV), April, pp 3ff.

Mosely, Ray.

1980   "Conformity, Intolerance Grip Revolutionary Iran." *Detroit Free Press,* November 25, pp 3f.

Munk, Erica.

1991   "The New Face of Techno-War." *The Nation,* May 6, pp 583ff.

Munro, Winsome.

1982   "Women Disciples in Mark?" *Catholic Biblical Quarterly* 44, pp 225ff.

Mydans, Seth.
1990 "Clash of Cultures Grows Amid American Dream." *New York Times,* March 26, p A12.
1988 "Aborigines Cast a Shadow over Australia's Party." *New York Times,* January 26.

Myers, Ched.
1993 "Vision Quest: Why We Must Re-member What Has Been Dis-membered." *The Other Side,* 29:2 (March–April): 8ff.
1992a "Looking for Justice, Holding the Peace." *Sojourners,* November, pp 30ff.
1992b "Framed in Black and White: To Live and Die in a City of Angels." *Sojourners,* July, pp 38ff.
1991a "We're All in the Same Boat: A Reflection on Gospel Journeys and the Quincentennial." *Sojourners,* October, pp 30ff.
1991b "A Gethsemane Awakening: Gospel Discernment in the Apocalypse of War." *Sojourners,* April, pp 14ff.
1988 *Binding the Strong Man: A Political Reading of Mark's Story of Jesus.* Maryknoll, NY: Orbis.
1986a "The Eye of a Geopolitical Storm: Nuclear Politics in the South Pacific." *Sojourners,* March, pp 8ff.
1986b "Deadly Paradises: Encounters with War and Love in the Pacific." *National Outlook* (Sydney, Australia), January.
1985a "The Church Works for a Non-Violent Revolution in New Caledonia." *National Outlook,* July.
1985b "Nuclear Colonialism: France in New Caledonia." *Pacific News* (Sydney, Australia), May–June.
1983a "The Wind That Diverts the Storm: The Nuclear Free and Independent Pacific Movement." *Sojourners,* August, pp 10ff.
1983b "By What Authority? The Bible and Civil Disobedience." *Sojourners,* May, pp 11ff.
1982 "The Broadening Middle: The Question of War in Catholicism." *Sojourners,* February, 36f.
1981 "Storming the Gates of Hell: Reflections on Christian Evangelism in Nuclear Security Areas." *The Christian Century,* September 16, pp 898ff.
1980a "Armed with the Gospel of Peace: The Vision of Ephesians." *Theology News and Notes* (Pasadena, CA), March, pp 17ff.
1980b "Vision from a Blind Man: The Naming of Bartimaeus Community." *Sojourners,* March, pp 25f.

Myers, William A.
1976 *Trolleys to the Surf: The Story of the Los Angeles Pacific Railway.* Glendale, CA: Interurban Press.

Nabokov, Peter.
1987 "Present Memories, Past History." In *The American Indian and the Problem of History,* edited by C. Martin. New York: Oxford University Press, pp 144ff.

Nakagawa, Gordon.
1992 "The Loyalty Oath and the 'No, No Boys.'" In *50 Year Remembrance: Japanese American Internment,* edited by S. Embrey, J. Matsuura, G. Nak-agawa, and K. Wada. Conference held February 15 at the Japanese American Cultural and Community Center, pp 10f.

Nakanishi, Don, ed.
1993   "Japanese American Internment: Fiftieth Anniversary Commemorative Issue." *Amerasia Journal* 19:1.
Nakawatese, Ed.
1989   "Report on 'Seventy Years of U.S. Communism.'" Conference sponsored by the Research Group on Socialism and Democracy, November 10. Unpublished paper, Philadelphia: AFSC.
National Council of Churches, USA.
1984   "Policy Statement on Racial Justice." Adopted by Governing Board, November 10. New York: NCC USA.
National Geographic.
1991   "1491: America before Columbus." Special issue, October.
Nazario, Sonia.
1993   "Hunger, High Food Costs Found in Inner-City Area." *Los Angeles Times,* June 11, pp A1f.
Neal, Mary A.
1977   *A Socio-theology of Letting Go: The Role of a First World Church Facing Third World Peoples.* New York: Paulist Press.
Needleman, Ruth.
1988   "Women Workers: A Force for Rebuilding Unionism." Special issue. *Labor Research Review* 11 (Spring): 1ff.
Nelson, Alan.
1981   *Psychology for Peace and Survival.* Santa Cruz, CA: Resource Center for Nonviolence.
Nelson-Pallmeyer, Jack.
1992   *Brave New World Order: Must We Pledge Allegiance?* Maryknoll, NY: Orbis.
1989   *War against the Poor: Low-Intensity Conflict and Christian Faith.* Maryknoll, NY: Orbis.
Neusner, Jacob.
1990   *A Midrash Reader.* Minneapolis: Fortress Press.
Newhagen, John.
1992   "Images of Fear." *Washington Journalism Review,* July–August, p 27.
Newman, Katherine.
1988   *Falling from Grace: The Experience of Downward Mobility in the American Middle Class.* New York: Free Press.
Newmann, Peter.
1991   "Sustainable Settlements: Restoring the Commons." *The Urban Ecologist,* Fall.
Newton, Edmund.
1993   "Coalition Geared to Averting Riot Not Eager to Disband." *Los Angeles Times,* April 25, pp J1ff.
Nichols, May, and Stanley Young.
1991   *The Amazing L.A. Environment: A Handbook for Change.* Los Angeles: Natural Resources Defense Council/Living Planet Press.
Niebuhr, Reinhold.
1961   "Intellectual Autobiography." In *Reinhold Niebuhr: His Religious, Social and Political Thought,* edited by C. Kegley and R. Bretall. New York: Macmillan Co.

1956   *An Interpretation of Christian Ethics.* New York: Charles Scribner's Sons.
1960   *Moral Man and Immoral Society.* New York: Charles Scribner's Sons.

Nietschmann, Bernard.
1988   "Third World War: The Global Conflict over the Rights of Indigenous Nations." *Utne Reader,* November–December, pp 84ff.

Njeri, Itabari.
1992   "Window into Time: Photos Show Facets of Black Life Long Ignored." *Los Angeles Times,* August 23, pp E1f.
1991a   "Rocking the Cradle of Classical Civilization." *Los Angeles Times,* February 1, pp E1ff.
1991b   "Beyond the Melting Pot," and "The World State." *Los Angeles Times,* January 13, pp E8.

Noble, David.
1977   *America by Design: Science, Technology and the Rise of Corporate Capitalism.* Oxford: Oxford University Press.

Nolan, Albert.
1985   *The Service of the Poor and Spiritual Growth.* London: Catholic Institute for International Relations.

Norris, Christopher.
1992   *Uncritical Theory: Postmodernism, Intellectuals and the Gulf War.* Amherst: University of Massachusetts Press.

Nouwen, Henri.
1972   *The Wounded Healer: Ministry in Contemporary Society.* New York: Doubleday & Co.

Nunley, Jan.
1992   "The Second Reformation: Interview with Steve Charleston." *The Witness* 75:10 (October): 28.

Oakman, Douglas.
1986   *Jesus and the Economic Questions of His Day.* Studies in the Bible and Early Christianity, vol 8. Lewiston, NY: Edwin Mellen Press.

Obayashi, H.
1975   "The End of Ideology and Politicized Theology." *Cross Currents,* Winter, pp 383ff.

O'Brien, John.
1991   *Theology and the Option for the Poor.* Collegeville, MN: Michael Glazier Books.

O'Connor, Elizabeth.
1969   *Journey Inward, Journey Outward.* New York: Harper & Row.

O'Hare, William, and Judy Felt.
1991   *Asian Americans: America's Fastest Growing Minority Group.* Population Trends and Public Policy no. 19. Washington, DC: Population Reference Bureau.

O'Neill, Stephanie.
1992   "L.A. Stories: A City Ablaze Casts a Glaring Light on the Press." *Columbia Journalism Review,* July–August, pp 23ff.

Oreskes, Michael.
1990   "Drug War Underlines Fickleness of Public." *New York Times,* September 9.

Ortíz, Alphonso et al.
1991   "Origins: Through Tewa Eyes." *National Geographic,* October, pp 6ff.
Ortíz y Pino, Jerry.
1992   "Man's War on Woman." *Radical Grace* (Albuquerque, NM) 5: 5 (October–November): 5.
Otaguro, Janice.
1992   "Beat the Drum Slowly: Next Year Marks the 100th Anniversary of the Overthrow of Queen Liliuokalani." *Honolulu Magazine,* June, pp 31ff.
Owensby, Walter.
1988   *Economics for Prophets: A Primer on Concepts, Realities and Values in Our Economic System.* Grand Rapids, MI: William B. Eerdmans.
Pacosz, Christina.
1985   *Some Winded, Wild Beast.* Detroit: Black & Red Press.
Paige, Glenn, and Sarah Gilliat.
1991   *Nonviolence in Hawaii's Spiritual Traditions.* Spark Matsunaga Institute for Peace. Honolulu: University of Hawai'i.
Palmer, Thomas.
1990   "P & G will Resume Ads on Channel 7 in '91." *Boston Globe,* December 12.
Parenti, Michael.
1986   *Inventing Reality: The Politics of the Mass Media.* New York: St. Martin's Press.
Parks, Rosa, with Jim Haskins.
1992   *Rosa Parks: My Story.* New York: Dial Books.
Passell, Peter.
1990   "So Much for Assumptions about Immigrants and Jobs." *New York Times,* April 15.
Patterson, Orlando.
1982   *Slavery and Social Death: A Comparative Study.* Cambridge, MA: Harvard University Press.
Patterson, William, ed.
1971   *We Charge Genocide.* New York: International Publishers.
Pavlik, Bruce, Pamela Muick, Sharon Johnson, and Marjorie Popper.
1991   *Oaks of California.* Los Olivos, CA: Cachuma Press.
Peck, M. Scott.
1983   *People of the Lie: The Hope for Healing Human Evil.* New York: Touchstone.
Peele, Stanton.
1989   "Ain't Misbehavin': Addiction Has Become an All-Purpose Excuse." *The Sciences,* July–August, pp 14ff.
Penn, William.
1970   *William Penn's Own Account of the Lenni Lenape or Delaware Indians.* Edited by A. Myers. Wilmington, DE: Middle Atlantic Press.
Perkins, John.
1976   *Let Justice Roll.* Glendale: Regal Books.
Peter-Raoul, Mar, Linda Forcey and Robert Hunter.
1990   *Yearning to Breathe Free: Liberation Theologies in the U.S.* Maryknoll, NY: Orbis.

Peters, Cynthia, ed.
1992   *Collateral Damage: The New World Order at Home and Abroad.* Boston:
          South End Press.
Peterson, Jonathan.
1991   "Industrial Blues in the Southland." *Los Angeles Times,* July 27, pp A1ff.
Pierre, Andrew.
1982   *The Global Politics of Arms Sales.* Princeton, NJ: Princeton University
          Press.
Pilgrim, Walter.
1981   *Good News to the Poor: Wealth and Poverty in Luke-Acts.* Minneapolis:
          Augsburg Publishing House.
Pinderhughes, Elaine.
1990   "Legacy of Slavery: The Experience of Black Families in America." In
          The Social and Political Contexts of Family Therapy, edited by M. Mirkin.
          Boston: Allyn & Bacon, pp 289ff.
Pine, Art.
1990   "High-Tech Sales Strictures Shift to Third World." *Los Angeles Times,*
          June 24, pp A1f.
Pinsky, Mark.
1987   "The Mexican-Hindu Connection." *Los Angeles Times,* December 21,
          pp V:1ff.
Pitt, Leonard.
1966   *The Decline of the Californios: A Social History of the Spanish-Speaking
          Californians, 1846–1890.* Berkeley: University of California Press.
Plant, Judith, ed.
1991   *Healing the Wounds: The Promise of Ecofeminism.* Philadelphia: New
          Society Publishers.
Plevin, Nancy.
1991   "Latinos Find a Hidden Jewish Heritage." *Los Angeles Times,* May 11,
          pp F16f.
Pollitt, Katha.
1992   "Are Women Morally Superior to Men?" *The Nation,* December 28,
          pp 799ff.
Pool, Bob.
1993   "Angel Feud: Rift over High-Rise's 'Unity' Mural." *Los Angeles Times,*
          February 12, pp B1f.
Potter, George Ann.
1988   *Dialogue on Debt: Alternative Analyses and Solutions.* Washington, DC:
          Center of Concern.
Prinz, Joachim.
1973   *The Secret Jews.* New York: Random House.
Quigley, Margaret, and Chip Bertlet.
1992   "Traditional Values, Racism and Christian Theocracy: The Right-wing
          Revolt against the Modern Age." *The Public Eye,* December, pp 1ff.
Rader, W.
1978   *The Church and Racial Hostility: A History of the Interpretation of Eph
          2: 11–22.* Tübingen: J. C. B. Mohr.

Ramachandran, G., and T. K. Mahadevan, eds.
1967   *Gandhi: His Relevance for Our Times.* Berkeley, CA: World Without War Council.

Ramírez, Anthony.
1990   "Proctor and Gamble Pulls Some TV Ads over Slur to Coffee." *New York Times,* May 12, pp A1f.

Ramos-Horta, José.
1987   *Funu: The Unfinished Saga of East Timor.* Trenton, NJ: Red Sea Press.

Ramsey, William.
1992   "Media Study: Post-Gulf War Coverage." *Middle East Peace Notes* (AFSC, Denver, CO), March, pp 3ff.

Raphael, David, ed.
1992   *The Expulsion 1492 Chronicles: An Anthology of Medieval Chronicles Relating to the Expulsion of the Jews from Spain and Portugal.* North Hollywood, CA: Carmi House Press, pp iiiff.

Raskin, Marcus.
1991   "The Road to Reconstruction: Rethinking the Left." *The Nation,* April 22, 512ff.

Rasmussen, Cecilia.
1993   "The City Then and Now." *Los Angeles Times,* June 7, p B3.

Rausch, Thomas.
1990   *Radical Christian Communities.* Collegeville, MN: Liturgical Press.

Rauschenbusch, Walter.
1945   *A Theology for the Social Gospel.* Nashville: Abingdon.

Read, Phyllis, and Bernard Witlieb.
1992   *The Book of Women's Firsts.* New York: Random House.

Recinos, Harold.
1992   *Jesus Weeps: Global Encounters on Our Doorstep.* Nashville: Abingdon.

Redclift, Michael.
1987   *Sustainable Development: Exploring the Contradictions.* London: Methuen.

Reed, Adolph and Julian Bond, eds.
1991   "The Assault on Equality: Race, Rights and the New Orthodoxy." Special Issue. *The Nation,* December 9.

Reid, Alastair.
1992   "Reflections: Waiting for Columbus." *New Yorker,* February 24, pp 57ff.

Religious Network for Equality for Women.
1988   "Learning Economics: Empowering Women for Action." Women's Collective Project in Economic Literacy. New York: RNEW.

Rich, Adrienne.
1987   "Resisting Amnesia: History and Personal Life." *Ms,* March, pp 66f.

Richard, Pablo.
1991   "1492: The Violence of God and the Future of Christianity." Translated by F. McDonagh. *Concilium,* October, pp 59ff.

Richardson, Bill.
1985   "Hispanic American Concerns." *Foreign Policy,* Fall, pp 30ff.

Richardson, Herbert, ed.
1974   *Religion and Political Society.* New York: Harper & Row.

Richter, Peyton, ed.
  1971   *Utopias: Social Ideals and Communal Experiments.* Boston: Holbrook
           Press.
Ringe, Sharon.
  1985   *Jesus, Liberation, and the Biblical Jubilee.* Overtures to Biblical Theology
           19. Philadelphia: Fortress Press.
Ringle, Ken.
  1992   "Freeing the Slaves and His Conscience: How 500 Gained Liberty through
           a Little-Known Baptist Emancipator." *Baptist Peacemaker* 12:3–4 (Fall-
           Winter): 8f.
Rios-Bustamante, Antonio, and Pedro Castillo.
  1986   *An Illustrated History of Mexican Los Angeles, 1781–1985.* Monograph
           no. 12. Los Angeles: Chicano Studies Research Center Publications.
Rioux, Caroline.
  1992   "Who Can You Trust with Your Money?" *Blueprint for Social Justice*
           (New Orleans) 45:8 (April): 1ff.
Risen, James.
  1992   "One Issue That Bush and Clinton Won't Touch: Bailout." *Los Angeles
           Times,* October 11, p D1f.
Roberts, Nanette.
  1993   "Special Issue on the UCC Resolution of Self-Governance of Native
           Hawaiians." *New Conversations* 15:1 (Spring).
Robinson, John.
  1991   *The San Gabriels.* Arcadia, CA: Big Santa Anita Historical Society.
Robinson, W. W.
  1948   *Land in California: The Story of Mission Lands, Ranchos, Squatters,
           Mining Claims, Land Scrip and Homesteads.* Berkeley: University of
           California Press.
Rodriguez, Luis, Cle Sloan, and Kershaun Scott.
  1992   "Gangs: The New Political Force in Los Angeles." *Los Angeles Times,*
           September 13, pp M1f.
Rodriguez, Primitivo, ed.
  1993   *From Global Pillage or Global Village: A Perspective from Work-
           ing People of Color on the North American Free Trade Agreement.*
           Unpublished paper. Philadelphia: AFSC.
Rohr, Richard.
  1993   *Near Occasions of Grace.* Maryknoll, NY: Orbis.
Rohr, Richard, and Andreas Ebert.
  1990   *Rediscovering the Enneagram: An Ancient Tool for a New Spiritual
           Journey.* New York: Crossroad.
Romero, C. Gilbert.
  1991   *Hispanic Devotional Piety: Tracing the Biblical Roots.* Maryknoll, NY:
           Orbis.
Romo, Ricardo.
  1983   *East Los Angeles: History of a Barrio.* Austin: University of Texas Press.
Rose, Stephen.
  1986   *The American Profile Poster: Who Owns What, Who Makes How Much,
           Who Works Where, and Who Lives with Whom.* New York: Pantheon.

Rose, Wendy.
1992   "For Some, It's a Time of Mourning." In *Without Discovery: A Native Response to Columbus,* edited by R. Gonzalez. Seattle: Broken Moon Press, pp 3ff.

Rose, Willie Lee, ed.
1976   *A Documentary History of Slavery in North America.* New York: Oxford University Press.

Rosenau, Pauline Marie.
1992   *Post-Modernism and the Social Sciences: Insights, Inroads, and Intrusions.* Princeton, NJ: Princeton University Press.

Rosentiel, Thomas.
1989   "Viewers Found to Confuse TV Entertainment with News." *Los Angeles Times,* August 17, p A17.

Ross, Andrew.
1990   "Do-It-Yourself Weaponry." *The Bulletin of the Atomic Scientists* 46:4 (May): 20ff.

Ruether, Rosemary Radford.
1992   *Gaia and God: An Ecofeminist Theology of Earth Healing.* San Francisco: Harper San Francisco.
1986   *Women-Church: Theology and Practice of Feminist Liturgical Communities.* San Francisco: Harper & Row.
1985   *WomanGuides: Readings Toward a Feminist Theology.* Boston: Beacon Press.

Ruether, Rosemary Radford, and Rosemary Keller.
1983   *Women and Religion in America: A Documentary History.* San Francisco: Harper & Row.

Russell, D. S.
1978   *Apocalyptic, Ancient and Modern.* Philadelphia: Fortress Press.

Russell, Elbert.
1979   *The History of Quakerism.* Richmond, IN: Friends United Press.

Russell, Letty.
1993   *Church in the Round: Feminist Interpretation of the Church.* Louisville, KY: Westminster/John Knox.
1992   *Household of Freedom: Authority in Feminist Theology.* Louisville, KY: Westminster/John Knox.
1990   *Feminist Interpretation of the Bible.* Louisville, KY: Westminster/John Knox.
1986   *Human Liberation in a Feminist Perspective.* Louisville, KY: Westminster/John Knox.

Russell, Letty, Kwok Pui-lan, Ada Isasi-Díaz, and Katie Cannon, eds.
1988   *Inheriting Our Mothers' Gardens: Feminist Theology in Third World Perspective.* Louisville, KY: Westminster/John Knox.

Rutschman, LaVerne.
1981   "Anabaptism and Liberation Theology." *Mennonite Quarterly Review* 55:3 (July): 255ff.

Sabath, Bob.
1980   "A Community of Communities: The Growing Ecumenical Network." *Sojourners,* January, pp 17ff.

Sakatani, Bacon.
    1992   "Let's Tell the Truth about Heart Mountain." *United Methodist Monitor* (newsletter of the General Commission of Religion and Race) 36 (Spring): 6f.

Sale, Kirkpatrick.
    1988   "Devolution, American-Style: Decentralism Hits Home." *Utne Reader,* November–December, pp 95ff.
    1985   *Dwellers in the Land: The Bioregional Vision.* San Francisco: Sierra Club.
    1990   *The Conquest of Paradise: Christopher Columbus and the Columbian Legacy.* New York: Alfred A. Knopf.

Salvorsen, Julie.
    1993   "The Mask of Solidarity: Theatre of the Oppressed and Popular Education as 'Naming the Moment.'" In *Playing Boal,* edited by J. Cohen-Cruz and M. Schutzman. London: Routledge.

Sanderlin, George.
    1992   *Witness: Writings of Bartolomé de Las Casas.* Maryknoll, NY: Orbis.

Sanders, James.
    1969   "Outside the Camp." *Union Seminary Quarterly Review* 24:3 (Spring): 239ff.

Sanders, Ronald.
    1992   *Lost Tribes and Promised Lands: The Origins of American Racism.* New York: Harper Collins.

Sandman, Peter, and JoAnn Valenti.
    1986   "Scared Stiff — or Scared into Action." *The Bulletin of the Atomic Scientists,* January, pp 12ff.

Sanford, John, and George Lough.
    1988   *What Men Are Like: The Psychology of Men for Men and the Women Who Live with Them.* New York: Paulist.

San Juan, E.
    1992   *Racial Transformations/Critical Transformations: Articulations of Power in Ethnic and Racial Studies in the United States.* Atlantic Highlands, NJ: Humanities Press International.

Sanks, T.
    1980   "Liberation Theology and the Social Gospel: Variations on a Theme." *Theological Studies* 41:4 (December): 668ff.

Santiago, Daniel.
    1990   "The Aesthetics of Terror, the Hermeneutics of Death." *America,* March 24, pp 292ff.

Sassen, Saskia.
    1989   "America's Immigration 'Problem.'" *World Policy Journal,* pp 812ff; excerpt from *The Mobility of Labor and Capital: A Study in International Investment and Labor Flow.* New York: Cambridge University Press, 1988.

Saville-Troike, Muriel.
    1978   *A Guide to Culture in the Classroom.* Rosslyn, VA: National Clearinghouse for Bilingual Education.

Schaaf, Gregory.
    1990   *Wampum Belts and Peace Trees: George Morgan, Native Americans and Revolutionary Diplomacy.* Golden CO: Fulcrum Publishing.

Schachter, Jim.
1990   "Marciano Brothers' Time of Trial." *Los Angeles Times Magazine,* January 21, pp D1ff.
Schaef, Anne Wilson.
1987   *When Society Becomes an Addict.* San Francisco: Harper & Row.
Schaef, Anne Wilson, and Diane Fassel.
1988   *The Addictive Organization.* San Francisco: Harper & Row.
Schaper, Donna.
1993   "Liturgies Where Women Matter." *Christianity and Crisis,* March 1, pp 70ff.
Schimmel, Julie.
1991   "Inventing 'the Indian.'" In *The West as America: Reinterpreting Images of the Frontier, 1820–1920,* edited by W. Truettner. Washington, DC: Smithsonian Institution Press, pp 149ff.
Schmidt, Daryl.
1990   *The Gospel of Mark: The Scholars Bible.* Sonoma, CA: Poleridge Press.
Schneider, William.
1993   "Bush's Pardons Break All the Rules." *Los Angeles Times,* January 3, pp M2f.
Schreiter, Robert.
1985   *Constructing Local Theologies.* Maryknoll, NY: Orbis.
Schuck, Peter, and David Rieff.
1991   "America and the New Immigrant Experience: Coming Together, Coming Apart." *Los Angeles Times,* May 5, pp M1ff.
Schulman, Bruce.
1991   "Dark Side of American Dream: When Reinventing Past Means Forgetting It." *Los Angeles Times,* November 3, pp M1f.
Schüssler Fiorenza, Elisabeth.
1985   *The Book of Revelation: Justice and Judgment.* Philadelphia: Fortress Press.
1983   *In Memory of Her: A Feminist Theological Reconstruction of Christian Origins.* New York: Crossroad.
Schwartz-Salant, Nathan.
1982   *Narcissism and Character Transformation: The Psychology of Narcissistic Character Disorders.* Toronto: Inner City Books.
Scialabba, George.
1991   Beyond Paradise: Christopher Lasch's Case against Progress." *L.A. Weekly,* May 31–June 6, pp 29ff.
Scott, David Clark.
1991   "US Trade Unionists Seek Mexican Allies." *Christian Science Monitor,* July 11.
Scott, Dick.
1975   *Ask That Mountain: The Story of Parihaka.* Auckland, NZ: Heinemann/ Southern Cross Press.
Segovia, Fernando, ed.
1985   *Discipleship in the New Testament.* Philadelphia: Fortress Press.
Segundo, Juan Luis.
1979   "Capitalism Versus Socialism: *Crux Theologica.*" In *Frontiers of Theology in Latin America,* edited by R. Gibellini. Maryknoll, NY: Orbis, pp 240ff.

Seid, Roberta.
    1989   *Never Too Thin: Why Women are at War with Their Bodies.* Englewood Cliffs, NJ: Prentice-Hall.

Sennett, Richard, and Jonathan Cobb.
    1973   *The Hidden Injuries of Class.* New York: Vintage.

Seriguchi, Karen, and Frank Abe, eds.
    1980   *Japanese America: Contemporary Perspectives on Internment.* Proceedings of conferences held January–March 1980 in the state of Washington. Seattle: AFSC.

Sewell, Marylin, ed.
    1991   *Cries of the Spirit: A Celebration of Women's Spirituality.* Boston: Beacon Press.

Shah, Sonia, ed.
    1992   *Between Fear and Hope: A Decade of Peace Activism.* New York: Nuclear Times Magazine.

Shamleffer, Doris et al.
    1989   *Borders and Quaker Values.* Philadelphia: AFSC.

Shannon, Thomas, ed.
    1980   *War or Peace? The Search for New Answers.* Maryknoll, NY: Orbis.

Sharp, Gene.
    1979   *Gandhi as a Political Strategist.* Boston: Porter Sargent Publishers.
    1973   *The Politics of Non-Violent Action.* 3 vols. Boston: Porter Sargent Publishers.

Shashaty, Andre.
    1992   "The Missing Beat." *Columbia Journalism Review,* July–August, pp 26.

Shaw, David.
    1992a   "Media Set Agenda But Often Misjudge Public's Interest." *Los Angeles Times,* October 26, pp A1ff.
    1992b   "The Media and the LAPD: From Coziness to Conflict." Four-part series, *Los Angeles Times,* May 24–27.

Sheehan, Michael.
    1983   *Beyond Majority Rule: Voteless Decisions in the Religious Society of Friends.* Westchester, PA: Philadelphia Yearly Meeting.

Sheine, Judith.
    1992   "Affordable Housing: 'Small Scale, Community Based.'" *Los Angeles Times,* October 26, p B5.

Shirley, Carol Bradley.
    1992   "Where Have You Been?" *Columbia Journalism Review,* July–August, pp 25f.

Shor, Ira, ed.
    1987   *Freire for the Classroom: A Sourcebook for Liberatory Teaching.* Portsmouth, NH: Boynton/Cook Publishers.

Shuger, Scott.
    1991   "Operation Desert Store: First the Air War, Then the Ground War, Now the Marketing Campaign." *Los Angeles Times Magazine,* September 29, pp 18ff.

Shuit, Douglas, and Patrick McDonnell.
    1992   "Calculating the Impact of California's Immigrants." *Los Angeles Times,* January 6, p A1.

Sibley, Mulford Q.

1970   *The Obligation to Disobey.* New York: Council on Religion and Inter-
        national Affairs.

Sidel, Ruth.

1990   *On Her Own: Growing up in the Shadow of the American Dream.* New
        York: Viking.

Sider, Ronald.

1977   *Rich Christians in an Age of Hunger: A Biblical Study.* Downers Grove,
        IL: Intervarsity Press.

Siegel, Barry.

1993   "Showdown at Rocky Flats." Two-part series, *Los Angeles Times Maga-
        zine,* August 8 and 15.

Silk, Leonard.

1992   "Next: Cold War of the Capitalists?" *New York Times,* March 6.

Silko, Leslie Marmon.

1977   *Ceremony.* New York: Penguin.

Silone, Ignazio.

1946   *Bread and Wine.* Translated by G. David and E. Mosbacher. New York:
        Penguin.

Silverstein, Stuart, and Sonni Efron.

1992   "Guess ? Accepts Pact to Curb Labor Violations." *Los Angeles Times,*
        May 8, pp A1f.

Simmons, Michael.

1987   "Review of *Black and Red: W. E. B. Du Bois and the Afro-American
        Response to the Cold War, 1944–1963* by Gerald Horne." *The Bulletin of
        the Atomic Scientists* 43:7 (September): 56f.

Simon, Julian.

1990   "Bring on the Wretched Refuse." *Wall Street Journal,* January 26.

Simon, Richard.

1993   "Anglo Vote Carried Riordan to Victory." *Los Angeles Times,* June 3,
        p A25.

Sindab, Jeane.

1990   "Blacks, Indigenous People and the Churches, 1992: Ending the Pain, Be-
        ginning the Hope." Paper presented to the Continental Forum on Racism
        in the Americas and Caribbean, September. Geneva: World Council of
        Churches.

Singer, Daniel.

1992   "Struggling with One Superpower." *Peace and Democracy News,* Winter,
        pp 31ff.

SIPRI (Stockholm International Peace Research Institute).

1992   *SIPRI Yearbook, 1992: World Armaments and Disarmament.* Oxford:
        Oxford University Press.

Sivard, Ruth.

1985   *World Military and Social Expenditures, 1985.* Washington, DC: World
        Priorities.

Sklar, Holly, ed.

1980   *Trilateralism: The Trilateral Commission and Elite Planning for World
        Management.* Boston: South End Press.

Slater, Philip.
    1983   *Wealth Addiction.* New York: E. P. Dutton.
    1977   *Footholds: Understand the Shifting Sexual and Family Tensions in Our Culture.* New York: E. P. Dutton.
Sloan, Robert.
    1977   *The Favorable Year of the Lord: A Study of Jubilary Theology in the Gospel of Luke.* Austin, TX: Schola.
Smith, D.
    1973   "The Two Made One: Eph 2: 14–18." *Ohio Journal of Religious Studies,* January, pp 35ff.
Smith, Gary, ed.
    1989   *Benjamin: Philosophy, History, Aesthetics.* Chicago: University of Chicago Press.
Smith, Hedrick.
    1992   *The Media and the Gulf War.* Cabin John, MD: Seven Locks Press.
Smith, Kenneth, and Ira Zepp, Jr.
    1986   *Search for the Beloved Community: The Thinking of Martin Luther King, Jr.* Washington, DC: University Press of America.
Smith, William.
    1969   *The Rhetoric of American Politics: A Study of Documents.* Westport, CT: Greenwood Publishing.
Smolich, Thomas.
    1990   "L.A.'s Day Laborers — The View 'From Below.'" *Desde la Base* (Newsletter of Proyecto Pastoral, Los Angeles), Summer, pp 2ff.
Snattman, Felix.
    1968   *With Grob in Toontown: Weedy Finds the Missing Piece.* Ashbourne, CA: Rumproast Press.
Snyder, Gary.
    1992   "Coming into the Watershed." Special Issue. *Wild Earth* (Cenozoic Society, Canton, NY), pp 65ff.
Snyder, T. Richard.
    1992   *Divided We Fall: Moving from Suspicion to Solidarity.* Louisville, KY: Westminster/John Knox.
Sobrino, Jon.
    1978   *Christology at the Crossroad: A Latin American Approach.* Translated by J. Drury. Maryknoll, NY: Orbis.
Sobrino, Jon, Ignacio Ellacuría, et al.
    1990   *Companions of Jesus: The Jesuit Martyrs of El Salvador.* Maryknoll, NY: Orbis.
Sochen, June.
    1973   *Movers and Shakers: American Women Thinkers and Activists, 1900–1970.* New York: New York Times Book Co.
Soelle, Dorothee.
    1991   *The Strength of the Weak: Toward a Christian Feminist Identity.* Louisville, KY: Westminster/John Knox.
    1979   "Resistance: Towards a First World Theology." *Christianity and Crisis,* June 23, pp 178ff.

Sofield, Loughlan, and Rosine Hammett.
    1981   "Experiencing Termination in Community." *Human Development* 2:2 (Summer): 24ff.

Soja, Edward.
    1989   *Postmodern Geographies: The Reassertion of Space in Critical Social Theory.* London: Verso.

Sonenshein, Raphael.
    1993   *Politics in Black and White: Race and Power in Los Angeles.* Princeton, NJ: Princeton University Press.

Song, C. S.
    1984   *Tell Us Our Names: Story Theology from an Asian Perspective.* Maryknoll, NY: Orbis.
    1979   *Third-Eye Theology: Theology in Formation in Asian Settings.* Maryknoll, NY: Orbis.

Southgate, Douglas, and John Disinger.
    1987   *Sustainable Resource Development in the Third World.* Boulder, CO: Westview.

Spicer, Edward.
    1962   *Cycles of Conquest: The Impact of Spain, Mexico and the United States on the Indians of the Southwest, 1533–1960.* Tucson: University of Arizona Press.

Stallard, Karin, et al.
    1983   *Poverty in the American Dream: Women and Children First.* Boston: South End Press.

Stammer, Larry.
    1993   "Rethinking Origins of Sin: Genetic Findings Prompt Religious Leaders to Take a New Look at Good and Evil." *Los Angeles Times,* May 15, pp A1ff.

Starr, Kevin.
    1973   *Americans and the California Dream, 1850–1915.* New York: Oxford University Press.

Stavenhagen, Rodolfo.
    1990   *The Ethnic Question: Conflicts, Development and Human Rights.* Tokyo: United Nations University Press.

Steere, Douglas, ed.
    1984   *Quaker Spirituality: Selected Writings.* Classics of Western Spirituality. New York: Paulist Press.

Stegner, Wallace.
    1992   "Where the Bluebird Sings." *American Way,* December 15, pp 26ff.

Stein, Benjamin.
    1990   "Ultimate American Weapon: Television." *Los Angeles Times,* March 31.

Steinberg, Stephen.
    1991   "Occupational Apartheid." *The Nation,* December 9, pp 744ff.

Steiner, Frederick.
    1991   *The Living Landscape: An Ecological Approach to Landscape Planning.* New York: McGraw-Hill.

Stephens, Mitchell.
    1993   "Pop Goes the World." *Los Angeles Times Magazine,* January 17, pp 22ff.

Stephenson, Carolyn.
1991   *Peace Studies: The Evolution of Peace Research and Peace Education.*
          Spark Matsunaga Institute for Peace Occasional Paper no. 1. Honolulu:
          University of Hawai'i.
Stevenson, Sandra.
1989   "The Effects of Experiences of Torture on Guatemalan and Salvadoran
          Immigrant Families: Implications for Family Therapy." Master's thesis,
          Family Study Center, Burbank, CA.
Stevick, Daniel.
1971   *Civil Disobedience and the Christian.* New York: Seabury.
Stewart, Jocelyn.
1992   "Civil Rights Groups Out of Touch, Many Believe." *Los Angeles Times,*
          August 31, pp A1f.
Styron, William.
1970   *The Confessions of Nat Turner.* London: Panther Books.
Sugden, John.
1991   *Sir Francis Drake.* New York: John MacRae/Henry Holt.
Suzuki, Lester.
1979   *Ministry in the Assembly and Relocation Centers of World War II.*
          Berkeley, CA: Yardbird Publications.
Swomley, John.
1972   *Liberation Ethics.* New York: Macmillan Co.
Tachibana, Judy.
1986   "California's Asians: Power from a Growing Population." *California
          Journal,* November, pp 535ff.
Tamez, Elsa.
1990   *Faith without Works is Dead: The Scandalous Message of James.* New
          York: Crossroad.
1982   *Bible of the Oppressed.* Maryknoll, NY: Orbis.
Tannen, Deborah.
1990   *You Just Don't Understand: Women and Men in Conversation.* New York:
          Ballantine Books.
Taylor, John V.
1975   *Enough Is Enough.* London: SCM.
Taylor, Mark Kline.
1990   *Remembering Esperanza: A Cultural-Political Theology for North Ameri-
          can Praxis.* Maryknoll, NY: Orbis.
Taylor, Stuart, Ched Myers, Cindy Moe-Lobeda, and Marie Dennis Grosso.
1991   *The American Journey, 1492–1992: A Call to Conversion.* Erie: Pax
          Christi.
Taylor, Vincent.
1963   *The Gospel According to St. Mark.* London: Macmillan & Co.
Thomas, Guboo Ted.
1987   "The Land is Sacred: Renewing the Dreaming in Modern Australia." In
          The Gospel is Not Western: Black Theologies from the Southwest Pacific,
          edited by G. Trompf. Maryknoll, NY: Orbis, pp 90ff.
Thomas, Hugh.
1961   *The Spanish Civil War.* New York: Harper & Brothers.

Thomson, James C., Jr., Peter Stanley, and John Perry.
1981   *Sentimental Imperialists: The American Experience in East Asia.* New York: Harper Colophon.

Thornton, Russell.
1987   *American Indian Holocaust and Survival: A Population History Since 1492.* Norman: University of Oklahoma Press.

Thurber, James.
1964   *The Thurber Carnival.* New York: Dell Publishing Co./Delta Books.

Tinker, George.
1993   *Missionary Conquest: The Gospel and Native American Cultural Genocide.* Minneapolis: Fortress Press.

Tinker, George, and Marie Therese Archambault.
1992   "A Native-American Reading of *Basileia tou Theou.*" Paper delivered at the Cassassa Conference, Loyola Marymount University, Los Angeles, CA, March 20.

Tolbert, Mary Ann.
1989   *Sowing the Gospel: Mark's World in Literary-Historical Perspective.* Minneapolis: Fortress Press.

Toth, Robert.
1990   "U.S. Fears a New Arms Race — In Third World." *Los Angeles Times,* April 3.

Trainer, F. E.
1985   *Abandon Affluence!* London: Zed.

Treviño, Jesús.
1991   "The *Pluribus* that Makes the *Unum:* A Review of *The American Kaleidoscope: Race, Ethnicity and the Civic Culture* by Lawrence Fuchs." *Los Angeles Times,* February 10.

Trible, Phyllis.
1984   *Texts of Terror: Literary-Feminist Readings of Biblical Narratives.* Overtures to Biblical Theology 13. Philadelphia: Fortress Press.

Truettner, William, ed.
1991   *The West as America: Reinterpreting Images of the Frontier, 1820–1920.* Washington, DC: Smithsonian Institution Press.

Turan, Kenneth.
1990   "Where America Came From: A Newly Restored Ellis Island Reminds Visitors That We Are All Refugees." *Los Angeles Times,* November 18, pp L1ff.

Uchitelle, Louis.
1990   "In the Ancient Land of the Aztecs, the Hurrah for Columbus is Muted." *New York Times* national edition. September 6, 1990, p A12.

Ulansey, David.
1991   "The Heavenly Veil Torn: Mark's Cosmic Inclusio." *Journal of Biblical Literature* 110:1 (Spring): 123ff.

Usdansky, Margaret.
1992   "Immigrant Tide Surges in '80s" and " 'Diverse' Fits Nation Better than 'Normal.' " *USA Today,* May 29–31.

Utne Reader.
1988   "Are You Addicted to Addiction?" Special issue, November–December, pp 51ff.

Vallely, Paul.
1990   *Bad Samaritans: First World Ethics and Third World Debt.* Maryknoll,
           NY: Orbis.

Valle, Victor, and Rudy Torres.
1992   "Enough of the Great Melodrama of Race Relations in Los Angeles." *Los
           Angeles Times,* December 6, p M6.

Vecsey, Christopher.
1987   "Envision Ourselves Darkly, Imagine Ourselves Richly." In *The American
           Indian and the Problem of History,* edited by C. Martin. New York: Oxford
           University Press, pp 120ff.
1991   *Imagine Ourselves Richly: Mythic Narratives of North American Indians.*
           San Francisco: Harper San Francisco.

Ventura, Michael.
1993   "The World Riots." *L.A. Weekly,* January 1–7, pp 8ff.
1990   "Could Psychology Be Part of the Disease, Not Part of the Cure? A
           Conversation with Psychologist James Hillman." *L.A. Weekly,* June 1,
           pp 16ff.

Verhelst, Thierry.
1990   *No Life without Roots: Culture and Development.* Translated by B. Cum-
           ming. London: Zed.

Vidal, Gore.
1992   "Monotheism and Its Discontents." *The Nation,* July 13, pp 37ff.

Viereck, Jennifer.
1992   "Radiation: The Newest Smallpox Blanket." *The Nuclear Resister* 87
           (December 23): 6ff.

Vilchis, Leonardo.
1991   "Renewing the Church from Below." *Desde la Base* (Newsletter of
           Proyecto Pastoral, Los Angeles), Winter, pp 4f.

Vobejda, Barbara.
1991   "Asians, Hispanics Giving Nation more Diversity." *Washington Post,*
           June 12.

Wachtel, Paul.
1989   *The Poverty of Affluence: A Psychological Portrait of the American Way
           of Life.* Philadelphia: New Society Publishers.

Wagua, Aiban.
1992   "Religious Legacies of the European Invasion." *500 Years* (Latin American
           Council of Churches, Quito, Ecuador), February, pp 6ff.

Wallace, Amy.
1992   "Riots Changed Few Attitudes, Poll Finds." *Los Angeles Times,* Septem-
           ber 3, pp B1f.

Wallace, Michele.
1990   "Defacing History — A Review of *Facing History: The Black Image in
           American Art, 1710–1940.*" *Art in America,* December, pp 121ff.

Wallis, Jim.
1980   "Rebuilding the Church: A Reconciled People for the Sake of the World."
           Sojourners, January, pp 9ff.
1976   *Agenda for Biblical People.* New York: Harper & Row.

Wallis, Jim, ed.
1987   *The Rise of Christian Conscience: The Emergence of a Dramatic Renewal Movement in Today's Church.* San Francisco: Harper & Row.
1991   "1992: Rediscovering America." *Sojourners* Special issue, October.

Wallis, Jim, and Bob Hulteen, eds.
1992   *America's Original Sin: A Study Guide on White Racism.* Rev. ed. Washington, DC: Sojourners Magazine.

Wallis, Jim and Joyce Hollyday, eds.
1991   *Cloud of Witnesses.* Maryknoll, NY: Orbis/Sojourners.

Walzer, Michael.
1977   *Just and Unjust Wars: A Moral Argument with Historical Illustrations.* New York: Basic Books.

Warren, Jennifer.
1991   "Northern Discontent Fuels Drive for a California Split." *Los Angeles Times,* December 24, pp A1ff.

Warrior, Robert Allen.
1991   "An Interview with Marie Not Help Him." *Native Nations* 1:2 (February): 13ff.
1990   "North and South Tribes Come Together in Ecuador: 1992 to Mark 500 Years of Resistance." *The Lakota Times,* August 14, pp A3f.

Washington, James Melvin, ed.
1986   *A Testament of Hope: The Essential Writings and Speeches of Martin Luther King, Jr.* San Francisco: Harper & Row.

Weatherford, Jack.
1988   *Indian Givers: How the Indians of the Americas Transformed the World.* New York: Ballentine, Fawcett & Columbine.

Weimann, Robert.
1984   *Structure and Society in Literary History: Studies in the History and Theory of Historical Criticism.* Baltimore, MD: Johns Hopkins University Press.

Welch, Sharon.
1989   *A Feminist Ethic of Risk.* Minneapolis: Fortress Press.
1985   *Communities of Resistance and Solidarity: A Feminist Theology of Liberation.* Maryknoll, NY: Orbis.

West, Charles C.
1969   *Ethics, Violence and Revolution.* New York: Council on Religion and International Affairs.

West, Cornel.
1993   *Race Matters.* Boston: Beacon Press.
1982   *Prophesy Deliverance! An Afro-American Revolutionary Christianity.* Philadelphia: Westminster.

Wexler, Annette.
1991   "Priest Who Won Award Fights Things That 'Shouldn't Happen.'" *New York Times,* August 11.

Weyler, Rex.
1992   *Blood of the Land: The Government and Corporate War against First Nations.* Philadelphia: New Society Publishers.

White, Richard.
  1992   *It's Your Misfortune and None of My Own: A New History of the American West.* Norman: University of Oklahoma Press.
Whitney, Janet.
  1943   *John Woolman, Quaker.* London: George Harrap & Co.
Wilkinson, Tracy.
  1993   "Salvadoran Government OKs Blanket Amnesty." *Los Angeles Times,* March 21, pp A1f.
Williams, Patricia.
  1991   "Nothing But the Best; Review of G. Ezorsky's *Racism and Justice: The Case for Affirmative Action* and S. Carter's *Reflections of an Affirmative Action Baby.*" *The Nation,* November 18, pp 632–38.
Williams, Raymond.
  1977   *Marxism and Literature.* London: Oxford University Press.
Williams, William Appleman.
  1980   *Empire as a Way of Life.* New York: Oxford University Press.
Wink, Walter.
  1992   *Engaging the Powers: Discernment and Resistance in a World of Domination.* Minneapolis: Fortress Press.
  1984   *Naming the Powers: The Language of Power in the New Testament.* Philadelphia: Fortress Press.
  1986   *Unmasking the Powers: The Invisible Forces that Determine Human Existence.* Philadelphia: Fortress Press.
  1980   *Transforming Bible Study.* Nashville: Abingdon.
Winner, Langdon.
  1977   *Autonomous Technology: Technics-out-of-Control as a Theme in Political Thought.* Cambridge, MA: MIT Press.
Winnicott, D. W.
  1986   *Home Is Where We Start From: Essays by a Psychoanalyst.* New York: W. W. Norton.
Winter, James.
  1992   *Common Cents: Media Portrayal of the Gulf War and Other Events.* Montreal: Black Rose Books.
Wise, Tim.
  1991   "Affirmative Action and the Politics of White Resentment." *Blueprint for Social Justice* 45:2 (October).
Witvliet, Theo.
  1984   *A Place in the Sun: An Introduction to Liberation Theology in the Third World.* Maryknoll, NY: Orbis.
Wolf, Eric.
  1982   *Europe and the People without History.* Berkeley: University of California Press.
Wolfe, Alan.
  1980   "Capitalism Shows Its Face: Giving up on Democracy." In *Trilateralism: The Trilateral Commission and Elite Planning for World Management,* edited by H. Sklar. Boston: South End Press, pp 295ff.
Wolfe, Tom.
  1970   *Radical Chic and Mau-mauing the Flak-Catchers.* New York: Farrar, Straus & Giroux.

Wollenberg, Charles.
    1988   "Cultures in Transition: Immigration in the Central Valley." *California Council on the Humanities Newsletter,* June, pp 3ff.

Womack, Paula.
    1992   "Roger Williams and Native Americans." *God and Caesar* (General Conference Mennonite Church) 16:4 (December): 23.

Woolman, John.
    1989   *The Journal and Major Essays of John Woolman.* Edited by P. Moulton. Richmond, IN: Friends United Press.

Wright, Robin.
    1993   "Women and Power." *Los Angeles Times,* June 29, pp F1ff.

Wright, Ronald.
    1992   *Stolen Continents: The "New World" Through Indian Eyes.* New York: Houghton Mifflin.

Wylie, Jeanie.
    1992   "Exchanging Birthrights: A Nation of Esaus." *The Witness,* October, pp 5f.
    1991   *Poletown: Community Betrayed.* Chicago: University of Illinois Press.

Wylie, Jeanie, and Carter Heyward.
    1992   "Abortion Rights: A Conversation." *The Witness,* June–July, pp 17ff.

Yalom, Irvin.
    1989   *Love's Executioner and Other Tales of Psychotherapy.* New York: Basic Books.

Yoder, John Howard.
    1984   *When War is Unjust: Being Honest in Just-War Thinking.* Minneapolis: Augsburg Publishing House.
    1972   *The Politics of Jesus.* Grand Rapids, MI: William B. Eerdmans.
    1971a   *The Original Revolution.* Scottdale, PA: Herald Press.
    1971b   *Nevertheless.* Scottdale, PA: Herald Press.
    1970   *Karl Barth and the Problem of War.* New York: Abingdon.

Young, Pamela.
    1990   *Feminist Theology/Christian Theology.* Minneapolis: Fortress Press.

Zajovic, Stasa, ed.
    1993   *Women for Peace Anthology.* Translated by S. Bogoslavjevic. Belgrade: Women in Black.

Zashin, Elliot.
    1972   *Civil Disobedience and Democracy.* New York: Free Press.

Zikmund, Barbara Brown.
    1987   "The Trinity and Women's Experience." *The Christian Century,* April 15.

Zinn, Howard.
    1980   *A People's History of the United States.* New York: Harper & Row.
    1968   *Disobedience and Democracy: Nine Fallacies on Law and Order.* New York: Vintage/Random House.

Zipes, Jack.
    1979   *Breaking the Magic Spell: Radical Theories of Folk and Fairy Tales.* New York: Methuen.

Index of Scriptural References

HEBREW BIBLE

NEW TESTAMENT

Index of Names and Titles